ISBN 978-1-5281-5711-7
PIBN 10940786

This book is a reproduction of an important historical work. Forgotten Books uses
state-of-the-art technology to digitally reconstruct the work, preserving the original format
whilst repairing imperfections present in the aged copy. In rare cases, an imperfection in
the original, such as a blemish or missing page, may be replicated in our edition. We do,
however, repair the vast majority of imperfections successfully; any imperfections that
remain are intentionally left to preserve the state of such historical works.

LAWS

OF THE

STATE OF NEW YORK,

PASSED AT THE

ONE HUNDRED AND TWENTIETH SESSION

OF THE

LEGISLATURE,

BEGUN JANUARY SIXTH, 1897, AND ENDED APRIL TWENTY-
FOURTH, 1897, IN THE CITY OF ALBANY.

VOL. I.

BANKS & BROTHERS,
NEW YORK.   ALBANY, N. Y.
1897.

JAMES B. LYON,
PRINTER, ELECTROTYPER AND BINDER,
LYON BLOCK, ALBANY, N. Y.

CERTIFICATE.

OFFICE OF THE SECRETARY OF STATE
OF THE STATE OF NEW YORK,
ALBANY, *July* 1, 1897.

Pursuant to the directions of chapter 682, Laws of 1892, entitled " The Legislative Law," I hereby certify that the following volume of the Laws of this State was printed under my direction.

JOHN PALMER,
Secretary of State.

In this volume, every act which received the assent of a majority of all the members of the Legislature, three-fifths of all the members elected to either House thereof being present, pursuant to section 21 of article 3 of the Constitution of this State, is designated under its title by the words " passed, three-fifths being present." And every act which received the assent of a majority of all the members elected to each branch of the Legislature, pursuant to section 15 of article 3 of the Constitution of this State, is designated under its title by the words " passed, a majority being present." And every act which received the assent of two-thirds of all the members elected to each branch of the Legislature, pursuant to section 9 of article 1 of the Constitution of this State, is designated under its title by the words " passed by a two-thirds vote." [See " the Legislative Law," chapter 682, Laws of 1892, as amended by chapter 53, Laws of 1894.]

LIST OF OFFICERS.

"§ 45. Contents of published volumes of session laws.— The Secretary of State shall annually cause * * * a statement of the names and residences of the Governor, Lieutenant-Governor, Senators and Members of Assembly, and presiding officers of both Houses in office during each session * * * to be printed and bound. * * *." Laws of 1892, Chap. 683, Sec. 45.

NAMES AND RESIDENCES

Of the Governor, Lieutenant-Governor, Senators, Members of Assembly and Presiding Officers of Both Houses of the Legislature of the State of New York at the Time of the Passage of the Laws Contained in This Volume.

GOVERNOR.
FRANK S. BLACK.................. .... *Albany, Albany County.

LIEUTENANT-GOVERNOR.
TIMOTHY L. WOODRUFF .... Brooklyn, Kings County.

SENATORS.

District.	NAME.	County.	Address.
1.....	Richard Higbie............	Suffolk.........	Babylon.
2.....	Theodore Koehler.............	Queens.............	Long Island City.
3.....	Frank Gallagher.............	Kings.............	Brooklyn.
4.....	George W. Brush.............	Kings.............	Brooklyn.
5.....	Michael J. Coffey.............	Kings.............	Brooklyn.
6.....	Peter H. McNulty	Kings.............	Brooklyn.
7.....	Patrick H. McCarren	Kings.............	Brooklyn.
8.....	Albert A. Wray	Kings.............	Brooklyn.
9.....	Julius L. Wieman	Kings.......	Brooklyn.
10...	John F. Ahearn	New York	New York.
11.....	Timothy D. Sullivan	New York	New York.
12.....	Samuel J. Foley	New York	New York.
13.....	Bernard F. Martin	New York	New York.
14.....	Thomas Francis Grady.........	New York	New York.
15.....	Frank D. Pavey.............	New York	New York.
16.....	Louis Munzinger.............	New York	New York.
17.....	Charles B. Page	New York	New York.
18.....	Maurice Featherson............	New York	New York.
19.....	John Ford	New York	New York.
20.....	Jacob A. Cantor	New York	New York.
21... ...	Charles Lewis Guy.............	New York	New York.
22.....	James Irving Burns.............	Westchester.	Yonkers.
23.....	Clarence Lexow	Rockland	Nyack.
24.....	William C. Daley.............	Columbia	Chatham.
25.....	Charles Davis.................	Ulster........ ...	Saugerties.
26.....	John Grant...................	Delaware	Margaretville.
27.....	Hobart Krum.................	Schoharie	Schoharie.
28.....	Edgar T. Brackett	Saratoga	Saratoga Springs.
29.....	Myer Nussbaum	Albany	Albany.
30.....	LeGrand C. Tibbits.............	Rensselaer............	Hoosick.
31.....	George Chahoon	Essex	Ausable Forks.
32.....	George R. Malby.............	St. Lawrence........	Ogdensburg.
33.....	Walter L. Brown	Otsego	Oneonta.
34.....	Henry J. Coggeshall	Oneida...............	Waterville.

* Official residence.

MEMBERS OF ASSEMBLY — (Concluded).

District.	NAME.	County.	Address.
1.....	Henry E. Warner	Niagara	North Tonawanda.
2.....	Frank A. Dudley	Niagara	Niagara Falls.
1.....	George E. Philo	Oneida	Utica.
2.....	William Cary Sanger	Oneida	Sangerfield.
3.....	William B. Graves	Oneida	Taberg.
1. ..	William J. Bellen	Onondaga	Baldwinsville.
2.....	Edward G. Ten Eyck	Onondaga	Fabius.
3.....	Joseph Bondy	Onondaga	Syracuse.
4....	Edwin M. Wells	Onondaga	Syracuse.
	Murray Benham	Ontario	Hopewell Centre.
1. .	Louis F. Goodsell	Orange	Highland Falls.
2....	Louis Bedell	Orange	Goshen.
	Fred L. Downs	Orleans	Medina.
1.....	Lewis P. Taylor	Oswego	Oswego Centre.
2.....	Thomas M. Costello	Oswego	Altmar.
	Charles B. Gorham	Otsego	Burlington.
	Emmerson W. Addis	Putnam	Brewster.
1.....	Thomas F. Kennedy	Queens	Long Island City.
2.....	Harvey S. McKnight	Queens	Bayside, N. Y.
3.....	Morton Cromwell	Queens	Glen Cove.
1.....	Edward McGraw	Rensselaer	Valley Falls.
2.....	William Hutton, Jr	Rensselaer	Troy.
3.....	George Anderson	Rensselaer	Castleton.
	George Garby	Richmond	Port Richmond.
	Fred L. Whritner	Rockland	Suffern.
1.....	Ira C. Miles	St. Lawrence	Edwards.
2.....	Martin V. B. Ives	St. Lawrence	Potsdam.
	George W. Kavanaugh	Saratoga	Waterford.
	Thomas W. Winne	Schenectady	Niskayuna.
	George M. Palmer	Schoharie	Cobleskill.
	Oliver H. Budd..	Schuyler	Hector.
	Harry M. Glen	Seneca	Seneca Falls.
1.....	James S. Harrison	Steuben	Addison.
2.....	Joel E. Clark	Steuben	Cameron.
1.....	Erastus F. Post	Suffolk	Quogue.
2.....	Carll S. Burr	Suffolk	Commack.
	George M. McLaughlin	Sullivan	Monticello.
	Daniel P. Witter	Tioga	Richford.
	Frederick E Bates	Tompkins	Caroline Depot.
1.....	William S. Van Keuren	Ulster	Kingston.
2.....	Harcourt J. Pratt	Ulster	Highland.
	Taylor J. Eldridge	Warren	North Creek.
	William R. Hobbie	Washington	Bottenville.
	George S. Horton	Wayne	Wolcott.
1.....	Alfred E. Smith	Westchester	Bronxville.
2.....	Richard S. Emmett, Jr	Westchester	New Rochelle.
3....	James W. Husted	Westchester	Peekskill.
	Mortimer N. Cole	Wyoming	Castile.
	Miles W. Raplee	Yates	Dundee.

Speaker of the Assembly.

JAMES M. E. O'GRADY .... Rochester, N. Y.

Clerk of the Assembly.

ARCHIE E. BAXTER .... Elmira, N. Y.

GENERAL LAWS.

OF THE

STATE OF NEW YORK.

VOLUME I.

PASSED AT THE ONE HUNDRED AND TWENTIETH REGULAR SESSION OF THE
LEGISLATURE, BEGUN THE SIXTH DAY OF JANUARY, 1897, AND ENDED THE
TWENTY-FOURTH DAY OF APRIL, 1897, AT THE CITY OF ALBANY.

Chap. 1.

AN ACT making appropriation for contingent expenses of the legislature.

Became a law January 21, 1897, with the approval of the Governor.
Passed, three-fifths being present.

The People of the State of New York, represented in Senate and Assembly, do enact as follows:

Section 1. The sum of twenty-six thousand five hundred dollars is hereby appropriated, out of any moneys in the treasury not otherwise appropriated, for advances by the comptroller to the clerks of the senate and assembly for contingent expenses and clerical services for the legislature, as may be approved on the part of the senate by the chairman of the senate committee on finance and on the part of the assembly by the chairman of the assembly committee on ways and means. *Appropriation for contingent expenses.*

§ 2. This act shall take effect immediately.

Chap. 4.

AN ACT to legalize and confirm certain acts of the boards of supervisors of the several counties of this state.

Became a law January 28, 1897, with the approval of the Governor.
Passed, three-fifths being present.

The People of the State of New York, represented in Senate and Assembly, do enact as follows:

Acts in issuing tax warrants legalized.

Section 1. The acts of the boards of supervisors of the several counties of this state, in annual session for the year eighteen hundred and ninety-six, in issuing warrants for the collection of taxes, to the collectors of the several towns or tax districts thereof, so far as such acts may be affected, questioned or impaired by reason of such warrants having been issued to such collectors under the hands and seals of the individual members of said boards of supervisors respectively, or a majority thereof, are hereby legalized, ratified and confirmed, and made as effectual and valid as if such warrants had been issued under the seal of the county and signed by the chairman and clerk of said several boards of supervisors, as required by the " tax law " of this state.

Proviso.

§ 2. Nothing in this act contained shall affect any legal action or proceeding now pending.

§ 3. This act shall take effect immediately.

Chap. 6.

AN ACT making an appropriation for the use of the health officer of the port of New York, for the purpose of preventing the introduction of infectious and contagious diseases.

Became a law February 5, 1897, with the approval of the Governor.
Passed, three-fifths being present.

The People of the State of New York, represented in Senate and Assembly, do enact as follows:

Appropriation for disinfecting apparatus.

Section 1. The sum of five thousand dollars, or so much thereof as may be necessary, is hereby appropriated from any moneys in the treasury not otherwise appropriated, for the completion of necessary apparatus at the quarantine station of the port of New York for disinfecting purposes, to prevent the introduction of infectious and contagious diseases; the sum hereby appropriated shall be payable by the treasurer, upon the warrant of the comptroller, drawn in favor of the health officer of the port of New York, as required.

§ 2. This act shall take effect immediately.

Chap. 7.

AN ACT to provide for the representation of the state of New York, at the Tennessee centennial and international exhibition at Nashville, Tennessee, and making an appropriation therefor.

Became a law February 9, 1897, with the approval of the Governor. Passed, three-fifths being present.

The People of the State of New York, represented in Senate and Assembly, do enact as follows:

Section 1. The appointment by the governor of commissioners to represent the state of New York at the Tennessee centennial and international exhibition to be held at Nashville, pursuant to a concurrent resolution of the legislature of eighteen hundred and ninety-six is ratified and confirmed, and for the purposes of this act such commissioners are known as the "Tennessee centennial commissioners." Such commission shall encourage and promote a full and complete exhibit of the commercial, educational, industrial, artistic and other interest of the state and its citizens at such exhibition, and, in its discretion, may provide, furnish and maintain, during the exhibition, a building or room for a state exhibit and for the official headquarters of the state, and for the comfort and convenience of its citizens and its exhibitors. *Appointment of commissioners.* *Duty of commission.*

§ 2. The members of the commission shall receive no compensation for their services, but shall be entitled to their actual, necessary expenses while in the discharge of duties imposed upon them by the commission. Such commission may provide such clerical assistance and office facilities as it deems necessary, but no salaries or expenses shall be incurred for a longer period than ninety days after the close of the exhibition. *Expenses and salaries.*

§ 3. The sum of twelve thousand dollars, or so much thereof as may be necessary, is hereby appropriated out of any money in the treasury not otherwise appropriated, for the purposes of this act. *Appropriation.*

Such money shall be paid by the treasurer, on the warrant of the
comptroller, issued upon a requisition signed by the president and
secretary of the commission, accompanied by an estimate of the
expenses for the payment of which the money so drawn is to be
Report to comptroller. applied. Within ninety days after the close of the exhibition,
such commission shall make a verified report to the comptroller of
all disbursements made by it, and shall return to the state treasury
the unexpended balance of money drawn in pursuance of this act.

Report of proceedings. § 4. The commission shall make a report of its proceedings, from
time to time, to the governor, and within three months from the
close of the exhibition, shall make a final, detailed report to him, to
be transmitted by him to the legislature.

§ 5. This act shall take effect immediately.

Chap. 8.

AN ACT to reappropriate the unexpended balance of a former
appropriation.

Became a law February 9, 1897, with the approval of the Governor.
Passed, three-fifths being present.

*The People of the State of New York, represented in Senate
and Assembly, do enact as follows:*

Reappropriation for canal wall. Section 1. The sum of one thousand four hundred and seventy-
one dollars, being the unexpended balance of the sum of two thou-
sand five hundred dollars appropriated by chapter six hundred and
fifty-three of the laws of eighteen hundred and ninety-four for
repairing and extending the high retaining wall of the Erie canal
on the west side of South St. Paul street, in the city of Rochester,
New York, between the north line of Court street and the aqueduct
crossing the Genesee river, is hereby reappropriated for the same
purpose.

§ 2. This act shall take effect immediately.

Chap. 9.

AN ACT making an appropriation for the payment of the confidential clerks to the justices of the supreme court in the second judicial district, not including the county of Kings, pursuant to chapter eight hundred and ninety-two, laws of eighteen hundred and ninety-six.

Became a law February 10, 1897, with the approval of the Governor.
Passed, three-fifths being present.

The People of the State of New York, represented in Senate and Assembly, do enact as follows:

Section 1. The sum of ten thousand nine hundred and fifty dollars, or so much thereof as may be necessary, is hereby appropriated out of any money in the treasury not otherwise appropriated, for the payment of confidential clerks appointed by the justices of the supreme court in the second judicial district, not including the county of Kings, in full compensation from June first, eighteen hundred and ninety-six, to September thirtieth, eighteen hundred and ninety-seven, to be refunded to the treasury, as provided by chapter eight hundred and ninety-two, laws of eighteen hundred and ninety-six

§ 2. This act shall take effect immediately.

Appropriation for confidential clerks.

Chap. 15.

AN ACT providing for the sale of certain lands belonging to the state of New York.

Became a law February 11, 1897, with the approval of the Governor.
Passed, three-fifths being present.

The People of the State of New York, represented in Senate and Assembly, do enact as follows:

Section 1. The commissioners of the land office are hereby authorized and empowered to sell at public auction, and to convey to the highest bidder, so much of the land belonging to the people of the state of New York, in the city of Utica and county of Oneida, and distinguished on a map of part of Schuyler farm, Utica, as being lot number four, part of lot number three, part of lot number five, in block six, fronting on Knox street. Also lots number nineteen and twenty, in said block six, fronting on Chestnut street. Also lot number eight, part of lot number seven, and part of lot number

Sale of land authorized.

nine, in block seven, fronting on Chestnut street. Also lot number fifteen, part of lot number sixteen, and part of lot number fourteen, in said block seven, fronting on Walnut street. Also parts of lots numbers eleven and twelve, in block two, fronting on Schuyler and Walnut streets. Also that tract or parcel of land beginning at the intersection of the easterly line of Hicks street with the northerly line of Knox street, fronting on Hicks and Knox streets, as may be certified by the managers of the Utica state hospital as no longer necessary for hospital purposes.

Proceeds of sale.   § 2. The moneys arising from the sale of said lands shall be deposited with the state treasurer.

§ 3. This act shall take effect immediately.

Chap. 17.

AN ACT to change the corporate name of the New York Casualty Insurance Association.

Became a law February 13, 1897, with the approval of the Governor.
Passed, a majority being present.

The People of the State of New York, represented in Senate and Assembly, do enact as follows:

Section 1. The corporate name of the New York Casualty Insurance Association is hereby changed to the New York Casualty Company.

§ 2. This act shall take effect immediately.

Chap. 19.

AN ACT to amend the legislative law, and the acts amendatory thereof, relative to the distribution of the session laws.

Became a law February 18, 1897, with the approval of the Governor.
Passed, three-fifths being present.

The People of the State of New York, represented in Senate and Assembly, do enact as follows:

Act amended.   Section 1. Subdivision three of section forty-six of chapter six hundred and eighty-two of the laws of eighteen hundred and ninety-two, entitled "An act in relation to legislation, constituting chapter eight of the general laws," as amended by chapter two hundred and eighteen of the laws of eighteen hundred and ninety-four, is hereby amended to read as follows:

3. One copy to each of the following officers: Each town clerk, Distribu-
for the use of the town, each district attorney, the clerk of each tion of
board of supervisors, for the use of the board, each surrogate, ex- laws.
cept where the county judge acts as surrogate, for the use of the
surrogate's court, to the county treasurer of each county, to the
mayor of each city, for the use of the city, and to each village clerk.
Every such officer shall deliver such copy of the session laws to his
successor in office.

§ 2. This act shall take effect immediately.

Chap. 21.

AN ACT to amend chapter three hundred and sixty-nine of the
laws of eighteen hundred and ninety-five, entitled "An act creating a commissioner of jurors for each county of the state, having
a certain population, and regulating and prescribing his duties;
also providing in what manner jury lists shall be made up and
jurors drawn and notified in the courts of record in such counties,
and how they may be exempt or excused, and the length of
service of such jurors," and the acts amendatory thereof, in
relation to the preparation of ballots, and correction of errors in
original act.

Became a law February 18, 1897, with the approval of the Governor.
Passed, three-fifths being present.

*The People of the State of New York, represented in Senate
and Assembly, do enact as follows:*

Section 1. Section sixteen of chapter three hundred sixty-nine Act
of the laws of eighteen hundred ninety-five as amended by chapter amended.
ninety-seven of the laws of eighteen hundred ninety-six is hereby
amended to read as follows:

§ 16. When the annual jury list has been prepared and filed Destruc-
as prescribed in the last section, the ballots for jurors used in ballots
the previous year shall be destroyed by the commissioner of jurors, used.
except those which are required for the ensuing year. The ballots Prepara-
for the ensuing year shall be prepared by the commissioner, who tion of
may use for that purpose such of the ballots prepared for the ballots.
previous year as shall be in condition to be used again. The
ballots shall be uniform slips of paper, and the name of each
person on the jury list who is qualified and liable for jury duty,
with his residence, shall be written separately on one of said

Deposit of same in box

ballots. The ballots so prepared shall be deposited by the commissioner of jurors in the jury box kept by the commissioner of jurors for that purpose, and he shall place his seal upon the box. The commissioner of jurors shall not deposit in the jury box for service for the ensuing year the ballots containing the names of jurors who have served their legal term as jurors during the

Jury box.

preceding jury year. The box shall be constructed with an aperture large enough only to conveniently admit the hand of the person by whom the ballots are to be drawn, and the aperture shall be provided with a cover so arranged as to be securely sealed when closed. The jury box shall be cylindrical in form, and shall be provided with some apparatus by which the ballots can be thoroughly mixed without exposing them, and its form and construction shall be approved by the said judges, and may from time to time be changed with their approval.

§ 2. Section twenty-two of chapter three hundred sixty-nine of the laws of eighteen hundred ninety-five is hereby amended to read as follows:

Discharge of jurors after service.

§ 22. A person summoned as a juror, who has actually served as a trial juror in a court of record in any county embraced within this act for two complete calendar weeks, or, if his service shall not be for complete calendar weeks, then for twelve days of actual service, within that jury year, shall be discharged by the court; except that he shall not be so discharged until the close of a trial in which he may be serving when the said time expires. A person discharged as prescribed in this section, is thereafter, during the same jury year, prohibited from jury service in any county of the state. Whenever the certificate of one or more clerks of a court, made as prescribed in section twenty-seven of this act, show that a person is entitled to a discharge, as prescribed in this section, the commissioner of jurors must, upon request, certify to the fact.

Sections of act re-numbered.

§ 3. Chapter three hundred sixty-nine of the laws of eighteen hundred ninety-five is hereby amended so that the first section after section thirty of said act shall be numbered section thirty-one, and the amendment to subdivision six of section thirty-one of said act, made by chapter ninety-seven of the laws of eighteen hundred ninety-six, shall be deemed to be an amendment to the said first section after section thirty of said chapter three hundred sixty-nine of the laws of eighteen hundred and ninety-five, which said section is to be hereafter numbered section thirty-one.

§ 4. This act shall take effect immediately.

Chap. 23.

AN ACT to amend section thirty-three hundred and fourteen of the code of civil procedure, relative to fees of jurors.

Became a law February 24, 1897, with the approval of the Governor.
Passed, three-fifths being present.

The People of the State of New York, represented in Senate and Assembly, do enact as follows:

Section 1. Section thirty-three hundred and fourteen of the code of civil procedure is hereby amended to read as follows:

§ 3314. **Supervisors may make allowance to grand and trial jurors.**— In the county of New York, the common council, and in any other county, the board of supervisors, may direct that a sum, not exceeding two dollars, in addition to the fees prescribed in the last section, or in any other statutory provision, be allowed to each grand juror, and each trial juror, for each day's attendance at a term of a court of record, of civil or criminal jurisdiction, held within their county. If a different rate is not otherwise established as herein provided, each juror is entitled to five cents for each mile necessarily traveled by him in going to and returning from the term; but such common council or board of supervisors may establish a lower rate. A juror is entitled to mileage for actual travel once in each calendar week during the term. The sum so allowed or established must be paid by the county treasurer, upon the certificate of the clerk of the court, stating the number of days that the juror actually attended, and the number of miles traveled by him, in order to attend. The amount so paid must be raised in the same manner as other county charges are raised.

§ 2. This act shall take effect immediately.

Chap. 25.

AN ACT to amend chapter three hundred and forty-eight of the
laws of eighteen hundred and eighty-five, entitled "An act to
authorize the appointment of stenographers for grand juries,
and to fix the compensation of such stenographers," as amended
by chapter one hundred and thirty-one of the laws of eighteen
hundred and eighty-six, chapter eighty-two of the laws of eighteen hundred and ninety-four, and chapter six hundred and
sixty-one of the laws of eighteen hundred and ninety-five.

Became a law February 25, 1897, with the approval of the Governor.
Passed, three-fifths being present.

*The People of the State of New York, represented in Senate
and Assembly, do enact as follows:*

Act
amended.

Section 1. Section seven of chapter three hundred and forty-
eight of the laws of eighteen hundred and eighty-five, entitled
" An act to authorize the appointment of stenographers for grand
juries, and to fix the compensation of said stenographers," as
amended by chapter one hundred and thirty-one of the laws of
eighteen hundred and eighty-six, chapter eighty-two of the laws
of eighteen hundred and ninety-four, and chapter six hundred and
sixty-one of the laws of eighteen hundred and ninety-five, is hereby
amended so as to read as follows:

Compen-
sation of
stenogra-
phers.

§ 7. Each stenographer appointed as aforesaid, shall receive
such compensation for services rendered while engaged in taking
testimony before a grand jury as shall be determined by the board
of supervisors of the county in which he is appointed, excepting that
in the county of New York, such compensation shall be fixed by
the board of estimate and apportionment of the city of New York,
and such compensation shall not be less than five nor more than
ten dollars per day; and in addition thereto he shall be entitled to
and shall be allowed for a copy of testimony furnished to the district attorney, the same rate per folio as is now allowed to the stenographers of the county court or court of common pleas in their
respective counties. Such compensation shall be a county charge,
and shall be paid by the treasurer of such county upon the affidavit
of the stenographer and the certificate of the district attorney,

Salaries in
Monroe,
Albany and
Queens
counties.

specifying the number of days of actual service, and the number
of folios furnished; excepting, that in the county of Monroe, the
stenographer   known   as   the   first   stenographer   shall

receive an annual salary of fifteen hundred dollars, and the stenographer known as the second stenographer shall receive a salary of fifty dollars per month; and excepting that in the county of Albany said stenographer shall receive a salary of twelve hundred dollars per annum; and excepting that in the county of Queens, said stenographer shall receive a salary of one thousand dollars per annum. Such salaries shall be a county charge and shall be paid monthly by the treasurers of said counties in the same manner as the salaries of other county officers are paid.

§ 2. This act shall take effect immediately.

Chap. 28.

AN ACT to amend chapter nine hundred and fifty-seven of the laws of eighteen hundred and ninety-six, entitled "An act conferring jurisdiction upon the board of claims to hear, audit and determine the claim of Mortimer Murphy against the state," relative to appeals.

Became a law February 25, 1897, with the approval of the Governor.
Passed, three-fifths being present.

The People of the State of New York, represented in Senate and Assembly, do enact as follows:

Section 1. Section two of chapter nine hundred and fifty-seven of the laws of eighteen hundred and ninety-six is hereby amended to read as follows: *Act amended.*

§ 2. Either party may take an appeal to the appellate division of the supreme court for the third department from any award made under authority of this act, provided such an appeal be taken by service of a notice of appeal within thirty days after service of a copy of the award. *Appeal from award.*

§ 2. This act shall take effect immediately.

Chap. 29.

AN ACT to amend the insurance law, relating to assessments by
town and county co-operative insurance companies.

Became a law February 25, 1897, with the approval of the Governor.
Passed, three-fifths being present.

*The People of the State of New York, represented in Senate
and Assembly, do enact as follows:*

Section 1. Section two hundred and sixty-eight of the insurance
law, constituting chapter thirty-eight of the general laws, as enacted by chapter six hundred and ninety of the laws of eighteen
hundred and ninety-two, is hereby amended to read as follows:

§ 268. **Classification of risks; borrowing money; assessments.-**
Every such corporation may, if a fire insurance corporation, classify the property or buildings insured therein at the time of insurance and issue policies under different rates according to the risk
from fire, to which they may be subject. In the case of any corporation formed under this article or any act repealed by this chapter for the formation of town and county co-operative insurance
corporations, if the amount of any loss or damage ascertained exceeds in amount the cash on hand of the corporation, such of its
officers as may be authorized by the by-laws to do so, shall convene
the directors or executive committee, who may borrow money on
the credit of the corporation sufficient to pay the loss, or make an
assessment upon all the property insured, pro rata, according to the
classification or according to the amount insured, as may be provided in the by-laws, sufficient to pay what the cash in hand falls
short of paying, or for the whole loss or damages, as the directors
or executive committee may decide to be for the best interests of
the corporation. If the directors or executive committee deem
it to be for the interest of the corporation, they may make an estimate of such sums as in their judgment will be necessary to pay all
losses, damages and expenses for the current year and supply any
deficiency in the preceding year, and proceed to assess, levy and
collect the same of the members of the corporation, at such times
as in their discretion will be most advantageous to the corporation.
Such assessment shall be made pro rata upon all the property
at such time insured, according to its classification or according to
the amount insured, sufficient to pay the amount so estimated.
Not more than four such general assessments shall be made
in any one year, nor shall any such assessment be made if more

than ten per cent of any previous assessment shall be in the treasury of the corporation and not required for losses actually suffered. No assessment shall be invalid because made in whole or in part for the purpose of paying any money borrowed by the directors or executive committee, which has been used in the payment of any claim for loss or damage against the corporation.

§ 2. This act shall take effect immediately.

Chap. 32.

AN ACT authorizing the construction of a bridge over the Erie canal at Fitzhugh street in the city of Rochester.

Became a law February 26, 1897, with the approval of the Governor.
Passed by a two-thirds vote.

The People of the State of New York, represented in Senate and Assembly, do enact as follows:

Section 1. The superintendent of public works is hereby authorized to provide for the construction of a suitable bridge with a roadway thirty six feet in width and sidewalks each ten feet in width over the Erie canal in the city of Rochester where Fitzhugh street crosses said canal and for the necessary approaches thereto and the necessary machinery to operate such bridge as he shall deem to the best interest of the state upon plans and specifications to be prepared by the state engineer and surveyor the cost of said bridge not to exceed the sum of twenty thousand dollars and said bridge to be operated under the direction of the superintendent of public works. *Construction of canal bridge. Operation of bridge.*

§ 2. The sum of twenty thousand dollars, or so much thereof as may be necessary, is hereby appropriated for the purposes of this act, payable by the treasurer on the warrant of the comptroller to the order of the superintendent of public works for the purposes of this act. *Appropriation.*

§ 3. This act shall take effect immediately.

Chap. 35.

AN ACT for the relief of certain religious societies.

Became a law March 9, 1897, with the approval of the Governor. Passed, a majority being present.

The People of the State of New York, represented in Senate and Assembly, do enact as follows:

Recording of certificates legalized.

Section 1. That the recording of any certificate of a religious corporation organized under provisions of "An act to provide for the incorporation of religious societies," passed April fifth, eighteen hundred and thirteen, and of the acts amending the same, in the office of a clerk of a county prior to the passage of this act, instead of in the office of the register of such county, shall be regarded and construed and such recording is hereby declared to be of the same validity, force and effect as would have been the recording of such certificate in the proper office. And every act, deed, matter and thing done or performed by every such religious society or corporation since the recording of its certificate in the office of said county clerk is hereby ratified, confirmed and declared to be as valid in all respects as if the said certificate had been properly and appropriately recorded in the office of the register of the county in which said religious society or corporation was organized; but this act shall not affect any suit or proceeding already commenced arising out of such original mistake.

Acts of societies confirmed.

§ 2. This act shall take effect immediately.

Chap. 36.

AN ACT to revise, amend and consolidate the several acts relating to the board of claims, to establish a court of claims, to amend the code of civil procedure, and to repeal certain acts and parts of acts.

Became a law March 9, 1897, with the approval of the Governor. Passed, three-fifths being present.

The People of the State of New York, represented in Senate and Assembly, do enact as follows:

Section 1. Chapter three of the code of civil procedure is hereby amended by adding a title and article to be known as title three, article one, entitled "the court of claims," and to consist of sections numbered from two hundred and sixty-three to two hundred and eighty, inclusive, as follows:

§ 263. **Court of claims.**—The board of claims is continued, and shall hereafter be known as the court of claims. The court consists of the commissioners of claims now in office and their successors, who shall hereafter be known and designated as judges of the court of claims. Judges shall be appointed by the governor, by and with the advice and consent of the senate. Whenever the term of office of a judge shall expire, his successor shall be appointed for a full term of six years from the expiration of the preceding term, and all terms shall expire on the thirty-first day of December. Vacancies shall be filled in like manner for the remainder of the unexpired term. By an order to be filed in the office of the secretary of state the governor shall designate one of the judges as a presiding judge, who shall act as such during his term; two of the judges shall constitute a quorum for the transaction of business.

§ 264. **Jurisdiction.**— The court of claims possesses all the powers and jurisdiction of the board of claims. It also has jurisdiction to hear and determine a private claim against the state, which shall have accrued within two years before the claim is filed. It may also hear and determine any claim on the part of the state against the claimant, or against his assignor at the time of the assignment; and must render judgment for such sum as should be paid by or to the state. But the court has no jurisdiction of a claim submitted by law to any other tribunal or officer for audit or determination. Where jurisdiction to hear and determine a claim is conferred upon the court by a special law, the liability of the state is not thereby implied, but such a claim is subject to defense and counterclaim by the state in the same manner and to the same extent as if presented under a general law.

§ 265. **Rules and procedure.**— The court may establish rules for its government, and the regulation of practice therein; prescribe the forms and methods of procedure before it, vacate or modify judgments, and grant new trials.

§ 266. **Officers.**— The court shall appoint, and may at pleasure remove, a clerk, a deputy clerk, a stenographer, and a marshal, who shall also act as messenger; and they shall perform such duties as the court may prescribe. Before entering upon the duties of his office, the clerk shall make and file in the office of the comptroller, a bond for the faithful performance of his duties in an amount and with sufficient sureties to be approved by at least two of the judges, which approval shall be indorsed on said bond.

§ 267. **Seal of court.**— The court shall adopt and procure an official seal, with suitable device and inscription. A description of such seal, with an impression thereof, shall be filed in the office of the secretary of state. The expense of procuring such seal shall be paid out of the contingent fund of the court.

§ 268. **Sessions, duty of sheriff.**—The court shall hold at least four sessions in each year at the capitol in the city of Albany, and it may also hold adjourned or special sessions at such other times and places in the state as it may determine. It may also hold a session and take testimony where the claimant resides or where the claim is alleged to have arisen, or in the vicinity, and may view any premises affected by the proceeding. The sheriff of any county, except Albany, shall furnish for the use of the court suitable rooms in the court house of his county for any session ordered to be held thereat, and shall if required attend said session. His fees for attendance shall be paid out of the contingent fund of the court, at the same rate as for attending a term of the supreme court, in that county.

§ 269. **Judgments.**—The determination of the court upon a claim shall be by a judgment to be entered in a book to be kept by the clerk for that purpose, and signed and certified by him. Within ten days after the entry of the judgment, the clerk shall serve a certified copy thereof on the claimant or his attorney and also upon the attorney-general. If the claim arises in a case where the state seeks to appropriate or has appropriated land for a public use, the judgment shall contain a description of such land. A transcript of a judgment in favor of the state, certified by the clerk of the court, may be filed and docketed in the clerk's office of any county; and upon being so docketed shall become and be a lien upon the property of the claimant in that county, to the same extent and enforceable by execution in the same manner, as a judgment of the supreme court. A final judgment against the claimant on any claim prosecuted as provided in this article shall forever bar any further claim or demand against the state arising out of the matters involved in the controversy.

§ 270. **Duty of attorney-general and superintendent of public works.**— The attorney-general shall represent the state in all proceedings relating to claims. In all cases of canal claims the superintendent of public works on request from the attorney-general, shall furnish such assistance as he may require in subpoenaing witnesses and preparing the cases for trial. The attorney-general may designate a clerk in his office to assist in the preparation of cases for trial, and to attend a term of the court. His reasonable and necessary expenses while engaged in such duty, except in Albany, when approved by the attorney-general, shall be audited by the court and paid out of its contingent fund.

§ 271. **Record of proceedings; report**—The court shall keep a record of its proceedings, and, at the commencement of each session of the legislature, and at such other times during the session as it may deem proper, or as the senate or assembly may request, report to the legislature the claims upon which it has finally acted, with a statement of the judgment rendered in each case.

§ 272. **Expense of procuring testimony on commission.**—When testimony is taken on commission at the instance of the claimant, the expense thereof including the fees of the commissioner, shall be paid by the claimant; and when taken at the instance of the state, such fees and all expense incurred by the attorney-general shall be paid out of the contingent fund of the court.

§ 273. **Annual report to comptroller.**— On the first day of January in each year, the clerk shall report, to the comptroller, under oath, a detailed statement of his disbursements made under the direction of the court from its contingent fund during the preceding year.

§ 274. **Cost not to be taxed.**— Costs, witnesses fees and disbursements shall not be taxed, nor shall counsel or attorney fees be allowed by the court to any party.

§ 275. **Appeals.**—Either party may appeal from an order or judgment of the court of claims to the appellate division of the supreme court of the third department. The appeal from a judgment may be taken upon questions of law or of fact, or both, or for an alleged excess or insufficiency of the judgment. Upon such appeal, the court may affirm, reverse, or modify the judgment, or dismiss the appeal, or grant a new trial. The provisions of this code relating to appeals in the supreme court apply, so far as practicable, to appeals from orders or judgments of the court of claims, except as modified in this article.

§ 276. **Time and manner of taking appeal.**— An appeal must be taken within thirty days after the entry and service of the order, or the service by the clerk of a certified copy of the judgment, by serving upon the claimant or his attorney, or upon the attorney-general, and upon the clerk, in like manner as in the supreme court, a written notice to the effect that the appellant appeals from the order or from the judgment or from a specified part thereof, and briefly stating the grounds of the appeal.

§ 277. **Case on appeal.**—With the notice of appeal from a judgment, the appellant shall serve upon the adverse party a case containing so much of the evidence as the appellant may deem necessary to present the questions raised by the appeal. Within ten days after the service of the case, the respondent may propose and serve amendments thereto, and the case may be settled upon five days' notice by any judge of the court. Notice of the settlement may be served by either party, within ten days after service of the proposed amendments. The court or a judge thereof may extend the time for serving a case or amendments.

§ 278. **Preference on appeals.**—An appeal taken after the calendar for a term of the appellate court is prepared may be placed thereon upon the application of the attorney-general at any time during the then current term, and brought on for hearing as a preferred cause upon a notice of fourteen days.

§ 279. **Salary of judge of court of claims.**— Each judge of the court of claims shall receive an annual compensation of five thousand dollars, payable monthly, and also his necessary expenses, not exceeding five hundred dollars per annum.

§ 280. **Salaries of officers of court of claims.**— Each officer of the court of claims shall receive an annual salary, payable monthly, and other compensation as follows:

1. The clerk, four thousand dollars.

2. The deputy clerk, two thousand five hundred dollars.

3. The stenographer, two thousand five hundred dollars and five cents a folio for copies of minutes and testimony furnished at the request of the claimant.

4. The marshal, including also his services as messenger, twelve hundred dollars. The clerk, deputy clerk, stenographer and marshal shall be paid their actual expenses while in the discharge of their respective duties, elsewhere than in the city of Albany, to be audited by the court and paid from the contingent fund. No charge shall be made against the state by the clerk or the stenographer for copies of minutes, testimony or papers, furnished to the attorney-general or to the court, or filed in the office of the clerk.

§ 2. Section two of the code of civil procedure is hereby amended by adding a subdivision thereto, numbered fifteen, as follows:

15. The court of claims.

§ 3. The terms of office of the two commissioners of claims in office when this act takes effect, who by their appointment have the shortest time to serve, shall expire on the thirty-first day of December, eighteen hundred and ninety-seven. The term of the other commissioner shall expire on the thirty-first day of December, eighteen hundred and ninety-nine. Their successors shall be appointed in the manner provided by section two hundred and sixty-three of the code of civil procedure. The officers of the board of claims in office when this act takes effect shall respectively continue as officers of the court of claims until changed pursuant to section two hundred and sixty-six of the code of civil procedure.

§ 4. The laws enumerated in the schedule hereto annexed are repealed. Such repeal shall not revive a law repealed by any law hereby repealed, but shall include all laws amendatory of the laws hereby repealed.

§ 5. The repeal of a law, or any part of it, specified in the annexed schedule, shall not affect or impair any act done or right accruing, accrued or acquired under or by virtue of the laws so repealed, but the same may be asserted, enforced or prosecuted as fully and to the same extent, as if such laws had not been repealed; and all actions or proceedings commenced under or by virtue of the laws so repealed, or otherwise, and pending in the board of claims when this act takes effect, may be prosecuted and defended to final effect in the court of claims, in the same manner as if instituted in that court, unless it shall be otherwise specially provided by law; and all records of the board of claims are hereby transferred to and shall become and be the records of the court of claims.

§ 6. This act shall take effect immediately.

SCHEDULE OF LAWS REPEALED.

Laws of —	Chapter.	Sections.	Subject.
1883......	205....	All....	Establishing board of claims and defining its powers and duties.
1884......	60....	All....	Amends L. 1883, ch. 205, §§ 2, 4, 6, 7, 9-11, 13.
1884......	85....	All....	Jurisdiction relative to claims for animals killed.
1885......	355....	All....	Returns on appeals from decisions of old board of canal appraisers.
1887......	507....	All....	Amends L. 1883, ch. 205, § 10.
1888......	365....	All....	Amends L. 1883, ch. 205, §§ 2, 3, 5, 16.
1889......	68....	All....	Amends L. 1883, ch. 205, §§ 2, 13.
1889......	522....	All....	Salary of marshal of board of claims.
1890......	403....	All....	Amends L. 1883, ch. 205, § 2.
1893......	425....	All....	Amends L. 1883, ch. 205, § 12.
1896......	451....	All....	Amends L. 1883, ch. 205, §§ 10, 11.

Chap. 37.

AN ACT to amend the code of civil procedure, relative to the right of inheritance of illegitimate children.

Became a law March 9, 1897, with the approval of the Governor. Passed, a majority being present.

The People of the State of New York, represented in Senate and Assembly, do enact as follows:

Section 1. Section twenty-seven hundred and thirty-two of the code of civil procedure is hereby amended by adding thereto a new subdivision to be known as subdivision fifteen, and to read as follows:

15. If a woman die, leaving illegitimate children, and no lawful issue, such children inherit her personal property as if legitimate.

§ 2. This act shall take effect immediately.

Chap. 38.

AN ACT to amend section twelve hundred and seventy-three of the code of civil procedure, with respect to confessions of judgment by married women.

Became a law March 9, 1897, with the approval of the Governor. Passed, a majority being present.

The People of the State of New York, represented in Senate and Assembly, do enact as follows:

Section 1. Section twelve hundred and seventy-three of the code of civil procedure is hereby amended so as to read as follows:

§ 1273. A judgment by confession may be entered, without action, either for money due or to become due, or to secure a person against contingent liability in behalf of the defendant, or both, as prescribed in this article. A married woman may confess such a judgment.

§ 2. This act shall take effect September first, eighteen hundred and ninety-seven.

Chap. 40.

AN ACT to amend section seven hundred and ninety-seven of the code of civil procedure.

Became a law March 9, 1897, with the approval of the Governor. Passed, a majority being present.

The People of the State of New York, represented in Senate and Assembly, do enact as follows:

Code amended.
Section 1. Section seven hundred and ninety-seven of the code of civil procedure is hereby amended so as to read as follows:

§ 797. Where the service is not personal, it may be made as follows:

Service of papers. mode of.
1. Upon a party or an attorney, through the post-office, by depositing the paper, properly inclosed in a post-paid wrapper, in the post-office or in any post-office box regularly maintained by the government of the United States and under the care of the post-office of the party, or the attorney serving it, directed to the person to be served at the address, within the state, designated by him for that purpose, upon the preceding papers in the action; or, where he has not made such a designation, at his place of residence, or the place where he keeps an office, according to the best information which can conveniently be obtained concerning the same.

2. Upon an attorney, during his absence from his office, by leaving the paper with his partner or clerk therein, or with a person having charge thereof.

3. Upon an attorney, if there is no person in charge of his office, and the service is made between six o'clock in the morning and nine o'clock in the evening, either by leaving it, in a conspicuous place in his office, or by depositing it, inclosed in a sealed wrapper, directed to him in his office letter-box; or, if the office is not open, so as to admit of leaving the paper therein, and there is no office letter-box, by leaving it at his residence, within the state, with a person of suitable age and discretion.

4. Upon a party, by leaving the paper at his residence within the state, between six o'clock in the morning and nine o'clock in the evening, with a person of suitable age and discretion.

§ 2. This act shall take effect September first, eighteen hundred and ninety-seven.

Chap. 42.

AN ACT to amend the penal code by adding a section to be known as section four hundred and twelve.

Became a law March 9, 1897, with the approval of the Governor. Passed, a majority being present.

The People of the State of New York, represented in Senate and Assembly, do enact as follows:

Section 1. The following section is hereby added to and made a part of the penal code to be known as section four hundred and twelve thereof. *Code amended.*

§ 412, subdivision 1. A person (other than a duly licensed physician or surgeon engaged in the lawful practice of his profession) who has in his possession any narcotic or anaesthetic substance, compound or preparation, capable of producing stupor or unconsciousness, with intent to administer the same or cause the same to be administered to another, without the latter's consent, unless by direction of a duly licensed physician, is guilty of a felony, punishable by imprisonment in the state prison for not more than ten years. *Possession or administering of narcotic substance, etc.*

2. The possession by any person (other than as exempted in the foregoing subdivision) of any such narcotic or anaesthetic substance or compound, concealed or furtively carried on the person, is presumptive evidence of an intent to administer the same or cause the same to be administered in violation of the provisions of this section.

§ 2. This act shall take effect immediately.

Chap. 43.

AN ACT to reappropriate the unexpended balance of the appropriation for the improvement of the Erie, Champlain and Oswego canals; and to provide for the increase of the sinking fund.

Became a law March 9, 1897, with the approval of the Governor. Passed, three-fifths being present.

The People of the State of New York, represented in Senate and Assembly, do enact as follows:

Reappropriation.

Section 1. The sum of three million one hundred and seventy-nine thousand one hundred and twelve dollars and fifty-five cents, being the unexpended balance of the sum of four million dollars appropriated by chapter seventy-nine of the laws of eighteen hundred and ninety-five, for the improvement of the Erie, Champlain and Oswego canals, is hereby reappropriated for the same purpose.

Transfer of interest to sinking fund.

§ 2. In addition to the provision which the comptroller is required to make for the sinking fund created by the second section of said act, he shall transfer to the said sinking fund the interest accruing on deposits of moneys received from the sale of the bonds therein authorized.

§ 3. This act shall take effect immediately.

Chap. 45.

AN ACT to confer upon the board of claims jurisdiction to hear, audit and determine the claim of the village of Watkins, for moneys expended in improving Glen creek in said village.

Became a law March 10, 1897, with the approval of the Governor. Passed, three-fifths being present.

The People of the State of New York, represented in Senate and Assembly, do enact as follows:

Jurisdiction to hear claim.

Section 1. Jurisdiction is hereby conferred upon the board of claims to hear, audit and determine the alleged claim of the village of Watkins for moneys expended in improving Glen creek in said village.

Determination and award.

§ 2. If the facts proved before the board of claims shall establish a just claim in favor of the village of Watkins, against the state, for moneys so expended in improving said creek, the board shall determine the amount of money so expended, and shall award therefor such sum as may be just and equitable not exceeding the sum of two thousand dollars. Such claim must be filed within one year after passage of this act.

§ 3. Either party may take an appeal to the appellate division of *Appeal from award.* the supreme court of the third department, from any award made under the authority of this act, provided such appeal be taken by service of a notice of appeal within thirty days after service of a copy of the award.

§ 4. This act shall take effect immediately.

Chap. 47.

AN ACT to amend section one of chapter four hundred and sixty-eight of the laws of eighteen hundred and ninety-four, being "An act to provide for the establishment of a home for the aged and dependent veteran and his wife, veterans' mothers, widows, and army nurses, residents of New York," and making an appropriation therefor.

Became a law March 10, 1897, with the approval of the Governor.
Passed, three-fifths being present.

The People of the State of New York, represented in Senate and Assembly, do enact as follows:

Section 1. Section one of chapter four hundred and sixty-eight *Act amended.* of the laws of eighteen hundred and ninety-four is hereby amended so as to read as follows:

§ 1. There shall be established in this state a home for the aged *Establishment of home.* dependent veteran and his wife, veterans' mothers, widows, and army nurses, which shall be located within the state at a point which shall be determined as hereinafter provided, said home to be known as "New York State Woman's Relief Corps Home."

§ 2. The sum of seven thousand dollars, or so much thereof as *Appropriation for maintenance.* may be necessary, is hereby appropriated out of any money in the treasury not otherwise appropriated, to be paid by the treasurer on the warrant of the comptroller, for the maintenance of said institution for the fiscal year ending September thirty, eighteen hundred and ninety-seven.

§ 3. This act shall take effect immediately.

Chap. 48.

AN ACT to amend the poor law, in relation to temporary or out-door relief.

**Became a law March 11, 1897, with the approval of the Governor.
Passed, three-fifths being present.**

The People of the State of New York, represented in Senate and Assembly, do enact as follows:

Section 1. Section thirteen of chapter two hundred and twenty-five of the laws of eighteen hundred and ninety-six, entitled " An act in relation to the poor, constituting chapter twenty-seven of the general laws," is hereby amended to read as follows:

§ 13. **Supervisors and members of town boards may direct as to temporary or out-door relief to the poor.**—The board of supervisors of any county may make such rules and regulations as it may deem proper in regard to the manner of furnishing temporary or out-door relief to the poor in the several towns in said county, and provided the board of supervisors shall have failed to make any such rules and regulations the town board of any town may make such rules and regulations as it may deem proper in regard to furnishing temporary or out-door relief to the poor in their respective towns, by the overseer or overseers of the poor thereof, and also in regard to the amount such overseer or overseers of the poor may expend for the relief of each person or family, and after the board of supervisors of any county, or the town board of any town, shall have made such rules and regulations, it shall not be necessary for the overseers of the poor of the towns in said county, where such rules and regulations were made by the board of supervisors, or if in a town by the said town board, to procure an order from the supervisor of the town, or the sanction of the superintendent of the poor to expend money for the relief of any person or family, unless the board of supervisors of such county or the town board of such town shall so direct; but this section shall not apply to the counties of New York and Kings.

§ 2. This act shall take effect immediately.

Chap. 54.

AN ACT to amend the general municipal law, relative to the rate of interest on bonds refunding municipal indebtedness.

Became a law March 17, 1897, with the approval of the Governor.
Passed, three-fifths being present.

The People of the State of New York, represented in Senate and Assembly, do enact as follows:

Section 1. Section seven of chapter six hundred and eighty-five of the laws of eighteen hundred and ninety-two, entitled "An act in relation to municipal corporations, constituting chapter seventeen of the general laws," as amended by chapter four hundred and sixty-six of the laws of eighteen hundred and ninety-three, is hereby amended to read as follows:

§ 7. **Funded and bonded debts.**—The bonded indebtedness of a municipal corporation, including interest due or unpaid, or any part thereof, may be paid up or retired by the issue of the new substituted bonds for like amounts by the board of supervisors or supervisor, board, council or officers having in charge the payment of such bonds. Such new bonds shall only be issued when the existing bonds can be retired by the substitution of the new bonds therefor, or can be paid up by money realized by the sale of such new bonds. Where such bonded indebtedness shall become due within two years from the issue of such new bonds, such new bonds may be issued and sold to provide money in advance to pay up such existing bonds when they shall become due. Such new bonds shall contain a recital that they are issued pursuant to this section, which recital shall be conclusive evidence of their validity and of the regularity of the issue; shall be made payable not less than one or more than thirty years from their date; shall bear date and draw interest from the date of the payment of the existing bonds, or the receipt of the money to pay the same, at not exceeding the rate of five per centum per annum, payable quarterly, semi-annually or annually; and an amount equal to not less than two per centum of the whole amount of such new bonds shall be payable each year after the issue thereof. Such new bonds shall be sold and negotiated at the best price obtainable, not less than their par value; shall be valid and binding on the municipal corporation issuing them; and until payable shall be exempt from taxation for town, county, municipal or state purposes. All bonds and coupons retired or paid shall be immediately canceled. A certificate shall be issued by the officer, board or body issuing such new bonds. stating the amount of existing bonds, and of the new bonds so issued. which shall be forthwith filed in the office of the county clerk. Except as provided in this section, new bonds shall not be issued in pursuance thereof, for bonds of a municipal corporation adjudged invalid by the final judgment of a competent court. A majority of the taxpayers of a town, voting at a general town meeting, or special town meeting duly called, may authorize the issue in pursuance of this section of new bonds for such invalid bonds, and each new bond so issued shall contain substantially the following recital: " The issue of this bond is duly authorized by a vote of the taxpayers of the said town," which shall be conclusive evidence of such fact. The payment, adjustment or compromise of a part of the bonded indebtedness of a municipal corporation shall not be deemed an admission of the validity or a recognition of any part of the bonded indebtedness of such municipal corporation not paid, adjusted or compromised.

§ 2. This act shall take effect immediately.

Chap. 62.

AN ACT to authorize the appointment of a county detective in counties of more than one hundred and twenty-five thousand inhabitants and to fix the compensation of such detective.

Became a law March 18, 1897, with the approval of the Governor.
Passed, three-fifths being present.

The People of the State of New York, represented in Senate and Assembly, do enact as follows:

Appointment of county detective.

Section 1. It shall be lawful for the county judge of any county in this state, which by the last federal census contained a population of not less than one hundred and twenty-five thousand inhabitants, and which adjoins a county containing a population of not less than one million inhabitants to appoint a detective to be known as the county detective for such county. Such appointment shall be in writing and signed by the county judge and filed in the office of the clerk of the county. Before entering upon the duties of his office, such county detective shall make and file the constitutional oath of office and shall enter into an undertaking to the people of the county conditioned for the faithful discharge of his duties as such county detective. The county detective so appointed shall continue in office for the period of three years from the date of his appointment and may be removed by the county judge after a hearing upon charges duly made by the district attorney, and shall receive for compensation the sum of fifteen hundred dollars per annum, payable monthly, and also his traveling and other necessary expenses, which shall be approved and audited by the district attorney, and such salary and traveling and other expenses shall be a

Oath of office and bond.

Term.

Compensation.

county charge and shall be paid monthly by the treasurer of such county in the same manner as the salaries of other county officers are paid. The provisions of this act shall not apply to the county Exemption. of Westchester.

§ 2. This act shall take effect immediately.

Chap. 64.

AN ACT to amend the fisheries, game and forest law, and the act amendatory thereof, relating to the shooting of web-footed wild fowl, in Long Island sound, Great South bay, Shinnecock and Peconic bays.

Became a law March 18, 1897, with the approval of the Governor. Passed, three-fifths being present.

The People of the State of New York, represented in Senate and Assembly, do enact as follows:

Section 1. Section one hundred and sixty-two of chapter four hundred and eighty-eight of the laws of eighteen hundred and ninety-two, the title to which was amended by chapter three hundred and ninety-five of the laws of eighteen hundred and ninety-five, to read, "An act relating to game, fish and wild animals and to the forest preserve and Adirondack park, constituting chapter thirty-one of the general laws, and to be known as the fisheries, game and forest law," as amended by chapter nine hundred and seventy-four of the laws of eighteen hundred and ninety-five, is hereby amended to read as follows:

§ 162. **Exceptions as to wild fowl.**—Floating devises may be used for the purpose of shooting web-footed wild fowl therefrom in Long Island sound, Great South bay, Shinnecock and Peconic bays, and in any part of said counties said birds may be pursued and killed from boats propelled by hand, and from any sailboats in Long Island sound, Gardiner and Peconic bays. Whoever shall violate or attempt to violate the provisions of this section shall be deemed guilty of a misdemeanor, and in addition thereto shall be liable to a penalty of twenty-five dollars for each bird killed or possessed contrary to the provisions of this section.

§ 2. This act shall take effect immediately.

Chap. 65.

AN ACT to release to Charles A. Engfer and Ottillia Engfer, his
wife, the right, title and interest of the people of the state of
New York to certain real estate situate in the city of Rochester,
county of Monroe.

Became a law March 18, 1897, with the approval of the Governor.
Passed, three-fifths being present.

*The People of the State of New York, represented in Senate and
Assembly, do enact as follows:*

Release of
interest of
state.

Section 1. All the estate, right, title and interest of the people
of the state in and to all that certain piece or parcel of land situate in
the city of Rochester, and county of Monroe, known as lot number
ninety-five on a map of a subdivision of part of the Colvin tract
made by F. J. M. Cornell, surveyor for John H. Martindale and
George F. Danforth and recorded in Monroe county clerk's office
in liber one hundred and nineteen of deeds at page four hundred
and ninety-eight; said lot being on the west side of Colvin street
and being forty feet front and rear and one hundred and sixty-five
feet deep. Excepting however so much of said lot number ninety-
five as was taken by the city of Rochester for the purpose of extending Syke street, being seven feet in width and extending the full
depth of said lot, more particularly described in the report of the
commissioners to extend Syke street filed in Monroe county clerk's
office February fifth, eighteen hundred and eighty-four; thus leaving
the premises hereby intended to be conveyed situate on the northwest corner of Colvin and Syke streets, being thirty-three feet front
on Colvin street and same in rear and extending back of equal width
westerly along the north line of Syke street one hundred and sixty-
five feet, is hereby released to Charles A. Engfer and Ottillia Engfer,
his wife, of the town of Chili, county of Monroe, and to his heirs
and assigns forever.

Proviso.

§ 2. Nothing herein contained shall be construed to impair, release
or discharge any claim, right or interest of any heir at law, devisee
or grantee, purchaser or creditor by judgment, mortgage or otherwise
in and to said premises or any part or parcel thereof.

§ 3. This act shall take effect immediately.

Chap. 71.

AN ACT conferring jurisdiction upon the board of claims to hear and determine the claim of Frederick C. Withers and Walter Dickson, composing the firm of Withers and Dickson, against the state, and to make an award therefor.

Became a law March 18, 1897, with the approval of the Governor.
Passed, three-fifths being present.

The People of the State of New York, represented in Senate and Assembly, do enact as follows:

Section 1. Jurisdiction is hereby conferred upon the board of claims to hear and determine the alleged claim of Frederick C. Withers and Walter Dickson, composing the firm of Withers and Dickson, against the state for work, labor and services alleged to have been performed, and money paid out and expended by them as architects, in preparing and drafting upon the request and under the authority of the managers of the Hudson River State Hospital at Poughkeepsie, plans and studies for the following buildings proposed to be erected on the grounds of the said Hudson River State Hospital, viz.: Annex to main building; infirmary; pavilion for convalescent women; hospital for Falkill farm; and to award thereon such sum as the said board shall deem just and reasonable, although such claim may have accrued more than two years prior to the time when it is filed. *Jurisdiction to hear claim.*

§ 2. Either party may take an appeal to the appellate division of the supreme court of the third department from any award made under authority of this act, provided such an appeal be taken by service of a notice of appeal within thirty days after service of a copy of the award. *Appeal from award.*

§ 3. This act shall take effect immediately.

Chap. 78.

AN ACT to amend the public buildings law, relating to the completion of the capitol.

Became a law March 22, 1897, with the approval of the Governor.
Passed, three-fifths being present.

The People of the State of New York, represented in Senate and Assembly, do enact as follows:

Section 1. Sections six, seven, eight, nine, ten and eleven of chapter two hundred and twenty-seven of the laws of eighteen hundred and ninety-three, entitled "An act relating to public buildings, constituting chapter fourteen of the general laws," as amended by chapter seven hundred and thirty-seven of the laws of eighteen hundred and ninety-five, are hereby amended to read as follows:

§ 6. **Capitol commissioner.**— The governor, by and with the advice and consent of the senate, shall appoint, and may at his pleasure remove, an officer to be known as the capitol commissioner, who shall receive an annual salary of seven thousand five hundred dollars. Before entering on the duties of his office, he shall execute an official undertaking in the sum of fifty thousand dollars with sufficient sureties approved by the comptroller and filed in his office. In addition to his other duties, the capitol commissioner shall, without additional compensation, prepare the plans and specifications, and act as architect of all buildings constructed at the expense of the state.

§ 7. **Completion of capitol.**— The construction and completion of the unfinished portions of the capitol, and all its approaches, and the care and custody of the unfinished portions, and the laying out of the capitol grounds, shall be under the supervision of the superintendent of public works. He shall examine the drawings and specifications for such work as prepared and submitted by the capitol commissioner, alter the same, and if, in his judgment, desirable, approve such drawings and specifications, and indorse his approval thereof when completed to his satisfaction. He shall see that the materials furnished and the work performed are in accordance with such plans and specifications. He may continue in his employment any of the clerks and assistants appointed by the capitol commission under chapter seven hundred and thirty-seven of the laws of eighteen hundred and ninety-five, and may employ other assistants as he deems necessary.

§ 8. **Contracts** — The work of completing the construction of the capitol and its approaches shall be done by contract in accordance with plans and specifications which the capitol commissioner must prepare and which must be approved by the superintendent of public works, who may determine whether such work shall be done by one contract or by two or more contracts, and may make contracts accordingly. Before letting any contract, the superintendent of public works shall publish an advertisement therefor, not less than two or more than four weeks in ten newspapers so distributed that such advertisement shall not be published in more than one newspaper in the same city, except in the city of New York, where it may be published in not more than four newspapers. Except as herein provided, a contract shall be made with the lowest responsible bidder, who will furnish security approved by the superintendent of public works for the faithful performance thereof, but such superintendent may accept such bids as he deems most favorable to the state, or he may reject all bids, if deemed unfavorable or disadvantageous to the state, or if there shall appear to be collusion between the parties, and may advertise anew for such work. Such contracts on behalf of the state shall be made by the superintendent of public works, but no contracts shall be valid unless approved by the governor, and each contract must reserve to the governor the right to declare it forfeited when, in his judgment, it is not being performed for the best interest of the state.

§ 9. **Payments on contracts.**— Payments for work done or materials furnished shall be made upon the certificate of the capitol commissioner, approved by the superintendent of public works, and audited by the comptroller. Payment for work done or materials furnished under a contract shall not exceed eighty per centum of the value thereof, until the contract is completed.

§ 10. **Powers and duties of capitol commissioner.**— The capitol commissioner, under the direction of the superintendent of public works, shall have the supervision of the work of constructing the unfinished portions of the capitol and its approaches, shall see that the work is performed in accordance with the plans and specifications under which the contract is made, and that the interests of the state are fully protected.

§ 11. **Accounts.**— The superintendent of public works shall keep and render to the comptroller monthly an accurate account of all his expenses and obligations. The account shall be audited by the comptroller and the amount allowed by him shall be paid upon his warrant by the treasurer, who shall take proper receipts and vouchers therefor, which shall be kept on file in his office.

§ 2. Nothing herein contained shall be construed to affect any valid contract made by the capitol commission created by chapter seven hundred and thirty-seven of the laws of eighteen hundred and ninety-five. That commission is hereby abolished and all its powers and responsibilities are transferred to, vested in and imposed upon the superintendent of public works, except as otherwise provided in this act.

§ 3. This act shall take effect immediately.

Chap. 80.

AN ACT to amend the tax law.

Became a law March 22, 1897, with the approval of the Governor.
Passed, three-fifths being present.

The People of the State of New York, represented in Senate and Assembly, do enact as follows:

Section 1. Subdivision six of section four of chapter nine hundred and eight of the laws of eighteen hundred and ninety-six, being chapter twenty-four of the general laws, is hereby ameded so as to read as follows: Tax law amended.

6. Bonds of this state to be hereafter issued by the comptroller to carry out the provisions of chapter seventy-nine of the laws of eighteen hundred and ninety-five, and bonds of a municipal corporation heretofore issued for the purpose of paying up or retiring the bonded indebtedness of such corporation.

§ 2. This act shall take effect immediately.

Chap. 81.

AN ACT in relation to the New York law library and the library of the supreme court in the first district.

Became a law March 22, 1897, with the approval of the Governor.
Passed, three-fifths being present.

The People of the State of New York, represented in Senate and Assembly, do enact as follows:

Section 1. There is hereby appropriated, and shall be paid by the state treasurer, upon the warrant of the state comptroller, to the presiding justice of the appellate division of the supreme court in the first department, the sum of five thousand dollars for the purchase and binding of books for the law library of the appellate division of the supreme court in the first department, and the law library of the supreme court in the first district, the books so purchased to be distributed between these two libraries as shall be directed by the justices of the appellate division in said department.

§ 2. This act shall take effect immediately.

Chap. 83.

AN ACT providing for the audit and payment, by cities, of moneys due by reason of the termination of licenses on June thirtieth, eighteen hundred and ninety-six.

Became a law March 22, 1897, with the approval of the Governor.
Passed, three-fifths being present.

The People of the State of New York, represented in Senate and Assembly, do enact as follows:

Section 1. The officer or board in each city charged by law with the duty of auditing claims against such city, is hereby authorized and directed, upon the presentation of a claim therefor, to audit and allow within thirty days after the passage of this act, to any person who on the thirtieth day of June, eighteen hundred and ninety-six, was the holder of a valid license for the sale of strong or spirituous liquors, wines, ale or beer, granted under the provisions of any law in force on the twenty-second day of March, eighteen hundred and ninety-six, and which license by virtue of the provisions of section four of chapter one hundred and twelve of the laws of eighteen hundred and ninety-six, known as the liquor tax law, was terminated on the said thirtieth day of June, such sum as he may be entitled to receive under said section four. Claims not presented within thirty days as herein prescribed, may be audited and allowed by such officer or board at any time in the same manner and within the same time as other claims against the city.

§ 2. The officer or board making such audit shall immediately make a certificate thereof in duplicate, showing the name of the claimant and the amount claimed and allowed, and shall deliver one of such certificates to the claimant and file the other with the disbursing officer of the city. *Certificate of audit.*

§ 3. The amount allowed upon such a claim shall be paid by the disbursing officer, on demand, from any moneys belonging to the city heretofore or hereafter received under the liquor tax law. *Payment of claims.*

§ 4. This act shall take effect immediately.

Chap. 84.

AN ACT to amend the town law, authorizing town boards to borrow the amount of a special appropriation for use prior to raising the same in the annual tax levy.

Became a law March 22, 1897, with the approval of the Governor.
Passed, three-fifths being present.

The People of the State of New York, represented in Senate and Assembly, do enact as follows:

Section 1. Article seven of chapter five hundred and sixty-nine of the laws of eighteen hundred and ninety, entitled "An act in relation to towns, constituting chapter twenty of the general laws," known as the town law, is hereby amended by adding thereto a new section, following section one hundred eighty-three, to be known as section one hundred and eighty-four and to read as follows: *Town law amended.*

§ 184. Whenever a town meeting shall vote a special appropriation of money in the sum of five hundred dollars or more, or an appropriation for highway purposes or for the support of the poor during the current year, to be levied upon the taxable property of the town, the town board shall have power to borrow the sum so appropriated upon the faith and credit of the town, and to issue therefor a certificate or certificates of indebtedness, bearing interest and payable at such date or dates as may be fixed by said board, and the proceeds *Borrowing of amount of special appropriations.*

Certifica-
tion and
raising of
of same.

of such loan shall be placed to the credit of the public officers charged by law with the expenditure of said moneys. A statement of the amount maturing on such certificate of indebtedness shall be certified by the town board at its second meeting and delivered to the supervisor of the town, to be by him presented to the board of supervisors of his county at its annual meeting, and the said board of supervisors shall cause the amount specified in such certified statement to be levied and raised upon the taxable property of the town in the same manner as they are directed to levy and raise other town charges. .

§ 2. This act shall take effect immediately.

Chap. 85.

AN ACT to provide for the representation of the state of New York in the Negro department of the Tennessee centennial at Nashville, and to amend chapter seven of the laws of eighteen hundred and ninety-seven.

Became a law March 22, 1897, with the approval of the Gover or.
Passed, three-fifths being present.

The People of the State of New York, represented in Senate and Assembly, do enact as follows:

Appointment of delegates confirmed.

Section 1. The appointment by the governor of delegates to represent the state of New York in the negro department of the Tennessee centennial and international exhibition to be held at Nashville, is ratified and confirmed, and for the purposes of this act, such delegates shall be known as the "New York commission to the negro department of the Tennessee centennial." Such commission shall encourage and promote a full exhibit of the commercial, educational, industrial, artistic and other interest of the colored citizens of this state at such exhibition and, in its discretion, may provide during the exhibition a room or rooms for the official headquarters, and for the comfort and convenience of citizens and exhibitors at an expense not exceeding the sum hereinafter named.

Powers and duties of commission.

Appropriation for expenses.

§ 2. The sum of three thousand dollars is hereby appropriated out of any money in the treasury not otherwise appropriated for the purposes of this act. Such money shall be paid by the treasurer, on the warrant of the comptroller, issued upon a requisition signed by the president and secretary of the commission, accompanied by an estimate of the expenses for the payment of which the money so drawn is to be applied. Within ninety days after the close of the exposition, this commission shall make a verified report to the comp-

Reports of commis-

troller of all disbursements made by it, and shall make a report within three months from the close of the exhibition to the governor, to be transmitted by him to the legislature.

§ 3. Section three of chapter seven of the laws of eighteen hundred and ninety-seven is hereby amended to read as follows: *Appropriation for expenses.*

§ 3. The sum of nine thousand dollars, or so much thereof as may be necessary, is hereby appropriated out of any money in the treasury not otherwise appropriated, for the purposes of this act. Such money shall be paid by the treasurer, on the warrant of the comptroller, issued upon a requisition signed by the president and secretary of the commission, accompanied by an estimate of the expenses for the payment of which the money so drawn is to be applied. Within ninety days after the close of the exhibition such commission shall *Reports of commission.* make a verified report to the comptroller of all disbursements made by it, and shall return to the state treasury the unexpended balance of money drawn in pursuance of this act.

§ 4. This act shall take effect immediately.

Chap. 92.

AN ACT to amend section ninety-four of the code of civil procedure, relating to the appointment of interpreters in Kings county.

Became a law March 23, 1897, with the approval of the Governor.
Passed, three-fifths being present.

Accepted by the city.

The People of the State of New York, represented in Senate and Assembly, do enact as follows:

Section 1. Section ninety-four of the code of civil procedure is hereby amended so as to read as follows:

§ 94. The justices of the supreme court for the second judicial *Court interpreters.* district, residing in Kings county or a majority of them, may appoint an interpreter or interpreters to attend the terms of the courts of record, except the county court and surrogate's court, held in that county, at which issues of fact are triable, and fix the salaries of such interpreters who shall hold office during good behavior.

§ 2. This act shall take effect immediately.

Chap. 93.

AN ACT for the protection of state nets while in use in any of the
waters of this state.

**Became a law March 23, 1897, with the approval of the Governor.
Passed, three-fifths being present.**

*The People of the State of New York, represented in Senate and
Assembly, do enact as follows:*

Protection
of nets.
Section 1. It shall not be lawful for any person or persons, except
those in charge of state nets, at any time to handle or take out any
fish while confined in a state net, or for any person or persons to
fish in any manner within one hundred feet of any leader or net
Penalty for
violation.
while in use by the state. Whoever shall violate, or attempt to
violate the provisions of this act, shall be deemed guilty of a misdemeanor; and in addition thereto shall be liable to a penalty of
one hundred dollars for each violation thereof.

§ 2. This act shall take effect immediately.

Chap. 94.

AN ACT to amend the fisheries, game and forest law in relation
to fishing in the Saint Lawrence river.

**Became a law March 23, 1897, with the approval of the Governor.
Passed, three-fifths being present.**

*The People of the State of New York, represented in Senate and
Assembly, do enact as follows:*

Game law
amended.
Section 1. Section three hundred and ten of article fifteen of the
fisheries, game and forest law, as provided for by chapter five hundred and thirty-one of the laws of eighteen hundred and ninety-six,
is hereby amended to read as follows:

Applica-
tion of
article.
§ 310. Article to apply to the Saint Lawrence river between Tibbett's Point lighthouse and Saint Regis. This article applies exclusively to the waters of the Saint Lawrence river lying between
an imaginary line drawn from Tibbett's Point lighthouse, about four
miles southwest from Cape Vincent to the Snake Island lighthouse,
about four miles southwest from the city of Kingston, in Ontario,
and the boundary line between the state of New York and the
Dominion of Canada at Saint Regis and to be known for the purpose
of this article as "the waters of the Thousand Islands."

§ 2. This act shall take effect immediately.

Chap. 97.

AN ACT to continue free instruction in natural history, geography
and kindred subjects in certain institutions, and making an appropriation therefor.

Became a law March 23, 1897, with the approval of the Governor.
Passed, three-fifths being present.

*The People of the State of New York, represented in Senate and
Assembly, do enact as follows:*

Section 1. The state superintendent of public instruction is hereby Agreement
authorized to enter into an agreement with the American museum tinuing in-
of natural history, in the city of New York, for continuing the struction.
instruction of natural history, geography and kindred subjects in
the several state normal schools, the normal college of the city of
New York, the training school for teachers in the city of Brooklyn,
the teachers' institutes in the different counties of the state, and
to the teachers in the common schools of the city of New York,
Brooklyn and vicinity, authorized by chapter four hundred and
twenty-eight of the laws of eighteen hundred and eighty-six, by
chapter three hundred and thirty-seven of the laws of eighteen hundred and eighty-eight, by chapter forty-three of the laws of eighteen
hundred and ninety-one, and by chapter six of the laws of eighteen
hundred and ninety-three, for the further term of four years from
the first day of January, eighteen hundred and ninety-seven.

§ 2. Said instruction may include free illustrated lectures to Lectures
artisans, mechanics and other citizens, on such legal holidays as the holidays.
state superintendent and museum authorities may agree upon.

§ 3. The sum of eighteen thousand dollars, payable from the free Appropria-
school fund, is hereby appropriated for the preparation for and the tion.
support and maintenance of said course of instruction, for the year
beginning on the first day of January, eighteen hundred and ninety-
seven; and the sum of eighteen thousand dollars shall be appropriated annually thereafter in the general appropriation bill for the
preparation for and the support and maintenance of said course of
instruction during the term of the agreement authorized by this act.

Chap. 104.

AN ACT to amend section twenty-six hundred and fifty-three-a of
the code of civil procedure, relating to the actions to determine
the validity of probate of wills.

Became a law March 23, 1897, with the approval of the Governor.

Passed, three-fifths being present.

*The People of the State of New York, represented in Senate and
Assembly, do enact as follows:*

Amend-
ment.

Section 1. Section twenty-six hundred and fifty-three-a of the
code of civil procedure is hereby amended so as to read as follows:

Actions to
determine
validity of
probate of
will.

§ 2653a. Any person interested as devisee, legatee or otherwise,
in a will or codicil admitted to probate in this state, as provided
by the code of civil procedure, or any person interested as heir-at-
law, next of kin or otherwise, in any estate, any portion of which
is disposed of, or affected, or any portion of which is attempted to
be disposed of, or affected, by a will or codicil admitted to probate
in this state, as provided by the code of civil procedure, may cause
the validity of the probate thereof to be determined in an action in
the supreme court for the county in which such probate was had.
All the devisees, legatees and heirs of the testator and other interested persons, including the executor or administrator must be parties to the action. Upon the completion of service of all parties,
the plaintiff shall forthwith file the summons and complaint in the
office of the clerk of the court in which said action is begun and
the clerk thereof shall forthwith certify to the clerk of the surrogate's court in which the will has been admitted to probate, the fact
that an action to determine the validity of the probate of such will
has been commenced, and on receipt of such certificate by the surrogate's court, the surrogate shall forthwith transmit to the court in
which such action has been begun a copy of the will, testimony
and all papers relating thereto, and a copy of the decree of probate
attaching the same together, and certifying the same under the seal

Issue of
pleadings
confined.

of the court. The issue of the pleadings in such action shall be
confined to the question of whether the writing produced is or is
not the last will and codicil of the testator, or either. It shall be
tried by a jury and the verdict thereon shall be conclusive, as to
real or personal property, unless a new trial be granted or the judgment thereon be reversed or vacated. On the trial of such issue,

Trial by
jury

the decree of the surrogate admitting the will or codicil to probate
shall be prima facie evidence of the due attestation, execution and
validity of such will or codicil. A certified copy of the testimony
of such of the witnesses examined upon the probate, as are out of
the jurisdiction of the court, dead, or have become incompetent
since the probate, shall be admitted in evidence on the trial. The

party sustaining the will shall be entitled to open and close the evidence and argument. He shall offer the will in probate and rest. The other party shall then offer his evidence. The party sustaining the will shall then offer his other evidence and rebutting testimony may be offered as in other cases. If all the defendants make default in pleading, or if the answers served in said action raise no issues, then the plaintiff may enter judgment as provided in article two of chapter eleven of the code of civil procedure in the case of similar defaults in other actions. If the judgment to be entered in an Judg-ments. action brought under this section is that the writing produced is the last will and codicil, or either, of the testator, said judgment shall also provide that all parties to said action, and all persons claiming under them subsequently to the commencement of the said action, be enjoined from bringing or maintaining any action or pro-ceeding, or from interposing or maintaining a defence in any action or proceeding based upon a claim that such writing is not the last will or codicil, or either, of the testator. Any judgment heretofore entered under this section, determining that the writing produced is the last will and codicil, or either, of the testator, shall, upon ap-plication of any party to said action, or any person claiming through or under them, and upon notice to such persons as the court at special term shall direct, be amended by such court so as to enjoin all parties to said action, and all persons claiming under the parties to said action subsequently to the commencement thereof, from bring-ing or maintaining any action or proceeding impeaching the validity of the probate of the said will and codicil, or either of them, or based upon a claim that such writing is not the last will and codicil, or either, of the testator, and from setting up or maintaining such impeachment or claim by way of answer in any action or proceeding. When final judgment shall have been entered in such action, a copy thereof shall be certified and transmitted by the clerk of the surro-gate's court in which such will was admitted to probate. The action Limitation of action. brought as herein provided shall be commenced within two years after the will or codicil has been admitted to probate, but persons within age of minority, of unsound mind, imprisoned, or absent from the state, may bring such action two years after such disability has been removed.

§ 2. This act shall take effect September first, eighteen hundred When take effect. and ninety-seven, and shall not affect any action or proceeding now pending.

Chap. 105.

AN ACT to provide for the construction of a hoist-bridge over the Erie canal at the head of Railroad street in the village of Ilion, Herkimer county, and making an appropriation therefor.

Became a law March 23, 1897, with the approval of the Governor.

Passed, three-fifths being present.

The People of the State of New York, represented in Senate and Assembly, do enact as follows:

Construction of bridge.

Section 1. The superintendent of public works is hereby authorized to remove the bridge over the Erie canal in Railroad street, in the village of Ilion, and to provide for the construction of a lift or hoist bridge over the Erie canal at that point in said village, for the necessary approaches thereto, and the necessary machinery to operate such bridge upon plans and specifications to be drawn up and prepared by the state engineer and surveyor immediately after the passage of this act. Such plans and specifications shall provide for the construction of such bridge for a sum not to exceed eighteen thousand dollars. Such bridge shall be operated under the direction of the superintendent of public works at the expense of the village of Ilion.

Plans.

Operation of bridge.

Commencement of work.

§ 2. Upon the completion of such plans and specifications, the superintendent of public works is authorized to proceed as soon as practicable with the construction of such bridge, the approaches thereto and machinery therefor, in accordance with such plans and specifications; but before any money appropriated for the above work shall be expended, except for plans, specifications and advertising, the said work shall be let by contract to the lowest responsible bidder after duly advertising therefor, as public works are usually let by contract.

Contracts.

Appropriation.

§ 3. The sum of eighteen thousand dollars is hereby appropriated for the purposes of this act, payable by the treasurer, on the warrant of the comptroller, to the order of the superintendent of public works.

§ 4. This act shall take effect immediately.

Chap. 106.

AN ACT making appropriation and authorizing the expenditure of certain moneys for the completion of the interior work and equipment of the mess halls, chapels, hospitals, kitchens, storehouses, bathhouses, laundry and state shops contained in the new buildings at Sing Sing state prison, authorized by chapter four hundred and eighty-seven of the laws of eighteen hundred and ninety-four, and by chapter ninety-six of the laws of eighteen hund~ed and ninety-five.

Became a law March 23, 1897, with the approval of the Governor.
Passed, three-fifths being present.

The People of the State of New York, represented in Senate and Assembly, do enact as follows:

Section 1. The sum of forty-five thousand dollars, or so much thereof as may be necessary, is hereby authorized to be expended by the superintendent of state prisons out of the moneys received by the agent and warden of said Sing Sing prison, as the proceeds of the labor of the prisoners and the sales of articles manufactured by them, now standing to the credit of the said agent and warden in the bank or banks designated for such deposits, in completing the interior work and equipping the mess halls, chapels, hospitals, kitchens, storehouses, bathhouses, laundry, and state shops contained in the new buildings authorized to be built by chapter four hundred and eighty-seven, laws of eighteen hundred and ninety-four, and chapter ninety-six of the laws of eighteen hundred and ninety-five, also in completing the addition to the clerk's office of said prison. *Expenditures for improvements authorized.*

§ 2. The work and labor in completing and equipping said buildings under the provisions of this act shall, as far as practicable, be done by the convicts confined in said prison, and the moneys authorized to be expended under the first section of this act will be drawn from the bank and accounted for in the same manner as moneys drawn for the maintenance of the industries carried on in the said prison and as provided by the laws relating thereto. *Work by convicts.* *Moneys, how drawn and accounted for.*

§ 3. This act shall take effect immediately.

Chap. 113.

AN ACT to provide for the building of a bridge over the Oswego canal in the village of Fulton and county of Oswego, and making an appropriation therefor.

Became a law March 25, 1897, with the approval of the Governor.
Passed, three-fifths being present.

The People of the State of New York, represented in Senate and Assembly, do enact as follows:

Erection of bridge.

Section 1. The superintendent of public works is hereby authorized and directed to remove the bridges now spanning the Oswego canal on the lines of Oneida street and First street in the village of Fulton, and erect in place thereof one modern steel bridge, with

Plans.

suitable foundations therefor and approaches thereto, upon plans and specifications to be prepared or approved by the state engineer and surveyor.

Appropriation.

§ 2. The sum of thirty thousand dollars, or as much thereof as may be needed, is hereby appropriated for the purposes of this act, payable by the treasurer on the warrant of the comptroller to the order of the superintendent of public works.

§ 3. This act shall take effect immediately.

Chap. 119.

AN ACT to amend section thirteen hundred and thirty-one of the code of civil procedure, relative to the possession of real property

Became a law March 25, 1897, with the approval of the Governor.
Passed, three-fifths being present.

The People of the State of New York, represented in Senate and Assembly, do enact as follows:

Section 1. Section thirteen hundred and thirty-one of the code of civil procedure is hereby amended to read as follows:

§ 1331. Id; on judgment, etc., for the possession of real property.—If the judgment or order directs the sale or the delivery of the possession of real property, or entitles the respondent to the immediate possession thereof, an appeal does not stay the execution of the judgment or order until the appellant gives a written undertaking to the effect that he will not, while in possession of the property, commit, or suffer to be committed, any waste thereon; and if the property is in his possession or under his control, the undertaking must also provide that if the judgment or order is affirmed or the appeal is dismissed, and there is a deficiency upon a sale, he will pay the value of the use and occupation of such property, or tne part thereof as to which the judgment or orders is affirmed, from the time of taking the appeal until the delivery of the possession thereof, pursuant to the judgment or order, not exceeding a specified sum fixed by a judge of the court below. If the judgment directs a sale of real property upon the foreclosure of a mortgage, and an appeal is taken by a party against whom payment of the deficiency is awarded by such jugdment, the undertaking must also provide that if the judgment is affirmed or the appeal is dismissed, the appellant will pay any deficiency which may occur upon the sale, with interest and costs, and all expenses chargeable against the proceeds of the sale, not exceeding a sum fixed by a judge of the court below.

§ 2. This act shall take effect September first, eighteen hundred and ninety-seven.

Chap. 120.

AN ACT to provide for the payment of the balance due newspapers for publication of the general laws of the state for the year eighteen hundred and ninety-six.

Became a law March 25, 1897, with the approval of the Governor.

Passed, three-fifths being present.

The People of the State of New York, represented in Senate and Assembly, do enact as follows:

Section 1. The sum of seventy thousand dollars, or so much thereof as may be necessary, is hereby appropriated out of any money in the treasury not otherwise appropriated, payable by the treasurer on the warrant of the comptroller, for the payment of the balance due newspapers in the various counties in this state for the publication of the general laws of the state for the year 1896. Appropriation for newspapers.

§ 2. This act shall take effect immediately.

Chap. 121.

AN ACT to amend section two hundred and twenty of the code of criminal procedure, relative to justices' criminal docket.

Became a law March 25, 1897, with the approval of the Governor.

Passed, three-fifths being present.

The People of the State of New York, represented in Senate and Assembly, do enact as follows:

Section 1. Section two hundred and twenty of the code of criminal procedure is hereby amended so as to read as follows:

§ 220. **Justices' criminal docket.** — Every justice of the peace and every police or other special justice appointed or elected in ℭ

city, village or town other than in the city and county of New York,
shall forthwith enter correctly at the time thereof, full minutes of
all business done before him as such justice and as a court of special
sessions in criminal actions and in criminal proceedings and including cases of felony, in a book to be furnished to him by the clerk
of the city, village or town where he shall reside, and which shall
be designated "justices' criminal docket," and shall be at all times
open for inspection to the public. Such docket shall be and remain
the property of the city, village or town of the residence of such
justice, and at the expiration of the term of office of such justice
shall be forthwith filed by him in the office of the clerk of said city,
village or town. The minutes in every such docket shall state the
names of the witnesses sworn and their places of residence, and if
in a city, the street and house number; and every proceeding had
before him. Any justice of the peace or police or other special
justice who shall willfully fail to make and enter in such docket
forthwith, the entries by this section required to be made or to
exhibit the docket when reasonably required, shall be guilty of a
misdemeanor and shall, upon conviction, in addition to the punishment provided by law for a misdemeanor forfeit his office.

§ 2. This act shall take effect immediately.

Chap. 122.

AN ACT to amend section nine hundred and seven of the code of
criminal procedure, relating to the discharge of disorderly persons.

Became a law March 25, 1897, with the approval of the Governor.
Passed, three-fifths being present.

*The People of the State of New York, represented in Senate and
Assembly, do enact as follows:*

Section 1. Section nine hundred and seven of the code of criminal
procedure is hereby amended so as to read as follows:

§ 907. **Defendant committed for not giving security; how discharged.**—A person committed as a disorderly person, on failure to
give security, may be discharged by the committing magistrate, or
by any two justices of the peace, or police justices or magistrates,
or the county judge of the county, upon giving security as originally
required, pursuant to section nine hundred and one.

§ 2. This act shall take effect September one, eighteen hundred
and ninety-seven.

Chap. 124.

AN ACT to confer jurisdiction upon the board of claims of the state of New York to hear, audit and determine the amount of the claim of Joseph Stickley, as administrator of the goods, chattels and credits of the estate of Alfred Stickley, deceased, against the state of New York, and to make an award thereon.

**Became a law March 25, 1897, with the approval of the Governor.
Passed, three-fifths being present.**

The People of the State of New York, represented in Senate and Assembly, do enact as follows:

Section 1. Jurisdiction is hereby conferred upon the board of claims Jurisdiction to hear claim. of the state of New York to hear, audit and determine the alleged claim of Joseph Stickley, as administrator of the goods, chattels and credits of the estate of Alfred Stickley, deceased, against the State of New York, for alleged damages arising from the death of said Alfred Stickley, on or about the fifth day of June, eighteen hundred and ninety-six, at Bath-on-the-Hudson, Rensselaer county, New York, caused and produced, as is alleged, by the wrongful act, neglect or default of the state of New York or its agents or servants in constructing and maintaining and continuing a rifle range in the village of Bath-on-the-Hudson, or by the wrongful act, neglect or default of its agents and servants negligently and wrongfully assigning and designating to the said Alfred Stickley a dangerous and unsafe place in which he was to discharge his duties as a marker on said rifle range, and to award such damage and compensation as the board of claims shall deem just and reasonable upon said claim, which shall not exceed ten thousand dollars.

§ 2. Either party may appeal to the appellate division of the Appeal from award. supreme court of the third department from any award made under the authority of this act if the amount in controversy exceeds five hundred dollars; provided, such appeal be taken by the service of a notice of appeal and exceptions within thirty days after the service of a copy of the award.

§ 3. This act shall take effect immediately.

Chap. 126.

AN ACT to authorize the state board of claims to hear, audit and determine the claims of the Presbyterian church society, the Methodist Episcopal church, and the Welsh Congregational church, all religious corporations located at New York Mills, Oneida county, against the state, for moneys paid by said religious corporations to the county treasurer of the county of Oneida, for the use of the state, under the law imposing a tax upon legacies known as the collateral inheritance tax law.

Became a law March 25, 1897, with the approval of the Governor.
Passed, three-fifths being present.

The People of the State of New York, represented in Senate and Assembly, do enact as follows:

Jurisdiction to hear claims. Section 1. The state board of claims is hereby authorized and empowered to hear, audit and determine the alleged claims of the Presbyterian church, the Methodist Episcopal church and the Welsh Congregational church, all religious corporations located at New York Mills, Oneida county, their successors or assigns, against the state, for the sum of two hundred and eighty dollars, one hundred and five dollars, and thirty-five dollars, respectively, paid by said religious corporations to the county treasurer of the county of Oneida, the said Presbyterian church and the said Methodist Episcopal church on the fourth day of October, eighteen hundred and ninety-three, and the said Welsh Congregational church on the twenty-fourth day of February, eighteen hundred and ninety-three, for the use of the state, under the laws of the state imposing a tax upon legacies known as the collateral inheritance tax law, and to make an award therefor.

Appeal from award. § 2. Either party may take an appeal to the appellate division of the supreme court of the state for the third judicial department, from any award made under authority of this act, provided such appeal be taken by service of a notice of appeal within thirty days after service of a copy of the award.

§ 3. This act shall take effect immediately.

Chap. 128.

AN ACT making an appropriation for the promotion of agriculture by the college of agriculture of Cornell university.

Became a law March 25, 1897, with the approval of the Governor. Passed, three-fifths being present.

The People of the State of New York, represented in Senate and Assembly, do enact as follows:

Section 1. For the promotion of agricultural knowledge through- *Appropriation.* out the state, the sum of twenty-five thousand dollars, or so much thereof as may be necessary, is hereby appropriated out of any money in the treasury not otherwise appropriated to be paid to the college of agriculture at Cornell university to be expended in giving instruction throughout the state by means of schools, lectures and other university extension methods, or otherwise, and in conducting investigations and experiments; in discovering the diseases of plants and remedies; in ascertaining the best method of fertilization of fields, gardens and plantations; and best modes of tillage and farm management and improvement of live stock; and in printing leaflets and disseminating agricultural knowledge by means of lectures or otherwise; and in preparing and printing for free distribution the results of such investigations and experiments; and for republishing such bulletins as may be useful in the furtherance of the work; and such other information as may be deemed desirable and profitable in promoting the agricultural interests of the state. Such college of *Employment of teachers and experts.* agriculture may, with the consent and approval of the commissioner of agriculture, employ teachers and experts and necessary clerical help to assist in carrying out the purposes of this bill. Such teachers, experts and clerical help may be removed by the college of agriculture in its discretion; and may be paid for their services such sum or sums as may be deemed reasonable and proper and as shall be approved by the commissioner of agriculture. All of such work by such teachers and experts who shall be employed under this bill shall be under the general supervision and direction of the commissioner of agriculture. The sum appropriated by this act shall be paid by the *Payment of appropriation.* treasurer of the state upon the warrant of the comptroller to the treasurer of Cornell university, upon such treasurer filing with the comptroller a bond in such sum and with such sureties as the comptroller may approve, conditioned for the faithful application of such sum to the purposes for which the same is hereby appropriated. Such sum shall be payable by the treasurer of Cornell university upon vouchers approved by the officers or agents of such university having charge of such college of agriculture, and such vouchers shall be filed by the treasurer of Cornell university in the office of the comptroller of the state.

§ 2. This act shall take effect immediately.

Chap. 129.

AN ACT to amend chapter one hundred and thirty-three of the laws of eighteen hundred and forty-seven, entitled "An act authorizing the incorporation of rural cemetery associations," as amended by chapter three hundred and eighty-nine of the laws of eighteen hundred and eighty-nine, in relation to powers of boards of supervisors in relation to cemeteries.

Became a law March 25, 1897, with the approval of the Governor.

Passed, three-fifths being present.

The People of the State of New York, represented in Senate and Assembly, do enact as follows:

Act amended.

Section 1. Section three of chapter one hundred and thirty-three of the laws of eighteen hundred and forty-seven, as amended by chapter three hundred and eighty-nine of the laws of eighteen hundred and eighty-nine, is hereby amended to read as follows:

Powers of board of supervisors.

§ 3. It shall not be lawful for any rural cemetery hereafter incorporated under the act hereby amended, to take by deed, devise or otherwise, any land in either of the counties of Westchester, Kings, Queens, Rockland or Suffolk, or set apart any ground for cemetery purposes therein, without the consent of the board of supervisors of such county first had and obtained as provided for by this act; nor shall it be lawful for any person or incorporation not incorporated under said act to take, as aforesaid, or set apart or use any land or ground in either of said counties for cemetery purposes without the consent of the board of supervisors of such county first had and obtained in like manner as provided for in this act; and said board of supervisors in granting such consent may annex thereto such conditions, regulations and restrictions as such board may deem the public health or the public good to require.

§ 2. This act shall take effect immediately.

Chap. 134.

AN ACT to amend the banking law, in relation to the salary of superintendent.

Became a law March 29, 1897, with the approval of the Governor.

Passed, three-fifths being present.

The People of the State of New York, represented in Senate and Assembly, do enact as follows:

Section 1. Section three of chapter six hundred and eighty-nine of the laws of eighteen hundred and ninety-two, entitled "An act in relation to banking corporations," and known as the banking law, is hereby amended so as to read as follows:

§3. **The banking department; superintendent.**—There shall continue to be a banking department charged with the execution of the laws relating to the corporations and individuals to which this chapter is applicable. The chief officer of such department shall continue to be the superintendent thereof, to be known as the superintendent of banks, who shall be appointed by the governor, by and with the advice and consent of the senate, and shall hold his office for the term of three years. He shall not either directly or indirectly be interested in any such corporation, or as an individual banker. He shall receive an annual salary of seven thousand dollars, to be paid monthly in the first instance out of the treasury on the warrant of the comptroller. He shall, within fifteen days from the time of notice of his appointment, take and subscribe the constitutional oath of office and file the same in the office of the secretary of state, and execute to the people of the state a bond in the penalty of fifty thousand dollars, with two or more sureties to be approved by the comptroller and treasurer of the state, conditioned for the faithful discharge of the duties of his office.

§ 2. This act shall take effect immediately.

Chap. 136.

AN ACT to amend the real property law, relating to·uses and trusts.

Became a law March 30, 1897, with the approval of the Governor.
Passed, three-fifths being present.

The People of the State of New York, represented in Senate and Assembly, do enact as follows:

Section 1. Section eighty-five of the real property law is hereby amended so as read as follows:

§ 85. **When trustee may convey trust property.**— If the trust is expressed in the instrument creating the estate, every sale, conveyance or other act of the trustee in contravention of the trust, except as provided in this section, shall be absolutely void. The supreme court may by order, on such terms and conditions as seem just and proper, authorize any such trustee to mortgage or sell such real property or any part thereof whenever it appears to the satisfaction of the court that said real property, or some portion thereof, has become so unproductive that it is for the best interest of such estate or that it is necessary or for the benefit of the estate to raise funds for the purpose of preserving it by paying off incumbrances or of improving it by erecting buildings or making other improvements, or that for other peculiar reasons, or on account of other peculiar circumstances, it is for the best interest of said estate, and whenever the interest of the trust estate in any real property is an undivided part or share thereof, the same may be sold if it shall appear to the court to be for the best interest of such estate.

§ 2. Section eighty-seven of the real property law is hereby amended so as to read as follows:

§ 87. **Notice to beneficiary and other persons interested where real property affected by a trust is conveyed, mortgaged or leased and procedure thereupon.** — The supreme court shall not grant an order under either of the last two preceding sections unless it appears to the satisfaction of such court that a written notice stating the time and place of the application therefor has been served upon the beneficiary of such trust, and every other person in being having an estate vested or contingent in reversion or remainder in said real property at least eight days before the making thereof, if such beneficiary or other person is an adult within the state or if a minor, lunatic, person of unsound mind, habitual drunkard or absentee until proof of the service on such beneficiary or other person of such notice as the court or a justice thereof prescribes. The court shall appoint a guardian ad litem for any minor and for any lunatic, person of unsound mind or habitual drunkard who shall not be represented by a committee duly appointed. The application must be by petition duly verified which shall set forth the condition of the trust estate and the particular facts which make it necessary or proper that the application should be granted. After taking proof of the facts, either before the court or a referee and hearing the parties and fully examining into the matter, the court must make a final order upon the application. In case the application is granted, the final order must authorize the real property affected by the trust or some portion thereof, to be mortgaged, sold or leased, upon such terms and conditions as the court may prescribe. In case a mortgage or sale of any portion of such real property is authorized, the final order must direct the disposition of the proceeds of such mortgage or sale and must require the trustee to give bond in such amount and with such sureties as the court directs, conditioned for the faithful discharge of his trust and for the due accounting for all moneys received by him pursuant to said order. If the trustee elects not to give such bond, the final order must require the proceeds of such mortgage or sale to be paid into court to be disposed of or invested as the court shall specially direct. Before a mortgage, sale or lease can be made pursuant to the final order, the trustee must enter into an agreement therefor, subject to the approval of the court and must report the agreement to the court under oath. Upon the confirmation thereof, by order of the court he must execute as directed by the court a mortgage, deed or lease. A mortgage, conveyance or lease made pursuant to a final order granted as provided in this and the last two preceding sections shall be valid and effectual against all minors, lunatics, persons of unsound mind, habitual drunkards and persons not in being interested in the trust or having estates vested or contingent in reversion or remainder in said real property, and against all other persons so interested or having such estates who shall consent to such order, or who having been made parties to such proceeding as herein provided, shall not appear therein and object to the granting of such order.

§ 3. This act shall take effect immediately.

Chap. 138.

AN ACT to amend the public health law, relating to local boards of health.

Became a law March 30, 1897, with the approval of the Governor.
Passed, three-fifths being present.

The People of the State of New York, represented in Senate and Assembly, do enact as follows:

Section 1. Section twenty-two of chapter six hundred and sixty-one of the laws of eighteen hundred and ninety-three entitled " An act in relation to the public health, constituting chapter twenty-five of the general laws," as amended by chapter six hundred and seventy-nine of the laws of eighteen hundred and ninety-four, is hereby amended to read as follows:

§ 22. **Vital statistics.**— Every such local board shall supervise and make complete the registration of all births, marriages and deaths occurring within the municipality, and the cause of death and the finding of coroners' juries, in accordance with the methods and forms prescribed by the state board of health, and, after registration, promptly forward the certificates of such births, marriages and deaths to the state bureau of vital statistics. Every physician or midwife attending at the birth of a child, and no physician or midwife being in attendance, the parent or custodian of a child born, and every groom, officiating clergyman or magistrate at every marriage shall cause a certificate of such birth or marriage to be returned within thirty days thereafter to the local board of health or person designated by it to receive the same, which shall be attested, if a birth, by the physician or midwife, if any in attendance, no physician or midwife being in attendance, by the parent or custodian of a child born, and, if a marriage, by the officiating clergyman or magistrate. The person making such certificate shall be entitled to the sum of twenty-five cents therefor, which shall be a charge upon, and paid by the municipality where such birth, marriage or death occurred. The cost of such registration, not exceeding twenty-five cents for the complete registered record of a birth, marriage or death, shall be a charge upon the municipality. The charge for a copy thereof shall be fixed by the board, not exceeding the same sum for a complete copy of a single registered record and the additional sum of twenty-five cents if certified to. Such copies shall be furnished upon request of any person, and when certified to be correct by the president or secretary of the board or local registering officer designated by it shall be presumptive evidence in all courts and places of the facts therein stated.

§ 2. This act shall take effect immediately.

Chap. 141.

AN ACT to amend the benevolent orders law, being chapter three hundred and seventy-seven of the laws of eighteen hundred and ninety-six.

Became a law March 30, 1897, with the approval of the Governor. Passed, a majority being present.

The People of the State of New York, represented in Senate and Assembly, do enact as follows:

Amendment. Section 1. Section three of chapter three hundred and seventy-seven of the laws of eighteen hundred and ninety-six is hereby amended so as to read as follows:

Powers of trustees. § 3. Such trustees may take, hold and convey by and under the direction of such lodge, chapter, commandery, consistory, council, temple or post, all the temporalities and property belonging thereto, whether real or personal, and whether given, granted or devised directly to it or to any person or persons for it, or in trust for its use and benefit, and may sue for and recover, hold and enjoy all the debts, demands, rights and privileges, and all buildings and places of assemblage, with the appurtenances, and all other estate and property belonging to it in whatsoever manner the same may have been acquired, or in whose name soever the same may be held, as fully as if the right and title thereto had been originally vested in them; and may purchase and hold for the purpose of the lodge, chapter, commandery, consistory, council, temple or post or other real and personal property, and demise, lease and improve the same. **Issue of bonds.** They may also issue their bonds or other evidences of indebtedness in such amounts and for such time and in such form as they shall determine for the exclusive purpose of raising money to pay for any real estate purchased and held by them, and for the improvement of the same, as hereinabove provided, and may mortgage such **Mortgaging of property.** real estate to a trustee or trustees named by them, for the purpose of securing the bonds or other evidences of indebtedness so issued by them. The proceeds of such bonds or other evidences of indebtedness shall be applied exclusively to pay for such real estate and the improvement thereof. Every such lodge, chapter, commandery, consistory, council, temple or post may make rule and regulations, not inconsistent with the laws of this state, or with the constitution or general rules or laws of the grand lodge or other governing body to which it is subordinate, for managing the temporal affairs thereof, and for the disposition of its property and other temporal concerns and revenue belonging to it, and the secretary and treasurer thereof, duly elected and installed according to its constitution and general regulations and law, shall, for the time being, be ex-officio its secretary and treasurer. No board of trustees for any lodge, chapter, commandery, consistory, council, temple or post filing the certificate aforesaid, shall be deemed to be dissolved for any neglect or omission to elect a trustee annually or fill any vacancy or vacancies that may occur or exist at any time in said board, but it shall and may be lawful for said lodge, chapter, commandery, consistory, council, temple or post to fill such vacancy or vacancies at any regular communication thereafter to be held, and till a vacancy arising from the expiration of the term of office of a trustee is filled, as aforesaid, he shall continue to hold the said office and perform the duties thereof. *[margin: Rules and regulations. Secretary and treasurer. Vacancies in board.]*

§ 2. Section five of the said act is hereby amended so as to read as follows:

§ 5. Such trustees shall have the care, management and control of all the temporalities and property of the lodge, chapter, commandery, consistory, council, temple or post, and they shall not sell, convey, mortgage or dispose of any property except by and under its direction, duly had or given at a regular or stated communication, convocation, encampment or meeting thereof, according to its constitution and general regulations. They shall at all times obey and abide by the directions, orders and resolutions of such lodge, chapter, commandery, consistory, council, temple or post, duly passed at any regular or stated communication, convocation, encampment or meeting thereof not in conflict with the constitution and laws of this state or of the grand body to which it shall be subordinate, or of such lodge, chapter, commandery, consistory, council, temple or post. If a lodge of Free and Accepted Masons, or a chapter of Royal Arch Masons, surrender its warrant to the grand body to which it is subordinate, or is expelled or becomes extinct, according to the general rules or regulations of such body, the trustees then in office shall, out of the property belonging to such lodge or chapter, satisfy all just debts due from it and transfer the residue of its property to the "trustees of the Masonic hall and asylum fund," a corporation created by chapter two hundred *[margin: Care, etc., of property. Trustees to obey orders. Satisfaction of debts of certain masonic lodges, etc. Transfer of residue of property.]*

and seventy-two of the laws of eighteen hundred and sixty-four, entitled "An act to incorporate the trustees of the Masonic hall and asylum fund," and unless reclaimed by such lodge or chapter within three years from such transfer, in accordance with the constitution and general regulations of such grand body, the same, with the avails or increase thereof, shall be applied by the "trustees of the Masonic hall and asylum fund" to the benevolent purposes for which such trustees were created in and by such act.

§ 3. This act shall take effect immediately.

Chap. 144.

AN ACT to amend chapter seven hundred and twenty-three of the laws of eighteen hundred and ninety-five, entitled "An act in relation to religious corporations, constituting chapter forty-two of the general laws."

Became a law March 31, 1897, with the approval of the Governor.
Passed, a majority being present.

The People of the State of New York, represented in Senate and Assembly, do enact as follows:

Section 1. Section five of said act is hereby amended to read as follows:

§ 5. **General powers and duties of trustees of religious corporations.**—The trustees of every religious corporation shall have the custody and control of all the temporalities and property, real or personal, belonging to the corporation and of the revenues therefrom, and shall administer the same in accordance with the discipline, rules and usages of the religious denomination or ecclesiastical governing body, if any, with which the corporation is connected, and with the provisions of law relating thereto, for the support and maintenance of the corporation, or provided the members of the corporation at a meeting thereof shall so authorize, of some religious, charitable, benevolent or educational object conducted by said corporation or in connection with it, or with such denomination, and they shall not use such property or revenues for any other purpose or divert the same from such uses. By-laws duly adopted at a meeting of the members of the corporation shall control the action of its trustees. But this section does not give to the trustees of an incorporated church any control over the calling, settlement, dismissal or removal of its minister, or the fixing of his salary; or any power to fix or change the times, nature or order of the public or social worship of such church, except when they are also the spiritual officers of such church. And this section does not, nor does any provision of this act authorize the calling, settlement, dismissal or removal of a minister, or the fixing or changing of his salary, and a meeting of such corporation for any such purpose shall be called, held, moderated, conducted, governed and notice of such meeting given, and person to preside thereat ascertained and the qualification of voters thereat determined, not as required by any provision of this act, but only according to such aforesaid laws, regulations, practice, discipline, rules and usages of such religious denomination or ecclesiastical governing body. And this section does not, nor does any provision of this act authorize the fixing or changing of the times, nature or order of public or social or other worship of any such church in any other manner or by any other authority than in the manner and by the authority provided in the laws, regulations, practice, discipline, rules and usages of the religious denomination or ecclesiastical governing body, if any, with which the church corporation is connected.

§ 2. Said act is further amended by inserting in said act, and after section ninety-three thereof, an additional section to be known as section ninety-four, and to be in the following words and figures, viz.:

§ 94. Nothing contained in this act shall prevent the qualified voters at any meeting held pursuant to this act or in this act described, from choosing a person to preside at any such meeting, other than the person or officer designated in this act to preside thereat, and when such other person shall be chosen he shall exercise all the powers in this act conferred upon the presiding officer of such meeting.

§ 3. This act shall take effect immediately.

Chap. 145.

AN ACT to amend chapter eight hundred and ninety-three of the laws of eighteen hundred and ninety-six, entitled "An act to provide for the appointment of clerks to certain justices of the supreme court of the fifth judicial district."

Became a law March 31, 1897, with the approval of the Governor.
Passed, three-fifths being present.

The People of the State of New York, represented in Senate and Assembly, do enact as follows:

Section 1. Section one of chapter eight hundred and ninety-three Act amended. of the laws of eighteen hundred and ninety-six, entitled "An act to provide for the appointment of clerks to certain justices of the supreme court of the fifth judicial district," is hereby amended so as to read as follows:

Confiden-
tial clerks
to justices.   Section 1. Each of the resident trial justices of the supreme court in the fifth judicial district, except those resident in cities in said district in which there is now a resident supreme court stenographer, may appoint, and at pleasure remove, a confidential clerk to said justice, by an instrument in writing under his own hand, to be filed in the office of the secretary of state. Each of said clerks shall receive an annual salary of eighteen hundred dollars, to be paid by the comptroller of the state in equal quarterly payments upon the certificate of the said justice. Each of the other trial justices of said court resident and doing work in said district at the time this act takes effect other than those above provided for, may appoint and at pleasure remove, a confidential clerk to said justice by an instrument in writing under his own hand to be filed in the office of the secretary of state. Each of said clerks shall receive an annual salary of twelve hundred dollars to be paid by the comptroller of the state in equal quarterly payments upon the certificate of said justice. And said salaries shall be a charge upon the fifth judicial district.

§ 2. This act shall take effect immediately.

Chap. 146.

AN ACT amending section twenty-nine hundred and ninety of the code of civil procedure, in relation to a demand for jury trial in justices' courts.

Became a law March 31, 1897, with the approval of the Governor.
Passed, three-fifths being present.

The People of the State of New York, represented in Senate and Assembly, do enact as follows:

Section 1. Section twenty-nine hundred and ninety of the code of civil procedure is hereby amended to read as follows:

§ 2990. **Demanding jury trial.**— At the time when an issue of fact is joined either party may demand a trial by jury, and unless so demanded at the joining of issue a jury trial is waived. The party demanding a trial by jury shall thereupon pay to the justice the statutory fees for the attendance of each person to be summoned and for the jurors to serve upon the trial, and also the fees to which the constable is entitled for notifying the persons to be drawn as jurors. The fees so deposited shall be delivered by the justice to the constable serving the venire, and by him shall be paid out as required by law. In default of a deposit as aforesaid the justice shall proceed as if no demand for trial by jury had been made. And the town clerk of every town in this state shall deliver to each of the justices of the peace in his town a certified copy of the list filed with him, in pursuance of section one thousand and thirty-seven of this code, and he shall also deliver to each of said justices a certified copy of any such list hereafter filed with him, within ten days after the same shall be filed. The town clerk is entitled to a fee of one dollar for each copy of said list so delivered. Any town clerk who shall neglect to deliver a copy of the list to each of the justices of the town within the time above prescribed, shall forfeit ten dollars for each failure, to be sued for and recovered by the overseers of the poor of said town for the use of the poor of said town.

§ 2. This act shall take effect September first, eighteen hundred and ninety-seven.

Chap. 148.

AN ACT to amend chapter two hundred and seventy-one of the laws of eighteen hundred and ninety-six, entitled "An act to regulate the practice of horseshoeing in the cities of the state of New York having a population of fifty thousand inhabitants or more."

Became a law April 1, 1897, with the approval of the Governor.
Passed, three-fifths being present.

The People of the State of New York, represented in Senate and Assembly, do enact as follows:

Section 1. The several sections hereinafter specified of chapter two hundred and seventy-one of the laws of eighteen hundred and ninety-six, entitled "An act to regulate the practice of horseshoeing in the cities of the state of New York, having a population of fifty thousand inhabitants or more," are hereby amended to read as follows: *Act amended.*

§ 3. Any person who has been practicing as a master or journeyman horseshoer in any such city of this state, for a period of not less than three years preceding the passage of this act, may register as herein provided within thirty days after the passage of this act, upon making and filing with the clerk of the county in which he practices, an affidavit stating that he has been practicing horseshoeing for the period hereinbefore prescribed, and upon complying with this section, shall be exempt from the provisions of this act requiring an examination. *Registration of horseshoers.*

§ 4. A state board of examiners, consisting of one veterinarian and two master horseshoers and two journeyman horseshoers, is hereby created, all of whom shall be citizens and residents of cities *State board of examiners.*

of the first or second class, whose duty it shall be to carry out the
provisions of this act. The members of said board shall be appointed by the governor, and the term of office shall be for five
years, except that the members of said board first appointed shall
hold office for the term of one, two, three, four and five years, as
designated by the governor, and until such time as their successors shall be duly appointed. The board of examiners shall hold
sessions for the purpose of examining applicants desiring to practice horseshoeing as master or journeyman horseshoers, in each city
affected by this act, as often as shall be necessary, and shall grant
a certificate to any person showing himself qualified to practice,
and shall receive as compensation a fee of five dollars from each
person examined. Three members of said board shall constitute
a quorum.

Certain
acts a misdemeanor.
§ 6. Any person who shall present to the clerk of any county
for the purpose of registration as herein provided, a false affidavit,
or any certificate which has been fraudulently obtained, or shall
practice as a master or journeymen horseshoer without conforming to
the requirements of this act, or shall otherwise violate or neglect
to comply with any of the provisions of this act, shall be guilty of
a misdemeanor, and on conviction thereof shall be punished by a
fine of not more than twenty-five dollars or imprisonment for not
Fines for
violation.
more than ten days, or by both such fine and imprisonment. All
fines imposed or collected for violations of the provisions of this act
must be paid to the state board of examiners herein to defray the
expenses of said board.

Repeal.
§ 2. All acts and parts of acts inconsistent with this act are
hereby repealed.

§ 3. This act shall take effect immediately.

Chap. 149.

AN ACT to amend the code of civil procedure, relating to the
appointment of committees for incompetent persons who are
inmates of State institutions.

Became a law April 1, 1897, with the approval of the Governor.
Passed, three-fifths being present.

*The People of the State of New York, represented in Senate and
Assembly, do enact as follows:*

Section 1. Section twenty-three hundred and twenty-three-a of
the code of civil procedure, is hereby amended to read as follows:

§ 2323a. **Application when incompetent person is in a state
institution; petition, by whom made; contents and proceedings
upon presentation thereof.**— Where an incompetent person has

been committed to a state institution in any manner provided by law, and is an inmate thereof, the petition may be presented on behalf of the state by a state officer having special jurisdiction over the institution where the incompetent person is confined or the superintendent or acting superintendent of said institution; the petition must be in writing and verified by the affidavit of the petitioner or his attorney, to the effect that the matters therein stated are true to the best of his information or belief; it must show that the person for whose person or property, or both, a committee is asked has been legally committed to a state institution over which the petitioner has special jurisdiction, or of which he is superintendent or acting superintendent, and is at the time an inmate thereof; it must also state the institution in which he is an inmate, the date of his admission, his last known place of residence, the name and residence of the husband or wife, if any, of such person, and if there be none, the name and residence of the next of kin of such person living in this state so far as known to the petitioner; the nature, extent and income of his property, so far as the same is known to the petitioner, or can with reasonable diligence be ascertained by him. The petition may be presented to the supreme court at any special term thereof, held either in the judicial district in which such incompetent person last resided, or in the district in which the state institution in which he is committed is situated, or to a justice of the supreme court at chambers within such judicial district. Notice of the presentation of such petition shall be personally given to such person, and also to the husband or wife, if any, or if none to the next of kin named in the petition, and to the officer in charge of the institution in which such person is an inmate. Upon the presentation of such petition, and proof of the service of such notice, the court or justice may, if satisfied of the truth of the facts required to be stated in such petition, immediately appoint a committee of the person or property, or both, of such incompetent person or may require any further proof which it or he may deem necessary before making such appointment.

§ 2. This act shall take effect April first, eighteen hundred and ninety-seven.

Chap. 150.

AN ACT to amend chapter four hundred and eighty-eight of the laws of eighteen hundred and ninety-two the title to which was amended by chapter three hundred and ninety-five of the laws of eighteen hundred and ninety-five to read "An act relating to game, fish and wild animals, and to the forest preserve and Adirondack park, constituting chapter thirty-one of the general laws, and to be known as the fisheries, game and forest law," as amended by chapter nine hundred and seventy-four of the laws of eighteen hundred and ninety-five, relating to trout, close season.

Became a law April 1, 1897, with the approval of the Governor.
Passed, three-fifths being present.

The People of the State of New York, represented in Senate and Assembly, do enact as follows:

Section 1. Section one hundred and five of article five of chapter four hundred and eighty-eight of the laws of eighteen hundred and ninety-two, the title to which was amended by chapter three hundred and ninety-five of the laws of eighteen hundred and ninety-five to read "An act relating to game, fish and wild animals, and to the forest preserve and Adirondack park, constituting chapter thirty-one of the general laws, and to be known as the fisheries, game and forest law," as amended by chapter nine hundred and seventy-four of the laws of eighteen hundred and ninety-five, is hereby amended so as to read as follows:

§ 105. **Trout; close season.**— Trout of any kind shall not be fished for, caught, killed or possessed except from the sixteenth day of April to the thirty-first day of August, both inclusive, except as provided by section one hundred and sixty-six and in Spring Brook creek, situated in the counties of Monroe and Livingston, trout shall not be fished for, caught, killed or possessed except from the twenty-ninth day of March to the thirty-first day of August, both inclusive. Whoever shall violate or attempt to violate the provisions of this section shall be deemed guilty of misdemeanor and in addition thereto shall be liable to a penalty of twenty-five dollars for each violation and ten dollars for each fish so caught or possessed.

§ 2. This act shall take effect immediately.

Chap. 151.

AN ACT to amend the fisheries, game and forest law, and the act amendatory thereof, relating to trout fishing.

Became a law April 1, 1897, with the approval of the Governor.
Passed, three-fifths being present.

The People of the State of New York, represented in Senate and Assembly, do enact as follows:

Section 1. Section one hundred and sixty-six of chapter four hundred and eighty-eight of the laws of eighteen hundred and ninety-two, the title to which was amended by chapter three hundred and ninety-five of the laws of eighteen hundred and ninety-five to read " An act relating to game, fish and wild animals, and to the forest preserve and Adirondack park, constituting chapter thirty-one of the general laws and to be known as the fisheries, game and forest law," as amended by chapter nine hundred and seventy-four of the laws of eighteen hundred and ninety-five is hereby amended to read as follows:

§ 166. **Trout; close season.**—Trout shall not be fished for, caught, killed or sold as food except from the twenty-ninth day of March to the thirty-first day of August, both inclusive. But trout so caught or killed under the provisions and limitations of this article, between the twenty-ninth day of March and the sixteenth day of April, may be sold anywhere in the city of New York and Long Island. Whoever shall violate or attempt to violate the provisions of this section shall be deemed guilty of a misdemeanor, and in addition thereto shall be liable to a penalty of twenty-five dollars for each violation thereof and ten dollars for each fish so caught.

§ 2. This act shall take effect immediately.

Chap. 153.

AN ACT to protect purchasers on sales of real estate of infants, by special guardian, prior to January first, eighteen hundred and seventy-two.

Became a law April 1, 1897, with the approval of the Governor.
Passed, three-fifths being present.

The People of the State of New York, represented in Senate and Assembly, do enact as follows:

Section 1. All sales of real estate belonging to infant owners, Sale of real estate made by special guardian under the orders of the supreme court, confirmed. county court, or late court of chancery, prior to January first, eighteen hundred and seventy-two, and the conveyance therefor, executed by said special guardian, are hereby ratified and confirmed, notwithstanding the omission by any such special guardian, to affix his or her title as special guardian or to sign the name of the infant or infants whose real estate was thus conveyed to such deed of conveyance; provided, that the person who executed such conveyance was the duly appointed special guardian of such infant or infants, and such conveyance was in other respects executed in conformity to the order of the court in which the proceedings for such sale were had.

Proviso.

Rights, etc., not affected.

§ 2. This act shall not affect the rights of any party to any suit or legal proceeding, commenced before the passage thereof, in consequence of the irregularity of any proceeding, or the invalidity of any deed which by the foregoing section is legalized and made valid.

§ 3. This act shall take effect immediately.

Chap. 154.

AN ACT providing for completing the erection of a new kitchen and for other improvements at Auburn prison, as contemplated by chapter two hundred and seventy-nine of the laws of eighteen hundred and ninety-six.

Became a law April 1, 1897, with the approval of the Governor. Passed, three-fifths being present.

The People of the State of New York, represented in Senate and Assembly, do enact as follows:

Expenditures authorized.

Section 1. The superintendent of state prisons is hereby authorized to expend out of the moneys received by the agent and warden of Auburn prison, " as the proceeds of the labor of the prisoners and the sales of articles manufactured by them," and standing to the credit of such agent and warden in banks at Auburn, the sum of sixty-five hundred dollars, or so much thereof as may be necessary, for completing the erection of a new kitchen and for purchasing an engine for the new execution room, and for other improvements at Auburn prison, as contemplated by chapter two hundred and seventy-nine of the laws of eighteen hundred and ninety-six.

Moneys, how drawn, etc.

§ 2. The moneys hereby authorized to be expended shall be drawn and accounted for in the same manner as moneys drawn for the purchase of materials for manufacturing purposes.

§ 3. This act shall take effect immediately.

Chap. 155.

AN ACT conferring jurisdiction upon the board of claims to hear, audit and determine the claim of Thomas Killam against the state of New York.

Became a law April 1, 1897, with the approval of the Governor. Passed, three-fifths being present.

The People of the State of New York, represented in Senate and Assembly, do enact as follows:

Section 1. Jurisdiction is hereby conferred upon the board of claims to hear, audit and determine the claim of Thomas Killam against the state of New York for damages alleged to have been sustained by him, arising from or in consequence of the failure of title to land situate in the so-called Canastota tract in the county of Madison and state of New York, granted to Daniel Cady under the great seal of the state by letters patent dated the twenty-sixth day of July, one thousand eight hundred and forty-five, and recorded in the office of the secretary of state in book of patents number thirty-five, at page one hundred and eighty-nine, including the actual costs and expenses incurred by the said Thomas Killam in defending such title; provided such claim shall have been filed with the said board on or before the first day of January, one thousand eight hundred and ninety-eight. If the facts proved before said board shall establish that damages have been sustained by said claimant, arising or resulting as hereinbefore stated, said board shall determine the amount of such damages and award to him such sum therefor as shall be just and equitable.

§ 2. This act shall take effect immediately.

Jurisdiction to hear claim.

Award.

Chap. 157.

AN ACT conferring upon the board of claims, jurisdiction to hear, audit and determine the claim of Fletcher F. Williams against the state.

Became a law April 3, 1897, with the approval of the Governor. Passed, three-fifths being present.

The People of the State of New York, represented in Senate and Assembly, do enact as follows:

Section 1. Jurisdiction is hereby conferred upon the board of claims to hear, audit and determine the claim of Fletcher F. Williams against the state of New York for damages alleged to have been sustained by him by a fall in the senate chamber of the capitol, in the year eigh-

Jurisdiction to hear claim.

teen hundred and ninety-five, while in the employ of the state, alleged to have been caused by reason of loose and insecure and defective part of the building and work furnished by said state, and by the alleged carelessness and negligence of the officers and agents of the state.

Award of damages. § 2. If the facts proved before said board shall establish that damages have been sustained by said claimant, arising or resulting as hereinbefore stated for which a master or•employer would be liable under like circumstances, said board shall determine the amount of such damages and award to him such sum therefor as shall be just and reasonable.

Appeal from award. § 3. Either party may take an appeal to the appellate division of the supreme court of the state of New York, third department, from any award made under authority of this act, provided such appeal be taken by service of a notice of appeal within thirty days after service of a copy of the award.

§ 4. This act shall take effect immediately.

Chap. 160.

AN ACT to authorize the board of claims to hear, audit and determine the claim of Carter H. Morgan, against the state for alleged damage to his property caused by the construction and maintenance of a channel (part of the way) from Oil Creek reservoir to the Genesee Valley canal, in the town of Cuba, New York, and for work and materials furnished therefor.

Became a law April 3, 1897, with the approval of the Governor.
Passed, three-fifths being present.

The People of the State of New York, represented in Senate and Assembly, do enact as follows:

Jurisdiction to hear claims. Section 1. The board of claims is hereby empowered to hear, audit and determine the claim or claims of Carter H. Morgan, or his assigns, against the state of New York for the value of certain real estate situate in Cuba, New York, alleged to have been taken and used by the said state in the construction and maintenance of a new channel or conduit from (part of the way) Oil Creek reservoir, in said town, to the Genesee Valley canal, and for loss and damage alleged to have been sustained by him resulting from such construction and maintenance, and for work and labor alleged to have been done and materials alleged to have been furnished by the said Carter H. Morgan for the said state by direction and at the request of an engineer or other officer in the employment of said state, in and about such construction and maintenance and work connected therewith, and to make an award therefor, as if such claim had accrued within two years prior to the time of such hearing.

§ 2. Either party may appeal to the third appellate division of Appeal from award. the supreme court from any award made under authority of this act, provided such appeal be taken by service of a notice of appeal within thirty days after service of a copy of the award.

§ 3. This act shall take effect immediately.

Chap. 164.

AN ACT appropriating money to erect an equestrian statue of Major-General Henry Warner Slocum, deceased, on the battlefield of Gettysburg.

Became a law April 8, 1897, with the approval of the Governor.
Passed by a two-thirds vote.

The People of the State of New York, represented in Senate and Assembly, do enact as follows:

Section 1. The sum of twenty-two thousand dollars is hereby Appropriation for statue. appropriated for the erection of a bronze equestrian statue of Major-General Henry Warner Slocum, late of the city of Brooklyn, deceased, on the battlefield of Gettysburg, being the balance of the sum of twenty-five thousand dollars, as authorized and provided for by chapter two hundred and three of the laws of eighteen hundred and ninety-six, on the site selected by the commissioners appointed by and pursuant to chapter three hundred and seventeen of the laws of eighteen hundred and ninety-five. The said money How payable. or so much thereof as may be necessary, to be paid by the treasurer on the warrant of the comptroller, on proper vouchers, duly certified by the presiding officer of said board of commissioners.

§ 2. This act shall take effect immediately.

Chap. 168.

AN ACT to amend chapter three hundred and eighty-four of the laws of eighteen hundred and ninety-five, entitled "An act in relation to the drainage of agricultural lands," and acts amendatory thereof.

Became a law April 8, 1897, with the approval of the Governor.
Passed, three-fifths being present.

The People of the State of New York, represented in Senate and Assembly, do enact as follows:

Section 1. Said act is hereby further amended by adding thereto two sections, to be numbered, respectively, seventeen and eighteen, to read as follows:

§ 17. **May borrow money for construction; issue evidence of indebtedness.**—In case it shall be necessary to raise funds for construction of said ditches or channels, drains or dykes, or for land damages before the assessment hereinbefore provided for can be made and collected, the said commissioners are hereby empowered from time to time, with the approval of the court in which the proceeding was instituted or is pending, to borrow so much money as may be necessary therefor, upon such evidence of indebtedness as they may deem proper, bearing interest at a rate of not more than six per centum per annum, payable upon the completion of such assessment and collection, and the interest accruing thereon shall be assessed as other expenses for the said construction. Such evidences of indebtedness shall not be issued for less than par, and shall be receivable in payment of such assessments.

§ 18. **Acts of commissioners legalized.**—The acts of any commissioners heretofore appointed under said chapter three hundred and eighty-four of the laws of eighteen hundred and ninety-five, or acts amendatory thereof, which acts have been performed since the passage of said act or acts and before the passage of this act, so far as such acts might be affected, impaired or questioned by reason of the failure of said commissioners to make the assessment and collection of said tax before the construction of said drains, ditches, dykes or payments of land damages, wherein they have acted in good faith, are hereby legalized and confirmed and made as effectual and valid as if the power herein conferred upon them to borrow funds for cost of construction and for payment of land damages, were expressly given under the original act itself.

§ 2. **When to take effect.**—This act shall take effect immediately.

Chap. 169.

AN ACT to amend the public health law, relating to local boards of health.

Became a law April 3, 1897, with the approval of the Governor.
Passed, three-fifths being present.

The People of the State of New York, represented in Senate and Assembly, do enact as follows:

Section 1. Section twenty-nine of chapter six hundred and sixty-one of the laws of eighteen hundred and ninety-three entitled "An act in relation to the public health, constituting chapter twenty-five of the general laws," is hereby amended to read as follows:

§ 29. **Jurisdiction of town and village boards.**—A town board of health shall not have jurisdiction over any city or incorporated village or part of such city or village in such town if such city or village has an organized board of health. The boards of health of any town and the incorporated villages therein, or any two or more towns and the incorporated villages therein, may unite, with the written approval of the state board of heath, in a combined sanitary and registration district, and appoint for such district one health officer and registering officer, whose authority in all matters of general application shall be derived from the boards of health appointing him; and in special cases not of general application arising within the jurisdiction of but one board shall be derived from such board alone. When one or more towns and the incorporated villages therein unite in one registration district, the registrar of vital statistics of such combined district will be required to make separate returns to the state board of health of village and town certificates of births, marriages and deaths.

§ 2. This act shall take effect immediately.

·

Chap. 171.

AN ACT to amend chapter six hundred and eighty-six of the laws of eighteen hundred and ninety-two, entitled "An act in relation to counties, constituting chapter eighteen of the general laws," and known as the county law, relating to the payment of orders for sheep killed by dogs.

Became a law April 3, 1897, with the approval of the Governor. Passed, three-fifths being present.

The People of the State of New York, represented in Senate and Assembly, do enact as follows:

Section 1. Section one hundred and twenty-one of chapter six hundred and eighty-six of the laws of eighteen hundred and ninety-two, known as the county law, is hereby amended to read as follows:

§ 121. **Tax to pay orders for sheep killed.**— Whenever the amount of the orders for damages, given by the town board to the owners of sheep killed or injured by dogs, shall exceed the amount of the dog fund in the hands of the supervisor of such town, the town board may, in its discretion, add to the accounts of such town, the amount of such orders then due and unpaid, but the amount so added shall not exceed the sum of three hundred dollars in any one year.

§ 2. This act shall take effect immediately.

Chap. 174.

AN ACT for the protection of purchasers of coal in cities of the first and second class, and providing for the enforcement thereof, and to repeal chapter five hundred and thirty-nine of the laws of eighteen hundred and eighty-eight.

Became a law April 3, 1897, with the approval of the Governor.
Passed, three-fifths being present.

The People of the State of New York, represented in Senate and Assembly, do enact as follows:

Legal ton. Section 1. In all transactions relating to the sale or delivery of coal, two thousand avoirdupois pounds in weight shall constitute a legal ton.

Attempting to deliver or sell less than 1 gal weight. § 2. Any person, firm or corporation, in any of the cities of the first and second class, violating the provisions of section one of this act, whereby it is attempted to sell or deliver less than two thousand pounds by weight to a ton, or a proper proportion thereof to quantities less than a ton, shall be liable to a penalty of not exceeding fifty dollars, provided that in all cases thirty pounds to the ton shall be allowed for the variation in scales and wastage.

Delivery tickets. § 3. It shall be unlawful for any person, firm or corporation delivering coal in cities of the first and second class, to deliver or cause to be delivered, any quantity or quantities of coal which shall have been sold by weight, without each such delivery being accompanied with a delivery ticket and a duplicate thereof, on each of which shall be in ink, or other indelible substance, distinctly expressed in pounds the quantity or quantities of coal contained in the cart, wagon or other vehicle used in such delivery, with the name of the purchaser thereof and the name of the dealer from whom purchased. One of such tickets shall be delivered to the purchaser of the coal specified thereon, and the other of such tickets shall be retained by the seller Proviso as to delivery of entire cargo. of the coal. The foregoing provisions of this section shall not apply to coal delivered by the entire cargo direct from the vessels containing the same, to one destination and accepted by the purchaser on the original bill of lading as proof of weight; but with every such delivery of an entire cargo of coal in any city of the first and second Delivery of bill of lading. class, there shall be delivered to the purchaser thereof one of the original bills of lading issued by the person, firm or corporation by whom the coal was loaded into the vessel from which such coal is delivered to the purchaser of the entire cargo thereof, on each of which bills of lading there shall be in ink or other indelible substance distinctly expressed, the date and place of loading such cargo and the Penalty. number of pounds contained therein. Any person, firm or corporation, who shall violate any of the provisions of this section shall be liable to a penalty of not exceeding fifty dollars.

§ 4. There may be designated by the respective mayors of the cities Scales, designation of, etc. of the first and second class in this state, stationary or movable scales, suitable for the purpose of weighing coal, the owners of which may tender the same for public use, in different parts of the city, in such convenience in number and locality as shall be deemed necessary, on which the coal or coal vehicle with or without coal, may be weighed at the request of the purchaser thereof. The scales so designated shall be provided at the expense of the owners thereof with test weights, and shall be subject at all times to the inspection and supervision of the sealers or inspectors of weights and measures in such city, who shall inspect such scales at least once in each month. Such scales shall also be provided by the owner thereof, with a competent weigh-master. The owner of such scales shall be entitled to charge for weighing coal and coal vehicles containing coal, at such scales, a fee of not exceeding fifteen cents per ton of coal; empty vehicles returning to such scales after delivery of the coal so weighed therein, shall be reweighed without further charge. The owner of such scales Owners to give bonds. so designated, shall enter into a bond with the city in which such scales are situated, in the sum of five hundred dollars with two sufficient sureties, conditioned that the said scales shall be kept in such condition as at all times to properly register the weight of coal, and that the person weighing coal thereat shall perform his duties faithfully and furnish correct certificates to all persons having coal or coal vehicles weighed at such scales. The amount of such bond shall be recoverable at the suit of the city, upon proof that any of the conditions thereof have not been complied with. The designation of Publication of designation. such scales shall be in writing signed by the mayor of the city in which such scales are situated, and a copy thereof inserted in any official publication in said city, and if there be none, in a newspaper published therein. Any owner of such scales, or any agent or representative of his, or any weigh-master employed by him thereat, who shall be in any manner concerned in any fraudulent weighing of coal Penalty for fraudulent weigh. at such scales, shall be guilty of a misdemeanor, and shall be punishable by a fine of not exceeding five hundred dollars or by imprisonment for one year or by both such fine and imprisonment. Every Memorandum book to be kept. owner of such scales shall keep a book in which shall be entered in ink a memorandum of every load of coal weighed at such scales, showing the name of the person, firm or corporation delivering said coal, the net weight thereof as shown by the delivery ticket thereof of such person, firm or corporation, the name of the purchaser thereof, the gross and net weight of the coal so weighed, and the date of the weighing thereof. Such book shall be the book of original entries, and all certificates delivered by the owner of such scales shall be copies of the entries contained therein, and such books shall be open to the inspection of any citizen.

Right of purchaser to have coal reweighed, etc.

§ 5. It shall be the right of every purchaser of coal in any of the cities of the first and second class, before accepting the delivery of the same, to have any of the deliveries of said coal weighed at his expense, at any of the scales designated under the provisions of section four of this act, provided such scales are within half a mile of the place of loading or of the place of delivery of the coal, and for this purpose to require that any vehicle containing coal purchased by him shall be taken by the driver or other person in charge thereof, to such scales for the purpose of having the same weighed, and, after the delivery of the coal, to require that the vehicles from which such coal so purchased shall have been delivered, shall be taken by the driver thereof, or any other person in charge thereof, to the said scales to be weighed at the expense of the purchaser thereof; and a certificate of the weight of such coal so weighed as aforesaid, shall thereupon be furnished to the purchaser of such coal by the owner of the scales at which such coal is so weighed.   The refusal of any seller of coal to permit coal purchased from him to be reweighed at the request of the purchaser thereof, as aforesaid, or of any driver or other person in charge of a vehicle containing coal, or from which coal has been delivered, to take the same at the request of the purchaser of such coal to such scales for the purpose of having the same weighed, provided, however, that the purchaser of such coal shall have first paid to the owner of the said scales, or to the seller of such coal, or to the driver or other person in charge of the vehicle containing such coal, an amount sufficient to meet the charges for weighing such coal, shall render the person, firm or corporation selling the said coal, liable to a penalty not to exceed the sum of fifty dollars.

Certificate of weight.

Penalty for refusal to permit coal to be reweighed, etc.

Recovery and disposition of penalties.

§ 6. The penalties provided by this act shall be recoverable at the suit of the city in which such penalties are incurred, and the amount so collected, as well as any amount collected in suits brought to recover the amounts due on bonds given under the provisions of section four of this act, shall be paid over, one-half to any police pension or relief fund in such city, and one-half to any firemen's pension or relief fund therein.

Bills of lading, penalty for altering, etc.

§ 7. A person guilty of altering, with intent to defraud, any original bill of lading issued by the person, firm or corporation by whom the coal was loaded into the vessel in which such coal is transported to any city of the first class in this state, or of uttering any such bill of lading so altered, or who is guilty of making, preparing, subscribing or uttering, a false or fraudulent manifest, invoice or bill of lading thereof, or removing any part of said cargo of coal without having the amount thereof certified to in writing on the said original bill of lading, by the person, firm or corporation receiving the coal so removed, and by the captain of the vessel containing such cargo, is punishable by imprisonment in the state prison not exceeding three years, or by a fine not exceeding one thousand dollars, or both, and the delivery of any fraudulent bill of lading to any purchaser of coal shall be presumptive evidence of uttering the same with criminal intent.

§ 8. Chapter five hundred and thirty-nine of the laws of eighteen Repeal. hundred and eighty-eight, is hereby repealed.

§ 9. This act shall take effect immediately.

Chap. 176.

AN ACT to amend section three hundred and sixty-one of the code of civil procedure, relating to stenographers of certain county courts.

Became a law April 3, 1897, with the approval of the Governor.
Passed, three-fifths being present.

The People of the State of New York, represented in Senate and Assembly, do enact as follows:

Section 1. Section three hundred and sixty-one of the code of civil procedure is hereby amended so as to read as follows:

§ 361. **Stenographers.**— The county judge in either of the counties of Livingston, Niagara, Monroe, Onondaga, Oswego or Cortland, where issues of fact are triable, may employ a stenographer to take stenographic notes upon trials thereat, who is entitled to a compensation to be certified by the judge, not exceeding ten dollars for each day's attendance at the request of the judge. The stenographer's compensation is a charge upon the county, and in the county of Livingston must be audited, allowed and paid as other county charges; and in the counties of Onondaga, Monroe, Niagara, Oswego and Cortland must be paid by the county treasurer, on an order of the court, granted on the affidavit of the stenographer, and the certificate of the judge that the services were rendered. The county judge of Erie county, and the county judge of Oneida county may each appoint and may at pleasure remove a stenographer of said court, who must attend each term of the said court where issues of fact in civil and criminal cases are triable, and who shall each receive therefor a salary of fifteen hundred dollars per annum, together with his necessary expenses for stationery, to be paid by the treasurer of said county of Erie, and the treasurer of the said county of Oneida, in equal monthly installments, on the certificates of said judges of Erie and Oneida counties, that the services have been actually performed or the expenses necessarily incurred. Said stenographers shall also report and transcribe opinions for the said county judges, as well as special proceedings where a stenographer is required, without additional compensation.

§ 2. This act shall take effect on the first day of September, eighteen hundred and ninety-seven.

Chap. 177.

AN ACT to amend the code of civil procedure, relating to applications for probate of wills and for granting of letters of administration.

Became a law April 3, 1897, with the approval of the Governor.
Passed, a majority being present.

The People of the State of New York, represented in Senate and Assembly, do enact as follows:

Section 1. Section twenty-six hundred and fourteen of the code of civil procedure is hereby amended to read as follows:

§ 2614. **Who may propound will.**—A person designated in a will as executor, devisee, or legatee, or any person interested in the estate, or a creditor of the decedent, or any party to an action brought or about to be brought, and interested in the subject thereof, in which action the decedent, if living, would be a proper party, may present to the surrogate's court having jurisdiction, a written petition, duly verified, describing the will, setting forth the facts, upon which the jurisdiction of the court to grant probate thereof depends, and praying that the will may be proved, and that the persons, specified in the next section, may be cited to attend the probate thereof. Upon the presentation of such a petition, the surrogate must issue a citation accordingly.

§ 2. Section twenty-six hundred and sixty of the code of civil procedure, as amended by chapter five hundred and three of the laws of eighteen hundred and ninety-four, is hereby further amended to read as follows:

§ 2660. **When entitled to letters of administration.**—Administration in case of intestacy must be granted to the relatives of the deceased entitled to succeed to his personal property, who will accept the same, in the following order:

1. To the surviving husband or wife.
2. To the children.
3. To the father.
4. To the mother.
5. To the brothers.
6. To the sisters.
7. To the grandchildren.
8. To any other next of kin entitled to share in the distribution of the estate.
9. To an executor or administrator of a sole legatee named in a will, whereby the whole estate is devised to such deceased sole legatee.

If a person entitled is a minor, administration must be granted to his guardian, if competent, in preference to creditors or other persons. If no relative, or guardian of a minor relative, will accept the same, the letters must be granted to the creditors of the deceased; the creditor first applying, if otherwise competent, to be entitled to preference. If no creditor applies, the letters must be granted to any other person or persons legally competent. Letters of administration shall also be granted to an executor or administrator of a deceased person named as sole legatee in a will. The public administrator in the city of New York has preference after the next of kin and after an executor or administrator of a sole legatee named in a will whereby the whole estate is devised to such deceased sole legatee over creditors and all other persons. In other counties, the county treasurer shall have preference next after creditors over all other persons. If several persons of the same degree of kindred to the intestate are entitled to administration, they must be preferred in the following order: First, men to women; second, relatives of the whole blood to those of the half blood; third, unmarried women to married. If there are several persons equally entitled to administration, the surrogate may grant letters to one or more of such persons, and administration may be granted to one or more competent persons, although not entitled to the same, with the consent of the person entitled to be joined with such person or persons; which consent must be in writing, and filed in the office of the surrogate. If a surviving husband does not take out letters of administration on the estate of his deceased wife, he is presumed to have assets in his hands sufficient to satisfy her debts, and is liable therefor. A husband is liable as administrator for the debts of his wife only to the extent of the assets received by him. If he dies leaving any assets of his wife unadministered, except as otherwise provided by law, they pass to his executors or administrators as part of his personal property, but are liable for her debts in preference to the creditors of the husband. If, in an action, brought or about to brought, the intestate, if living, would be a proper party thereto, any party to such action, interested in the subject thereof, may apply to the surrogate's court for the granting of letters of administration to himself, or some other qualified person, and upon the jurisdictional facts being satisfactorily shown, and no relative, or guardian of a minor relative, and no creditor, county treasurer or public administrator consenting to such administration, some legally competent person must be appointed administrator.

§ 3. This act shall take effect immediately.

Chap. 182.

AN ACT to amend the game law, and the act amendatory thereof, relating to taking fish in Canandaigua lake.

Became a law April 6, 1897, with the approval of the Governor. Passed, three-fifths being present.

The People of the State of New York, represented in Senate and Assembly, do enact as follows:

Section 1. Chapter four hundred and eighty-eight of the laws of eighteen hundred and ninety-two, the title to which was amended by chapter three hundred and ninety-five, of the laws of eighteen hundred and ninety-five to read "An act relating to game, fish and wild animals and to the forest preserve and Adirondack park, constituting chapter thirty-one of the general laws, and to be known as the fisheries, game and forest law," as amended by chapter nine hundred and seventy-four of the laws of eighteen hundred and ninety-five, is hereby amended by adding a new section following section one hundred and forty-one and to be known as section one hundred forty-two to read as follows:

§ 142. **Taking whitefish; eels and other fish in the waters of Canandaigua lake.**— No fish, shall be fished for, caught or killed in any manner or by any device except angling in the waters of Canandaigua lake except as herein provided. It shall be lawful to fish with set lines, no line to exceed six hundred feet in length, one end thereof to le attached at the shore, in the waters of Canandaigua lake, no person to own or operate more than two lines. Whoever shall violate or attempt to violate the provisions of this section shall be deemed guilty of a misdemeanor and in addition thereto shall be liable to a penalty of one hundred dollars for each violation thereof.

§ 2. All acts and parts of acts inconsistent with this act are hereby repealed.

§ 3. This act shall take effect immediately.

Chap. 183.

AN ACT to amend section six hundred and thirty-five of the penal code, relative to injuries to railroad tracks and other injuries to and interference with property.

Became a law April 6, 1897, with the approval of the Governor.
Passed, a majority being present.

The People of the State of New York, represented in Senate and Assembly, do enact as follows:

Section 1. Section six hundred and thirty-five of the penal code is hereby amended so as to read as follows:

§ 635. A person who wilfully:

1. Displaces, loosens, removes, injures or destroys any rail, sleeper, switch, bridge, viaduct, culvert, embankment or structure or any part thereof, attached, appertaining to or connected with any railway, or by any other means attempts to wreck, destroy, or so damage any car, tender, locomotive or railway train or part thereof, while moving or standing upon any railway track in this state, as to render such car, tender, locomotive or railway train wholly or partially unfitted for its ordinary use, whether operated by steam, electricity or other motive power; or

2. Places any obstruction upon the track of any such railway; or

3. Wilfully destroys or breaks any guard erected or maintained by a railroad corporation as a warning signal for the protection of its employes; or

4. Wilfully discharges a loaded firearm or projects, or throws a stone or other missile at a railway train, or at a locomotive, car or vehicle standing or moving upon a railway; or

5. Wilfully displaces, removes, cuts, injures or destroys any wire, insulator, pole, dynamo, motor, locomotive, or any part thereof, attached, appertaining to or connected with any railway operated by electricity, or wilfully interferes with or interrupts any motive power used in running such road, or wilfully places any obstruction upon the track of such railroad, or wilfully discharges a loaded firearm, or projects or throws a stone or any other missile at such railway train or locomotive, car or vehicle, standing or moving upon such railway; or

6. Removes a journal brass from a car while standing upon any railroad track in this state, without authority from some person who has a right to give such authority, is punishable as follows: First. If thereby the safety of any person is endangered, by imprisonment for not more than twenty years. Second. In every other case by imprisonment for not more than five years.

§ 2. This act shall take effect September first, eighteen hundred and ninety-seven.

Chap. 185.

AN ACT in relation to a library for the appellate division of the supreme court for the second department, and making an appropriation therefor.

Became a law April 6, 1897, with the approval of the Governor.
Passed, three-fifths being present.

The People of the State of New York, represented in Senate and Assembly, do enact as follows:

Appropriation for books.

Section 1. There is hereby appropriated out of any moneys in the treasury not otherwise appropriated, to be paid by the state treasurer upon the warrant of the comptroller, to the presiding justice of the appellate division of the supreme court of the state of New York for the second department, the sum of three thousand dollars, or so much thereof as said presiding justice shall certify to be necessary for the purpose of purchasing books for a law library for the said appellate division of the supreme court of the second department.

Law library created.

The books so purchased shall constitute the law library for the appellate division of the supreme court of the second department, and shall be under the custody and control of the justices of said court.

§ 2. This act shall take effect immediately.

Chap. 186.

AN ACT to extend the time in which the Elevated Railroad Passenger insurance company may complete its organization and make the necessary deposit.

Became a law April 6, 1897, with the approval of the Governor.
Passed, three-fifths being present.

The People of the State of New York, represented in Senate and Assembly, do enact as follows:

Section 1. The period during which the Elevated Railroad Passenger Insurance company may deposit the sum of one hundred thousand dollars in proper securities with the superintendent of the insurance department of the state, in conformity with the laws under which it was organized, is hereby extended to December thirty-first, eighteen hundred and ninety-seven.

§ 2. This act shall take effect immediately.

Chap. 187.

AN ACT to remedy irregularities in, and to confirm, the entry of judgments heretofore filed for entry.

Became a law April 6, 1897, with the approval of the Governor. Passed, a majority being present.

The People of the State of New York, represented in Senate and Assembly, do enact as follows:

Section 1. Every interlocutory or final judgment heretofore filed for entry shall be deemed to have been duly entered, as required by law, as of the time of such filing, and the entry of every such judgment is hereby confirmed.

§ 2. This act shall take effect immediately.

Chap. 188.

AN ACT to amend section twelve hundred and thirty-six of the code of civil procedure, relating to the entry of judgment

Became a law April 6, 1897, with the approval of the Governor. Passed, a majority being present.

The People of the State of New York, represented in Senate and Assembly, do enact as follows:

Section 1. Section twelve hundred and thirty-six of the code of civil procedure is hereby amended so as to read as follows:

§ 1236. **Entry of judgment.**— Every interlocutory judgment or final judgment shall be signed by the clerk and filed in his office, and such signing and filing shall constitute the entry of the judgment. The clerk shall, in addition to the docket-books required to be kept by law, keep a book, styled the "judgment-book," in which he shall record all judgments entered in his office.

§ 2. This act shall take effect immediately.

Chap. 189.

AN ACT to amend section twenty-four hundred and fifty-eight of
the code of civil procedure, relative to the right of a judgment-
creditor to maintain special proceedings.

Became a law April 6, 1897, with the approval of the Governor.
Passed, a majority being present.

*The People of the State of New York, represented in Senate and
Assembly, do enact as follows:*

Code
amended.
Section 1. Section twenty-four hundred and fifty-eight of the
code of civil procedure is hereby amended so as to read as follows:

Right of
judgment-
creditor to
maintain
special pro-
ceedings.
§ 2458. In order to entitle a judgment-creditor to maintain either
of the special proceedings authorized by this article, the judgment
must have been rendered upon the judgment debtor's appearance
or personal service of the summons upon him, for a sum not less than
twenty-five dollars or substituted service of the summons upon him
in accordance with section four hundred and thirty-six of the code
of civil procedure; and the execution must have been issued out of
a court of record; and either:

1. To the sheriff of the county where the judgment debtor has,
at the time of the commencement of the special proceedings, a place
for the regular transaction of business in person; or,

2. If the judgment debtor is then a resident of the state, to the
sheriff of the county where he resides; or,

3. If he is not then a resident of the state, to the sheriff of the
county where the judgment-roll is filed unless the execution was
issued out of a court other than that in which the judgment was
rendered, and, in that case, to the sheriff of the county where the
transcript of the judgment is filed.

When takes
effect.
§ 2. This act shall take effect September first, eighteen hundred
and ninety-seven.

Chap. 190.

AN ACT to reappropriate money to improve and repair the state
armory at Catskill, New York, as provided for by chapter eight
hundred and forty-four of the laws of eighteen hundred and
ninety-five.

Became a law April 6, 1897, with the approval of the Governor.
Passed, three-fifths being present.

*The People of the State of New York, represented in Senate and
Assembly, do enact as follows:*

Appropria-
tion for
repairs.
Section 1. The sum of five thousand dollars remaining in the
treasury unexpended, appropriated by chapter eight hundred and

forty-four of the laws of eighteen hundred and ninety-five, providing for improving and repairing the state armory at Catskill, New York, is hereby appropriated for the same purpose; and the comptroller is directed from time to time to pay the same, or so much thereof as may be necessary for the aforesaid purpose, out of the money in the treasury not otherwise appropriated, on the written requisition of the commission appointed by and under chapter eight hundred and forty-four of the laws of eighteen hundred and ninety-five.

§ 2. This act shall take effect immediately.

Chap. 192.

AN ACT to amend chapter eighty-eight of the laws of eighteen hundred and sixty-four, entitled "An act to incorporate the Missionary Society of the Most Holy Redeemer in the state of New York."

Became a law April 7, 1897, with the approval of the Governor.
Passed, a majority being present.

The People of the State of New York, represented in Senate and Assembly, do enact as follows:

Section 1. Section two of chapter eighty-eight of the laws of eigh- Charter teen hundred and sixty-four, entitled "An act to incorporate the amended. Missionary Society of the Most Holy Redeemer in the state of New York," is hereby amended so as to read as follows:

§ 2. The persons named in the first section of this act shall be the Trustees of first trustees of said corporation and all vacancies by death, resigna- corpora-tion, removal or otherwise of any of the said trustees and all vacancies that may hereafter occur for any cause among the trustees, shall be filled without unnecessary delay by the remaining trustees, by the election of some person who shall be a recognized member in good standing of the Redemptorist Order in the United States, which is also known as the Congregation of the Most Holy Redeemer, stationed in the state of New York, to fill such vacancy, and at least four votes shall be necessary for the election of any trustee. The provincial for the time being of said Redemptorist Order in the United States shall be one of said trustees. The said trustees may by by-laws increase their number to ten, but there shall never be less than five trustees. The said trustees shall hold a regular meeting at least once each year to transact such business as may be necessary.

§ 2. Section five of said chapter eighty-eight, is hereby amended so as to read as follows:

§ 5. The objects of said corporation shall be the religious instruc- Objects of tion of the people, especially of poor and neglected persons; taking corpora-tion.

care temporarily of small congregations not able to support a clergy-man; the erecting, maintaining and conducting of churches of the Roman Catholic faith to enable the members of said churches to meet for divine worship or other religious observances; the erecting, maintaining and conducting of schools and colleges; the giving of missions and to impart a moral education to poor and orphan children.

§ 3. This act shall take effect immediately.

Chap. 193.

AN ACT in relation to the consolidation of domestic and foreign rail-road corporations.

Became a law April 7, 1897, with the approval of the Governor.
Passed, three-fifths being present.

The People of the State of New York, represented in Senate and Assembly, do enact as follows:

Consolidation not deemed invalid.

Section 1. The consolidation heretofore effected of a domestic railroad corporation with a foreign railroad corporation, shall not be deemed invalid because such roads at the time of the consolidation did not form a connected and continuous line, if, when the consolidation was effected, an intermediate line, by purchase or by a lease, of not less than ninety-nine years became, with the consolidated roads, a continuous and connecting line of railroad, and such consolidation is hereby ratified and confirmed.

§ 2. This act shall take effect immediately.

Chap. 194.

AN ACT creating a commissioner of jurors for each county of the state having a population of more than one hundred and fifty thousand and less than one hundred and ninety thousand, and regulating and prescribing his duties.

Became a law April 7, 1897, with the approval of the Governor.
Passed, three-fifths being present.

The People of the State of New York, represented in Senate and Assembly, do enact as follows:

Act amended.

Section 1. The office of commissioner of jurors is hereby created for each county of the state, having a population of more than one hundred and fifty thousand and less than one hundred and ninety thousand, according to the last preceding state enumeration of inhabitants; but this act shall not apply to the county of Albany.

§ 2. Within twenty days after the passage of this act, at a time *Commissioner of jurors, appointment of.* and place to be designated by the county judge, by a notice in writing, the justices of the supreme court residing in each county embraced within this act, and the county judge of such county, shall meet, and they, or a majority of them, shall thereupon, or within twenty days thereafter, appoint a suitable person to be commissioner of jurors for such county, who shall be a resident of the county, and if a lawyer, shall not while holding such office, directly or indirectly, engage in the practice of law. Such appointment shall be made in writing, and shall be signed by the judges making the same, or a majority of them, and filed in the office of the clerk of such county. The commissioner so appointed shall, unless removed, hold office for five years and until his successor shall be appointed and qualify. The said *Removal for cause.* judges, or a majority of them, may, for cause, at any time remove such commissioner by an instrument in writing to be filed in the county clerk's office of the county for which said commissioner was appointed, and which shall state the cause of such removal; and may in like *Vacancy in office.* manner, as hereinbefore provided, appoint a successor and fill any vacancy which may occur in that office.

§ 3. Within ten days after his appointment such commissioner *Oath of office.* shall take the usual oath of office, before a justice of the supreme court, and said oath shall be filed by him with the clerk of the county for which he is appointed; and he shall thereupon be entitled to enter upon the discharge of his duties.

§ 4. The commissioner of jurors in each county embraced within *Annual salary.* this act shall receive an annual salary of fifteen hundred dollars, payable in monthly installments by the county treasurer of each of said counties, to be raised by tax by the board of supervisors thereof. The board of supervisors of each county embraced within this act shall also *Rooms and supplies.* provide suitable rooms and accommodations for the office of said commissioner, and shall also provide for the payment for books, stationery, printing, and all necessary expenses incurred by him in the discharge of the duties of his office, which expenses shall be first audited by a board consisting of the chairman of the board of supervisors of the county for which said commissioner is appointed, or if not in session, by the chairman of the preceding board of supervisors, and the treasurer and sheriff of said county, and shall be paid by the treasurer of said county. The said commissioner, until the board of *Use of county clerk's office.* supervisors shall make provisions therefor, shall use the county clerk's office of his county to transact the necessary duties of his office, and shall be supplied by the county clerk with necessary books and supplies, which shall be a county charge.

§ 5. The supervisors and assessors of each of the towns, and the *Officials to make and file lists of persons qualified.* supervisor of each of the wards in each county embraced within this act shall within sixty days after written notice given by such commissioner requesting the same (which notice may be served upon said officers by mail), prepare, certify and file with such commissioner a list of all persons residing within such town or ward qualified under the laws of this state to serve as grand and trial jurors. At any time thereafter, whenever required by said commissioner, said supervisor and assessors, or said supervisor, shall make an additional list of persons residing in such town or ward qualified to serve as grand and trial jurors. On the failure of any such officials to make and file such list, the said commissioner shall make and file the same in his office.

Jury list, commissioner to prepare.

§ 6. The said commissioner, from the lists filed as provided in section five of this act, and from such other sources of information as he may find available, shall on or before the first day of November in each year make a list of not less than four hundred and fifty names of persons residing within the county for which he is commissioner who are qualified to act as grand jurors, and who are of approved integrity, fair character, sound judgment, and well informed, apportioned' among the several towns and wards of such county in proportion to the population of the same. The said commissioner shall also from the lists filed, as provided in section five, and from such other sources of information as he may find available, on or before the first day of November in each year, make a list of not less than three thousand names of persons residing within the county for which he is commissioner, who are qualified to act as trial jurors, and who are of approved integrity, fair character, sound judgment, and well informed.

Record and publication of lists.

§ 7. The said commissioner shall on or before the tenth day of November in each year cause such list of names of grand and trial jurors to be alphabetically arranged and entered in a separate book kept by him for that purpose, and shall give, in addition to the name and age, the residence and occupation of each person, which book shall at all reasonable times be open to public inspection; and shall cause the list of grand jurors to be published in at least two newspapers published within said county at least once a week for three

Revision of same.

successive weeks. The said commissioner, on or before the first day of December in each year may revise said list or lists, so prepared, by striking therefrom the name of any person or persons thereon who it shall appear to him are for any good and sufficient reason not qualified to act as grand or trial jurors. Such commissioner shall give notice of a hearing for the proof of exemptions by mailing a notice thereof to each person whose name appears on said revised list to appear at a time and place designated in said notice; and any person who shall not claim or prove his exemption shall be deemed to have

Addition of names

waived the same, and may not thereafter claim it. And in case the number of names upon the lists, as originally prepared by said commissioner, as aforesaid, are reduced, it shall be his duty in the same manner as provided by section six hereof, to add such further or additional names as are required to make the full list of jurors, as provided under section six of this act, and which said lists of additional names shall be subject to revision and correction, and to the addition of other names in the same manner hereinbefore provided for the original lists, until the full lists of jurors, as above provided, are obtained.

§ 8. On or before the fifteenth day of December in each year said commissioner shall file the lists, so prepared and corrected by him, with the county clerk of the county for which he is commissioner, and such corrected list shall constitute the lists of grand and trial jurors for the year beginning on the first day of January then following; the names of said grand and trial jurors are to be prepared for drawing, drawn and summoned in all respects in accordance with the general statutes now in force. *Annual filing of lists. Drawing of jurors.*

§ 9. The county clerk of each county embraced within this act shall on or before the first day of November in each year return to the commissioner a list of names of persons, who have served as grand or trial jurors, or who have been excused by any court by reason of not being qualified, and the reason for such excuse. *Return of county clerk.*

§ 10. Any person who shall do any act whereby he or another shall be placed, or attempted to be placed, upon the jury list, or omitted therefrom, or attempted to be omitted from said list, contrary to the provisions of this act, shall be guilty of a misdemeanor. *Misdemeanor.*

§ 11. This act shall not be deemed to repeal or supercede any general act of this state relating to grand jurors, or to trial jurors except so far, and so far only, as it may be inconsistent with such general act or acts. *Construction of act.*

§ 12. The trial and grand jurors of the counties embraced within this act shall continue to be drawn from the list heretofore prepared pursuant to law and in the manner now prescribed until the first Monday of December, one thousand eight hundred and ninety-seven. *Drawing of jurors from former lists.*

§ 13. This act shall take effect immediately.

Chap. 195.

AN ACT to amend the consolidated school law, in relation to tax for text books.

Became a law April 7, 1897, with the approval of the Governor. Passed, three-fifths being present.

The People of the State of New York, represented in Senate and Assembly, do enact as follows:

Section 1. Section thirteen of article three, title eight of chapter five hundred and fifty-six of the laws of eighteen hundred and ninety-four, entitled "An act to revise, amend and consolidate the *School law amended.*

general acts relating to public instruction," and known as the consolidated school law, is hereby amended by adding thereto a new
subdivision, to be known as subdivision three, to read as follows:

Tax for
text books.
3. The qualified voters of any union free school district present
at any annual school meeting therein, for which a notice has been
duly given that the vote hereinafter mentioned will be taken, or at
any special school meeting therein, duly and legally called for that
purpose, shall have power, by a majority vote, to be ascertained by
taking and recording the ayes and noes, to vote a tax for the purchase of all text books used, or to be used, in the schools of the
district. If such tax shall be voted it shall be the duty of the board
of education of such district, within ninety days thereafter, to purchase and furnish free text books to all the pupils attending the
Rules for
use, etc., of
books.
schools in such district. Such board of education shall have power
to establish such rules and regulations concerning the use by the
pupils of such text books, and the care, preservation and custody
thereof as it shall deem necessary.

§ 2. This act shall take effect immediately.

Chap. 201.

AN ACT to release the right, title and interest of the people of the
state acquired by escheat, in and to certain real estate situate in
the city of Utica.

Became a law April 7, 1897, with the approval of the Governor.
Passed by a two-thirds vote.

*The People of the State of New York, represented in Senate and
Assembly, do enact as follows:*

Interest of
state re-
leased.
Section 1. All the right, title and interest of the people of the
state acquired by escheat in and to real estate situate in the city of
Utica, owned by Sebastian Hoeflinger, deceased, at his decease, is
hereby released unto Anna Hoeflinger, of Nordlingen, Germany,
and Johann Schiele, of Holheim, Germany. Said real estate is
described as being that building lot shown on a map of the Schuyler
farm filed in the Oneida county clerk's office, September twenty-sixth,
eighteen hundred and forty-seven, as lot number thirty-one in block
number one, fronting on Schuyler street, and being forty feet wide
in front and rear, and one hundred feet deep, with the appurtenances thereto belonging, being the property conveyed by Thomas
Chapman and wife to said Sebastian Hoeflinger and his wife
Barbara, as tenants by entireties by deed dated December sixth,
eighteen hundred and sixty-two, recorded in said clerk's office on the
twentieth day of December, eighteen hundred and sixty-two, in

liber two hundred and thirty-nine of deeds at page three hundred and forty-one, to which deed, or the record thereof, reference is hereby made for a more full and accurate description of said property.

§ 2. Nothing in this act contained shall be construed to impair Proviso. or effect the right in the said real estate of any heir at law, devisee, grantee or creditor, by mortgage, judgement or otherwise.

§ 3. This act shall take effect immediately.

Chap. 203.

AN ACT to amend the poor law, relating to the loss of settlement by a poor person.

Became a law April 7, 1897, with the approval of the Governor.
Passed, a majority being present.

The People of the State of New York, represented in Senate and Assembly, do enact as follows:

Section 1. Chapter two hundred and twenty-five of the laws of eighteen hundred and ninety-six, entitled " An act in relation to the poor, constituting chapter twenty-seven of the general laws," is hereby amended by inserting therein a new section to be known as section fifty-seven, and to read as follows:

§ 57. **Settlement, how lost.**— A person who has gained a settlement in a town or city loses the same by a continuous residence elsewhere for one year.

§ 2. This act shall take effect immediately.

Chap. 204.

AN ACT to amend sections fourteen and eighty of the highway law, in relation to the use and dedication of highways.

Became a law April 7, 1897, with the approval of the Governor.
Passed, three-fifths being present.

The People of the State of New York, represented in Senate and Assembly, do enact as follows:

Section 1. Sections fourteen and eighty of chapter five hundred and sixty-eight of the laws of eighteen hundred and ninety, entitled " An act in relation to highways constituting chapter nineteen of the general laws," is hereby amended to read as follows:

§ 14. **Drainage, sewer and water pipes in highways.**—The commissioners of highways may upon written application of any resident of their town, grant permission to lay and maintain drainage, sewer and water pipes and hydrants under ground, within the portion therein described, of any highway within the town, but not under the traveled part of the highway, except to cross the same, for the purposes of sewerage, draining swamps or other lands, and supplying premises with water, upon condition that such pipes and hydrants shall be so laid as not to interrupt or interfere with public travel upon the highway. The consent of the commissioner shall be executed in duplicate, signed by him and indorsed with the written approval of the supervisor and the acceptance of the applicant, and one of such duplicates shall be delivered to the applicant and the other filed with the town clerk. The consent shall also contain a provision to the effect that it is granted on the condition that the applicant will replace all earth removed, and leave the highway in all respects in as good condition as before the laying of said pipes; that the applicant will keep such pipes and hydrants in repair and save the town harmless from all damages which may accrue by reason of their location in the highway; that upon notice by the commissioner, the applicant will make any repairs required for the protection or preservation of the highway; that upon his default such repairs may be made by the commissioner at the expense of the applicant, and that such expense shall be a lien prior to any other lien upon the land benefited by the use of the highway for such pipes or hydrants; and that the commissioner may also, upon the applicant's default, revoke the permission for the use of the highway, and remove therefrom such pipes or hydrants.

§ 80. **Highways by dedication.**—Whenever land is dedicated to a town for highway purposes therein, the commissioners of highways in such town may, either with or without a written application therefor, and without expenses to the town, make an order laying out such highway, upon filing and recording in the town clerk's office with such order a release of the land from the owner thereof. A highway so laid out must not be less than two rods in width. Section ninety of this chapter does not apply to a highway by dedication. Such commissioners of highways may also, upon written application and with the written consent of the town board, make an order laying out or altering a highway in their town, upon filing and recording in the town clerk's office, with such application, consent and order, a release from all damages from the owners of the lands taken or affected thereby, when the consideration for such release, as agreed upon between such commissioners and owners, shall not in any one case, from any one claimant, exceed one hundred dollars, and from all claimants five hundred dollars. An order of the commissioners as herein provided shall be final.

§ 2. This act shall take effect immediately.

Chap. 205.

AN ACT to amend chapter five hundred and fifty-nine of the laws of eighteen hundred and ninety-five, entitled "An act relating to membership corporations," constituting chapter forty-three of the general laws.

Became a law April 7, 1897, with the approval of the Governor. Passed, three-fifths being present.

The People of the State of New York, represented in Senate and Assembly, do enact as follows:

Section 1. Section thirty-one of chapter five hundred and fifty-nine of the laws of eighteen hundred and ninety-five, entitled "An act relating to membership corporations," constituting chapter forty-three of the general laws, is hereby amended so as to read as follows:

§ 31. **Certificates of incorporation.**—Five or more persons may become a membership corporation for any one of the purposes for which a corporation may be formed under this article or for any two or more of such purposes of a kindred nature, by making, acknowledging and filing a certificate, stating the particular objects for which the corporation is to be formed, each of which must be such as is authorized by this article; the name of the proposed corporation; the territory in which its operations are to be principally conducted; the town, village or city in which its principal office is to be located, if it be then practicable to fix such location; the number of its directors, not less than three or more than thirty; and the names and places of residence of the persons to be its directors until its first annual meeting. Such certificate shall not be filed without the written approval, indorsed thereupon or annexed thereto, of a justice of the supreme court. If such certificate specify among such purposes the care of orphan, pauper or destitute children, the establishment or maintenance of a maternity hospital or lying-in asylum where women may be received, cared for or treated during pregnancy or during or after delivery, or for boarding or keeping nursing children, the written approval of the state board of charities shall also be indorsed thereupon or annexed thereto, before the filing thereof. On filing such certificate, in pursuance of law, the signers thereof, their associates and successors, shall be a corporation in accordance with the provisions of such certificate.

§ 2. This act shall take effect immediately.

Chap. 207.

AN ACT authorizing the reconstruction of the bridge over the
Erie canal at Monroe avenue, in the city of Rochester, and making
an appropriation therefor.

Became a law April 7, 1897, with the approval of the Governor.
Passed, three-fifths being present.

*The People of the State of New York, represented in Senate and
Assembly, do enact as follows:*

Reconstruction of bridge   Section 1. The superintendent of public works is hereby authorized to remove the iron bridge now spanning the Erie canal, in the
city of Rochester, at Monroe avenue, including the substructure
thereof, and to erect in its place a new masonry substructure, with
a new steel bridge surmounting the same.

Plans and specifications.   § 2. The plans and specifications of all the parts of said bridge
shall be furnished by the state engineer and surveyor. They shall
include the immediate construction of all the masonry of the substructure. For the superstructure, the said plans and specifications
shall include ultimate provision for two properly-supported asphalt
roadways, with sidewalks on the outside, the roadways to be twenty-
five feet in width and sidewalks eight feet wide; but for immediate
purposes only one roadway and sidewalk to be constructed at one
side of the street; all of which shall be duly defined in the said plans
and specifications.

Appropriation.   § 3. The sum of thirty-two thousand dollars, or so much thereof
as may be necessary, is hereby appropriated for the purposes specified in this act out of any moneys in the treasury not otherwise
appropriated, to be paid by the treasurer, on the warrant of the
comptroller, to the superintendent of public works.

§ 4. This act shall take effect immediately.

Chap. 208.

AN ACT to provide life saving medals for heroic conduct in saving
life on the waters of the state.

Became a law April 7, 1897, with the approval of the Governor.
Passed, three-fifths being present.

*The People of the State of New York, represented in Senate and
Assembly, do enact as follows:*

Medals of honor.   Section 1. That the state comptroller is hereby directed to cause
to be prepared medals of honor with suitable devices, to be distinguished as life-saving medals of the first and second class, which

shall be bestowed by him upon persons who shall hereafter endanger their own lives in saving or endeavoring to save lives from perils of the sea or waters, within or adjacent to the state of New York, at such times and in such manner as he shall prescribe.

§ 2. Medals of the first class shall be confined to cases of extreme Award of and heroic daring, and medals of the second class shall be given in medals. cases of less distinguished conduct, but no award of either medal shall be made to any person until sufficient evidence of his heroism shall have been filed with the state comptroller and entered upon the records of the department.

§ 3. The sum of one hundred dollars is hereby appropriated out Appropria- of any money in the treasury of the state not otherwise appropri- tion. ated, to defray the expenses of carrying into effect the provisions of this act.

§ 4. This act shall take effect immediately.

Chap. 216.

AN ACT to amend section sixty-seven of title two of chapter three of part four of the revised statutes, as amended by chapter three hundred and eighty-two of the laws of eighteen hundred and eighty-nine, and chapter two hundred and eight of the laws of eighteen hundred and ninety-four, to give the warden of Clinton prison control of all lands owned by the state within ten miles of said prison.

Became a law April 7, 1897, with the approval of the Governor.
Passed, three-fifths being present.

The People of the State of New York, represented in Senate and Assembly, do enact as follows:

Section 1. Section sixty-seven of title two of chapter three of Amend- part four of the revised statutes, relating to state prisons, and for ment. other purposes connected therewith, as amended by and superseded by chapter three hundred and eighty-two of the law of eighteen hundred and eighty-nine, and chapter two hundred and eight of the laws of eighteen hundred and ninety-four, is hereby amended so as to read as follows:

§ 67. All lands belonging to the state of New York, or which may Lands re- hereafter become the property of said state, and which shall be tained for use of situated within ten miles of the Clinton prison, shall be withdrawn prison. from sale, and shall be retained by the state for the use of said prison.

§ 2. This act shall take effect immediately.

Chap. 217.

AN ACT to amend the executive law, relating to the second deputy comptroller and to legalize and confirm certain acts of such deputy.

Became a law April 8, 1897, with the approval of the Governor.
Passed, a majority being present.

The People of the State of New York, represented in Senate and Assembly, do enact as follows:

Amendment.

Section 1. Section thirty-one of chapter six hundred and eighty-three of the laws of eighteen hundred and ninety-two, entitled "An act in relation to executive officers, constituting chapter nine of the general laws," is hereby amended to read as follows:

Deputies of comptroller.

§ 31. **Deputies.**— The comptroller shall appoint a deputy who shall be paid an annual salary of four thousand dollars and who may perform any of the duties of the comptroller, except the drawing of warrants on the treasury, the auditing of public accounts, and the duties of the comptroller as commissioner of the land office, commissioner of the canal fund, and as state canvasser. The comptroller shall also appoint one of his clerks as second deputy, who shall assist the deputy comptroller in performing any and all of the duties of that position as the comptroller shall direct, and such second deputy comptroller shall not receive any extra salary by reason of such appointment.

Acts of second deputy legalized.

§ 2. All the acts performed since the first day of October, eighteen hundred and ninety-six by the clerk in the office of the state comptroller appointed as a second deputy comptroller, pursuant to section three of chapter thirteen of the laws of eighteen hundred and ninety-five, which was repealed by chapter five hundred and forty-six of the laws of eighteen hundred and ninety-six, are hereby legalized, ratified and confirmed, and shall be of the same force and effect as if section three of such chapter thirteen of the laws of eighteen hundred and ninety-five had not been so repealed.

§ 3. This act shall take effect immediately.

Chap. 218.

AN ACT to amend the insurance law and the act amendatory thereof, relative to capital and surplus.

**Became a law April 8, 1897, with the approval of the Governor.
Passed, three-fifths being present.**

The People of the State of New York, represented in Senate and Assembly, do enact as follows:

Section 1. Section sixteen of chapter six hundred and ninety of the laws of eighteen hundred and ninety-two, entitled "An act in relation to insurance corporations, constituting chapter thirty-eight of the general laws," and known as the insurance law, as amended by chapter nine hundred and seventeen of the laws of eighteen hundred and ninety-five, is hereby amended so as to read as follows:

§ 16. **Investment of capital and surplus.**— The cash capital of every domestic insurance corporation required to have a capital, to the extent of the minimum capital required by law, shall be invested and kept invested in the kinds of securities in which deposits with the superintendent of insurance are required by this chapter to be made. The residue of the capital and the surplus money and funds of every domestic insurance corporation over and above its capital, and the deposit that it may be required to make with the superintendent, may be invested in or loaned on the pledge of any of the securities in which deposits are required to be invested, or in the public stocks or bonds of any one of the United States, or except as herein provided, in the stocks, bonds or other evidence of indebtedness of any solvent institution incorporated under the laws of the United States or of any state thereof, or in such real estate as it is authorized by this chapter to hold; but no such funds shall be invested in or loaned on its own stock or the stock of any other insurance corporation carrying on the same kind of insurance business. Any domestic insurance corporation may, by the direction and consent of two-thirds of its board of directors, managers or finance committee, invest, by loan or otherwise, any such surplus moneys or funds in the bonds issued by any city, county, town, village or school district of this state, pursuant to any law of this state. Any corporation organized under the ninth subdivision of section seventy of the insurance law, for guaranteeing the validity and legality of bonds issued by any state, or by any city, county, town, village, school district, municipality or other civil division of any state, may invest by loan or otherwise any of such surplus moneys or funds in the bonds which they are authorized to guarantee. Every such domestic corporation doing business in other states of the United States or in foreign countries, may invest the funds required to meet its obligation incurred in such other states

or foreign countries and in conformity to the laws thereof, in the
same kind of securities in such other states or foreign countries that
such corporation is by law allowed to invest in, in this state. Any
life insurance company may lend a sum not exceeding the lawful
reserve which it holds upon any policy, on the pledge to it of such
policy and its accumulations as collateral security. But nothing in
this section shall be held to authorize one insurance corporation to
obtain, by purchase or otherwise, the control of any other insurance
corporation.

§ 2. Section ninety-two of said chapter is hereby amended so as
to read as follows:

§ 92. **No forfeiture of policy without notice** —No life insurance
corporation doing business in this state shall within one year after
the default in payment of any premium, installment or interest
declare forfeited or lapsed, any policy hereafter issued or renewed
and not issued upon the payment of monthly or weekly premiums,
or unless the same is a term insurance contract for one year or less,
nor shall any such policy be forfeited, or lapsed, by reason of non-
payment when due of any premium, interest or installment or any
portion thereof required by the terms of the policy to be paid, within
one year from the failure to pay such premium, interest or installment
unless a written or printed notice stating the amount of such premium, interest, installment, or portion thereof, due on such policy,
the place where it shall be paid, and the person to whom the same is
payable, shall have been duly addressed and mailed to the person
whose life is insured, or the assignee of the policy, if notice of the
assignment has been given to the corporation, at his or her last known
post-office address in this state, postage paid by the corporation, or
by any officer thereof, or person appointed by it to collect such premium, at least fifteen and not more than forty-five days prior to the
day when the same is payable. The notice shall also state that unless such premium, interest, installment or portion thereof, then due,
shall be paid to the corporation, or to the duly appointed agent or
person authorized to collect such premium by or before the day it
falls due, the policy and all payments thereon will become forfeited
and void except as to the right to a surrender value or paid-up
policy as in this chapter provided. If the payment demanded by
such notice shall be made within its time limited therefor, it shall
be taken to be in full compliance with the requirements of the
policy in respect to the time of such payment; and no such policy
shall in any case be forfeited or declared forfeited, or lapsed, until
the expiration of thirty days after the mailing of such notice. The
affidavit of any officer, clerk, or agent of the corporation, or of any
one authorized to mail such notice that the notice required by this
section, has been duly addressed and mailed by the corporation
issuing such policy shall be presumptive evidence that such notice

has been duly given. No action shall be maintained to recover under a forfeited policy, unless the same is instituted within one year from the day upon which default was made in paying the premium, installment, interest or portion thereof for which it is claimed that forfeiture ensued.

§ 3. This act shall take effect immediately.

Chap. 219.

AN ACT making an appropriation for the attendance of the national guard and naval militia of the state of New York at the ceremonies for the dedication of the tomb of General Ulysses S. Grant, on the twenty-seventh of April, eighteen hundred and ninety-seven.

Became a law April 8, 1897, with the approval of the Governor.
Passed, three-fifths being present.

The People of the State of New York, represented in Senate and Assembly, do enact as follows:

Section 1. There is hereby appropriated out of any money in the treasury not otherwise appropriated, the sum of twenty-five thousand dollars, or so much thereof as may be necessary, to pay the transportation, subsistence and other necessary expenses of the national guard and naval militia of the state of New York, in attending the ceremonies for dedicating the tomb of General Ulysses S. Grant, on the twenty-seventh of April, eighteen hundred and ninety-seven. Such money shall be paid by the treasurer on the warrant of the comptroller, upon the certificate and audit of the adjutant-general. approved by the commander-in-chief. *Appropriation.* *How payable.*

§ 2. This act shall take effect immediately.

Chap. 220.

AN ACT to provide for the acquisition of land in the territory embraced in the Adirondack park and making an appropriation therefor.

Became a law April 8, 1897, with the approval of the Governor.
Passed, three-fifths being present.

The People of the State of New York, represented in Senate and Assembly, do enact as follows:

Section 1. The governor, within twenty days after this act takes effect, shall appoint from the commissioners of fisheries, game and forest and the commissioners of the land office, by and with the advice and consent of the senate, three persons to constitute a board *Forest preserve board.*

to be known as "the forest preserve board." The members of such
board may be removed by the governor at his pleasure. Vacancies
shall be filled in like manner as an original appointment. The members of the board shall not receive any compensation for their services under this act, but shall receive their actual and necessary
Assistants. expenses to be audited by the comptroller. The board may employ
such clerical and other assistants as it may deem necessary. The
Annual report. forest preserve board annually in the month of January shall make
a written report to the governor showing in detail all its transactions
under this act during the preceding calendar year.

Acquisition of lands, etc., for state. § 2. It shall be the duty of the forest preserve board and it is
hereby authorized to acquire for the state, by purchase or otherwise,
land, structures or waters or such portion thereof in the territory
embraced in the Adirondack park, as defined and limited by the
fisheries, game and forest law, as it may deem advisable for the
interests of the state.

Entry upon and appropriation of lands. § 3. The forest preserve board may enter on and take possession
of any land, structures and waters in the territory embraced in the
Adirondack park, the appropriation of which in its judgment shall
be necessary for the purposes specified in section two hundred and
ninety of the fisheries, game and forest law, and in section seven of
article seven of the constitution.

Description of lands to be appropriated. § 4. Upon the request of the forest preserve board an accurate
description of such lands so to be appropriated shall be made by the
state engineer and surveyor, or the superintendent of the state
land survey, and certified by him to be correct, and such
board or a majority thereof shall indorse on such description a
certificate stating that the lands described therein have been appropriated by the state for the purpose of making them a part of the
Adirondack park; and such description and certificate shall be filed
Notice of appropriation. in the office of the secretary of state. The forest preserve board
shall thereupon serve on the owner of any real property so appro-
priated a notice of the filing and the date of filing of such description
and containing a general description of the real property belonging to
such owner which has been so appropriated; and from the time of
such service, the entry upon and appropriation by the state of the
real property described in such notice for the uses and purposes above
specified shall be deemed complete, and thereupon such property
shall be deemed and be the property of the state. Such notice shall
be conclusive evidence of an entry and appropriation by the state.
Record and service thereof. The forest preserve board may cause duplicates of such notice with an
affidavit of due service thereof on such owner to be recorded in the
books used for recording deeds in the office of the clerk of any
county of this state where any of the property described therein
may be situated, and the record of such notice and of such proof of
service shall be evidence of the due service thereof.

§ 5. Claims for the value of the property taken and for damages caused by any such appropriation may be adjusted by the forest preserve board if the amount thereof can be agreed upon with the owners of the land appropriated. The board may enter into an agreement with the owner of any land so taken and appropriated, for the value thereof, and for any damages resulting from such appropriation. Upon making such agreement the board shall deliver to the owner a certificate stating the amount due to him on account of such appropriation of his lands, and a duplicate of such certificate shall also be delivered to the comptroller. The amount so fixed shall be paid by the treasurer upon the warrant of the comptroller. *Adjustment of claims by board.*

§ 6. If the forest preserve board is unable to agree with the owner for the value of property so taken or appropriated, or on the amount of damages resulting therefrom, such owner, within two years after the service upon him of the notice of appropriation as above specified, may present to the court of claims a claim for the value of such land and for such damages, and the court of claims shall have jurisdiction to hear and determine such claim and render judgment thereon. Upon filing in the office of the comptroller a certified copy of the final judgment of the court of claims, and a certificate of the attorney-general that no appeal from such judgment has been or will be taken by the state, or, if an appeal has been taken a certified copy of the final judgment of the appellate court, affirming in whole or in part the judgment of the court of claims, the comptroller shall issue his warrant for the payment of the amount due the claimant by such judgment, with interest from the date of the judgment until the thirtieth day after the entry of such final judgment, and such amount shall be paid by the treasurer. *Presentation of claims to board of claims. Payment of award.*

§ 7. The owner of land to be taken under this act may, at his option, within the limitations hereinafter prescribed, reserve the spruce timber thereon ten inches or more in diameter at a height of three feet above the ground. Such option must be exercised within six months after the service upon him of a notice of the appropriation of such land by the forest preserve board, by serving upon such board a written notice that he elects to reserve the spruce timber thereon. If such a notice be not served by the owner within the time above specified, he shall be deemed to have waived his right to such reservation, and such timber shall thereupon become and be the property of the state. In case land is acquired by purchase, the spruce timber and no other may be reserved by agreement between the board and the owner, subject to all the provisions of this act in relation to timber reserved after an appropriation of land by the forest preserve board. The presentation of a claim to the court of claims before the service of a notice of reservation, shall be deemed a waiver of the right to such reservation. *Reservation of spruce timber.*

§ 8. The reservation of timber and the manner of exercising and consummating such right are subject to the following restrictions, limitations and conditions:

1. The reservation does not include or affect timber within twenty rods of a lake, pond or river, and such timber can not be reserved. Roads may be cut or built across or through such reserved space of twenty rods, under the supervision of the forest preserve board, for the purpose of removing spruce timber from adjoining land, and the reservation of spruce timber within such space shall be deemed a reservation by the owner, his assignee or representative, of the right to cut other timber necessary in constructing such road, but such reservation does not confer a right to remove such other timber so cut, or to use it otherwise than in constructing a road.

2. The timber reserved must be removed from the land within fifteen years after the service of notice of reservation, or the making of an agreement subject to regulations to be prescribed by the forest preserve board; but such land shall not be cut over more than once, and the said board may prescribe regulations for the purpose of enforcing this limitation. All timber reserved and not removed from the land within such time shall thereupon become and be the property of the state, and all the title or claim thereto by the original owner, his assigns or representatives, shall thereupon be deemed abandoned.

§ 9. A person who reserves timber as herein provided is not entitled to any compensation for the value of his land purchased or taken and appropriated by the state, nor for any damages caused thereby, until:

1. The timber so reserved is all removed and the object of the reservation fully consummated; or

2. The time limited for the removal of such timber has fully elapsed, or the right to remove any more timber is waived by a written instrument filed with the forest preserve board; and

3. The forest preserve board is satisfied that no trespass on state lands has been committed by such owner or his assigns or representatives; that no timber or other property of the state not so reserved has been taken, removed, destroyed or injured by him or them, and that a cause of action in behalf of the state does not exist against him or them for any alleged trespass or other injury to the property or interests of the state; and

4. That the owner, his assignee, or other representative has fully complied with all rules, regulations and requirements of the forest preserve board concerning the use of streams or other property of the state for the purpose of removing such timber.

§ 10. A warrant shall not be drawn by the comptroller for the amount of compensation agreed upon between the owner and the forest preserve board, nor for the amount of a judgment rendered

Marginal notes:

Limitations and conditions of reservation.

Reserver not entitled to compensation until, etc.

Certificate to be filed before drawing warrant.

by the court of claims, until a further certificate by the board is filed with him to the effect that the owner has not reserved any timber or that he, his assignee, or other representative, has complied with the provisions of this act, or has otherwise become entitled to receive the amount of the purchase price, award or judgment.

§ 11. The forest preserve board may settle and adjust any claims *Claims for* for damages due to the state on account of any trespasses or other *trespass.* injuries to property or interests of the state, or penalties incurred by reason of such trespasses or otherwise, and the amount of such damages or penalties so adjusted shall be deducted from the original compensation agreed to be paid for the lands, or for damages, or from a judgment rendered by the court of claims on account of the appropriation of such land. A judgment recovered by the state for such a trespass or for a penalty shall likewise be deducted from the amount of such compensation or judgment.

§ 12. If timber is reserved upon land purchased or appropriated *Interest* as provided by this act, interest is not payable upon the purchase price *not pay-* *able in cer-* or the compensation which may be awarded for the value of such *tain cases.* land or for damages caused by such appropriation, except as provided in section six.

§ 13. Persons entitled to cut and remove timber under this act *Use of* may use streams or other waters belonging to the state within *waters for* *removing* the forest preserve for the purpose of removing such timber, under *timber.* such regulations and conditions as may be prescribed or imposed by the forest preserve board. The persons using such waters shall be liable for all damages caused by such use.

§ 14. If timber be reserved, its value at the time of making an *Value of* agreement between the owner and the forest preserve board for the *timber to* *be taken* value of the land so appropriated and the damages caused thereby, *into con-* *sideration.* or at the time of the presentation to the court of claims of a claim for such value and damages, shall be taken into consideration in determining the compensation to be awarded to the owner on account of such appropriation either by such agreement or by the judgment rendered upon such a claim.

§ 15. The forest preserve board may appoint inspectors to examine *Inspectors* the lands upon which timber is reserved and ascertain and report to *to examine* *lands.* the board, from time to time, or whenever required, whether such timber is being removed in accordance with the provisions of this act, whether any trespasses or other violations of this act are being committed, and whether the persons entitled to the use of such waters for the purpose of removing timber have complied with the regulations and conditions relating thereto, prescribed or imposed by the board.

§ 16. The forest preserve board shall fix the compensation of all *Pay of* clerks, inspectors or other assistants employed by it, which com- *clerks, in-* *spectors,* pensation shall be paid by the treasurer, upon the certificate of the *etc.*

Removal. board and the audit and warrant of the comptroller. A person so appointed may be removed at the pleasure of the board.

Perfection of title. § 17. The forest preserve board shall take such measures as may be necessary or proper to perfect the title to any lands in the forest preserve now held by the state, and for that purpose may pay and discharge any valid lien or incumbrance upon such land, or may acquire any outstanding or apparent right, title, claim or interest which, in its judgment, constitutes a cloud on such title. The amounts necessary for the purposes of this section shall be paid by the treasurer upon the certificate of the board and the audit and warrant of the comptroller.

Costs and disbursements. § 18. If an offer is made by the forest preserve board for the value of land appropriated, or for damages caused by such appropriation, and such offer is not accepted, and the recovery in the court of claims exceeds the offer, the claimant is entitled to costs and disbursements as in an action in the supreme court, which shall be allowed and taxed by the court of claims and included in its judgment. If in such a case the recovery in the court of claims does not exceed the offer, costs and disbursements to be taxed shall be awarded in favor of the state against the claimant and deducted from the amount awarded to him, or if no amount is awarded judgment shall be entered in favor of the state against the claimant for such costs and disbursements. If an offer is not accepted, it can not be given in evidence on the trial.

Liens to be stated in judgment. § 19. When a judgment for damages is rendered for the appropriation of any lands or waters for the purposes specified in this act, and it appears that there is any lien or incumbrance upon the property so appropriated, the amount of such lien shall be stated in the judgment, and the comptroller may deposit the amount Deposit of award. awarded to the claimant in any bank in which moneys belonging to the state may be deposited, to the account of such judgment, to be paid and distributed to the persons entitled to the same as directed by the judgment.

Actions for despoiling trees, etc. § 20. If a person cuts down or carries off any wood, bark, underwood, trees or timber, or any part thereof, or girdles or otherwise despoils a tree in the forest preserve, without the permission of the forest preserve board, an action may be maintained against him by the board in its name of office and in such an action the board Forfeiture for trees cut down, etc. may recover treble damages if demanded in the complaint. Every such person also forfeits to the state the sum of twenty-five dollars for every tree cut down or carried away by him or under his direction, to be recovered in a like action by the forest preserve board. All sums recovered in any such action shall be paid by the board to the state treasurer, and credited to the general fund.

Service of notice. § 21. Service of a notice by the forest preserve board under section four must be personal if the person to be served can be found

in the state. The provisions of the code of civil procedure relating
to the service of a summons in an action in the supreme court, except
as to publication, apply, so far as practicable, to the service of such
a notice. If a person to be served can not with due diligence be
found in the state, a justice of the supreme court may, by order,
direct the manner of such service, and service shall be made accordingly.

§ 22. The court of claims, if requested by the claimant or the Examina-
attorney-general, shall examine the real property affected by the court of
claim and take the testimony in relation thereto in the county where claims.
such property or a part thereof is situated. The actual and necessary expenses of each judge and of each officer of the court in making
such examination and in so taking testimony shall be audited by
the comptroller and paid from the money appropriated for the purposes of this act.

§ 23. The power to appropriate real property, vested in the forest Limitation
preserve board by section four, is subject to the following limitations: to appro-
Such real property must adjoin land already owned or appropriated property.
by the state at the time the description and certificate are filed in
the office of the secretary of state, except that timber land not so
adjoining state land may be appropriated whenever in the judgment
of the board timber thereon other than spruce, pine or hemlock is
being cut or removed to the detriment of the forest, or the interests
of the state.

§ 24. The sum of six hundred thousand dollars, or so much thereof Appropria-
as may be necessary, is hereby appropriated for the purposes speci- tion.
fied in this act, out of any moneys in the treasury not otherwise
appropriated.   In addition to the amount above appropriated, the
comptroller, upon the written request of the forest preserve board,
is hereby authorized and directed to borrow, from time to time, not Issue of
exceeding in the aggregate the sum of four hundred thousand dol- certifi-
lars for the purposes specified in this act, and to issue bonds or cates.
certificates therefor payable within ten years from their date, bearing interest at a rate not exceeding five per centum per annum, and
which shall not be sold at less than par. The sums so borrowed
are hereby appropriated, payable out of the moneys realized from
the sale of such bonds or certificates, to be expended under the direction of the forest preserve board for the purposes of this act, and to
be paid by the treasurer or the warrant of the comptroller.

§ 25. All acts and parts of acts inconsistent with this act are hereby Repeal.
repealed.

§ 26. This act shall take effect immediately.

Chap. 221.

AN ACT to amend the code of civil procedure, in relation to clerks
and offices for judges of the court of appeals.

Became a law April 8, 1897, with the approval of the Governor.
Passed, three-fifths being present.

*The People of the State of New York, represented in Senate and
Assembly, do enact as follows:*

Section 1. The code of civil procedure is hereby amended by adding two sections to be numbered two hundred and two and two
hundred and three and to read as follows:

§ 202. **Clerks for judges of the court of appeals.**—Each judge of
the court of appeals may appoint and at pleasure remove a clerk,
who shall perform such services as the judge appointing him may
require. He shall be entitled to a compensation to be fixed by such
judge, not exceeding twelve hundred dollars a year, to be paid
monthly by the comptroller upon the certificate of the judge.

§ 203. **Offices for judge of the court of appeals.**—The board of
supervisors of a county in which a law library is maintained by the
state shall, upon the request of a judge of the court of appeals who
resides therein, provide and maintain for his use, suitable and com-
modious offices, approved by him. In case of the refusal or neglect
of the board to comply with such request, the judge may rent and
maintain at his place of residence offices suitable for his use and
the expense thereof shall be a county charge. A judge of said
court who resides in a county where there is no such library, may
rent and maintain at his place of residence offices suitable for his
use, and the necessary expense thereof shall be paid by the state
treasurer upon the audit and warrant of the comptroller.

§ 2. This act shall take effect immediately.

Chap. 222.

AN ACT to amend the poor law, relating to books of accounts and
reports of overseers of the poor.

Became a law April 8, 1897, with the approval of the Governor.
Passed, a majority being present.

*The People of the State of New York, represented in Senate and
Assembly, do enact as follows:*

Section 1. Section twenty-six of chapter two hundred and twenty-
five of the laws of eighteen hundred and ninety-six, entitled "An
act in relation to the poor, constituting chapter twenty-seven of the
general laws," is hereby amended to read as follows:

§ 26. **Overseers to keep books of accounts.**—Overseers of the poor, who receive and expend money for the relief and support of the poor in their respective towns and cities, shall keep books to be procured at town or city expense, in which they shall enter the name, age, sex and native country of every poor person who shall be relieved or supported by them, together with a statement of the causes, either direct or indirect, which shall have operated to render such relief necessary, so far as the same can be ascertained. They shall also enter upon such books a statement of the name and age, and of the names and residences of the parents of every child who is placed by them in a family, with the name and address of the family with whom every such child is placed, and the occupation of the head of the family. They shall also enter upon books so procured, a statement of all moneys received by them, when and from whom, and on what account received, and of all moneys paid out by them, when and to whom paid and on what authority, and whether to town, city or county poor; also a statement of all debts contracted by them as such overseers, the names of the persons with whom such debts were contracted, the amount and consideration of each item, the names of the persons for whose benefit the debts were contracted, and if the same have been paid, the time and manner of such payment. The overseers shall lay such books before the board of town auditors or the common council of the city, at its first annual meeting in each year and, upon being given ten days' notice thereof, at any adjourned or special meeting of such board or council, together with a just, true and verified itemized account, of all moneys received and expended by them for the use of the poor since the last preceding annual meeting of said board, and a verified statement of debts contracted by them as such overseer and remaining unpaid. The board or council shall compare said account with the entries in the book, and shall examine the vouchers in support thereof, and may examine the overseers of the poor, under oath, with reference to such account. They shall thereupon audit and settle the same, and state the balance due to or from the overseer, as the case may be. Such account shall be filed with the town or city clerk, and at every annual town meeting, the town clerk shall produce such town account for the next preceding year, and read the same, if it be required by the meeting. The overseers of the town shall have such books present each year at the annual town meeting, subject to the inspection of the voters of the town, and the entries thereon for the preceding year shall there be read publicly at the time reports of other town officers are presented, if required by a resolution of such meeting. No credit shall be allowed to any overseers for moneys paid, unless it shall appear that such payments were made necessarily or pursuant to a legal order.

§ 2. This act shall take effect immediately.

AN ACT to amend chapter ninety-nine of the laws of eighteen hundred and ninety-six, entitled "An act to authorize the justices of the appellate division of the supreme court in the second judicial department to appoint a clerk, a deputy clerk and attendants, and to provide for their compensation."

Became a law April 8, 1897, with the approval of the Governor.
Passed, three-fifths being present.

The People of the State of New York, represented in Senate and Assembly, do enact as follows:

Act amended. Section 1. Section one of chapter ninety-nine of the laws of eighteen hundred and ninety-six, entitled "An act to authorize justices of the appellate division of the supreme court in the second judicial department to appoint a clerk, a deputy clerk and attendants, and to provide for their compensation," is hereby amended so as to read as follows:

Clerk, deputy and attendants. § 1. The justices of the appellate division of the supreme court in the second judicial department are authorized to apoint and at pleasure remove a clerk, a deputy clerk and five attendants. One of such attendants shall act as crier when directed by the said justices. **Salaries.** The salary of the clerk of said appellate division shall be five thousand dollars per annum, and shall be paid quarterly by the comptroller of the state out of the public treasury. The salary of the deputy clerk shall be three thousand five hundred dollars per annum and of each of said attendants twelve hundred dollars per annum, and shall be paid quarterly by the comptroller of the state out of the moneys to be raised in the manner provided in the next section.

§ 2. This act shall take effect immediately.

Chap. 224.

AN ACT to amend chapter four hundred and sixty-six of the laws of eighteen hundred and sixty-six, entitled "An act in regard to normal schools," relative to quorum of local boards.

Became a law April 8, 1897, with the approval of the Governor.
Passed, three-fifths being present.

The People of the State of New York, represented in Senate and Assembly, do enact as follows:

Act amended. Section 1. Section three of chapter four hundred and sixty-six of the laws of eighteen hundred and sixty-six, entitled "An act in regard to normal schools," is hereby amended so as to read as follows:

§ 3. When the said commission shall have accepted proposals and determined the location of any one of such schools, and when suitable grounds and buildings have been set apart and appropriated for such schools, and all needful preparations made for opening same in accordance with the proposals accepted, the commission shall certify the same in writing, and then their power under this act in relation to such school shall cease, and thereupon the superintendent of public instruction shall appoint a local board, consisting of not less than three persons, who shall, respectively, hold their offices until removed by the concurrent action of the chancellor of the university and the superintendent of public instruction, and who shall have the immediate supervision and management of such school, subject, however, to his general supervision and to his direction in all things pertaining to the school. Such local boards shall have power to appoint one of their number chairman, and another secretary, of the board. A majority of each of said boards shall form a quorum for the transaction of business, and in the absence of any officer of the board, another member may be appointed pro tempore to fill his place and perform his duties. It shall be the duty of such board to make and establish, and from time to time to alter and amend, such rules and regulations for the government of such schools under their charge, respectively, as they shall deem best, which shall be subject to the approval of the superintendent of public instruction. They shall also severally transmit through him, and subject to his approval, a report to the legislature on the first day of January in each year, showing the condition of the school under their charge during the year next preceding, and which report shall be in such form and contain such an account of their acts and doings as the superintendent shall direct, including, especially, an account in detail of their receipts and expenditures, which shall be duly verified by the oath or affirmation of their chairman and secretary.

§ 2. This act shall take effect immediately.

Chap. 225.

AN ACT making an appropriation for the expense of the unusual and extraordinary repairs and alterations in the capitol under the direction of the superintendent of public buildings, and for the maintenance of that department.

Became a law April 8, 1897, with the approval of the Governor.

Passed, three-fifths being present.

The People of the State of New York, represented in Senate and Assembly, do enact as follows:

Appropria-
tion.

Section 1. The treasurer shall pay on the warrant of the comptroller, from any monies not otherwise appropriated, to the superintendent of public buildings, for the unusual alterations, repairs, changes and improvements in the public buildings already made under his charge and for deficiency now existing in the appropriation for care, cleaning, labor, lights, services and other necessary expenses of said department, the sum of eighty-five thousand dollars,

Audit of
claims.

or so much thereof as may be necessary. No such warrant shall be issued except for wages until the amounts claimed shall have been duly audited and allowed by the comptroller.

§ 2. This act shall take effect immediately.

Chap. 226.

AN ACT to legalize the official acts of certain justices of the peace and authorizing them to execute and file official bonds, et cetera.

Became a law April 8, 1897, with the approval of the Governor.

Passed, three-fifths being present.

The People of the State of New York, represented in Senate and Assembly, do enact as follows:

Official
acts legal-
ised.

Section 1. The official acts of every justice of the peace heretofore done and performed, duly elected or appointed to office, so far as such official acts may be affected, impaired or questioned, by reason of the failure of any such justice to take and subscribe the official oath, or give an official bond as required by law, are hereby legalized, ratified and confirmed, and any justice of the peace heretofore elected or appointed to the office who has neglected to file an official bond or undertaking or take the oath of office within the time prescribed by law, may take such oath and file such bond or undertaking within sixty days from and after the passage of this act, and the same shall have all the force, effect and validity as if the same had been

Proviso.

done within the time required by law. Nothing herein contained shall affect any action or proceeding now pending.

§ 2. This act shall take effect immediately.

Chap. 227.

AN ·ACT to amend the highway law and the town law, in relation to abatement of taxes for watering troughs.

Became a law April 8, 1897, with the approval of the Governor.
Passed, three-fifths being present.

The People of the State of New York, represented in Senate and Assembly, do enact as follows:

Section 1. Section forty-eight of chapter five hundred and sixty-eight of the laws of eighteen hundred and ninety, entitled "An act in relation to highways, constituting chapter nineteen of the general laws," is hereby amended to read as follows:

§ 48. **Abatement of tax for watering trough.**—The commissioners of highways shall annually abate three dollars from the highway tax of any inhabitant of a highway district, who shall construct on his own land therein, and keep in repair a watering trough beside the public highway, well supplied with fresh water, the surface of which shall be two or more feet above the level of the ground, and easily accessible for horses with vehicles; but the number of such watering troughs in the district, and their location, shall be designated by the commissioners. In a town in which the highways are worked or repaired by the money system of taxation, the commissioners of highways shall annually issue to each person to whom such an abatement is allowed, a certificate specifying the amount thereof.

§ 2. Section one hundred and eighty of chapter five hundred and sixty-nine of the laws of eighteen hundred and ninety entitled " An act in relation to towns, constituting chapter twenty of the general laws," is hereby amended by adding at the end thereof a new subdivision to be subdivision eight thereof and to read as follows:

8. Every sum allowed by the highway commissioners of a town in which the highways are worked and repaired by the money system of taxation in abatement of highway taxes for the maintenance of watering troughs.

§ 3. This act shall take effect immediately.

Chap. 228.

AN ACT to confer jurisdiction upon the board of claims to hear, audit and determine the alleged claims of Alonzo Denton and N. G. Waterbury (comprising the firm of Denton and Waterbury), William E. Syphert and Albert Harrig (comprising the firm of Syphert and Harrig), Woodhull Lumber Company, Forestport Lumber Company, and James Gallagher, junior, against the state, arising from damages alleged to have been sustained by reason of the building of the state reservoir at Forestport.

Became a law April 8, 1897, with the approval of the Governor.
Passed, three-fifths being present.

The People of the State of New York, represented in Senate and Assembly, do enact as follows:

Jurisdic-
tion to hear
claims.

Section 1. Jurisdiction is hereby conferred upon the board of claims to hear, audit and determine the alleged claims of Alonzo Denton and N. G. Waterbury (comprising the firm of Denton and Waterbury), William E. Syphert and Albert Harrig (comprising the firm of Syphert and Harrig), Woodhull Lumber company, Forestport Lumber company, and James Gallagher, junior, for all damages alleged to have been sustained by them respectively by reason of the building of the state reservoir at Forestport, during the six years last past, and award thereto such sums as a reasonable compensation therefor as, in the judgment of said board, shall be just and equitable.

Appeals
from
awards.

§ 2. Either party may appeal to the appellate division of the supreme court of the third judicial department from any award made under authority of this act, provided such appeal be taken by service of notice of appeal within thirty days of the service of the copy of the award.

§ 3. This act shall take effect immediately.

Chap. 232.

AN ACT to amend chapter six hundred and eighty-six of the laws of eighteen hundred and ninety-two, entitled "An act in relation to counties, constituting chapter eighteen of the general laws."

Became a law April 14, 1897, with the approval of the Governor. Passed,
three-fifths being present.

The People of the State of New York, represented in Senate and Assembly, do enact as follows:

Salary of
county
judge and
rate.

Section 1. Subdivision forty-nine of section two hundred and twenty-two of chapter six hundred and eighty-six of the laws of eighteen hundred and ninety-two, entitled "An act relating to counties, constituting chapter eighteen of the general laws," is hereby amended so as to read as follows:

Subd.	Name of county.	Salary of county judge.	Salary of surrogate.
49	Suffolk.	$1,500 00	$3,000 00

§ 2. This act shall take effect on the first day of January, eighteen hundred and ninety-eight.

Chap. 233.

AN ACT to amend chapter nine hundred and eight of the laws of eighteen hundred and ninety-six, entitled "An act in relation to taxation, constituting chapter twenty-four of the general laws," relative to the purchases by the comptroller for state.

Became a law April 14, 1897, with the approval of the Governor. Passed, three-fifths being present.

The People of the State of New York, represented in Senate and Assembly, do enact as follows:

Section 1. Section one hundred and twenty-three of chapter nine hundred and eight of the laws of eighteen hundred and ninety-six, entitled "An act in relation to taxation, constituting chapter twenty-four of the general laws," is hereby amended to read as follows:

§ 123. Purchases by the comptroller for state or county.—The comptroller shall bid in for the state all lands of the state, and also all lands which may have been bid in by or for the state at any tax sale which has not been canceled, or from which said lands have not been duly redeemed, liable to be sold at any tax sale held by him, or lands that are then mortgaged to the commissioners for loaning certain moneys of the United States, and for each county, all lands belonging to such county liable to be sold at such sale, and also all lands which may have been bid in by or for such county at any tax sale which has not been canceled or from which said lands have not been duly redeemed; and to reject any and all bids made for any of such lands. The comptroller shall make certificates of sales for all lands so bid in by him, describing the lands purchased and specifying the time when a deed therefor can be obtained. Such purchases shall be subject to the same right of redemption as purchases by individuals; and if the land so sold shall not be redeemed, the comptroller's deed therefor shall have the same effect and become absolute in the same time, and on the performance of the like conditions, as in the case of sales and conveyances to individuals. The comptroller shall charge to each county, on the books of his office, the amount for which it may be liable, by reason of any purchase made in accordance with this section, and such amount shall become due on the last day of each tax sale, and shall be payable in the same manner as the state tax is required by law to be paid. The comptroller shall, as soon as practicable, after each tax sale, transmit the certificates of sale for such lands to the treasurer of each of such counties, on receipt of which the county treasurer shall enter the same, in their proper order, in a book to be kept by him for such purpose, and unless otherwise directed by the board of supervisors of his county, shall have full power and authority, until the expiration of one year from the last day of such sale, to sell and assign any of such certificates for any land not at the time owned by his county, on payment therefor, into the county treasury, of the amount for which the land described therein was sold at such tax sale, with interest thereon, from the date of such tax sale to the date of such sale and assignment by him. All such sales and assignments shall be duly and fully entered by such county treasurer in such book, which book shall be a part of the records of the county. If any such tax sale certificate shall not have been sold or assigned by the respective county treasurers on or before the expiration of one year from the last day of such sale, each of such county treasurers shall then transmit such unsold certificate or certificates to the comptroller, who shall issue to the board of supervisors of each county, respectively, a deed or deeds for all of the lands described thereon then remaining unredeemed, or the sale for which has not been canceled. The title thus acquired by the boards of supervisors shall be held by them in trust for their respective counties, and may be disposed of by them at such times and on such terms as shall be determined by a majority of such board at any regular or special meeting thereof.

§ 2. This act shall take effect immediately.

Chap. 235.

AN ACT to amend the railroad law, and the act amendatory thereof, in relation to change of route, grade or terminus.

Became a law April 14, 1897, with the approval of the Governor. Passed, three-fifths being present.

The People of the State of New York, represented in Senate and Assembly, do enact as follows:

Section 1. Section thirteen of chapter five hundred and sixty-five of the laws of eighteen hundred and ninety, entitled "An act in relation to railroads constituting chapter thirty-nine of the general laws," and known as the railroad law as amended by chapter six hundred and seventy-six of the laws of eighteen hundred and ninety-two, is hereby amended so as to read as follows:

§ 13. Change of route, grade or terminus.—Every railroad corporation, except elevated railway corporations, may, by a vote of two-thirds of all its directors, alter or change the route or any part of the route of its road or its termini, or locate such route, or any part thereof, or its termini, in a county adjoining any county named in its certificate of incorporation, if it shall appear to them that the line can be improved thereby, upon making and filing in the clerk's office of the proper county a survey, map and certificate of such alteration or change. If the same is made after the corporation has commenced grading the original route, compensation shall be made to all persons for injury done by such grading to any lands donated to the corporation. But neither terminus can be changed, under this section, to any other county than one adjoining that in which it was previously located; nor can the route or terminus of any railroad be so changed in any town, county or municipal corporation, which has issued bonds and taken any stock or bonds in aid of the construction of such railroad without the written consent of a majority of the taxpayers appearing upon the last assessment roll of such town, county or municipal corporation, unless such terminus, after the change, will remain in the same village or city as theretofore. No alteration of the route of any railroad after its construction shall be made, or new line or route of road laid out or established, as provided in this section, in any city or village, unless approved by a vote of two-thirds of the common council of the city or trustees of the village. Any railroad corporation whose road as located terminates at any railroad previously constructed or located, whereby communication might be had with any incorporated city, of the state, may amend its certificate of incorporation so as to terminate its road at the point of its intersection with any railroad subsequently located to intersect it, and thereby, by itself or its connection, afford communication with such city, with the consent of the stockholders owning two-thirds of the stock of the corporation. Any railroad corporation may, by a vote of its directors, change the grade of any part of its road, except that in the city of Buffalo such change must conform to the general plan heretofore adopted and filed by the grade crossing commissioners of said city, or any modification thereof, within the territory covered by said general plan, in such manner as it may deem necessary to avoid accidents and facilitate the use of such road; and it may by such vote alter the grade of its road, for such distance and in such manner as it may deem necessary, on each or either side of the place where the grade of its road has been changed by direction of the superintendent of public works, at any point where its road crosses any canal or canal feeder, except that in the city of Buffalo such change must conform to the general plan heretofore adopted and filed by the grade crossing commissioners of said city, or any modification thereof, within the territory covered by said general plan. The superintendent of public works shall have a general and supervisory power over that part of any railroad which passes over, or approaches within ten rods of any canal or canal feeder belonging to the state so far as may be necessary to preserve the free and perfect use of such canals or feeders, or to make any repairs, improvements or alterations, in the same. Any railroad corporation whose tracks cross any of the canals of the state, and the grade of which may be raised by direction of the superintendent of public works, with the assent of such superintendent, may lay out a new line of road to cross such canal at a more favorable grade, and may extend such new line and connect the same with any other line of road owned by such corporation upon making and filing in the clerk's office of the proper county a survey map and certificate of such new or altered line. No portion of the track of any railroad, as described in its certificate of incorporation, shall be abandoned under this section.

§ 2. This act shall take effect immediately.

Chap. 238.

AN ACT to amend chapter seven hundred and twenty-three of the laws of eighteen hundred and ninety-five, entitled "An act in relation to religious corporations, constituting chapter forty-two of the general laws," as amended by chapter three hundred and thirty-seven of the laws of eighteen hundred and ninety-six, relative to the Baptist missionary convention.

Became a law April 14, 1897, with the approval of the Governor. Passed, three-fifths being present.

· *The People of the State of New York, represented in Senate and Assembly, do enact as follows:*

Section 1. Section fifteen of chapter seven hundred and twenty-three of the laws of eighteen hundred and ninety-five, known as the "religious corporations law" as amended by chapter three hundred and thirty-seven of the laws of eighteen hundred and ninety-six, is hereby amended so as to read as follows:

§ 15. **Property of extinct churches.**—Such incorporated governing body may decide that a church, parish or society in connection with it or over which it has ecclesiastical jurisdiction, has become extinct, if it has failed for two consecutive years next prior thereto, to maintain religious services according to the discipline, customs and usages of such governing body, or has had less than thirteen resident attending members paying annual pew rent, or making annual contribution toward its support, and may take possession of the temporalities and property belonging to such church, parish or religious society, and manage; or may, in pursuance of the provisions of law relating to the disposition of real property by religious corporations, sell or dispose of the same and apply the proceeds thereof to any of the purposes to which the property of such governing religious body is devoted, and it shall not divert such property to any other object. The New York Eastern Christian Benevolent and Missionary Society shall be deemed the governing religious body of any extinct or disbanded church of the Christian denomination situated within the bounds of the New York Eastern Christian conference; and the New York Christian Association, of any other church of the Christian denomination, and any other incorporated conference shall be deemed the governing religious body of any church situated within its bounds. By Christian denomination is meant only the denomination especially termed " Christian," in which the Bible is declared to be the only

rule of faith, Christian their only name, and Christian character
their only test of fellowship, and in which no form of baptism is
made a test of Christian character.

§ 2. This act shall take effect immediately.

Chap. 241.

AN ACT making an appropriation for the Thomas asylum for orphan,
and destitute Indian children.

Became a law April 15, 1897, with the approval of the Governor.
Passed, three-fifths being present.

*The People of the State of New York, represented in Senate and
Assembly, do enact as follows:*

Appropria-
tion for
improve-
ments.

Section 1. So much of the following sums as may be necessary, is
hereby appropriated for the uses and purposes of the Thomas asylum for orphan and destitute Indian children, from any moneys in
the treasury not otherwise appropriated: For a new main building,
twenty-five thousand dollars. For moving present main building
and converting the same into a boys' building and dormitory, one
thousand five hundred dollars. For improved electric light
equipment, engine, dynamo, boiler, lights and wiring, one thousand eight hundred dollars. For addition to laundry and
altering the present room suitably for an engineroom, one thousand
dollars. For mangler and other laundry machinery, five hundred
dollars. For furnishing the family kitchen and children's kitchen,
six hundred dollars. For sewer extensions and repairs, one thous-
and dollars. For changing the location of the present building,
used for small boys, seven hundred dollars. For improvements
needed in water supply, eight hundred dollars. For new cow barn,
one thousand dollars. For milkhouse, two hundred dollars. For
new icehouse, two hundred dollars

Plans and
specifica-
tions.

§ 2. Such buildings and improvements shall be erected and constructed in accordance with plans and specifications prepared by
the capitol commissioner under the provisions of chapter seven
hundred and eighty-four of the laws of eighteen hundred and

Payment of
appropria-
tion.

ninety-five. The treasurer of the state shall, on the warrant of the
comptroller, pay to the treasurer of such asylum the sums so appropriated as required for the erection of such buildings and the
making of such improvements. Before such warrant is issued
an itemized statement shall be made to the comptroller showing

the purposes for which the money is required. Such statement shall be signed by a majority of the board of managers and verified by the superintendent.

§ 3. This act shall take effect immediately.

Chap. 244.

AN ACT to extend the time of the New York Connecting Railroad Company, to begin construction of its road and expend thereon ten per centum of the amount of its capital, and finish and put the same in operation.

Became a law April 15, 1897, with the approval of the Governor. Passed, a majority being present.

The People of the State of New York, represented in Senate and Assembly, do enact as follows:

Section 1. The time of the New York Connecting Railroad Company for beginning the construction of its road, and expending thereon ten per centum of the amount of its capital, is hereby extended to the first day of May in the year eighteen hundred and ninety-nine, and the time for said company to finish its road and put it in operation, is hereby extended five years from said date. Time for completion of road extended.

§ 2. This act shall take effect immediately.

Chap. 247.

AN ACT to permit examination of dental students matriculated prior to January first, eighteen hundred and ninety-six, under the conditions as to preliminary education in force at the date of their matriculation.

Became a law April 15, 1897, with the approval of the Governor. Passed, three-fifths being present.

The People of the State of New York, represented in Senate and Assembly, do enact as follows:

Section 1. Any student who had matriculated in a registered dental school prior to January first, eighteen hundred and ninety-six, in compliance with the requirements as to preliminary education announced in the catalogue, prospectus or announcement of such dental school for that year shall on completing his full course of professional study, passing satisfactory examinations thereon, Examination of certain dental students permitted.

and in all other respects complying with the requirements of the
faculty and trustees of said dental school, be entitled to receive his
degree in dentistry from said dental school without other requirements as to preliminary education, and shall on application be cer-
Proviso. tified by the regents to the state board of dental examiners for
examination for license to practice dentistry; providing that said
application shall in all respects, other than preliminary education,
meet the present requirements of said regents and said board.

§ 2. This act shall take effect immediately.

Chap. 248.

AN ACT to amend section twenty-six hundred and six of the code
of civil procedure, relating to accounting by executor, et cetera,
of deceased executor.

Became a law April 15, 1897, with the approval of the Governor.
Passed, three-fifths being present.

*The People of the State of New York, represented in Senate and
Assembly, do enact as follows:*

Section 1. Section twenty-six hundred and six of the code of
civil procedure is hereby amended to read as follows:

§ 2606. **Accounting by executor, et cetera, of deceased executor.**—Where an executor, administrator, guardian or testamentary trustee dies, the surrogates' court has the same jurisdiction,
upon the petition of his successor, or of a surviving executor, administrator or guardian, or of a creditor, or person interested in the
estate, or of a guardian's ward, or the legal representative of a
deceased ward, or a surety upon the official bond of the decedent,
or the legal representative of a deceased surety, to compel the
executor or administrator of the decedent to account, which it
would have against the decedent if his letters have been revoked
by a surrogate's decree. And an executor or administrator of a
deceased executor, administrator, guardian, or testamentary
trustee may voluntarily account for any of the trust property which
comes to his possession, and upon his petition such successor or
surviving executor, administrator, or guardian or other necessary
party shall be cited and required to attend such settlement. With
respect to the liability of the sureties in, and for the purpose of
maintaining an action upon the decedent's official bond, a decree
against his executor or administrator, rendered upon such an ac-

counting, has the same effect as if an execution issued upon a surrogate's decree against the property of decedent had been returned unsatisfied during decedent's life-time. So far as concerns the executor or administrator of decedent, such a decree is not within the provisions of section twenty-five hundred and fifty-two of this act. The surrogate's court has also jurisdiction to compel the executor or administrator at any time to deliver over any of the trust property which has come to his possession or is under his control, and if the same is delivered over after a decree, the court must allow such credit upon the decree as justice requires.

§ 2. This act shall take effect September first, eighteen hundred and ninety-seven.

Chap. 249.

AN ACT to further amend chapter eight hundred and eighty-eight of the laws of eighteen hundred and sixty-nine, entitled "An act to amend title sixteen, chapter eight, part three, of the revised statutes, relative to proceedings for the drainage of swamps, marshes, and other low or wet lands, and for draining farm lands," and acts amendatory thereof and supplementary thereto.

Became a law April 15, 1897, with the approval of the Governor. Passed, three-fifths being present.

The People of the State of New York, represented in Senate and Assembly, do enact as follows:

Section 1. Section eleven of chapter eight hundred and eighty-eight of the laws of eighteen hundred and sixty-nine, entitled "An act to amend title sixteen, chapter eight, part three of the revised statutes, relative to proceedings for the drainage of swamps, marshes and other low and wet lands, and for draining farm lands," as amended by section two, of chapter three hundred and twenty-one of the laws of eighteen hundred and ninety-two, is hereby further amended so as to read as follows: *Act amended.*

§ 11. The said commissioners shall within thirty days after filing said statement, in case the same is not appealed from, and within thirty days after notice of the final determination of the appellate court thereon, in case the same is appealed from, levy the assessments herein provided for in one sum or annually thereafter until said sum is paid, and proceed to collect the same. In cases where any persons have been awarded land damages, such damages shall be deducted from the assessment, and only the balance shall *Levy and collection of assessments.*

Towns and villages may borrow money.

be collected. In case it is determined that any town or village shall pay any part of such sum, the supervisor of such town, or the board of trustees of such village, is authorized to borrow money on the credit of the town or village, as the case may be, to pay the same, or any instalment thereof, and the board of supervisors shall at their next ensuing annual meeting include the amount assessed on any town in the next tax levy on said town, together with any sum to be paid by said county, which shall be included in the sum to be raised for such county. Money so borrowed shall be upon obligation of the village or town issued at not less than par, bearing interest at six per centum, payable out of the moneys raised by tax levy as aforesaid, and receivable in payment of such taxes.

Annual assessments.

In case it is determined that said assessments shall be levied annually, the said commissioners shall also determine the amount of each annual assessment, and shall certify such amounts to the supervisor of the town in which the lands to be assessed are located,

Issue and sale of bonds.

and the supervisor of such town shall thereupon immediately issue bonds of the town to the total amount named in said statement filed by said commissioners, and so certified by them to him, such bonds to bear interest at six per centum per annum, to be sold for not less than par, and shall be paid out of the moneys collected from the assessments against said lands as determined by said commissioners and included in their said statement filed as aforesaid, and the amounts of such assessments shall be collected annually from the property assessed, in such instalments as determined by said commissioners, together with the interest accrued on such town bonds for such amounts as other town taxes are collected. Such bonds shall be issued in several series, each series made payable at such time and equal to such amount, as shall correspond with the annual instalments as certified to said supervisor by said commissioners. Said bonds or the proceeds from the sale of said bonds as said commissioners shall direct in writing, shall immediately be delivered by said supervisor to the treasurer of said commission, and said commissioners shall thereupon be discharged of all duty respecting the collection of said annual instalments and shall thereupon im-

Application of proceeds from sale of bonds.

mediately, from the proceeds derived from the sale of said bonds at not less than par, pay all obligations incurred by them for draining said lands, authorized by this act, included in the statement filed by them, including such evidences of indebtedness as they may have theretofore issued in pursuance of the authority contained in section eight of this act. The court in which the proceeding is pending shall have jurisdiction, by mandamus, upon the petition of any party aggrieved to enforce the prompt compliance of any of the provisions of this section on the part of any official charged therewith.

Power of court to enforce compliance.

§ 2. This act shall apply to all proceedings instituted in pursuance of chapter eight hundred and eighty-eight of the laws of eighteen hundred and sixty-nine, prior to the passage of this act and not concluded at the time of its passage, as well as to all such proceedings that may hereafter be instituted.

Application act.

Chap. 250.

AN ACT to amend the fish, game and forest law, in relation to fishing in certain waters in Warren county.

Became a law April 15, 1897, with the approval of the Governor. Passed, three-fifths being present.

The People of the State of New York, represented in Senate and Assembly, do enact as follows:

Section 1. Chapter four hundred and eighty-eight of the laws of eighteen hundred and ninety-two, the title to which was amended by chapter three hundred and ninety-five of the laws of eighteen hundred and ninety-five, to read "An act relating to game, fish and wild animals, and to the forest preserve and Adirondack park, constituting chapter thirty-one of the general laws, and to be known as the fisheries, game and forest law," as amended by chapter nine hundred and seventy-four of the laws of eighteen hundred and ninety-five, is hereby amended by adding thereto, after section one hundred and thirty-two, a new section to be numbered one hundred and thirty-three and to read as follows:

§ 133. **Fishing in certain waters in Warren county.**—No person or persons shall attempt to fish, catch or attempt to catch fish of any kind in any manner or with any device whatever in or from any of the following named waters, viz.: East brook and West brook, or from any of the tributaries of said East brook or to said West brook, in the town of Caldwell, Harris or Edmund brook, Indian brook and Finkle brook in the town of Bolton, Warren county, at any time within two years after the passage of this act. No person or persons shall fish or attempt to fish in any manner or with any device in or from the waters of Lake George or in or from Glen lake or from any of the tributaries of said lakes in Warren county, any pike-perch or any great northern pike, between the first day of January and the fifteenth day of June in each year, or bull-heads, between the first day of January and the first day of July of each year, nor black bass or Oswego bass from any of the waters in the town of Horicon, between the first day of January and the tenth day of July of each year. Provided, however, that perch may be caught by angling in the waters of Lake George at any time. Whoever shall violate or attempt to violate any of the provisions of this section shall be deemed guilty of a misdemeanor and in addition thereto shall be liable to a penalty of fifty dollars for each violation and ten dollars for each fish caught, killed or possessed contrary to any of the provisions of this section.

§ 2. All acts and parts of acts inconsistent with this act are hereby repealed.

§ 3. This act shall take effect immediately.

Chap. 251.

AN ACT conferring jurisdiction upon the board of claims to hear, audit and determine the claim of Hannah E. Gilbert against the state for damages from flooding and otherwise injuring the lands owned by her, caused by a change in the bed and course of Newtown creek.

Became a law April 15, 1897, with the approval of the Governor.
Passed, three-fifths being present.

The People of the State of New York, represented in Senate and Assembly, do enact as follows:

Jurisdiction to hear claim.

Section 1. Jurisdiction is hereby granted to and conferred upon the board of claims to hear, audit and determine the claim of Hannah E. Gilbert, owner of lands situate in the village of Horseheads, Chemung county, New York, for damages caused by the flooding of said lands, injuring and destroying foundations of buildings and embankments thereon and compelling the erection of new embankments for her protection, at the expense of said owner, alleged to have been occasioned by changing the course and bed of Newtown creek, in said village of Horseheads, by the officers and agents of the state, and by their negligent acts, and negligent failure to properly dock said creek and protect said owner and her property adjacent thereto, from injury by the waters thereof.

§ 2. If the facts proved before said board shall establish a just *Award of damages.* and equitable claim against the state for damages caused as aforesaid, the said board shall determine the amount of said damages, and award such sum therefor as may be just and equitable.

§ 3. Either party may take an appeal to the appellate division *Appeal from award.* of the supreme court of the third department from any award made under authority of this act, provided such appeal be taken by service of a notice of appeal within thirty days of the service of a copy of the award.

§ 4. This act shall take effect immediately.

Chap. 252.

AN ACT to amend the town law, relative to the compensation of town officers.

Became a law April 15, 1897, with the approval of the Governor. Passed, three-fifths being present.

The People of the State of New York, represented in Senate and Assembly, do enact as follows:

Section 1. Section one hundred and seventy-eight of chapter five hundred and sixty-nine of the laws of eighteen hundred and ninety, entitled "An act in relation to towns, constituting chapter twenty of the general laws," is hereby amended to read as follows:

§ 178. Compensation of town officers.—Town officers shall be entitled to compensation at the following rates for each day actually and necessarily devoted by them to the service of the town in the duties of their respective offices, when no fee is allowed by law for the service, as follows:

1. The supervisor, except when attending the board of supervisors, town clerks, assessors, commissioners of highways, justices of the peace and overseers of the poor, each, two dollars per day.

2. If a different rate is not otherwise established as herein provided, each inspector of election, ballot clerk and poll clerk is entitled to two dollars per day; but the board of supervisors may establish in their county a higher rate, not exceeding six dollars per day.

§ 2. This act shall take effect immediately.

Chap. 255.

AN ACT to amend sections forty-one and forty-one-a of title five of chapter six hundred and seventy-six of the laws of eighteen hundred and eighty-one, as amended, entitled the penal code of the state of New York, relating to primaries and conventions.

Became a law April 15, 1897, with the approval of the Governor.

Passed, a majority being present.

The People of the State of New York, represented in Senate and Assembly, do enact as follows:

Section 1. Sections forty-one and forty-one-a of title five of chapter six hundred and seventy-six of the laws of eighteen hundred and eighty-one are hereby amended so as to read as follows:

§ 41. **Misdemeanor at political caucuses, primaries and conventions.**— Any person who:

1. Votes or attempts to vote at a political caucus, primary or convention without being entitled to do so; or

2. By bribery, menace or other corrupt means, directly or indirectly, attempts to influence the vote of any person entitled to vote at such caucus, primary or convention, or obstructs such person in voting, or prevents him from voting thereat; or

3. Fraudulently or wrongfully does any act tending to affect the result of an election at such caucus, primary or convention; or,

4. Being an officer, teller or canvasser thereof, willfully omits, refuses or neglects to do any act required by the election law, or refuses to permit any person to do any act authorized thereby, or makes or attempts to make any false canvass of the ballots cast at such caucus, primary or convention, or statement of the result of a canvass of the ballots cast thereat; or

5. Induces or attempts to induce any officer, teller or canvasser of such caucus, primary or convention to do any act in violation of his duty; or,

6. Directly or indirectly, by himself or through any other person, pays, or offers to pay, money or other valuable thing to any person to induce any voter or voters to vote or refrain from voting at such caucus, primary or convention for any particular person or persons; or

7. Directly or indirectly, by himself or through any other person, receives money or other valuable thing, before, at or after such caucus, primary or convention, for voting or refraining from voting for or against any person at such caucus, primary or conven-

tion, is guilty of a misdemeanor, punishable by imprisonment for not more than one year.

§ 41a. Any person who causes his name to be placed upon any list or register of voters in more than one election district for the same election or upon a list or register of voters knowing that he will not be a qualified voter in the district at the election for which such list or register is made, or who causes his name to be placed upon the rolls of a party organization of one party while his name is by his consent or procurement upon the rolls of a party organization of another party, or aids or abets any such act, is punishable by a fine of five hundred dollars and imprisonment for not more than five years.

§ 2. This act shall take effect immediately.

Chap. 256.

AN ACT to prohibit the sale or gift of tobacco to minors in reformatories, penitentiaries or house of refuge.

Became a law April 15, 1897, with the approval of the Governor.
Passed, three-fifths being present.

The People of the State of New York, represented in Senate and Assembly, do enact as follows:

Section 1. A person or officer who sells or gives any cigar, cigarette, snuff or tobacco in any of its forms to any minor undergoing confinement or sentence in any reformatory, penitentiary or house of refuge in this state is guilty of a misdemeanor.

§ 2. This act shall take effect immediately.

Chap. 259.

AN ACT to authorize the state to acquire title to certain lands of the county of Ulster lying within the forest preserve.

Became a law April 15, 1897, with the approval of the Governor.
Passed, three-fifths being present.

The People of the State of New York, represented in Senate and Assembly, do enact as follows:

Section 1. The county treasurer of the county of Ulster shall, Statement of lands within thirty days after the passage of this act, transmit to the acquired at tax sale. board of fisheries, game and forest, a full and complete statement,

until the expiration of the term for which he was appointed at an annual salary of one thousand five hundred dollars and shall give an official undertaking within ten days after this act takes effect in the sum of thirty thousand dollars with at least five sufficient sureties for the faithful performance of his duties to be approved by and filed in the office of the comptroller.

§ 6. **Powers of the superintendent.**—Such superintendent shall:

1. Have the possession, government and management of all lands, wood, timber, trees, buildings, erections, pumps and machinery of every kind, and of all water courses, conduits, wells, aqueducts, springs and other property belonging to the state on the Onondaga reservation, and the Montezuma salt springs.

2. Superintend and have charge of the salt springs and of the manufacture and inspection of salt and regulate and control the delivery of salt water to salt manufacturers.

3. Daily examine or cause to be examined the cisterns attached to the several manufactories in order to discover any leaks or waste of salt water therefrom or from the logs or conduits leading the water to them and to discover any leak or waste of salt water, either by negligence or design whether in the cisterns, logs or conduits or in the use of the water in any manufactory, or in letting the same into the cistern or in any other manner; and shall order the owner or other person occupying such manufactory or his agents or servants who may be present to immediately stop such leak or waste.

4. Cause any person wrongfully possessed of any land or property on the Onondaga reservation or the Montezuma salt springs to remove therefrom and take possession of the same and may sue in his name of office for the recovery of, damages for any injury to such lands or property according to the nature of such injury.

5. Keep in each of his offices regular books of entry in which all of his accounts and transactions shall be entered.

6. Provide suitable books of entry, blank books, blank inspection bills, returns, forms and other stationery for the use of himself and his deputies for the performance of their official duties.

7. Receive all moneys payable to the state for the duties, rents, fines or penalties specified in this chapter or arising from the salt springs or property of the state connected with the salt manufactory.

8. Deposit each week to the credit of the state treasurer in such bank or banks as may be designated by the comptroller all moneys received by him as superintendent, and transmit every Monday

to the comptroller a statement showing the amount of the revenues collected, received and deposited during the preceding week.

9. Forward a statement to the comptroller on the first Monday in each month exhibiting the whole amount of revenue collected during the preceding month and the amount in each week, with a transcript of the receiver's books in each of the manufacturing districts.

10. Prosecute in the name of the state all persons who shall knowingly trespass upon or injure any of the lands or property belonging to the state who shall wilfully damage any of the machinery, erections, fixtures or other property of the state and for the recovery of all such sums forfeited to the state.

11. Make a report annually to the comptroller on September thirtieth or within ten days thereafter, stating the quantity of salt inspected during the previous year, the amount of revenues accruing thereon and from other sources, the expenditures made by the superintendent, and the amount which, in his judgment, will be necessary for the support of the salt springs for the ensuing year.

12. Make a report annually to the legislature on or before January fifteenth, of his doings during the preceding year, embracing such information in regard to the manufacture of salt and the situation of public work, and submitting such recommendations for their further improvement and extension as he shall deem necessary and proper. If the superintendent neglect to make the monthly return required by this section, or to make or transmit the certificate of such deposits to the comptroller, the comptroller shall order the superintendent in bonds to be put in suit for the recovery of any moneys which may be in his hands belonging to the state, and such neglect or omission of duty shall be deemed cause for the removal of such superintendent by the governor.

§ 7. **Further powers and duties of superintendent.—** The superintendent may:

1. Administer oaths to his deputies, foreman and employes in regard to the return of check rolls and other matters relating to their duties when he shall deem it necessary.

2. Require the officers appointed by him to perform such duties and services in behalf of the state as he may consider appropriate and necessary and remove them or either of them from office.

3. Establish and from time to time alter the boundaries of the inspection districts so as to allow of the inspection of salt at the

offices most convenient to the officers in charge and to the owners of the salt works.

§ 8. **Rules and regulations** – The superintendent shall, annually, in the month of April, adopt rules and regulations for the guidance and direction of the salt manufacturers for the ensuing year, and may also, from time to time, establish such rules and regulations, not inconsistent with law, as he may deem expedient respecting:

1. The manufacture and inspection of salt and the collection of duties thereon.

2. The manner and order of receiving salt water from the state reservoirs and aqueducts, the mode of conducting it to the respective manufactories and the erections and securing it from waste and loss.

3. The examination of the several salt works and manufactories by his deputies to determine whether the provisions of the law are properly complied with.

4. The loading of salt in bulk, or otherwise, into boats to be transported upon the canals or the shipment of salt by railway, or otherwise, to be conveyed to market.

5. Such matters as shall tend to the more perfect execution of the provisions of this chapter, such rules and regulations shall take effect upon the expiration of one week from the time they are made and published, and shall be enforced until they are revoked or others are established in their stead.

§ 9. **Penalties, rules and penalties to be posted.**—The superintendent may prescribe specific penalties not exceeding one hundred dollars for each offense for any violation of the rules and regulations established by him and recover the same in the name of the state with costs, and shall stop all communication between any salt block or manufactory and the state reservoir, if the person in charge of such block or manufactory shall refuse to comply with the provisions of law or the rules and regulations of the superintendent so that no salt water shall come to such block or manufactory until such provisions are complied with. Such rules and regulations and the several penalties prescribed thereby and by law shall be printed and posted conspicuously in the several offices of the superintendent, in all the fine salt manufactories and in the storehouses for coarse salt, and in the mills for grinding salt, and in such other places as shall be deemed expedient for the information of the public.

§ 10. **Habitual neglect to comply with rules.**—The superintendent shall suspend for such length of time as he may deem proper,

not exceeding three months at any one time, the right of any salt
manufacturer to carry on his manufactory if such manufacturer
shall habitually neglect the rules and regulations prescribed by the
superintendent or by law, or shall be in the habit of making bad
salt, or if the quantity of salt inspected from his manufactory shall
be found materially less than is usually produced from a manufactory of the same capacity of kettles for the time it is actually in
operation.

§ 11. Officers not to be concerned in manufacturing.—No officer
or employe connected with the salt springs shall be in any way concerned in the manufacture or sale of salt or have any interest whatever, directly or indirectly, in any salt manufactory or erection for
the manufacture of salt, or in the profits of any such manufactory,
or in any labor or materials, or contracts for doing any work on the
salt reservations which may be done under the provisions of this
chapter.

§ 12. Deputies and inspectors.—The superintendent may by a
written order filed in the clerk's office of Onondaga county appoint
the following deputies and assistants: One deputy superintendent,
who shall be the receiver and chief clerk and in the case of the
death, removal or resignation of the superintendent, possess his
powers and discharge his duties until another shall be appointed;
one chief engineer, one chief inspector of salt, each of whom shall
receive an annual salary of twelve hundred dollars; three inspectors of salt, who shall receive an annual salary of six hundred dollars; three block inspectors, each of whom shall receive a salary of
sixty dollars for not more than eight months in each year; two re
ceivers, who shall receive an annual salary of eight hundred and
forty dollars; one receiver, who shall receive an annual salary of five
hundred and forty dollars; one overseer of pumps, who shall receive
an annual salary of six hundred dollars; three overseers of pumps,
who shall each receive the sum of fifty dollars a month for not
more than eight months in each year; one superintendent of aque
ducts and reservoirs, who shall receive an annual salary of six
hundred and sixty dollars; three such superintendents, who shall
each receive an annual salary of four hundred and eighty dollars;
one chief inspector of barrels, who shall receive an annual salary of
eight hundred and forty dollars; three assistant barrel inspectors,
who shall each receive a salary of fifty dollars a month while employed; two assistant barrel inspectors, who shall each receive
fifty dollars a month for such time as their services are necessary

and such additional assistants, pumpers, inspectors, weigners and overseers as may be necessary during the business part of the season, who shall receive not more than fifty dollars a month for not more than eight months a year. Before entering upon the duties of his office, each person appointed by the superintendent shall execute and deliver, to him an official undertaking in amounts with sufficient sureties for the faithful performance of his duties and for the faithful and punctual payment to such superintendent of all moneys which such person shall from time to time receive, and as often and at such stated periods as may be required of him. A list of the names of all officers appointed by the superintendent shall be kept conspicuously posted in each of the receivers' offices in the several districts.

§ 13. Inspection of salt.—The superintendent and his deputies charged with the inspection of salt shall carefully and constantly superintend its manufacture in the several fine and coarse salt manufactories, and examine and inspect such salt in the various stages of its production in the kettles, vats, bins and storehouses; and require inferior or impure salt to be separated from salt suitable for passing inspection, and to be either destroyed or returned to the cisterns to be dissolved or deposited in some proper place and disposed of as salt of second quality. No salt shall pass as good unless it is manufactured as directed by this chapter and by the rules and regulations of the superintendent, and is well made, free from dirt, filth, stones, admixtures of lime, ashes of wood, and other substances injurious thereto, fully drained from pickle and bitterns, properly extracted therefrom. The superintendent shall allow salt made from the brine of the springs to be manufactured without extracting the bitterns or impurities therefrom, provided all such salt, whether shipped loose or in bags, barrels or packages shall be designated and branded as impure and agricultural salt. Salt shall not be packed in casks, barrels, sacks or other vessels, or taken from the salt house in bulk or otherwise, until it has remained in the bin or storehouse at least fourteen days, and the inspectors shall have determined upon an actual examination that it is sufficiently drained of pickle and fit for inspection. No inspection shall be made after sundown or before sunrise, and no salt manufacturer shall retail or deliver any uninspected salt after sundown or before sunrise. No person shall remove or attempt to remove from the reservation or from any salt manufactory, storehouse or other place of deposit, any salt before it shall have been inspected, and the duties paid thereon, with intent to evade the inspection thereof or the payment of the duties thereon. Every person so removing or attempting to remove any salt shall forfeit to the state such salt, with the bag, barrel or other vessel in which it shall be contained, and five dollars for every bushel so removed or attempted to be removed; and the boat, vessel, cart, wagon, sled or other vehicle, in or by which the same shall be removed or attempted to be removed, with the apparel, tackle and team belonging thereto, shall be taken to be the property of such person and be liable to the payment of such penalty.

§ 14. **Persons who may execute process.**—The superintendent or any of his deputies may enter every barn, storehouse, enclosure or other place of deposit which he may suspect to contain salt so removed or attempted to be removed, and every boat, vessel, cart, wagon, sled or other vehicle in or by which such salt shall have been removed or attempted to be removed and seize such salt, with the bag, barrel, or other vessel containing it, and sell the same at public auction for the use of the people of the state after giving six days notice of the time and place of sale. The officer or person making such seizure may also seize such boat, vessel, cart, wagon, sled or other vehicle, with the tackle, apparel and the team belonging thereto and retain the same until the determination of any suit which may be brought for the penalty so imposed. The owner of the property so seized may obtain possession thereof by giving a bond to the superintendent with sureties to be approved by him for the return of such property to the officer if judgment for the plaintiff shall be recovered in the suit brought for the forfeiture incurred, and to secure which such seizure shall have been made.

§ 15. **By whom inspection shall be made.**—Persons desiring to have salt inspected shall apply to the inspector in the district where such salt shall be, who shall thereupon actually examine it in the bag, barrel or vessel in which it is contained. In order to facilitate its examination, the person offering it shall unhead or bore the barrel or open the bag or other vessel containing it as directed by the inspector so as to expose the salt to his touch, view and examination, and shall in all cases provide the necessary assistance to lift the salt while the inspector weighs or measures it.

§ 16. **Examination of kettles.**—The inspectors shall daily examine in their respective districts all kettles used in the manufacture of fine salt and shall require their removal if damaged or defective so as to be unsuitable for the manufacture of good salt and if not removed upon his order, the superintendent may withhold brine from such manufacturer until such order shall be complied with.

§ 17. **Damaged salt; penalties.**—The superintendent shall erase his inspection brand from packages containing salt which, after it has been inspected and the duties paid, shall have suffered any damage so as to reduce its weight or impair its quality and require that it shall be repacked, if reduced in weight only, or destroyed, if impaired in quality, by returning it to the cisterns from which the owner or manufacturer thereof shall draw his supplies of brine for his works. Salt of any inferior quality, dirty, damaged or condemned, may be sold loose or in bulk at the works by the manufacturer thereof, the inspector designating quantity by weight in the inspection bill as in ordinary cases, and distinguishing the same as "second quality," and the person having it inspected paying the duty thereon. Such inferior salt shall not be mixed with other salt which is to be ground or prepared as table salt, or for the packing of provisions, nor shall it be packed in a manner calculated to deceive an innocent purchaser as to its real quality, and if packed in barrels in the ordinary manner it shall be branded in plain letters, "second quality." Every person violating the provisions of this section relating to mixing such salt with other salt or the preparing of it for table use or for packing purposes shall for every such violation forfeit to the people of the state the sum of one hundred dollars. The inspector or deputy who shall have inspected and branded any Onondaga salt put up in barrels or sacks which on being opened are found to contain salt of a quality inferior to that required by law, and the maker and manufacturer whose name is branded on any such barrel or painted on any such sack, shall forfeit to the purchaser injured thereby the sum of one dollar for each bushel so found inferior.

§ 18. **Deleterious ingredients prohibited.**—No salt manufacturer or other person shall put any article or ingredient into the salt water in his cisterns or while evaporating other than such as shall be allowed and approved of by the superintendent in the general rules and regulations which he shall adopt in relation thereto. Every person violating any provision of this section shall for every such offense forfeit to the state the sum of fifty dollars.

§ 19. **Bittern Pans.**—Every manufacturer shall keep one good bittern pan for each kettle or pan used in the manufacture of salt for the purpose of removing the feculent matter and other foreign substances held in solution in the brine during the process of making salt. The superintendent shall, in the rules and regulations adopted by him, regulate the manner of using such pans and of removing the impurities contained in the salt water during the process of manufacturing the same into salt, and the manner of cleansing the kettles and pans.

§ 20. **Salt in barrels.**—The superintendent shall cause all salt barrels to be inspected before salt is packed therein, under such rules and regulations as shall from time to time be adopted and published by him, and all salt shall be rejected when offered for inspection in barrels not inspected or in inspected barrels not properly secured after the salt is packed therein so as to preserve it from waste or injury, and all barrels so used shall be such as are approved by the superintendent. Salt in barrels shall not be marked unless the barrels are thoroughly seasoned, stout and well made, with a sufficient number of good, strong hoops, to be well nailed and secured, not burned or colored on the inside or dirty on the outside, nor without having the holes made for inspection or the knot holes, if any, well and securely plugged up. If the salt upon examination shall prove not to be thoroughly drained, or if, when the barrels are standing on end, water shall exude therefrom, such barrels shall not be branded by the inspector, but the salt therein shall forthwith be emptied back into the bins where it shall remain for a further period of fourteen days before it shall be lawful again to pack the same.

§ 21. **Quantity of salt in barrels.**—The superintendent shall from time to time specify the quantity of salt that barrels or other packages offered for inspection shall contain, and shall prohibit the inspector's brand from being placed upon any package that does not correspond with such regulation. He shall require that all ground salt manufactured at the Onondaga springs and put up for the market in barrels, kegs, boxes, sacks or bags, shall be legibly marked in letters at least half an inch in length, on each barrel, keg, box, sack or bag, with the word " solar " or " boiled " as the fact may be.

§ 22. **Name of manufacturer to be branded on package.**—Every manufacturer shall brand or mark with durable paint every barrel or other package of salt manufactured by him with the name of the district in which his block of kettles is located, the surname at full length of the proprietor or owner of the manufactory at which the salt shall have been made, and the initial letter of his christian name. If the salt shall have been manufactured for a

company or association of individuals, he shall mark or brand in
like manner upon every such barrel or other package, the name of
the firm by which the company is so called; and no inspector shall
inspect or pass any barrel or other package of salt which shall not
be so marked or branded, nor shall the superintendent affix his
brand to any such barrel or other package.

§ 23. Boat sunk in canal—The owner or agent of any boat laden
in whole or in part with salt which shall be sunk or partly im-
mersed in the canals or navigable waters of this state or filled
with water so as to damage any part of the cargo of salt on board,
shall not sell or otherwise dispose of the salt in the original package. Such salt shall be emptied from the barrels or sacks containing it and sold or disposed of after having been exposed to
public inspection so that its quality and condition shall be known.
Salt so injured shall not be again packed in barrels bearing the
inspector's brand nor shipped or transported beyond the bounds of
the state. Every person violating the provisions of this section
shall forfeit the sum of two hundred and fifty dollars for every
violation.

§ 24. Duplicate inspection bills.—The superintendent shall, after
the inspector has ascertained the quantity of salt in any parcel
offered for inspection, and is satisfied that it is of such quality
that it ought to pass inspection, deliver duplicate inspection bills
thereof, dated and signed by him to the person applying for the
inspection. Such bills shall contain the name of the manufacturer
and the person at whose instance the inspection is had, the number
of bushels and pounds of salt contained in the parcel and the number of bags, barrels or other vessels in which it shall be contained,
with a certificate of the inspector stating that he has inspected the
salt specified in such bill. The person applying for inspection
shall thereupon deliver such duplicate inspection bills to the receiver or person in charge of his office in the district where the
salt is inspected and pay the duties on the salt mentioned therein.

§ 25. Receiver's duties.— The receiver shall:

1. Mark such inspection bills with the numbers in the order in
which they are presented, placing the same number on each duplicate bill of the same parcel, and commencing anew with the commencement of every month.

2. Enter upon his books an account of the parcels of salt in
  shall state the number of the parcel, the name of the man-
  d of the person at whose instance the salt shall have
  d, the number of bushels and pounds of salt in the

parcel, the number of bags, barrels or other vessels in which it is contained, the amount of duties thereon and when the same are paid.

3. Sign a receipt at the foot of each duplicate inspection bill and deliver the same to the person paying the duties.

§ 26. **Delivery of bills to the inspector.**— The person receiving the bills shall forthwith deliver one to the inspector by whom the salt was inspected, to be entered in a book kept by him, and retain the other as evidence of payment of the duties thereon. Such inspector shall thereupon brand or mark with durable paint the barrel or cask containing the salt so inspected with his surname at length and the first letter of his christian name, with the addition of the word " inspector " in letters of at least one inch in length; and shall mark upon the head of the barrel or cask with durable paint, the number of pounds of salt contained therein, Barrels, sacks or other packages in which salt shall have been packed and inspected, shall not be again used for the packing of salt therein until the marks or brands made by the superintendent shall be first effaced. The inspection shall not be deemed complete nor the payment of the duties consummated until one of the inspection bills so receipted shall have been returned to the superintendent, and the salt, in cask headed up, shall have been so marked or branded. Every person violating the provisions of this section relating to the package of salt in barrels, sacks or other packages, before the marks or brands made by the superintendent shall have been effaced, shall forfeit to the state for every bushel of salt so packed the sum of five dollars.

§ 27. **Wells, pumps and lines of aqueducts.**--The superintendent shall keep the present wells, pumps, reservoirs, aqueducts and machinery in necessary repair; but no repair involving any aggregate expenditure of more than five hundred dollars shall be made or undertaken without the approval of the comptroller, to be indorsed upon detailed statements. Said superintendent may enter upon the lands of any individual or company or upon any leased land and carry the salt across the same in the same manner as hitherto, and by suitable and proper aqueducts or conduits, paying to the owner or lessee of such lands the damages sustained by him, to be ascertained by mutual agreement, or by the appraisement of three commissioners appointed as prescribed in the condemnation law.

§ 28. **Ascertainment of quantity of water.**—The superintendent shall cause the quantity of water required for the efficient work-

ing of the pumps or other machinery for raising salt water from
the wells and reservoirs now or hereafter to be constructed in any
district, to be ascertained by competent engineers, and shall certify
the same to the superintendent of public works, who on receiving
such certificate shall cause such quantity of water to be at all
times supplied to the Syracuse level of the canal, in addition to that
usually required or supplied for the purpose of navigation, except
when it shall be necessary to withdraw the water from such level
for repairs. The certificate shall be filed in the office of the superintendent of public works and the amount of water thus ascertained
to be necessary may be drawn from the canal for such purposes
by the superintendent of the Onondaga salt springs, provided the
navigation of the canal be not thereby impeded. All bulkheads,
gates and other appurtenances required for taking and regulating
the flow of such water shall be constructed and maintained by the
superintendent of the Onondaga salt springs; and any property
taken by virtue of this section shall be paid for by agreement or
appraisement in the manner prescribed in the condemnation law.

§ 29. **Numerical list of salt blocks to be kept.**— The superintendent shall keep on file in each of the receivers' offices a numerical
list of all the fine salt blocks containing the name of the owner
or occupant of each, the several manufactories entitled to the first
use of the water, and the date of any additional erections entitled
to the surplus water, in the order of their erection. A similar
list shall also be kept of the coarse salt erections entitled to the first
use of the water, including the number of covers or rooms; and
of all subsequent erections entitled to supplies from the surplus.

§ 30. **Distribution of brine.**—No distinction in the furnishing and
distribution of brine to the fine and coarse salt erections from the
Onondaga salt springs or wells shall be made between the works
situated on the state lands and those built on private lands. If
there be an insufficiency of brine to supply all such erections,
the superintendent shall so classify them as to furnish a full supply of water to each in an equal portion of the time while such
shall, during the months of July and August, so classify to the erections for the manufacture of solar salt, but such classifications shall
not give such erections a supply for more than an equal portion of
the time. The superintendent shall not furnish brine to any erection for the manufacture of fine or coarse salt erected after April
fifteenth, eighteen hundred and fifty-nine, either upon vacant lands
or by doubling the blocks on lots then used and occupied for manu-

facturing purposes, until the quantity of brine raised and distributed by the state shall be sufficient for fully supplying all the works through the manufacturing season, without classifying the same for any part of the time.

§ 31. Cisterns; repair of buildings.—Every salt manufacturer who shall provide an earth reservoir for the storage of salt water may have such reservoir filled by the superintendent from any surplus not required for immediate distribution, and shall be allowed to use the same in addition to the ordinary supply to which such manufacturer may be entitled according to the provisions of this chapter. Every manufacturer of fine salt shall have two cisterns or reservoirs attached to and adjoining his manufactory. Such cisterns or reservoirs shall be well made, and as free from leaks as may be, and shall each be of sufficient capacity to contain as much salt water as can be boiled or evaporated in such manufactory from the kettles or pans set therein, in two days. No manufacturer of fine salt who shall neglect to provide such reservoirs or cisterns or to keep the same in good repair so as to save the water from undue or unnecessary waste shall be entitled or permitted to receive any salt water from the state reservoirs. Every manufacturer shall keep his buildings, cisterns and appurtenances for the manufacture of salt in thorough repair, so that the salt manufactured by him shall not suffer damage or be impaired in quality after the same shall have been deposited in the bins or storehouses. If any such manufacturer shall neglect or refuse, upon the requisition of the superintendent to place his works in such a state of repair or to put them in a proper condition for the manufacture and preservation of good air, he shall forfeit his right to the use of the salt water, and the superintendent may disconnect the communications between the state aqueducts and his cisterns until such manufacturer shall comply with the requisitions of the superintendent.

§ 32. Unauthorized communications.—No manufacturer or other person shall open or aid, assist, counsel or advise in opening the communication between any manufactory or salt work and the logs or conduits leading to or connecting with the state reservoirs without the consent of the superintendent or one of his deputies. Every person violating the provisions of this section shall forfeit to the state the sum of one hundred dollars for every such violation. The owners of any salt works surreptitiously receiving a supply of salt water by such means shall forfeit and pay to the state a like sum on demand of the superintendent; and in default of payment shall be deprived of his supply of water until such demand shall be complied with.

§ 33. **Discharge of laborers for neglect.**—The superintendent shall require the discharge of every boiler, packer or other laborer employed by any manufacturer who shall neglect or refuse to obey his or his deputies directions in and about any salt works or manufactory respecting the manufacture, packing or care of salt produced by such manufacturer, and to be offered for inspection; and each person so discharged shall not be again employed by any person in the manufacture of salt without the consent of the superintendent.

§ 34. **Earthworks.**—The superintendent may, whenever the construction of any earthwork requiring the services of an engineer shall be undertaken by him, apply to the state engineer for the services of an engineer, who may, by a written order, if in his judgment, the interests of the state will be promoted thereby, direct the resident engineer of either the Oswego or Erie canal to assume the charge of such work under the direction of the superintendent of the Onondaga salt springs, and to make surveys, maps, profiles, estimates and measurements thereof.

§ 35. **Charges against the state; estimates to be made out.**—All charges against the state or liabilities incurred for, the support and maintenance of the Onondaga salt springs shall be audited and paid by the superintendent from the moneys advanced to him from time to time by the treasurer, upon the warrant of the comptroller. Before drawing any money from the treasury to be expended by him, the superintendent shall make out in minute detail an estimate of the necessary expenses to be incurred so far as they can reasonably be forseen for a period of two months, commencing with the month of January and forward the same to the comptroller who shall thereupon authorize the superintendent to make his draft upon the treasurer for the amount of such estimate or such portion thereof as he shall think necessary and proper. To meet any extraordinary expenditure, the superintendent may, in like manner, make special estimates, upon which the comptroller shall advance in like manner if the same be approved by him, but the superintendent shall not receive from the treasury a larger sum than the amount of the appropriation made by the legislature for the support of the salt springs. At the expiration of each period of two months the superintendent shall make a full and perfect abstract of the vouchers in his possession to which his affidavit shall be attached, to the effect that he has deposited in the bank designated by the comptroller all the moneys received by him for duties on salt, rents, fines or penalties, or for other property of the state, that such abstract is a true abstract of all the vouchers taken by him as superintendent for such two months; that the moneys specified in the receipts referred to in the abstract, has been actually paid as specified in such receipts; and that all the receipts were filled up as they then appear, and were read or the amount distinctly stated, to the signer of each, when signed, according to his best knowledge and belief. The report and vouchers shall be returned to the comptroller and if satisfactory to him, he shall enter his approval on the abstract and audit and allow the accounts of the superintendent. The superintendent shall make out a report showing the expenditures for the two preceding months, corresponding in its detail of items to the estimate presented before an advance is authorized to be made by the comptroller. If any such vouchers are objectionable, the comptroller shall enter his disapproval on the particular voucher and not audit and allow the same until satisfied of its legality and propriety.

§ 36. Sale of lands on the Onondago Salt Springs Reservation.— The commissioners of the land office shall cause to be appraised and sell and convey in fee any of the lands of the Onondaga Salt Springs Reservation upon the request of any of the lessees of said lands, or their legal representatives, upon their releasing absolutely all right to have, demand or receive from the state any money by way of damages either on account of the termination of the leases by which such lots are held or on account of the destruction or removal of any salt blocks, their appurtenances or any other property or buildings therefrom. Such lessees or their legal representatives after the appraisement of the value of such lands is returned to and approved by the commissioners of the land office may for thirty days after the date of such approval become the purchasers of such lands at the appraised value thereof, but if the lessee or his legal representatives does not purchase such lands at such appraisal within said thirty days, the title thereof shall vest and be in the people of the state released and discharged from the terms and conditions of any leases, and such lands shall be advertised and sold under the direction and control of the commissioners of the land office to the highest bidder in accordance with the provisions of the public lands law, but the lessee or his legal repre-

sentatives, may, for thirty days after such sale, remove therefrom
the buildings and other property placed thereon by him. In case of
failure to so remove such buildings or other property within said
time, the same shall be considered as given up and abandoned and
shall become and be the property of the person or persons so purchasing said land.

§ 37. The title of all lands of the Onondaga Salt Springs Reservation which shall not have been sold or disposed of in accordance with the foregoing provisions of this chapter on or before the
first day of March, eighteen hundred and ninety-eight, shall vest
and be in the people of the state released and discharged from the
terms and conditions of any leases and the buildings, structures
and property thereon shall be deemed abandoned and shall become
and be the property of the people of the state of New York.

§ 38. **Moneys arising from sale.**—All moneys arising from the
sale of the Onondaga Salt Springs Reservation or any part thereof,
by virtue of the foregoing provisions of this chapter, shall be placed
by the comptroller in the state treasury. The state shall cease to
furnish brine at any expense to said state on or before the
first day of January, eighteen hundred and ninety-nine, and
shall cease to operate its works at any expense to the state
upon the Onondaga Salt Springs Reservation on or before
the first day of January, eighteen hundred and ninety-nine, and
the commissioners of the land office are authorized and directed to
sell all of the right, title and interest of the state, or the people
thereof, at public or private sale, in or to any or all of the personal
property upon said Onondaga Salt Springs Reservation or connected therewith. The lessees of any such personal property, if
any there be, shall have the first opportunity of purchasing the
same, but all such personal property which shall not have been
disposed of on or before the first day of April, eighteen hundred and
ninety-eight, shall vest absolutely in the people of the state of New
York free from all claims in behalf of any lessee or his legal representatives.

§ 39. **Affecting appointments already made.**—This act shall not
affect any appointment or term of office heretofore made by the
present superintendent of the Onondaga Salt Springs Reservation.

§ 40. **Laws repealed.**—All acts or parts of acts inconsistent with
or repugnant to the provisions of this act are hereby repealed.

§ 41. **When to take effect.**—This act shall take effect immediately.

Chap. 264.

AN ACT to amend chapter one hundred and seven of the laws of eighteen hundred and eighty-eight, entitled "An act for the incorporation of the Grand Lodge of the United States of the Independent Order Free Sons of Israel," relative to provisions by means of endowments.

Became a law April 15, 1897, with the approval of the Governor.
Passed, three-fifths being present.

The People of the State of New York, represented in Senate and Assembly, do enact as follows:

Section 1. Section two of chapter one hundred and seven of the laws of eighteen hundred and eighty-eight, entitled "An act for the incorporation of the Grand Lodge of the United States of the Independent Order Free Sons of Israel," is hereby amended so as to read as follows: Charter amended.

§ 2. The objects of said organization are hereby declared to be for the cultivation and promotion of charity and benevolence, and moral, mental and social culture among its members, their mutual benefit in case of sickness or distress, proper interment for their dead, and provisions by means of endowments for their widows and orphans, parents and such beneficiaries as may be duly designated by the members of said organization in accordance with the laws and rules as such organization may adopt. The principal business office of said corporation shall be located in the city of New York. Objects of organization. Principal office.

§ 2. This act shall take effect immediately.

Chap. 266.

AN ACT to amend chapter four hundred and sixty-six of the laws of eighteen hundred and seventy-seven, entitled "An act in relation to assignments of the estates of debtors for the benefit of creditors," as amended by chapter three hundred and twenty-eight of the laws of eighteen hundred and eighty-four.

Became a law April 15, 1897, with the approval of the Governor.
Passed, three-fifths being present.

The People of the State of New York, represented in Senate and Assembly, do enact as follows:

Section 1. Section twenty-nine of chapter four hundred and sixty-six of the laws of eighteen hundred and seventy-seven, en- Act amended.

titled " An act in relation to assignments of the estates of debtors for the benefit of creditors " is hereby amended to read as follows:

Preference of employees. § 29. In all assignments, made in pursuance of this act, the wages or salaries actually owing to the employes of the assignor or assignors at the time of the execution of the assignment, shall be preferred before any other debt; and should the assets of the assignor or assignors not be sufficient to pay in full all the claims preferred, pursuant to this section, they shall be applied to the payment of the **Sums due truckmen and cartmen.** same pro rata to the amount of each such claim. All sums due to truckmen or cartmen for the payment of freight and for the carriage of goods, wares and merchandise shall be deemed and treated as wages for the purposes of this act.

§ 2. This act shall take effect immediately.

Chap. 267.

AN ACT to amend section six hundred and fifty-two of the penal code, relative to side-paths.

Became a law April 15, 1897, with the approval of the Governor. Passed, three-fifths being present.

The People of the State of New York, represented in Senate and Assembly, do enact as follows:

Section 1. Section six hundred and fifty-two of the penal code is hereby amended so as to read as follows:

§ 652. **Driving vehicles, et cetera, on sidewalks.**—A person who willfully and without authority or necessity drives any team, vehicle, cattle, sheep, horse, swine or other animal along upon a sidewalk is punishable by a fine of fifty dollars, or imprisonment in the county jail not exceeding thirty days, or both.

Subdivision 1. A person who willfully and without authority or necessity drives any team or vehicle, except a bicycle, upon a side path, or wheelway, constructed by or exclusively for the use of bicyclists, and not constructed in a street of a city, is punishable by a fine of not more than fifty dollars, or imprisonment not exceeding thirty days, or both.

§ 2. This act shall take effect immediately.

Chap. 268.

AN ACT to amend the code of civil procedure, relating to judges
sitting when interested parties.

Became a law April 15, 1897, with the approval of the Governor.
Passed, three-fifths being present.

*The People of the State of New York, represented in Senate and
Assembly, do enact as follows:*

Section 1. Section forty-six of article one, title two, of the code
of civil procedure, is hereby amended so as to read as follows: *Amendment.*

§ 46. A judge shall not sit as such in, or take any part in the
decision of, a cause or matter to which he is a party, or in which
he has been attorney or counsel, or in which he is interested, or if he
is related by consanguinity, or affinity to any party to the controversy within the sixth degree. The degree shall be ascertained
by ascending from the judge to the common ancestor, and descending to the party, counting a degree for each person in both lines,
including the judge and party, and excluding the common ancestor. But a judge of the court of appeals shall not be disqualified from taking part in the decision of an action or special proceeding in which an insurance company is a party or is interested, by
reason of his being a policyholder therein. A judge other than a
judge of the court of appeals, or of the appellate division of the
supreme court, shall not decide or take part in the decision of a
question, which was argued orally in the court, when he was not
present and sitting therein as a judge. *Judge not to sit when interested party, etc.*

§ 2. This act shall take effect September first, eighteen hundred
and ninety-seven. *When takes effect.*

Chap. 269.

AN ACT to provide for the construction and maintenance of bridges
over the waters between cities and towns or incorporated villages in
said towns.

Accepted by the city.

Became a law April 15, 1897, with the approval of the Governor.
Passed, three-fifths being present.

*The People of the State of New York, represented in Senate and
Assembly, do enact as follows:*

Section 1. Whenever the highway commissioners having power
in the premises under this act shall decide that the public con- *Construction of bridges.*

venience requires a bridge to be constructed over the stream or waters dividing a city from a town or any incorporated village in said town, the same shall be constructed under and according to the provisions of the highway law for the construction of bridges between towns, being article five of chapter nineteen of the general laws, the common council of the city being the highway commissioners of said city, and the board of village trustees of any incorporated village in the town being the highway commissioners of said village.

Purchase of lands for approaches.

§ 2. Any land required for the approaches to said bridges for a distance not exceeding three hundred feet from the bridge, may be bought by the commissioners of highway constructing the bridge, the approaches constructed and the cost thereof included in the cost of the bridge.

Condemnation of land.

§ 3. When an agreement can not be made as to the price to be paid for the land for such approaches, the said land shall be condemned in the manner as provided by chapter ninety-five, laws of eighteen hundred and ninety, with the acts amendatory thereof. The expenses of said condemnation proceedings shall be included in and be a part of the cost of the bridge.

Issue of bonds.

§ 4. In order to pay for the said bridges, the city, the town, if the bridge is in an unincorporated section of the town, or an incorporated village in said town, if the bridge is in said incorporated village, shall have the power to issue bonds to be known as bridge bonds of the said city, town or village, as the case may be, by the officers thereof, and in the manner provided by law for the issue of other bonds of said city, town or village, to an amount necessary to pay its proportion of the cost of said bridges. The total amount of such bonds to be issued by the city shall not exceed thirty thousand dollars, or by a town or incorporated village fifteen thousand

Sale and application of proceeds.

dollars. Said bonds shall not be sold for less than the par value thereof and accrued interest, if any; shall mature and be payable at a time not over twenty years from date; be of such denominations and bear such interest, not exceeding five per centum per annum, as the common council of the city, in case of a city; the board of village trustees, in case of a village, or the town board, in the case of the town, shall determine. The proceeds of the said bonds shall be paid to the proper officer for receiving funds of each municipality, and credited to a fund which shall be known as the bridge fund, and shall only be paid out by warrants, as other funds of said city, town or village are paid out.

§ 5. This act shall apply only to towns from which at least one- Application of act. quarter of the territory thereof has heretofore been taken for park purposes, and which also adjoin a city containing at the time of the taking of the last federal census a population of one and one-half million.

§ 6. This act shall take effect immediately.

Chap. 273.

AN ACT for acquiring lands in "The state reservation on the Saint Lawrence," for improving and maintaining state lands in such reservation, and making an appropriation therefor.

Became a law April 15, 1897, with the approval of the Governor.
Passed, three-fifths being present.

The People of the State of New York, represented in Senate and Assembly, do enact as follows:

Section 1. The sum of thirty thousand dollars, or so much thereof Appropriation for land and improvements. as may be necessary, is hereby appropriated out of any moneys in the treasury, not otherwise appropriated, to be paid by the treasurer on the warrant of the comptroller, to the commissioners of fisheries, game and forests, to be expended by such board in the purchase of islands, points of land on the main shore or on islands within such reservation, created and described by chapter eight hundred and two of the laws of eighteen hundred and ninety-six, for building wharves, piers and necessary buildings on the lands so acquired, and for otherwise maintaining and improving the lands of the state within such reservation.

§ 2. This act shall take effect immediately.

Chap. 274.

AN ACT providing for the sale of certain lands belonging to the state.

Became a law April 15, 1897, with the approval of the Governor.
Passed, three-fifths being present.

The People of the State of New York, represented in Senate and Assembly, do enact as follows:

Section 1. The commissioners of the land office are hereby au- Sale of hospital lands authorized. thorized and empowered to sell at public auction, and to convey to the highest bidder, so much of the land belonging to the people of the state, in the city of Utica and county of Oneida, and distinguished on a map of part of Hamilton farm, Utica, as being parts of lots numbers eleven and twelve in block number two, described as follows, viz.: Beginning at the intersection of the southerly line of Walnut with the westerly line of Schuyler street and running thence southerly along Schuyler street eighty feet; thence westerly at right angles to Schuyler street fifty-four feet; thence northerly parallel with Schuyler street eighty feet to Walnut street and thence easterly along Walnut street fifty-four feet to the place of beginning. Also part of lots numbers four and five, block eight, as represented on said map described as follows, viz.: Beginning at the intersection of the easterly line of Schuyler, with the northerly line of Hickory street and running thence northerly along Schuyler street eighty feet, thence easterly at right angles to Schuyler street, forty feet; thence southerly parallel with Schuyler street, eighty feet to Hickory street; thence westerly along Hickory street, forty feet to the place of beginning. Also part of lots numbers one and two in block number nine, as represented on said map described as follows, viz.: Beginning at a point in the southerly line of Hickory street, sixty-six feet easterly from the easterly line of Schuyler street, and running thence easterly along the line of Hickory street, seventy-five and one-quarter feet to Hamilton avenue; thence southerly along the westerly line of said avenue sixty-two feet; thence westerly at right angles to said avenue to a point at right angles to Hickory street from the place of beginning, and thence to the place of beginning. Also lot number eleven, and the southerly half of lot number twelve in block number ten, as represented on said map, making a piece of land sixty feet wide in front and rear extending from Hamilton avenue to the line of land appropriated by the people of the state, for the construction of the Chenango canal, as may be certified by the managers of the Utica State Hospital as no longer necessary for hospital purposes.

Proceeds of sale. § 2. The moneys arising from the sale of said lands shall be deposited with the state treasurer.

§ 3. This act shall take effect immediately.

Chap. 277.

AN ACT to amend the real property law, being chapter five hundred and forty-seven of the laws of eighteen hundred and ninety-six, relating to forms of conveyances.

Became a law April 15, 1897, with the approval of the Governor.
Passed, three-fifths being present.

The People of the State of New York, represented in Senate and Assembly, do enact as follows:

Section 1. Subdivision one of section two hundred and nineteen of the real property law is hereby amended so as to read as follows:

1. **Agreement that whole sum shall become due.**— The words " and it is hereby expressly agreed that the whole of the said principal sum shall become due at the option of said mortgagee or obligee after default in the payment of any installment of principal or of interest for .... days, or after default in the payment of any tax or assessment for.......... days after notice and demand," must be construed as meaning that should any default be made in the payment of any installment of principal or any part thereof, or in the payment of the said interest, or of any part thereof, on any day whereon the same is made payable, or should any tax or assessment, which now is or may be hereafter imposed upon the premises hereinafter described, become due or payable, and should the said interest remain unpaid and in arrear for the space of .... days, or such tax or assessment remain unpaid and in arrear for .... days after written notice by the mortgagee or obligee, his executors, administrators, successors or assigns, that such tax or assessment is unpaid, and demand for the payment thereof, then and from thenceforth, that is to say, after the lapse of either one of said periods, as the case may be, the aforesaid principal sum, with all arrearage of interest thereon, shall, at the option of the said mortgagee or obligee, his executors, administrators, successors or assigns, become and be due and payable immediately thereafter, although the period above limited for the payment thereof may not then have expired, anything thereinbefore contained to the contrary thereof in anywise notwithstanding.

§ 2. Schedule C of section two hundred and twenty-three of the real property law is hereby amended so as to read as follows:

SCHEDULE C — MORTGAGE.

This indenture, made the .... day of ...., in the year eighteen hundred and ...., between ...., of ...., party of the first part, and ...., of ...., party of the second part.

Whereas, the said .... is justly indebted to the said party of the second part in the sum of .... dollars, lawful money of the United States, secured to be paid by his certain bond or obligation, bearing even date herewith, conditioned for the payment of the said sum of .... dollars, on the .... day of ...., eighteen hundred and ...., and the interest thereon, to be computed from .... at the rate of .... per centum per annum, and to be paid ....

It being thereby expressly agreed that the whole of the said principal sum shall become due after default in the payment of any installment of principal, interest, taxes or assessments, as hereinafter provided.

Now, this indenture witnesseth, that the said party of the first part, for the better securing the payment of the said sum of money mentioned in the condition of the said bond or obligation, with interest thereon, and also for and in consideration of one dollar, paid by the said party of the second part, the receipt whereof is hereby acknowledged, doth hereby grant and release unto the said party of the second part, and to his heirs (or successors) and assigns forever (description), together with the appurtenances, and all the estate and rights of the party of the first part in and to said premises. To have and hold the above granted premises unto the said party of the second part, his heirs and assigns forever. Provided, always, that if the said party of the first part, his heirs, executors or administrators, shall pay unto the said party of the second part, his executors, administrators or assigns, the said sum of money mentioned in the condition of the said bond or obligation, and the interest thereon, at the time and in the manner mentioned in the said condition, that then these presents, and the estate hereby granted, shall cease, determine and be void. And the said party of the first part covenants with the party of the second part as follows:

1. That the said party of the first part will pay the indebtedness as hereinbefore provided, and if default be made in the payment of any part thereof, the party of the second part shall have power to sell the premises therein described according to law.

2. That the said party of the first part will keep the buildings on the said premises insured against loss by fire for the benefit of the mortgagee.

3. And it is hereby expressly agreed that the whole of said principal sum shall become due at the option of the said party of the second part after default in the payment of any installment of principal or of interest for .... days, or after default in the payment of any tax or assessment for .... days after notice and demand.

In witness whereof, the said party of the first part hath hereunto set his hand and seal, the day and year first above written.

In the presence of........

§ 3. This act shall take effect immediately.

Chap. 279.

AN ACT to provide for acquiring lands to commemorate the battle of Lake George.

Became a law April 15, 1897, with the approval of the Governor. Passed, three-fifths being present.

The People of the State of New York, represented in Senate and Assembly, do enact as follows:

Section 1. The comptroller of the state is hereby authorized and empowered to purchase such lands as he may deem proper, not to exceed fifty acres, at or near where the battle of Lake George was fought, in Warren county, at such point as he may deem just, and at a price not exceeding five thousand dollars, and acquire title thereto in the name of the people of the state according to law. _{Acquisition of land authorized.}

§ 2. The sum of five thousand dollars or so much thereof as may be necessary, is hereby appropriated out of any moneys not otherwise appropriated, to carry into effect the intents and purposes of this act. _{Appropriation.}

§ 3. The lands acquired under this act shall be exempt from taxation, and shall belong to the state forever, and shall be under the care of the comptroller of the state. _{Exemption from taxation.}

§ 4. This act shall take effect immediately.

Chap. 281.

AN ACT to amend section three hundred and ninety-four of the code
of civil procedure, relating to limitation of actions against directors,
et cetera.

Became a law April 16, 1897, with the approval of the Governor.
Passed, three-fifths being present.

*The People of the State of New York, represented in Senate and
Assembly, do enact as follows:*

Section 1. Section three hundred and ninety-four of the code of
civil procedure is amended so as to read as follows:

§ 394. This chapter does not affect an action against a director
or stockholder of a moneyed corporation, or banking association, to
recover a penalty or forfeiture imposed, or to enforce a liability
created by the common law or by statute; but such an action must
be brought within three years after the cause of action has accrued.

§ 2. This act shall take effect September first, eighteen hundred
and ninety-seven.

Chap. 282.

AN ACT to amend the public health law, relating to local boards of
health.

Became a law April 16, 1897, with the approval of the Governor.
Passed, three-fifths being present.

*The People of the State of New York, represented in Senate and
Assembly, do enact as follows:*

Section 1. Section twenty of chapter six hundred and sixty-one
of the laws of eighteen hundred and ninety-three, entitled "An act
in relation to the public health, constituting chapter twenty-five
of the general laws," as amended by chapter five hundred and
eighty-four of the laws of eighteen hundred and ninety-five, is
hereby amended to read as follows:

§ 20. Local boards of health.— There shall continue to be local
boards of health and health officers in the several cities, villages
and towns of the state. In the cities except New York, Brooklyn,
Buffalo, Albany and Yonkers, the board shall consist of the mayor
of the city, who shall be its president, and, at least six other persons, one of whom shall be a competent physician, who shall be
appointed by the common council, upon the nomination of the
mayor, and shall hold office for three years. Appointments of

members of such boards shall be made for such shorter terms as at any time may be necessary, in order that the terms of two appointed members shall expire annually. The board shall appoint a competent physician, not one of its members, to be the health officer of the city. In villages the board shall consist of not less than three nor more than seven persons, not trustees of the village, who shall be appointed at the first meeting of the board of trustees of such village, after the next annual election of the village; the members of said board of health shall at their first meeting divide themselves by lot into three classes, whose terms of office shall expire respectively in one, two and three years from the annual election held prior to their appointment; from and after the appointment of said board as above provided, the appointment of the successors of said members shall be made immediately after the annual elections of said village and shall continue in office until their successors are appointed unless removed therefrom; provided, however, that upon failure to appoint such board of health at such first meeting such appointment may be made at any subsequent meeting, in the event of no appointment having been made by the county judge as hereinafter provided. Every such village board shall elect a president and appoint a competent physician, not a member of the board, to be the health officer of the village. In towns the board of health shall consist of the town board and another citizen of the town of full age, annually appointed by the town board at a meeting thereof after each annual town meeting, for the term of one year from and after such town meeting and until his successor is appointed. Such board of health shall annually appoint a competent physician to be the health officer of the town. If the proper authorities shall not fill any vacancies occurring in any local board within thirty days after the happening of such vacancy, the county judge of the county shall appoint a competent person to fill the vacancy for the unexpired term, which appointment shall be immediately filed in the office of the county clerk, and a duplicate thereof filed with the clerk of the municipality for which such appointment is made. Notice of the membership and organization of every local board of health shall be forthwith given by such board to the state board of health. The term " municipality," when used in this article, means the city, village or town for which any such local board may be or is appointed.

§ 2. This act shall take effect immediately.

Chap. 284.

AN ACT to amend certain sections of article ten of chapter nine hundred and eight of the laws of eighteen hundred and ninety-six, entitled "An act in relation to taxation, constituting chapter twenty-four of the general laws," relating to taxable transfers of property.

Became a law April 16, 1897, with the approval of the Governor.
Passed, three-fifths being present.

The People of the State of New York, represented in Senate and Assembly, do enact as follows:

Section 1. The following sections of chapter nine hundred and eight of the laws of eighteen hundred and ninety-six, entitled "An act in relation to taxation, constituting chapter twenty-four of the general laws," relating to taxable transfers of property, are hereby amended to take effect immediately, and to read as follows:

§ 2. Section two hundred and twenty of said act is hereby amended so as to read as follows:

§ 220. **Taxable transfers.**— A tax shall be and is hereby imposed upon the transfer of any property, real or personal, of the value of five hundred dollars or over, or of any interest therein or income therefrom, in trust or otherwise, to persons or corporations not exempt by law from taxation on real or personal property, in the following cases:

1. When the transfer is by will or by the intestate laws of this state from any person dying seized or possessed of the property while a resident of the state.

2. When the transfer is by will or intestate law, of property within the state, and the decedent was a nonresident of the state at the time of his death.

3. When the transfer is of property made by a resident or by a nonresident when such nonresident's property is within this state, by deed, grant, bargain, sale or gift made in contemplation of the death of the grantor, vendor or donor, or intended to take effect in possession or enjoyment at or after such death.

4. (Such tax shall be imposed) When any such person or corporation becomes beneficially entitled, in possession or expectancy, to any property or the income thereof by any such transfer, whether made before or after the passage of this act.

5. Whenever any person or corporation shall exercise a power of appointment derived from any disposition of property made either before or after the passage of this act, such appointment

when made shall be deemed a transfer taxable under the provisions of this act in the same manner as though the property to which such appointment relates belonged absolutely to the donee of such power and had been bequeathed or devised by such donee by will; and whenever any person or corporation possessing such a power of appointment so derived shall omit or fail to exercise the same within the time provided therefor, in whole or in part, a transfer taxable under the provisions of this act shall be deemed to take place to the extent of such omissions or failure, in the same manner as though the persons or corporations thereby becoming entitled to the possession or enjoyment of the property to which such power related had succeeded thereto by a will of the donee of the power failing to exercise such power, taking effect at the time of such omission or failure.

6. The tax imposed thereby shall be at the rate of five per centum upon the clear market value of such property, except as otherwise prescribed in the next section.

§ 3. Section two hundred and twenty-two of said act is hereby amended so as to read as follows:

§ 222. **Lien of tax and payment thereof.**— Every such tax shall be and remain a lien upon the property transferred until paid and the person to whom the property is so transferred, and the administrators, executors and trustees of every estate so transferred shall be personally liable for such tax until its payment. The tax shall be paid to the treasurer or the comptroller of the county of the surrogate having jurisdiction as herein provided; and said treasurer or comptroller shall give, and every executor, administrator, or trustees, shall take duplicate receipts from him of such payment, one of which he shall immediately send to the comptroller of the state, whose duty it shall be to charge the treasurer or comptroller so receiving the tax with the amount thereof and to seal said receipt with the seal of his office and countersign the same and return it to the executor, administrator or trustee, whereupon it shall be a proper voucher in the settlement of his accounts; but no executor, administrator or trustee shall be entitled to a final accounting of an estate in settlement of which a tax is due under the provisions of this act, unless he shall produce a receipt so sealed and countersigned by the state comptroller or a copy thereof certified by him, or unless a bond shall have been filed as prescribed by section two hundred and twenty-six of this chapter. All taxes imposed by this article shall be due and payable at the time of the transfer, except as hereinafter provided. Taxes upon the transfer of any estate, property or interest therein limited, conditioned, dependent or determinable upon the happening of any contingency or future event by reason of which the fair market value thereof can not be ascertained at the time of the transfer as herein provided, shall accrue and become due and payable when the persons or corporations beneficially entitled thereto shall come into actual possession or enjoyment thereof.

§ 4. Section two hundred and twenty-five of said act is hereby amended so as to read as follows:

§ 225. **Refund of tax erroneously paid.**— If any debts shall be proven against the estate of a decedent after the payment of any legacy or distributive share thereof, from which any such tax has been deducted or upon which it has been paid by the person entitled to such legacy or distributive share, and such person is required by order of the surrogate having jurisdiction, on notice to the state comptroller, to refund the amount of such debts or any part thereof, an equitable proportion of the tax shall be repaid to him by the executor, administrator or trustee, if the tax has not been paid to the county treasurer, or comptroller of the city of New York, or if such tax has been paid to such treasurer or comptroller of the city of New York, he shall refund out of the funds in his hands or custody to the credit of such taxes such equitable proportion of the tax, and credit himself with the same in his quarterly account rendered to the comptroller of the state under this act. If after the payment of any tax in pursuance of an order fixing such tax, made by the surrogate having jurisdiction, such order be modified or reversed, on due notice to the comptroller of the state, the state comptroller shall, by order, direct and allow the treasurer of the county, or the comptroller of the city of New York, to refund to the executor, administrator, trustee, person or persons, by whom such tax had been paid, the amount of any moneys paid or deposited on account of such tax in excess of the amount of the tax fixed by the order modified or reversed, out of the funds in his hands or custody, to the credit of such taxes, and to credit himself with the same in his quarterly account rendered to the comptroller of the state under this act; but no application for such refund shall be made after one year from such reversal or modification, and the comptroller of the state, shall deduct from the fees allowed by this article to the comptroller of the city of New York or the county treasurer the amount theretofore allowed bim upon such overpayment. Where it shall be proved to the satisfaction of the surrogate who has assessed the tax upon the transfer of property under this article that deductions for debts were allowed upon the appraisal, since proved to have been erroneously allowed, it shall be lawful for such surrogate to enter an order assessing the tax upon the amount wrongfully or erroneously deducted.

§ 5. Section two hundred and twenty-six of said act is hereby amended so as to read as follows

§ 226. **Deferred payment.**—Any person or corporation beneficially interested in any property chargeable with a tax under this article, and executors, administrators and trustees thereof may elect within eighteen months from the date of the transfer thereof as herein provided, not to pay such tax until the person or persons beneficially interested therein shall come into the actual possession or enjoyment thereof. If it be personal property, the person or persons so electing shall give a bond to th· state in penalty of three times the amount of any such tax, with such sureties as the surrogate of the proper county may approve, conditioned for the payment of such tax and interest thereon, at such time or period as the person or persons beneficially interested therein may come into the actual possession or enjoyment of such property, which bond shall be filed in the office of the surrogate. Such bond must be executed and filed and a full return of such property upon oath made to the surrogate within one year from the date of transfer thereof as herein provided, and such bond must be renewed every five years.

§ 6. Section two hundred and thirty of said act is hereby amended so as to read as follows:

§ 230. **Appointment of appraisers.**—The surrogate, upon the application of any interested party, including the state comptroller, county treasurers, or the comptroller of New York city, or upon his own motion, shall, as often as, and whenever occasion may require, appoint a competent person as appraiser, to fix the fair market value (at the time of the transfer thereof) of property of persons whose estates shall be subject to the payment of any tax imposed by this article. If the property upon the transfer of which a tax is imposed shall be an estate, income or interest, or shall be a remainder or reversion or other expectancy, real or personal, the title to which is fixed, absolute and indefeasible, such estate or estates shall be appraised immediately after such transfer, or as soon thereafter as may be practicable, at the fair and clear market value thereof at that time; provided, however, that when such estate, income or interest shall be of such a nature that its fair and clear market value can not be ascertained at such time, it shall be appraised in like manner at the time when such value first becomes ascertainable. Estates in expectancy which are contingent or defeasible shall be appraised at their full, undiminished value when the persons entitled thereto shall come into the beneficial enjoyment or possession thereof, without diminution for or on account of any valuation theretofore made of the particular estates for purposes of taxation, upon which said estates in expectancy may have been limited. The value of every future or limited estate, income, interest or annuity dependent upon any life or lives in being, shall be determined by the rule, method and standard of mortality and value employed by the superintendent of insurance in ascertaining the value of policies of life insurance and annuities for the determination of liabilities of life insurance companies, except that the rate of interest for making such computation shall be five per centum per annum. In estimating the value of any estate or interest in property, to the beneficial enjoyment or possession whereof there are persons or corporations presently entitled thereto, no allowance shall be made in respect of any contingent incumbrance thereon, nor in respect of any contingency upon the happening of which the estate or property or some part thereof or interest therein might be abridged, defeated or diminished; provided, however, that in the event of such incumbrance taking effect as an actual burden upon the interest of the beneficiary, or in the event of the abridgment, defeat or diminution of said estate or property or interest therein as aforesaid, a return shall be made to the person properly entitled thereto of a proportionate amount of such tax in respect of the amount or value of the incumbrance when taking effect, or so much as will reduce the same to the amount which would have been assessed in respect of the actual duration or extent of the estate or interest enjoyed. Such return of tax shall be made in the manner provided by section two hundred and twenty-five of this article. Where any property shall, after the passage of this act, be transferred subject to any charge, estate or interest, determinable by the death of any person, or at any period ascertainable only by reference to death, the increase of benefit accruing to any person or corporation upon the extinction or determination of such charge, estate or interest shall be deemed a transfer of property taxable under the provisions of this act in the same manner as though the person or corporation beneficially entitled thereto had then acquired such increase of benefit from the person from whom the title to their respective estates or interests is derived.   When property is devised or bequeathed in trust for persons in succession who are all liable to taxation at the same rate, it shall be lawful for the trustees thereof to pay out of the principal of the trust fund or property the taxes to which the particular estates and the expectant estates limited thereon may be respectively liable; and when such remainders or expectant estates shall be of such a nature or so disposed and circumstanced that the taxes thereon shall not be presently payable under the provisions of this act, or when property is devised or bequeathed in trust for persons in succession who are not liable at the same rate; or where some of the persons taking in succession are exempt, it shall, nevertheless, be lawful for county treasurers and the comptroller of New York city, by and with the consent of the comptroller of the state, expressed in writing, to agree with such trustees and to compound such taxes upon such terms as may be deemed equitable and expedient and to grant discharges to said trustees upon payment of the taxes provided for in such compositions; provided, however, that no such composition shall be conclusive in favor of such trustees as against the interest of such cestuis que trustent as may possess either present rights of enjoyment or fixed, absolute and indefeasible rights of future enjoyment, or of such as would possess such rights in the event of the immediate termination of particular estates, unless they consent thereto, either personally when competent, or by guardian or committee. Such compositions when made shall be executed in triplicate and one copy shall be filed in the office of the comptroller of the state, one copy in the office of the surrogate and one copy be delivered to the trustees who shall be parties thereto.

§ 7. Section two hundred and thirty-two of said act is hereby amended so as to read as follows:

§ 232. Determination of surrogate.—The report of the appraiser shall be made in duplicate, one of which duplicates shall be filed in the office of the surrogate and the other in the office of the state comptroller. From such report and other proof relating to any such estate before the surrogate, the surrogate shall forthwith, as of course determine the cash value of all estates and the amount of tax to which the same are liable; or the surrogate may so deter-

mine the cash value of all such estates and the amount of tax to
which the same are liable, without appointing an appraiser. The
superintendent of insurance shall, on the application of any surrogate, determine the value of any such future or contingent estates,
income or interest therein limited, contingent, dependent or determinable upon the life or lives or persons in being, upon the facts
contained in any such appraiser's report, and certify the same to
the surrogate, and his certificate shall be conclusive evidence that
the method of computation adopted therein is correct. The comptroller of the state of New York or any person dissatisfied with the
appraisement or assessment and determination of tax, may appeal
therefrom to the surrogate, within sixty days from the fixing, assessing and determination of tax by the surrogate as herein provided,
upon filing in the office of the surrogate a written notice of appeal,
which shall state the grounds upon which the appeal is taken. The
surrogate shall immediately give notice, upon the determination by
him as to the value of any estate which is taxable under this article,
and of the tax to which it is liable, to all parties known to be interested therein, including the state comptroller. Within two years
after the entry of an order or decree of a surrogate determining the
value of an estate and assessing the tax thereon, the comptroller
of the state may, if he believes that such appraisal, assessment or
determination has been fraudulently, collusively, or erroneously
made, make application to a justice of the supreme court of the
judicial district in which the former owner of such estate resided,
for a reappraisal thereof. The justice to whom such application
is made may thereupon appoint a competent person to reappraise
such estate. Such appraiser shall possess the powers, be subject to
the duties and receive the compensation provided by sections two
hundred and thirty and two hundred and thirty-one of this article,
Such compensation shall be payable by the county treasurer or
comptroller, out of any funds he may have on account of any tax
imposed under the provisions of this article, upon the certificate of
the justice appointing him. The report of such appraiser shall
be filed with the justice by whom he was appointed, and thereafter
the same proceedings shall be taken and had by and before such
justice as herein provided to be taken and had by and before the
surrogate. The determination and assessment of such justice shall
supersede the determination and assessment of the surrogate, and
shall be filed by such justice in the office of the state comptroller
and a certified copy thereof transmitted to the surrogate's court of
the proper county.

Chap. 286.

AN ACT to provide for the widening and improving of highways in towns having a total population of eight thousand or more inhabitants and containing an incorporated village having a total population of not less than eight thousand and not more than fifteen thousand inhabitants.

Became a law April 16, 1897, with the approval of the Governor.

Passed, three-fifths being present.

The People of the State of New York, represented in Senate and Assembly, do enact as follows:

Section 1. In any town, having a total population of eight thous- Petition and or more inhabitants and containing an incorporated vil- missioners, lage having a total population of not less than eight etc. thousand and not more than fifteen thousand inhabitants, except in the county of Madison, any five or more persons owning lands adjoining or abutting on any highway, which extends within the limits of such town and without the limits of such incorporated village for a distance of at least two and one-half miles, may present to the supreme court, at a special term thereof to be held in the county containing said town, a petition for the appointment of three commissioners for the purpose of widening and improving such highway or a certain specified portion thereof not less than two miles and a half in length, such portion being wholly without the limits of such incorporated village. Such petition shall describe Contents the part of the highway proposed to be widened and improved by stating its location and the length and limits of the portion thereof proposed to be widened and improved, and shall state the width of the proposed widening and the character of the proposed improvement, and shall also state and give the exterior lines of said portion of said highways as proposed to be made by such widening, and shall have annexed thereto a diagram or map showing such proposed exterior lines. Such petition shall be signed by all of the petitioners and verified by at least three of them. Notice Notice of of the presentation of such petition to such court shall be given by tion of the petitioners by publishing such notice in two newspapers published in such town, if there be such newspapers published therein, and if not in two newspapers published in such county, once in each week for two weeks successively preceding the day of such presentation. Such notice shall be signed by at least three of said petitioners and shall set forth the time and place when such presentation will be made and that the same will be made pursuant to this act. Upon such presentation such court shall, after hearing any

Appointment of commissioners. person interested or claiming to be interested in any land within such town, who may appear, appoint three disinterested persons, who shall not reside or be freeholders within such town, as commis-

Vacancies. sioners. And in case any of such commissioners shall at any time decline to serve or die or for any cause become disqualified or disabled from serving as such, the said court, at a similar special term, may upon similar notice and application and hearing, appoint another or other persons similarly qualified to fill the vacancy or vacancies and to act in their place and stead.

Oath of office. § 2. The said commissioners shall take the oath of office prescribed by the constitution of this state, which oath shall be filed in the office of the town clerk of said town, and a copy thereof, certified

Examination of highway. by such clerk, in the office of the county clerk of such county. The commissioners shall then proceed with all reasonable diligence to examine such highway and the portion thereof proposed by said petition to be widened and improved and the lands adjoining or abutting on such portion, and may enter upon said lands for such purpose. After having made such examination they shall appoint a time and place within said town for a meeting to hear all persons

Notice of hearing. interested in such widening and improving. They shall cause notice of such meeting to be given by publishing a notice, stating the time and place of such meeting, in at least two newspapers published in said town, if such there be, and if not, in two newspapers published in said county once in each week for two weeks successively next preceding the day of such meeting. At such meeting they shall hear the proofs and allegations of any party interested or claiming to be interested who may appear ; and they shall have power to

Decision of commissioners. adjourn such meeting from time to time for such purpose. The said commissioners shall thereafter and with all reasonable diligence determine whether or not such proposed widening and improving shall be made. They shall make and sign duplicate certificates of their decision and file one of such certificates in the town clerk's office of said town and the other in the county clerk's office of such county.

Duties cease upon adverse decision. § 3. If the said decision of such commissioners shall be against the making of such widening and improvement, their duties under this act shall cease and they shall be entitled to receive from and be paid by such town for their services at the rate of five dollars a day

Proceedings upon favorable decision. not to exceed one hundred dollars; but if such decision shall be in favor of the making of said widening and improvement, then the said commissioners shall continue in the discharge of their duties as hereinafter provided.

§ 4. The said commissioners shall prepare a map showing the present lines and boundaries of said portion of such highway before being widened and also the lines and boundaries of such portion as to be widened, and also designating the several lots, pieces or parcels of land necessary to be taken for such widening and for such purposes may enter upon such lands. They shall sign said map and file the same in the office of the town clerk of such town. *Map of lines and boundaries.*

§ 5. Said commissioners shall then cause a notice to be published, in two such newspapers as aforesaid once in each week for two weeks successively next preceding the day of the meeting mentioned in such notice, that at a stated time and place within said town they will meet for the purpose of hearing any and all parties interested or claiming to be interested in the amount of damages to be awarded for the lands to be taken for such widening. Said notice shall also state the fact that said map has been filed as aforesaid. At the time and place of said meeting and at any adjournment thereof, which said commissioners may publicly make, they shall hear the proofs and allegations of any and all parties interested or claiming to be interested in the amount of said damages. The said commissioners shall therefore make and sign a report in writing, in which they shall assess, allow and state the amount of damages to be sustained by the owners of the several lots, pieces and parcels of land to be taken for said widening. Such report shall contain the names of such owners; except that in case the commissioners are unable after due diligence to ascertain the name or names of the owner or owners of any parcel of land to be taken for said widening as aforesaid, they may, in place of the name of such undiscovered parties, insert the words " unknown owner " in their said report. The said commissioners shall then file their said report in the office of the town clerk of said town. After said report shall have been completed and filed as aforesaid, the commissioners shall cause a notice to be published in two such newspapers as aforesaid once in each week for two weeks successively that their said report has been completed and filed and that they will meet at a time or place in said town therein specified, not less than ten days from the first publication of said notice, to review their report, and that at said time and place any person interested or claiming to be interested, may offer objections in writing to such report and accompany the same with such affidavits as he may think *Notice of hearing.* *Hearing.* *Report of commissioners.* *Notice of review*

Review and correction of report.

proper. The commissioners at such meeting shall hear the proofs and allegations of any party interested or claiming to be interested, who may appear, and they shall have power to adjourn such meeting from time to time for such purpose. The commissioners shall thereupon review their said report and correct the same, where they shall deem proper, and shall thereafter refile the same with the said town clerk; and the commissioners shall thereupon, after publishing a notice in like manner as that provided in the first section hereof for the publication of the notice therein provided for, apply to the supreme court, at a special term thereof to be held

Confirmation of report by court.

in such county, to have the said report confirmed. Upon the hearing of such application for confirmation such court shall hear in opposition only the objections in writing and the accompanying affidavits, which have been presented to the commissioners as above provided. If no sufficient reason to the contrary shall appear, the court shall affirm the said report. Otherwise it may refer the same back to the said commissioners for revision or correction; and after such revision or correction the same proceedings shall be taken as are hereinbefore provided for at and after the first meeting of the commissioners for the revision or correction of such report. The commissioners shall thereupon, in the same manner as hereinbefore provided for, make renewed application for the confirmation of such report and the court shall thereupon affirm or refer back the said report; and such proceedings shall be repeated until a report shall be presented, which shall be confirmed by the said court.

Payment of award.

§ 6. Within six months after the report of said commissioners shall be refiled and confirmed as aforesaid, the supervisor of such town shall out of the proceeds of the bonds hereinafter mentioned, pay to the several and respective persons named in such report respectively the amounts awarded to them for damages as aforesaid with six per centum interest thereon from the day of the confirmation of said report, which amounts with such interest are hereby made and declared to be charges upon said town; except in cases where the persons named in such report shall be liable to be assessed for the improvements herein, in which cases the amount of the assessment hereinafter provided for shall be first

Deposit of award.

deducted and the balance only (if any) paid to the owners. And in case there are any unknown owners named in said report, the said supervisor shall deposit the amounts awarded to them with like interest in some trust company in such manner as the said court shall in the order of confirmation direct, such amounts to be paid out upon the application of said unknown owners when discovered. From the date of the confirmation of such report by _{Title to lands.} the order of the said court the title of all the lands therein designated to be taken for the said widening shall vest in such town for the purposes of a highway forever.

§ 7. After the confirmation of the said report the supervisor of _{Issue of bonds.} the said town shall from time to time, upon the written requisition of the said commissioners, for the purpose of paying the said land damages and the expenses of the said improvement, make, execute and issue in due form the bonds of the said town for not to exceed* the aggregate sum of seventy-five thousand dollars principal, in denominations of one thousand dollars each. The faith and credit of the said town is hereby pledged for the payment of the said bonds, principal and interest. The said bonds shall bear interest at not to exceed five per centum per annum, such interest to be payable semi-annually. They shall become due and payable, the first two thousand dollars thereof at the expiration of ten years from the day of their issue and two thousand dollars thereof in each and every year after said ten years, until all of the same shall have become due and payable. Each of said bonds shall contain a recital that it is issued under the provisions of this act; and such recital shall be conclusive evidence in any court of the validity of such bond and of the regularity of its issue. Each such bond shall be signed by the supervisor of such town and countersigned by the town clerk thereof. All of such bonds shall be numbered consecutively and a record thereof shall be kept by such town clerk showing the number, date, amount and date of maturity of each. The said bonds shall _{Sale and application of proceeds.} be sold by the supervisor for not less than their par value and accrued interest, if any. All moneys derived from the sale of said bonds shall be kept in a separate fund by the said supervisor and shall be paid out by him only upon orders signed by the said commissioners and shall be applied only to meet and defray disbursements under this act, except that the said supervisor shall, without any order signed by said commissioners, out of the said funds, pay to the parties entitled thereto or to such trust company as above provided the amounts awarded in such report as confirmed for damages for lands taken or to be taken; and the said supervisor shall be entitled to receive and shall receive one per centum, and all necessary expenses or disbursements, on all moneys disbursed by him hereunder.

Designation of depositories.

§ 8. In case the town board of said town shall deem it necessary or proper so to do, they may make an order to be entered on their minutes, designating one or more good and solvent bank, bankers or banking associations in said county for the deposit of all moneys received by the supervisor upon the sale of said bonds; and said commissioners shall have power and authority to agree with any such bank, banker or banking association so designated, upon a rate of interest per annum to be paid on the money when deposited; and the accrued interest thereon shall as often as once in six months be credited by such depository or depositories to

Supervisors to deposit proceeds with same.

the account of such funds; and it shall be the duty of said supervisor, upon the making of such order of said board, to forthwith deposit all sums of money received by him from the sale of such bonds with such depository or depositories so selected by said board; and thereupon said supervisor shall be relieved and released from all liabilities occasioned from any loss of said money while upon deposit with such depository or depositories, but nothing herein contained shall be held to relieve said supervisor of responsibility for the loss of any such moneys, while they are in his hands.

Plans, etc., for work and material.

§ 9. The said commissioners, after the completion of said report, shall make and sign the necessary plans and specifications for the work and materials necessary for making said widening and improvement, and shall file the same in the office of said town clerk. They shall then publish, in the manner provided in section one

Proposals and contracts.

hereof for the publication of the notice therein provided for, a notice, that they will receive at a time and place therein designated, sealed proposals for such work and materials. All bids or proposals received in response to said advertisements shall be publicly opened at such meeting of the said commissioners; and they shall award each contract for which bids and proposals have been so advertised for, as aforesaid, to the lowest bidder therefor; or they may reject any or all bids, and readvertise as often as they may deem it to be best so to do, and shall continue to do so until bids acceptable to said commissioners shall have been received. Said contract or contracts when awarded, shall be executed by the supervisor of such town under the direction of the aforesaid commissioners in behalf of said town. All contracts when awarded shall be executed in writing and in duplicate by the contractor or contractors on the one part, and said supervisor and commissioners acting for such town on the other part. One of said original con-

tracts shall be delivered to the said contractor or contractors and
the other shall be filed in the town clerk's office of said town. The Supervis-
work and materials called for by said contractor or contractors ion of work.
shall be done and furnished under the direction and supervision,
and subject to the inspection of said commissioners ; and in no
event shall such town be held in any action brought or had under Liability of
any contract so made to any other or greater liability than that town.
expressed therein, nor required to pay out or otherwise dispose
of any sum of money for the doing of such work or the furnishing
of such materials greater than is stipulated in said contract, nor
otherwise than in strict conformity with the stipulations thereof.
In case any work shall be abandoned by any contractor, or his con- Reletting
tract terminated pursuant to the provisions thereof, it shall be tract. of con-
readvertised and relet in the manner in this act provided for the
original letting of said work. No extra work or materials shall be Extra
done or furnished or allowed for unless the same is allowed by said work.
commissioners or a majority of them in writing before the same is
done. Each bidder to whom a contract or contracts is awarded as Bond of
hereinbefore provided, shall give a bond to said town with two or tors. contrac-
more sureties for the faithful performance of his contract in such
sum as shall be prescribed by said commissioners ; and the said
town may bring and maintain action upon any such bond.

§ 10. No surface railway shall be constructed on any said high- Surface
way so widened, except within eleven feet on each side of the railway.
center line of said highway, and no such railway shall be operated
by horse or horses. A distance of not less than twenty feet on
each side of such twenty-two feet so reserved for railroad purposes
shall be improved for highway purposes and not less than sixteen
feet of said twenty feet shall be of macadam. Sidewalks shall be Sidewalks.
graded on each side of said highway to a width of not less than
fifteen feet each.

§ 11. The said commissioners may employ counsel and an engineer Counsel,
and other assistants to advise and assist them in the discharge of and assis-
their duties under this act. The compensation of such counsel, tants.
engineer and assistants shall be audited and fixed by the commissioners and shall be a charge upon the said town and shall be
paid by the supervisor of such town out of the proceeds of said
bonds, upon the order or orders of said commissioners, except
that in case the decision of said commissioners, provided for in
sections two and three of this act, be against the widening and
improving of such highway, then the compensation of such coun-

the overflow of such lands; and nothing in this act shall be construed as a recognition or assumption of any liability on the part of the state for any damage done by the washing out of soil by said stream.

Appropria-
tion.   § 4. The sum of five thousand dollars, or as much thereof as may be necessary. is hereby appropriated out of any moneys in the treasury not otherwise appropriated, for the purposes specified in this act, to be paid by the treasurer upon warrant of the comptroller to the order of the superintendent of public works.

§ 5. This act shall take effect immediately.

Chap. 292.

AN ACT to provide for the erection of a suitable monument in commemoration of the soldiers of the One Hundred and Fourteenth regiment, New York Volunteer infantry, who were engaged in the battle of Winchester and Cedar Creek, Virginia, September nineteenth and October nineteenth, eighteen hundred and sixty-four, and making an appropriation therefor.

Became a law April 16, 1897, with the approval of the Governor.
Passed, three-fifths being present.

The People of the State of New York, represented in Senate and Assembly, do enact as follows:

Committee
appointed.   Section 1. Oscar H. Curtis, Samuel S. Stafford, William C. Reddy, Charles B. Dudley, Adelbert F. Coope, W. M. Rexford, Charles W. Underhill, William H. Longwell, Dennis Thompson, James L. Talbot, Alonzo B. Merchant and Harrison Brand, are hereby appointed a committee of the surviving members of the One Hundred and Fourteenth regiment, New York State Volunteer infantry, which was engaged in the battles of Winchester and Cedar Creek, Virginia, September nineteenth and October nineteenth, eighteen hundred and sixty-four, for the purposes hereinafter required.

Erection of
monu-
ment.   § 2. The committee appointed pursuant to section one of this act is hereby authorized and directed to erect a monument in the National cemetery, at Winchester, in the state of Virginia, in commemoration of the distinguished services and sacrifices of the soldiers of the One Hundred and Fourteenth regiment, New York State Volunteer infantry, upon the site which may be hereafter designated by the proper authorities in charge of said cemetery, and, if practicable, upon the plot where the dead of said regiment

are buried; but prior to the erection of such monument the said ^{Permission} committee shall secure permission for the use of the ground upon ^{grounds,} which said monument shall rest, to the memorial purpose for which said monument shall be erected, with the right of free access thereto by the public, subject, nevertheless, to the rules and regulations prescribed by said authorities for the protection and preservation of said grounds and the monument to be erected thereon.

§ 3. The said committee shall have full control in every respect Control and selec- of the selection and erection of said monument, except that said tion of monu- monument shall bear upon some conspicuous part thereof the ment. coat of arms of the state of New York, and so far as practicable a statement of the principal movements made and losses sustained by said regiment during said battles. The said committee Organiza- tion of is hereby directed to organize by electing a chairman, secretary committee. and treasurer, and to prescribe rules and regulations to cover the consideration and determination of the matter relating thereto.

§ 4. The sum of twenty-five hundred dollars is hereby appro- Appropria- tion for priated out of any money in the treasury not otherwise appro- monu- priated, payable by the treasurer, on the warrant of the comp- ment. troller, to the order of the treasurer of the committee appointed by section one of this act, for the purpose of the completion of the monument authorized by section two of this act, to be disbursed only upon the order of the committee, countersigned by the chairman and secretary of said committee.

§ 5. This act shall take effect immediately.

Chap. 293.

AN ACT to amend the consolidated school law, relating to separate neighborhoods.

Became a law April 16, 1897, with the approval of the Governor.
Passed, three-fifths being present.

The People of the State of New York, represented in Senate and Assembly, do enact as follows:

Section 1. Section fifty-one of title fifteen of chapter five hundred School law amended. and fifty-six of the laws of eighteen hundred and ninety-four, entitled "An act to revise, amend and consolidate the general acts relating to public instruction," and known as the consolidated school law, is hereby amended to read as follows:

Separate neighborhoods may be set apart.

§ 51. Each school commissioner in respect to the territory within his district shall have the power, with the approval of the state superintendent of public instruction, to set off by itself any neighborhood adjoining any other state of the union, where it shall be found most convenient for the inhabitants to send their children to a school in such adjoining state, and to deliver to the town clerk of the town in which it lies, in whole or in part, a description of each such separate neighborhood. He shall also prepare a notice, describing such neighborhood, and appointing a time and place for the first neighborhood meeting, and deliver such notice to a taxable inhabitant of such neighborhood. It shall be the duty of such inhabitant to notify every other inhabitant of the neighborhood, qualified to vote at the meeting, by reading the notice in his hearing, or, in case of his absence from home, by leaving a copy thereof, or so much thereof as relates to the time, place and object of the meeting, at the place of his abode, at least six days before the time of the meeting. In case such meeting shall not be held, and in the opinion of the commissioner it shall be necessary to hold such meeting before the time herein fixed for the first annual meeting, he shall deliver another such notice to a taxable inhabitant of the neighborhood, who shall serve it as hereinbefore provided.

Notice of first meeting

§ 2. Title fifteen of said act is hereby amended by adding thereto the following sections:

Annual neighborhood meeting.

§ 52. The annual meeting of each neighorhood shall be held on the first Tuesday of August in each year, at the hour and place fixed by the last previous neighborhood meeting; or, if such hour and place has not been so fixed, then at the hour and place of such last meeting; or, if such place be no longer accessible, then at such other place as the trustee, or, if there be no trustee, the clerk, shall in the notices designate. The proceedings of no neighborhood meeting, annual or special, shall be held illegal for want of a due notice to all the persons qualified to vote thereat, unless it shall appear that the omission to give such notice was wilful and fraudulent. The inhabitants of any neighborhood, entitled to vote, when assembled in any annual meeting or any special meeting called by the commissioner as above provided, shall have power, by a majority vote of those present, to appoint a chairman for the time being, and to choose a neighborhood clerk and one trustee, and to fill vacancies in office. The provisions of sections ten, eleven, twelve and thirteen of article one of title seven of this act, shall apply to and govern such meeting, so far as the same can in substance be

Officers may be chosen.

Application of provisions of sections.

applied to the proceedings; and the provisions of sections twenty-two, twenty-three, twenty-four, twenty-five, twenty-seven, twenty-nine, thirty, thirty-one and thirty-two of title seven of this act shall apply to and govern the officers of such neighborhood, so far as the same can in substance be applied thereto.

§ 53. The neighborhood clerk shall keep a record of the proceedings of his neighborhood, and of the reports of the trustees, and deliver the same to his successor. In case such neighborhood shall be annexed to a district within this state its records shall be filed in the office of the clerk of such district. The trustee shall, between the twenty-fifth day of July and the first day of August in every year, make his annual report to the school commissioner, and file it in the office of the clerk of the town of which the neighborhood is a part. Such report shall specify the whole amount of public moneys received during the year and from what public officer, and the manner in which it was expended; the whole number of such children as can be included in the district trustees' report residing in the neighborhood on the thirtieth day of June prior to the making of such report; and any other matters which the superintendent of public instruction may require.

§ 54. The superintendent of public instruction shall apportion to each separate neighborhood which shall have duly reported, such fixed sum as will, in his opinion, be equitably equivalent to its portion of all the state school moneys upon the basis of distribution established by this act; such sum to be payable out of the contingent fund hereinbefore established. The school commissioner or commissioners shall set apart and credit from the state and other school moneys apportioned to each separate neighborhood the amount apportioned to it by the state superintendent. The amount so apportioned shall be set apart to the town in which such neighborhood is situated, and the commissioner or commissioners shall certify the same to the supervisor thereof; and the same shall be paid over to the supervisor for distribution by him as a part of the school moneys of the town in the manner provided by article two of title two of this act. It shall be the duty of such supervisor to disburse said moneys upon the order of the trustee of such neighborhood in favor of any teacher of a school in an adjoining state, recognized by him and patronized by the inhabitants of such neighborhood; and to include a statement thereof in the account required by this act to be made by him of the school moneys received by him and the disbursement thereof.

§ 3. This act shall take effect immediately.

Chap. 294.

AN ACT to amend the consolidated school law, relating to contracts between common school districts.

Became a law April 16, 1897, with the approval of the Governor.
Passed, three-fifths being present.

The People of the State of New York, represented in Senate and Assembly, do enact as follows:

School law amended.

Section 1. Sections fourteen and fifteen of article four of title fifteen of chapter five hundred and fifty-six of the laws of eighteen hundred and ninety-four, entitled "An act to revise, amend and consolidate the general acts relating to public instruction," and known as the consolidated school law, as amended by chapter two hundred and sixty-four of the laws of eighteen hundred and ninety-six, is hereby amended so as to read respectively as follows:

Contract between common school districts.

§ 14. Whenever any school district, by a vote of a majority of the qualified voters present and voting thereon, shall empower the trustees thereof, the said trustees shall enter into a written contract with the trustees or boards of education consenting thereto, or any other district, village or city, whereby all the children of such district may be entitled to be taught in the public schools of such city, village or school district for a period of not less than

Effect of filing copy of contract

one hundred and sixty days in any school year, upon filing a copy of such contract, duly certified by the trustees of each of such school districts, or by the secretary of the board of education of such city or village in the office of the state superintendent of public instruction. Such school district shall be deemed to have employed a competent teacher for such period, and shall be entitled to receive one distributive district quota each year, during which such contract shall be continued.

Reports by boards of education and trustees.

§ 15. The board of education of any city or village, and the trustees of any school district so contracting with any other school district, shall report the number of persons of school age in such district, together with those resident in said city, village or school district, the same as though they were actual residents thereof, and shall report for the pupils attending such schools from such adjoining districts to the superintendent of public instruction, the same as though they were residents of such city, village or school district.

§ 2. This act shall take effect immediately.

Chap. 297.

AN ACT to amend the public health law, in relation to the sale of domestic remedies.

Became a law April 16, 1897, with the approval of the Governor.
Passed, three-fifths being present.

The People of the State of New York, represented in Senate and Assembly, do enact as follows:

Section 1. Section one hundred and eighty-seven of chapter six hundred and sixty-one of the laws of eighteen hundred and ninety-three, entitled, " An act in relation to the public health, constituting chapter twenty-five of the general laws, is hereby amended to read as follows:

§ 187. Application of article limited.—This article shall not apply to the business of a practitioner of medicine who is not the proprietor of a store for the retailing of drugs, medicines or poisons and shall not prevent practitioners of medicine from supplying their patients with such articles as they may deem proper, nor shall it apply to persons who sell medicines or poisons at wholesale, or to the sale of Paris green, white hellebore and other poisons for destroying insects, or any substance for use in the arts, or to the manufacture and sale of proprietary medicines, or to the sale by retail dealers or merchants of ammonia, bicarbonate of soda, borax, camphor, castor oil, cream tartar, dye-stuffs, epsom salts, essence ginger, essence peppermint, essence wintergreen, glauber's salts, glycerine, licorice, olive oil, rochelle salts, sal-ammoniac, saltpetre, salts of tartar, sal-soda and sulphur, or to the sale of the usual domestic remedies by retail dealers in the rural districts.   The term " usual domestic remedies," here employed, means medicines, a knowledge of the properties of which and dose has been acquired for common use and includes only such remedies as may be safely employed without the advice of a physician, such as paragoric, magnesia, aloes, myrrh, guaiac, arnica, rhubarb, senna, squills, ipecac and preparations of the same, spirits of nitre, essence anise and other like remedies, but does not include opium, morphine, laudanum, strychnine, arsenic, belladonna, aconite and other poisons requiring knowledge and pharmaceutical skill to safely dispense, unless they are sold in original packages, or packages put up by and bearing the label of a licensed pharmacist.   The term " rural districts " here employed, shall apply only to small villages and country districts having no store where pharmacy is practiced. The term " practice of pharmacy," when used in this article, means the compounding of prescriptions or of any United States pharmacopaeial preparation, or of any drug or poison, to be used as medicines, or the retailing of any drug or poison, except as provided for in this section.

§ 2. This act shall take effect immediately.

Chap. 302.

AN ACT amending the code of civil procedure relative to actions by certain specified officers.

Became a law April 16, 1897, with the approval of the Governor. Passed, three-fifths being present.

The People of the State of New York, represented in Senate and Assembly, do enact as follows:

Section 1. Section nineteen hundred twenty-six of the code of civil procedure is hereby amended to read as follows:

§ 1926. **Actions by certain specified officers.**— An action or special proceeding may be maintained, by the trustee or trustees of a school district; the overseer or overseers of the poor of a village, or city; the county superintendent or superintendents of the poor; or the supervisors of a county, upon a contract, lawfully made with those officers or their predecessors, in their official capacity; to enforce a liability created, or a duty enjoined, by law, upon those officers, or the body represented by them; to recover a penalty or a forfeiture, given to those officers, or the body represented by them; or to recover damages for an injury to the property or rights of those officers, or the body represented by them; although the cause of action accrued before the commencement of their term of office.

. § 2. This act shall take effect September first, eighteen hundred ninety-seven.

Chap. 305.

AN ACT to amend chapter four hundred and twenty-one of the laws of eighteen hundred and fifty-five, entitled "An act to regulate the liability of hotel keepers," and the title of such act, relating to iiabilities of owners and managers of steamboats navigating the waters of this state.

Became a law April 16, 1897, with the approval of the Governor.
Passed, three-fifths being present.

The People of the State of New York, represented in Senate and Assembly, do enact as follows:

Section 1. Section one of chapter four hundred and twenty-one Act amended. of the laws of eighteen hundred and fifty-five, entitled "An act to regulate the liability of hotel keepers," as amended by chapter two hundred and eighty-four of the laws of eighteen hundred and ninety-two, is hereby further amended to read as follows:

§ 1. Whenever the proprietor or manager of any hotel, inn or When not liable for steamboat shall provide a safe in the office of such hotel or steam- loss of valuables. boat, or other convenient place for the safe keeping of any money, jewels or ornaments belonging to the guests of or travelers in such hotel, inn or steamboat, and shall notify the guests or travelers thereof by posting a notice stating the fact that such safe is provided, in which such money, jewels, or ornaments may be deposited, in a public and conspicuous place and manner in the office and public rooms, and in the public parlors of such hotel or inn, or saloon of such or steamboat; and if such guest or traveler shall neglect to deliver such money, jewels or ornaments, to the person in charge of such office for deposit in such safe, the proprietor or manager of such hotel or steamboat shall not be liable for any loss of such money, jewels or ornaments, sustained by such guest or traveler by theft or otherwise; but no hotel or steamboat pro- Deposits for safe prietor, manager or lessee shall be obliged to receive property on keeping and liabil- deposit for safe keeping exceeding five hundred dollars in value; ity for loss limited. and if such guest or traveler shall deliver such money, jewels or ornaments to the person in charge of such office, for deposit in such safe, said proprietor, manager or lessee shall not be liable for any loss thereof, sustained by such guest or traveler by theft or otherwise in any sum exceeding the sum of two hundred and fifty dollars unless by special agreement in writing with such proprietor, manager or lessee.

Title of act amended.
§ 2. The title of such chapter four hundred and twenty-one of the laws of eighteen hundred and fifty-five is hereby amended to read as follows: "An act to regulate the liability of hotel keepers and owners and managers of steamboats navigating the waters of this state."

§ 3. This act shall take effect immediately.

Chap. 306.

AN ACT making appropriations for the support of government.

Became a law April 19, 1897, with the approval of the Governor.
Passed by a two-thirds vote.

The People of the State of New York, represented in Senate and Assembly, do enact as follows:

Appropriations for fiscal year.
Section 1. The several amounts named in this act are hereby appropriated and authorized to be paid from the several funds indicated, to the respective public officers, and for the several purposes specified, for the fiscal year beginning on the first day of October, in the year eighteen hundred and ninety-seven namely:

FROM THE GENERAL FUND.
EXECUTIVE DEPARTMENT.

Executive department.
For the governor, for salary, ten thousand dollars.

For lieutenant-governor, for salary, five thousand dollars.

For the private secretary of the governor, for salary, four thousand dollars.

For clerks, stenographer and messenger in the executive department, including the military secretary and messenger, for full compensation, ten thousand five hundred dollars.

For blanks and other books necessary for the use of the executive department, binding, blanks, printing, stationery, telegraphing and other incidental expenses thereof, five thousand dollars.

For the apprehension of criminals and fugitives from justice, one thousand dollars.

For repairs, furniture and incidental expenses of the executive mansion and rent of stable, three thousand dollars, to be paid by the comptroller on the certificate of the governor.

For compensation, expenses and fees of witnesses and sheriffs, upon application for executive clemency, pursuant to chapter two hundred and thirteen of the laws of eighteen hundred and eighty-seven, five hundred dollars.

JUDICIARY.
COURT OF APPEALS.

For the judges of the court of appeals, for salaries and expenses, eighty-four thousand five hundred dollars. Court of appeals.

For the state reporter, for salary, five thousand dollars; for clerk hire and additional assistance, seven thousand dollars, and for office expenses, one thousand dollars.

For clerk of the court of appeals, for salary, five thousand dollars.

For the deputy clerk of the court of appeals, for salary, three thousand dollars.

For clerks in the office of the clerk of the court of appeals, for salaries, six thousand five hundred dollars.

For the messenger to the clerk of the court of appeals, for salary, eight hundred dollars.

For furniture, books, binding, blanks, printing, calendars, and other necessary expenses of the office of the clerk of the court of appeals, two thousand five hundred dollars.

For compensation of the crier and attendants of the court of appeals, twelve thousand nine hundred and fifty dollars.

For the messenger to attend to the judges of the court of appeals, for salary, seven hundred and fifty dollars.

For keeping up the state library used by the judges of the court of appeals, twenty-five hundred dollars.

For the payment of services of the librarians of the court of appeals libraries at Rochester, and Syracuse, heretofore paid from the chancery fund, each six hundred dollars, to be paid on vouchers approved by the secretary of the regents of the university.

SUPREME COURT.

For the justices of the supreme court, for salaries and expenses, four hundred and twenty thousand dollars. Supreme court.

For the compensation of deputy clerk and attendants of the appellate division of the supreme court in the second judicial department, eight thousand dollars, to be refunded to the treasury as provided by chapter ninety-nine of the laws of eighteen hundred and ninety-six.

For the justices of the supreme court in the second judicial district, not residing in the county of Kings, for additional compensation, pursuant to chapter seven hundred and sixty-five of the laws of eighteen hundred and sixty-eight, as amended by

All fees of every name and nature received by said clerk or
any of his deputies or employes shall be covered into the state
treasury, and all laws allowing fees of any kind to said clerk or
his deputies are hereby repealed.

OFFICE OF THE SECRETARY OF STATE.

Secretary
of state.

For the secretary of state, for salary, five thousand dollars.

For the deputy secretary of state and clerk of the commissioners of the land office, for salary and for indexing the session
laws and making marginal notes thereof, four thousand dollars.

For clerks and messengers in the office of the secretary of state,
for salaries, twenty-nine thousand five hundred dollars.

For furniture, books, binding, blanks, printing and other necessary expenses of the office of the secretary of state, four thousand
dollars.

For deficiency in appropriation for office expenses, and for cataloguing and indexing maps and records, and for the preservation
of the same, in the office of the secretary of state, two thousand
dollars, or so much thereof as may be necessary.

OFFICE OF THE COMPTROLLER.

Comp-
troller.

For the comptroller, for salary, six thousand dollars.

For the deputy comptroller, for salary, four thousand
dollars.

For clerks in the office of the comptroller, for salaries, fifty-two
thousand five hundred dollars.

For messenger in the office of the comptroller, for salary, eight
hundred dollars.

For furniture, books, binding, blanks, printing and other necessary expenses of the office of the comptroller, five thousand dollars.

For the expenses of making an examination of the accounts of
the several county treasurers of the state, as required by chapter
six hundred and fifty-one of the laws of eighteen hundred and
ninety-two, for the expenses and disbursements incurred by him
in the supervision and administration of the funds paid into court
as may be necessary and required by said act, eight thousand
dollars.

For the comptroller, to pay the expenses of serving notices on
occupants or despoilers of land now owned by the state, or bid in
therefor at the comptroller's tax sales; or protecting the state's
title to such lands by discharging them from the taxes due thereon,
or bidding them in at, or redeeming them from county treasurer's

tax sales; of preparing and recording deeds and certificates protecting the state's title to such lands; of definitely locating, appraising and examining them as may be required; of protecting them from trespassers or despoilers, and prosecuting all such offenders, and generally of guarding, preserving the value of, and protecting such lands, three thousand five hundred dollars.

OFFICE OF THE TREASURER.

For the treasurer, for salary, five thousand dollars.   Treasurer.

For the deputy treasurer, for salary, four thousand dollars.

For clerks and messengers in the office of the treasurer, for salaries, fourteen thousand dollars.

For the new capitol paymaster in the office of the treasurer, for salary, two thousand five hundred dollars.

For furniture, books, binding, blanks, printing and other necessary expenses of the office of the treasurer, two thousand dollars.

DEPARTMENT OF PUBLIC INSTRUCTION.

For the superintendent of public instruction, for salary, five thousand dollars.   Department of public instruction.

For the deputy superintendent of public instruction, for salary, four thousand five hundred dollars.

For clerks and other employes in the office of the superintendent of public instruction, for salaries, twenty thousand dollars.

For furniture, books, binding, blanks, printing and other necessary expenses of the office of the superintendent of public instruction, five thousand dollars.

For traveling expenses which may be incurred in the visitation of common schools, normal schools, teachers' institutes, Indian schools and other institutions under the supervision of this department and educational associations, one thousand dollars.

For superintendent of public instruction, for printing circulars and programs relating to the observance of Arbor Day for distribution among the school districts of the state, and for the expenses relating to the observance of that day, pursuant to the provisions of chapter five hundred and fifty-six of the laws of eighteen hundred and ninety-four, one thousand dollars, or so much thereof as may be necessary.

For the purpose of carrying out the provisions of chapter six hundred and seventy-one of the laws of eighteen hundred and

ninety-four, as amended by chapter nine hundred and eighty-eight of the laws of eighteen hundred and ninety-five, and for the payment of salaries of assistants, expenses and blanks, the sum of ten thousand dollars.

OFFICE OF THE STATE ENGINEER AND SURVEYOR.

State engineer and surveyor.

For the state engineer and surveyor, for salary, five thousand dollars.

For the deputy state engineer and surveyor, for salary, four thousand dollars.

For clerks in the office of the state engineer and surveyor, for salaries, nine thousand two hundred dollars.

For furniture, books, binding, blanks, printing and other necessary expenses of the office of the state engineer and surveyor, two thousand one hundred dollars.

RAILROAD COMMISSIONERS.

Railroad commissioners.

For the board of railroad commissioners, for salaries, and expenses, as provided in section one hundred and seventy, article six, chapter five hundred and sixty-five of the laws of eighteen hundred and ninety, as amended by chapter five hundred and thirty-four of the laws of eighteen hundred and ninety-two, and chapter four hundred and fifty-six, of the laws of eighteen hundred and ninety-six, sixty thousand dollars.

For printing and binding the additional reports of the board of railroad commissioners, as provided in section one hundred and sixty-six, article six, chapter five hundred and sixty-five of the laws of eighteen hundred and ninety, twenty-five hundred dollars, or so much thereof as may be necessary.

For services and expenses of deputies and clerks in the office of the attorney-general, in proceedings or litigation, for or on account of railroad companies, or in which railroad companies were parties, one thousand dollars, or so much thereof as may be necessary, as may be certified by the attorney-general to the comptroller, which amount is hereby appropriated and authorized to be paid.

The amounts stated in the last three items shall be refunded to the treasury by the several corporations owning or operating railroads in this state, in such manner and proportion as is prescribed by law.

BANKING DEPARTMENT.

For the superintendent of banks, for salary, five thousand Banking department. dollars. And the superintendent of banks shall receive the sum of one thousand five hundred dollars annually, payable monthly, in lieu of and in full for all expenses and disbursements incurred by him.

For clerk hire, office rent and for books, binding, blanks, printing and other necessary expenses of the office of the superintendent of banks, nineteen thousand dollars.

The amounts required for the aforesaid salary, clerk hire and other expenses, above mentioned, shall be refunded to the treasury by the several banks, individual bankers, savings banks and trust companies in this state, in whose behalf they are incurred, pursuant to chapter six hundred and eighty-nine of the laws of eighteen hundred and ninety-two.

For carrying out the provisions of chapter six hundred and eighty-nine of the laws of eighteen hundred and ninety-two, providing for reports concerning the dormant accounts in savings banks, one thousand dollars, to be assessed upon and collected from the savings banks making such reports, as provided in said chapter.

For carrying out the provisions of the banking law, chapter six hundred and eighty-nine of the laws of eighteen hundred and ninety-two, as amended, in reference to the supervision and visitation of mortgage, loan or investment companies, and of co-operative savings and loan associations, and foreign co-operative savings and loan associations, and other similar associations required by the law to report to said superintendent of banks, seven thousand five hundred dollars, to be assessed and collected from said associations and corporations, and refunded to the state treasury, as provided in said banking law.

INSURANCE DEPARTMENT.

For the superintendent of the insurance department, for salary, Insurance department. seven thousand dollars.

For the first and second deputy superintendents of the insurance department, for salaries, nine thousand five hundred dollars.

For clerk hire, furniture, books, binding, blanks, printing and other necessary expenses of the office of the superintendent of insurance, sixty-eight thousand five hundred dollars. The superintendent of insurance shall receive the further sum of one thousand seven hundred dollars, and the first deputy superintendent, two thousand three hundred dollars annually, payable monthly, in lieu of and in full for all expenses and disbursements incurred by them.

For additional examinations made by the direction of the superintendent of the insurance department, to be used in his discretion, five thousand dollars.

The amount required for the aforesaid salaries, clerk hire, · and other expenses of the insurance department, and such additional sum as may be certified to the comptroller by the attorney-general as a reasonable compensation for the services and expenses of deputies and clerks in his office in proceedings or litigation for or on account of insurance companies, or in which insurance companies were parties, not exceeding the sum of one thousand dollars, which sum is hereby appropriated, shall be refunded to the treasury by the several insurance companies, associations, persons and agents to whom said chapter six hundred and ninety of the laws of eighteen hundred and ninety-two applies.

BOARD OF TAX COMMISSIONERS.

Board of tax commissioners. For the salaries of the tax commissioners the sum of seven thousand five hundred dollars. For the salary of the clerk, two thousand dollars. For clerical help, traveling and other expenses of the board of tax commissioners, five thousand five hundred dollars.

COMMISSIONERS OF QUARANTINE.

Quarantine. For the commissioners of quarantine, for salaries, seven thousand five hundred dollars.

LAND OFFICE.

Land office. For assessments and other expenses of the public lands, and for mileage and expenses of the speaker of the assembly for attendance as commissioner of the land office, five thousand dollars.

PUBLIC OFFICES.

Public offices. For postage or expressage on official letters, documents and other matter sent by mail or express by the governor, secretary of state, comptroller, treasurer, attorney-general, state engineer and surveyor, superintendent of public instruction, regents of the university, adjutant-general, clerk of the court of appeals, state board of charities, state board of health, civil service commission and bureau of labor statistics, ten thousand dollars; and for stationery for the aforesaid offices and departments, ten thousand dollars.

PUBLIC BUILDINGS.

For the care, cleaning, labor, lights, salary of the superintendent of public buildings, services of orderlies and watchmen, and all necessary expenses of the public buildings, pursuant to the provisions of chapter two hundred and twenty-seven of the laws of eighteen hundred and ninety-three, one hundred and fifty thousand dollars; provided that the orderlies and watchmen and persons employed in positions, which on March first, eighteen hundred and eighty-six, were designated on the books of the superintendent of public buildings, as those of orderlies and watchmen, who shall receive any portion of said sum of one hundred and fifty thousand dollars for their services, shall be persons who are citizens of the state of New York, and who served in the Union army or navy during the late war, and have been honorably discharged therefrom, and such honorably discharged persons shall not be subject to civil service rules of examination. *Public buildings.*

UNIVERSITY OF THE STATE OF NEW YORK.
REGENTS' OFFICE.

For salaries of secretary, chief clerk, bookkeeper, clerks in charge of reports, statistics and printing, stenographer, typewriter, messenger and other office assistants, for traveling expenses of regents, officers and inspectors in visitation of institutions and attending meetings, and for furniture, fittings, supplies, printing, telegraphing, repairs and other incidental expenses of the regents' office, pursuant to the provisions of chapter three hundred and seventy-eight of the laws of eighteen hundred and ninety-two, twenty-one thousand dollars. *Regents' office.*

For the academic department of union schools, to be appropriated as provided by chapter three hundred and seventy-eight of the laws of eighteen hundred and ninety-two, sixty thousand dollars.

For dividends to be apportioned by the regents for the benefit of the academies of the university by chapter three hundred and forty-one of the laws of eighteen hundred and ninety-five, one hundred and thirty-nine thousand one hundred and twelve dollars and nine cents.

STATE LIBRARY.

State library.

For books, serials and binding, pursuant to chapter three hundred and seventy-eight of the laws of eighteen hundred and ninety-two, fifteen thousand dollars; three thousand dollars thereof to be paid to the regents on the first day of October next, and the balance in such sums, from time to time, as shall be required by them, upon vouchers to be approved by the comptroller.

For salaries of the officers and employes, including the keeper of the records, for assistance required for supervision of the reading-rooms, for cataloguing and classifying the books, and for keeping the library open evenings and holidays, and for maintaining the duplicate department, and for furniture, fittings, supplies, printing, telegraphing, repairs and other incidental expenses, pursuant to chapter three hundred and seventy-eight of the laws of eighteen hundred and ninety-two, twenty-two thousand nine hundred dollars.

STATE MUSEUM.

State museum.

For the preservation and increase of the collection of the State museum, and for salaries and official expenses of the botanist and entomologist and other employes, pursuant to chapter three hundred and seventy-eight of the laws of eighteen hundred and ninety two, ten thousand dollars; and for the department of geology and paleontology, for services and expenses, pursuant to chapter four hundred and eighty-eight of the laws of eighteen hundred and ninety-three, twelve thousand four hundred and eighty dollars, payable upon the certificate of the state geologist and the audit of the comptroller.

DEPARTMENT OF AGRICULTURE.

Department of agriculture.

For the promotion of agriculture in this state, seventy-six thousand dollars: twenty thousand dollars thereof shall be distributed in premiums by the New York state agricultural society; of the remaining fifty-six thousand dollars there shall be distributed by the commissioners of agriculture among the American institute of the city of New York, town, county and other agricultural societies, fairs, clubs and expositions the amount they are entitled thereto by virtue of the provisions of section eighty-nine of the agricultural law; seventy per centum of the said remainder shall be apportioned among the county agricultural societies, fairs or associations, the American institute of the city of New York or to the societies, fairs or associations entitled thereto in counties where there are no such county agricultural societies, and thirty per centum thereof shall be apportioned to the various town and other agricultural societies, clubs or exhibitions, to be distributed in the manner provided by section eighty-eight of the agricultural law.

For the necessary expenditures of the agricultural experiment station at Geneva, for salaries, labor, repairs, laboratory, farm implements, dairy, expense of board of control, meteorological instruments, and all other necessary expenses at the station, pursuant to chapter seven hundred and two of the laws of eighteen hundred and eighty-one, chapter four hundred and thirteen of the laws of eighteen hundred and eighty-six, and chapter one hundred and forty-four of the laws of eighteen hundred and ninety-one, and chapter three hundred and thirty-eight of the laws of eighteen hundred and ninety-three, fifty thousand dollars.

For the department of agriculture, for salary of commissioner and for the salaries of the assistant commissioners and clerks, the employment of experts, chemist, agents and counsel, pursuant to chapter three hundred and thirty-eight of the laws of eighteen hundred and ninety-three, and for all the necessary expenses in prosecuting the business of this department, one hundred thousand dollars.

No more than ten assistant commissioners shall be employed by the commissioner of agriculture for said department. The assistant residing in the city of Albany shall receive as salary the sum of two thousand five hundred dollars, and the assistant commissioner residing in the city of New York shall receive an annual salary of two thousand five hundred dollars, and such expenses as may be necessary, when they are away from the city of Albany or New York respectively, on business of said department. The other assistant commissioners shall receive such salaries as shall be fixed by the commissioner of agriculture, and all necessary expenses incurred in the performance of their duties.

COMMISSIONER OF THE NEW CAPITOL.

For the commissioner of the new capitol, for salary, seven thousand five hundred dollars.

Commissioner of new capitol.

LEGISLATURE.

Legisla-
ture.

For the compensation and mileage of members and officers of the legislature, four hundred and fifty thousand dollars.

For advances by the comptroller to the clerks of the senate and assembly, for contingent expenses, twenty-five thousand dollars.

For postage, expenses of committees, compensation of witnesses, legislative manual, Croswell's manual, clerk's manual, indexing the bills, journals and documents of the senate and assembly, and other contingent expenses of the legislature, thirty thousand dollars.

STATE PRINTING.

State
printing.

For the legislative printing of the state, including binding, mapping, lithographing and engraving, one hundred thousand dollars.

SESSION LAWS AND OFFICIAL CANVASS.

Session
laws.

For the publication of the session laws and the official canvass and official notices provided by law, which are subjects of contract, twenty-five thousand dollars.

PUBLICATION OF GENERAL LAWS.

Publica-
tion of gen-
eral laws.

For the payment of newspapers in the various counties in this state for the publication of the general laws of the state pursuant to chapter seven hundred and fifteen of the laws of eighteen hundred and ninety-two, ninety thousand dollars.

STATE PRISONS.

State
prisons.

For the support and maintenance of the several state prisons, pursuant to chapter three hundred and eighty-two of the laws of eighteen hundred and eighty-nine, and for the ordinary repairs of the prisons and supplying water therefor, three hundred thousand dollars.

For the superintendent of state prisons, for salary, six thousand dollars.

For the necessary traveling expenses of the superintendent and his clerk, five hundred dollars.

For necessary clerk hire and copying and a messenger, and for postage, stationery and other incidental expenses, six thousand five hundred dollars.

For compensation of sheriffs, for the transportation of convicts to prisons, asylum for insane criminals, penitentiaries, houses of refuge and reformatories, twelve thousand dollars.

For the maintenance of convicts sentenced to penitentiaries, in pursuance of chapter one hundred and fifty-eight of the laws of eighteen hundred and fifty-six, chapter five hundred and eighty-four of the laws of eighteen hundred and sixty-five, chapter six hundred and sixty-seven of the laws of eighteen hundred and sixty-six, chapter five hundred and seventy-four of the laws of eighteen hundred and sixty-nine, chapter two hundred and forty-seven of the laws of eighteen hundred and seventy-four, chapter five hundred and seventy-one of the laws of eighteen hundred and seventy-five, chapter four hundred and ninety of the laws of eighteen hundred and eighty-five, chapter one hundred and fifteen of the laws of eighteen hundred and ninety-one and chapter five hundred and eighty-seven, laws of eighteen hundred and ninety-two, one hundred thousand dollars.

For the support and maintenance of the state prison for women, at Auburn, pursuant to chapter three hundred and six of the laws of eighteen hundred and ninety-three, for ordinary repairs, supplying water therefor and for the transportation of women prisoners, thirty thousand dollars.

MATTEAWAN STATE HOSPITAL FOR INSANE CRIMINALS.

For the support and maintenance of the Matteawan state hospital for insane criminals and for the ordinary repairs of the hospital, fifty thousand dollars. Hospital for insane criminals.

For the resident officers of the Matteawan state hospital for insane criminals, for salaries, eight thousand nine hundred dollars.

INDIAN AFFAIRS.

For the payment of the annuities to the several Indian tribes, as follows: Indian affairs.

To the Onondagas, two thousand four hundred and thirty dollars.

To the Cayugas, two thousand three hundred dollars.

To the Senecas, five hundred dollars.

To the Saint Regis, two thousand one hundred and thirty-one dollars and sixty-seven cents.

For the relief of the Onondaga Indians, three hundred dollars.

For compensation of the agent of the Onondaga Indians, two hundred dollars.

For compensation of the agent of the Onondaga Indians, pur-

SOLDIERS AND SAILORS' HOME.

Soldiers and sailors' home.   For the support and maintenance of the New York state soldiers and sailors' home, for the transportation of applicants for admission and for ordinary repairs, one hundred and eighty-five thousand dollars.

STATE REFORMATORY.

State reformatory.   For the New York state reformatory, at Elmira, for maintenance and ordinary repairs, and for the purchase of material, and for expenses of manufacturing, pursuant to chapter seven hundred and eleven of the laws of eighteen hundred and eighty-seven, two hundred and fifteen thousand dollars.

STATE BOARD OF HEALTH.

State bo.rd of health.   For the state board of health, for the maintenance of its work, in administering the several laws with which it is charged, thirty-five thousand dollars.

DEAF AND DUMB.

Deaf and dumb.   For the support and instruction of two hundred and fifty pupils at the institute for deaf and dumb in New York city, sixty-five thousand dollars.

For the support and instruction of one hundred and twenty pupils at the institution for the improved instruction of deaf-mutes in New York city, thirty-one thousand two hundred dollars.

For the support and instruction of seventy-five pupils at the Le Couteulx Saint Mary's institution for the improved instruction of deaf-mutes at Buffalo, nineteen thousand five hundred dollars.

For the support and instruction of one hundred and fifteen pupils at the Central New York institution for the improved instruction of deaf-mutes at Rome, twenty-nine thousand nine hundred dollars.

For the support and instruction of one hundred and eighty pupils at Saint Joseph's institution for the improved instruction of deaf-mutes at Fordham, forty-five thousand dollars.

For the support and instruction of ninety-five pupils at the western New York institution at Rochester for the improved instruction of deaf-mutes, twenty-four thousand seven hundred dollars.

For the support and instruction of sixty-five pupils at the northern New York institution for deaf-mutes at Malone, sixteen thousand nine hundred dollars.

A proportionate amount for a shorter period of time than one year, or for a smaller number of pupils in each case, shall be allowed in each of the last seven items, and paid by the comptroller, upon certificate verified by oath of the president and secretary of such institution, and upon the approval of the superintendent of public instruction.

ASYLUMS AND HOSPITALS.
THOMAS ASYLUM.

For the Thomas asylum for orphan and destitute Indian children, for maintenance, salaries of officers and teachers, and ordinary repairs, twenty thousand dollars. <small>Thomas asylum.</small>

BLIND.

For the support and instruction of one hundred and eighty pupils, one year, at the New York institution for the blind, forty-five thousand dollars, or a proportionate amount for a shorter period of time than one year, or for a smaller number of pupils, as shall be duly verified by the affidavits of the president and secretary of the institution. <small>Blind.</small>

For the maintenance and instruction of the inmates of the state school for the blind, at Batavia, and for the ordinary repairs of buildings, forty thousand dollars.

CRAIG COLONY FOR EPILEPTICS.

For the salary of officers and employes of the Craig colony for epileptics, for the maintenance of the institution and for ordinary repairs, fifty thousand dollars. <small>Craig colony.</small>

JUVENILE DELINQUENTS.

For the society for the reformation of juvenile delinquents in the city of New York, for maintenance and rewards to inmates and repairs and betterments of tools and equipment and furniture and for repairs to buildings and for necessary tools to properly conduct the trade schools and common schools and military system and photographing of inmates, one hundred and sixty-five thousand dollars. <small>Juvenile delinquents.</small>

STATE INDUSTRIAL SCHOOL.

State in-
dustrial
school.
For the state industrial school at Rochester, for maintenance and rewards to inmates and repairs and betterments of tools and equipment and furniture and for repairs to buildings and for necessary tools to properly conduct the trade schools and common schools and military system and photographing of inmates, one hundred ninety thousand dollars.

SYRACUSE STATE INSTITUTION FOR FEEBLE-MINDED CHILDREN.

Institution
for feeble-
minded
children.
For the Syracuse state institution for feeble-minded children, for maintenance and ordinary repairs, seventy-five thousand dollars.

CUSTODIAL ASYLUM.

Custodial
asylum.
For the support and maintenance of the inmates of the Newark custodial asylum; for the service of the attendants therein, and for other necessary expenses, and the ordinary repairs of the asylum, fifty thousand dollars.

ROME STATE CUSTODIAL ASYLUM.

Rome cus-
todial
asylum.
For the support and maintenance of the inmates of the Rome state custodial asylum; for the services of attendants therein and for other necessary expenses and the ordinary repairs of the asylum. fifty-five thousand dollars.

HOUSE OF REFUGE FOR WOMEN.

House of
refuge for
women.
For the compensation of officers and employes of the house of refuge for women, at Hudson; for the maintenance of the institution and for the transportation of the convicts, sixty-eight thousand dollars.

For the compensation of officers and employes of the western house of refuge for women, at Albion; for the maintenance of the institution and for the transportation of convicts, thirty thousand dollars.

HOME FOR VETERANS.

Home for
veterans.
For the home for veterans, for maintenance and ordinary repairs, fifteen thousand dollars, pursuant to chapter four hundred and sixty-eight, laws of eighteen hundred and ninety-four.

STATE COMMISSION OF PRISONS.

For the secretary of state commission of prisons, for salary, three State commission of prisons. thousand dollars; and for traveling expenses of the commissioners and secretary, office expenses and clerk hire, ten thousand dollars.

STATE BOARD OF CHARITIES.

For the secretary of the state board of charities, for salary, three State board of charities. thousand five hundred dollars; and for the traveling expenses of the commissioners and secretary, for the office expenses and clerk hire, twenty-five thousand dollars.

For the support, care and removal of state, alien and Indian poor, pursuant to chapter five hundred and forty-nine of the laws of eighteen hundred and eighty, chapter two hundred and twenty-five of the laws of eighteen hundred and ninety-six, and chapter five hundred and forty-six, laws of eighteen hundred and ninety-six, forty thousand dollars; and it shall be the duty of said board, in their annual report to the legislature, to give a complete and itemized statement of the expenditures for state paupers during the preceding fiscal year.

WEIGHTS AND MEASURES.

For the superintendent of weights and measures, for salary, Weights and measures. three hundred dollars.

CORNELL UNIVERSITY.

For payment to Cornell university, being the interest at five per Cornell university. centum on the proceeds of the college land scrip fund pursuant to chapter seventy-eight of the laws of eighteen hundred and ninety-five, thirty-four thousand four hundred and twenty-eight dollars and eighty cents.

For the state veterinary college at Cornell university, for maintenance, equipment and necessary material to conduct the same, twenty-five thousand dollars, payable to the treasurer of Cornell university on the warrant of the comptroller.

STATE HISTORIAN.

For the state historian, for salary, four thousand five hundred State historian. dollars; for the salary of a stenographer, one thousand dollars; and for stationery and other office expenses three hundred and fifty dollars.

FACTORY INSPECTORS.

Factory inspectors.

For the factory inspector, assistant and deputy factory inspectors and employes, for salaries, and for actual and necessary expenses, pursuant to the provisions of chapter four hundred and nine of the laws of eighteen hundred and eighty-six, as amended by chapter four hundred and sixty-two of the laws of eighteen hundred and eighty-seven, chapter five hundred and sixty of the laws of eighteen hundred and eighty-nine, chapter three hundred and ninety-eight of the laws of eighteen hundred and ninety, chapter six hundred and seventy-three of the laws of eighteen hundred and ninety-two, chapter one hundred and seventy-three of the laws of eighteen hundred and ninety-three, chapter five hundred and eighteen of the laws of eighteen hundred and ninety-five, chapter three hundred and ninety-four of the laws of eighteen hundred and ninety, chapter three hundred and eighty-eight of the laws of eighteen hundred and ninety, chapter seven hundred and seventeen of the laws of eighteen hundred and ninety-three, chapter seven hundred and ninety-one of the laws of eighteen hundred and ninety-five, and chapter nine hundred and ninety-one, laws of eighteen hundred and ninety-six, eighty thousand dollars.

STATE BOARD OF MEDIATION AND ARBITRATION.

Board of mediation.

For the members, officers and employes of the state board of mediation and arbitration, for salaries and actual and necessary expenses, sixteen thousand dollars.

NIAGARA RESERVATION.

Niagara reservation.

For the commissioners of the state reservation at Niagara, for salaries and for actual and necessary expenses, twenty-five thousand dollars.

STATE EXCISE DEPARTMENT.

State excise department.

For salaries and expenses of state excise department, pursuant to chapter one hundred and twelve of the laws of eighteen hundred and ninety-six, namely: Salary of state commissioner of excise, five thousand dollars; expenses and disbursements, which shall be allowed him in lieu and in full of expenses, eighteen hundred dollars; salary of deputy commissioner, four thousand dollars; expenses and disbursements, which shall be allowed him in lieu and in full of expenses, twelve hundred dollars; for salary of three special deputy commissioners (New York, Brooklyn and Buffalo), clerk hire (including counsel for Albany, New York, Brooklyn and Buffalo offices), salaries and expenses of sixty special agents, printing certificates, books (including books for county treasurers), law cases, blanks, et cetera, office equipments, stationery and office supplies, rentals for New York, Brooklyn and Buffalo offices, telegraphing, telephoning, expressing (including telephone rentals), expenses of enumeration and examining county treasurers' excise accounts, attorneys' fees and disbursements, as per section ten, furniture, fittings, supplies, postage and other incidental expenses necessary to carry out the provisions of said law, the sum of two hundred and eighty-eight thousand dollars.

For the state commissioner of excise, one hundred and seventy-five thousand dollars, to pay refunds upon surrender of liquor tax certificates, under the provisions of the liquor tax law, to be paid by the state treasurer from excise moneys in his hands upon the certificate of the comptroller.

ONONDAGA SALT SPRINGS.

For the salary of superintendent, compensation of clerks and other persons employed, and necessary expenses of the Onondaga salt springs, fifty thousand dollars, pursuant to chapter six hundred and eighty-four of the laws of eighteen hundred and ninety-two. To be available only upon the passage of an act which shall provide that on or before January first, eighteen hundred and ninety-nine, all the interest of the state in any real property of the Onondaga Salt Springs Reservation be sold or the title thereof vested in the people of the state of New York, free from all claims, in behalf of any lessee or his legal representatives; that all personal property connected therewith be sold, and that the state shall cease to furnish brine or operate such works at an expense to the state.

Salt springs.

MISCELLANEOUS.

For supplying other states with reports of the court of appeals and the supreme court, pursuant to section twenty-seven of the executive law as amended by chapter two hundred and forty-eight of the laws of eighteen hundred and ninety-three, one thousand dollars.

Court reports.

For the expenses of the board of pilot commissioners, three thousand five hundred dollars.

Pilot commissioners.

Inspectors of gas meters. For the inspector of gas meters, for salary and salaries of deputies, as provided for by chapter three hundred and eighty-five of the laws of eighteen hundred and ninety-three, nine thousand five hundred dollars, which sum hereby appropriated shall be refunded to the treasury by the several gas-light corporations in this state in amounts proportionate to the amount of the capital stock of such corporation respectively, to be ascertained and assessed by the comptroller of the state in accordance with the provisions of chapter three hundred and eighty-five of the laws of eighteen hundred and ninety-three.

Washington's headquarters. For the trustees of Washington's headquarters, at Newburgh, for compensation of the superintendent, and for the care, maintenance, repairs and improvements of the grounds, one thousand dollars.

Gate tenders for state dam. For the compensation of gate tenders for the state dams upon the Beaver and Moose rivers, as provided by chapter one hundred and sixty-eight of the laws of eighteen hundred and ninety-four, the sum of one thousand one hundred dollars, to be paid by the comptroller on the certificate of the commissioners appointed under said act, or a majority thereof.

Senate house. For the trustees of public buildings, for the salary of the keeper of the senate-house property, at Kingston, pursuant to chapter two hundred and twenty-seven of the laws of eighteen hundred and ninety-three, six hundred dollars.

Port wardens. For the expenses of the board of port wardens of the port of New York, pursuant to chapter one hundred and forty-two of the laws of eighteen hundred and ninety-one, forty-five hundred dollars.

Superintendent state land survey. For the compensation of the superintendent of the state land survey, pursuant to chapter five hundred and eighty-nine of the laws of eighteen hundred and ninety-five, five thousand dollars; and for continuing the work of the state land survey, pursuant to chapter five hundred and eighty-nine of the laws of eighteen hundred and ninety-five, twenty-five thousand dollars, and which shall be immediately available.

Janitor Saratoga monument. For salary of janitor of the Saratoga monument, five hundred dollars, per chapter nine hundred and fifty-five, laws of eighteen hundred and ninety-five.

Draw-bridge tender. For the compensation of the tender and for the maintainance and operation of the draw-bridge over Minneceongo creek, Rockland county, the sum of seven hundred dollars. The sum of five thousand dollars, or so much thereof as may be necessary, is hereby appropriated from the canal fund to pay for the services and disbursements incurred by the agent employed by the superintendent of public works on request of the attorney-general, as provided in section two hundred and seventy of the code of civil procedure, in defense of claims against the state, on account of the canals; such sum to be advanced to said agent by the comptroller, upon his filing with the comptroller a good and sufficient bond in the sum of ten thousand dollars, for the same. But no account for such services, disbursements and expenses shall be paid until the same has been presented to and approved by the canal board. *Agent of superintendent of public works.*

PAYABLE FROM THE FREE SCHOOL FUND.

For the support of the common schools of the state, three million five hundred thousand dollars. *Normal schools*

For the support and maintenance of the state normal and training schools, located as follows:

At Albany, twenty-nine thousand dollars.

At Buffalo, twenty-one thousand dollars.

At Brockport, twenty-five thousand dollars.

At Cortland, twenty-six thousand dollars.

At Fredonia, twenty-three thousand five hundred dollars.

At Geneseo, twenty-eight thousand dollars.

At New Paltz, twenty thousand dollars.

At Oswego, twenty-five thousand dollars.

At Oneonta, twenty-five thousand dollars.

At Plattsburgh, twenty thousand eight hundred dollars.

At Potsdam, twenty-five thousand dollars.

At Jamaica, twenty thousand dollars.

For the support and education of Indian youth at the normal schools of the state in pursuance of chapter eighty-nine of the laws of eighteen hundred and fifty, one thousand dollars, or so much thereof as may be necessary, payable on the audit of the state superintendent of public instruction. *Indian youth, support of.*

For the maintenance of teachers' institutes, pursuant to chapter five hundred and fifty-six of the laws of eighteen hundred and ninety-four, and for the preparation of question papers, and the supervision of examinations for state certificates and uniform commissioners' certificates by institute conductors, thirty-five thousand dollars. *Teachers' institutes.* *Examinations.*

For the department of public instruction for defraying the expenses of the examination of answer papers submitted under the *Answer papers* uniform system of examinations of commissioners' certificates as provided for by chapter five hundred and fifty-six of the laws of eighteen hundred and ninety-four, fifteen thousand dollars, or so much thereof as may be necessary.

School commissioners.

For the commissioners of common schools, for salaries, one hundred and thirteen thousand dollars.

School registers and reports.

For the department of public instruction, for printing and binding fifteen thousand school registers, pursuant to chapter five hundred and fifty-six of the laws of eighteen hundred and ninety-four, and for printing and binding twenty-five thousand copies of trustees' reports, and for packing and boxing the same, five thousand two hundred dollars.

Teachers' classes.

For instruction and supervision of classes of common school teachers in the academies and union schools designated by the superintendent of public instruction, pursuant to chapter five hundred and fifty-six of the laws of eighteen hundred and ninety-four, sixty thousand dollars.

School examinations.

Certificates.

For the expense of holding examinations for commissioners' certificates, common school examinations in connection with the course of study adopted by school commissioners and approved by the superintendent of public instruction, state certificates and state scholarships in Cornell university, and for preparing and printing blanks, circulars, question papers and certificates necessary for such examinations, and for printing graduates' certificates issued by the superintendent of public instruction, pursuant to chapter five hundred and fifty-six of the laws of eighteen hundred and ninety-four, eight thousand dollars.

PAYABLE FROM THE COMMON SCHOOL FUND.
CAPITAL.

Investment of fund.

For investment of the capital of the common school fund, pursuant to chapter fifty of the laws of eighteen hundred and eighty-nine, fifty thousand dollars, or so much thereof as may be necessary.

REVENUE.

Dividends to schools.

For dividends to common schools, revised statutes, volume one, page five hundred and thirty-eight, one hundred and seventy thousand dollars.

Indian schools.

For support of Indian schools, chapter seventy-one of the laws of eighteen hundred and fifty-six, six thousand dollars.

REVENUE.

For dividends to be apportioned by the regents for the benefit Dividends to academies. of the academies of the university, chapter three hundred and seventy-eight of the laws of eighteen hundred and ninety-two, twelve thousand dollars.

PAYABLE FROM THE UNITED STATES DEPOSIT FUND.
CAPITAL.

For investment of the United States deposit fund, in pur- Investment of fund. suance of chapter one hundred and fifty of the laws of eighteen hundred and thirty-seven, and chapter fifty of the laws of eighteen hundred and eighty-nine, fifty thousand dollars, or so much thereof as may be necessary.

REVENUE.

For dividends to common schools, chapter five hundred and Dividends to schools. fifty-six of the laws of eighteen hundred and ninety-four, and chapter five hundred and seventy-three of the laws of eighteen hundred and ninety-two, as amended by chapter five hundred and forty-six of the laws of eighteen hundred and ninety-five, seventy-five thousand dollars.

For dividends to be apportioned by the regents for the benefit Dividends to academies. of the academies of the university, chapter three hundred and seventy-eight of the laws of eighteen hundred and ninety-two, thirty-four thousand dollars.

For apportionment of public library money by the regents of Public library money. the university, for the benefit of free libraries and the purchase of books to be lent in accordance with sections fourteen, forty-seven and fifty of chapter three hundred and seventy-eight of the laws of eighteen hundred and ninety-two, twenty-five thousand dollars.

For amount to be added to the capital of the common school Capital of school fund. fund, article nine of constitution, twenty-five thousand dollars.

For establishing and conducting examinations in accordance Examination of medical and law students. with chapter four hundred and twenty-five of the laws of eighteen hundred and seventy-seven, and for conducting preliminary examinations for law students, as prescribed by the rules of the court of appeals, in pursuance of section one hundred and ninety-three of the code of civil procedure, and for medical students,

as prescribed by section one hundred and forty-five of chapter
six hundred and sixty-one of the laws of eighteen hundred and
ninety-three, twenty-six thousand five hundred dollars.

PAYABLE FROM THE MILITARY RECORD FUND.
REVENUE.

Bureau of military records. For the adjutant-general for the expenses of the bureau of military records, two thousand dollars.

Appropriation. how paid. The several amounts herein appropriated shall be paid by the treasurer from their respective funds, as specified, and the salaries named shall be established and fixed by this act, for the several officers for whom they are designated, but the comptroller **Drawing of warrant.** shall not draw his warrant for the payment of the several amounts hereinbefore named, except for salaries and other expenditures and appropriations. the amounts of which are duly established and fixed by law, until the persons demanding them **Detailed statement required.** shall present to him a detailed statement thereof, in items, and shall make all reports required of them by law; and if such accounts shall be for services, it must show when, where and under what authority they were rendered; if for expenditures, when, where and under what authority they were made; if for articles furnished, when and where they were furnished, to whom they were delivered, and under what authority, and if the demand be for traveling expenses, the account must also specify the distance traveled, the places of starting and destination, the duty or business, and all the dates and items of expenditure. **Personal expenses.** But no payments shall be made to any salaried state officer or commissioner, except to commissioners of the land office and the trustees of public buildings, for personal expenses incurred by them while in the discharge of their duties as such **Verification of accounts.** commissioners or trustees at Albany. All accounts must be verified by affidavit to the effect that the account is true, just and correct, and that no part thereof has been paid, but is actually **Bills to be receipted.** due and owing. On all accounts for transportation, furniture, blanks, and other books purchased for the use of offices, binding, blanks, printing, stationery, postage, cleaning and other necessary and incidental expenses provided for by this act, a bill duly receipted must also be furnished; and it shall be the duty of the treasurer to report annually to the legislature the details of the several expenditures.

The superintendent or other managing officers of each of the state charitable and reformatory institutions other than the state prisons, and state hospitals for the insane for the support of which provision is herein made, shall on or before the fifteenth day of each month, commencing with the month of September, eighteen hundred and ninety-five, cause to be prepared and delivered to the comptroller a statement in detail, of the expenses estimated to be necessary for such institution for the next succeeding month, and for an amount in gross not exceeding two hundred and fifty dollars, for a contingent fund to meet unexpected emergencies during each succeeding month. Such statement shall be made in such form as the comptroller shall direct. The comptroller may revise such statement as to the quantity of supplies, estimate the cost thereof and as to such gross amount. The expenditures in each such institution during each succeeding month, for any purpose, shall not exceed the total amount of the estimate therefor as so revised by the comptroller, unless in case of extraordinary emergencies the comptroller may authorize an expenditure in excess of said amount.

Monthly estimates by institutions.

Expenditures restricted.

The treasurer or other fiscal officer of each such institution, provision for the support of which is herein made, shall, on or before the fifteenth day of each month commencing with the month of November, eighteen hundred and ninety-five, make to the comptroller an itemized statement, duly verified, of all the receipts and expenditures of such institution for the next preceding month, in such form as the comptroller shall direct.

Statement of receipts and expenditures.

No manager, trustee or other officer of any state, charitable or other institution receiving moneys under this act from the state treasury for maintenance and support shall be individually interested in any purchase, sale or contract made by any officer for any of said institutions.

Interest in purchases, etc prohibited.

All institutions receiving moneys under this act from the state treasury for maintenance, in whole or in part, shall deposit all their funds in some responsible bank, banks or banking-house, in pursuance of the provisions of chapter three hundred and twenty-six of the laws of eighteen hundred and eighty-eight, and the comptroller, in addition to the liability of said bank, shall require for all such funds so deposited the bond of said bank, with such good and sufficient sureties, to be approved by him as to form and amount as he shall deem necessary, and all state institutions

Deposit of funds in banks.

Payment of earnings into treasury. and departments, except charitable institutions, reformatories, houses of refuge and state industrial schools, shall pay into the treasury quarterly, all receipts and earnings other than receipts from the state treasury.

Annual inventory to be filed. All charitable institutions, reformatories, houses of refuge and the state industrial school, receiving moneys under this act, shall file with the comptroller on or before the twentieth of October of each year, a certified inventory of all articles of maintenance on hand at the close of the preceding year, naming in such inventory the kind and amount of such articles of maintenance.

Form of accounts. The comptroller is hereby authorized and empowered to devise a form of accounts to be observed in every state charitable institution, reformatory, houses of refuge, state industrial school, or department receiving moneys under this act, which shall be accepted and followed by such institutions and departments after thirty days' notice thereof has been submitted to them by the comptroller, and such form of accounts shall include such a uniform method of bookkeeping, filing and rendering of accounts as may insure a uniform mention of purchase of like articles, whether by weight, measure or otherwise, as the interest of the public service requires. Such form shall also include a uniform rate of allowance in reporting in such institutions and departments, the amount in value of all produce and other articles of maintenance raised upon lands of the state, or which may enter into the maintenance of such institutions or departments.

Duty of clerk or bookkeeper. It shall be the duty of the clerk or bookkeeper in each state charitable institution, reformatory, house of refuge, state industrial school or any state department receiving moneys under this act, to receive and examine all articles purchased by the proper officer or received for the maintenance thereof, to compare them with the bill therefor, to ascertain whether they correspond in weight, quantity and quality, and to inspect the supplies thus received; and the said clerk or bookkeeper shall also enter each bill of goods thus received in the book of the institution or department in which he is employed at the time of the receipt of the articles; and if any discrepancy is found between such bill and the articles received, he shall make a note thereof, whether it be in weight, quality or quantity, and no goods or other articles of purchase, or farm or garden production of lands of the institution, shall be received unless an entry thereof be made in the books of accounts of the institution, with the proper bill, invoice or mention, according to the form of accounts and record prescribed by the comptroller.

In accounts for repairs or new work provided for in this act the name of each workman, the number of days he is employed, and the rate and amount of wages paid to him shall be given. If contracts are made for repairs or new work, or for supplies, a duplicate thereof, with specifications, shall be filed with the comptroller.

Accounts for repairs.

Contracts.

Chap. 308.

AN ACT to release to Jane G. Peters all the right, title and interest of the people of the state of New York in and to certain real estate in the city of Brooklyn, county of Kings and state of New York.

**Became a law April 19, 1897, with the approval of the Governor.
Passed by a two-thirds vote.**

The People of the State of New York, represented in Senate and Assembly, do enact as follows:

Section 1. All the estate, right, title and interest of the people of the state of New York in and to all those two certain lots, pieces or parcels of land, situate, lying and being in the town of New Lots, county of Kings and state of New York, which are known and distinguished on a certain map of the Rapalye property on the Brooklyn and Jamaica Railroad and Turnpike, made by Martin G. Johnson and filed in the Kings county register's office as lots numbers two hundred and thirty-one and two hundred and thirty-two, which taken together are bounded and described as follows, namely: Commencing at a point on the westerly line of Locust street, distant eleven hundred and fifty feet northerly from the northwest corner of Locust and Second streets; running thence northerly along Locust street fifty feet; thence westerly one hundred and fifty feet; thence southerly fifty feet, and thence easterly and parallel with Second street one hundred and fifty feet to Locust street at the point or place of beginning. Being the same premises conveyed to Alexander Lockhart by deed dated the fifteenth day of May, eighteen hundred and seventy-three, and recorded in Kings county register's office in liber eleven hundred and eight of conveyances, at page one hundred and ninety on the twenty-first day of May, eighteen hundred and seventy-three, and from said Alexander Lockhart to Albert Peters by deed dated September

Interest of state released.

first, eighteen hundred and seventy-four, and recorded in the Kings
county register's office, in liber eleven hundred and seventy-four
of conveyances, at page five hundred and seventy-four on September twelfth, eighteen hundred and seventy-four, is hereby released
to Jane G. Peters of the city of Brooklyn, county of Kings and
state of New York, her heirs and assigns forever.

Proviso.   § 2. Nothing herein contained shall be construed to impair, release or discharge any right, claim or interest of any purchaser,
heir-at-law, devisee or grantee, or any creditor by judgment, mortgage or otherwise in said real estate.

§ 3. This act shall take effect immediately.

Chap. 309.

AN ACT to release to Hannah Kilfoy all the right, title and interest
of the people of the state of New York in and to certain real estate in the city of Brooklyn.

Became a law April 19, 1897, with the approval of the Governor.
Passed by a two-thirds vote.

*The People of the State of New York, represented in Senate and
Assembly, do enact as follows:*

Interest of   Section 1. All the right, title and interest of the people of the
state re-
leased.   State of New York in and to all that certain lot, piece or parcel
of land situate, lying and being in the ninth ward of the city of
Brooklyn, being butted and bounded as follows, viz.: Beginning
at a point which is on the south side of President street, being two
hundred and seventy-five feet westerly from the southwest corner
of New York avenue and President street; thence southerly one
hundred and twenty-seven feet, nine and one-half inches; thence
westerly, parallel to President street, fifty feet; thence northerly,
parallel with New York avenue, and along the land of the late Maria
E. Kindergan, one hundred and twenty-seven feet, nine and one-half
inches, to President street, and from thence easterly along the
southerly side of President street, fifty feet, to the place of beginning, are hereby granted, conveyed and released to Hannah
Kilfoy, of the city of Brooklyn, county of Kings, and state of New
York, and to her heirs and assigns forever.

Proviso.   § 2. Nothing in this act shall be construed to impair or affect the
right of any heir-at-law, devisee, grantee or creditor by mortgage,
judgment or otherwise.

§ 3. This act shall take effect immediately.

Chap. 312.

AN ACT to amend chapter one hundred and twelve of the laws of eighteen hundred and ninety-six, entitled "An act in relation to the traffic in liquors, and for the taxation and regulation of the same, and to provide for local option, constituting chapter twenty-nine of the general laws."

**Became a law April 20, 1897, with the approval of the Governor.
Passed, three-fifths being present.**

The People of the State of New York, represented in Senate and Assembly, do enact as follows:

Section 1. Section two, of chapter one hundred and twelve, of the laws of eighteen hundred and ninety-six, entitled "An act in relation to the traffic in liquors, and for the taxation and regulation of the same, and to provide for local option, constituting chapter twenty-nine of the general laws," is hereby amended so as to read as follows:

§ 2. **Definitions.**— The term " liquors," as used in this act, includes and means all distilled or rectified spirits, wine, fermented and malt liquors. The term " association " includes any combination of two or more persons, not incorporated nor constituting a copartnership. " Trafficking in liquors," within the meaning of this act, is:

1. A sale of less than five wine gallons of liquor; or,

2. A sale of five wine gallons or more of liquor, in which less than five gallons of any one kind and quality is included; or,

3. A sale of five wine gallons or more of liquor, any portion of which is intended or permitted to be drunk on the premises where sold; or,

4. A sale of five wine gallons or more of liquor, when the liquor so sold is delivered, or agreed to be delivered, in a less quantity than five wine gallons at one time; or,

5. The distribution of liquor by, between or on behalf of members of a corporation, association or copartnership, to a member thereof or to others, in quantities less than five wine gallons.

§ 2. Section six of the said chapter is hereby amended so as to read as follows:

§ 6. **State commissioner of excise.**— Within ten days after the passage of this act the governor, by and with the advice and consent of the senate, shall appoint a state commissioner of excise who shall hold his office for the term of five years, and until his successor is appointed and has qualified. A commissioner shall in like manner be appointed upon the expiration of the term. If a vacancy occurs in the office of commissioner it shall be filled in like manner for the residue of the term. The commissioner shall execute and file with the comptroller of the state a bond to the people of the state in the sum of twenty thousand dollars, with sureties to be approved by the comptroller, conditioned for the faithful performance of his duties, and for the due accounting for all moneys received by him as such commissioner. The commissioner shall receive an annual salary of five thousand dollars and the further sum of eighteen hundred dollars in lieu and in full of his expenses, which salary and expenses shall be payable in equal monthly installments. The state commissioner shall make an annual report to the legislature on or before the second Monday in each year, which shall contain such statements, facts and explanations as will disclose the actual workings of the liquor tax law in its bearings upon the welfare of the state, including all receipts and revenues collected under the law, and all expenses and disbursements incurred, and also such suggestions as to the general policy of the state and such amendments of this law as the commissioner shall deem appropriate. The state commissioner shall also cause the accounts and vouchers of all excise moneys collected and paid over to the state and to the several localities by each county treasurer and special deputy commissioner in the state, and the records of all transactions by them under the liquor tax law to be carefully examined, and the result of such examination certified to the state comptroller at least once in every year between the first day of May and the first day of October; and in addition to such annual examination, said commissioner may, whenever in his discretion he shall deem it necessary, examine said accounts, vouchers and records.

§ 3. Section eight of said chapter is hereby amended so as to read as follows:

§ 8. **Deputy commissioner; secretary; clerks.**— The state commissioner of excise shall appoint a deputy commissioner who shall receive an annual salary of four thousand dollars and the further sum of fifteen hundred dollars in lieu and in full of his necessary expenses, which salary and expenses shall be payable in equal monthly installments. During the absence or inability to act of the state commissioner, the deputy commissioner shall have and exercise all the powers conferred by this chapter upon the state commissioner. The deputy commissioner shall give a bond to the people of the state in the sum of twenty thousand dollars and with such sureties as shall be approved by the commissioner. The commissioner shall appoint a secretary, who shall receive an annual salary of two thousand dollars, payable in equal monthly installments, and a financial clerk, who shall receive an annual salary of eighteen hundred dollars payable in equal monthly installments. Such clerk, under the direction of the commissioner, shall have charge of the disbursement of the moneys appropriated for the expenses of the office, and shall give a bond to the people of the state, in such sum and with such sureties as shall be approved by the commissioner. Each of the officers provided for by this section, shall take and subscribe the constitutional oath of office before entering upon the performance of his duties, and may be removed by the commissioner, who may in like manner appoint his successor. The commissioner may also appoint such clerical force in his office as may be necessary.

§ 4. Section nine of the said chapter is hereby amended so as to read as follows:

§ 9. Special deputy commissioners in certain counties.— The state commissioner of excise shall appoint a special deputy in each of the counties containing a city of the first class, who shall hold office during his pleasure. The special deputy for the county of New York shall receive an annual salary of four thousand dollars; for the county of Kings and for the county of Erie three thousand dollars each Such salaries shall be payable in equal monthly installments. Each of such special deputies shall take and subscribe the constitutional oath of office, execute and file in the office of the comptroller, a bond to the people of the state, in such sum and with such sureties as shall be approved by the commissioner. The commissioner shall appoint in the office of each of such deputies such clerical force as may be necessary, or as may be provided by law. Each of such deputies shall be furnished with an office, and furniture, fixtures and appliances therefor, as may be necessary. They shall perform such duties as may be required by the commissioner, or as may be provided by law. Each of such special deputies shall perform, in the county for which he is appointed, all the duties heretofore conferred upon boards of excise or excise commissioners in such county under any law repealed by this act, during the continuance of any license heretofore granted as to the transfer, surrender or revocation thereof, or as to prosecuting offenses for violations of law under any law existing immediately prior to the passage of this act.

§ 5. Section ten of the said chapter is hereby amended so as to read as follows:

§ 10. Special agents; attorneys.— The state commissioner of excise shall appoint not more than sixty special agents, each of whom shall receive an annual salary of twelve hundred dollars, payable in equal monthly installments, together with the necessary expenses incurred by direction of the state commissioner in the performance of the duties of his office. Each of such special agents shall execute and file in the office of the comptroller, a bond to the people of the state in such sum and with such sureties as the commissioner shall require, conditioned for the faithful performance of the duties of his office. Such special agents shall be deemed the confidential agents of the state commissioner, and shall, under the direction of the commissioner, and as required by him, investigate all matters relating to the collection of liquor taxes and penalties under this act and in relation to the compliance with law by persons engaged in the traffic in liquors. Any such special agent may enter any place where liquors are sold at any time when the same is open, and may examine any liquor tax certificate granted or purported to have been granted in pursuance of law. He may investigate any other matters in connection with the sale of liquor and shall make complaints of violations of this act as provided for other officers in section thirty-seven hereof. He shall be liable for penalties as provided in section thirty-eight of this act, for neglect by public officers. The state commissioner of excise may designate for any county in which there is not a special deputy commissioner, one of such special agents to perform the duties conferred upon special deputies in relation to the transfer, surrender or revocation of a license existing at the time this act takes effect and as to prosecuting violations of laws repealed by this act. The state commissioner may designate an attorney or attorneys, to act with the special deputy of such county or a special agent, designated by the commissioner, as provided by this section, in the prosecution of all actions or proceedings under any law repealed by this chapter and pending when this chapter shall take effect, who shall have such authority as was conferred by law upon attorneys for boards of excise under the laws in force immediately prior to the passage of this chapter, whose compensation shall be paid by the county or city in whose behalf such prosecutions, actions or proceedings may be or shall have been instituted. The state commissioner may employ necessary counsel in the department of excise, and may likewise designate and appoint an attorney or attorneys to represent him or to act with the special deputy, special agent or county treasurer in the prosecution or defense of any action or proceeding brought under the provisions of this act. They shall be paid by the state treasurer, on the warrant of the comptroller, such compensation as shall be agreed upon by the state commissioner. All officers appointed or employed under the provisions of sections eight, nine and ten of this act may be removed by the state commissioner, who may appoint their successors, as provided by law.

§ 6. Section eleven of the said chapter is hereby amended so as to read as follows:

§ 11. **Excise taxes upon the business of trafficking in liquors; enumeration** — Excise taxes upon the business of trafficking in liquors shall be of six grades, and assessed as follows:

Subdivision 1. Upon the business of trafficking in liquors to be drunk upon the premises where sold, or which are so drunk, whether in a hotel, restaurant, saloon, store, shop, booth or other place, or in any out-building, yard or garden appertaining thereto or connected therewith, there is assessed an excise tax to be paid by every corporation, association, copartnership or person engaged in such traffic, and for each such place where such traffic is carried on by such corporation, association, copartnership or person if the same be in a city having by the last state census a population of fifteen hundred thousand or more, the sum of eight hundred dollars; if in a city having by said census a population of less than fifteen hundred thousand, but more than five hundred thousand, the sum of six hundred and fifty dollars; if in a city having by said census a population of less than five hundred thousand, but more than fifty thousand, the sum of five hundred dollars; if in a city or village having by said census a population of less than fifty thousand, but more than ten thousand, the sum of three hundred and fifty dollars; if in a city or village having by said census a population of less than ten thousand, but more than five thousand, the sum of three hundred dollars; if in a village having by said census a population of less than five thousand, but more than twelve hundred, the sum of two hundred dollars; if in any other place, the sum of one hundred dollars. The holder of a liquor tax certificate under this subdivision is entitled also to traffic in liquors as though he held a liquor tax certificate under subdivision two of this section, subject to the provisions of section sixteen of this act.

Subdivision 2. Upon the business of trafficking in liquors in quantities less than five wine gallons, no part of which shall be drunk on the premises where sold, or in any outbuilding, yard, booth or garden appertaining thereto or connected therewith, there is assessed an excise tax to be paid by every corporation, association, copartnership or person engaged in such traffic, and for each such place where such traffic is carried on by such corporation, association, copartnership or person, if the same be in a city having by the last state census a population of fifteen hundred thousand or more, the sum of five hundred dollars; if in a city having by the said census a population of less than fifteen hundred thousand, but more than five hundred thousand, the sum of four hundred dollars; if in a city having by said census a population of less than five hundred thousand, but more than fifty thousand, the sum of three hundred dollars; if in a city or village having by said census a population of less than fifty thousand, but more than ten thousand, the sum of two hundred dollars; if in a city or village having by said census a population of less than ten thousand, but more than five thousand, the sum of one hundred dollars; if in a village having by said census a population of less than five thousand, but more than twelve hundred, the sum of seventy-five dollars; if in any other place, the sum of fifty dollars. The holder of a liquor tax certificate under this subdivision, who is a duly licensed pharmacist, and the corporation, association or copartnership of which he is a member is subject to the provisions of exception one of section thirty-one of this act, and to the provisions of section sixteen of this act.

Subdivision 3. Upon the business of trafficking in liquors by a duly licensed pharmacist, which liquors can only be sold upon the written prescription of a regularly licensed physician, signed by such physician, which prescription shall state the date of the prescription, the name of the person for whom prescribed, and shall be preserved by the vendor, pasted in a book kept for that purpose, and be but once filled, and which liquors shall not be drunk on the premises where sold, or in any outbuilding, yard, booth or garden appertaining thereto or connected therewith, there is assessed an excise tax to be paid by such duly licensed pharmacist or the corporation, association or copartnership of which he is a member, engaged in such traffic, and for each such place where such traffic is carried on by such pharmacist, or by such corporation, association or copartnership of which he is a member, the sum of five dollars. The holder of a liquor tax certificate under this subdivision may sell alcohol, to be used for medicinal, mechanical or chemical purposes, without a prescription, except during prohibited hours.

Subdivision 4. Upon the business of trafficking in liquors upon any car, steamboat or vessel within this state, to be drunk on such car or on any car connected therewith, or on such steamboat or vessel, or upon any boat or barge attached thereto, or connected therewith, there is assessed an excise tax, to be paid by every corporation, association, copartnership or person engaged in such traffic, and for each car, steamboat or vessel, boat or barge, upon which such traffic is carried on, the sum of two hundred dollars.

Subdivision 5. The holder of a liquor tax certificate under subdivision two of section eleven of this act, who is engaged in the business of bottling malt liquors, or who bottles the same, and who sells such malt liquors at any place other than that stated in such liquor tax certificate, in quantities of less than five wine gallons, may sell and deliver from a vehicle to the occupant of a store or other building at such place of occupancy, malt liquors in bottles in a quantity of less than five wine gallons, but of not less than three gallons (or twenty-four pint bottles) at a time, provided he shall have obtained for each vehicle from which he so sells and delivers a special tax certificate permitting such traffic from such vehicle. There is assessed for each vehicle so employed an excise liquor tax of one hundred dollars. The state commissioner of excise shall prepare and issue such special liquor tax certificate as shall be necessary to carry out the provisions of this subdivision, and such certificate shall at all times be carried with each such vehicle, or posted therein or thereon, in such manner as the state commissioner of excise shall direct. No sale or delivery of malt liquor under the provisions of this subdivision shall be permitted in any town in which, under section sixteen of this act, the sale of liquor, under subdivision two of section eleven, is prohibited.

Subdivision 6. Upon the business of trafficking in alcohol in quantities of less than five gallons, which alcohol can only be sold between the hours of seven o'clock in the morning and seven o'clock in the evening, on any day except Sunday, for use for mechanical, medicinal or scientific purposes, by dealers who neither keep nor sell any liquors of any kind other than alcohol, there is assessed an excise tax to be paid by every corporation, association, copartnership or person engaged in such traffic, and for each such place where such traffic is carried on by such corporation, association, copartnership or person, if the same be in a city having by the last state census a population of fifteen hundred thousand or more, the sum of twenty-five dollars; if in a city having by said census a population of less than fifteen hundred thousand, but more than five hundred thousand, the sum of twenty dollars; if in a city having by said census a population of less than five hundred thousand, but more than fifty thousand, the sum of fifteen dollars; if in a city or village having by said census a population of less than fifty thousand, but more than ten thousand, the sum of ten dollars; if in any other place, the sum of five dollars. No liquor tax certificate issued under subdivisions three, five or six of this section, shall be transferred or assigned, and no rebate shall be allowed or paid upon the surrender or cancellation thereof. If there be more than one bar, room or place on the premises, car, steamboat, vessel, boat or barge, at which the traffic in liquors is carried on under any subdivision of this section, a like additional tax is assessed for each such additional bar, room or place.

Subdivision 7. **Enumeration.**— When the population of a city or village is not shown by the last state census, it shall be determined for the purposes of this act by the last United States census, and if not shown by reason of the incorporation of a new city or village, or by reason of not having been separately enumerated, the state commissioner of excise is authorized and directed to cause an enumeration of the inhabitants to be taken in such city or village, if the commissioner has any doubt as to the number of the population as affecting the amount of the excise tax assessed therein. He may also cause to be taken an enumeration of the inhabitants of any hamlet or unincorporated village, after first having established a limit or boundary line around such hamlet or unincorporated village, within which limit or boundary line such enumeration may be taken. Whenever a limit or boundary line shall have been established around any hamlet or unincorporated village, such limit or boundary line shall be described and certified to by the

state commissioner of excise and be entered of record and become
part of the records of the state department of excise, and such limit
or boundary line shall not be changed for a period of five years
after the date of recording the same, except such hamlet or unincorporated village become an incorporated village with corporate
limits and boundary lines different from those established by the
state commissioner of excise, in which case such newly incorporated
village may be enumerated as hereinbefore provided in this section.
If, since the latest state enumeration was taken, the boundaries of
a city shall have been changed by the addition of territory not in
the same judicial district, such annexed territory shall not be
deemed to be a part of such city for the purposes of determining the
amount of excise tax assessed therein by this act; but the inhabitants
of such annexed territory shall be enumerated for purposes of so
determining such excise tax and, except as to the amount of the excise tax so determined, all the provisions of this act shall be applicable to such annexed territory and the excise tax assessed in such
annexed territory shall be paid to the city to which such territory
shall have been annexed.   The excise tax assessed in each place
enumerated under this subdivision shall be the same as that provided in subdivisions one, two, three and six of this section, for
places containing the same population.

§ 7.   Section thirteen of the said chapter is hereby amended so as
to read as follows:

§ 13.   Officers to whom the tax is to be paid and how distributed. — The taxes assessed and all fines and penalties incurred
under this act in counties containing a city of the first class shall be
collected by and paid to the special deputy commissioner for such
county, and in all other counties by and to the county treasurer of
the county in which the traffic is carried on, except that the taxes
assessed under subdivisions four and five of section eleven of this
act, and all fines and penalties in connection therewith, shall be collected by and paid to the state commissioner of excise and by him
to the state treasurer.   One-third of the revenues resulting from
taxes, fines and penalties under the provisions of this act, less the
amount allowed for collecting the same, shall be paid by the county
treasurer, and by the several special deputy commissioners receiving the same within ten days from the receipt thereof, to the treasurer of the state of New York, to the credit of the general fund, as
a part of the general tax revenue of the state and shall be appropriated to the payment of the current general expenses of the state
and the remaining two-thirds thereof, less the amount allowed for
collecting the same, shall belong to the town or city in which the
traffic was carried on from which the revenues were received, and
shall be paid to the county treasurer of such county, and by the
special deputy commissioners to the supervisor of such town, or to

the treasurer or fiscal officer of such city, within ten days from the receipt thereof. At the time of making such payment the special deputy commissioner or county treasurer shall furnish to the officer of such city or town to whom such payment is made a written statement under oath stating when such money was received and from whom received; and that the statement includes all the moneys received to a date named in such statement. Such revenues shall be appropriated and expended by such town or city, in such manner as is now or may hereafter be provided by law for the appropriation and expenditure of sums received for excise licenses, or in such other manner as may hereafter be provided by law; and any portion of such revenues not otherwise specifically appropriated by law may be applied to the ordinary expenses of the city or town. Any special deputy commissioner or county treasurer who shall neglect or refuse to apportion and pay over such moneys, as above provided, shall, in addition to the fines and penalties otherwise provided in this act, be liable to a penalty of fifty dollars for each and every offense, to be recovered in an action by the officer entitled to receive such excise moneys, brought by such officer in the name of the city or town entitled thereto, with costs, in addition to the money unlawfully withheld; and if any special deputy commissioner or county treasurer shall willfully make and verify a false statement under this section, he shall be guilty of perjury.

§ 8. Section fifteen of the said chapter is hereby amended so as to read as follows:

§ 15. **Books and blanks to be furnished by the state commissioner of excise.**— Immediately upon the passage of this act the state commissioner of excise shall cause to be prepared the necessary books for his office and shall also cause to be prepared and furnish to each special deputy commissioner and to each county treasurer in counties not containing a city of the first class, the necessary and proper books of record, and books in which accounts shall be kept of all taxes, or other moneys accruing and collected under the provisions of this act, and the necessary blanks for reports, and the blanks necessary for the application for liquor tax certificates, and the blank bonds and liquor tax certificates provided for in this act, which books, blanks and certificates shall be uniform throughout the state. Such books of record and account and all reports, applications and bonds, when filed, shall be public records. The necessary expenses of preparing such books and blanks and certificates shall be paid out of the treasury of the state from any funds not otherwise appropriated. He shall furnish to each county treasurer in counties not containing a city of the first class, and to each special deputy commissioner, who shall keep the same, a record book showing the following facts:

1. The name of each corporation, association, copartnership or

person upon which or whom a tax is assessed under the provisions
of this act.

2. The name of each corporation, association, copartnership or
person paying a tax under the provisions of this act.

3. The name of each corporation, association, copartnership or
person to which, or to whom, a certificate of the payment of such
tax is issued.

4. Under which of the subdivisions of section eleven of this act
such certificate of the payment of such tax is issued.

5. The date when such tax is assessed and the date of the commencement of the term for which issued.

6. The term for which such certificate is issued and the date of
the ending thereof.

7. The amount of the tax assessed.

8. The amount of tax paid.

9. The date when paid.

10. The location of the premises where the traffic is carried on.

11. The name and residence of each surety or corporation on the
bond of the corporation, association, copartnership or person to
whom the tax certificate is issued.

12. The amount of each fine or penalty and the costs if any.

13. The amount collected.

14. The amount of the expenses of such collection.

15. The date of the surrender or cancellation of any tax certificate and the cause therefor.

16. The amount of tax refunded, if any, upon such surrender or
cancellation.

17. Said special deputy commissioner or county treasurer shall
keep a separate and distinct account of all excise moneys received
and paid over by him; and if such moneys shall be deposited in
a bank or other depository, they shall be kept in a separate account,
in the official name of such officer, and shall also be entitled
"Liquor tax moneys." Such officer shall also keep all such books
of account and in such form as the state commissioner of excise
shall provide and direct, and shall render to such commissioner
such reports and exhibit such records, accounts and vouchers as he
may from time to time require, which reports shall be verified
if the state commissioner shall so direct. The willful making of
a false statement under oath in any such report shall be perjury,
and in addition thereto shall subject the person guilty to the
penalty and punishment prescribed in section thirty-eight of this
act.

§ 9. Section sixteen of the said chapter is hereby amended so as to
read as follows:

§ 16. **Local option, to determine whether liquors shall be
sold under the provisions of this act.**— In order to ascertain

the will of the qualified electors of each town, it shall be the duty of each officer of a town charged by the election law, or by any special act relating to election in any town, with the duty of preparing official ballots, to have prepared at the time fixed by law for preparing the ballots for the annual town meeting occurring next after March twenty-third, eighteen hundred and ninety-six, the ballots required by the election law for voting upon any constitutional amendment, proposition or question, in the form and of the number required by the election law. Upon the face of the ballot to be voted at such town meeting, by all persons who may legally vote thereat, shall be printed the following questions submitted:

1. **Selling liquor to be drunk on the premises where sold.—** Shall any corporation, association, copartnership or person be authorized to traffic in liquors under the provisions of subdivision one of section eleven of the liquor tax law in (here insert the name of the town)?

2. **Selling liquor not to be drunk on the premises where sold.—** Shall any corporation, association, copartnership or person be authorized to traffic in liquor under the provisions of subdivision two of section eleven of the liquor tax law in (here insert the name of the town)?

3 **Selling liquor as a pharmacist on a physician's prescription** — Shall any corporation, association, copartnership or person be authorized to traffic in liquor under the provisions of subdivision three of section eleven of the liquor tax law in (here insert the name of the town)?

4. **Selling liquor by hotelkeepers.—** Shall any corporation, association, copartnership or person be authorized to traffic in liquors under subdivision one of section eleven of the liquor tax law, but only in connection with the business of keeping a hotel in (here insert the name of the town), if the majority of the votes cast on the first question submitted are in the negative? At such town meeting, the several questions may be voted upon by the electors who may legally vote thereat. A return of the votes so cast and counted shall be made as provided by law, and if the majority of the votes shall be in the negative on either of such questions, no corporation, association, copartnership or person shall thereafter so traffic in liquors or apply for or receive a liquor tax certificate under the subdivision or subdivisions of section eleven, upon which the majority of the votes have been cast in the negative, that is against so authorizing the traffic in liquors within such town, but if the majority of the votes cast on the fourth question submitted are in the affirmative, and a majority of the votes cast on the first question submitted are in the negative, a liquor tax certificate may be granted under subdivision one of

section eleven to the keepers of hotels who may traffic in liquor to be drunk in the hotel and off the premises, though the majority of the votes cast on the second question submitted are in the negative. If the majority of the votes cast on the second question submitted shall be in the affirmative, the holder of a liquor tax certificate under subdivision two of section eleven, who is a pharmacist, shall not sell as a pharmacist if the majority of the votes cast on the third question submitted are in the negative. Such action shall not, however, shorten the term for which any liquor tax certificate may have been given under the provisions of this act, nor affect the rights of any person thereunder. The same questions shall be again submitted in the same way at the annual town meeting held in every second year thereafter, provided the electors of the town to the number of ten per centum of votes cast at the next preceding general election shall, by written petition, signed and acknowledged by such electors before a notary public or other person authorized to take acknowledgments or administer oaths and duly filed with the officer charged with the duty of furnishing ballots for the election, request such submission. If for any reason the four propositions provided to be submitted herein to the electors of a town shall not have been properly submitted at such annual town meeting, such propositions shall be submitted at a special town meeting duly called, and in such case the time for the resubmission of such propositions shall be reckoned from the date of holding the regular town meeting at which they should have been submitted. A certified copy of the statement of the result of the vote, upon each of such questions submitted, shall, immediately after such submission thereof be filed by the town clerk or other officer with whom returns of town meetings are required to be filed by the election law, with the county treasurer of the county, and with the special deputy commissioner for counties containing a city of the first class, which also contains a town, and no liquor tax certificate shall thereafter be issued by such officers to any corporation, association, copartnership or person to traffic in liquor in said town under such subdivision of section eleven of this act upon which a majority of the votes may have been cast in the negative, except as otherwise provided in this act. It is further provided that in any town in which at the time this act shall become a law there is no license, it shall not be lawful for the county treasurer, or special deputy commissioner to issue any liquor tax certificate provided for by this act, until such town shall have voted upon the questions provided to be submitted by this section, and then to issue such liquor tax certificate only, as may be in accordance with the vote of a majority of the electors on the questions submitted.

§ 10. Section seventeen of the said chapter is hereby amended so as to read as follows:

§ 17. **Statements to be made upon application for liquor tax certificates.**— Every corporation, association, copartnership or person liable for a tax under subdivisions one, two, three or six of section eleven of this act shall, on or before the first day of May of each year, or if now holding a license legally granted by any board of excise, then on or before the termination of such license, prepare and make upon the blank which shall be furnished by the county treasurer of the county and in counties containing a city of the first class by the special deputy commissioner for such county, upon application therefor, a statement which shall be given to such county treasurer or special deputy, signed and sworn to by such applicant or applicants, or by the person making such application in behalf of a corporation or association, stating:

1. The name of each applicant, and if there be more than one and they be partners, also their partnership name, and the age and residence of the several persons so applying, and the fact as to his citizenship.

2. The name and residence of every person interested or to become interested in the traffic in liquors for which the statement is made, unless such applicant be a corporation or association, in which case the person making the application in behalf of the corporation or association shall set forth, instead, the name of the corporation or association, the state under the laws of which it is organized, and the nature of his authority to act for such corporation or association.

3. The premises where such business is to be carried on, stating the street and number, if the premises have a street and number, and otherwise such apt description as will reasonably indicate the locality thereof, and also the specific location on the premises of the bar or place at which liquors are to be sold.

4. Under which subdivision of section eleven of this act the traffic in liquors is to be carried on, and what, if any, other business is to be carried on in connection therewith, or on the same premises, by the applicant or any other person; and also what, if any, other business is to be carried on by the applicant or by another in any room adjoining, which is not entirely separated from the room in which the traffic in liquors is to be carried on, by solid partition at least three inches thick extending from floor to ceiling, without any opening therein.

5. And a statement that such applicant has not been convicted of a felony; has not had a license revoked under the laws in force immediately prior to March twenty-third, eighteen hundred and ninety-six, by reason of a violation of such laws; has not been

convicted of a violation of this law within five years prior to the date of such application; does not, as owner or agent, carry on, or permit to be carried on, nor is interested in any traffic, business or occupation, the carrying on of which is a violation of law, and may lawfully carry on such traffic in liquors upon such premises, under such subdivision, and is not within any of the prohibitions of this act.

6. There shall also be so filed simultaneously with said statement, a consent in writing that such traffic in liquors be so carried on in such premises, executed by the owner of the premises, or by his duly authorized agent, and acknowledged as are deeds entitled to be recorded; except in cases where such traffic in liquors was actually lawfully carried on in said premises as described in said statement on the twenty-third day of March, eighteen hundred and ninety-six, in which case such consent shall not be required.

7. If such traffic is to be carried on in any building or place owned by the public, or in any building or place situate on land owned by the public such applicant or applicants shall at the same time file with such county treasurer, or special deputy, the written consent of the authorities having the custody and control of such building, and of the land on which it is situated for the traffic in liquors therein.

8. When the nearest entrance to the premises described in said statement as those in which traffic in liquor is to be carried on is within two hundred feet, measured in a straight line, of the nearest entrance to a building or buildings occupied exclusively for a dwelling, there shall also be so filed simultaneously with said statement a consent in writing that such traffic in liquors be so carried on in said premises during a term therein stated, executed by the owner or owners, or by the duly authorized agent or agents of such owner or owners of at least two-thirds of the total number of such buildings within two hundred feet so occupied as dwellings, and acknowledged as are deeds entitled to be recorded, except that such consent shall not be required in cases where such traffic in liquor was actually lawfully carried on in said premises so described in said statement on the twenty-third day of March, eighteen hundred and ninety-six, nor shall such consent be required for any place described in said statement which was occupied as a hotel on said last-mentioned date, notwithstanding such traffic in liquors was not then carried on thereat. Whenever the consent required by this section shall have been obtained and filed as herein provided, unless the same be given for a limited term, no further or other consent for trafficking in liquor on such premises shall be required so long as such premises shall be continuously occupied for such traffic.

9. If the traffic in liquors is to be carried on in connection with

the business of keeping a hotel, the applicant shall also show by his application that all the requirements of section thirty-one hereof, defining hotels, have been complied with.

10. When such applicant shall be a duly licensed pharmacist desiring to traffic in liquors as such, under subdivision three of section eleven of this act, he shall file with such county treasurer, or special deputy commissioner, in addition to the other statements required by this act, a verified statement also showing that said applicant is a licensed pharmacist in good standing, actually carrying on and doing business as a pharmacist on his own account at the place or store where he desires to so traffic in liquor, that the principal business which will be transacted by said applicant in said place or store, during the period to be covered by the certificate applied for, is the dispensing and retailing of drugs and medicines, that said applicant has not, during the year last past, allowed any liquor sold on said place or store to be drunk therein, or otherwise violated any of the provisions of this act. Every corporation, association, copartnership or person liable for a tax under subdivision four of section eleven of this act shall, on or before the first day of May of each year, or if now holding a license from the comptroller of the state, then on or before the termination of such license, prepare and make upon a blank, which shall be furnished by the state commissioner of excise, such statements in regard to carrying on such traffic as the commissioner may require, including the statements required under clauses one, two and five of this section.

§ 11. Section eighteen of the said chapter is hereby amended so as to read as follows:

§ 18. **Bonds to be given.**— Each corporation, association, copartnership or person taxed under this act, shall, at the time of making the application provided for in section seventeen of this act, file in the office of the county treasurer of the county in which such traffic is to be carried on, or if in a county containing a city of the first class with the special deputy commissioner for such county, or if the application be under subdivision four of section eleven of this act, with the state commissioner of excise, a bond to the people of the state of New York, in the penal sum of twice the amount of the tax for one year upon the kind of traffic in liquor to be carried on by such applicant, where carried on, but in no case for less than five hundred dollars, conditioned that if the tax certificate applied for is given, the applicant or applicants will not, while the business for which such tax certificate is given shall be carried on, suffer or permit any gambling to be done in the place designated by the tax certificate in which the traffic in liquors is to be carried on, or in any yard, booth, garden or any other place appertaining thereto or connected therewith, or suffer or permit

such premises to become disorderly, and will not violate any of
the provisions of the liquor tax law; and that all fines and penalties
which shall accrue during the time the certificate applied for is
held, and any judgment or judgments recovered therefor, will be
paid, together with all costs taxed or allowed. Such bond shall
be executed by each such applicant, and if given by a corporation
or association, by some person or persons duly authorized so to
do as principal, and by at least two sureties residents of the town
or city in which the premises are where such traffic is to be carried
on, one of whom shall be a freeholder, or instead of such sureties,
by a corporation duly authorized to issue surety bonds by the laws
of this state. The bond, if given by two sureties, shall have annexed thereto or indorsed thereon the affidavit of each surety that
he is worth double the penal sum named in such bond over and above
his property exempt by law from levy and sale upon an execution
and over and above his just debts and liabilities. The state commissioner of excise may at any time without previous prosecution
or conviction for violation of any provision of the liquor tax law,
or for the breach of any condition of said bond, commence and
maintain an action, in his name, as such commissioner, in any
court of record in any county of the state, for the recovery of the
penalty for the breach of any condition of any bond, or for any
penalty or penalties incurred or imposed for a violation of the
liquor tax law, and all moneys recovered in such actions shall be
paid over and accounted for in the same manner as are moneys
collected under subdivision four of section eleven of this act.

§ 12. Section nineteen of said chapter is hereby amended so as to
read as follows:

§ 19. The payment of the tax and issuing of the tax certificate.— When the provisions of sections seventeen and eighteen of
this act have been complied with and the application provided for
in section seventeen is found to be correct in form, and does not
show on the face thereof that the applicant is prohibited from
trafficking in liquor under the subdivision of section eleven under
which he applies, nor at the place where the traffic is to be carried
on, and the bond required by section eighteen is found to be
correct as to its form and the sureties thereon are approved as
sufficient by the county treasurer, or if in a county containing a
city of the first class by the special deputy commissioner for such
county, then upon the payment of the taxes levied under section
eleven of this act the county treasurer of the county, and in a
county containing a city of the first class, the special deputy commissioner for such county, or if the application be made under subdivisions four or five of section eleven of this act, the state commissioner of excise, shall at once prepare and issue to the corporation, association, copartnership or person making such application

and filing such bond and paying such tax, a liquor tax certificate in the form provided for in this act, unless it shall appear by a certified copy of the statement of the result of an election held on the question of local option, pursuant to section sixteen of this act, in and for the town where the applicant proposes to traffic in liquors under the certificate applied for, that such liquor tax certificate can not be lawfully granted, in which case the application shall be refused.

§ 13. Section twenty-one of said chapter is hereby amended so as to read as follows:

§ 21. **Posting liquor tax certificates.**— Before commencing or doing any business for the time for which the excise tax is paid and the certificate is given, the said liquor tax certificate shall be posted up and at all times displayed in a conspicuous place in the room or bar where the traffic in liquors for which the tax was paid is carried on, so that all persons visiting such place may readily see the same, but if there be a door opening from the street into the room or bar room where the traffic in liquors is carried on and a window facing the street upon which such door opens, such certificate shall be displayed in such window, so it may be readily seen from the street. It is provided, however, that when the holder of an unexpired license under the law in force prior to the passage of this act, or the holder of a liquor tax certificate under this act, shall have presented the application and bond as required by sections seventeen and eighteen of this act, and paid the tax assessed by this act, not less than fifteen days before the time fixed for the expiration of such license or tax certificate, such holder of such license or tax certificate may continue to traffic in liquors pending the issue of the tax certificate, until notified in writing, by the officer charged with the duty of issuing such tax certificate, that such tax certificate so applied for will not be issued. If the application is refused the moneys thus paid shall be returned to the applicant within ten days from the receipt of the same, with said notice, by the said certificate-issuing officer. To continue to traffic in liquor after such notice is received is a violation of this law and subjects the person violating to the penalties prescribed for trafficking in liquors without having a liquor tax certificate.

§ 14. Section twenty-two of the said chapter is hereby amended so as to read as follows:

§ 22. **Restrictions on the traffic in liquors in connection with other business.**— No corporation, association, copartnership or person engaged in carrying on the business of selling dry goods or groceries, or provisions, or drugs as a pharmacist, shall be assessed under subdivision one of section eleven of this act, or receive a liquor tax certificate under such subdivision, unless it be to carry on the traffic in liquors under such subdivision one at some other building entirely distinct and separate from, and not communicating with the place where, and in which, such business of selling dry goods, groceries, provisions or drugs as a pharmacist is carried on, or if in the same building, then only in a room which is separated by partitions at least three inches thick, extending from floor to ceiling, with no opening or means of entrance or communication between the room where the traffic in liquors is carried on and the store or rooms in which the selling of dry goods, groceries, provisions or drugs as a pharmacist is carried on, so that it is necessary to go into a public street before the one place can be entered upon leaving the other.

§ 15. Section twenty-three of the said chapter is hereby amended so as to read as follows:

§ 23. Persons who shall not traffic in liquors, and persons to whom a liquor tax certificate shall not be granted.

1. No person who has been or shall be convicted of a felony, or knowingly has in his employ a person who has been so convicted.

2. No person under the age of twenty-one years.

3. No person not a citizen of the United States and a resident of the state of New York.

4. No corporation or association incorporated or organized under the laws of another state or country; provided, however, that if such corporation or association be acting as a common carrier in this state it may be granted a liquor tax certificate under subdivision four of section eleven of this act.

5. No copartnership, unless one or more of the members of such copartnership, owning at least one-half interest in the business thereof, shall be a resident of this state and a citizen of the United States.

6. No corporation, association, copartnership or person which or who has had a license revoked under the laws in force immediately prior to the passage of this act by reason of a violation of such laws.

7. No corporation, association, copartnership or person who has been or shall be convicted for a violation of this act, nor the agent of such corporation, association, copartnership or person, until five years from the date of such conviction.

8. No corporation organized under chapter five hundred and fifty-nine of the laws of eighteen hundred and ninety-five, and the acts amendatory thereof, which traffics in liquors with any person other than the members thereof.

9. No corporation, association, copartnership or person who as owner or agent carries on or permits to be carried on or is interested in any traffic, business or occupation, the carrying on of

which is a violation of law, shall traffic in liquors or be granted a liquor tax certificate or be interested therein.

§ 16. Section twenty-four of the said chapter, as amended by chapter four hundred and forty-five of the laws of eighteen hundred and ninety-six, is hereby further amended so as to read as follows:

§ 24. **Places in which traffic in liquor shall not be permitted.**— Traffic in liquor shall not be permitted:

1. In any building or upon any premises established as a penal institution, protectory, industrial school, asylum, state hospital, colony or institution established for the care or treatment of epileptics, or poorhouse, and if such building or premises, other than a county jail or state prison, be situated in a town and outside the limits of an incorporated village or city, not within one-half mile of any building or premises so occupied, provided there be such distance of one-half mile between such building and premises, and the nearest boundary line of such village or city; nor

2. Under the provisions of subdivision one of section eleven of this act, in any building, yard, booth or other place which shall be on the same street or avenue and within two hundred feet of a building occupied exclusively as a church or schoolhouse; the measurements to be taken in a straight line from the center of the nearest entrance of the building used for such church or school to the center of the nearest entrance of the place in which such liquor traffic is desired to be carried on; provided, however, that this prohibition shall not apply to a place which on the twenty-third day of March, eighteen hundred and ninety-six, was lawfully occupied for a hotel, nor to a place in which such traffic in liquors was actually lawfully carried on at that date, nor to a place which at such date was occupied, or was in process of construction, by a corporation or association which traffics in liquors solely with the members thereof, nor to a place within such limit to which a corporation or association trafficking in liquors solely with the members thereof at such date may remove; but none of the exceptions under subdivision two of this section shall apply to subdivision one of this section; nor

3. In any form, in, upon or from any vehicle, except as provided in subdivisions four and five of section eleven of this act.

4. Upon any premises used for and as a cemetery.

§ 17. Section twenty-five of the said chapter is hereby amended so as to read as follows:

§ 25. **Surrender and cancellation of liquor tax certificates; payment, of rebates.** — If a corporation, association, copartnership or person holding a liquor tax certificate and authorized to sell liquors under the provisions of this act, against which or whom no complaint, prosecution or action is pending on account of any violation thereof, shall voluntarily, and before arrest or indictment for a violation of the liquor tax law, cease to traffic in liquors during the term for which the tax is paid under such certificate, such corporation, association, copartnership or person or their duly authorized attorney may surrender such tax certificate to the officer who issued the same or to his successor in office provided that such tax certificate shall have at least one month to run at the time of such surrender; and provided that no rebate shall be allowed or paid upon the surrender and cancellation of a certificate issued under subdivisions three, five or six of section eleven of this act, and provided further, that the rebate thereon shall be computed for full months, commencing with the first day of the month succeeding the one in which such certificate is surrendered, unless such surrender be on the first day of the month; and at the same time shall present to such officer a verified petition setting forth all facts required to be shown upon such application. Said officer shall thereupon compute the amount of pro rata rebate then due on said certificate for the unexpired term thereof, and shall execute duplicate receipts therefor showing the name of the corporation, association, copartnership or person to whom or which such certificate was issued, the number thereof, date when issued, amount of tax paid therefor, and the date when surrendered for cancellation, together with the amount of rebate due thereon at such date as computed by him, the name of the person entitled to receive the rebate, the locality liable for two-thirds of such rebate, and the name and title of the fiscal officer thereof. One of such receipts said officer shall deliver to the person entitled thereto, and the other of such receipts he shall immediately transmit, with the surrendered certificate and the petition for the cancellation thereof, to the state commissioner of excise. If within thirty days from the date of the receipt of such certificate by the state commissioner of excise, the person surrendering such certificate shall be arrested or indicted for a violation of the liquor tax law, or proceedings shall be instituted for the cancellation of such certificate, or an action shall be commenced against him for penalties, such petition shall not be granted until the final determination of such proceedings or action; and if the said petitioner be convicted, or said action or proceedings be determined against him, said certificate shall be cancelled and all rebate thereon shall be forfeited; but if such petitioner be acquitted, and such proceedings or action against him be dismissed on the merits, then the state commissioner of excise shall prepare two orders for the payment of such rebate, one order for the one-third thereof, directed to the state treasurer, to be paid by him, on the certificate of the comptroller, and one order for the two-thirds of such rebate, directed to the fiscal officer of the proper locality, to be paid by such fiscal officer out of any excise or other moneys of such locality applicable thereto. If he have no such moneys of such locality in his possession or under his control, then the said fiscal officer shall at once borrow enough money upon the credit of the locality, and he is hereby authorized so to do, to pay said order, and shall pay the same. The money so borrowed shall be a lawful claim against such locality, to be paid as are other legal claims. The aforesaid orders, or the order on the said fiscal officer and the check of the state treasurer for said one-third of such rebate moneys, shall be transmitted to the officer who issued such cancelled certificate, or to his successor in office, to be delivered to the holder of the duplicate receipt upon the surrender of such receipt, which receipt shall be immediately transmitted to the said state commissioner. Any rebate moneys due on the cancellation of certificates issued by the state commissioner of excise under subdivision four of section eleven of this act, shall be paid by the state treasurer from any moneys applicable thereto, on the certificate or check of the state commissioner of excise, countersigned by the comptroller. All outstanding receipts issued and given for liquor tax certificates heretofore surrendered and cancelled, shall also be paid in the manner above provided for the payment of rebate moneys upon certificates hereafter surrendered and cancelled, upon the order of the said state commissioner, to be issued by the said commissioner upon the surrender of such receipt to him, accompanied by the verified petition of the holder of such receipt, setting forth the facts that the holder of said cancelled certificate at the time of the surrender and cancellation thereof, had not violated any of the provisions of the liquor tax law, and has not been arrested or indicted for any such violation; provided, however, that the holder of such receipt for rebate due upon a liquor tax certificate surrendered and cancelled prior to January first, eighteen hundred and ninety-seven, who is an applicant for a new liquor tax certificate, to traffic in liquors in the same town or city where such cancelled certificate was held, shall be entitled to have the same applied as cash in payment for such new certificate at the time of the application therefor. If a corporation, association or copartnership holding a liquor tax certificate shall be dissolved, or a receiver or assignee be appointed therefor or a receiver, assignee or a committee of the property of a person holding a liquor tax certificate be appointed during the time for which such certificate was granted, or a person holding a liquor tax certificate shall die during the term for which such tax certificate was given, such corporation, association, copartnership or receiver or assignee, or the administrator or executor of the estate of such person, or the person or persons who may succeed to such business, or a committee of the property of a person adjudged to be incompetent, may in like manner surrender such liquor tax certificate; or they may continue to carry on such business, upon such premises, for the balance of the term for which such tax was paid and the certificate given, with the same right and subject to the same restrictions and liabilities as if such persons had been the original applicant for and the original owners of such liquor tax certificate, upon filing a statement and bond, as provided by sections seventeen and eighteen of this act, and not otherwise; but the liquor tax certificate under which such business is carried on shall have written or stamped across the face of the same, over the signature of the officer who issued the same or his successor in office, the words " (herein insert the name of the person), is permitted to traffic in liquor as (here insert the representative capacity whether as assignee, receiver, executor, administrator or otherwise) of the original owner of this certificate for the unexpired term thereof."

§ 18. Section twenty-seven of said chapter is hereby amended so as to read as follows:

§ 27. **Voluntary sale of a liquor tax certificate.** — The corporation, association, copartnership or person to which or to whom any liquor tax certificate is issued, except a certificate issued under subdivisions three, five or six of section eleven of this act, or their duly authorized attorney, may sell, assign and transfer such liquor tax certificate during the time for which it was granted to any corporation, association, copartnership or person not forbidden to traffic in liquors under this act, nor under the subdivision of section eleven under which such certificate was issued, which or who may thereupon carry on the business for which such liquor tax certificate was issued upon the premises described therein, if such traffic is not prohibited therein by this act, during the balance of the term of such tax certificate, with the same rights, and subject to the same liabilities as if such corporation, association, copartnership or person were an original applicant for such certificate and the original owner thereof, upon the making and filing of a new application and bond by such purchaser in the form and as provided for by sections seventeen and eighteen of this act, and the presentation of the tax certificate to the officer who issued the same or to his successor in office, who shall write or stamp across the face of the certificate over his signature the words " consent is hereby given for the transfer of this liquor tax certificate to (and here insert the name of the corporation, association, copartnership or person to which or to whom the same is transferred) ; " provided, however, that no such sale, assignment or transfer shall be made except in accordance with the provisions of the liquor tax law, nor permitted by any holder of a certificate who shall have been convicted, or be under indictment, or against which or whom a complaint under oath shall have been made, and be pending,

for violating the provisions of this act or who shall have violated
any provision of the liquor tax law.   For each endorsement under
sections twenty-five, twenty-six and twenty-seven of this act, the
officer making the same shall charge and receive the sum of ten
dollars to be paid by the applicant, which sum shall be apportioned
and accounted for as are taxes, as provided in sections thirteen and
fourteen of this act.

§ 19. Section twenty-eight of the said chapter is hereby amended
30 as to read as follows:

§ 28. Subdivision 1. **Certiorari upon refusal to issue or transfer liquor tax certificates, and of the revocation and cancellation of a liquor tax certificate.**— Whenever any officer charged
with the duty of issuing or consenting to a transfer of a liquor tax
certificate under the provisions of this act shall refuse to issue or
transfer the same, such officer shall indorse upon the application
therefor, or attach thereto a statement of his reasons for such
determination, and shall, if requested, furnish to the applicant a
copy of such statement.   Such applicant shall have the right to
a writ of certiorari to review the action of such officer.   The writ
may be issued by, returnable to, and heard by a county judge of
the county, or a justice of the supreme court of the judicial district in which the premises are situated in which the applicant
desires to carry on the business of trafficking in liquors.   If the
writ be granted, the officer to whom it is directed shall in his return
thereto, include copies of all the papers on which his action was
based, and a statement of his reasons for refusing to grant such
application.   If such judge or justice shall upon the hearing
determine that such application for a liquor tax certificate or for
a transfer has been denied by such officer without good and valid
reasons therefor, and that under the provisions of this act such
liquor tax certificate should be issued or transferred, such judge
or justice may make an order commanding such officer to grant
such application and to issue or transfer such liquor tax certificate
to such applicant upon the payment of the tax or fee therefor.

Subdivision 2. At any time after a liquor tax certificate has
been granted to any corporation, association, copartnership or person in pursuance of this act, under subdivision one, two, three or
six of section eleven, any citizen of the state may present a verified
petition to a justice of the supreme court, or a special term of the
supreme court of the judicial district in which such traffic in
liquors is authorized to be carried on, or in which the holder of
such certificate resides, or if such holder of a liquor tax certificate
is authorized to traffic in liquor under subdivision four or five of
section eleven of this act, to a justice of the supreme court of the
judicial district in which the principal office within this state of
the corporation, association, copartnership or person is located, for

an order revoking and cancelling such certificate upon the ground that material statements in the application of the holder of such certificate were false, or that he was not entitled to receive or is not entitled, on account of the violation of any provisions of this law, conviction for which would cause a forfeiture of such certificate, or for any other reason, to hold such certificate. Such petition shall state the facts upon which such allegations are based. Upon the presentation of the petition, the justice or court shall grant an order requiring the holder of such certificate, and the officer who granted the same, or his successors in office, to appear before him, or before a special term of the supreme court of the judicial district, on a day specified therein, not more than ten days after the granting thereof; and said order shall also contain an injunction restraining the said certificate-holder from transferring or surrendering such certificate until the final determination of the proceedings. A copy of such petition and order shall be served upon the holder of such certificate, and the officer granting the same, or his successor in office, in the manner directed by such order, not less than five days before the return day thereof. On the day specified in such order, the justice or court before whom the same is returnable shall hear the proofs of the parties, and may, if deemed necessary or proper, take testimony in relation to the allegations of the petition, or appoint a referee to take proofs in relation thereto, and report the evidence to such justice or court. If the justice or court is satisfied that material statements in the application of the holder of such certificate were false, or that the holder of such certificate was not entitled to receive, or is not entitled to hold such certificate, an order shall be granted revoking and cancelling such certificate. Said order shall also provide that the holder of said liquor tax certificate, or any other person having such certificate in his possession or under his control, shall forthwith surrender said certificate to the officer who issued the same, or to his successor in office. Upon the entry of such order in the county clerk's office of the county in which the traffic in liquors is authorized to be carried on under the certificate so revoked, and filing a copy thereof with the officer who issued such certificate, or his successor in office, and the service of a certified copy thereof upon the holder of said liquor tax certificate, or such substituted service as the court or justice may direct, all the rights of the holder of said liquor tax certificate under such certificate, to traffic in liquors or to any rebate thereon under this act, shall cease; and the holder of said liquor tax certificate, or any other person having such certificate in his possession or under his control, upon whom service of a certified copy of said order shall be made in like manner, shall immediately surrender said certificate to the officer who issued the same, or to his successor in office.

The neglect or refusal on the part of any person to surrender said certificate in pursuance of such order immediately upon the service thereof, shall be a contempt of court, punishable in the manner provided by the code of civil procedure.   Costs upon such proceedings may be awarded in favor of and against any party thereto, in such sums as in the discretion of the justice or court before which the petition is heard, may seem proper.

§ 20. Section twenty-nine of the said chapter is hereby amended so as to read as follows:

§ 29. **Injunction for unlawfully trafficking in liquors or without liquor tax certificate.**— If any corporation, association, copartnership or person shall unlawfully traffic in liquor without obtaining a liquor tax certificate, as provided by this act, or shall traffic in liquors contrary to any provision of this act, the state commissioner of excise, the deputy commissioner, special deputy commissioners, special agents or, except in counties containing a city of the first class, the county treasurer of the county in which the principal office of such corporation, association or copartnership is located, or in which such person resides or traffics in liquor, or any taxpayer residing in the county, may present a verified petition to a justice of the supreme court or a special term of the supreme court of the judicial district in which such county is situated, for an order enjoining such corporation, association, copartnership or person from trafficking in liquor thereafter.   Such petition shall state the facts upon which such allegations are based.   Upon the presentation of the petition, the justice or court shall grant an order requiring such corporation, association, copartnership or person to appear before him, or before a special term of the supreme court of the judicial district, on the day specified therein, not more than ten days after the granting thereof, to show cause why such corporation, association, copartnership or person should not be permanently enjoined from trafficking in liquor, until a liquor tax certificate has been obtained, in pursuance of law, or why such corporation, association, copartnership or person should not be permanently enjoined from trafficking in liquors contrary to the provisions of the liquor tax law.   A copy of such petition and order shall be served upon the corporation, association, copartnership or person, in the manner directed by such order, not less than five days before the return day thereof.   On the day specified in such order, the justice or court before whom the same is returnable shall hear the proofs of the parties, and may, if deemed necessary or proper, take testimony in relation to the allegations of the petition, or appoint a referee to take proofs in relation thereto, and report the evidence to such justice or court.   If the justice or court is satisfied that such corporation, association, copartnership or person is unlawfully trafficking in liquor without having obtained a liquor tax certificate, as provided by this act, or contrary to the provisions of this act, an order shall be granted enjoining such corporation, association, copartnership or person from thereafter trafficking in liquor, contrary to the provisions of the liquor tax law, or without obtaining a liquor tax certificate. If, after the entry of such order in the county clerk's office of the county in which the principal place of business of the corporation, association or copartnership is located, or in which the person so enjoined resides or traffics, and the service of the copy thereof upon such corporation, association, copartnership or person, or such substituted service as the court may direct, such corporation, association, copartnership or person shall, in violation of such order, traffic in liquor, such traffic shall be deemed a contempt of court and punishable in the manner provided by the code of civil procedure. Costs upon the application for such injunction may be awarded in favor of and against the parties thereto in the discretion of the justice or court before which the petition is heard. If awarded against the people of the state of New York, such costs shall be payable by the county treasurer, special deputy or state commissioner, upon the certificate of such justice or court, out of any moneys which may be in his hands, or that may thereafter come into his hands, on account of the tax provided for by this act. No proceeding under this section shall be taken, however, for a violation of section twenty-one of the liquor tax law, against any holder of a liquor tax certificate, who shall have made proper application for a new certificate, during the days of grace allowed under the provisions of said section twenty-one.

§ 21. Section thirty of the said chapter is hereby amended so as to read as follows:

§ 30. **Persons to whom liquor shall not be sold or given away.**— No corporation, association, copartnership or person, whether taxed under this act or not, shall sell, deliver or give away or cause or permit or procure to be sold, delivered or given away any liquors to:

1. Any minor under the age of eighteen years; nor to such minor for any other person;

2. To any intoxicated person;

3. To any habitual drunkard;

4. To any Indian;

5. To any person to whom such corporation, association, copartnership or person may be forbidden to sell by notice in writing from the parent, guardian, husband, wife or child of such person over sixteen years of age, or by a magistrate or overseer of the poor of the town; provided, however, that such notice in writing by a magistrate or overseer of the poor of the town shall apply only in

the case of a person who is wholly or partly a charge upon the town, which fact shall be stated in such notice;

6. To any person confined in or committed to a state prison, jail, penitentiary, house of refuge, reformatory, protectory, industrial school, asylum or state hospital, or any inmate of a poor-house, or any patient in any colony or institution established for the care or treatment of epileptics, except upon a written prescription from a physician to such institution, specifying the cause for which such prescription is given, the quantity and kind of liquor which is to be furnished, the name of the person for whom and the time or times at which the same shall be furnished. Such prescription shall not be made unless the physician is satisfied that the liquor furnished is necessary for the health of the person for whose use it is prescribed, and that fact must be stated in the prescription.

§ 22. Section thirty-one of the said chapter is hereby amended so as to read as follows:

§ 31. **Other illegal sales and selling; definitions of " hotel " and " guest; " exceptions; special liquor tax certificates in cities of the first and second class.**— It shall not be lawful for any corporation, association, copartnership or person which, or who, has not paid a tax as provided in section eleven of this act and obtained and posted the liquor tax certificate as provided in this act to sell, offer or expose for sale, or give away liquors in any quantity less than five wine gallons at a time; nor, without having paid such tax and complied with the provisions of this act, to sell, offer or expose for sale or give away liquor in any quantity whatever, any part of which is to be drunk on the premises of such vendor or in any outbuilding, booth, yard or garden appertaining thereto or connected therewith. It shall not be lawful for any corporation, association, copartnership or person, whether having paid such tax or not, to sell, offer or expose for sale, or give away, any liquor:

a. On Sunday; or before five o'clock in the morning on Monday; or

b. On any other day between one o'clock and five o'clock in the morning; or

c. On the day of a general or special election, or city election or town meeting, or village election, within one-quarter of a mile of any voting place, while the polls for such election or town meeting shall be open: or

d. Within two hundred yards of the grounds or premises upon which any state, county, town or other agricultural or horticultural fair is being held, unless such grounds or premises are within the limits of a city containing one hundred and fifty thousand inhabitants or more; or

e. To sell or expose for sale or have on the premises where liquor is sold, any liquor which is adulterated with any deleterious drug, substance or liquid which is poisonous or injurious to health; or

f. To permit any girl or woman, not a member of his family, or to knowingly permit any person who has been convicted of a felony, to sell or serve any liquor upon the premises; or

g. To have open or unlocked any door or entrance from the street, alley, yard, hallway, room or adjoining premises to the room or rooms where any liquors are sold or kept for sale during the hours when the sale of liquors is forbidden, except when necessary for the egress or ingress of the person holding the liquor tax certificate authorizing the traffic in liquors at such place, or members of his family, or his servants, for purposes not forbidden by this act; or to admit to such room or rooms any other person during hours when the sale of liquor is forbidden; or

h. To have during the hours when the sale of liquor is forbidden any screen or blinds, or any curtain or article or thing covering any part of any window, or to have in any window or door any opaque or colored glass that obstructs or in any way prevents a person passing from having a full view from the sidewalk, alley, or road in front of, or from the side, or end of the building, of the bar and room, or any part of such bar and room, in such building where liquors are sold or kept for sale; or to traffic in liquors in any interior bar or room or place not having in the principal door of entrance to such room or bar, a section of such door fitted with clear glass, through which, during prohibited hours and times, a clear, unobstructed view of the bar and room where liquors are sold and kept for sale can be had. And it shall be unlawful to have at any time in the room where liquors are sold any enclosed box or stall or any obstruction which prevents a full view of the entire room by every person present therein; or

i. For the holder of a liquor tax certificate under subdivision four of section eleven to sell liquor except to passengers in actual transit; or

j. To sell liquor in any quantity in a town in which a liquor tax certificate is prohibited under subdivisions one, two and four of section sixteen of this act, as the result of a vote upon "questions submitted;" provided, however, that a grower of fruit or a manufacturer of any liquor produced therefrom, in such town, may sell such liquor in quantities of five gallons or more, but only for delivery outside of such town; or

k. To solicit, accept or procure an order to deliver or send to another, or for another, liquor in any quantity, when the person for whom such liquor is procured, and the person soliciting, accepting or procuring such order, resides in a town in which a liquor tax certificate is prohibited under subdivisions one, two and four of section sixteen of this act, as the result of a vote on " questions submitted."

The provisions of clauses " a," " b," " c," and " d " of this section are subject, however, to the following exception: The holder of a liquor tax certificate under subdivision two or three of section eleven of this act who is a legally licensed pharmacist may sell liquor for medicinal purposes, only upon the prescription of a duly licensed physician, which prescription shall be preserved by the vendor and pasted in a book and be but once filled, and that only on the day when dated and given, which book shall be kept in the same room where the traffic in liquors is carried on, and shall be open to the inspection of any special agent or peace officer, and such liquors so sold shall not be drunk on the premises where sold, or in any outbuilding, yard, booth or garden appertaining thereto or connected therewith, except when such physician prescribes it to be used upon such premises in case of an accident, and provided further that the physician giving such prescription, shall not be the pharmacist himself nor a member of the corporation, association or copartnership selling such liquor, nor in his or their employ, and such prescription shall not be given unless the physician is satisfied that the liquor to be furnished is necessary for the health of the person for whom it is prescribed, which fact must be stated in the prescription. Clauses " a," " c " and " d " of this section are subject to the following exception:

The holder of a liquor tax certificate under subdivision one of section eleven of this act who is the keeper of a hotel, may sell liquor to the guests of such hotel, except to such persons as are described in clauses one, two, three, four, five and six of section thirty of this act, with their meals, or in their rooms therein, except between the hours of one o'clock and five o'clock in the morning, but not in the barroom or other similar room of such hotel; and the term " hotel " as used in this act shall mean a building regularly used and kept open as such for the feeding and lodging of guests, where all who conduct themselves properly and who are able and ready to pay for their entertainment, are received if there be accommodations for them, and who, without any stipu lated engagement as to the duration of their stay, or as to the rate of compensation, are, while there, supplied, at a reasonable charge, with their meals, lodgings, refreshment and such service and attention as are necessarily incident to the use of the place as a temporary home, and in which the only other dwellers shall be the family and servants of the hotel keeper; and which shall conform to the following requirements, if situate in a city, incorporated village of twelve hundred or more inhabitants, or within two miles of the corporate limits of either:

1. The laws, ordinances, rules and regulations relating to hotels

and hotel keepers, including all laws, ordinances, rules and regulations of the state or locality pertaining to the building, fire and health departments in relation to hotels and hotel keepers, shall be fully complied with.

2. Such building shall contain at least ten bedrooms above the basement, exclusive of those occupied by the family and servants, each room properly furnished to accommodate lodgers, and separated by partitions at least three inches thick, extending from floor to ceiling, with independent access to each room by a door opening into a hallway, each room having a window or windows with not less than eight square feet of surface opening upon a street or open court, light-shaft or open air, and each having at least eighty square feet of floor area, and at least six hundred cubic feet of space therein; a dining-room with at least three hundred square feet of floor area, which shall not be a part of the barroom, with tables, and having suitable table furniture and accommodations for at least twenty guests therein at one and the same time, and a kitchen and conveniences for cooking therein sufficient to provide bona fide meals at one and the same time for twenty guests. The same requirements shall apply to a hotel situate in any other place, except that the number of bedrooms for guests shall not be less than six, and the dining-room shall have not less than one hundred and fifty square feet of floor area, and the kitchen accommodations shall be sufficient for at least ten guests. A guest of a hotel, within the meaning of this exception to section thirty-one of this act, is:

1. A person who in good faith occupies a room in a hotel as a temporary home, and pays the regular and customary charges for such occupancy, but who does not occupy such room for the purpose of having liquor served therein; or

2. A person who, during the hours when meals are regularly served therein, resorts to the hotel for the purpose of obtaining, and actually orders and obtains at such time, in good faith, a meal therein.

And it is further provided that a corporation or association, organized in good faith under chapter five hundred and fifty-nine of the laws of eighteen hundred and ninety-five, or under any law which, prior to May sixth, eighteen hundred and ninety-five, provided for the organization of societies or clubs for social, recreative or similar purposes, and which corporation or association was actually lawfully organized, and, if a corporation, its certificate of incorporation duly filed, prior to March twenty-third, eighteen hundred and ninety-six, and which at such date trafficked in or distributed liquors among the members thereof, is excepted from the provisions of clauses " a," " b." " c " and " d " of this section. And the provisions of clause " b " of this section is subject to the following exception: In cities on the presentation by the holder of a liquor tax ceretificate under subdivision one of section eleven of a permit for trafficking in liquor during the designated hours of one or more specified days, except Sunday, and at a place specified, granted and signed by the mayor of the city and the chief of police, and the payment of a tax of ten dollars for each day, the county treasurer or special deputy commissioner charged with the duty of issuing liquor tax certificates shall issue a special liquor tax certificate for the sale of liquor at the place and during the time so specified, which certificate shall be in the form prescribed and furnished by the state commissioner of excise.

§ 23. Section thirty-two of said chapter is hereby amended so as to read as follows:

§ 32. **Sales and pledges; when void.**—No recovery shall be had in any civil action, to recover the purchase price of any sale on credit of any liquor, to be drunk on the premises, where the same shall be sold. All securities given for such debts shall be void. Any person taking such security, with intent to evade this section, shall forfeit a penalty of fifty dollars for each offense. Each assignment, sale or pledge of articles or property exempt, by law, from execution, and every levy or sale of such articles or property by virtue of an execution by consent of the defendant therein, shall be void, where the consideration, or any part thereof, for which such assignment, sale or pledge was made, or for the debt on which judgment was rendered in any court and on which such execution was issued, was for the sale of liquors.

§ 24. Section thirty-four of the said chapter is hereby amended so as read as follows:

§ 34. **Penalties for violation of this act.**—1. Any corporation, association, copartnership or person trafficking in liquors, who is prohibited from so doing or who so traffics without having lawfully obtained a liquor tax certificate; or contrary to the provisions of section sixteen of this act; or who shall neglect or refuse to make application for a liquor tax certificate, or give the bond, or pay the tax imposed as required by this act, shall be guilty of a misdemeanor, and upon conviction therefor shall be punished by a fine of not less than two hundred dollars nor more than one thousand dollars, provided such fine shall equal at least the amount of tax for one year, imposed by this act upon the kind of traffic in liquors carried on, where carried on, or which would be so imposed if such traffic were lawful, and may also be imprisoned in a county jail or penitentiary for the term of not more than one year.

2. Any corporation, association, copartnership or person, who shall make any false statement in the application required to be presented to the county treasurer or other officer to obtain a liquor tax certificate, or to obtain a transfer thereof, or who shall

violate the provisions of this act by trafficking in liquors contrary to the provisions of sections eleven, twenty-two, twenty-three, twenty-four, thirty or thirty-one, shall be guilty of a misdemeanor, and upon conviction therefor shall be punished by a fine of not more than five hundred dollars or by imprisonment in a county jail or penitentiary for a term of not more than one year, or by both such fine and imprisonment, and shall forfeit the liquor tax certificate, and be deprived of all rights and privileges thereunder, and of any right to a rebate of any portion of the tax paid thereon, and such certificate shall be surrendered to the officer who issued it, or to his successor in office, who shall immediately forward the same to the state commissioner of excise for cancellation, and if the corporation, association, copartnership or person convicted be a pharmacist holding a license issued by the board of pharmacy, the said board of pharmacy shall, in addition to said penalties, immediately revoke said license, and no liquor tax certificate shall be issued to any corporation, association, copartnership or person to traffic in liquors at said store or place, under subdivision three of section eleven of this act for the term of one year from the date of said conviction; but this clause does not apply to violations of section thirty-one of this act, the punishment for which is provided in the first clause of this section.

3. If there shall be two convictions of clerks, agents, employes, or servants of a holder of a liquor tax certificate, for a violation of any provision of this act, the liquor tax certificate of the principal shall be forfeited, and the said principal shall be deprived of all rights and privileges thereunder, and of any right to any rebate of any portion of the tax paid thereon, and such certificate shall be surrendered to the officer who issued it or to his successor in office, who shall immediately forward the same to the state commissioner of excise for cancellation.

4. No liquor tax certificate shall be issued to any person convicted of a violation of the liquor tax law within five years from the date of such conviction, nor shall any such person have any interest therein, or become a surety on any bond, required under section eighteen of this act, during such period.

5. Any wilful violation by any person of any provision of this act, for which no punishment or penalty is otherwise provided, shall be a misdemeanor.

§ 25. Section thirty-five of said chapter is hereby amended so as to read as follows:

§ 35. **Jurisdiction of courts; reports of magistrates.**

Subdivision 1. Except as otherwise provided by this act, all proceedings instituted for the punishment of any violations of the provisions of this act, the penalties for which are prescribed in subdivisions one, two, three or four of section thirty-four, shall be prosecuted by indictment by the grand jury of the county in which the crime was committed, and by trial in a court of record having jurisdiction for the trial of crimes of the grade of felony; except that a magistrate shall issue a warrant of arrest upon information and depositions and examine the case as now provided by law, but if it shall appear upon such examination that a crime, not triable by a court of special sessions has been committed, and that there is sufficient cause to believe that the person or persons charged with such crime is guilty thereof, such magistrate shall admit such person or persons to bail, in a sum not less than one thousand dollars, and in default of bail shall commit him or them to the sheriff of the county or if in the city of New York to the keeper of the city prison of the city of New York. A magistrate by whom any person charged with a violation of the provisions of the liquor tax law, shall be admitted to bail or committed to the sheriff or other proper officer of the county, upon such charge shall immediately notify the state commissioner of excise in writing of the fact of such arrest and the result of such examination, stating the name and residence of each person accused; the date when admitted to bail or committed; the name, residence and address of the complainant, and of each witness sworn in support of the charge in case a preliminary examination shall have been had, and shall at the same time transmit a duplicate copy of such report to the district attorney of the county.

Subdivision 2. Courts of special sessions shall have exclusive jurisdiction to try and determine, according to law, all complaints for violations of sections forty and forty-one of this act and also all violations of the liquor tax law defined by subdivision five of section thirty-four as a misdemeanor. Any person convicted in a court of special sessions for violation of any of the provisions of the liquor tax law, shall be punished according to the provisions of this act.

§ 35a. **Jurisdiction of courts of special sessions in the city and county of New York.**—After a person has been held to bail or committed to the keeper of the city prison by a magistrate, upon a complaint for a violation of any of the provisions of the liquor tax law in the city and county of New York, as provided in section thirty-one, all further and subsequent proceedings instituted for the purposes mentioned in section thirty-five of this act shall be prosecuted in the court of special sessions in and for said city and county in the manner prescribed by law for the trial of misdemeanors committed therein. Upon the conviction in such court of special sessions of any person charged with a violation of any of the provisions of the liquor tax law, judgment shall be pronounced by the said court pursuant to the provisions of this act, and all fines imposed shall be collected and paid over to the special deputy commissioner of the county to be apportioned and disposed of as provided by section thirteen.

§ 26. Section thirty-six of said chapter is hereby amended so as to read as follows:

§ 36. **Collection of fines and penalties and forfeitures of bonds; reports of county clerks.**— Upon conviction and sentence of any corporation, association or copartnership and upon the conviction and sentence of any person or persons whether as officer of a corporation or as member of a copartnership or as an individual, for a violation of the provisions of this act, the penalty for which is prescribed in sections twenty-eight, twenty-nine or thirty-four hereof, the court or officer imposing the sentence, or the clerk of the court if there be a clerk, shall forthwith make and file in the office of the clerk of the county in which such conviction shall have been had a certified statement of such conviction and sentence, and the clerk of said county shall immediately thereupon enter in the docket book, kept by said clerk for the docketing of judgments in said office, the account of the penalty or fine and costs imposed, as a judgment against the person or persons, corporation, association or copartnership so convicted or sentenced, and in favor of the state commissioner of excise, and said county clerk shall also enter in the docket of said judgment a brief statement setting forth the fact that said judgment is for a fine or penalty imposed for a violation of the " liquor tax law," and said county clerk shall immediately mail or deliver to the state commissioner of excise a duly certified transcript of said judgment. If the fine and costs imposed be paid into court, the said officer or clerk of the court shall at once pay the same to the county treasurer or special deputy commissioner of the county, who shall give his receipt therefor, and shall, at once notify the state commissioner of excise of the payment of such judgment, who shall thereupon execute a satisfaction thereof and forward the same to the said county treasurer or special deputy commissioner, to be delivered to the judgment debtor. If said judgment shall not be paid within five days after such conviction and sentence, the clerk of said county shall issue an execution against the property of such judgment debtor or debtors, against whom said judgment is docketed, directed to the sheriff of the county and at once deliver the said execution to the said sheriff, who shall forthwith proceed to collect the amount due on said judgment, together with his legal fees and costs, by levy and sale, in the manner now provided by law for the collection of executions against property, of any goods, chattels, furniture, fixtures, and leasehold interest, or other property of such judgment debtor or debtors, whenever found. Such levy shall take precedence over any and all liens, mortgages, conveyances, or incumbrances taken or had on such property, subsequent to the docketing of said judgment in said clerk's office, and no property of said judgment debtor or debtors shall be exempt from such levy and sale. All moneys collected upon execution under the provisions of this section shall be paid by the officer collecting the same, less his legal fees and costs thereon, to such county treasurer or special deputy commissioner who shall apportion and account for the same as provided by this act. In case such judgment debtor or debtors shall have given the bond provided for in section eighteen of this act, the state commissioner of excise may forthwith proceed to collect from the sureties thereon the amount of such judgment, together with the costs of collection, by due process of law, and the issuing of an execution under the provisions of this act shall not be a condition precedent to the enforcement of the provisions and penalties of any bond given by such judgment debtor or debtors pursuant to the provisions of this act. At the end of each month, every county clerk shall make under his hand and official seal and forward to the state commissioner of excise a written report of all orders or judgments filed or entered in his office during such month, in favor of or against the state commissioner of excise, and also a report of all orders or judgments entered in said office in favor of or against any person illegally trafficking in liquor or the holder of a liquor tax certificate in any proceeding or action instituted or brought for the purpose of compelling the surrender and cancellation of a liquor tax certificate, or in favor of or against any county treasurer or special deputy commissioner on account of his having issued or transferred or refused to issue or transfer any liquor tax certificate. Such report shall contain the title of the action or proceeding in which each of said orders or judgments was obtained, the date of each order or judgment, also when filed and entered and also the substance or purport of such order or judgment; also all indictments for violations of the liquor tax law, and all judgments of conviction thereon. Such report shall state the date when each indictment was found, the name of the defendant, the time and place when and where the crime was committed, and the particular offense charged; and in case of a conviction shall state the name of the defendant, the date of the conviction, and the judgment pronounced thereon, and if the fine imposed shall have been paid in court a statement of that fact. All sealed indictments shall be included in the first report made by such county clerk after the defendant therein shall have been arrested or admitted to bail. Said county clerk shall also furnish a complete certified copy of any such order, indictment, judgment or record upon the request of the state commissioner of excise. The first report made under this section shall include and contain a statement of all orders, judgments, indictments and convictions, and the judgments pronounced thereon in said county, under the liquor tax law, filed or entered in said clerk's office from the twenty-third day of March, eighteen hundred and ninety-six, to and including the date of the said report. The fees or compensation of such clerk for making such report and for making and furnishing a certified copy of any such order, judgment, indictment or record, at the request of the state commissioner of excise, shall be a legal charge against the county in which the office of the said clerk is situated, and shall be audited and paid as are other lawful claims.

§ 27. Section thirty-seven of the said chapter is hereby amended so as to read as follows:

§ 37. Duties of public officers in relation to complaints and prosecutions under this act.— It shall be the duty of the special deputy commissioners and special agents and of every county treasurer, sheriff, deputy sheriff, police officer or constable, having notice or knowledge of any violation of the provisions of this act, to immediately notify the district attorney of the county in which such violation occurs, by a statement under oath of the fact of such violation, and it shall be the duty of such district attorney when complaint on oath is made of such violation, forthwith to cause the arrest and attend the examination personally or by an assistant, of each person so complained of, unless a term of court with a grand jury in attendance shall be appointed to be held in such county within ten days from the time of the receipt by the district attorney of such verified complaint, or unless such accused persons shall have been examined upon such charge and admitted to bail or committed thereon. It shall be the duty of the district attorney to prepare and present to the grand jury of the county all evidence tending to show a violation in each case within his knowledge, or reported to him pursuant to the provisions of this section, or reported to him by the verified complaint of any reputable citizen, except that said district attorney shall prosecute such violations as are specified in subdivision two of section thirty-five in the court of special sessions having jurisdiction thereof and the said district attorney shall prosecute any person violating any of the provisions of this act, and for each and every violation thereof. All officers authorized to make arrests in any city, town or village, and the special agents appointed under section ten of this act may in the performance of their duties enter upon any premises where the traffic in liquors is carried on or liquors are exposed for sale at any time when such premises are open, except that places occupied by membership corporations incorporated prior to the twenty-third day of March, eighteen hundred and ninety-six, which traffic in liquors solely with the members thereof, shall not be entered for inspection by any officer unless such entry and inspection is expressly authorized and directed by the state commissioner of excise by written instructions.

§ 28. Section forty of the said chapter is hereby amended so as to read as follows:

§ 40. **Intoxication in a public place.**—Any person intoxicated in a public place is guilty of a misdemeanor, and may be arrested without warrant while so intoxicated, and shall be punished by a fine of not less than three nor more than ten dollars, or by imprisonment not exceeding six months or by both such fine and imprisonment. The purchase or procurement of liquor for any person to whom it is forbidden to sell liquor under section thirty of this act, is a misdemeanor, punishable upon conviction, by a fine of not less than ten dollars or by imprisonment not exceeding six months, or by both such fine and imprisonment.

§ 29. Section forty-two of the said chapter is hereby amended so as to read as follows:

§ 42. **Penalties; actions to recover.**—Any corporation, association, copartnership or person who shall traffic in liquor contrary to the provisions of the liquor tax law, or who shall make a false statement upon application for a liquor tax certificate, or upon application for the transfer or surrender and cancellation thereof, or who shall violate any of the provisions of sections eleven, thirteen, twenty-one, twenty-two, twenty-three, twenty-four, twenty-five, twenty-six, twenty-seven, twenty-eight, twenty-nine, thirty, thirty-one, thirty-two, thirty-five, thirty-six, or thirty-seven of said law, in addition to the punishment and penalties in this act otherwise imposed and provided, shall be liable to a penalty of fifty dollars for each and every violation, to be recovered by the state commissioner of excise in an action brought in his name as such commissioner, in any court of record in any county of the state, provided that two or more penalties may be sued for and recovered in the same action; and if such corporation, association, copartnership or person be the holder of a liquor tax certificate, such certificate shall be forfeited. When an action is brought in any county other than the county wherein the defendant resides, or in an adjoining county, the place of trial of such action may be changed to any county adjoining the county wherein the defendant resides, for cause shown as provided by the code of civil procedure. If judgment be recovered against the holder of a liquor tax certificate in any action for penalties, such judgment shall provide, in addition to the penalties included therein, that such certificate and all rights thereunder of the holder thereof, including all rebate moneys upon cancellation, be forfeited, and that the defendant, or any person having such certificate in his possession or under his control, shall surrender said certificate to the officer who issued the same, or to his successor in office, im-

mediately upon the service ot a certified copy of said judgment;
and neglect or refusal of any person to surrender said certificate
in pursuance of the provisions of any such judgment shall be a
contempt of court, punishable in the manner provided by the
code of civil procedure.   All moneys recovered in any such action
or actions shall be paid over and accounted for in the same manner
as are moneys collected under subdivision four of section eleven
of this act.   The state commissioner of excise may also in like
manner bring an action in his name as such commissioner to recover
the penalty provided for by section thirty-eight of this act and
the provisions of this section shall apply to the commencement
and prosecution of such action and the disposition of all moneys
recovered as penalties therein.

§ 30. **When to take effect.**— This act shall take effect immediately.

Chap. 315.

AN ACT to provide for the erection and equipment of a building for
experiments and investigations in dairying, and for other purposes,
at the State Agricultural Station at Geneva, and making an appropriation therefor.

Became a law April 21, 1897, with the approval of the Governor.
Passed, three-fifths being present.

*The People of the State of New York, represented in Senate and
Assembly, do enact as follows:*

Appropria-
tion for
building.

Section 1. For the purpose of erecting and equipping a suitable
building for experiments and investigations in dairying in all its
relations, in horticulture, in plant diseases and insect pests, the
sum of forty-one thousand dollars, or so much thereof as may be
necessary, is hereby appropriated from any moneys in the treasury
not otherwise appropriated, to be paid by the treasurer on the warrant of the comptroller, to the New York Agricultural Experiment Station at Geneva, upon vouchers approved by the commis-

Approval
of plans.

sioner of agriculture.   No part of such moneys so appropriated
shall be expended until plans and specifications for the construction of such buildings shall have been approved by the state architect, nor until the state architect has certified that in his judgment
the cost of the completion of such building, in accordance with
such plans and specifications, will not exceed the amount of such
appropriation.   Such approval and certificate shall be filed with
the commissioner of agriculture.

§ 2. This act shall take effect immediately.

Chap. 317.

AN ACT to legalize the acts and services of Charles N. Hoffman while acting as school commissioner for the second district of Niagara county, performed by him between January first, eighteen hundred and ninety-four, and December thirty-first, eighteen hundred and ninety-six, and permitting the board of claims to hear and audit his claim for services.

Became a law April 21, 1897, with the approval of the Governor.

Passed, three-fifths being present.

The People of the State of New York, represented in Senate and Assembly, do enact as follows:

Section 1. The acts and services of Charles N. Hoffman while acting as school commissioner for the second district of Niagara county, actually performed by him between January first, eighteen hundred and ninety-four and the time when he was finally judicially declared not to have been elected to said office, are hereby ratified, legalized and confirmed. *Acts and services legalized.*

§ 2. Jurisdiction is hereby conferred upon the board of claims to hear, audit, and determine, the alleged claim of Charles N. Hoffman, the person named in section one hereof, or his legal representatives or assigns. The said board of claims is hereby empowered to award such compensation for such services rendered, and for expenditures incurred by said Charles N. Hoffman as school commissioner for the second district of Niagara county, between the first day of January, eighteen hundred and ninety-four and the time when he was finally judicially declared not to have been elected to said office, as may be just and equitable, not exceeding the amount which he would have received for the time during which he performed the duties of the office had he been duly elected, and all technical and legal objections to the ascertainment of the value of such services, and the amount of said disbursements by the said board of claims are hereby expressly waived. *Jurisdiction to hear claims.*

§ 3. Either party may appeal to the third appellate division of the supreme court from any award made under authority of this act; provided such appeal be taken by service of a notice of appeal within thirty days after the service of a copy of the award. *Appeal from award.*

§ 4. This act shall take effect immediately.

Chap. 322.

AN ACT to amend the game law, relating to woodcock in Richmond
county.

Became a law April 23, 1897, with the approval of the Governor.
Passed, three-fifths being present.

*The People of the State of New York, represented in Senate and
Assembly, do enact as follows:*

Section 1. Chapter four hundred and eighty-eight of the laws of
eighteen hundred and ninety-two, the title of which was amended
by chapter three hundred and ninety-five of the laws of eighteen
hundred and ninety-five, to read " An act relating to game, fish and
wild animals and to the forest preserve and Adirondack park constituting chapter thirty-one of the general laws to be known as the
fisheries, game and forest law," is hereby amended by adding the
following section to be number fifty-six to read as follows:-

§ 56. Closed season for woodcock in Richmond county.—Woodcock shall not be pursued, shot at, hunted, killed or possessed, in
Richmond county, except from the fourth day of July to the thirty-
first day of December, both inclusive. Whoever shall violate or attempt to violate the provisions of this section shall be deemed
guilty of misdemeanor, and in addition thereto shall be liable to a
penalty of twenty-five dollars for each woodcock killed, trapped
or possessed contrary to the provisions of this section. Anything
contained in sections seventy-four, seventy-five and seventy-six of
this act relating to woodcock, effecting Richmond county as to
closed season on woodcock, is hereby repealed.

§ 2. This act is to take effect immediately.

Chap. 323.

AN ACT to amend the town law, relative to the filing and lien of collectors' undertakings, and providing for filing a satisfaction thereof.

Became a law April 23, 1897, with the approval of the Governor.
Passed, three-fifths being present.

*The People of the State of New York, represented in Senate and
Assembly, do enact as follows:*

Section 1. Section fifty-three of article three of chapter five hundred and sixty-nine of the laws of eighteen hundred and ninety,
entitled " An act in relation to towns, constituting chapter twenty

of the general laws," known as the town law, is hereby amended to
read as follows:

§ 53. **Filing and lien of collectors' undertaking.**—The supervisor
shall, within six days thereafter, file the undertaking with his approval indorsed thereon, in the office of the county clerk, who shall
make an entry thereof in a book to be provided for the purpose,
in the same manner as judgments are entered of record; and every
such undertaking shall be a lien on all the real estate held jointly or
severally by the collector or his sureties within the county at the
time of the filing thereof, and shall continue to be such lien, until
its condition, together with all costs and charges which may accrue
by the prosecution thereof, shall be fully satisfied. Upon a settlement in full between the county treasurer and collector, a certificate of payment shall be executed in duplicate by the county
treasurer, one copy to be delivered to the collector and one copy of
such certificate shall be filed by the county treasurer in the office
of the county clerk, and said county clerk shall then enter a satisfaction thereof in the book in which the filing of said bond is entered
and opposite said entry of filing.

§ 2. This act shall take effect immediately.

Chap. 326.

AN ACT to amend the game law, and the act amendatory thereof,
relating to taking minnows for bait.

Became a law April 23, 1897, with the approval of the Governor.
Passed, three-fifths being present.

*The People of the State of New York, represented in Senate and
Assembly, do enact as follows:*

Section 1. Section one hundred forty-five of chapter four hundred and eighty-eight of the laws of eighteen hundred and ninety-
two, the title to which was amended by chapter three hundred and
ninety-five of the laws of eighteen hundred and ninety-five, to read
"An act relating to game, fish, and wild animals and to the forest
preserve and Adirondack park, constituting chapter thirty-one of
the general laws, and to be known as the fisheries, game and forest
law," as amended by chapter nine hundred and seventy-four of the
laws of eighteen hundred and ninety-five, is hereby amended to read
as follows:

§ 145. **Taking minnows for bait.**—The provisions of this act prohibiting the use or placing of nets and certain other devices in

waters of the state shall not apply to taking minnows for bait, but
nets for that purpose must not exceed forty feet in length and four
feet in depth, with ropes at either end for hauling not exceeding
thirty feet in length.   This section shall not authorize the placing
or use of nets or any other devices of a kind used for catching fish
in streams inhabited by trout, nor the taking of trout by means of
nets or other devices except angling in any waters.   If any black
bass, Oswego bass, muscalonge, great northern pike, sometimes
called pickerel, wall-eyed pike, or whitefish or minnows thereof are
taken in nets used for catching minnows for bait, they shall be
returned to the water at once without injury.   Whoever shall
violate or attempt to violate the provisions of this section by placing, drawing, using or maintaining any device of any kind in
streams inhabited by trout whereby fish can be taken other than
that of angling, which shall mean by hook and line or rod held in
hand, shall be deemed guilty of misdemeanor and in addition
thereto shall be liable to a penalty of one hundred dollars for each
violation thereof and five dollars for each and every fish caught,
killed or possessed, taken contrary to the provisions of this section.
. § 2. All acts and parts of acts inconsistent with this act are
hereby repealed.

§ 3. This act shall take effect immediately.

Chap. 327.

AN ACT to amend chapter five hundred and fifty-nine of the laws
   of eighteen hundred and ninety-five, relating to membership
   corporations.

Became a law April 23, 1897, with the approval of the Governor.
Passed, three-fifths being present.

*The People of the State of New York, represented in Senate and
Assembly, do enact as follows:*

Act
amended.

Section 1. Article ten of chapter five hundred and fifty-nine of
the laws of eighteen hundred and ninety-five, entitled "An act relating to membership corporations, constituting chapter forty-three
of the general laws," is hereby amended by adding to said article
immediately after section one hundred and twenty-two an additional section to read as follows:

§ 123. Any unincorporated association which shall have been or- Transfer of funds of unincorporated monument associations. ganized solely for the purpose of raising funds to be devoted to the erection of a monument or memorial to perpetuate the memory of the soldiers and sailors who served in the defense of the union in the late war, may by a majority vote of all its members who shall be present and voting at a meeting thereof, called as in this section provided, transfer to and vest in any incorporated association which shall have been organized under a general statute, or under the foregoing sections of this article for the sole purpose of erecting a like monument or memorial in the same town or village where such unincorporated association is located, any or all money which it shall have accumulated for such object, except as hereinafter provided, provided that such transfer does not conflict with any provision of the constitution or by-laws of such association, and that it shall be made and the money so transferred shall be accepted by such incorporated association in trust to apply the same, or the income thereof, exclusively for the purposes mentioned in section one hundred and twenty-one of this article. Any member of such unincorporated as- Right of members to receive contributions paid. sociation who shall have contributed individually to the fund so raised, and paid such contribution into the treasury of such association, the same appearing upon the books of the treasurer, shall be entitled to demand and receive the amount of such contribution from the treasurer of such association, in case such transfer shall be made and before the same shall be consummated upon filing with the president or secretary of such unincorporated association his or her affidavit to the effect that he or she has not approved of such transfer by vote or otherwise. No Vote upon question of transfer. vote upon the question of transferring the funds of such unincorporated association as hereinbefore provided for shall be had or taken except at a meeting of such association especially called for that purpose by the president or secretary or other managing officer thereof, upon notice given at least ten days before the time fixed for such meeting, personally or by mail to each member of such association whose residence or post-office address is known, which notice shall state the object of the meeting to be the consideration of making such transfer pursuant to this section.

§ 2. This act shall take effect immediately.

Chap. 329.

AN ACT to amend chapter six hundred and eighty-six of the laws of eighteen hundred and ninety-two, entitled "An act in relation to counties, constituting chapter eighteen of the general laws," and the act amendatory thereof, relating to fire districts.

Became a law April 23, 1897, with the approval of the Governor.
Passed, three-fifths being present.

The People of the State of New York, represented in Senate and Assembly, do enact as follows:

Section 1. Section thirty-seven of chapter six hundred and eighty-six of the laws of eighteen hundred and ninety-two as amended by chapter nine hundred and two of the laws of eighteen hundred and ninety-six is hereby amended so as to read as follows:

§ 37. **Fire districts outside of incorporated villages.**— Each board of supervisors may, on the written, verified petition of the taxable inhabitants of a proposed fire district outside of an incorporated village or city, and within the county, whose names appear on the last preceding assessment-roll of the town within which such proposed fire district is located, as owning or representing more than one-half of the taxable real property of such district, or as owning or representing more than one-half of the taxable real property of such district owned by the residents thereof, establish such district as a fire district. No such district shall extend in any direction to exceed one mile from the nearest engine or hook or ladder-house located within the district. When any such fire district has been established in the manner above provided, the legal voters thereof may elect not less than three nor more than five residents thereof to be the fire commissioners, for a term of five years, or such less term as a majority of such voters at the time of any such election may express on their ballots; and may also elect a treasurer in such fire district for a term of three years, who shall be entitled to receive and have the custody of the funds of the district and pay out the same for the purposes herein provided for, on the order of the fire commissioners, which treasurer before entering on the duties of his office, shall give such security as the board of supervisors may require. The first election for such fire commissioners and treasurer, shall be called by the clerk of the town within which any such district shall be established, within thirty days from the establishment of such district, and upon such notice, and in the same manner as required for by special town meetings. All subsequent elections shall be called in the same manner by the clerk of the town, not less than thirty days prior to the expiration of the term of office of any such commissioners or of the treasurer; special elections to fill any vacancies shall be called in the same manner, within thirty days after any such vacancy shall occur. Any such district, when established, shall be known by such name as the fire commissioners thereof may adopt at their first meeting for organization, and thereafter such fire commissioners shall be authorized and empowered to purchase apparatus for the extinguishment of fires therein; rent or purchase suitable real estate and buildings for the keeping and storing of the same; and to procure supplies of water, and have control and provide for the maintenance and support of a fire department in such district; and shall have the power to organize fire, hook, hose, ladder, axe and bucket fire patrol companies; and to appoint a suitable number of able and respectable inhabitants of said district as firemen, and to prescribe the duties of the firemen and the rules and regulations for the government of such companies and of the fire department; and who shall have power to make any and all contracts within the appropriations voted by the resident taxpayers of the district for the purpose of carrying out the authorization and powers herein granted. Whenever the fire commissioners in any such fire district shall submit a request in writing for an appropriation of any sum of money for the purposes herein authorized, the clerk of the town in which such fire district shall be located, shall call a meeting of the resident taxpayers of the district for the purpose of voting upon the question of appropriating such money; such meeting to be called by a notice posted conspicuously in at least two of the most public places in such fire district, at least ten days before the holding of any such meeting, which notices shall state the time, place and purposes of the meeting. At any such meeting such resident taxpayers may appropriate the amount requested by the fire commissioners, or any less amount, and when any such appropriation is made, the amount appropriated shall be assessed, levied and collected on such district, in the same manner, at the same time and by the same officers as the taxes of the town in which the district is located are assessed, levied and collected, and when collected shall be paid over immediately by the supervisor of the town to the treasurer of the fire district;

and the town shall be responsible for any and all sums
so collected until the same shall be paid over to such
treasurer. All meetings of any such district called for the
election of officers, or for the appropriation of money, shall be
presided over by a resident taxpayer to be designated by the fire
commissioners, except at the first meeting after any such fire
district shall have been established shall be presided over by a
resident taxpayer selected by the legal voters at the meeting; and
all elections for fire commissioners and for treasurer shall be by
ballot, in the same manner as is provided for the election of other
town officers. The board of supervisors in any county in which
any such fire district shall have been heretofore or shall be hereafter established, may at any time, upon the written verified petition of the taxable inhabitants of any such district, whose names
appear upon the last preceding assessment-roll of the town within
which such district is located as owning or representing more
than one-half of the taxable real property of such district, or as
owning or representing more than one-half of the taxable real
property in such district owned by the residents thereof, discontinue such district as a fire district, and upon such action being
taken by the supervisors, the fire commissioners of such district,
where it is wholly within a village incorporated since said district
was formed shall turn over to any fire corporation organized by
the trustees of said village all the property thereof, such village
to pay all the debts thereof, and in other than such last named
districts the fire commissioners shall proceed to sell the property
belonging to such district at public sale; three notices of such sale
shall be posted conspicuously in three of the most public places
in the district, for a period of thirty days prior to the sale, and
the proceeds of such sale shall be paid over by the treasurer of
the district to the supervisor of the town, and the sum so paid over
shall be credited to the taxable real property located in such district, in the next succeeding assessment of town taxes. Whenever any portion of any such fire district heretofore or hereafter
established shall be incorporated into the corporate limits of any
incorporated village or city, the board of supervisors of the county
in which such district is located upon the written verified petition
of more than one-half in assessed valuation of the taxable inhabitants of such incorporated portion of the fire district, change the
boundaries of such district in such manner as shall exclude such
incorporated portion of the district, and thereafter such incor-

porated portion of the district shall not be entitled to the protection, nor liable to be assessed or taxed for the support of the fire department of such district. Where any two fire districts not within any incorporated village adjoin each other, the boundary line between such districts may be changed by the board of supervisors of the county in which they are located, upon a written verified petition of the taxable inhabitants of the portion of the fire district applied to be changed, whose names appear upon the last preceding assessment-roll of the town within which said portion of said fire district is located, as owning or representing more than one-half of the taxable property of such portion of said fire district, provided the taxable inhabitants of both said fire districts and within the county, whose names appear upon the last preceding assessment-roll of the town or towns, owning or representing more than one-half of the taxable property of said district shall consent in writing to such change.

§ 2. This act shall take effect immediately.

Chap. 330.

AN ACT to amend the fisheries, game and forest law, and the act amendatory thereof, in regard to use of nets.

Became a law April 23, 1897, with the approval of the Governor. Passed, three-fifths being present.

The People of the State of New York, represented in Senate and Assembly, do enact as follows:

Section 1. Section one hundred and thirty-four of chapter four hundred and eighty-eight of the laws of eighteen hundred and ninety-two, the title to which was amended by chapter three hundred and ninety-five of the laws of eighteen hundred and ninety-five to read "An act relating to game, fish and wild animals, and to the forest preserve and Adirondack park, constituting chapter thirty-one of the general laws and to be known as the fisheries, game and forest law," as amended by chapter nine hundred and seventy-four of the laws of eighteen hundred and ninety-five, is hereby amended to read as follows:

§ 134. **Meshes of nets used in Lakes Erie and Ontario and Cattaraugus creek.**—The meshes of nets used in Lake Erie and Lake Ontario and Cattaraugus creek shall not be less than one and one-eighth inch bar. It shall be lawful for fishermen holding license from the fisheries, game and forest commission to fish with nets in said lakes, to hang or reel the said licensed nets for the purpose of cleaning and drying, on the shores of said lakes, or on the shores of any island therein, or on the shores of any of the harbors of said lakes or of any island therein. Whoever shall violate or attempt to violate the provisions of this section shall be guilty of misdemeanor and in addition thereto shall be liable to a penalty of one hundred dollars for each violation thereof.

§ 2. This act shall take effect immediately.

Chap. 331.

AN ACT making an appropriation for the payment of confidential clerks to certain justices of the supreme court in the fifth judicial district, pursuant to chapter eight hundred and ninety-three, laws of eighteen hundred and ninety-six.

Became a law April 23, 1897, with the approval of the Governor.
Passed, three-fifths being present.

The People of the State of New York, represented in Senate and Assembly, do enact as follows:

Appropriation for confidential clerks. Section 1. The sum of four thousand seven hundred and ninety-five dollars, or so much thereof as may be necessary, is hereby appropriated out of any money in the treasury not otherwise appropriated, for the payment of confidential clerks to resident trial justices of the supreme court in the fifth judicial district, excepting those resident in cities in said district, in which there is now a resident supreme court stenographer, from May thirtieth, eighteen hundred and ninety-six, to September thirtieth, eighteen hundred ninety-seven, to be refunded to the treasury, pursuant to the provisions of chapter eight hundred ninety-three, laws of eighteen hundred ninety-six.

§ 2. This act shall take effect immediately.

Chap. 332.

AN ACT to amend chapter two hundred and ninety-one of the laws of eighteen hundred and seventy, entitled "An act for the incorporation of villages," as amended by chapter five hundred and three of the laws of eighteen hundred and ninety-three, in relation to powers of boards of supervisors.

Became a law April 23, 1897, with the approval of the Governor.
Passed, three-fifths being present.

The People of the State of New York, represented in Senate and Assembly, do enact as follows:

Section 1. Section thirty-three of chapter two hundred and nine- Act amended. ty-one of the laws of eighteen hundred and seventy, entitled "An act for the incorporation of villages," as amended by chapter eight hundred and seventy of the laws of eighteen hundred and seventy-one, and chapter five hundred and three of the laws of eighteen hundred and ninety-three, is hereby amended to read as follows:

§ 33. The board of supervisors of a county, having as shown Powers of super- by the then last preceding federal or state enumeration, a popula- visors to extend tion of not more than two hundred thousand inhabitants, are bound- aries. hereby authorized and empowered to extend the boundaries of any incorporated village within such county, upon the petition of the president and a majority of the board of trustees of such village and of one-half of the electors resident within the portion of territory sought to be included, who shall be liable to be assessed for the ordinary and extraordinary expenditures of such village, if so extended, by a vote of a majority of all the supervisors elected, to be taken by yeas and nays, provided, that no act, ordinance or resolution for such purpose shall be valid and operative unless it shall receive the affirmative vote of the supervisors of the town or towns from which the additional territory is to be taken, in which such village is situated, and of the supervisor or supervisors, if any, of such village. And the said boards of supervisors are also author- Power to diminish ized and empowered to diminish the boundaries of any incorporated bound- aries. village within their respective counties, so as to exclude from such incorporation any portion of the territory embraced therein, upon the petition of two-thirds of the electors resident within the portion of territory sought to be so excluded, who shall be liable to be assessed for the ordinary and extraordinary expenditures of such village, by a vote of a majority of all the supervisors elected, to be taken by yeas and nays, provided, that no act, ordinance or resolution for such purpose shall be valid and operative unless it shall receive the affirmative vote of the supervisor or supervisors, if any,

Petition where there is no resident population. of such village. Where, in any territory proposed to be included in or excluded from any such incorporated village, there is no resident population, the petition for changing the boundaries of such village shall be signed by a majority of the electors residing within the village, who shall be liable to be assessed for the ordinary and extraordinary expenditures of such village.

§ 2. This act shall take effect immediately.

Chap. 334.

AN ACT to amend the highway law, relative to commutations of labor on highways.

Became a law April 23, 1897, with the approval of the Governor. Passed, three-fifths being present.

The People of the State of New York, represented in Senate and Assembly, do enact as follows:

Highway law amended. Section 1. Section sixty-two of chapter five hundred and sixty-eight of the laws of eighteen hundred and ninety, constituting chapter nineteen of the general laws, as amended by chapter nine hundred and seventy-three of the laws of eighteen hundred and ninety-six, is hereby amended so as to read as follows:

Commutations of labor. § 62. Every person and corporation shall work the whole number of days for which he or it shall have been assessed, except such days as shall be commuted for, at the rate of one dollar per day, and such commutation money shall be paid to the overseers of highways of the district in which the labor shall be assessed, within at least twenty-four hours before the time when the person or corporation is required to appear and work on the highways; but any corporation must pay its commutation money to the commissioners of highways of the town, who shall pay the same to the overseers of the districts respectively, in which the labor commuted for was assessed, except in the counties of Chemung, Onondaga, Columbia, Wayne, Erie, Franklin, Sullivan, Tioga, Saratoga, Broome and Orange, where such commutation money shall be paid on or before the first day of June of each year, to the commissioner or commissioners of highways of the town in which the labor shall be assessed, and such commutation money shall be expended by the commissioner or commissioners of highways upon the roads and bridges of the town as may be directed by the town board.

§ 2. This act shall take effect immediately.

Chap. 335.

AN ACT to release to Mary Ann Connolly, the right, title and interest and estate of the people of the state, in and to certain real estate in the city of Brooklyn, county of Kings.

Became a law April 23, 1897, with the approval of the Governor.
Passed, three-fifths being present.

The People of the State of New York, represented in Senate and Assembly, do enact as follows:

Section 1. All the right, title and interest of the people of the state, acquired by escheat in and to all that certain lot or parcel of land situate in the seventeenth ward of the city of Brooklyn, county of Kings, bounded and described as follows, viz.: Beginning at a point on the southerly side of K street (now called Kent street) distant four hundred and twenty-five feet easterly from the corner formed by the intersection of the southerly line of said Kent street with the easterly line of Union avenue (now called Manhattan avenue) running thence easterly along the southerly side of said Kent street, twenty-five feet, thence southerly parallel with Union avenue (now called Manhattan avenue) one hundred feet; thence westerly parallel with said Kent street, twenty-five feet, and thence northerly parallel with Union avenue (now called Manhattan avenue) one hundred feet to the point or place of beginning, is hereby released to Mary Ann Connolly, of the city of Brooklyn, county of Kings and state of New York and to her heirs and assigns forever. *Interest of state released.*

§ 2. Nothing in this act shall be construed to impair or affect the right in said real estate of any heir-at-law, devisee, grantee or creditor by mortgage, judgment or otherwise. *Proviso.*

§ 3. This act shall take effect immediately.

senting the application to the commissioners of highways, and after at least five days' notice to said commissioners of the time and place of the application to the county court, in this section provided for, by verified petition showing the applicant's right to so present the same, and that such application has been in good faith presented, and if the county judge require, on such notice to such parties interested as he shall direct, apply to the county court of the county where such highway shall be, for the appointment of three commissioners to determine upon the necessity of such highway proposed to be laid out or altered, or to the uselessness of the highway proposed to be discontinued and to assess the damages by reason of the laying out, opening, altering or discontinuing of such highway. Such application to the county court shall be accompanied by the written undertaking of the applicant executed by one or more sureties, approved by the county judge, to the effect that if the commissioners appointed determine that the proposed highway or alteration is not necessary or that the highway proposed to be discontinued is not useless, the sureties will pay to the commissioners their compensation at the rate of four dollars for each day necessarily spent and all costs and expenses necessarily incurred in the performance of their duties, which amount shall not exceed the sum of fifty dollars.

§ 2. Section ninety-two of chapter five hundred and sixty-eight of the laws of eighteen hundred and ninety is hereby amended to read as follows:

§ 99. Costs, by whom paid.—In all cases of assessments of damages by commissioners appointed by the court, the costs thereof shall be paid by the town except when reassessment of damages shall be had on the application of the party for whom the damages were assessed, and such damages shall not be increased on such reassessment, the costs shall be paid by the party applying for the reassessment; and when application shall be made by two or more persons for the reassessment of damages, all persons who may be liable for costs under this section shall be liable in proportion to the amount of damages respectively assessed to them by the first assessment, and may be recovered by action in favor of any person entitled to the same. Each commissioner appointed by the court, for each day necessarily employed as such, shall be entitled to four dollars and his necessary expenses.

§ 3. This act shall take effect immediately.

Chap. 345.

AN ACT to amend the insurance law, in relation to the exemption from execution of money or aid provided by life or casualty insurance corporations upon the co-operative or assessment plan.

Became a law April 23, 1897, with the approval of the Governor.
Passed, three-fifths being present.

The People of the State of New York, represented in Senate and Assembly, do enact as follows:

Section 1. Section two hundred and twelve of chapter six hundred and ninety of the laws of eighteen hundred and ninety-two, entitled "An act in relation to insurance corporations, constituting chapter thirty-eight of the general laws," is hereby amended to read as follows:

§ 212 Exemption from execution.—The money or other benefit, charity, relief or aid, paid or to be paid, provided or rendered by any such corporation, association or society shall not be liable to be seized, taken or appropriated by any legal or equitable process, to pay any debt or liability of a member, or any debt or liability of the widow of a deceased member of such corporation designated as the beneficiary thereof, which was incurred before such money was paid to her or such benefit, charity, relief or aid was provided or rendered.

§ 2. This act shall take effect immediately.

Chap. 346.

AN ACT creating the office of commissioner of jurors for each of the counties of the state of New York having a population of more than two hundred thousand and less than three hundred thousand.

Became a law April 23, 1897, with the approval of the Governor.
Passed, three-fifths being present.

The People of the State of New York, represented in Senate and Assembly, do enact as follows:

Section 1. The office of commissioner of jurors is hereby created, Office created. for each county of the state having a population of more than two hundred thousand and less than three hundred thousand, as appears by the last enumeration of the inhabitants of the state.

Appointment and term of commissioners.

§ 2. Within thirty days after the passage of this act, the justices of the supreme court residing in any such county, and the county judge thereof, or a majority of them, shall appoint a suitable person to be commissioner of jurors, who shall be a resident of the county, and, if a lawyer, shall not, while holding such office, directly or indirectly, engage in the practice of law. The appointment shall be made in writing, and signed by the judges making the same, and filed in the office of the clerk of such county. The commissioner, so appointed, shall, unless removed, hold office for five years and until his successors shall be appointed and qualified. The said judges may at any time remove such commissioner, and appoint a successor, and they shall appoint a commissioner to fill any vacancy that may occur in that office. The said commissioner may also be removed at any time by an order of any court of record in such county, except the surrogate's court, after notice to such commissioner, for a failure to perform his duties, as required by this act. The said commissioner, when so appointed, shall be an officer of the courts of record in such county.

Removal.

Annual salary.

§ 3. The commissioner shall receive an annual salary, to be fixed by the judges aforesaid, or a majority of them, not to exceed three thousand dollars, payable in monthly installments, by the county treasurer of such county.

Rooms and supplies.

§ 4. The commissioner, until the board of supervisors shall make suitable provision therefor, shall procure suitable rooms and accommodations, and the necessary supplies for his office, with all books, blanks, stationery and printing required for the proper discharge of his duties; and all expenses incurred by him in his office, including the expense of summoning jurors for examination, shall be audited by the judges having the power of appointment, or by any two of them, and shall be paid by the treasurer of such county.

Expenses.

Lists of persons liable to jury duty.

§ 5. The supervisor of each of the wards and towns of such county, within thirty days after written notice to him, given by such commissioner, shall prepare, certify and file with such commissioner, a list of all persons, residing within his town or ward, qualified to serve as trial jurors. At any time thereafter, whenever required by said commissioner, the supervisor of each ward and town shall make an additional list of persons liable to jury duty in his town or ward. On failure of any supervisor to make and file such list, the commissioner shall have power to make it.

Oath of office.

§ 6. Before entering upon the discharge of the duties of his office, the commissioner shall take and subscribe the oath of office prescribed by the constitution, and file the same with the clerk of such county. He shall make and enter, in alphabetical order, in a book kept for that purpose, a list of all persons returned to him by the supervisors of such county, as persons qualified for jury duty, and all such other persons as said commissioner shall, from time to time, ascertain or believe to be qualified for jury duty in such county. *Record of lists of persons qualified.*

§ 7. The commissioner shall have power, upon a notice of not less than three days, to summon, or cause to be summoned, before him, at such time and place in the town or city where the person so summoned resides, as he shall deem expedient, every person whose name shall be upon the list aforesaid, and shall examine such person, under oath, as to his qualifications to serve as a juror, and shall himself investigate and report such facts as he may learn as to the qualification for, and liability to, jury duty of any person on the said list, and shall preserve such examination and information, and file the same in his office as a public record. No exemption from liability to serve as a juror shall be allowed, unless claimed on such examination. *Examinations as to qualifications.*

§ 8. On or before the first Monday of November in each year the commissioner shall revise the list of jurors by striking therefrom the names of all persons found to be entitled to exemption from jury duty and all persons found to be not qualified for jury duty, subject to such revision from time to time by the justices of the supreme court residing in such county, and the county judge of such county, or a majority of them, as they deem proper. The commissioner shall then make and file in his office a revised list of all the names of persons so found qualified and liable for jury duty. The same shall thereafter be a public record, and shall be the list from which all jurors shall thereafter be drawn for trial of issues of fact in civil and criminal cases, and for grand jurors in such county until a new list shall be filed. All persons whose names are on the list as qualified for trial jurors shall be deemed to be qualified to serve as grand jurors in such county. *Revision of lists.* *Revised list.* *Grand jurors.*

§ 9. When such list is completed, the commissioner shall cause the name and residence of each person thereon to be written or printed upon a separate slip of paper, and shall deposit said slips in a box prepared therefor, which shall then be, in the presence of at least two of said judges, sealed and locked and delivered to the clerk of such county, and, from it, or the names remaining therein, *Preparation and deposit of slips.*

Drawing of juries. all trial and grand jurors for service in courts of record, in such county, shall thereafter be drawn, as provided by law. Such partial lists as may be made under the provisions of this act may be used instead of the completed lists herein provided for, until the completion of such lists.

Boxes and lists for towns and cities. § 10. The commissioner of jurors shall provide and furnish to the clerk of each town in such county, and to the clerk of any court, not of record, in any city of such county, a box containing slips as aforesaid, of the names of such persons, from the county list, as shall be liable to jury duty in such town or city, together with a list, alphabetically arranged, of the names in the box so furnished.

Drawing of juries for courts therein. All juries in both civil and criminal cases, in the courts of such towns and cities shall be drawn, as provided by law, from the names so furnished for such towns and cities.

Certain acts contempt of court. § 11. A person who willfully refuses or neglects to obey any lawful mandate, order or direction of the commissioner of jurors, or who shall hinder, delay, or obstruct the service of any process issued by said commissioner, or who shall willfully refuse or neglect to appear, or who shall refuse to answer any question touching his qualifications as a juror, shall be deemed guilty of a contempt of court, and shall be punishable accordingly.

Certain acts misdemeanors. § 12. Any person who shall do any act, whereby he or another shall be placed, or attempted to be placed, upon the jury list, or omitted from, or attempted to be omitted from, said list, contrary to the provisions of this act, and not specified in section eleven, shall be guilty of a misdemeanor.

Continuation of drawings under law. § 13. The trial and grand jurors of such counties shall continue to be drawn as now prescribed by law, until the first Monday of November, eighteen hundred and ninety-seven.

Repeal. § 14. All acts, or parts of acts, inconsistent with this act, and applicable to such counties, are hereby repealed.

§ 15. This act shall take effect immediately.

Chap. 347.

AN ACT to amend the tax law, in relation to the exemption from taxation of real property purchased with the proceeds of a pension.

Became a law April 23, 1897, with the approval of the Governor.
Passed, three-fifths being present.

The People of the State of New York, represented in Senate and Assembly, do enact as follows:

Section 1. Subdivision five of section four of chapter nine hundred and eight of the laws of eighteen hundred and ninety-six, entitled " An act in relation to taxation, constituting chapter twenty-four of the general laws," is hereby amended to read as follows. Tax law amended.

5. All property exempt by law from execution, other than an exempt homestead. But real property purchased with the proceeds of a pension granted by the United States for military or naval services, and owned and occupied by the pensioner, or by his wife or widow, is subject to taxation as herein provided. Such property shall be assessed in the same manner as other real property in the tax districts. At the meeting of the assessors to hear the complaints concerning assessments, a verified application for the exemption of such real property from taxation may be presented to them by or on behalf of the owner thereof, which application must show the facts on which the exemption is claimed, including the amount of pension money used in or toward the purchase of such property. If the assessors are satisfied that the applicant is entitled to the exemption, and that the amount of pension money used in the purchase of such property equals or exceeds the assessed valuation thereof, they shall enter the word " exempt " upon the assessment-roll opposite the description of such property. If the amount of such pension money used in the purchase of the property is less than the assessed valuation, they shall enter upon the assessment-roll the words " exempt to the extent of .... dollars " (naming the amount) and thereupon such real property, to the extent of the exemption entered by the assessors, shall be exempt from state, county and general municipal taxation, but shall be taxable for local school purposes, and for the construction and maintenance of streets and highways. If no application for exemption Exemption and assessment of property purchased with pension money.

be granted, the property shall be subject to taxation for all purposes. The entries above required shall be made and continued in each assessment of the property so long as it is exempt from taxation for any purpose. The provisions herein, relating to the assessment and exemption of property purchased with a pension apply and shall be enforced in each municipal corporation authorized to levy taxes.

§ 2. This act shall take effect immediately.

Chap. 348.

AN ACT to amend the code of civil procedure, relative to the seizure and sale of real property purchased with the proceeds of a pension.

Became a law April 23, 1897, with the approval of the Governor. Passed, three-fifths being present.

The People of the State of New York, represented in Senate and Assembly, do enact as follows:

Section 1. Section thirteen hundred and ninety-three of the code of civil procedure, is hereby amended to read as follows:

§ 1393. **Military pay, rewards, et cetera, exempt from execution and other legal proceedings.**–The pay and bounty of a non-commissioned officer, musician or private in the military or naval service of the United States or the state of New York; a land warrant, pension or other reward heretofore or hereafter granted by the United States, or by a state, for military or naval services; a sword, horse, medal, emblem or devise of any kind presented as a testimonial for services rendered in the military or naval service of the United States or a state; and the uniform, arms and equipments which were used by a person in that service, are also exempt from levy and sale, by virtue of an execution, and from seizure for non-payment of taxes, or in any other legal proceeding; except that real property purchased with the proceeds of a pension granted by the United States for military or naval services, and owned by the pensioner, or by his wife or widow, is subject to seizure and sale for the collection of taxes or assessments lawfully levied thereon.

§ 2. This act shall take effect September first, eighteen hundred and ninety-seven.

Chap. 349.

AN ACT conferring upon the board of claims jurisdiction to hear, audit and determine the claim of George F. Gallagher against the state and to make an award therefor.

Became a law April 23, 1897, with the approval of the Governor.
Passed, three-fifths being present.

The People of the State of New York, represented in Senate and Assembly, do enact as follows:

Section 1. Jurisdiction is hereby conferred upon the board of claims to hear, audit and determine the alleged claim of George F. Gallagher against the state for the purchase price of three Gallagher settings and furnaces sold, delivered and furnished to the state industrial school at Rochester on the sixth day of June, eighteen hundred and ninety-two, upon the request and under the authority of the superintendent and managers of the said state industrial school, and award thereon such sums as the said board shall deem just and reasonable, although said alleged claim may have accrued more than two years prior to the time when it is filed. · [Jurisdiction to hear claim.]

§ 2. Either party may take an appeal to the appellate division of the supreme court, third department, from the award made under authority of this act, provided said appeal is taken by service of a notice of appeal within thirty days after service of a copy of the award. [Appeal from award.]

§ 3. This act shall take effect immediately.

Chap. 350.

AN ACT conferring jurisdiction upon the court of claims to hear, audit and determine the claim of George H. Pierce and Clement B. Brun, composing the firm of Pierce and Brun, against the state.

Became a law April 23, 1897, with the approval of the Governor.
Passed, three-fifths being present.

The People of the State of New York, represented in Senate and Assembly, do enact as follows:

Section 1. Jurisdiction is hereby conferred upon the court of claims to hear, audit and determine the alleged claim of George H. Pierce and Clement B. Brun, composing the firm of Pierce and [Jurisdiction to hear claim.]

Brun against the state, for work, labor and services performed,
and for property and materials furnished either or both
and for money alleged to have been paid, laid out and expended by
them, in the preparation and furnishing of sketches, plans, specification and working drawings for the state normal school at
Jamaica, and award thereon such sums as a reasonable compensation as, in the judgment of said court shall be just and equitable not
exceeding forty-five hundred dollars, although such claim may have
accrued more than two years prior to the time when it is filed; provided, however, that such claim shall be filed with said court within
one year after the passage of this act.

Appeal
from
award.

§ 2. Either party may take an appeal from any award made under
authority of this act, to the appellate division of the supreme court
of the third department provided such appeal be taken by service
of a notice of appeal within thirty days of a service of a copy of the
award.

§ 3. This act shall take effect immediately.

Chap. 351.

AN ACT conferring upon the board of claims jurisdiction to hear,
audit and determine the claim of William Foster Kelly against
the state and to make an award therefor.

Became a law April 23, 1897, with the approval of the Governor.
Passed, three-fifths being present.

*The People of the State of New York, represented in Senate and
Assembly, do enact as follows:*

Jurisdic-
tion to
hear claim.

Section 1. Jurisdiction is hereby conferred upon the board of
claims to hear, audit and determine the alleged claim of William Foster Kelly against the state for work, labor and services performed
and money paid out and expended by him as architect in preparing
and draughting, upon the request and under the authority
of the managers of the Western House of Refuge for Women at
Albion, plans, studies and specifications in competition for the
construction of the building erected by the state for the uses and purposes of such Western House of Refuge for Women, and to award
thereon such sums as said board shall deem just and reasonable,
although such claim may have accrued more than two years prior
to the time when it is filed.

§ 2. Either party may take an appeal to the appellate division of the supreme court, third department, from the award made under authority of this act, provided said appeal is taken by service of a notice of appeal within thirty days after service of a copy of the award. *Appeal from award.*

§ 3. This act shall take effect immediately.

Chap. 352.

AN ACT making an appropriation for continuing work on the capitol.

Became a law April 23, 1897, with the approval of the Governor.
Passed, three-fifths being present.

The People of the State of New York, represented in Senate and Assembly, do enact as follows:

Section 1. The sum of one million two hundred and fifty thousand dollars, or so much thereof as may be necessary, is hereby appropriated out of any money in the treasury belonging to the general fund, not otherwise appropriated, for continuing work on the capitol in pursuance of any contract or contracts heretofore entered into by the capitol commissioners, pursuant to the provisions of chapter seven hundred and thirty-seven of the laws of eighteen hundred and ninety-five, or which may hereafter be entered into by the superintendent of public works, pursuant to the provisions of chapter seventy-eight of the laws of eighteen hundred and ninety-seven, for the construction and completion of the unfinished portions of the capitol and the laying out of the capitol grounds, and for the payment of the sums due or to become due on any such contracts heretofore or hereafter made. Eight hundred thousand dollars of the sum hereby appropriated shall be available immediately, but the balance, four hundred and fifty thousand dollars, shall not be available until May first, eighteen hundred and ninety-eight. Such money shall be payable by the treasurer upon the audit and warrant of the comptroller, on certificates of the capitol commissioner approved by the superintendent of public works. *Appropriation for work on capitol.* *When available.*

§ 2. This act shall take effect immediately.

Chap. 354.

AN ACT authorizing the superintendent of banks to issue a certificate to do business to the First State bank of Canisteo, New York.

Became a law April 23, 1897, with the approval of the Governor.
Passed, a majority being present.

The People of the State of New York, represented in Senate and Assembly, do enact as follows:

Section 1. The superintendent of banks is hereby authorized to accept and file the certificate of incorporation of the First State bank at Canisteo, New York, and to issue a certificate, under the banking laws, authorizing such bank to do business, notwithstanding the fact that the capital of such bank does not exceed twenty-five thousand dollars, and that the population of such village as appears by the last federal census is more than two thousand.

§ 2. This act shall take effect immediately.

Chap. 367.

AN ACT to amend the code of civil procedure, relative to an assistant clerk.

Became a law April 24, 1897, with the approval of the Governor.
Passed, three-fifths being present.

The People of the State of New York, represented in Senate and Assembly, do enact as follows:

Code amended.

Section 1. Section two hundred and twenty-one of the code of civil procedure is hereby amended by adding thereto two subdivisions, to read as follows:

Assistant clerk for fourth appellate division.

Subd. 1. The presiding justice of the appellate division of the fourth department shall, with the approval of the other justices of said department, have power to appoint and remove an assistant to the clerk of said appellate division, who shall be paid an annual salary of one thousand dollars. A certificate of the appointment of such assistant clerk, signed by the justices of the said fourth department, shall be filed with the comptroller of the state, and the salary hereby established for such assistant clerk shall be paid by the said comptroller to such appointee quarterly.

Subd. 2. The clerk of the appellate division of the fourth depart- _{Compen-
sation for} ment, in addition to the salary herein provided, shall be entitled to _{clerk and
assistant.} receive his necessary disbursements for postage, telephone, telegraph and express charges, to be certified by the presiding justice of said department and to be paid in the same manner as his salary. And the compensation herein provided for said clerk and said assistant clerk shall be in lieu of all fees and charges, and neither said clerk nor assistant clerk shall hereafter be permitted to charge or receive any fee whatever in addition to his salary, for any official service rendered by him.

§ 2. This act shall take effect immediately.

Chap. 368.

AN ACT to amend section eighty-nine of the code of criminal procedure, in relation to undertakings.

**Became a law April 24, 1897, with the approval of the Governor.
Passed, a majority being present.**

The People of the State of New York, represented in Senate and Assembly, do enact as follows:

Section 1. Section eighty-nine of the code of criminal procedure _{Amend-
ment.} is hereby amended so as to read as follows:

§ 89. If, however, there be just reason to fear the commission _{Undertak-
ings.} of the crime, the person complained of may be required to enter into an undertaking, in such sum, not exceeding one thousand dollars, as the magistrate may direct, with one or more sufficient sureties, to abide the order of the next county court of the county, held for the trial of indictments, and in the meantime to keep the peace toward the people of this state, and particularly toward the complainant.

§ 2. This act shall take effect September first, eighteen hundred _{When
takes
effect.} and ninety-seven.

Chap. 369.

AN ACT to amend the tax law, in relation to the payment of organization tax by railroad corporations.

Became a law April 24, 1897, with the approval of the Governor.
Passed, three-fifths being present.

The People of the State of New York, represented in Senate and Assembly, do enact as follows:

Section 1. Section one hundred and eighty of chapter nine hundred and eight of the laws of eighteen hundred and ninety-six, entitled "An act in relation to taxation, constituting chapter twenty-four of the general laws," is hereby amended to read as follows:

§ 180. **Organization tax.**— Every stock corporation incorporated under any law of this state shall pay to the state treasurer a tax of one-eighth of one per centum upon the amount of capital stock which the corporation is authorized to have, and a like tax upon any subsequent increase. Such tax shall be due and payable upon the incorporation of such corporation or upon the increase of its capital stock. Except in the case of a railroad corporation, neither the secretary of state nor county clerk shall file any certificate of incorporation or article of association, or give any certificate to any such corporation or association until he is furnished a receipt for such tax from the state treasurer, and no stock corporation shall have or exercise any corporate franchise or powers, or carry on business in this state until such tax shall have been paid. In case of the consolidation of existing corporations into a corporation, such new corporation shall be required to pay the tax hereinbefore provided for only upon the amount of its capital stock in excess of the aggregate amount of capital stock of said corporations. This section shall not apply to state and national banks or to building, mutual loan, accumulating fund and co-operative associations. A railroad corporation need not pay such tax at the time of filing its certificate of incorporation, but shall pay the same before the railroad commissioners shall grant a certificate, as required by the railroad law, authorizing the construction of the road as proposed in its articles of association, and such certificate shall not be granted by the board of railroad commissioners until it is furnished with a receipt for such tax from the state treasurer.

§ 2. This act shall take effect immediately.

Chap. 371.

AN ACT to amend chapter nine hundred and eight of the laws of eighteen hundred and ninety-six, entitled "An act in relation to taxation, constituting chapter twenty-four of the general laws."

Became a law April 24, 1897, with the approval of the Governor.
Passed, three-fifths being present.

The People of the State of New York, represented in Senate and Assembly, do enact as follows:

Section 1. Subdivision seven of section four of chapter nine hundred and eight of the laws of eighteen hundred and ninety-six, entitled "An act in relation to taxation, constituting chapter twenty-four of the general laws," is hereby amended so as to read as follows:

7. The real property of a corporation or association organized exclusively for the moral or mental improvement of men or women, or for religious, bible, tract, charitable, benevolent, missionary, hospital, infirmary, educational, scientific, literary, library, patriotic, historical or cemetery purposes, or for the enforcement of laws relating to children or animals, or for two or more such purposes, and used exclusively for carrying out thereupon one or more of such purposes; and the personal property of any such corporation shall be exempt from taxation. But no such corporation or association shall be entitled to any such exemption if any officer, member or employe thereof shall receive or may be lawfully entitled to receive any pecuniary profit from the operations thereof except reasonable compensation for services in effecting one or more of such purposes, or as proper beneficiaries of its strictly charitable purposes; or if the organization thereof, for any such avowed purposes be a guise or pretense for directly or indirectly making any other pecuniary profit for such corporation or association, or for any of its members or employes, or if it be not in good faith organized or conducted exclusively for one or more of such purposes. The real property of any such corporation or association entitled to such exemption held by it exclusively for one or more of such purposes and from which no rents, profits or income are derived, shall be so exempt, though not in actual use therefor by reason of the absence of suitable buildings or improvements thereon, if the construction of such buildings or improvements is in progress, or is in good faith contemplated by such corporation or association. The real property of any such corporation not so

Tax law amended.

Exemption of property of religious, etc., corporations.

Proviso as to exemption.

Exemption of property not in actual use.

Exemption of leased property. used exclusively for carrying out thereupon one or more of such purposes, but leased or otherwise used for other purposes, shall not be exempt, but if a portion only of any lot or building of any such corporation or association is used exclusively for carrying out thereupon one or more such purposes of any such corporation or association, then such lot or building shall be so exempt only to the extent of the value of the portion so used, and the remaining or other portion to the extent of the value of such remaining or other portion shall be subject to taxation; pro-

Proviso as to hospital property. vided, however, that a lot or building owned, and actually used for hospital purposes, by a free public hospital, depending for maintenance and support upon voluntary charity shall not be taxed as to a portion thereof leased or otherwise used for the purposes of income, when such income is necessary for, and is actually applied to, the maintenance and support of such hospital.

Property held by officers of religious corporation. Property held by any officer of a religious denomination shall be entitled to the same exemptions, subject to the same conditions and exceptions, as property held by a religious corporation.

§ 2. This act shall take effect immediately.

Chap. 373.

AN ACT to amend chapter nine hundred and eight of the laws of eighteen hundred and ninety-six, entitled "An act in relation to taxation, constituting chapter twenty-four of the general laws," in relation to notices of tax sales.

Became a law April 24, 1897, with the approval of the Governor.

Passed, three-fifths being present.

The People of the State of New York, represented in Senate and Assembly, do enact as follows:

Section 1. Section one hundred and thirty-eight of chapter nine hundred and eight of the laws of eighteen hundred and ninety-six, is hereby amended to read as follows:

§ 138. **Lien of mortgage not affected by tax sale.** — The lien of a mortgage, duly recorded or registered at the time of the sale of any lands for non-payment of any tax or assessment thereon, shall not be destroyed, or in any manner affected, except as provided in this section. The purchaser at any such sale shall give to the mortgagee a written notice of such sale within one year from the expiration of the time to redeem, and in case of tax sales heretofore held, where the time of redemption by mortgagees has not

expired, within three years from the passage of this act, requiring
him to pay the amount of purchase-money, with interest at the
rate allowed by law in case of redemption by occupants, within
six months after giving the notice. Such notice may be given
either personally or in the manner required by law in respect to
notices of non-acceptance or non-payment of notes or bills of exchange, and a notarial certificate thereof shall be presumptive evidence of the fact that may be recorded in the county in which the
mortgage was recorded, in the same manner and with the same
effect as a deed or other evidence of title of real property.

§ 2. Section one hundred and thirty-nine of said act is hereby
amended to read as follows:

§ 139. **Redemption by mortgagee before notice.**— The holder of
any mortgage which is duly recorded at the time of the sale, may,
at any time after the sale of all or any part of the mortgaged premises for unpaid taxes, and before the expiration of six months from
the giving of the notice required by this article to be given to a
mortgagee, redeem the premises so sold, or any part thereof from
such sale. The redemption shall be made by filing with the comptroller a written description of his mortgage, and by paying to
the state treasurer, upon the certificate of the comptroller, for the
use of the purchaser, his heirs or assigns, the sum mentioned in
his certificate, with interest at the rate allowed by law in case of
redemption by occupants from the date of such certificate. The
holder of such mortgage shall have a lien upon the premises redeemed for the amount so paid with interest from the time of payment, in like manner as if it had been included in the mortgage.
Provided, however, that the notice required to be given under this
and the last preceding section shall be directed only to such persons as shall within two years from the time of such sale, and in
case of all sales heretofore held where the time allowed by law for
redemption by mortgagees has not expired, within two years from
the passage of this act, file in the office of the comptroller a notice,
stating the names of the mortgagor and mortgagee, the date of
the mortgage, and the amount claimed to be due thereon, and the
county, town and tract in which the mortgaged premises are situated, with the number of the lot on which said mortgage is claimed
to be a lien, with the name of the person or persons claiming notice,
their residence, and the post-office to which such notice shall be
addressed.

§ 3. This act shall take effect immediately.

Chap. 377.

AN ACT to amend subdivision ten of section four of chapter thirty-nine of the general laws, known as the railroad law, so as to enable stockholders to assent to mortgages thereby authorized.

Became a law May 3, 1897, with the approval of the Governor.
Passed, three-fifths being present.

The People of the State of New York, represented in Senate and Assembly, do enact as follows:

Railroad law amended.

Section 1. Subdivision ten of section four of chapter thirty-nine of the general laws, known as the "railroad law," is hereby amended so as to enable stockholders to assent to mortgages thereby authorized, and so as to read as follows, namely:

Power to borrow money and mortgage property.

10. From time to time to borrow such sums of money as may be necessary for completing and finishing or operating its railroad, and to issue and dispose of its bonds for any amount so borrowed, and to mortgage its property and franchises to secure the payment of any debts contracted by the company for the purposes aforesaid.

Assent of stockholders.

But no such mortgage, except purchase money mortgages, shall be issued without either the consent of the stockholders owning at least two-thirds of the stock of the corporation, which consent shall be in writing, and shall be filed and recorded in the office of the clerk or register of the county where it has its principal place of business; or else the consent by their votes of stockholders owning at least two-thirds of the stock of the corporation which is represented and voted upon in person or by proxy at a meeting called for that purpose upon a notice stating the time, place and object of the meeting, served at least three weeks previously upon each stockholder personally, or mailed to him at his postoffice address, and also published at least once a week for three weeks successively in some newspaper printed in the city, town or county where such corporation has its principal office; and a certificate of the vote at such meeting, signed and sworn to by the chairman and secretary of such meeting, shall be filed and recorded as aforesaid.

§ 2. This act shall take effect immediately.

Chap. 379.

AN ACT to amend chapter nine hundred and nine of the laws of eighteen hundred and ninety-six, known as the election law, and entitled " An act in relation to the elections, constituting chapter six of the general laws."

Became a law May 6, 1897, with the approval of the Governor.
Passed, three-fifths being present.

The People of the State of New York, represented in Senate and Assembly, do enact as follows:

Section 1. Section five of chapter nine hundred and nine of the laws of eighteen hundred and ninety-six, being an act entitled " An act in relation to the elections, constituting chapter six of the general laws," is hereby amended to read as follows:

NOTICE OF ELECTIONS BY SECRETARY OF STATE AND COUNTY CLERK.

§ 5. The secretary of state shall, at least three months before each general election, make and transmit to the county clerk of each county, and the police board of The City of New York, a notice under his hand and official seal, stating the day upon which such election shall be held, and stating each officer, except city, village and town officers, who may be lawfully voted for at such election by the electors of such county or any part thereof. If any such officer is to be elected to fill a vacancy, the notice shall so state. The secretary of state shall forthwith, upon the filing in his office of the governor's proclamation ordering a special election, make and transmit to each county clerk and to the police board of The City of New York, a like notice of the officers to be voted for at such special election in such county or city or any part thereof, and cause such proclamation to be published in the newspapers published in such county having large circulation therein, at least once a week until such election shall be held. Each county clerk shall forthwith, upon the receipt of either such notice, file and record it in his office, and shall cause a copy of such notice to be published once in each week until the election therein specified in the newspapers designated to publish election notices. He shall also publish as a part of such notice, each city, village and town officer who may lawfully be voted for at such election by the electors of such county or any part thereof.

§ 2. Section six of said act is hereby amended so as to read as follows:

NOTICE OF SUBMISSION OF PROPOSED CONSTITUTIONAL AMENDMENTS OR
OTHER PROPOSITIONS OR QUESTIONS.

§ 6. Every amendment to the constitution proposed by the legislature, unless otherwise provided by law, shall be submitted to the
people for approval at the next general election, after action by
the legislature in accordance with the constitution; and whenever
any such proposed amendment to the constitution or other proposition, or question provided by law to be submitted to a popular vote,
shall be submitted to the people for their approval, the secretary
of state shall include in his notice to the county clerk and the police
board of The City of New York, of the general election, a copy of
such amendment, proposition or question, and if more than one
such amendment, proposition or question is to be voted upon at
such election, such amendment, proposition or question, respectively, shall be separately and consecutively numbered. If such
amendment, proposition or question is to be submitted at a special
election, the secretary of state shall, at least twenty days before the
election, make and transmit to each county clerk and the police
board of The City of New York a like notice. Each county clerk
shall, forthwith upon the receipt of such notice, file and record it in
his office, and shall cause a copy of such notice to be published
once a week until the election therein specified, in the newspapers
designated to publish election notices.

§ 3. Section eight of said act is hereby amended so as to read as
follows:

CREATION, DIVISION AND ALTERATION OF ELECTION DISTRICTS.

§ 8. Every town, or ward of a city, not subdivided into election
districts shall be an election district. The town board of every
town containing more than four hundred electors, and the common
council of every city except New York, in which there shall be a
ward containing more than four hundred electors, shall, on or before the first day of July in each year, whenever necessary so to do,
divide such town or ward respectively into election districts, each
of which shall be compact in form, wholly within the town or ward,
and shall contain respectively as near as may be, four hundred
electors, but no such ward or town shall be again divided into
election districts until, at some general election, the number of
votes cast in one or more districts thereof shall exceed six hundred;
and in such a case the redivision shall apply only to the town or
ward in which such district is situated. If any part of a city shall
be within a town, the town board shall divide into election districts

only that part of the town which is outside of the city. No election
district including any part of a city shall include any part of a
town outside of a city. A town or a ward of a city containing less
than four hundred electors may, at least thirty days before the
election or appointment (where appointment is directed to be made
by law) of inspectors of election of such town or ward, be divided
into election districts by the board or other body charged with such
duty when, in the judgment of such board or body, the
convenience of the electors shall be promoted thereby. The
creation, division or alteration of an election district outside of a
city shall take effect immediately after the next town meeting,
and at such next town meeting inspectors of election shall be
elected for each election district as constituted by such creation,
division or alteration. If the creation, division or alteration of
an election district is rendered necessary by the creation or alteration of a town, or ward of a city, it shall take effect immediately,
but a new town or ward shall not be created, and no
new town or ward shall be subdivided into election districts between the first day of August of any year, and the day of the general election next thereafter. If inspectors are not elected or appointed for such district outside of a city before September the first
next thereafter, the town board of the town shall appoint four inspectors of election for such district. If a town shall include a
city, or a portion of a city, only such election districts as are wholly
outside of the city shall be deemed election districts of the town,
except for the purpose of town meetings. The police board of The
City of New York shall divide such city into election districts on or
before the first day of July in any year whenever necessary so to
do as hereinafter provided. The election districts existing pursuant to the provisions of law in the year eighteen hundred and
ninety-seven in the counties of New York and Kings shall continue with their present boundaries until at some general election
for the office of governor the number of registered electors therein
shall exceed six hundred, provided, however, that any election district containing less than seventy-five electors in such counties,
made necessary by the crossing of congressional lines with other
political divisions, may be consolidated with contiguous election districts in any year when no representative in congress is to be voted
for in such districts. On or before the first day of July in the year
eighteen hundred and ninety-eight the police board of The City of
New York shall divide that portion of such city that is outside the

counties of New York and Kings into election districts which shall
be compact in form and shall contain as near as may be four hundred electors as shown by the registration of electors for the general
election held therein in the year eighteen hundred and ninety-seven.
Such election districts so established in The City of New York shall
not again be changed until at some general election for the office
of governor the number of registered electors therein shall exceed
six hundred, except where changes are made necessary by a change
in the boundaries of congressional, senate or assembly districts or
ward lines, provided, however, that when the number of registered
electors in any election district shall for two consecutive years, be
less than two hundred and fifty, such district may be consolidated
with contiguous election districts in the discretion of said police
board.   In that portion of The City of New York within the county
of New York each election district shall be compact in form entirely
within an assembly district and numbered in consecutive order
therein respectively.   In that portion of The City of New York outside of the county of New York each election district shall be compact in form, entirely within a ward and numbered in consecutive
order therein respectively.   Except as heretofore provided no election district shall contain portions of two counties, or two congressional, senate or assembly districts or two wards.   Each town and
each part of a town included in The City of New York, as constituted by the Greater New York charter, shall be respectively
deemed to be a ward within the meaning of this section.

§ 4. Section ten of said act is hereby amended so as to read as
follows:

DESIGNATION OF PLACES FOR REGISTRY AND VOTING, PUBLICATION OF SAME,
AND PROVISION OF FURNITURE THEREFOR.

§ 10. On the first Tuesday of September in each year, the town
board of each town, and the common council of each city, except
New York, and the police board of The City of New York, shall designate the place in each election district in the city or town at
which the meeting for the registration of electors and the election
shall be held during the year.   Each room so designated shall be of
a reasonable size, sufficient to admit and comfortably accommodate at least ten electors at a time outside of the guard rails.   No
building, or part of a building, shall be so designated in any city if
within thirty days before such designation, intoxicating liquors,
ale or beer, shall have been sold in any part thereof.   No room
shall be designated elsewhere in a city, if within thirty days before

such designation, intoxicating liquors, ale or beer, shall have been sold in such room, or in a room adjoining thereto, with a door or passage-way between the two rooms. No intoxicating liquors, ale or beer shall be sold in such building in a city or such room or adjoining room elsewhere after such designation and before the general election next thereafter, or be allowed in any room in which an election is held during the day of the election or the canvass of the votes. Any person or persons violating the provisions of this section shall be deemed guilty of a misdemeanor. If any place so designated shall thereafter and before the close of the election be destroyed, or for any reason become unfit for use, or can not for any reason be used for such purpose, the officers charged with the designation of a place for such election shall forthwith designate some other suitable place for holding such election. Not more than one polling place shall be in the same room, and not more than two polling places shall be in the same building. The officers authorized to designate such places in any town or city, shall provide for each polling place at such election, the necessary ballot and other boxes, guard rails, voting booths and supplies therein, and the other furniture of such polling place, necessary for the lawful conduct of each election thereat, shall preserve the same when not in use, and shall deliver all such ballot and other boxes for each polling place, with the keys thereof, to the inspectors of election of each election district at least one-half hour before the opening of the polls at each election. The officers authorized to designate the registration and polling places in any city, except The City of New York, shall cause to be published in two newspapers within such city a list of such places so designated, and the boundaries of each election district in which such registration and polling place is located. Such publication shall be made in the newspapers so selected upon each day of registration and the day of election, and on the day prior to each such days. One of such newspapers so selected shall be one which advocates the principles of the political party polling the highest number of votes in the state at the last preceding election for governor, and the other newspaper so designated shall be one which advocates the principles of the political party polling the next highest number of votes for governor at said election. The police board of The City of New York shall cause to be published in two newspapers in each county wholly or partly within such city a list of the registration and polling places so designated in each borough in such respective counties and the boundaries of each election district therein in which such registration and polling place is located; except that in the borough of Brooklyn, such publication shall be made in the newspapers designated to publish corporation notices therein. Such publication shall be made in such newspapers upon each day of registration and the day of election and on the day prior to each of such days. Such publications shall be made in the newspapers published in such counties which shall respectively advocate the principles of the political parties which at the last preceding election for governor respectively cast the largest and next largest number of votes in the state'for such office. The said police board shall also cause to be published in the City Record on or before the first day of registration in each year a complete list of all the registration and polling places so designated and the boundaries of the election districts in which such places are located arranged in numerical order under the designation of the respective boroughs in which they are located. In selecting the newspapers in which such publications are to be made the said board shall keep in view the object of giving the widest publicity thereto.

§ 5. Section twelve of said act is hereby amended so as to read as follows:

APPOINTMENT AND QUALIFICATIONS OF ELECTION OFFICERS IN CITIES.

§ 12. On or before the first day of October in each year, the police board of The City of New York and the mayor of each other city, shall select and appoint the election officers for each election district in their respective cities; and shall severally have the power to fill all vacancies which may arise before the opening of the polls on election day. To insure the bipartisan character of such board or body of election officers required by the election law, each political party entitled to representation in such board or body shall have the right, not later than the first day of August in each year, to prepare and file with the board or officer empowered to make the appointments as herein provided, a list of persons, members of such party, duly qualified to serve as election officers, together with a supplemental list of persons, members of such party, duly qualified to serve as election officers, from which the said mayor or board may select and appoint persons to fill vacancies occurring in the representation of such party in such board or body of election officers. In The City of New York such list shall be authenticated and filed by the chairman of the executive committee of the county committee of the party in the respective counties wholly or partly within such city, as constituted by the Greater New York charter; in other cities, by the chairman and secretary of the general, city or county committee of such party, if there be such a committee, or, if not, then by the corresponding officers (by whatever name known) of any committee performing the usual functions of a city or county committee; provided, however, that if in any city more than one such list be submitted in the name or on behalf of the same political party, only that list shall be accepted which is authenticated by the proper officer or officers of the faction or section of such party, which was recognized as regular by the last preceding state convention of such party; or, where no such convention has been held within the year, by the proper officer of the faction or section of said party which, at the time of the filing of said list, is recognized as regular by the state committee of such party, which was organized by or pursuant to the direction of the last preceding state convention of such party. All persons so proposed for appointment may be examined as to their qualifications by or under the direction of the board or officer charged with the duty of making the appointment; and if found duly qualified they shall be appointed to the respective positions for which they were recommended. If any of them are found disqualified, notice in writing of that fact shall be promptly given to the person or persons by whom the list embracing their names was authenticated, and the vacancy shall be filled by the appointment of a qualified person named in the supplemental list of party representatives heretofore provided for. If either party entitled to propose election officers, as herein provided, shall fail to authenticate and file such lists on or before the first day of August, or if any of the persons named therein shall be found disqualified, and if no supplemental list be filed, as herein provided, or if, one or more persons named in such supplemental list be found disqualified, then such board or officer shall, if necessary, proceed to select in such manner as may seem to them or him feasible from the members of the party or parties in default, or whose nominees have been found disqualified, and shall appoint suitable persons to act as election officers. In The City of New York the members of the board charged with the duty of appointing election officers, who represent the same political party, shall have the exclusive right and be charged with the exclusive duty of selecting from the lists submitted, or in lieu of persons named on such list who shall have been found disqualified, the members of such party who are to be appointed as election officers. Every person appointed as an election officer shall, within five days after notice of his appointment, take and subscribe the constitutional and statutory oaths of office, which shall be administered, if in The City of New York, by the superintendent of elections or by the chief of the branch bureau of elections in the borough in which they are appointed to serve, or the chief clerk, or assistant clerk of such bureau designated by the police board to perform such duty; and if in any other city, by the mayor thereof, or by any person or persons designated by him for that purpose; and all of said officers, and every clerk or person so designated by them or him for that purpose, shall be and is hereby authorized and empowered to administer such oaths. Every person so sworn as an election officer shall receive a certificate of appointment and qualification, signed by the person who administered the oath, in such form as may be approved by the board or officer by which or whom he was appointed, and specifying the capacity and the election district in which he is to serve, and the date of the expiration of his term of office. Any election officer so appointed may be removed for cause, by the board or mayor making the appointment, in which case such removal, unless made while such officer is actually on duty on the day of registration, revision of registration or election, and for improper conduct as an election officer, shall only be made after notice in writing to the officer to be removed, which notice shall set forth clearly and distinctly the reason for his removal. The said board of police may delegate to the superintendent of elections of The City of New York, and to the chief of a branch bureau of elections, the power to remove election officers for cause, on any day of registration or election. Any election officer who shall at any time be appointed to fill a vacancy, which fact shall be stated in the certificate of appointment, shall hold office only during the unexpired term of his predecessor, and provided that no election officer shall be transferred from one election district to another after he has entered upon the performance of his duties. The chairman of each board of inspectors of each election district shall, within twenty-four hours after any election, furnish to the mayor or board appointing such officers, if required so to do by such mayor or board, under his hand, a certificate stating the number of days of actual service of each member of such board, the names of the persons who served as poll clerks and ballot clerks on election day, and the number of days during which the store or building hired for registration and election purposes was actually used for such purposes. Any person acting as such chairman, who shall willfully make a false certificate, shall be deemed guilty of a misdemeanor. Every person appointed as an election officer, failing to take and subscribe the oath of office as hereinbefore provided, or who shall willfully neglect or refuse to discharge the duties to which he was appointed, shall, in addition to the other penalties prescribed by law, be liable to a fine of one hundred dollars, to be sued for and recovered by the mayor or board making the appointment in a court of record, for the use and benefit of the treasury of such city. Any election officer who, being removed for cause, shall fail upon demand to deliver over to his successor the register of electors, or any tally sheets, book, paper, memorandum or document relating to the election in his possession, so far as he has made it, shall be liable to a like penalty to be recovered in a like manner for the benefit of such city. All persons appointed and serving as election officers on each of the days of registration and of election and of canvass of the votes in cities of the first class shall be exempt from jury duty for one year from the date of the general election at which they serve.

§ 6. Section eighteen of said act is hereby amended so as to read as follows :

PAYMENT OF ELECTION EXPENSES.

§ 18. The expense of providing polling places, voting booths, supplies therefor, guard rails and other furniture of the polling place, and distance markers, and the compensation of the election officers in each election district, shall be a charge upon the town or city in which such election district is situated except that such expenses incurred for the purpose of conducting a village election, not held at the same time as a general election, shall be a charge upon the village. The expense of printing and delivering the official ballots, sample ballots and cards of instruction, poll books, tally sheets, return sheets for inspectors and ballot clerks, and distance markers to be used at a town meeting, city or village elections not held at the same time as a general election, and of printing the list of nominations therefor shall be a charge upon the town, city or village in which the election is held. The expense of printing and delivering the official ballots, sample ballots and cards of instruction, poll books, tally sheets, return sheets for inspectors and ballot clerks, and distance markers to be

used in any county, except such counties or portions thereof as are
included within The City of New York, at any other election, if
no town meeting, city or village election be held at the same time
therewith, and of printing the lists of nominations therefor, shall
be a charge upon such county. The expense of printing and delivering the official ballots, sample ballots and cards of instruction,
poll books, tally sheets, return sheets for inspectors and ballot
clerks and distance markers, to be used in any such county at any
such other election, and of printing the lists of nominations
therefor, if the town meeting, city or village election be held in
such county at the same time therewith, shall be apportioned by
the county clerk between such town, city or village and such
county, in the proportion of the number of candidates for town,
city or village officers on such ballots, respectively, to the whole
number of candidates thereon, and the amount of such expense
so apportioned to each such municipality shall be a charge thereon.
All expenses relating to or connected with elections lawfully
incurred by the police board of The City of New York shall be a
charge on such city, and after being audited by the proper officer,
shall be paid by the comptroller of said city upon the certificate of
such board. The county clerk of each county, not salaried, shall
be paid by such county a reasonable compensation for his services
in carrying out the provisions of this chapter, to be fixed by the
board of supervisors of the county, or the board acting as such
board of supervisors. The town clerk of each town shall be paid
by such town a reasonable compensation for his services in carrying out the provisions of this chapter, to be fixed by the other
members of the town board of the town. Ballot clerks, and persons acting as such, shall receive the same compensation for their
attendance at an election, as inspectors of election for the election,
and be paid in like manner. Poll clerks shall receive the same
compensation for their attendance at an election and canvass of
the votes as inspectors of election and shall be paid in like manner.
An inspector of election, except in The City of New York, lawfully
required to file papers in the county clerk's office, shall, unless he
resides in the city or town in which such office is situated, be
entitled to receive as compensation therefor five dollars, and also
four cents a mile for every mile actually and necessarily traveled
between his residence and such county clerk's office in going to and
returning from such office. In cities of the first class, the persons
appointed and serving as inspectors of election shall receive five

dollars for the hours fixed by law for each day of registration, and of revision of registration for a special election, and five dollars for the hours fixed by law for the election, and five dollars for the canvass and return of the votes. The poll clerks in such city shall each receive the same compensation as inspectors for the election and for the canvass of the votes, and the ballot clerks shall receive five dollars each. Such officers shall be paid by the comptrollers of the respective cities upon the certificate of the board appointing them.

§ 7. Section nineteen of said act is hereby amended so as to read as follows:

DELIVERY OF ELECTION LAWS TO CLERKS, BOARDS AND ELECTION OFFICERS.

§ 19. The secretary of state shall at least sixty days before each general election held after this act takes effect cause to be prepared a compilation of all the laws relating to elections in cities, towns, and villages then in force with annotations and explanatory notes and blank forms, properly indexed, and shall procure the same to be printed wherever he deems it desirable for the best interests of the state, and transmit to the county clerk of each county, except New York, Kings and Richmond counties, and to the superintendent of elections located in the borough of Manhattan and to the chief of the branch bureau of elections in each other borough of The City of New York a sufficient number of copies thereof, to furnish one such copy to the county clerk and to said superintendent and to each of said chiefs of bureaus of elections and one to each town, village and city clerk and to each election officer in such county and said boroughs, together with such number of extra copies as may in his judgment be necessary to replace lost or mutilated copies before delivery thereof to election officers. The county clerk of each county, except those counties the whole of which are included within The City of New York, shall forthwith transmit one of such copies to each of such officers in such county, and not in The City of New York, and said superintendent and the chief of each branch bureau of elections of the boroughs of The City of New York shall forthwith transmit one of such copies to each such officer in his borough. Each copy so received by each such officer shall belong to the office of the person receiving it. Every incumbent of the office shall preserve such copy during his term of office, and upon the expiration of his term or removal from office deliver it to his successor.

§ 8. Subdivision three of section thirty-two of said act is hereby amended so as to read as follows:

Subdivision 3. In cities of the first and second classes, the board of inspectors of each election district shall, immediately after the close of the last day of registration, make and complete one list of all persons enrolled in their respective districts, in the numerical order of the street numbers thereof which list shall be signed and certified by the board of inspectors. Such list shall be delivered by the chairman of the board of inspectors to the police captain of the precinct in which the election district is located, or an officer thereof, who shall forthwith deliver the same, if in The City of New York, to the superintendent of elections as to each election district in the borough of Manhattan, and to the chief of the branch bureau of elections of each other borough in which the election district is located, and if in any other of the cities of the first or second class, to the city clerk. The police board of The City of New York and the city clerk of other cities of the first and second class shall, as soon as possible after the delivery of such lists, and before the day of election, print in pamphlet form for each assembly district or ward within such respective cities not less than fifty times as many copies of said lists as there are election districts in such assembly district or ward, so that each assembly district or ward pamphlet shall contain the lists of the several election districts in such assembly district or ward. Upon the written application of the chairman of the executive committee of the county committee of any political party entitled to a separate column upon the official ballot to be voted in such city at the election for which the registration is made, the said police board and said city clerk shall respectively deliver to such chairman five copies of each assembly district or ward pamphlets for each election district within such assembly district or ward in such county. Two pamphlets containing the lists of the registered persons in the election districts within his precinct shall be furnished to each police captain in such cities, and it shall be the duty of such police captains to cause an investigation of each name registered therein to be made and to report to his commanding officer any case of false registration found in his precinct. The remaining pamphlets so printed shall be distributed in the discretion of the said police board, and said city clerk, who shall have respectively the power to charge for each pamphlet a sum not exceeding ten cents a copy and any moneys resulting from the sale thereof shall be paid to the comptroller of the city for the benefit of the treasury of such city. Such lists shall be made and printed as near as may be in the following form, to wit:

GRAND STREET.

Residence number or other designation.	Name of voter.
14.	Smith, John M.
15.	Jones, Charles M.

§ 9. Subdivision two of section thirty-five of said act is hereby amended so as to read as follows:

Subdivision 2. The register of electors made by the chairman of the board of inspectors shall be, and shall be known, as the public copy of registration. Such public copy shall be left in a prominent position in the place of registration from the first day of registration until election day, and shall at all reasonable times be open to public inspection and for making copies thereof. Each other inspector shall carefully preserve his register of electors and shall be responsible therefor, until the close of the canvass of the votes on election day, except as hereinafter provided for in cities of the first class. At the close of each day of registration the inspectors shall draw a line in ink immediately below the name of the elector last entered upon each page of each such register. Upon the succeeding day of registration, they shall enter the names of electors in the alphabetical order of the first letter of the surname below the line so drawn upon the proper page after the close of the previous day of registration. Upon the close of the last day of registration, the inspectors shall again carefully compare all the books of registration, to see that they are identical as to their contents, and (after making and completing the separate list of the electors in cities of the first class, as provided in subdivision three of section thirty-two of the election law), shall certify as a board in the proper place provided therefor upon each such register that such register is a true and correct register of the persons enrolled by them in such district for the next ensuing election, and shall state the whole number of such persons so enrolled. In cities of the first class, at the close of the last day of registration, the chairman of the board of inspectors shall take from an inspector of op-

posite political faith from himself, the register of electors made by
such inspector, and shall file the same on the Monday after the
last day of registration, if in The City of New York, with the superintendent of elections in the borough of Manhattan and with the
chief of the branch bureau of elections of each other borough in
which the election district is located, and if in the city of Buffalo
with the city clerk. Such register so filed, shall be a part of the records of the offices in which it is filed. The two other inspectors of
opposite political faith from each other shall each retain their respective registers of electors for use on election day. All registers
of electors shall at all reasonable hours be accessible for public
examinations and making copies thereof, and no charge of any
kind shall be made for such examination or for any elector making
a copy thereof. In cities of the first class the public copy of registration shall be used, if necessary, on election day by the inspector
whose register was filed as herein provided by said chairman. Any
person who shall alter, mutilate, destroy or remove from the place
of registration the public copy of such registration, shall be guilty
of a felony, and shall be punished upon conviction thereof by imprisonment in a state prison for not less than two nor more than
five years. unless otherwise provided by law. If, in cities of the
first class, the board of inspectors shall meet on the second Saturday before the election for the purpose of revising and correcting
the register of electors in pursuance of an order of the supreme
court, a justice thereof or a county judge, as provided in section
thirty-one of the election law, the inspectors shall certify forthwith
to the officer with whom the copy of the register is filed, the change
or changes made upon such register in pursuance of such order.
At any revision of registration for an election other than a general election, the quadruplicate register of electors for the last
preceding general election shall be furnished to the inspectors of
election by the officer or board having the custody thereof, and
the inspectors shall certify to the officer or board in cities of the
first class with whom the registers are filed, the changes, additions
or alterations made in such registers for such election. In the
cities of the first class at the close of the canvass of the votes of
any election, or within twenty-four hours thereafter the two copies
of the register of electors used by the inspectors and the public
copy thereof shall be filed respectively with the superintendent of
elections in the borough of Manhattan and with the chief of the
branch bureau of elections in each other borough of The

City of New York, in which the election district is located, and with the city clerk of Buffalo. In all election districts other than in cities of the first class, one copy of the register used on election day by the inspectors shall within twenty-four hours after the close of the election be filed in the office of the town or city clerk of the town or city in which such election district is, and the other copies with the county clerk. Such register of electors shall be carefully preserved for use at any election which may be ordered or held in either of such counties or cities, respectively, prior to the next ensuing general election, at which they may be required.

§ 10. Subdivision one of section thirty-six of said act is hereby amended so as to read as follows:

DELIVERY OF BLANK BOOKS FOR REGISTRATION, CERTIFICATES AND INSTRUCTIONS.

§ 36. Subdivision 1. The secretary of state shall purchase wherever he deems it desirable for the best interests of the state, a suitable number of blank books for register of electors, with blank certificates and brief instructions for registering the names of electors therein, in the forms respectively provided in subdivisions one and two of section thirty-two of the election law, at least four of such books for each board of inspectors in the state, and such number of extra copies thereof as in his judgment may be necessary for each county or city to replace lost or damaged registers before delivery to the inspectors. Such register of electors shall have the leaves thereof indexed with the letters of the alphabet, beginning with the letter "A" for the first leaf, and so on. He shall transmit such registers, certificates and instructions to the county clerk of each county, except those counties the whole of which are included within The City of New York; to each such county clerk a sufficient number thereof for the use of the boards of inspectors within his county and not within The City of New York, and to the superintendent of elections of The City of New York, located in the borough of Manhattan, and to the chief of the branch bureau of elections in each other borough within The City of New York a sufficient number thereof for the use of each board of inspectors within said respective boroughs at least twenty days prior to the first day of registration for a general election in each year. The county clerk shall deliver such books to the town clerks of each town, and to the city clerk of each city in such county, by mail or otherwise, at least five days prior to the first day of registration, and such town clerks and city clerks, and the said superintendent and chiefs of bureaus of elections in The City of New York shall deliver such books to the inspectors of said boroughs, respectively, before the hour set for registering the names of electors on the first day of registration. On each day of registration, the police board of The City of New York, and the city clerk of Buffalo shall furnish to each board of inspectors in their respective cities, blanks for the list of electors provided for in subdivision three of section thirty-two of the election law.

§ 11. Section fifty-eight of said act is hereby amended so as to read as follows:

PLACES OF FILING CERTIFICATES OF NOMINATION.

§ 58. Certificates of nomination of candidates for office to be filled by the electors of the entire state, or of any division or district greater than a county, shall be filed with the secretary of state, except that each certificate of nomination of a candidate for member of assembly for the assembly district composing the counties of Fulton and Hamilton, shall be filed in the office of the county clerk of Fulton county, and a copy thereof certified by the county clerk of Fulton county, shall be filed in the office of the county clerk of Hamilton county, so long as the said counties constitute one assembly district, and except that certificates of nomination of candidates for offices to be filled only by the electors or a portion of the electors of The City of New York shall be filed with the police board of The City of New York, in the office of the superintendent of elections. Certificates of nomination of candidates for offices to be filled only by the votes of electors, part of whom are of New York city, and part of whom are of a county not wholly within The City of New York shall be filed with the clerk of such county and in the office of the superintendent of elections and with the police board of said city. Certificates of nomination of candidates for offices of any other city, or for officers of a village or town to be elected at a different time from a general election, shall be filed with the clerk of such city, village or town, respectively. All other certificates of nomination shall be filed with the clerk of the county in which the candidates so nominated are to be voted for. All certificates and corrected certificates of nomination, all objections to such certificates and all declination of nominations are hereby declared to be public records; and it shall be the duty of every officer or board to exhibit without delay, every such paper or papers to any person who shall request to see the same. It shall also be the duty of each such officer or board to keep a book which shall be open to public inspection, in which shall be correctly recorded the names of all candidates nominated by certificates filed in the office of such officer or board, or certified thereto, the title of the office for which any such nomination is made, the political or other name and emblem of the political party or independent body making such nomination; and in which shall also be stated all declinations of nominations or objections to nominations, and the time of filing each of the said papers.

§ 12. Section fifty-nine of said act is hereby amended so as to read as follows:

THE TIMES OF FILING CERTIFICATES OF NOMINATION.

§ 59. The different certificates of nomination shall be filed within the following periods before the election for which the nominations are made, to wit: Those required to be filed with the secretary of state, if party nominations, at least thirty and not more than forty days; if independent nominations, at least twenty-five and not more than forty days; those required to be filed with a county clerk, or the police board of The City of New York, or with the city clerk of any other city, if party nominations, at least twenty-five and not more than thirty-five days; if independent nominations, at least twenty, and not more than thirty-five days; those required to be filed with a town or village clerk, if party nominations, at least fifteen and not more than twenty days; if independent nominations, at least ten and not more than twenty days. In case of a special election ordered by the governor under the provisions of section four of the election law, the certificates of nominations for the office or offices to be filled at such special election shall be filed with the proper officer or board not less than fifteen days before such special election.

§ 13. Section sixty of said act is hereby amended so as to read as follows:

CERTIFICATION OF NOMINATIONS BY SECRETARY OF STATE.

§ 60. The secretary of state shall, fourteen days before the election, certify to the county clerk of each county, except those counties the whole of which are within The City of New York, and to the police board of The City of New York, the name, residence and place of business, if any, of each candidate nominated in any certificate so filed for whom the electors of any such county or said city, respectively, may vote, the title of the office for which he is nominated, the party or other political name specified in such certificate, and the emblem or device chosen to represent and distinguish the candidates of the political party or independent body making such nominations.

§ 14. Section sixty-one of said act is hereby amended so as to read as follows:

PUBLICATION OF NOMINATIONS.

§ 61. At least six days before an election to fill any public office, the county clerk of each county, except those counties which are wholly within The City of New York, shall cause to be published in not less than two or more than four newspapers within such county, a list of all nominations of candidates for offices to be filled at such election, certified to such clerk by the secretary of state, or filed in the office of such clerk. The police board of The City of New York shall, within the same time before an election to fill any public office, cause to be published in not less than two, nor more than four newspapers published in each county wholly or partly within such city a list of the nominations of candidates for offices to be voted for at such election in such counties respectively, which were certified to such board by the secretary of state, or filed in the office of such board; except that in the borough of Brooklyn such publications shall be made in the newspapers designated to publish corporation notices therein. Such publication shall contain the name and residence, and if in a city, the street number of the residence and place of business, if any, and the party or other designation of each candidate, the office for which he was nominated, specifying the political division in which he is to be voted for, and a fac-simile of the emblems or devices selected and designated as prescribed by the fifty-sixth and fifty-seventh sections of this act, to represent and distinguish the candidates of the several political parties or independent bodies. The city clerk of each city, except New York, and the police board in said city, shall at least six days before an election of city officers thereof, held at a different time from a general election, cause like publication to be made as to candidates for offices to be filled at such city election in a like number of newspapers published in said city. One of such publications shall be made in a newspaper which advocates the principles of the political party that, at the last preceding election for governor, cast the largest number of votes in the state for such office; and another of such publications shall be made in a newspaper which advocates the principles of the political party that at the last preceding election for governor cast the next largest number of votes in the state for such office. The clerk or board, in selecting the papers for such publications, shall select those which, according to the best information he can obtain, have a large circulation within such county or city. In making additional publications, the clerk or board shall keep in view the object of giving information, so far as possible, to the voters of all political parties; and in no event shall additional publications be made in two newspapers representing the same political party. The clerk or board shall make such publication twice in each newspaper so selected in a county or city in which daily newspapers are published; but if there be no daily newspaper published within the county, one publication only shall be made in each of such newspapers. Should the county clerk find it impracticable to make the publication six days before election day in counties where no daily newspaper is printed, he shall make the same at the earliest possible day thereafter, and before the election.

§ 15. Section sixty-two of said act is hereby amended so as to read as follows:

LISTS FOR TOWN CLERKS AND ALDERMEN.

§ 62. The county clerk of each county, except those counties which are wholly within The City of New York, shall at least six days before election day, send to the town clerk of each town, and to an alderman of each ward in any city in the county, at least five and not more than ten printed lists for each election district in such town or ward, containing the name and residence, and if in a city, the street number of residence, and place of business, if any, and the party or other designation, and also a fac-simile of the emblem or device of each political party, or independent body nominating candidates to be voted for by the electors of the respective towns and wards. Such lists shall, at least three days before the day of election be conspicuously posted by such town clerk or alderman in one or more public places in each election district of such town or ward, one of which shall be at each polling place.

§ 16. Section sixty-four of said act is hereby amended so as to read as follows:

DECLINATION OF NOMINATION.

§ 64. The name of a person nominated for any office shall not be printed on the official ballot if he notifies the officer with whom the original certificate of his nomination is filed, in a writing signed by him and duly acknowledged, that he declines the nomination, or if nominated by more than one political party, or independent body, the name of a person so nominated shall not be printed on the ticket of a party or independent body whose nomination he shall in like manner decline. If the declination be of a party nomination filed with the secretary of state, such notification shall be given at least twenty-five days, and if an independent nomination, at least twenty days before the election. If the declination be of a party nomination filed with a county clerk or the police board of The City of New York, or with the city clerk of any other city, such notification shall be given at least twenty days, and if of an independent nomination, at least eighteen days before the election. If the declination be of a party nomination filed with a town or village clerk, such notification shall be given at least ten days, and if of an independent nomination, at least seven days before the election. The officer to whom such notification is given, shall forthwith inform by mail or otherwise, the committee, if any, appointed on the face of such certificate as permitted by sections fifty-six and fifty-seven of this act, and otherwise one or more persons whose names are attached to such certificate, that the nomination conferred by such certificate has been declined, and if such declination be filed with the secretary of state, such officer shall also give immediate notice by mail or otherwise, that such nomination has been declined, to the several county clerks or other officers, authorized by law to prepare official ballots for election districts affected by such declination.

§ 17. Subdivision one of section sixty-six of said act is hereby amended so as to read as follows:

FILLING VACANCIES IN NOMINATIONS, AND CORRECTION OF CERTIFICATE.

§ 66. Subdivision 1. If a nomination is duly declined, or a candidate regularly nominated dies before election day, or is found to be disqualified to hold the office for which he is nominated, or if any certificate of nomination is found to be defective but not wholly void, the committee appointed on the face of such certificate of nomination, as permitted by sections fifty-six and fifty-seven of this act, may make a new nomination to fill the va-

cancy so created, or may supply such defect, as the case may be, by
making and filing with the proper officer a certificate setting forth
the cause of the vacancy or the nature of the defect, the name of
the new candidate, the title of the office for which he is nominated, the name of the original candidate, the name of the
political party or other nominating body which was inscribed
on the original certificate, and such further information as
is required to be given by an original certificate of nomination;
except that where a certificate is filed pursuant to this section
to fill a vacancy it shall not be lawful to select a new emblem or
device, but the emblem or device chosen to represent or distinguish
the candidate nominated by the original certificate shall be used to
represent and distinguish the candidate nominated, as provided
by this section. The certificate so made shall be subscribed and
acknowledged by a majority of the members of the committee, and
the members of the committee subscribing the same shall make
oath before the officer or officers before whom they shall severally
acknowledge the execution of the said certificate that the matters
therein stated are true to the best of their information and belief.
Except in a case as provided for in subdivision two of this section,
the said certificate shall be filed in the office in which the original
certificate was filed, at least six days before the election, if filed in
the office of a town or village clerk; at least fifteen days before
the election if filed with the county clerk or the police board of The
City of New York, or the city clerk of any other city; and at least
fifteen days if filed with the secretary of state, and upon being so
filed shall have the same force and effect as an original certificate
of nomination. When such certificate is filed with the secretary
of state, he shall, in certifying the nomination to the various county
clerks and other officers, insert the name of the person who has
been nominated as prescribed by this section, instead of that of the
candidate nominated by the original certificate, or, if he has already
sent forward his certificate, he shall forthwith certify to the proper
clerks and other officer, the name of the person nominated as prescribed by this section, and such other facts as are required to be
stated in a certificate filed pursuant to this section. When no
nomination shall have been originally made by a political party,
or by an independent body for an office, or where a vacancy shall
exist, it shall not be lawful for any committee of such party or independent body authorized to make nominations, or to fill vacancies, to nominate or substitute the name of a candidate of another

party, or independent body for such office; it being the intention
of this act that when a candidate of one party is nominated and
placed on the ticket of another party or independent body, such
nomination must be made at the time and in the manner provided
for making original nominations by such party or independent
body.

§ 18. Section eighty-six of said act is hereby amended so as to
read as follows:

OFFICERS PROVIDING BALLOTS AND STATIONERY.

§ 86. The clerk of each county, except those counties the whole of
which are within The City of New York, shall provide the requisite
number of official and sample ballots, cards of instruction, two pollbooks, distance markers, two tally sheets, inspectors' and ballot
clerks' return sheets (three of each kind, and one of each to be
marked " original "), pens, penholders, ink, pencils having black
lead, blotting paper, sealing wax and such other articles of stationery as may be necessary for the proper conduct of the election,
and the canvass of the votes, for each election district in such
county and not within The City of New York, for each election to be
held thereat, except that when town meetings, city or village elections and elections for school officers are not held at the same time
as a general election the clerk of such town, city or village, respectively, shall provide such official and sample ballots and stationery
for such election or town meeting. And the police board of The
City of New York shall provide such articles for each election to be
held in said city. Each officer or board charged with the duty of
providing official ballots for any polling place, shall have sample
ballots and official ballots provided, and in the possession of such
officer or board, and open to public inspection as follows: The sample ballots five days before the election, and the official ballots
four days before the election for which they are prepared unless
prepared for a village election or town meeting held at a different
time from a general election, in which case the official ballot shall
be so printed and in possession at least one day, and the sample
ballots at least two days before such election or town meeting.
During the times within which the same are open for inspection
as aforesaid, it shall be the duty of the officer or board charged
by law with the duty of preparing the same, to deliver a sample
ballot of the kind to be voted in his district to each qualified elector
who shall apply therefor, so that each elector who may
desire the same may obtain a sample ballot, similar except

vo e.

§ 19. Section eighty-seven of said act is hereby amended so as to read as follows:

DISTRIBUTION OF BALLOTS AND STATIONERY.

§ 87. The county clerk of each county except those counties which are wholly within The City of New York, shall deliver at his office to each town or city clerk in such county, except in New York city, on the Saturday before the election at which they may be voted, the official and sample ballots, cards of instructions and other stationery required to be provided for each polling place in such town or city for such election. It is hereby made the duty of each such town or city clerk to call at the office of such county clerk at such time and receive such ballots and stationery. In The City of New York the board required to provide such ballots and stationery shall cause them to be delivered to the board of inspectors of each election district at least one-half hour before the opening of the polls on each day of election. Each kind of official ballots shall be arranged in a package in the consecutive order of the numbers printed on the stubs thereof, beginning with number one. All official and sample ballots provided for such election shall be in separate sealed packages, clearly marked on the outside thereof with the number and kind of ballots contained therein and indorsed with the designation of the election district for which they were prepared. The instruction cards and other stationery provided for each election district shall also be enclosed in a sealed package or packages, with a label on the outside thereof showing the contents of each such package. Each such town and city clerk receiving such packages shall cause all such packages so received and marked for any election district to be delivered unopened and with the seals thereof unbroken to the inspectors of election of such election district one-half hour before the opening of the polls of such election therein. The inspectors of election receiving such packages shall give to such town or city clerk, or board, delivering such packages a receipt therefor specifying the number and kind of packages received by them, which receipt shall be filed in the office of such clerk or board. Town, city and village clerks required to provide the same for town meetings, city and village elections held at different times from a general election, and the board of The City of New York required to provide the same for elections held therein, respectively, shall in like manner, deliver to the inspectors or presiding officers of the election at each polling place at which such meetings and elections are held, respectively, the official ballots, sample ballots, instruction cards and other stationery required for such election or town meeting, respectively, in like sealed packages marked on the outside in like manner, and shall take and file receipts therefor in like manner in their respective offices.

§ 20. Section one hundred and thirteen of said act is hereby amended so as to read as follows:

DELIVERY AND FILING OF PAPERS RELATING TO THE ELECTION.

§ 113. Subdivision 1. If the election be other than an election of town, city, village or school officers, held at a different time from a general election, the chairman of the board of inspectors of each election district, except in The City of New York, shall forthwith upon the completion of such certified original statement of the result, deliver one certified copy thereof to the supervisor of the town in which the election, if outside of a city, is situated, and if in a city, to one of the supervisors of said city. If there be no supervisor, or he be absent or unable to attend the meeting of the county board of canvassers, such certified copy shall be forthwith delivered to an assessor of such town or city. One certified copy of such original statement of the result of the canvass, the pollbooks of such election, and one of the tally sheets, shall be forthwith filed by such inspectors, or by one of them deputed for that purpose, with the town clerk of such town, or the city clerk of such city, as the case may be. The original certified statement of the result of the canvass, with the original ballot returned, prepared by the ballot clerk, attached, the sealed package of void and protested ballots, the record as to challenged and assisted voters, and the sealed packages of detached stubs and unvoted ballots, and one of the tally sheets shall, within twenty-four hours after the completion of such canvass, be filed by the chairman of the board of inspectors, with the county clerk of the county in which the election district is situated. The register of electors and public copy thereof shall be filed as prescribed in section thirty-five of this act.

Subdivision 2. In The City of New York the original statement of canvass and the sealed package of void and protested ballots shall be filed by the chairman of the board of inspectors within twenty-four hours after the completion of the canvass with the county clerk of the county within

ment of canvass not used at the canvass and the sealed packages of void and protested ballots shall be retained in the office in which or by the officer with whom they were filed. The sealed packages of void and protested ballots shall be retained inviolate in the office in which they are filed subject to the order and examination of a court of competent jurisdiction and may be destroyed at the end of six months from the time of the completion of such canvass, unless otherwise ordered by a court of competent jurisdiction.

§ 24. Section one hundred and thirty-six of said act is hereby amended so as to read as follows:

DECISIONS OF COUNTY BOARD AS TO PERSONS ELECTED.

§ 136. Upon the completion of the statements required by section one hundred and thirty-five of this act the board of canvassers for each county shall determine what person has by the greatest number of votes been so elected to each office of member of assembly to be filled by the electors of each county for which they are county canvassers if constituting one assembly district, or in each assembly district therein, if there be more than one, and each person elected by the greatest number of votes to each county office of such county to be filled at such election, and if there be more than one school commissioner district in such county, each person elected by the greatest number of votes to the office of school commissioner to be filled at such election in each such district. The county clerk of the county of Hamilton shall forthwith transmit to the county clerk of the county of Fulton, a certified copy of the statement so filed and record it in his office, of the county board of canvassers of Hamilton county, as to all the votes so cast in Hamilton county for all the candidates and for each of the candidates for the office of member of assembly of the assembly district composed of Fulton and Hamilton counties; and the county clerk of Fulton county shall forthwith deliver the same to the Fulton county board of canvassers, who shall from such certified copy, and from their own statement as to the votes so cast for such office in Fulton county, determine what person was at such election, elected by the greatest number of votes to such office. Such board of each county shall determine whether any proposition or question submitted to the electors of such county only, has by the greatest number of votes been adopted or rejected. All such determinations shall be reduced to writing, and signed by the members of such board, or a majority of them, and filed and recorded in the office of

osition or question upon which only the electors of such county were entitled to vote at such election.

8. In the counties wholly or partly within The City of New York, the respective county boards shall make a separate statement as to the votes, if any, so cast upon any proposition or question upon which only the electors of such city were entitled to vote at such election in such county or portion thereof. Each such statement shall set forth, in words written out at length, all such votes cast for all the candidates for each such office; and if any such office was to be filled at such election by the electors of a portion only of such county all the votes cast for all . the candidates for each office in any such portion of the county, designating by its proper district number or other appropriate designation, the names of each such candidate and the number of votes so cast for each, the whole number of votes so cast upon any proposed constitutional amendment or other proposition or question, and of all the votes so cast in favor of and against the same respectively. In the counties wholly or partly within The City of New York the respective county boards shall make a separate statement of the votes cast for all the city offices voted for by the electors of such city or any portion thereof, within such counties. If, upon such canvass, in any original statement or duly certified copy of an original statement of the result of the canvass of the votes of any election district in such county or city, there shall be included any ballot indorsed by the inspectors to the effect that it was objected to as marked for identification, the county and city boards of canvassers shall add to each statement in which the counting of any such ballot or any portion thereof is included, a statement of the whole number of ballots so indorsed and counted. If, upon such canvass, in any original statement or duly certified copy of an original statement of the result of the canvass of the votes of any election district there shall be included any ballot indorsed by the inspectors to the effect that it was rejected as void, the county and city boards of canvassers shall add to each statement, a statement of the whole number of ballots so indorsed. The statements required by this section shall each be certified as correct over the signatures of the members of the board, or a majority of them, and shall be filed and recorded in the office of the county clerk of such county. When the whole canvass shall be completed, the original statements of canvass and certified copies used thereat shall be filed in the office of the secretary of the board. The certified copies of such original state-

ment of canvass not used at the canvass and the sealed packages of void and protested ballots shall be retained in the office in which or by the officer with whom they were filed. The sealed packages of void and protested ballots shall be retained inviolate in the office in which they are filed subject to the order and examination of a court of competent jurisdiction and may be destroyed at the end of six months from the time of the completion of such canvass, unless otherwise ordered by a court of competent jurisdiction.

§ 24. Section one hundred and thirty-six of said act is hereby amended so as to read as follows:

DECISIONS OF COUNTY BOARD AS TO PERSONS ELECTED.

§ 136. Upon the completion of the statements required by section one hundred and thirty-five of this act the board of canvassers for each county shall determine what person has by the greatest number of votes been so elected to each office of member of assembly to be filled by the electors of each county for which they are county canvassers if constituting one assembly district, or in each assembly district therein, if there be more than one, and each person elected by the greatest number of votes to each county office of such county to be filled at such election, and if there be more than one school commissioner district in such county, each person elected by the greatest number of votes to the office of school commissioner to be filled at such election in each such district. The county clerk of the county of Hamilton shall forthwith transmit to the county clerk of the county of Fulton, a certified copy of the statement so filed and record it in his office, of the county board of canvassers of Hamilton county, as to all the votes so cast in Hamilton county for all the candidates and for each of the candidates for the office of member of assembly of the assembly district composed of Fulton and Hamilton counties; and the county clerk of Fulton county shall forthwith deliver the same to the Fulton county board of canvassers, who shall from such certified copy, and from their own statement as to the votes so cast for such office in Fulton county, determine what person was at such election, elected by the greatest number of votes to such office. Such board of each county shall determine whether any proposition or question submitted to the electors of such county only, has by the greatest number of votes been adopted or rejected. All such determinations shall be reduced to writing, and signed by the members of such board, or a majority of them, and filed and recorded in the office of

osition or question upon which only the electors of such county were entitled to vote at such election.

8. In the counties wholly or partly within The City of New York, the respective county boards shall make a separate statement as to the votes, if any, so cast upon any proposition or question upon which only the electors of such city were entitled to vote at such election in such county or portion thereof. Each such statement shall set forth, in words written out at length, all such votes cast for all the candidates for each such office; and if any such office was to be filled at such election by the electors of a portion only of such county all the votes cast for all the candidates for each office in any such portion of the county, designating by its proper district number or other appropriate designation, the names of each such candidate and the number of votes so cast for each, the whole number of votes so cast upon any proposed constitutional amendment or other proposition or question, and of all the votes so cast in favor of and against the same respectively. In the counties wholly or partly within The City of New York the respective county boards shall make a separate statement of the votes cast for all the city offices voted for by the electors of such city or any portion thereof, within such counties. If, upon such canvass, in any original statement or duly certified copy of an original statement of the result of the canvass of the votes of any election district in such county or city, there shall be included any ballot indorsed by the inspectors to the effect that it was objected to as marked for identification, the county and city boards of canvassers shall add to each statement in which the counting of any such ballot or any portion thereof is included, a statement of the whole number of ballots so indorsed and counted. If, upon such canvass, in any original statement or duly certified copy of an original statement of the result of the canvass of the votes of any election district there shall be included any ballot indorsed by the inspectors to the effect that it was rejected as void, the county and city boards of canvassers shall add to each statement, a statement of the whole number of ballots so indorsed. The statements required by this section shall each be certified as correct over the signatures of the members of the board, or a majority of them, and shall be filed and recorded in the office of the county clerk of such county. When the whole canvass shall be completed, the original statements of canvass and certified copies used thereat shall be filed in the office of the secretary of the board. The certified copies of such original state-

ment of canvass not used at the canvass and the sealed packages of void and protested ballots shall be retained in the office in which or by the officer with whom they were filed. The sealed packages of void and protested ballots shall be retained inviolate in the office in which they are filed subject to the order and examination of a court of competent jurisdiction and may be destroyed at the end of six months from the time of the completion of such canvass, unless otherwise ordered by a court of competent jurisdiction.

§ 24. Section one hundred and thirty-six of said act is hereby amended so as to read as follows:

DECISIONS OF COUNTY BOARD AS TO PERSONS ELECTED.

§ 136. Upon the completion of the statements required by section one hundred and thirty-five of this act the board of canvassers for each county shall determine what person has by the greatest number of votes been so elected to each office of member of assembly to be filled by the electors of each county for which they are county canvassers if constituting one assembly district, or in each assembly district therein, if there be more than one, and each person elected by the greatest number of votes to each county office of such county to be filled at such election, and if there be more than one school commissioner district in such county, each person elected by the greatest number of votes to the office of school commissioner to be filled at such election in each such district. The county clerk of the county of Hamilton shall forthwith transmit to the county clerk of the county of Fulton, a certified copy of the statement so filed and record it in his office, of the county board of canvassers of Hamilton county, as to all the votes so cast in Hamilton county for all the candidates and for each of the candidates for the office of member of assembly of the assembly district composed of Fulton and Hamilton counties; and the county clerk of Fulton county shall forthwith deliver the same to the Fulton county board of canvassers, who shall from such certified copy, and from their own statement as to the votes so cast for such office in Fulton county, determine what person was at such election, elected by the greatest number of votes to such office. Such board of each county shall determine whether any proposition or question submitted to the electors of such county only, has by the greatest number of votes been adopted or rejected. All such determinations shall be reduced to writing, and signed by the members of such board, or a majority of them, and filed and recorded in the office of

shall have organized the secretary shall deliver to such board the certified copies of the statements of the county boards of canvassers of each county wholly or partly within such city of the votes cast for candidates for city office within such city and upon any proposition or question, if any submitted, to the electors of such city only and the said board shall proceed to canvass such statements. If a certified copy of any statement of any county board required to be delivered to said board shall not be delivered prior to the meeting and organization of said board, it may adjourn such meeting from day to day not exceeding a term of five days and it shall be the duty of the secretary to procure from the county clerk of such county the required certified copy of such statement. Upon the completion of such canvass said board shall make separate tabulated statements signed by the members of such board or a majority thereof, and attested by the secretary, of the whole number of votes cast for all the candidates for each office shown by such certified statements to have been voted for and of the whole number of votes cast for each of such candidates, indicating the number of votes cast in each county for them, and if the voters of not more than one county or portion of such county were entitled to vote for such candidates, the name and portion of such county and the name of each candidate, and the determination of the board of the persons thereby elected to such office by the greatest number of votes. The said board shall also make a separate similar tabulated statement of the vote cast upon any proposition or question submitted at the election to the electors of such city only and shall include a determination as to whether such proposition or question by the greatest number of votes has been adopted or rejected. Each such statement and determination shall be filed and recorded in the office of the clerk of the municipal assembly and the said board shall cause the publication of the same in at least two newspapers within such county wholly within such city and in the City Record. Upon the filing in his office of such statements and determination the clerk of the municipal assembly shall issue and transmit by mail or otherwise a certificate of election to each person shown thereby to be elected, such certificate to be countersigned by the mayor of The City of New York under the seal of The City of New York.

§ 27. Sections one hundred and thirty-eight, one hundred and thirty-nine, one hundred and forty and one hundred and forty-one of said act are hereby renumbered one hundred and thirty-nine, one hundred and forty, one hundred and forty-one and one hundred and forty-two, respectively.

§ 28. This act shall take effect on the first day of January in the year eighteen hundred and ninety-eight.

Chap. 380.

AN ACT to provide for boards of supervisors in counties wholly within the limits of a city but not comprising the whole of such city, and defining the powers and duties thereof.

Became a law May 6, 1897, with the approval of the Governor.
Passed, three-fifths being present.

The People of the State of New York, represented in Senate and Assembly, do enact as follows:

Section 1. In every county of the state wholly included within the limits of a city but not comprising the whole of such city, there shall be a board of supervisors to be composed of the members of the municipal assembly, board of aldermen, common council or other legislative body of such city who shall be elected as such and also as supervisors within the territorial limits of the county. *Board of supervisors.*

§ 2. Every such board of supervisors may act as a board of county canvassers, and shall, in case the county be entitled to more than one member of assembly, have the power of dividing the county into assembly districts as provided by section five of article three of the constitution. *County canvassers. Division of county into assembly districts.*

§ 3. Every such board of supervisors shall have no other or further powers of local legislation or administration, and shall have no power to incur any debt. *No power of local legislation, etc.*

§ 4. The members of every such board of supervisors shall serve as such without compensation and without other or further compensation than is received by them as members of the municipal assembly, board of aldermen, common council or other legislative body of the city within which the county is included. *Compensation.*

§ 5. The term of office of each member of every such board of supervisors shall be co-extensive with and no longer than his term of office as member of said municipal assembly, board of aldermen, common council or other legislative body of the city within which the county is located. *Term of office.*

§ 6. All acts and parts of acts heretofore passed by the legislature which are in any respect in conflict or inconsistent with the provisions hereof or any of them, are hereby repealed. *Repeal.*

Boards abolished.

§ 7. Each and every board of supervisors in existence prior to January first, eighteen hundred and ninety-eight, in any county of the state falling within the provisions of section one of this act, shall from and after said January first, eighteen hundred and ninety-eight, be abolished; and all the rights, powers and duties which by law were vested in any such board of supervisors prior to said January first, eighteen hundred and ninety-eight, are hereby wholly abrogated except as herein provided.

Rights, etc., abrogated.

When takes effect.

§ 8. This act shall take effect immediately save as otherwise herein provided.

Chap. 383.

AN ACT to prevent monopolies in articles or commodities of common use, and to prohibit restraints of trade and commerce, providing penalties for violations of the provisions of this act, and procedure to enable the attorney-general to secure testimony in relation thereto.

Became a law May 7, 1897, with the approval of the Governor.
Passed, three-fifths being present.

The People of the State of New York, represented in Senate and Assembly, do enact as follows:

Contracts, etc., creating monopolies, etc. illegal and void.

Section 1. Every contract, agreement, arrangement or combination whereby a monopoly in the manufacture, production or sale in this state of any article or commodity of common use is or may be created, established or maintained, or whereby competition in this state in the supply or price of any such article or commodity is or may be restrained or prevented, or whereby for the purpose of creating, establishing or maintaining a monopoly within this state of the manufacture, production or sale of any such article or commodity, the free pursuit in this state of any lawful business, trade or occupation is or may be restricted or prevented, is hereby declared to be against public policy, illegal and void.

Penalties for violations of provisions.

§ 2. Every person or corporation, or any officer or agent thereof, who shall make or attempt to make or enter into any such contract, agreement, arrangement or combination, or who within this state shall do any act pursuant thereto, or in toward or for the consummation thereof, wherever the same may have been made, is guilty of a misdemeanor, and on conviction thereof shall, if a natural person, be punished by a fine not exceeding five thousand dollars, or by imprisonment for not longer than one year, or by both such fine and imprisonment; and if a corporation, by a fine of not exceeding five thousand dollars.

§ 3. The attorney-general may bring an action in the name and in behalf of the people of the state against any person, trustee, director, manager, or other officer or agent of a corporation, or against a corporation, foreign or domestic, to restrain and prevent the doing in this state of any act herein declared to be illegal, or any act in, toward or for the making or consummation of any contract, agreement, arrangement or combination herein prohibited, wherever the same may have been made.

Actions and proceedings by attorney-general.

§ 4. The provisions of article one of title three of chapter nine of the code of civil procedure relating to the application for an order for the examination of witnesses before the commencement of an action and the conduct of such examination shall apply, so far as practicable, to an action or proceeding by the attorney-general instituted pursuant to this chapter; and for the purpose of determining whether an action or a proceeding should be commenced hereunder, the attorney-general may examine and procure the testimony of witnesses in the manner herein prescribed.

Application of civil code.

§ 5. Whenever the attorney-general deems it necessary or proper to procure testimony before beginning any action or proceeding under this chapter, he may present to any justice of the supreme court, an application in writing for an order directing such persons as the attorney-general may require to appear before a justice of the supreme court, or a referee designated in such order, and answer such relevant and material questions as may be put to them, concerning any alleged illegal contract, arrangement, agreement or combination, in violation of this chapter, if it appears to the satisfaction of the justice of the supreme court to whom the application for the order is made that such an order is necessary, then such order shall be granted. Such order shall be granted without notice, unless notice is required to be given by the justice of the supreme court to whom the application is made, in which event an order to show cause why such application should not be granted shall be made containing such preliminary injunction or stay as may appear to said justice to be proper or expedient, and shall specify the time when and place where the witnesses are required to appear and such examination shall be held either in the city of Albany or in the judicial district in which the witness resides or in which the principal office within this state of the corporation affected is located. The justice or referee may adjourn such examination from time to time and witnesses must attend accordingly.

Procedure for securing testimony.

Order for examination. § 6. The order for such examination must be signed by the justice making it and the service of a copy thereof, with an endorsement by the attorney-general signed by him, to the effect that the person named therein is required to appear and be examined at the time and place, and before the justice or referee specified in such endorsement, shall be sufficient notice for the attendance of witnesses. Such endorsement may contain a clause requiring such person to produce on such examination all books, papers and documents in his possession, or under his control, relating to the subject of such examination. The order shall be served upon the person named in the endorsement aforesaid, by showing him the original order, and delivering to and leaving with him, at the same time, a copy thereof endorsed as above provided, and by paying or tendering to him the fee allowed by law to witnesses subpoenaed to attend trials of civil actions in a court of record in this state.

Testimony of witness. § 7. The testimony of each witness must be subscribed by him, and all testimony taken by such justice or referee appointed must be certified and delivered to the attorney-general at the close of the examination. The testimony given by a witness in a proceeding or examination under this act shall not be given in evidence against him in any criminal action or proceeding, nor shall any criminal action or proceeding be brought against such witness on account of the testimony so given by him, nor shall any person be excused from answering any questions that may be put to him on the ground that it may tend to convict him of a violation of the provisions of this act.

Powers and duties of referee. § 8. A referee appointed as provided in this act possesses all the powers and is subject to all the duties of a referee appointed under section ten hundred and eighteen of the code of civil procedure, so far as practicable, and may punish for contempt a witness duly served as prescribed in this act for non-attendance or refusal to be sworn or to testify, or to produce books, papers and documents according to the direction of the endorsement aforesaid, in the same manner, and to the same extent as a referee appointed to hear, try and determine an issue of fact or of law.

Repeal. § 9. Chapter seven hundred and sixteen of the laws of eighteen hundred and ninety-three and chapter two hundred and sixty-seven of the laws of eighteen hundred and ninety-six, are hereby repealed.

§ 10. This act shall take effect immediately.

Chap. 384.

AN ACT to amend the stock corporation law, relating to annual reports and liabilities of officers, directors and stockholders of foreign stock corporations.

Became a law May 7, 1897, with the approval of the Governor. Passed, three-fifths being present.

The People of the State of New York, represented in Senate and Assembly, do enact as follows:

Section 1. Section seven of chapter five hundred and sixty-four of the laws of eighteen hundred and ninety, entitled "An act in relation to stock corporations, constituting chapter thirty-six of the general laws," as amended by chapter six hundred and eighty-eight of the laws of eighteen hundred and ninety-two, is hereby amended to read as follows:

§ 7. **Combinations abolished.**—No domestic stock corporation and no foreign corporation doing business in this state shall combine with any other corporation or person for the creation of a monopoly or the unlawful restraint of trade or for the prevention of competition in any necessary of life.

§ 2. Section thirty of article two of such act is hereby amended to read as follows :

§ 30. **Annual report.**—Every domestic stock corporation and every foreign stock corporation doing business within this state, except moneyed and railroad corporations, shall annually, during the month of January, or, if doing business without the United States, before the first day of May, make a report as of the first day of January, which shall state :

1. The amount of its capital stock, and the proportion actually issued.

2. The amount of its debts or an amount which they do not then exceed.

3. The amount of its assets or an amount which its assets at least equal.

Such report shall be signed by a majority of its directors, and verified by the oath of the president or vice-president and treasurer or secretary, and filed in the office of the secretary of state, and in the office of the county clerk of the county within this state where its principal business office may be located. If such report is not so made and filed, all the directors of the corporation shall jointly

and severally be personally liable for all the debts of the corporation then existing, and for all contracted before such report shall
be made. No director shall be liable for the failure to make and
file such report if he shall file with the secretary of state, within
thirty days after the first day of February, or the first day of May,
as the case may be, a verified certificate, stating that he has endeav-
ored to have such report made and filed, but that the officers or a
majority of the directors have refused and neglected to make and
file the same, and shall append to such certificate a report containing the items required to be stated in such annual report, so
far as they are within his knowledge or are obtainable from sources
of information open to him, and verified by him to be true to the
best of his knowledge, information and belief.

§ 3. Section fifty-three of such act is hereby amended to read as
follows :

§ 53. **Stock books of foreign corporations.**—Every foreign stock
corporation having an office for the transaction of business in this
state, except moneyed and railroad corporations, shall keep therein
a book to be known as a stock book, containing the names, alphabetically arranged, of all persons who are stockholders of the corporation, showing their places of residence, the number of shares
of stock held by them respectively, the time when they respectively
became the owners thereof, and the amount paid thereon. Such
stock book shall be open daily, during business hours, for the inspection of its stockholders and judgment creditors, and any officer
of the state authorized by law to investigate the affairs of any
such corporation. If any such foreign stock corporation has in
this state a transfer agent, whether such agent shall be a corporation
or a natural person, such stock book may be deposited in the office
of such agent and shall be open to inspection at all times during
the usual hours of transacting business, to any stockholder, judgment creditor or officer of the state authorized by law to investigate
the affairs of such corporation. For any refusal to allow such book
to be inspected, such corporation and the officer or agent so refusing shall each forfeit the sum of two hundred and fifty dollars to
be recovered by the person to whom such refusal was made.

§ 4. Article three of such act is hereby amended by adding at
the end thereof a new section to be known as section sixty, and to
read as follows :

§ 60. **Liabilities of officers, directors and stockholders of foreign
corporations.**—Except as otherwise provided in this chapter the

officers, directors and stockholders of a foreign stock corporation transacting business in this state, except moneyed and railroad corporations, shall be liable under the provisions of this chapter, in the same manner and to the same extent as the officers, directors and stockholders of a domestic corporation, for :

1. The making of unauthorized dividends;
2. The creation of unauthorized and excessive indebtedness;
3. Unlawful loans to stockholders;
4. Making false certificates, reports or public notices;
5. An illegal transfer of the stock and property of such corporation, when it is insolvent or its insolvency is threatened;
6. The failure to file an annual report.

Such liabilities may be enforced in the courts of this state, in the same manner as similar liabilities imposed by law upon the officers, directors and stockholders of domestic corporations.

§ 5. This act shall take effect immediately.

Chap. 385.

AN ACT to regulate the price of illuminating gas in cities of fifteen hundred thousand inhabitants.

Became a law May 7, 1897, with the approval of the Governor.
Passed, a majority being present.

The People of the State of New York, represented in Senate and Assembly, do enact as follows:

Section 1. A corporation, association, company, copartnership or person shall not charge or receive for illuminating gas in a city, as now constituted, which has a population of fifteen hundred thousand, sums to exceed, per thousand cubic feet, during the remainder of the year eighteen hundred and ninety-seven, one dollar and twenty cents; during the year eighteen hundred and ninety-eight, one dollar and fifteen cents; during the year eighteen hundred and ninety-nine, one dollar and ten cents; during the year nineteen hundred, one dollar and five cents, and during each year thereafter, one dollar. *Price of gas regulated.*

§ 2. Such a corporation, association, company, copartnership or person shall not charge for illuminating gas for the use of any such city, sums to exceed, per thousand cubic feet, during the remainder *Id.*

of the year eighteen hundred and ninety-seven, one dollar; during
the year eighteen hundred and ninety-eight, ninety-seven and a half
cents; during the year eighteen hundred and ninety-nine, ninety-five
cents; during the year nineteen hundred, ninety-two and a half

Act not applicable to certain localities. cents, and during each year thereafter, ninety cents, but this act
shall not apply to that portion of the city of New York which for-
merly constituted the town of Kingsbridge, or that portion of said
city which was annexed thereto by chapter nine hundred and
thirty-four of the laws of eighteen hundred and ninety-five, entitled "An act to annex to the city and county of New York, territory lying within the incorporated villages of Wakefield, East
Chester and Williamsbridge, the town of Westchester, and portions
of the towns of East Chester and Pelham."

Change of territory not to affect act. § 3. A change hereafter effected in the territory or boundaries of
such a city, either by annexation, consolidation or otherwise, shall
not be deemed to enlarge or change the territory within which the
price of gas is regulated as herein provided, but this act shall continue in force for the purpose of regulating the price of gas in such
city, as now constituted, notwithstanding any subsequent change of
territory, but shall not apply in or to territory not now in such city.

Standard of illuminating power. § 4. The illuminating gas furnished by any such corporation, association, company, co-partnership or person shall have an illum-
inating power of not less than twenty-two sperm candles of six to
the pound, burning at the rate of one hundred and twenty grains
of spermaceti per hour tested, at a distance of not less than one mile
from the place of manufacture, by a burner consuming five cubic
feet of gas per hour, and shall, as regards purity, comply with the
standard now or hereafter established by law.

Repeal. § 5. All acts and parts of acts inconsistent with this act are
hereby repealed.

When takes effect. § 6. This act shall take effect on the first day of May, eighteen
hundred and ninety-seven.

Chap. 386.

AN ACT to amend the banking law and the act amendatory thereof, relative to securities in which deposits may be invested.

Became a law May 7, 1897, with the approval of the Governor.
Passed, three-fifths being present.

The People of the State of New York, represented in Senate and Assembly, do enact as follows:

Section 1. Subdivision five of section one hundred and sixteen of chapter six hundred and eighty-nine of the laws of eighteen hundred and ninety-two, entitled "An act in relation to banking corporations," as amended by chapter four hundred and fifty-four of the laws of eighteen hundred and ninety-six, is hereby further amended to read as follows: *Banking law amended.*

5. In the stocks or bonds of the following cities: Boston, Worcester, Cambridge, Lowell, Fall River, Springfield and Holyoke in the state of Massachusetts; Saint Louis, in the state of Missouri; Cleveland, Cincinnati and Toledo in the state of Ohio; Detroit and Grand Rapids, in the state of Michigan; Providence in the state of Rhode Island; New Haven and Hartford in the state of Connecticut; Portland in the state of Maine; Philadelphia, Pittsburg, Allegheny, Reading and Scranton in the state of Pennsylvania; Minneapolis and Saint Paul in the state of Minnesota; Des Moines in the state of Iowa; Milwaukee in the state of Wisconsin; Louisville in the state of Kentucky; Paterson, Trenton, Newark and Camden in the state of New Jersey; Baltimore, in the state of Maryland. If at any time the indebtedness of any of said cities, less its water debt and sinking fund, shall exceed seven per centum of its valuation for purposes of taxation, its bonds and stocks shall thereafter, and until such indebtedness shall be reduced to seven per centum of the valuation for the purposes of taxation, cease to be an authorized investment for the moneys of savings banks, but the superintendent of the banking department may, in his discretion, require any savings bank to sell such bonds or stocks of said city, as may have been purchased prior to said increase of debt. *Investment of deposits.*

§ 2. This act shall take effect immediately.

Chap. 387.

AN ACT to amend the insurance law relating to credit guaranty
corporations.

Became a law May 7, 1897, with the approval of the Governor.
Passed, a majority being present.

*The People of the State of New York, represented in Senate and
Assembly, do enact as follows:*

Section 1. Section one hundred and seventy-eight of chapter six
hundred and ninety of the laws of eighteen hundred and ninety-two
is hereby amended so as to read as follows:

§ 178. **Powers of credit guaranty corporations.**—Any such credit
guaranty corporation shall have the right, power and authority to
guaranty from loss, and to agree to pay to merchants, manufacturers, dealers and persons engaged in business and giving credit, the
debt or debts owing to them, and to indemnify them from loss and
to charge and receive therefor such a sum or percentum as the
consideration for such agreement, guaranty and indemnity as shall
be agreed upon between such corporation and the persons guaranteed, and to buy, hold, own and take an assignment of any and all
claims, accounts and demands so' guaranteed, and to hold, own
and collect the same, and to enforce the collection thereof by action
the same as the original holder and owner thereof might or could
do; also to insure the payment of money for personal services
under contract of hiring. Any such corporation may use its capital
stock or its funds accumulated in the course of its business to purchase or pay for any claim or demand, the payment of which it has
or does guarantee; and such of its capital stock of funds as may
not be so used shall be invested in the securities in which the capital
and funds of insurance corporations are required by the provisions
of this chapter to be invested. When an examination is made by
the authority of the superintendent of insurance into the affairs of
any credit guaranty corporation doing business in this state, or
when such corporation renders a statement to the insurance department, there shall not be allowed as assets any investments which
are not held as prescribed by law at the date of such examination
or rendering such statement; but unpaid premiums on policies
written within three months shall be admitted as available resources. In estimating its liabilities, there shall be charged, in
addition to the capital stock and all outstanding claims, a sum

equal to the total unearned premiums on the policies in force, calculated on the gross sum without any deduction on any account,
charged to the policyholders on each respective risk from the date
of the issue of the policy.

§ 2. This act shall take effect immediately.

Chap. 388.

AN ACT to amend the fisheries, game and forest law, relating to
taking shad in the Hudson river.

Became a law May 7, 1897, with the approval of the Governor.
. Passed, a majority being present.

*The People of the State of New York, represented in Senate and
Assembly, do enact as follows:*

Section 1. Section one hundred and thirty-six of chapter four
hundred and eighty-eight of the laws of eighteen hundred and
ninety-two, the title to which was amended by chapter three hundred and ninety-five of the laws of eighteen hundred and ninety-
five, to read, " An act relating to game, fish and wild animals and
to the forest preserve and Adirondack park, constituting chapter
thirty-one of the general laws, and to be known as the fisheries,
game and forest law," as amended by chapter one hundred and
fifty-four of the laws of eighteen hundred and ninety-six, is hereby
amended to read as follows:

§ 136. **Taking shad, herring and other fish in the Hudson and
Delaware rivers, and other waters.**—Except as herein provided,
shad, herring and other fish shall not be taken from the Hudson
and Delaware rivers or Rondout creek with nets of any kind.
Between the fourteenth day of March and the fifteenth day of
June shad and herring may be taken from said waters by nets to
be operated by hand only; but said nets shall not be drawn nor
fish taken therefrom between sunset on Friday night and sunrise
on Monday morning, unless by reason of the inclemency of the
weather said nets can not be drawn prior to sunset on Friday
night, in which case it shall be lawful to take fish therefrom as
soon as the weather will permit on Saturday, and between the first
day of September and the thirtieth day of May following, bull-
heads, catfish, suckers, eels, pickerel, sturgeon, white and yellow
perch, carp and sunfish may be caught by means of hoop-nets,
fykes, dip-nets, scoop-nets, and gill-nets, in the Hudson river, Wall-

kill creek and in Rondout creek below the dam at Eddyville and in
Wappingers creek and in the Ten Mile river in the town of Dover.
Nets shall not be set or used north of the dam at Troy.   Between
June first and September first sturgeon may be taken in the waters
of the Hudson river with sturgeon nets of not less than eleven
inches mesh.   Nothing in this section shall be construed to prohibit the catching of fish with hook and line in Rondout creek at
any time.   Whoever shall violate or attempt to violate any of the
provisions of this section shall be deemed guilty of misdemeanor
and in addition thereto shall be liable to a penalty of fifty dollars
for each violation thereof.

§ 2. This act shall take effect immediately.

Chap. 390.

AN ACT to amend chapter four hundred and eighty-eight of the
laws of eighteen hundred and ninety-two, entitled "An act for
the protection, preservation and propagation of birds, fish and
wild animals in the state of New York and the different counties
thereof," as amended by chapter nine hundred and seventy-four
of the laws of eighteen hundred and ninety-five and by chapter
six hundred and fifty-four of the laws of eighteen hundred and
ninety-six.

Became a law May 10, 1897, with the approval of the Governor.
Passed, three-fifths being present.

*The People of the State of New York, represented in Senate and
Assembly, do enact as follows:*

Section 1. Section forty of chapter four hundred and eighty-
eight of the laws of eighteen hundred and ninety-two, as amended
by chapter nine hundred and seventy-four of the laws of eighteen
hundred and ninety-five and by chapter six hundred and fifty-four
of the laws of eighteen hundred and ninety-six, is hereby amended
so as to read follows:

§ 40. Deer, close season.— Wild deer shall not be caught, shot at,
hunted or killed except from the fifteenth day of August
to the fifteenth day of November, both inclusive.   No person shall
kill or take alive more than two deer in any season.   And in the
counties of Ulster, Greene and Delaware no wild deer shall be
caught, shot at, hunted or killed at any time within five years
from the passage of this act.   Deer may be taken alive in any
part of the state at any season of the year under the direction of the

fish, game and forest commission to be placed in the deer parks belonging to the state for the purpose of breeding. The provisions of this section as to the close season shall not apply to Long Island. This section shall not be so construed as to prevent any person from reclaiming alive any deer which may have escaped from a private park or inclosure. Whoever shall violate or attempt to violate the provisions of this section shall be deemed guilty of a misdemeanor, and in addition thereto shall be liable to a penalty of one hundred dollars for each wild deer caught, shot at, hunted or killed.

§ 2. Section forty-three of chapter four hundred and eighty-eight of the laws of eighteen hundred and ninety-two, as amended by chapter nine hundred and seventy-four of the laws of eighteen hundred and ninety-five and by chapter six hundred and fifty-four of the laws of eighteen hundred and ninety-six, is hereby amended so as to read as follows:

§ 43. Traps and artificial lights.— Traps or any device whatsoever, to trap or entice deer, including salt licks, shall not be made, set or used, and deer shall not be caught, hunted or killed by aid or use thereof. No jack-light or any other artificial light shall be used in hunting or killing or attempting to kill any deer for the term of five years from and after the first day of June, eighteen hundred and ninety-seven. Whosoever shall violate or attempt to violate the provisions of this section shall be deemed guilty of a misdemeanor, and in addition thereto shall be liable to a penalty of one hundred dollars for each violation thereof.

§ 3. Section forty-four of chapter four hundred and eighty-eight of the laws of eighteen hundred and ninety-two, as amended by chapter nine hundred and seventy-four of the laws of eighteen hundred and ninety-five and by chapter six hundred and fifty-two of the laws of eighteen hundred and ninety-six, is hereby amended so as to read as follows:

§ 44. Hounding.— Deer shall not be hunted, pursued or killed with any dog or bitch in this state for the term of five years from the first day of June, eighteen hundred and ninety-seven. Dogs of the breed commonly used for hunting deer shall not be permitted by the owner or person harboring the same to run at large for or during the said term of five years in the forests where deer inhabit. The provisions of this section as to the close season shall not apply to Long Island. If any dog or bitch of the breed used for hunting deer shall be found hunting, pursuing or killing any deer or running at large in the forests

of this state where deer inhabit, it shall be deemed prima
facie evidence of the violation of the foregoing section by the per.
son or persons owning, using, having or harboring such dog or
bitch. Whoever shall violate or attempt to violate the provisions
of this section shall be deemed guilty of a misdemeanor and in
addition thereto shall be liable to a penalty of one hundred dollars
for each violation thereof.

Chap. 391.

AN ACT authorizing the state engineer and surveyor to continue
to co-operate with the director of the United States geological
survey in making a topographic survey and map of the state of
New York, and making an appropriation therefor.

Became a law May 10, 1897, with the approval of the Governor.
Passed, three-fifths being present.

*The People of the State of New York, represented in Senate and
Assembly, do enact as follows:*

Co-opera-
tion with
United
States au-
thorized.

Section 1. In order to continue the execution and speedy completion of a topographic survey and map of this state, the state
engineer and surveyor is hereby authorized to confer with the
director of the United States geological survey and to accept the
co-operation of the United States with this state in the execution of topographic survey and map of this state, which is hereby
Details of
work.
authorized to be made; and the said state engineer and surveyor
shall have the power to arrange with the said director, or other
authorized representative of the United States geological survey,
concerning the details of said work, the method of its execution
and the order in point of time in which these surveys and maps
of different parts of the state shall be completed; provided that
the said director of the United States geological survey shall
agree to expend on the part of the United States upon said work
Maps re-
sulting
from sur-
vey.
a sum equal to that hereby appropriated for this purpose. In
arranging details heretofore referred to, the state engineer and
surveyor shall, in addition to such other provisions as he may
deem wise, require that the maps resulting from this survey shall
be similar in general design to the West Point sheet edition of
October, eighteen hundred and ninety-two, made by the United
States geological survey, shall show the outlines of all counties,
towns, and extensive wooded areas, as existing on the ground
at the time of the execution of the survey ; the location of

all roads, railroads, streams, canals, lakes, and rivers, and shall contain contour lines showing the elevation and depression for every twenty feet in vertical interval of the surface of the country; that the resulting map shall fully recognize the co-operation of the state of New York, and that as each manuscript sheet of the map is completed, the state engineer and surveyor shall be furnished by the United States geological survey with photographic copies of the same and as the engraving on each sheet is completed the state engineer and surveyor shall be furnished by the said director with transfers from the copper plates of the same. *State engineer to be furnished with maps.*

§ 2. The sum of fifteen thousand dollars, or so much thereof as may be necessary, is hereby appropriated for the purposes specified in this act, out of any moneys in the treasury not otherwise appropriated, to be paid by the treasurer upon the warrant of the comptroller to the order of the state engineer and surveyor. *Appropriation.*

§ 3. This act shall take effect immediately.

Chap. 392.

AN ACT to amend chapter nine hundred and eight of the laws of eighteen hundred and ninety-six, entitled "An act in relation to taxation," and constituting chapter twenty-four of the general laws.

Became a law May 10, 1897, with the approval of the Governor.
Passed, a majority being present.

The People of the State of New York, represented in Senate and Assembly, do enact as follows:

Section 1. Section one hundred and forty-one of article six of chapter nine hundred and eight of the laws of eighteen hundred and ninety-six, known as the tax law, is hereby amended so as to read as follows:

§ 141. **Setting aside cancellation of sale.**— The comptroller is hereby authorized and empowered and shall, upon the application of anyone whomsoever aggrieved thereby, set aside any cancellation of sale made by him, or by any of his predecessors in office, in either of the following cases:

First. When such cancellation was procured by fraud or misrepresentation.

Second. When it was procured by the suppression of any material fact bearing on the case.

Third. When it was made under a mistake of fact.

Fourth. When such cancellation was made upon an application which the comptroller, or any of his predecessors in office, had no jurisdiction or legal right to entertain at the time of such cancellation.

Eight days written notice of an application made under and pursuant to this section shall be served upon the person upon whose application such sale was cancelled, or his heirs or grantees, the county treasurer of the county or counties in which the lands affected by such application are situate and upon the attorney-general of the state of New York; in case any of the parties to be served are not residents of the state of New York, or can not after reasonable diligence be found within the state of New York, such notice may be served by the publication thereof in a newspaper published in the county or counties where the lands affected by such application are situate, and, also in the newspaper printed at Albany, in which legal notices are required to be published, once in each week for three weeks immediately preceding the day upon which such application is to be made, and also by mailing a copy of said notice to each of said parties at their last known place of residence; and on or before the day of the first publication all papers upon which such application is to be made shall be filed in the office of the comptroller. The comptroller shall in all cases specify the grounds upon which such cancellation is set aside, and every such cancellation set aside by the comptroller shall in every and all respects have the same force and effect as though no cancellation thereof had ever been made.

§ 2. This act shall take effect immediately.

Chap. 393.

AN ACT authorizing an exchange of arms on the part of the state with the United States government.

Became a law May 10, 1897, with the approval of the Governor. Passed, three-fifths being present.

The People of the State of New York, represented in Senate and Assembly, do enact as follows:

Exchange of arms and ammunition authorized. Section 1. The governor, as commander-in-chief of the military and naval forces of the state, is authorized to turn over to the war department such Remington rifles and carbines, and such ammunition for such rifles and carbines, as may be in possession of the state, property of the state, as he may deem proper, in exchange for new Springfield rifles and carbines, and such ammunition as required in exchange for a like quantity of ammunition as may be held by the state for the Remington rifles and carbines, without expense to the state except for transportation and expenses incidental thereto, whenever the war department of the United States is prepared to make such exchange.

§ 2. This act shall take effect immediately.

Chap. 394.

AN ACT in relation to the library of the appellate division of the supreme court for the third department.

Became a law May 10, 1897, with the approval of the Governor.
Passed, a majority being present.

The People of the State of New York, represented in Senate and Assembly, do enact as follows:

Section 1. In addition to the amount appropriated by chapter four hundred and thirty-four of the laws of eighteen hundred and ninety-six, there is hereby appropriated and shall be paid by the state treasurer upon the warrant of the comptroller to the presiding justice of the appellate division of the supreme court of the state of New York for the third department, the sum of three thousand dollars, or so much thereof as said presiding justice shall certify to be necessary for the purpose of purchase and binding books for the law library of said appellate division. _{Appropriation for books.}

§ 2. This act shall take effect immediately.

Chap. 395.

AN ACT providing for continuing the construction of buildings at Dannemora, adapted to the requirements of three hundred insane convicts, to be known as the Dannemora State Hospital for Insane Convicts.

Became a law May 10, 1897, with the approval of the Governor.
Passed, three-fifths being present.

The People of the State of New York, represented in Senate and Assembly, do enact as follows:

Section 1. The superintendent of state prisons is hereby authorized and directed to continue, by the use of convict labor so _{Construction of buildings to be continued.}

far as practicable, the construction of buildings, on the state
lands at Dannemora, suitable for the requirements of three hundred insane convicts, the erection of which was commenced under
the provisions of chapter nine hundred and forty-nine, of the laws
of eighteen hundred and ninety-six.

State Hos-
pital.
§ 2. The buildings, so constructed, shall be known as the Dannemora State Hospital for Insane Convicts.

Expendi-
tures au-
thorized.
§ 3. For the purpose of carrying out the provisions of this act
the superintendent of state prisons is hereby authorized to expend the sum of seventy-five thousand dollars from the
" capital fund " of Clinton prison and if, at any time, there should
not be sufficient money available in the " capital fund " of Clinton
prison, to provide for the expenditures necessary to carry out the
provisions of this act, the superintendent of state prisons shall
cause a sufficient sum of money to be transferred from the " capital fund " of Sing Sing or Auburn prison to provide for such expenditures.

Moneys,
how
drawn, etc.
§ 4. The moneys authorized to be expended under the provisions
of this act shall be drawn and accounted for in the same manner
as moneys drawn for carrying on the industries.

§ 5. This act shall take effect immediately.

Chap. 396.

AN ACT authorizing and directing the comptroller to pay to
George H. Blackman for services rendered as acting superin-
tendent of the New York State Soldiers and Sailors' home at
Bath, New York.

Became a law May 10, 1897, with the approval of the Governor.
Passed, three-fifths being present.

*The People of the State of New York, represented in Senate and
Assembly, do enact as follows:*

Section 1. The comptroller is hereby authorized and directed
to pay to George H. Blackman, and he is hereby authorized to receive the same, such sum for services rendered as acting superintendent of the New York State Soldiers and Sailors' home at
Bath, New York, as may be audited by the board of trustees of said
home, not exceeding the sum of eight hundred and thirty-three
dollars and thirty-three cents.

§ 2. This act shall take effect immediately.

Chap. 397.

AN ACT to authorize and enable the Volunteer Firemen's Associations of the city of New York to erect a monument upon the battlefield of Gettysburg, Pennsylvania, in commemoration of their fallen members, and making an appropriation therefor.

Became a law May 10, 1897, with the approval of the Governor. Passed, three-fifths being present.

The People of the State of New York, represented in Senate and Assembly, do enact as follows:

Section 1. The Volunteer Firemen's Associations of the city of New York are hereby authorized to erect a suitable monument to their comrades who fell at the battle of Gettysburg, Pennsylvania, said monument to be placed on the position in said battlefield occupied by the Seventy-third regiment, New York volunteers (Second regiment, New York Zouaves), and shall be so placed under the direction of the trustees hereinafter named in conjunction with the New York monuments commission for the battlefields of Gettysburg and Chattanooga. _{Erection of monument authorized.}

§ 2. The following named persons are hereby constituted a board of trustees for the purpose of carrying out the provisions of this act: Robert B. Nooney, president Exempt Firemen association; George W. Anderson, president Veteran Firemen association; Richard Cullen, president Volunteer Firemen association; Mathew Stewart, president of the Second New York Fire Zouaves Veteran association; Peter J. Hickey, Michael F. Wynn, Thomas Fair, chairman of the monument committee of the Seventy-third regiment, New York volunteers; John Sidell, secretary of the said committee, and Francis McCarthy, treasurer of said committee, all of the city of New York, who shall serve without compensation. _{Board of trustees.}

§ 3. The sum of three thousand five hundred dollars is hereby appropriated to aid in the erection of said monument, out of any public moneys not otherwise appropriated, and the comptroller of the state of New York is hereby directed to draw his warrant upon the state treasurer for said amounts payable to the order of said board of trustees and to deliver the same to said board of trustees for the purpose of carrying out the provisions of this act, upon satisfactory evidence of the designation of a site by said New York monuments commission for the battlefields of Gettysburg and Chattanooga, and their approval of the design for such monument, and that a contract has been made for the completion of a monument thereon. _{Appropriation for monument.}

§ 4. This act shall take effect immediately.

Chap. 398.

AN ACT making an appropriation to assist in the erection of a monument to the memory of the late Frederick Douglass, at his former place of residence within this state.

Became a law May 10, 1897, with the approval of the Governor.
Passed, three-fifths being present.

The People of the State of New York, represented in Senate and Assembly, do enact as follows:

Appropriation for monument.

Section 1. The sum of three thousand dollars is hereby appropriated out of any moneys in the treasury not otherwise appropriated for the purpose of assisting in the erection of a monument to the memory of the late Frederick Douglass at the city of Rochester, his former place of residence within this state for which contributions are now being publicly solicited of the citizens of this state by the colored people, and the comptroller is hereby authorized to pay the same to the committee having the same in charge whenever it shall be satisfactorily shown by such committee that the collectible subscriptions for such purpose together with the sum hereby appropriated will be sufficient to purchase and erect such monument.

Payment of same.

§ 2. This act shall take effect immediately.

Chap. 399.

AN ACT making an appropriation for paying the interest on the canal debt.

Became a law May 10, 1897, with the approval of the Governor.
Passed, three-fifths being present.

The People of the State of New York, represented in Senate and Assembly, do enact as follows:

Appropriation for interest on canal debt.

Section 1. The following sums are hereby appropriated from the canal debt sinking fund, for the payment of the interest on the said debt, namely: For the payment of the interest due on the first day of July next on bonds issued during the current fiscal year, the sum of sixty thousand dollars; for the payment of the interest on the said debt due in the fiscal year beginning on the first day of October, eighteen hundred and ninety-seven, the sum of one hundred and nty-three thousand one hundred dollars.

Chap. 400.

AN ACT to amend chapter one hundred and twenty-five of the laws of eighteen hundred and ninety-one, entitled "An act to provide for the publication of the colonial statutes from the foundation of the colony to the adoption of the first constitution of the state of New York," and making an appropriation for the purchase and distribution of additional copies of the report of the commissioners of statutory revision relating thereto.

Became a law May 10, 1897, with the approval of the Governor.
Passed, three-fifths being present.

The People of the State of New York, represented in Senate and Assembly, do enact as follows:

Section 1. Sections two, three and five of chapter one hundred and twenty-five of the laws of eighteen hundred and ninety-one, entitled "An act to provide for the publication of the colonial statutes from the foundation of the colony to the adoption of the first constitution of the state of New York," are hereby amended to read as follows: *Act amended.*

§ 2. The republication shall be in octavo volumes of not less than one thousand or more than thirteen hundred pages each, with an index to each volume, and of a material equal in style and quality to the session laws of eighteen hundred and eighty-four. *Republication of statutes.*

§ 3. The commissioners of statutory revision shall deliver to the state senate and assembly libraries two sets each of their report containing the republication of such statutes, and one set to each of the following persons, corporations and institutions: *Distribution.*

1. To the governor and lieutenant-governor.

2. To each member of the legislature of eighteen hundred and ninety-seven.

3. To the secretary of state, comptroller, attorney-general, state treasurer, state engineer and surveyor, and the deputies of such officers.

4. To each other state officer or member of a state board or commission, requesting the same.

5. To each judge of the court of appeals, each justice of the supreme court, each county judge, and each surrogate, except where the county judge acts as surrogate, and to each district-attorney.

6. To the libraries of the court of appeals and to each supreme court and county law library.

7. To the library of each incorporated college, university or normal school within the state.

8. To the library of each union school, having an academic department under the supervision of the regents.

9. To such other libraries and institutions as request the same.

Title page.   § 5. It shall appear on the title page of every volume that it was transmitted to the legislature by the commissioners of statutory revision, pursuant to chapter one hundred and twenty-five of the

Statute in report evidence.   laws of eighteen hundred and ninety-one, and a statute contained in such report shall be evidence in any action or proceeding, and of the same force and effect as though the original was produced, if it appears from such publication that such statute was copied from the original.

Appropriation for purchase and distribution of copies.   § 2. The sum of nine thousand dollars, or so much thereof as may be necessary, is hereby appropriated out of any money in the treasury, not otherwise appropriated, for purchasing and distributing two thousand sets bound in full sheep of the report of the commissioners of statutory revision, containing the colonial laws, such money to be paid by the treasurer on the warrant of the comptroller on the order of the chairman of the commission of statutory revision.

§ 3. This act shall take effect immediately.

Chap. 404.

AN ACT to amend the code of civil procedure, relative to buildings in which justices' courts may be held.

Became a law May 10, 1897, with the approval of the Governor.
Passed, a majority being present.

The People of the State of New York, represented in Senate and Assembly, do enact as follows:

Section 1. Section twenty-eight hundred and sixty-eight of the code of civil procedure is hereby amended to read as follows:

§ 2868. Justices to hold court; general powers.— A justice of the peace must hold, within his town or city, a court for the trial of any action or special proceeding, of which he has jurisdiction, brought before him; but such a court shall not be held in a building in any part of which trafficking in liquors is authorized. He must hear, try and determine the same according to law and equity, and for that purpose, where special provision is not otherwise made by law, the court is vested with all the necessary powers possessed by the supreme court.

§ 2. This act shall take effect immediately.

Chap. 405.

AN ACT to amend section eleven hundred and twenty-six of the code of civil procedure, and in relation to the qualification of grand and trial jurors in Kings county.

Became a law May 10, 1897, with the approval of the Governor.
Passed, a majority being present.

The People of the State of New York, represented in Senate and Assembly, do enact as follows:

Section 1. The second paragraph of section eleven hundred and twenty-six, of the code of civil procedure, is hereby amended so as to read as follows:

2. Not less than twenty-one, nor more than seventy years of age.

§ 2. This act shall take effect September first, eighteen hundred and ninety-seven.

Chap. 406.

AN ACT to amend section fifty-four of article three of chapter six hundred and eighty-six of the laws of eighteen hundred and ninety-two, entitled "An act in relation to counties, constituting chapter eighteen of the general laws," relating to clerks of boards of supervisors.

Became a law May 10, 1897, with the approval of the Governor.
Passed, a majority being present.

The People of the State of New York, represented in Senate and Assembly, do enact as follows:

Section 1. Section fifty-four of article three of chapter six hundred and eighty-six of the laws of eighteen hundred and ninety-two, entitled "An act in relation to counties, constituting chapter eighteen of the general laws," relating to clerks of boards of supervisors, is hereby amended so as to read as follows:

§ 54. Forfeiture.—1. Any such clerk, or any person or persons required under this article to make any report, return or statement who shall refuse or neglect to make the same, shall forfeit to the county the sum of one hundred dollars, to be recovered by the district attorney thereof in the name of the county, and whenever such failure or neglect is caused by any such clerk, person or persons required to make such report, return or statement under the provisions of section fifty-two of this article, such district attorney shall forthwith proceed to obtain such forfeiture on notice in writing by the state comptroller of such failure or neglect; but such clerk shall not be subject to such forfeiture, in case he certify to the said comptroller, on or before the second Monday in December, the name or names of such person or persons who have refused or neglected to furnish him with the information necessary to make such report, return or statement required by said section fifty-two of this article; provided, however, that any such report, return or statement, which may have been made after said second Monday in December, shall be furnished by said clerk to the comptroller immediately upon its receipt.

2. The costs awarded upon the collection of such recoveries may be retained by the district attorney for his own use.

§ 2. This act shall take effect immediately.

Chap. 407.

AN ACT to amend chapter six hundred and eighty-six of the laws of eighteen hundred and ninety-two, entitled "An act in relation to counties, constituting chapter eighteen of the general laws," relating to the salaries and expenses of county judges and surrogates.

Became a law May 10, 1897, with the approval of the Governor.
Passed, three-fifths being present.

The People of the State of New York, represented in Senate and Assembly, do enact as follows:

Section 1. Section two hundred and twenty-three of article twelve of chapter six hundred and eighty-six of the laws of eighteen hundred and ninety-two is hereby amended to read as follows:

§ 223. When and how paid.— Such salaries, except in the county of Kings, shall be paid quarterly, by the county treasurer of the respective counties. When a county judge of one county shall hold a county court, or preside at a court of sessions in any other county, he shall be paid the sum of five dollars per day for his expenses in going to, and from, and holding or presiding at such court, which shall be paid by the county treasurer of such other county, on the presentation of the certificate of the clerk of such court of the number of days.

§ 2. This act shall take effect immediately.

Chap. 408.

AN ACT to amend the domestic relations law, in relation to adoption.

Became a law May 10, 1897, with the approval of the Governor.
Passed, three-fifths being present.

The People of the State of New York, represented in Senate and Assembly, do enact as follows:

Section 1. Section sixty-four of chapter two hundred and seventy-two of the laws of eighteen hundred and ninety-six, entitled "An act relating to the domestic relations, constituting chapter forty-eight of the general laws," is hereby amended to read as follows:

§ 64. Effect of adoption.— Thereafter the parents of the minor are relieved from all parental duties toward, and of all responsibility for, and have no rights over such child, or to his property by descent or succession. Where a parent who has procured a divorce, or a surviving parent, having lawful custody of a child, lawfully marries again, or where an adult unmarried person who has become a foster parent and has lawful custody of a child, marries, and such parent or foster parent consents that the person who thus becomes the stepfather or the stepmother of such child, may adopt such child, such parent or such foster parent, so consenting, shall not thereby be relieved of any of his or her parental duties toward, or be deprived of any of his or her rights over said child, or to his property by descent or succession. The child takes the name of the foster parent. His rights of inheritance and succession from his natural parents remain unaffected by such adoption. The foster parent or parents and the minor sustain toward each other the legal relation of parent and child and have all the rights, and are subject to all the duties of that relation, including the right of inheritance from each other, except as the same is affected by the provisions in this section in relation to adoption by a stepfather or stepmother, and such right of inheritance extends to the heirs and next of kin of the minor, and such heirs and next of kin shall be the same as if he were the legitimate child of the person adopting, but as respects the passing and limitation over of real or personal property dependent under the provisions of any instrument on the foster parent dying without heirs, the minor is not deemed the child of the foster parent so as to defeat the rights of remaindermen.

§ 2. This act shall take effect immediately.

Chap. 409.

AN ACT to amend section two hundred and three of article ten of chapter six hundred and eighty-six of the laws of eighteen hundred and ninety-two, known as the county law.

Became a law May 10, 1897, with the approval of the Governor.
Passed by a two-thirds vote.

The People of the State of New York, represented in Senate and Assembly, do enact as follows:

Section 1. Section two hundred and three of article ten of chapter six hundred and eighty-six of the laws of eighteen hundred and ninety-two, is hereby amended so as to read as follows:

§ 203. **In Erie, Monroe and Rensselaer counties.**— The district attorneys of Erie and Monroe counties may each appoint, in and for their respective counties, in the manner provided in the last section, and with like powers, two assistants, to be called respectively the first and second assistant district attorneys, and a managing clerk, who shall severally take the constitutional oath of office before entering upon the duties thereof; and the district attorney shall be responsible for their acts. They may also appoint a person to act as interpreter at all sessions of the grand juries of the counties of Erie and Monroe, and of the city of Buffalo, whose compensation shall be fixed by the court in and for which such grand jury may be empaneled. The district attorneys of the counties of Erie and Monroe shall each be entitled to receive in addition to their salary, all costs collected by them in actions and proceedings prosecuted and defended by them. The county judge or the special county judge of the county of Monroe, or any supreme court judge, shall have power, on the application of the district attorney of Monroe county, to order and direct the county treasurer of Monroe county to pay to the district attorney any sum of money expended or incurred by him in the performance of his duties in his office, and the county judge of the county of Rensselaer, or any supreme court judge, shall have power, on the application of the district attorney of Rensselaer county to order and direct the county treasurer of Rensselaer county to pay to the district attorney any sum of money expended or incurred by him in the performance of his duties in his office.

Chap. 410.

AN ACT to amend chapter nine hundred and nine of the laws of eighteen hundred and ninety-six, entitled "In relation to the elections, constituting chapter six of the general laws," and known as the "election law," in relation to the designation, number and qualification of election officers.

Became a law May 10, 1897, with the approval of the Governor. Passed, three-fifths being present.

The People of the State of New York, represented in Senate and Assembly, do enact as follows:

Section 1. Section eleven of chapter nine hundred and nine of the laws of eighteen hundred and ninety-six, is hereby amended to read as follows:

§11. Election officers; designation, number and qualifications.— There shall be in every election district of this state the following election officers, namely, four inspectors, two poll clerks and two ballot clerks, whose term of office shall be for one year from the date of their appointment or election, and who shall serve at every general or special election held within their districts during such term. No person shall act as an inspector of election, poll clerk or ballot clerk who is not a qualified elector of the city, or of the election district of the town in which he is to serve, of good character, able to read and speak the English language understandingly, and to write it legibly, or who is a candidate for any office to be voted for by the electors of the district at the election at which he is to serve, except inspector of election; or, who has been convicted of a felony, or who holds any other public office or place of public trust, except notary public or commissioner of deeds, town or village assessor, justice of the peace, village trustee, water commissioner, officer of a school district, overseer of highway, who is employed in any public office or by any public officer whose services are paid for out of the public moneys. Each class of such officers shall be equally divided between the two political parties which, at the last preceding election for governor, polled the highest number of votes for such office in the state.

§ 2. This act shall take effect immediately.

Chap. 411.

AN ACT to amend the executive law, relating to the fees to be
paid for filing certain certificates of incorporation.

Became a law May 10, 1897, with the approval of the Governor.
Passed, a majority being present.

*The People of the State of New York, represented in Senate and
Assembly, do enact as follows:*

Executive
law
amended.
Section 1. Subdivision twelve of section twenty-six of chapter
six hundred and eighty-three of the laws of eighteen hundred and
ninety-two, entitled "An act in relation to executive officers, constituting chapter nine of the general laws," is hereby amended to
read as follows :

Fees of
secretary
of state.
12. For filing and recording the original certificate of incorporation of a railroad corporation for the construction of a railroad in
a foreign country, fifty dollars; for filing the original certificates
of every other railroad corporation, twenty-five dollars; for filing
the original certificate of any other stock corporation, ten dollars;
for filing any original certificate of incorporation drawn under
article two of the membership corporations law ten dollars.

§ 2. This act shall take effect immediately.

Chap. 413.

AN ACT relating to state finance, constituting chapter ten of the
general laws.

Became a law May 13, 1897, with the approval of the Governor.
Passed, three-fifths being present.

*The People of the State of New York, represented in Senate and
Assembly, do enact as follows:*

CHAPTER X OF THE GENERAL LAWS.
THE STATE FINANCE LAW.

Article 1. General fiscal provisions. (§§ 1-34.)

  2. The general fund. (§§ 50-51.)

  3. Canal fund and canal debt sinking fund. (§§ 60-66.)

  4. Education funds. (§§ 80-96.)

  5. Miscellaneous funds. (§§ 100-102.)

  6. Laws repealed ; when to take effect. (§§ 110-111.)

ARTICLE I.
GENERAL FISCAL PROVISIONS.

Section 1 Short title.— This chapter shall be known as the state finance law.

§ 2. Fiscal year.— The fiscal year of all offices, asylums, hospitals, charitable and reformatory institutions in this state shall begin with the first day of October and end with the next following thirtieth day of September. All books and accounts in the offices of the comptroller and treasurer shall be kept by fiscal years. All annual accounts required to be rendered to the comptroller or treasurer by any person shall be closed on the thirtieth day of September in each year, and rendered as soon thereafter as practicable, if no time is specially prescribed by law.

§ 3. Duties of treasurer.— The treasurer shall receive all moneys paid into the treasury of the state, pay all warrants drawn by the comptroller on the treasury, make no payment out of the treasury except on the warrant of the comptroller, unless otherwise provided by law, and annually report to the legislature an exact statement of the balance in the treasury, at the close of the preceding fiscal year, with a summary of the receipts into and payments from the treasury during such year.

§ 4. Duties of comptroller.—The comptroller shall:

1. Superintend the fiscal concerns of the state.

2. Keep, audit and state all accounts in which the state is interested, and keep accurate and proper books, showing their conditions at all times.

3. Examine, audit and settle the accounts of all public officers and other persons indebted to the state, and certify the amount or balance due thereon.

4. Examine, audit and liquidate the claims of all persons against the state, if payment thereof out of the treasury is provided for by law.

5. Draw warrants on the treasury for the payment of the moneys directed by law to be paid out of the treasury, but no such warrant shall be drawn unless authorized by law, and every such warrant shall refer to the law under which it is drawn.

6. Make a report to the legislature at its annual session, containing a complete statement of the funds of the state, its resources, public expenditures during the preceding fiscal year, a detailed estimate of the expenditures to be defrayed from the treasury for the fiscal year beginning October first following, a statement of each object of expenditure, the funds, if any, from which it is to be defrayed, and of all claims against the state presented to him where no provision or an insufficient provision for the payment thereof has been made by law, with the facts relating thereto and

his opinion thereon, and suggesting plans for the improvement and management of the public resources, and containing such other information and recommendations relating to the fiscal affairs of the state, as in his judgment should be communicated to the legislature.

7. Represent and vote for the state, either in person or by proxy at all meetings and on all occasions where the state is entitled to representation or vote as stockholder in a corporation or joint stock association.

§ 5. **Treasurer's checks and accounts** — The comptroller shall countersign and enter in the proper books of his department all checks drawn by the treasurer and all receipts for money paid to the treasurer. No such receipt shall be evidence of payment unless so countersigned. He shall keep an account between the state and the treasurer, and therein charge the treasurer with the balance in the treasury when he came into office, and with all moneys received by him, and credit him with all warrants drawn on and paid by him. He shall draw, in favor of the treasurer, on all corporations or companies in which the state may own stock, for the dividends on such stock as they become due. He shall procure from the books of the banks in which the treasurer makes his deposits, monthly statements of the moneys received and paid out of the same on account of the treasurer. On the first Tuesday of every month, or oftener if he deem it necessary, he shall carefully examine the accounts of the debts and credits in the bank books kept by the treasurer. If he discovers any irregularity or deficiency therein, he shall, unless rectified or explained to his satisfaction, forthwith report the same to the governor.

§ 6. **Custody of state securities.** — All leases, bonds, mortgages, certificates of stock and other securities belonging to the state, and all papers relating to the duties of the comptroller, or of the commissioners of the canal fund, or of the canal board, all deeds to the state, abstracts of title, and state contracts, unless otherwise specially directed, shall be deposited in the office of the comptroller.

§ 7. **Examination of state securities.** — The comptroller, from time to time, shall examine the securities on which money may be due to the state, and make inquiries relating to the sufficiency of the security for the payment of such money. He shall require the immediate payment of all interest due, and the payment of such part of the principal as he deems necessary for the security and interest of the state.

§ 8. Deposit in banks.— The state treasurer shall deposit all
moneys received by him on account of the state, except such as
belong to the canal fund, within three days after receiving the
same, in such banks, in the cities of Albany and New York, as
in the opinion of the comptroller and treasurer are secure and
pay the highest rate of interest to the state for such deposits.
The moneys so deposited shall be placed to the account of the
treasurer. He shall keep a bank-book in which shall be entered
his account of deposit in and moneys drawn from the banks in
which deposits are made by him, which he shall exhibit to the
comptroller for his inspection on the first Tuesday of every
month and oftener if required. The treasurer shall not draw
any moneys from such banks unless by checks subscribed by
him as treasurer and countersigned by the comptroller, unless otherwise provided by law. No moneys shall be paid by any such bank
out of any such deposit except upon such checks. Every such
bank shall transmit to the comptroller monthly statements of all
moneys received and paid by it on account of the treasurer.

§ 9. Monthly statement of balances in state depositories.— The
state treasurer shall cause to be published in the state paper,
on or before the tenth day of each month, a detailed statement of
the balances in the several banks designated by any state officer
or board as a depository of state funds. Such statement shall
contain the name of each bank and the amount subject to draft
at the close of the month preceding such publication. All officers,
departments, commissions or boards receiving fees or penalties
shall certify to the comptroller, on or before the tenth day of
January, April, July and October in each year, the amount of
moneys on their hands or on deposit at the close of the quarter
preceding, in the banks designated to receive such deposits, and
shall pay over such amount at once to the treasurer of the state.

§ 10. Deposit of moneys by state officers.— Every state officer
or other person except the state treasurer, receiving or disbursing
moneys belonging to the state, shall deposit and keep all the
moneys received by him, deposited to his official credit in some
responsible bank or banking house, to be designated by the comptroller, until such moneys are paid out or disbursed according to
law. Every such bank or banking house, when required by the
comptroller, shall execute and file in his office an undertaking to
the state in such sum and with such sureties as are required and
approved by him, for the safekeeping and prompt payment on
legal demand therefor of all such moneys held by or on deposit

in such bank or banking house, with interest thereon, on daily or monthly balances at such rate as the comptroller may fix. Every such undertaking shall have indorsed thereon, or annexed thereto, the approval of the attorney-general as to its form.

§ 11. **Deposit of moneys by charitable and benevolent institutions.**— All moneys received from the state by any charitable or benevolent institution, supported wholly or partly by moneys received from the state, shall be deposited in such national or state bank or trust company, as the comptroller may designate. Every such bank or trust company shall give an undertaking, as provided in the last section. The treasurer of such institution shall keep all the funds thereof which come into his possession from the state, deposited in his name as such treasurer in such bank or trust company.

§ 12. **Proofs required on audit by the comptroller.**— The comptroller shall not draw his warrant for the payment of any sum appropriated, except for salaries and other expenditures and appropriations, the amounts of which are duly established and fixed by law, until the person demanding the same presents to him a detailed statement thereof in items and makes all reports required of him by law. If such statement is for services rendered or articles furnished, it must show when, where, to whom and under what authority they were rendered or furnished. If for traveling expenses, the distance traveled, between what places, the duty or business for the performance of which the expenses were incurred, and the dates and items of each expenditure. If for transportation, furniture, blank and other books purchased for the use of offices, binding, blanks, printing, stationery, postage, cleaning and other necessary and incidental expenses, a bill duly receipted must be attached to the statement. Each statement of accounts must be verified by the person presenting the same to the effect that it is just, true and correct, that no part thereof has been paid, except as stated therein, and that the balance therein stated is actually due and owing. No payment shall be made to any salaried state officer or commissioner having an office established by law, for personal expenses incurred by him while in the discharge of his duties as such officer or commissioner at the place where such office is located. No manager, trustee or other officer of any state charitable or other institution, receiving moneys from the state treasury in whole or in part for the maintenance or support of such institution shall be interested in any purchase or sale by any of such officers.

§ 13. **Regulations for the transmission of public moneys.**— The comptroller may make such regulations and give such directions from time to time, respecting the transmission to the treasury of moneys belonging to the state from the several county treasurers and other public officers as in his judgment is most conducive to the interests of the state. He may, in his discretion, audit, allow and cause to be paid the expenses necessarily incurred under or in consequence of such regulations and directions or so much thereof as he deems equitable and just.

§ 14. **Temporary loans and revenue bonds.**—From time to time, as the legal demands on the treasury render it necessary, the comptroller may make such temporary loans at a rate of interest not exceeding five per centum per annum, as are necessary to discharge such demands, and may issue transfer certificates for the amount borrowed, with interest, payable semi-annually, and the principal payable at such time or times not exceeding seven years, at which in his opinion, the treasury will be in a conditon to pay the same from the revenues of the state applicable to their payment, and so much of such revenues as will be sufficient to pay the amount borrowed, are pledged to that object. He may issue bonds in anticipation of the state tax, authorized to be levied for the current expenses of the government, not exceeding fifty per centum of such tax to any one year, payable on or before May fifteenth following the date of issue, and drawing interest at the least rate obtainable by him. The proceeds of such bonds shall be applied in payment of the current expenses of the government and to no other object. When received into the treasury so much as may be necessary of the taxes in anticipation of which any such bonds are issued, shall be applied exclusively to the payment of the principal and interest of such bonds. He shall include in his annual report, a detailed statement of all such loans made and bonds issued during the year, and of his proceedings in relation thereto.

§ 15. **New in place of lost certificates.**—The comptroller may issue to the lawful owner of any certificate or bond issued by him in behalf of this state, which he is satisfied, by due proof filed in his office, has been lost or casually destroyed, a new certificate or bond, corresponding in date, number and amount with the certificate or bond so lost or destroyed, and expressing on its face that it is a renewed certificate or bond. No such renewed certificate or bond shall be issued unless sufficient security is given to satisfy the lawful claim of any person to the original certificate or bond, or to any interest therein. The comptroller shall report annually to the legislature the number and amount of all renewed certificates or bonds so issued.

§ 16. **Forms of state accounts.**—The comptroller shall prepare a form of accounts to be observed in every state charitable institution, reformatory, house of refuge, industrial school, department, board or commission, which shall be accepted and followed by them respectively, after thirty days' notice thereof. Such forms shall include such a uniform method of bookkeeping, filing and rendering of accounts as may insure a uniform statement of purchase of like articles, whether by the pound, measure or otherwise, as the interests of the public service may require, and a uniform method of reporting in such institutions and departments, the amount and value of all produce and other articles of maintenance raised upon the lands of the state, or manufactured in such institution, and which may enter into the maintenance of such institution or department. All purchases for the use of any department, office or work of the state government shall be for cash. Each voucher, whether for a purchase or for services or other charge shall be filled up at the time it is taken. Where payment is not made directly by the state treasurer, proof in some proper form shall be furnished on oath that the voucher was so filled up at the time it was taken, and that the money stated therein to have been paid, was in fact paid in cash or by check or draft on some specified bank.

§ 17. **Itemized and monthly accounts of public officers.**—The proper officer of each state hospital, asylum, charitable or reformatory institution, the state commission in lunacy, the state board of charities, the state board of health, the commissioners of fisheries, game and forestry and all other state commissions, commissioners and boards, shall, on/ or before the fifteenth day of each month, render to the comptroller a detailed and itemized account of all receipts and expenditures of such hospital, asylum, institution, commission, board of commissioners during the three months next preceding. Such accounts shall give in detail the • source of all receipts, including the sums received from any county, and be accompanied by original and proper vouchers for all funds paid from the state treasury, unless such vouchers have been previously filed with the comptroller and have appended or annexed thereto the affidavit of the officer making the same to the effect that the goods and other articles therein specified were purchased and received by him or under his direction or that the indebtedness was incurred under his direction; that the goods were purchased at a fair cash market price and that neither he, nor any person in his behalf, had any pecuniary or other interest in the articles purchased or in the indebtedness incurred; that he received no pecuniary or other benefit therefrom, nor any promises thereof; that the articles contained in such bill were received by him and that they conformed in all respects to the goods ordered by him or under his direction, both in quality and quantity.

§ 18. **Inspection of supplies and entry in books.**—The steward, clerk or bookkeeper in every such institution, board or commission shall receive and examine all articles purchased or received for the maintenance thereof, compare them with the bills for the same, ascertain whether they correspond in weight, quality or quantity, and inspect the supplies thus received. Such steward, clerk or bookkeeper shall enter each bill of goods thus received in the books of the institution or department at the time of receipt thereof. He shall make a full memorandum in the book of accounts of such institution of any difference in weight, quality or quantity of any article received from the bill thereof, and no goods or other articles of purchase or manufacture or farm or garden production of land of the institution shall be received unless so entered in such book with the proper bill, invoice or statement, according to the form of accounts and record prescribed by the comptroller. In accounts for repairs or new work, the name of each workman, the number of days employed and the rate and amount of wages paid to him shall be given. If contracts are made for repairs or new work, or for supplies, a duplicate thereof, with specifications, shall be filed with the comptroller. The steward of every such institution or other officer performing the duties of a steward under whatever name, shall take, subscribe and file with the comptroller, before entering on his duties, the constitutional oath of office, and may administer oaths and take affidavits concerning the business of such institution.

§ 19. **Deposit in banks of moneys received by state institutions.**—Every state institution supported, in whole or in part, by the state, shall deposit at interest, all its funds received from sources other than the state in a bank or trust company, which shall give a bond with sufficient sureties for the security of such deposit, to be approved by the comptroller. All state institutions or departments, except charitable institutions, state hospitals for the insane, reformatories, houses of refuge, and state industrial schools, shall pay into the treasury, quarterly, all receipts and earnings other than receipts from the state treasury.

§ 20. **Annual inventory and report of institutions.**—Every state charitable institution, state hospital, reformatory, house of refuge and industrial school shall file with the comptroller annually, on or before October twentieth, a certified inventory of all articles of maintenance on hand at the close of the preceding fiscal year, stating the kind and amount of each article. Every state charitable institution, state hospital, reformatory, house of refuge, state agricultural experiment station, and the quarantine commissioners, required by law to report annually to the legislature, shall state an inventory of each article of property, stating its kind and amount, except supplies for maintenance, belonging to the state and in their possession on October first of each year.

§ 21. **Rendition of accounts.**— The comptroller, from time to time, shall require all public officers and other persons receiving moneys or securities, or having the care and management of any property of the state, of which an account is or is required to be kept in his office, to render statements thereof to him; and all such officers or persons shall render such statements at such time and in such form as he requires, and at all times when required by law. He may require any one presenting to him an account or claim for audit or settlement, to be examined upon oath before him touching such account or claim, as to any facts relating to its justness or correctness. He may issue a notice to any person receiving moneys of the state for which he does not account or to the legal representatives of such a person, requiring an account and vouchers for the expenditure of such moneys to be rendered at a time to be fixed not less than thirty nor more than ninety days from the date of the service of the notice. Such notice shall be served by delivering a copy thereof to such person or representative or leaving such copy at his usual place of abode; and if such service is made by the sheriff of the county, where the person served resided, the certificate of such sheriff, and if made by any other person, the affidavit of such other person, shall be presumptive evidence of such service.

§ 22. **Statements of account not rendered.**— The comptroller shall state an account against every person who receives moneys belonging to the state for which he does not account when required, charging him with the amount received according to the best information which the comptroller may have in regard thereto, with interest at six per centum per annum from the time when the same was due and payable, and shall deliver a certified copy of such account to the attorney-general for prosecution, and such certified copy shall be presumptive evidence of the indebtedness of such person to the state for the amount stated therein. The person against whom an action is brought by the attorney-general on any such account, shall be liable for and pay the costs of the action whether final judgment therein shall be against him or in his favor, unless he is sued as the representative of the person originally accountable for such moneys.

§ 23. **Statements of accounts rendered.**—The comptroller shall immediately examine the accounts rendered by every public officer or other person receiving moneys belonging to the state, with the vouchers, and audit, adjust and make a statement thereof. If any necessary vouchers are wanting or defective, he shall give notice to such person to furnish proper vouchers within not less than thirty nor more than ninety days, and at the expiration of such time he shall audit, adjust and make a statement of such accounts on the vouchers and proofs before him. He shall transmit a copy of every account as settled to such persons, and if any balance is stated therein to be due the state, and is not paid to the treasurer within ninety days after its transmission to such person, the comptroller shall deliver a certified copy of such account to the attorney-general for prosecution. Such certified copy shall be presumptive evidence of the indebtedness of such person to the state for the balance so certified, and if on the trial of any action brought thereon, the defendant gives any evidence other than such as was produced to the comptroller before the statement of such accounts, and by means thereof, the balance so stated is reduced or no balance is found to be due, the defendant shall be liable for and pay the costs of such action.

§ 24. **Statement of joint accounts.**—The comptroller may, in his discretion, settle separately the accounts of one or more persons receiving moneys of the state for which they are accountable to the state. In such case no person shall plead as a defense to an action brought for a balance certified to be due from him, the non-joinder of any other person, or give in evidence upon the trial thereof the fact that any other person was concerned with him in the receipt or expenditure of such moneys.

§ 25. **Other remedies preserved.**—This article does not preclude the state from the enforcement of any other remedy, for the recovery of any debt due or to become due to the state.

§ 26. **Foreclosure of mortgages by the state**—The comptroller shall cause all mortgages belonging to the state upon which default is made in the payment of principal or interest, to be foreclosed, whenever, in his judgment, it may be necessary for the protection of the interest of the state. All actions or proceedings for that purpose shall be prosecuted or conducted by the attorney-general.

§ 27. **When comptroller shall bid in premises.**—If on a sale on any such foreclosure, there is not bid and paid or received the amount unpaid on the mortgage, for principal and interest and the costs and expenses of the foreclosure, the comptroller may cause the sale to be postponed and have the value of the premises appraised by two competent and disinterested persons selected by him. If the premises are appraised at a sum equal to or exceeding the amount unpaid to the state, including the costs of the foreclosure and expenses of the appraisal, the comptroller on the sale thereof, shall bid for the state such amount, if necessary to prevent a sale of the premises at a less sum. If the premises are appraised at a sum less than such amount, the comptroller may bid the amount of the appraisement and no more. If the premises are struck off for a sum less than such amount, no greater sum shall be credited to the mortgagor or any other person, on account of such sale than the sum bid for the premises sold, deducting therefrom all costs and expenses of the sale and appraisal. The appraisers shall receive a reasonable compensation for their services, to be allowed by the comptroller and paid out of the treasury.

§ 28. **Conditions of sale.**—At a sale under such foreclosure the comptroller shall require the purchaser to pay, at the time of the sale, the costs and expenses thereof, and at least one-fourth of the amount so unpaid; and for securing the remainder of the moneys due the state, on the execution of a deed or of the affidavits of sale to the purchaser, he may accept from the purchaser a bond and mortgage to the state on the premises sold, payable in six equal annual installments, with annual interest at six per centum. If the mortgaged premises sell for a greater sum than the amount so unpaid and the costs and expenses of the sale, the comptroller shall also require the purchaser at the time of sale to make payment of such surplus. The expense, incurred by the attorney-general in any action or proceeding for the foreclosure of any such mortgage, shall be paid to him out of the treasury.

§ 29. **Sale in parcels** —On any such foreclosure, if any person having title to a part of the mortgaged premises, by conveyance from or through the mortgagor, delivers to the comptroller an affidavit stating that he has such title, and describing with certainty such part, the comptroller on the sale under such foreclosure shall cause to be first sold that part of the mortgaged premises not specified in the affidavit. If the part so sold does not produce enough to satisfy the amount so unpaid and costs and expenses he shall immediately cause such part or parts of the premises as have been conveyed by the mortgagor and described in any such affidavit, to be sold, and if more than one part of such premises has been so conveyed, and an affidavit made as herein required, the comptroller shall cause such parts to be sold in the inverse order of the dates of such conveyances, if it is necessary to sell them, commencing with the part last conveyed by the mortgagor, and such sale shall cease when the proceeds of the sale are sufficient to satisfy the amount so unpaid and such costs and expenses.

§ 30. **Separate accounts for lands purchased or mortgaged.**— The comptroller on application to him for that purpose, shall open an account in his office against any person, for a part or subdivision of a lot of land purchased from or mortgaged to the state, for the proportionate part of the moneys on any such part or subdivision, and thereafter give credit on the several parts or subdivisions, as the persons making payments may require. He may credit any prior payment to a part or subdivision, if such payment appears by satisfactory proof to have been originally intended to be paid on such part or subdivision or by or for the use of the person claiming the credit, whether so expressed in the receipts or not. No part of any such payments shall be applied to the reduction of the principal unpaid on any such part or subdivision, unless the payments exceed the interest, calculated on the principal due on such part, or subdivision, to the day when such part or subdivision is to be paid off, or a new account opened therefor. If separate receipts be given by the treasurer, for any payments which are claimed to be credited to the account of any such part or subdivision, the receipts shall be delivered to the comptroller and filed in his office. Separate accounts shall not be opened under this section unless a map and survey of the whole lot is filed with the comptroller, showing particularly the part or subdivision for which such account is to be opened, and satisfactory proof furnished the comptroller that the residue of the lot is sufficient security for the sum remaining unpaid thereon.

§ 31. Discharge of mortgages.—The treasurer's receipt, countersigned by the comptroller, setting forth that the whole sum secured by the mortgage held by the state has been paid, shall be a sufficient discharge of the mortgage, and the officer in whose office such mortgage is recorded shall record such receipt as a satisfaction of the mortgage and satisfy the mortgage of record. When any part or subdivision of any lot mortgaged to or purchased from the state, for which a separate account has been opened, is paid, the comptroller shall execute a discharge of such part or subdivision from such mortgage.

If a map and survey of the whole lot is filed with the comptroller showing particularly a part or subdivision for which no separate account has been opened, and the owner thereof pays into the treasury its full proportion of principal and interest unpaid, and satisfactory proof is furnished the comptroller that the residue of the lot is sufficient security for the sum remaining unpaid, he may execute a like discharge of such part or subdivision.

§ 32. Surplus moneys on sale of lands mortgaged to the state.— If real property mortgaged to the state, or purchased for the benefit of the state, or for which a certificate has been given to a former purchaser, is sold by the comptroller, state engineer or the commissioners of the land office for a greater sum than the amount due to the state, with the costs and expenses of the foreclosure or resale, the surplus moneys received into the treasury after a conveyance has been executed to the purchaser, shall be paid to the person legally entitled to such real property at the time of the foreclosure or of the forfeiture of the original contract. On a sale of such real property by the comptroller, the state engineer or the commissioners of the land office, the comptroller shall give credit to the mortgagor on his bond or to the original purchaser on his contract, for the amount at which such property has been sold, after deducting therefrom all the costs, charges and expenses of the sale. If interfering claims to such surplus moneys be made, they shall be referred by the comptroller to the attorney-general, whose decision as to the rights of the respective claimants shall be final and conclusive as to any claim against the state. The comptroller shall not draw his warrant for any moneys authorized by this section to be refunded, except on satisfactory proof, by affidavit or otherwise, of the legal right of the person in whose favor such warrant is applied for.

§ 33. **Assignments of mortgages; releases from judgments.**—The comptroller, on the written request of the owner in actual possession of real property mortgaged to the state, may assign such mortgage, with the bond or other instrument accompanying the same, on payment into the treasury of the amount of principal and interest unpaid on such mortgage. The comptroller, with the consent of the attorney-general, if satisfied that the interests of the state will not be prejudiced thereby, may release any portion of any real property subject to a judgment in favor of the people of the state from the lien created by such judgment.

§ 34. **Compromise of old judgments and debts** —The attorney-general and comptroller, or either of them, may acknowledge satisfaction of judgment in favor of the people of the state when the same is settled or discharged. The comptroller, with the approval of the attorney-general, may compromise, settle, release and discharge any judgment or contract debt not in judgment in favor of the state, after the lapse of ten years since the recovery of the judgment, or since the debt became due, on such terms as the comptroller and attorney-general deem for the best interest of the state.

ARTICLE II.
THE GENERAL FUND.

Section 50. General fund.

51. Payments out of the general fund.

Section 50. **General fund.**—The stocks, debts and other property known as the general fund of this state, the income and revenues thereof, and the additions which may be made thereto, shall continue to be known as the general fund. All money paid into the treasury of the state, not belonging to any specific fund established by law, belongs to and is part of the general fund.

§ 51. **Payments out of the general fund.**—All moneys authorized by law to be paid out of the treasury of the state and not payable from any specific fund established by law shall be paid out of the general fund.

ARTICLE III.

CANAL FUND AND CANAL DEBT SINKING FUND.

Section 60. Canal fund.

61. Commissioners of the canal fund.

62. Deposit of funds.

63. Charges on the canal fund.

64. Rules and regulations.

65. When money may be borrowed for the canal fund.

Section 60. **Canal fund.**—The canal fund shall continué to consist of the following property:

1. Real property granted for the construction of the canals, by the state, by companies, or by individuals, and remaining unsold.

2. Debts due for portions of such real property heretofore sold.

3. All moneys received from the sale or use of the surplus waters of any canal.

4. All moneys recovered in suits for penalties or damages instituted under the canal law.

5. All moneys required by law to be paid into the canal fund.

§ 61. **Commissioners of the canal fund.**—The canal fund and the canal debt sinking fund shall continue to be superintended and managed by the commissioners of the canal fund, a majority of whom, including the comptroller, shall be a quorum for the transaction of business. The care and disposition of all lands belonging to the canal fund shall be vested in the commissioners of the land office. Investments for the canal fund and the canal debt sinking fund shall be made by the comptroller, subject to the approval of the commissioners of the canal fund, in such securities as he is authorized by law to invest the other funds of the state.

§ 62. **Deposit of funds.**—The commissioners of the canal fund may deposit the moneys belonging to such fund, or the canal debt sinking fund, with any safe incorporated moneyed institution or banking association in this state, and may make such contracts therewith for the interest on and the duration of such deposits as will best promote the interest of the funds.

§ 63. **Charges on the canal fund.**— All moneys expended in the construction, repair or improvement of the canals now authorized by law, or allowed or expended by the commissioners of the canal fund, or the superintendent of public works or other officer or assistant employed on such canals pursuant to law, with the compensation of such officers respectively, including the salary of the superintendent of public works, shall be charged to the canal fund unless otherwise expressly provided by law, and the comptroller shall also charge from time to time so much for the services of the clerks in his office, devoted to the accounts and revenues of the canals, as in his opinion is just.

§ 64. Rules and regulations.— The commissioners of the canal fund from time to time, shall prescribe such rules and regulations relative to the transfer of all or any of the public stocks of this state, constituting the debt known as the canal debt, and the division and consolidation of the certificates thereof, as they think advisable. They may require such returns to be made to the comptroller by the officer or person authorized by law to transfer such stocks, and pay the interest on any loan, as they deem reasonable.

§ 65. When money may be borrowed for the canal fund.— If the legislature, the canal board, the commissioners of the canal fund or the superintendent of public works, lawfully authorize or require the payment of any sum of money out of the canal fund, for any purpose connected with canal expenditures, and there is not money in such fund applicable to such purpose, the commissioners of the canal fund may borrow such sum of money, payable in such time not exceeding eighteen years, and bearing such rate of interest not exceeding five per centum, as they deem most beneficial to the interests of the state, and the comptroller may issue bonds therefor in the manner provided by law.

ARTICLE IV.
THE EDUCATION FUND.

Section 93. Certified copy of original mortgage.
94. Fees of loan commissioners.
95. Powers and duties of boards of supervisors as to loan mortgages.
96. Payments to Cornell University on account of the college land scrip fund.

Section 80. The education fund.— The common school fund, the literature fund, and the United States deposit fund, shall continue to consist of all moneys, securities or other property in the treasury of the state, or under the control of any state officer, and of all debts due the state, or real property owned by it, belonging to such fund. The proceeds of all lands which belonged to the state on January first, eighteen hundred and twenty-three, except the parts thereof reserved or appropriated to public use, or ceded to the United States, shall belong to the common school fund.

Of the income of the United States deposit fund, twenty-five thousand dollars shall annually be added to the capital of the common school fund. The remainder of such income, together with the income of the common school fund, and of the literature fund, and also such amounts as may be raised or received by taxation or otherwise or by transfer from any other fund shall constitute the education fund, and appropriations therefrom may be made annually for the support of the educational system of the state, to be distributed by the superintendent of public instruction, and the university of the state of New York, in the manner provided by law. It shall be the duty of the comptroller to transfer from the general fund at the close of each fiscal year such an amount to the revenue of the common school fund, United States deposit fund and literature fund, as may be necessary to reimburse the revenue of said funds by reason of the excess of appropriations over the revenue derived from the investment of the capital thereof. The moneys so transferred shall become and be a part of the education fund and be included in the amount raised by taxation for the next fiscal year. The comptroller is hereby authorized and directed to certify to the superintendent of public instruction the amount appropriated by the legislature for the support and maintenance of the common school system of the state, which amount so certified shall be payable from the treasury upon the warrant of the state superintendent of public instruction, countersigned by the comptroller, and nothing in this act shall be taken or construed as limiting or restricting the duties and powers now possessed by the superintendent of public instruction in the apportionment, distribution and payment of moneys appropriated by the legislature for the support and maintenance of the common school system of the state.   On the first working day of each month the superintendent of public instruction shall make to the comptroller a written statement of the condition of the fund so certified showing the amount paid therefrom during the preceding month, and the balance remaining on hand.

§ 81. **Investments.**—The comptroller shall invest and keep invested all moneys belonging to the common school, literature and United States deposit funds in the stocks and bonds of the United States and of this state, or for the payment of which, the faith and credit of the United States or of this state are pledged, or in the stocks or bonds of any county, town, city, village or school district of the state authorized to be issued by law.   The moneys belonging to the United States deposit funds now invested in mortgages in the several counties of the state, may continue to be so invested until such mortgages are paid or foreclosed, the amount received on such foreclosure or payment shall be paid into the state treasury to the credit of the United States deposit fund.   The comptroller, whenever he deems it for the best interests of such funds, or either of them, may dispose of any of the securities therein or investments thereof, in making other investments authorized by law, and he may exchange any such securities for those held in any other of such funds, and the comptroller may draw his warrant upon the treasurer for the amount required for such investments and exchanges.   The care and disposition of all lands belonging to the literature fund and the common school fund shall be vested in the commissioners of the land office.

§ 82. **The United States deposit fund.**—The part of the United States deposit fund received out of the surplus money of the treasury of the United States, under the thirteenth section of the act of congress, entitled "An act to regulate the deposits of the public money," passed June twenty-third, eighteen hundred and thirty-six, is held by the state on the terms, conditions and provisions specified in such act of congress, and the faith of the state is inviolably pledged for the safe-keeping and repayment of all moneys thus received from time to time, whenever the same shall be required by the secretary of the treasury of the United States, under the provisions of such act.   The comptroller and treasurer of the state shall keep the accounts of the moneys belonging to the United States deposit fund in the books of their respective offices, separate and distinct from the state funds, and in such manner as to show the amount of principal, of the fund, the amount received from the interest, the amount paid from the annual revenue and the objects to which the same has been applied. If there shall be any loss in the loans of the moneys belonging to the United States deposit fund, it shall be a charge on the interest derived from the loan of such moneys, and none of the interest moneys shall be paid out for any purpose until such loss has been made good thereon.

§ 83. Appointment and qualification of loan commissioners.— There shall continue to be two commissioners for loaning the moneys belonging to the United States deposit fund, in each county, where such moneys are now invested, who shall be known as loan commissioners. The term of office of each commissioner shall be two years. Such commissioners shall be appointed by the governor, with the advice and consent of the senate. Each commissioner shall reside in the county for which he is appointed and shall not be a supervisor. The office of such commissioners for each county shall be kept at the court-house of the county or at some convenient place near the same. The office of the commissioners appointed in the city and county of New York shall be at the office of the register of such city and county. The commissioners shall attend their offices annually on the first Tuesday of October, and thereafter on the Tuesday and Wednesday of each week for the space of three weeks to receive moneys to be paid to them by virtue of this chapter.

§ 84. Discharge and cancellation of mortgages by commissioners.— The comptroller may direct the commissioners to cancel and discharge any mortgage, on satisfactory proof that the moneys loaned and secured by such mortgage have been fully paid to either of the commissioners authorized to receive the same, if the mortgage remains uncanceled and undischarged of record. The commissioners, in pursuance of the order and direction of the comptroller, shall cancel and discharge such mortgage.

§ 85. Bond of commissioners.—Every such commissioner hereafter appointed, before entering on his official duties, shall execute to the people of the state of New York, an undertaking with two or more sufficient sureties, to be approved by the comptroller, in such sum as the comptroller directs, for the true and faithful performance of his duties as such commissioner. No commissioner shall receive any moneys under the provisions of this article until such undertaking has been executed, approved and filed in the office of the comptroller. The comptroller may require additional security at any time, and, if the same is not given when required, shall report the fact, with his reason for requiring additional security, to the governor.

§ 86. **Powers of single commissioner ; books and records.**— If there is but one commissioner in a county, or but one able or qualified to act, he shall have all the powers of two commissioners of the county until his associate has been appointed and qualified or has become able to act. If the two commissioners of the county disagree with reference to any matter requiring their action, either may apply to the supreme court for direction in the premises, on notice of eight days to his associate, and any order which the court may make on such application shall be observed and complied with by such commissioners. The book or books of mortgages executed to the commissioners when not in use by them shall remain in the clerk's office of the county, and in the city and county of New York in the office of the register. The commissioners shall keep a record of their proceedings in a book to be kept for that purpose, which, when not in use by them, shall be deposited in the clerk's or register's office of the county. During office hours any person may search and examine any book required to be kept by this article.

§ 87. **Supervision of existing loan office mortgages.**— Such commissioners in each county shall have charge of the mortgages heretofore executed to them or their predecessors in office, on lands in such county, which mortgages shall continue with the same force and effect as if this chapter were not enacted. The rate of interest on such mortgages shall be five per centum per annum.

Such commissioners shall collect and receive the interest arising on any such mortgage, and in case of failure to pay such interest when due, may foreclose such mortgage in the name of the people of the state of New York, by such actions or proceedings as other mortgages may be foreclosed. Such commissioners shall receive payment of the principal or any part thereof of any such mortgage on lands within their respective counties when tendered and immediately pay the same into the state treasury and shall satisfy and discharge the same by the execution and acknowledgment of a satisfaction piece in the usual form, which shall be recorded by the county clerk, who shall thereupon write upon the margin of such mortgage, in the book containing the same in his office, a statement to the effect that the same has been discharged and satisfied by such commissioners, giving the date thereof.

Such commissioners may allow any such mortgage to remain as a continuing security if all interest due thereon has been paid, and they are satisfied, on due inquiry, that the same is a first lien on the premises described therein, and that such premises are worth double the amount paid on the mortgage. If not so satisfied, they shall report the facts to the comptroller, and if directed so to do by him, they shall proceed to foreclose such mortgage and collect the principal and interest due thereon. On or before the first Tuesday in November in each year, the commissioners shall pay to the treasurer of the state the amount of moneys in their hands, received on account of the interest of the moneys in their charge, less the amount which they are entitled to retain for their compensation, costs, disbursements and expenses.

§ 88. **New accounts for parts of premises.**— If the owner of mortgaged premises sell a part thereof, the commissioners, on application and with the consent of the mortgagor and such owner shall open an account against the purchaser for his proportionate share of the moneys unpaid on the mortgage, but not for a less sum than one hundred dollars nor unless the part of the mortgaged premises remaining unsold, exclusive of buildings and prior liens, is worth double the residue of the mortgage debt not included in the new account. On full payment of the amount for which a separate account is opened, the commissioners shall discharge the part for which such account was opened by the execution of a release in the usual form, which, when acknowledged, shall be recorded by the county clerk and a minute thereof made upon a margin of the mortgage. Such discharge shall not affect or impair the obligation or liability of the mortgagor.

§ 89. **Power of commissioners to maintain actions.**— The commissioners may, at any time, before the sale of the mortgaged premises, bring an action in the name of the people to restrain the commission of waste by any person upon the mortgaged premises, or to correct any mistake or omission in the description thereof, or to recover the amount due on a mortgage. At any time after default, and before sale, if any person cuts or removes or injures the timber, fences, buildings or other fixtures, belonging to such mortgaged premises, or threatens so to do, they may maintain a like action for damages or an injunction. All actions or proceedings brought by the loan commissioners under this article shall be under the control and supervision of the attorney-general.

§ 90. **Foreclosure and redemption of loan office mortgages.—** If the interest due on any such mortgage shall not be paid on the first Tuesday of October of any year, or within twenty-three days thereafter, or the principal or any part thereof shall not be paid when due, the state shall be seized of an absolute estate in fee, in such lands, and the mortgagor, his heirs and assigns, shall be foreclosed and barred of all equity of redemption of the mortgaged premises; but shall be entitled to retain possession thereof, until sale under foreclosure, as herein provided; and shall, at any time before the purchaser at such sale receives his evidences of title on the foreclosure, be entitled to redeem the same by paying to the commissioners the principal unpaid on the mortgage and the interest to the time of redemption, and all the costs and expenses of the foreclosure and sale. On such redemption, the title to the mortgaged premises shall revert to and be vested in the mortgagor, his heirs or assigns. If, before redemption, the purchaser pays to the commissioners, the purchase money, or part thereof, the amount so paid shall be repaid to him.

§ 91. **Purchases for the state.—** If, on any such foreclosure, the property does not bring a sum sufficient to pay in full the amount of principal and interest unpaid on such mortgage, and the costs and expenses of the sale, the commissioners shall bid in the mortgaged property for the people of the state, and take title thereto in the name of the state, and transmit the original mortgage complete and other evidence of title to the comptroller, and thereafter such property shall belong to the state and form a part of the United States deposit fund. If the comptroller is satisfied that nothing more can be collected on account of any such mortgage so foreclosed, and that the deficiency has not been caused by the default or neglect of the commissioners, he shall credit them with the full amount due on the mortgage at the time of such sale. The commissioners, under the direction of the commissioners of the land office, shall continue to exercise supervision and care over such property until it is disposed of according to law, and may include the original amount loaned on the mortgage in the sum on which their commissions are estimated. In all such cases the commissioners, under the direction of the comptroller, shall sue for and collect any deficiency from any person liable to pay the same, and such sale and the purchase of the lands by the people shall not be a defense to the action or any part thereof. The commissioners shall be allowed by the comptroller the taxable costs and disbursements incurred in any action or proceeding for the foreclosure of any such mortgage, when the real property is bid in or conveyed to the state under this section, and any reasonable expenses incurred by them in such action to be fixed and approved by the comptroller; and any recovery which may be had against them in any action or proceeding where the comptroller is satisfied that such recovery was not had in consequence of any default or misconduct on their part, with their costs and expenses in such action or proceeding; and the amount of such costs, disbursements and expenses, when so fixed and approved, may be retained out of any moneys in the hands of the commissioners received by them under this article, or may be paid by the comptroller out of the revenues of the United States deposit fund.   No commissioners shall be directly or indirectly interested in the purchase of any mortgaged premises; if so interested such sale shall be void.

§ 92. **Report to comptroller**—Such commissioners, annually, on the first Tuesday of January, shall make a report to the comptroller, showing all their transactions under this article to the close of the calendar year then ending.   Such report shall contain:

1. A statement of the mortgages outstanding in the county, in numerical order, with the number of each mortgage, the names of the mortgagors, the dates of the mortgages, the amounts paid thereon, both principal and interest, the amount of property on which each is a lien and the estimated cash market value of such property.

2. The amount of interest received during such year, from whom received and on what mortgages, the names of the mortgagors and the number of each mortgage.

3. The amount of principal received during such year, from whom received, and on what mortgage, giving the name of the mortgagor and the number of each mortgage.

4. The amount retained for compensation.

5. A statement of all moneys retained for the costs, disbursements and expenses of foreclosures.

6. All other matters deemed material for the information of the comptroller, or required by him.

The comptroller may prescribe the form of such report, and may require a special report to be made at any time in regard to any matter under this article. At any time within one year from the rendition of such report, the comptroller, if dissatisfied with the same, may audit and adjust the account of any such commissioner for the moneys received, paid out or retained by him under this article, and fix and determine the amount due the state on account thereof, and make a certificate to that effect, which shall be presumptive evidence of the amount due the state in any action or proceeding against such commissioner or the sureties on his undertaking.

§ 93. Certified copy of original mortgage.— On the application of any person interested, the comptroller shall furnish a certified copy of any original mortgage which has been delivered to him pursuant to law, and the same may be recorded in the office of the clerk of the county where the mortgaged premises are situated.

§ 94. Fees of loan commissioners— The loan commissioners in each county may retain annually, as full compensation for their services under this article, three-fourths of one per centum on twenty-five thousand dollars or a less sum, committed to their charge during the preceding year, and one-half of one per centum on all sums over twenty-five thousand dollars, unless the whole amount exceeds fifty thousand dollars, in which case they may retain but one-half of one per centum on the whole sum; and in the city and county of New York, where they may retain but one-fourth of one per centum on the amount in excess of fifty thousand dollars, which compensation shall be retained out of the interest moneys collected and received.

§ 95. Powers and duties of boards of supervisors as to loan mortgages.—The loan commissioners in each county shall exhibit to the board of supervisors thereof at its annual meeting, all mortgages in their charge, together with their books of accounts, minutes and vouchers, so that such board of supervisors may ascertain whether the moneys committed to the charge of such commissioners are still outstanding as satisfactory loans, and that the money collected either as principal, interest or rent on property owned by the state has been paid by them into the state treasury, according to law. Such board of supervisors shall at its annual meeting, examine all such mortgages, books of accounts, minutes and vouchers, and shall give to such commissioners such directions as to taking additional security from the borrowers as the said board of supervisors shall deem proper and necessary. Such board shall certify to the comptroller as to the sufficiency of the securities for the money loaned, and as to whether or not the moneys collected by such commissioners on account of the principal or interest of such mortgages and the rent on property owned by the state has been paid into the state treasury, and as to what directions they have given to such commissioners as to taking additional security. If it shall appear to the comptroller from any such certificate that the moneys in the charge of such commissioners, or any part thereof, are not on loan or have not been paid by the state treasurer as required by law, he shall cause an action to be brought upon the bonds of the commissioners found to be in default. He shall also report to the governor the names of such commissioners who are in default.

§ 96. Payment to Cornell university on account of the college land scrip fund.—The acceptance by this state of the provisions of an act of the congress of the United States, approved July second, eighteen hundred and sixty-two, entitled "An act donating public lands to the several states and territories which may provide colleges for the benefit of agriculture and mechanic arts," and which acceptance is contained in chapter twenty of the laws of eighteen hundred and sixty-three, is continued in force, notwithstanding the repeal thereof by this chapter.

The money raised under chapter seventy-eight of the laws of eighteen hundred and ninety-five, by the sale or conversion into cash of the securities in which were invested the proceeds of the sales of lands and land scrip, formerly constituting the college land scrip fund, together with the money paid into the state treasury from the sale of lands or land scrip belonging to such fund, is held by the state as a part of the general fund for the benefit and use of Cornell university.

Five per centum of the amount of the proceeds so transferred to the general fund shall annually be paid to the Cornell university, pursuant to a certificate issued by the comptroller to such university, by virtue of chapter seventy-eight of the laws of eighteen hundred and ninety-five, which certificate is hereby ratified and confirmed.

Certificates shall also be issued by the state to such university from time to time, as the proceeds of the sales of the lands and land scrip are paid into the treasury, 'or the payment annually of five per centum upon such proceeds from the date of their receipt upon the same conditions as the original certificate.

The comptroller in his annual estimate of the appropriations required for the expenses of the government shall include the amount required to pay the interest on these certificates.

ARTICLE V.
MISCELLANEOUS FUNDS.

Section 100. The military record fund.

101. The mariners' fund.

102. Payments on account of chancery fund.

Section 100. **The military record fund.**—All moneys contributed and paid over to the treasurer of the state by towns, cities and individuals for the erection of a hall of military record belong to the military record fund. Such fund shall be invested in the same manner as other state funds and a separate account thereof shall be kept by the state treasurer. The interest arising from the investment of such fund shall be used in the maintenance of such quarters in the state capitol as shall be set apart for the safe-keeping of military records, books and property, and for the display of colors, standards, battle flags and relics, which is known as the hall of military record.

§ 101. **The mariners' fund.**—The loan of ten thousand dollars made by the comptroller to the trustees of the American Seamen's Friend Society in the city of New York, pursuant to chapter one hundred and seventy-three of the laws of eighteen hundred and forty, and continued by chapter thirty-seven of the laws of eighteen hundred and forty-five, shall constitute the mariners' fund. Such loan shall be secured by mortgage satisfactory to the comptroller and may be retained by such trustees, without payment of interest, as long as they shall faithfully use and apply the same to promote the benevolent objects of the sailors' home, erected for the boarding and accommodation of seamen in such city.

The trustees of such institution may mortgage the sailors' home for a term not less than seven years to secure the debts due from, or money loaned to, them for the lawful purpose of such institution, to an amount not exceeding fifteen thousand dollars. Such mortgage shall be a lien on such home prior to the lien held by the state to secure the loan mentioned in this section, provided all other liens and incumbrances on such home be discharged and canceled of record.

No sale of such sailors' home upon the foreclosure of any mortgage prior to the lien of the state shall be had without, at least, six weeks' previous notice of such sale served personally upon the comptroller.

§ 102. **Payments on account of chancery fund.**—All moneys, securities and real estate formerly under the control and in possession of the court of chancery, and transferred to the comptroller by the clerk of the court of appeals, pursuant to chapter one hundred and thirty-five of the laws of eighteen hundred and ninety four, is credited to the general fund and is a part thereof. The comptroller is authorized to convert into cash the securities, real estate and other property belonging to the fund so transferred, and may execute good and sufficient deeds for the conveyance of such real property.

A person claiming any portion of such property, shall apply to a court of competent jurisdiction after due notice to the comptroller of the time and place of making such application, for an order directing the payment of such portion to him. Upon such order and the warrant of the comptroller the treasurer shall pay such portion to him.

ARTICLE VI.

§ 110. **Laws repealed.**—Of the laws enumerated in the schedule hereto annexed that portion specified in the last column is repealed.

§ 111. **When to take effect.**—This chapter shall take effect on October first, eighteen hundred and ninety-seven.

SCHEDULE OF LAWS REPEALED.

Revised Statutes....	Part I, ch. VIII, title 3, articles 1, 2, 3..................	All, except §15.
Revised Statutes....	Part I, ch. VIII, title 4........	All.
Revised Statutes....	Part I, ch. IX, titles 2, 3, 4 and 6.....................	All.

Laws of—	Chapter.	Sections.
1830.................	184..............	All.
1830.................	242..............	All
1831.................	102..............	All.
1831.................	286..............	All.
1831.................	320..............	All.
1832.................	8..............	1, 2.
1832.................	296..............	All.
1833.................	56..............	All.
1834.................	284..............	All.
1835.................	260..............	All.
1836.................	356..............	All.
1837.................	2..............	All.
1837.................	150..............	All except § 43.
1837.................	360..............	All.
1838.................	58..............	All.
1838.................	193..............	All.
1838.................	237..............	All.
1839.................	381..............	All.
1840.................	294..............	All.
1841.................	264..............	All.
1842.................	310..............	All.
1843.................	44..............	All.
1844.................	326..............	All.
1845.................	37..............	All.
1845.................	267..............	All.
1847.................	8..............	All.
1847.................	258..............	All.
1847.................	476..............	All.
1848.................	162..............	All.
1848.................	215..............	All.
1848.................	366..............	All.
1849.................	228..............	All.

Laws of—	Chapter.	Sections.
1849	230	All.
1849	301	All.
1849	382	13.
1850	337	All.
1851	286	All.
1851	536	All.
1852	235	All.
1852	370	All.
1853	36	All.
1855	535	3.
1857	721	All.
1857	783	All.
1861	177	All.
1863	20	All.
1863	731	All except § 9.
1863	460	All.
1864	229	All.
1864	553	All.
1868	698	All.
1872	115	All.
1877	245	All.
1878	233	All.
1878	291	All.
1880	100	All.
1880	517	All.
1884	412	2, 3.
1887	245	All.
1888	326	All.
1888	464	All.
1889	50	All.
1889	136	All.
1891	181	All.
1893	672	All.
1894	135	All.
1894	678	All.
1895	78	All.
1895	818	All.
1896	191	All.

Chap. 414.

AN ACT in relation to villages, constituting chapter twenty-one of the general laws.

Became a law May 13, 1897, with the approval of the Governor.
Passed, three-fifths being present.

The People of the State of New York, represented in Senate and Assembly, do enact as follows:

CHAPTER XXI OF THE GENERAL LAWS.

THE VILLAGE LAW.

ARTICLE I.

INCORPORATION.

Section 1. **Short title.**— This chapter shall be known as the village law.

§ 2. **Requisite population.**— A territory not exceeding one square mile, or an entire town, containing in either case a population of not less than three hundred, and not including a part of a city or village, may be incorporated as a village under this chapter.

§ 3. **Proposition for incorporation.**— Twenty-five adult freeholders residing in such territory may institute a proceeding for the incorporation thereof as a village, by making and delivering to the supervisor of the town in which such territory is situated, or if situated in two or more towns, to the supervisor of each of such towns, a proposition in substantially the following form:

Proposition for the incorporation of the village of ....

The undersigned adult resident freeholders of the territory hereinafter described propose the incorporation thereof by the name of the village of ....

The territory proposed to be incorporated does not exceed one square mile and is bounded and described as follows: (or, the territory proposed to be incorporated is the entire town of ....)

Such territory contains a population of ...., as appears from the enumeration hereto attached.

Dated .

(Signatures and residences.)

The proposition shall be signed by the persons proposing such incorporation, with the addition of the town in which they respectively reside.

A list of the names of the inhabitants of such territory shall be attached to and accompany the proposition. At the time of the delivery of the proposition the sum of fifty dollars shall be deposited with one of the supervisors for the purpose specified in this article.

§ 4. Notice of hearing.— Within ten days after the receipt of such proposition the supervisor or supervisors shall cause to be posted in five public places in such territory and also published at least twice in each newspaper published therein, a notice, that a proposition for the incorporation of the village of (naming it) has been received by him or them, that at a place in such territory and on a day, not less than ten nor more than twenty days after the date of posting such notice, which place and date shall be specified therein, a hearing will be had upon such proposition; and that such proposition will be open for public inspection at a specified place in such territory until the date of such hearing.

§ 5. Proceeding on hearing.— The supervisor or supervisors shall meet at the time and place specified in such notice, and shall hear any objections which may be presented against such incorporation upon either of the following grounds:

1. That a person signing such proposition is not qualified therefor, or

2. That, if the territory is less than an entire town, it contains more than one square mile, or

3. That the population of the territory is less than three hundred.

All objections must be in writing and signed by one or more resident taxpayers of a town in which some part of the proposed village is situated. Testimony may be taken on such hearing, which shall be reduced to writing, and subscribed by the witnesses. The hearing may be adjourned, but must be concluded within ten days from the date fixed in the notice.

§ 6. Decision of supervisor.— Within ten days after such hearing is concluded the supervisor or supervisors shall determine whether the proposition complies with this chapter, and shall within such time make and sign a written decision accordingly, and file it or a duplicate thereof in the office of the town clerk of each town in which any part of such proposed village is situated.   The proposition for incorporation, a copy of the notice, the objections, testimony and minutes of proceedings taken and kept on the hearing, shall also be filed with such decision in one of such town clerk's offices. If the decision be adverse to the proposition, it shall contain a brief statement of the reasons upon which it is based.   If no appeal be taken from such decision within ten days from the filing thereof, it shall be final and conclusive.

§ 7. Notice of appeal from decision of supervisor.— If the decision sustains the proposition for incorporation, a resident taxpayer of a town in which any part of such proposed village is situated may appeal therefrom by serving a notice of appeal upon each town clerk with whom the decision was filed, and on at least three of the persons who signed the proposition.   If the decision be adverse, five of the persons who signed the proposition may join in an appeal therefrom, by serving a notice of appeal upon each town clerk with whom the decision was filed, and on each person who signed objections to the proposition.   All appeals shall be taken to the county court of the county in which the proposition, notice, objections and testimony are filed, and the notice of appeal must be served within ten days after the filing of the decision.

The town clerk with whom the proposition and other papers are filed must, within five days after service upon him of the notice of appeal, transmit all such papers to the county judge.

§ 8. Hearing and decision of appeal — A person, except a town clerk, by or upon whom the notice of appeal is served, may bring on the appeal for argument before the county court, upon a notice of not less than ten nor more than twenty days.   Such notice must be served upon all parties to the appeal, except a town clerk.

The county court shall hear such appeal, and, within ten days after the date fixed in the notice of argument, shall make and file an order affirming or reversing the decision.   The county judge shall file such order, together with the papers upon which the appeal was heard, with the town clerk by whom the papers were transmitted to him.   Such order shall be final and conclusive.   No costs of the appeal shall be allowed to any party.

§ 9. When election may be held.— An election to determine the question of incorporation upon such proposition shall be held in either of the following cases:

1. Where a decision has been made sustaining the proposition, and an appeal has not been taken therefrom.

2. Where an appeal has been taken from a decision sustaining the proposition, and such decision has been affirmed by the county court.

3. Where an appeal has been taken from an adverse decision, and the decision has been reversed by the county court.

§ 10. Notice of election.—Within five days after the right to an election is complete the town clerk with whom the proposition and other papers are filed shall give notice of an election to be held in such territory at a specified time and place. The notice shall be signed by the town clerk and posted in ten conspicuous places in such territory, and also published at least twice in each newspaper published therein, and it shall fix a time for such election, not less than fifteen nor more than twenty-five days from the date of the posting thereof. Such election shall be held at a convenient place in such territory between the hours of one o'clock in the afternoon and sunset, but shall not be held upon the day of a town meeting or of a general election in a town in which any part of the proposed village is situated.

§ 11. Conduct of election.— Such election shall be held at the time and place specified. The town clerk giving such notice shall serve a copy thereof upon the supervisor and town clerk of each town, in which any part of the proposed village is situated, at least ten days before the date fixed for such election. Two or more of such officers, including the town clerk giving such notice, shall constitute the board of inspectors to conduct such election. If only one of the officers attend at the time and place fixed for the election, he shall appoint an elector of such territory to act with him as an inspector of such election. If no officer attend, the electors present may choose two of their number to act as inspectors. The inspectors shall file the constitutional oath of office with the town clerk with whom the proposition was filed. Such inspectors of election shall possess all the powers conferred by law upon a board of inspectors of election at a town meeting, so far as the same are applicable. The ballot at such election may be either written or printed, and shall contain either the words " for incorporation," or " against incorporation."

§ 12. **Qualification of electors.**—Each elector qualified to vote at a town meeting, who has been a resident of such territory for at least thirty days next preceding such election, and who or whose wife is the owner of property within such territory which was assessed upon the last assessment-roll of the town, may vote at such election.

§ 13. **Ballot boxes where territory is in more than one town.**—If the proposed village is situated in more than one town, a separate ballot box shall be provided for each town, and the ballot of each person voting at such election shall be deposited in the ballot box assigned to the town in which he resides.

§ 14. **Canvass of election.**—Immediately after the closing of the polls of the election the board of inspectors shall canvass the ballots cast thereat, and make and sign a certificate of the holding of the election and of the canvass, showing, if the territory is wholly within one town, the whole number of such ballots, the number for incorporation, and the number against incorporation; or if it includes parts of two or more towns, showing such facts separately as to each town. Within three days after the election, the inspectors shall file such certificate in the office of the town clerk with whom the proposition and other papers are filed.

§ 15. **Appeal from election.**— If the certificate shows that a majority of the votes cast at such election in each town included in the territory is in favor of incorporation, a person qualified to vote at such election may appeal therefrom to the county court of the county in which the proposition and other papers are filed.

§ 16. **Notice of appeal and return.**—An appeal may be taken by serving a notice of appeal on the town clerk with whom the certificate of incorporation is filed, and by posting the same in five conspicuous places in such territory. The notice shall be signed by the appellant and must state briefly the grounds upon which the appeal is taken. It must be served and posted within ten days after the filing of the certificate of election.

The town clerk on whom the notice of appeal is served, must, within five days thereafter, transmit to the county judge a certified copy of such notice of appeal and of the certificate of election.

§ 17. **Hearing and decision of appeal.**—Upon such appeal the county court can only consider questions relating to the validity or regularity of the election. An appeal may be brought on for hearing by the service of a notice of argument by the appellant upon the town clerk, and by posting the same in five conspicuous places in such territory. The notice shall state the time of the hearing, which must be not less than ten days after the service and posting thereof. On such hearing, any number of qualified electors of the territory, not exceeding five, may appear in support of the validity or regularity of such election. The county court may take testimony, either orally or by affidavit, as it may determine. Such appeal must be heard and decided and the decision filed within thirty days after service of the notice of appeal; and the county court has no jurisdiction to consider the same after the expiration of that period. The county court may sustain or set aside the election. The decision must be filed by the county judge in the office of the town clerk on whom the notice of appeal was served. He shall also file a copy of the decision with the county clerk, together with the papers transmitted to him by the town clerk.

No costs shall be allowed to any party on such appeal.

§ 18. **Appeal to appellate division.**— If the county court sustains the election, an appeal may be taken from such decision to the appellate division of the supreme court. Such appeal brings up for review all proceedings in the county court, and a case on appeal must be made and settled by the county judge as on an appeal from a judgment of the county court. Such appeal shall be taken within ten days after the filing of the decision, by the service of a notice of appeal upon the county clerk with whom a copy of the decision is filed, and upon each person who appeared in support of the election in the county court.

The proceedings for bringing on the appeal and the hearing and decision thereof by the appellate division are regulated by the code of civil procedure.

The appellate division may affirm the decision of the county court or reverse the same and set aside the election.

Within ten days after the determination of the appeal by the appellate division, a certified copy of its decision or order must be filed in the office of the town clerk with whom the proposition is filed.

No costs shall be allowed to any party on appeal to the appellate division.

§ 19. **Stay on appeal.**—An appeal to the county court or to the appellate division stays all proceedings for the election of officers or otherwise in such proposed village until the determination of such appeal.

§ 20. **New election.**— If the election be set aside on appeal, a new election shall be held. The right to such an election shall be com-

plete upon the filing of the decision on appeal with the town clerk.
He shall thereupon give notice of another election. All the provisions herein contained regulating the first election apply to proceedings for a new election, including the service and posting of
notices, the conduct of the election, the canvass and certification of
the result, and appeals therefrom. A new election shall be held in
like manner if any election is set aside on appeal.

§ 21. **When village deemed incorporated.**— If the territory is
wholly within one town, and a majority of the votes cast is in favor
of incorporation, or if it includes parts of two or more towns and a
majority of the votes cast in each town is in favor of incorporation,
then such territory shall become and be an incorporated village
under this chapter from and after the date of such election, unless
the election is set aside on appeal as herein provided.

§ 22. **Report of incorporation.**—After ten and within fifteen days
from the filing of the certificate of election, if no appeal has been
taken, or within fifteen days after the filing of a final decision sustaining the election, the town clerk with whom such certificate is
filed shall deliver a certified copy thereof to the secretary of state
and to the county clerk of each county in which any part of such
village is situated, together with a statement of the population of
such village as it appears by the proposition for incorporation.

§ 23. **Compensation for services under this article.**—The following compensation is payable for services under this article:

1. To supervisors for services in connection with the proposition
for incorporation, two dollars for each day actually and necessarily
spent by them.

2. To town clerks, the compensation allowed by law for other
similar services, and for services the compensation for which is not
fixed by law, two dollars for each day actually and necessarily
spent by them.

3. To electors acting as inspectors of election, two dollars for each
day actually and necessarily spent in such service.

§ 24. **Payment of expenses if village not incorporated** — If the
incorporation of the proposed village be not effected by the proceedings authorized in this article, the fees and expenses of the town
officers or other persons performing official services shall be paid
from the fund deposited with the supervisor. If the persons making
such deposit and the officers and persons entitled to compensation
for services in such proceedings do not agree upon the amounts pay-

able therefor, such fees and expenses shall be taxed by the county judge of the county in which the proposition was filed, and the amounts taxed by him shall be paid to the persons entitled thereto.

The remainder of the sum deposited, if any, or if the proceedings result in the incorporation of the village, the whole of such deposit, shall be returned to the persons making it by the supervisor on demand.

§ 25. Payment of expenses of incorporation.—The following expenses incurred in the proceedings for incorporation shall be a charge against the village:

1. The reasonable necessary expenses incurred by the persons signing the proposition prior to the delivery thereof to the supervisor.

2. If on appeal from the decision of the supervisor the proposition for incorporation be sustained, the reasonable necessary expenses on such appeal, not exceeding fifty dollars, incurred by the persons signing the proposition.

3. The fees payable to town officers and to electors acting as inspectors of election for services performed by them under this article and their necessary disbursements.

§ 26. First election of officers, when held.—An election of officers of the village shall be held in either of the following cases:

1. After the lapse of ten days from the filing of the certificate of election showing the incorporation, unless an appeal has been taken therefrom.

2. If such an appeal has been taken, after the lapse of ten days from the filing of the decision of the county court sustaining the election, unless an appeal has been taken therefrom.

3. If an appeal has been taken from the decision of the county court, after the filing of the decision of the appellate division of the supreme court sustaining the election.

§ 27. Appointment of village clerk; inspectors of election.—Within five days after the right of an election of officers is complete, the town clerk with whom the proposition for incorporation was filed, shall appoint the following officers:

1. A village clerk, who shall serve until his successor is chosen.

2. Three qualified electors of the village to serve as inspectors of such election, not more than two of whom shall be members of the same political party.

The town clerk shall file such appointments in his office and deliver a copy thereof to each of the persons so appointed, who, within three days after their appointment, shall file with such town clerk the constitutional oath of office.

§ 28. Notice of election of officers.—Within five days after his appointment, the village clerk shall give notice for an election of officers. Such notice shall be posted in ten conspicuous places in the village and published in a newspaper therein, if any. It shall also contain the following particulars:

1. The place in such village where the election is to be held.

2. The date of such election, which shall be not less than ten nor more than fifteen days after the posting of such notice.

3. The hours for holding such election, which shall be for the space of at least four consecutive hours between ten o'clock in the forenoon and four o'clock in the afternoon.

4. The officers to be elected.

§ 29. Officers to be elected; terms of office —The following officers shall be chosen at such first election: A president, two trustees, a treasurer and a collector.

If such election be held after the date of an annual election under this chapter, and before the first day of October, the terms of all such officers shall expire at the end of the current official year. If such election be held after the thirtieth day of September, and on or before the date fixed for the next annual election, the president, one trustee, the treasurer and the collector shall hold their offices until the end of the next official year, and one trustee shall hold his office during the next two official years.

The terms of office of officers elected under this section commence as soon as they have qualified.

§ 30. Conduct of election.—All persons qualified to vote at town meetings, and who have been residents of the territory thirty days prior to such election may vote for such officers. The inspectors appointed by the town clerk or any two of them shall conduct such election. The provisions of this chapter relating to the election of village officers at an annual election, including the canvass and certification of the result, apply to such first election, so far as practicable.

§ 31. First meeting of board of trustees.—Within five days after such first election, the president and trustees elected thereat shall meet and appoint a clerk and a street commissioner. They may also appoint such other officers as are authorized by law.

§ 32. Temporary loan for expenses.—The board of trustees first elected may borrow not exceeding five hundred dollars upon the credit of the village for the purpose of raising funds to defray the expenses of incorporation, and such other necessary expenses as may be incurred before the collection of the first annual tax, and the amount so borrowed shall be included in the first tax levy.

ARTICLE II.

Officers and Elections.

Section 40. **Classification of villages.**—Villages are divided into classes according to their population as shown by the latest village enumeration as follows:

First class.— Villages containing a population of five thousand or more.

Second class.—Villages containing a population of three thousand and less than five thousand.

Third class.—Villages containing a population of one thousand and less than three thousand.

Fourth class.—Villages containing a population of less than one thousand.

§ 41. **Qualification of voters.**—A voter at a village election, other than the first, must possess the following qualifications:

1. To entitle him to vote for an officer, he must be qualified to vote at a town meeting of the town in which he resides, and must have resided in the village thirty days next preceding such election.

2. To entitle him to vote upon a proposition, he must be entitled to vote for an officer, and he or his wife must also be the owner of property in the village assessed upon the last preceding assessment-roll thereof.

§ 42. **Eligibility to office.**—A president or trustee, or a fire, water, light, sewer or cemetery commissioner must, at the time of his election and during his term, be the owner of property assessed upon the last preceding assessment-roll of the village; except that a president or trustee elected at the first village election, must be the owner of property assessed upon the last preceding town assessment-roll. Any resident elector is eligible to any other village office.

A resident woman, who is a citizen of the United States, and of the age of twenty-one years, is eligible to the office of village clerk or deputy clerk. A person shall not hold two village offices at the same time, except the offices of collector and police constable, or water and light commissioner.

§ 43. **List of village officers; mode of choosing; official year; terms of office.**— Every village shall have a president, not less than two trustees, a treasurer, a clerk and a street commissioner. Except as herein provided, every village shall also have a collector, but a village of the first class may, upon the adoption of a proposition therefor at a special election, determine that no collector shall thereafter be elected therein. A village of the first or second class may also have a deputy clerk, and any village may have a village engineer.

There shall be a board of health in each village, consisting of not less than three nor more than seven persons, appointed by the board of trustees of such village, in the manner provided by article two of the public health law. The president, trustees, treasurer, collector, police justice, and assessors shall be elective officers, except that in a village of the first or second class the treasurer may be appointed, upon the adoption of a proposition therefor at a village election. All other village officers shall be appointed by the board of trustees, except as otherwise provided herein.

An " official year " begins at noon on the first Monday after the third Tuesday of March, and ends at noon on the same Monday in the next calendar year.

The term of office of the president, treasurer, collector, clerk, street commissioner and inspectors of election shall be one official year; of each trustee elected for a full term, two official years, and of a police justice, four calendar years.

The term of each village officer, except police justice, begins at noon on the first Monday after the annual election. A full term of the police justice begins on the first day of January succeeding the annual election at which he was elected.

After the first election in a village subject to the provisions of this chapter one-half of the trustees shall be elected each year for a full term.

§ 44. **Number of trustees.**—Villages in the several classes shall elect trustees as follows:

1. In the first class, not less than two nor more than eight.
2. In the second class, not less than two nor more than six.
3. In the third class, two or four.
4. In the fourth class, two.

Each village shall always have an even number of trustees.

§ 45. **Changing number of trustees.**— Within the limitations herein prescribed, the number of trustees may be changed by adopting a proposition therefor at a special election. If the number be increased, the additional trustees shall be elected at the next annual election. One-half of the additional trustees shall be elected for one year and one-half for two years. If the number of trustees be reduced, such reduction shall not take effect until the expiration of the terms of the trustees then in office.

§ 46. **Readjustment of terms of trustees.**—The terms of the trustees in office at noon on the Monday next following the date of the annual election in the year eighteen hundred and ninety-eight shall then expire. At such election the whole number of trustees which the village is authorized to choose shall be elected, one-half for one year and one-half for two years. This section does not apply to villages hereafter incorporated, and in which an election of officers is held subsequent to September thirtieth, eighteen hundred and ninety-seven, and prior to the third Tuesday of March, eighteen hundred and ninety-eight.

§ 47. Determination of future number of trustees.—If when this chapter takes effect a village not in the fourth class has a greater or a less number of trustees than the number to which it is or may be entitled, a special election may be held therein prior to March fi.st, eighteen hundred and ninety-eight, to determine the number of trustees to be thereafter elected, within the limitations herein prescribed.

Such special election shall only be held upon the petition of twenty-five electors qualified to vote upon a proposition; and if it be not held, such village shall only elect two trustees at the annual election in eighteen hundred and ninety-eight, one of whom shall be elected for a term of one year and one for two years.

§ 48. Abolition of existing wards or districts.—All divisions of villages into districts, subdivisions or wards, for the purpose of electing trustees, made under a general law and in force when this chapter takes effect, are abolished.

§ 49. Election of trustees by wards.—A village of the first class may elect trustees by wards upon the adoption of a proposition therefor at a special election. If such a proposition be adopted, the board of trustees shall meet within twenty days thereafter and divide the village into wards of a number equal to one-half of the number of trustees which the village has a right to elect. Such wards shall contain a population as nearly equal as may be, and be of convenient and contiguous territory, in as compact form as practicable. The board of trustees shall make a certificate of such division, which shall contain a description of each ward, and shall file the same in the office of the village clerk, and publish it in each newspaper published in the village, at least twenty days before the next annual election. One trustee shall thereafter be elected annually in each ward, for a full term.

If after such a division into wards, the number of trustees in the village be changed, the board of trustees shall, in like manner, make a new division into wards.

§ 50. Election of police justice.—The office of police justice is con-tinued in every village in which it is now established. A village may establish the office of police justice by adopting a proposition there-for. A village, in which the office of police justice has been estab-lished, may abolish such office at an annual election, to take effect upon the expiration of the term of the police justice then in office

§ 51. Election of assessors.— The board of trustees shall act as assessors of the village, or may appoint of their number a committee for that purpose, unless separate assessors are appointed or elected as provided by this section. If twenty-five electors qualified to vote upon a proposition shall present a petition to the board of trustees for the election of separate assessors, it shall submit to the next annual election a proposition therefor, and if such proposition be adopted, shall appoint three persons to be assessors of such village for the terms of one, two and three years, respectively, and there-after at each annual election, one assessor shall be elected for a full term of three years. In a village of the first or second class, which now has no separate assessors, the board of trustees may, by resolution, direct that three assessors be elected at the next annual election, and they shall be elected accordingly for the terms of one, two and three years, respectively. At each annual election thereafter one assessor shall be elected for a full term of three years.

§ 52. Election districts.—A village, containing not more than eight hundred qualified electors, shall constitute a single election district for village elections. If at an annual election, the number of votes cast for village officers shall exceed eight hundred, the board of trustees may by resolution, adopted at least thirty days before the next annual election, divide such village into election districts, containing not more than eight hundred voters. Such resolution shall specify the boundaries of each district, but a ward shall not be divided in the formation thereof, except to make two or more elec-tion districts wholly within such ward. Such resolution shall be published and posted with a notice of such election.

§ 53. Officers to be elected at annual election.—Elective offices shall be filled at the annual election next preceding the expiration of the terms thereof. If a vacancy in an elective office occurs more than ten days prior to an annual election, at which a successor for a full term is not to be chosen, it shall be filled at such election for the remainder of the unexpired term.

§ 54. **Inspectors of election.**—If a village constitutes but one election district, the trustees and clerk of the village, after the first election of village officers, shall be inspectors of election for the village, and one or more of them shall preside at all elections. If a trustee or the clerk shall not be present, the electors may appoint a chairman to preside, who shall have all the powers of an inspector.

If a village is divided into election districts, the board of trustees shall, annually, at least thirty days before the annual election, appoint two inspectors of election for each district to preside at all village elections therein, until their successors are appointed. Such inspectors shall not both be chosen from the same political party. The board may also appoint for each district a poll clerk and a ballot clerk.

§ 55. **Annual elections.**—An annual election shall be held in each village on the third Tuesday in March, unless a town meeting of a town in which any part of the village is situated, or a general election, shall be held on such day, in which case the annual election shall be held upon the next day thereafter. All other village elections are special elections. The board of trustees shall, by resolution, adopted at least ten days before every village election, designate the hours of opening and closing the polls thereof, which shall include at least four consecutive hours between sunrise and sunset. The resolution shall also designate the place of holding the election, or if there is more than one election district in the village, the place of holding the election in each district. The board also shall, at least ten days before the election, cause notice thereof to be published at least once in the official paper, if such paper is published in the village, and a printed copy thereof conspicuously posted in at least six public places in the village, specifying the time and place, or places, of holding the election, the hours of opening and closing the polls thereof, the offices, if any, and the term to be filled, and setting forth in full all propositions to be voted upon. If the board neglects to appoint the place or places for the annual election, the election shall be held at the place or places of the last preceding annual election, and if it neglects to appoint the hours of opening and closing the polls thereof, such hours shall be the same as at the last preceding annual election. An annual election of the village officers shall not be invalid because of a failure to give such notice. A vote upon a proposition shall be void unless due notice of the election has been given.

If a village, constituting a single election district, is divided into wards and elects trustees by wards, separate ballot boxes shall be provided for each ward, and the ballots of the electors residing therein shall be deposited in the ballot box designated for such ward.

§ 56. **Canvass of annual election.**—The inspectors of election of each election district shall, immediately upon the closing of the polls of each annual election, proceed to canvass the votes cast thereat, and shall complete such canvass without adjournment. They shall, before nine o'clock in the forenoon of the following day, file with the village clerk their certificate setting forth the holding of the election, the total number of votes cast for each office, the number of votes cast for each person for such office, the total number of votes cast upon each proposition voted upon, and the number cast for and against it. If the village contains more than one election district, the board of trustees of such village shall meet at its usual place of meeting, at nine o'clock in the forenoon of the next day after the election. The village clerk shall produce at such meeting the returns of the inspectors of election, and the board of trustees shall canvass such returns, and file in the office of the village clerk a certificate declaring the result. The person eligible and receiving the highest number of votes for an office shall be elected thereto. If two or more persons receive an equal and the greatest number of votes for the same office, the board of trustees shall determine by lot which of them shall be deemed elected.

§ 57. **Failure to designate terms.**—No election of village officers, heretofore or hereafter held in any village, shall be invalid on account of the failure of the electors to designate in their ballots the respective terms of office of persons to be elected thereat, for the same office, for different terms; but the persons so to be elected to such office, who are eligible and receive the highest number of votes, shall be elected. The person first named on a ballot containing the names of more than one person for such an office, and not designating their respective terms, shall be deemed designated for the longest term, the second, for the next longest term, and so on to the end; and the inspectors of election shall count the ballots and certify the result accordingly. If the votes shall not be so counted and canvassed the board of trustees shall, at least twenty days before the expiration of the shortest term, determine by lot which of such officers shall hold office for each term, and thereupon such officers shall be deemed to have been elected accordingly.

§ 58. **Special elections of officers.**—Whenever the day fixed by law for an annual election shall have passed, and no election shall have been held thereon, the board of trustees shall, forthwith, give notice of a special election, to be held at the place of the omitted annual election. Such notice shall be given in like manner as a notice of an annual election, and a special election shall be held in the same manner as, and for the purposes of, an annual election. For the purpose of determining the terms of office of the officers elected thereat, the time therefrom to the beginning of the next official year shall be deemed one year.

§ 59. **Submission of propositions; special elections.**—The board of trustees may, upon its own motion, and shall, upon the petition of twenty-five electors, qualified to vote upon a proposition, cause to be submitted at a village election, a proposition upon any question which may be lawfully decided thereat. A separate board of fire, water, light, sewer, cemetery or other commissioners may present to the board of trustees a petition, requesting the submission of a specified proposition, relating to its department, at a village election. Upon the presentation of such petition, the board of trustees shall cause the proposition to be submitted accordingly. If a petition under this section be presented after the annual election and before the first day of January following, a special election shall be called, to be held not less than ten nor more than twenty days after the presentation of such petition. If a petition be presented at any other time, and more than ten days prior to the annual election, the proposition shall be submitted at such annual election. Except for the purpose of fixing or changing the number of trustees, or for the purpose of determining whether an officer shall be thereafter elected or appointed, no special election shall be held in the months of February or March. Notice of a special election for the submission of a proposition shall be given in the same manner as for an annual election. Such special election shall be held by the same officers, and conducted and the result canvassed in the same manner as an annual election.

§ 60. **Votes upon propositions to be by ballot.**—All votes upon a proposition submitted at a village election shall be by ballot; and, unless otherwise provided, the provisions of the election law, relating to ballots, apply to propositions submitted, under this chapter.

§ 61. **Official undertakings.**—The treasurer, collector, police justice, street commissioner, and such other officers as may be required by the board of trustees, shall, before they enter upon the duties of their respective offices, each execute to the village and file with the village clerk, an official undertaking in such sum and with such sureties as the board of trustees shall direct and approve. The board of trustees may at any time require any such officer to file a new official undertaking for such sum and with such sureties as the board shall approve.

§ 62. Notice to person chosen to a village office.—The clerk of the village shall, within three days after the election or appointment of a village officer, except the first election or appointment after the incorporation of the village, notify each person elected or appointed of his election or appointment and of the date thereof, and that he is required to file his oath of office with such clerk, before entering upon the duties thereof, and, if an official undertaking be required of him, by or in pursuance of law, that he is also required to file the same with such clerk, and that upon his failure so to do, he will be deemed to have declined the office. If an undertaking is required of a village officer, by or in pursuance of law, after entering upon the duties of his office, the clerk of the village shall thereupon serve upon such officer personally, a written notice that he is required to file such undertaking with the clerk, within ten days after the service of the notice, and that upon his failure to do so, his office will become vacant.

§ 63. Resignations and removals.—A village officer may resign to the board of trustees, and his resignation shall take effect upon the delivery thereof to the village clerk, unless a time be specified in such resignation for its taking effect thereafter, in which case, such resignation shall take effect at the time so specified.

In addition to the method provided by the public officers law, an officer, except a president or a trustee, appointed by the board of trustees of the village, may be removed by the board for misconduct, on notice to such officer and an opportunity given him to make his defense.

§ 64. Filling of vacancies.—Vacancies occurring otherwise than by expiration of term in a village office, other than that of health officer, shall be filled by the board of trustees, if the office be elective, until the end of the current official year, but if the office be appointive, for the balance of the unexpired term. If a vacancy in an elective office occurs within less than ten days prior to an annual election, and which office is not to be filled at such election, the appointment shall be for a term which will expire at the end of the next official year.

§ 65. **Refusal of officer to surrender his office.**—If a person who has been an officer of a village refuses or neglects to deliver to his successor in office, within ten days after notification and request, all the moneys, books, papers, records, property and effects of every description, which have come into his possession or under his control, by virtue of his office, and belonging to the village or appertaining to the office, he shall forfeit and pay to the village, the sum of twenty-five dollars for each and every day he shall so neglect or refuse, and also all damages, costs and expenses caused by such neglect or refusal.

§ 66. **Separate boards of commissioners.**—A village which has no separate board of fire, water, light, sewer or cemetery commissioners, by adopting a proposition therefor at an annual election, may establish such a board, or may establish a municipal board, with the powers, duties and responsibilities of two or more of such separate boards. In a village of the first class a board of commissioners or a municipal board may be composed of three or five members as shall be determined by the proposition. If such proposition be adopted, the board of trustees at its next annual meeting shall appoint such commissioners, for the terms of one, two and three years, respectively, or in a village which determines to have five commissioners, for the terms of one, two, three, four and five years, respectively; and at each annual meeting thereafter the board of trustees shall appoint one commissioner for the full term of three or five years, as the case may be.

§ 67. **Municipal boards; consolidation.**—Upon the adoption of a proposition therefor a village may establish a municipal board, possessing all the powers and subject to all the responsibilities of two or more of the boards named in this article. Such municipal board shall be composed of three members appointed by the board of trustees for the terms of one, two, and three years, respectively. Upon the filing of the certificate of the adoption of such proposition, all the powers, duties and responsibilities of such separate boards are transferred to the municipal board, and all property, records, books and papers in the possession of such separate boards shall, within fifteen days after such consolidation, be delivered to the municipal board. If the village has only one of the boards provided in this article, the powers and responsibilities of one

or more other boards, named therein, may be conferred upon such
existing board by the adoption of a proposition therefor at an annual election, and thereupon such existing board shall possess all
the powers and responsibilities of such other board or commission
consolidated with it, and shall thereafter be known as the municipal board of the village.

§ 68. **Continuance of separate boards.**—If a village now has a
separate board of fire, water, light, sewer or cemetery commissioners, such commissioners shall continue in office during their
respective terms, and no commissioner shall be hereafter appointed
until the whole number be reduced by expiration of term or otherwise to less than three, except that if a village of the first or second
class now has a board of commissioners composed of five members,
such number shall be continued. All such commissioners shall
hereafter be appointed by the board of trustees; and the terms shall
be so adjusted that one shall expire each official year.

§ 69. **Continuance of municipal board.**—A municipal board or
commission heretofore created and existing in a village under a
general law when this chapter takes effect is continued, and one
member of such board or commission shall be appointed by the
board of trustees each year for a full term, as provided by the law
relating to such board or commission in force on the day next preceding the day when this chapter takes effect, and such terms are
hereby established as the terms for the members of such board or
commission under this chapter. Such municipal board or commission so continued shall possess all the powers and responsibilities
and be subject to all the duties and liabilities herein conferred or
imposed upon the several separate boards named in this article,
except boards of cemetery commissioners.

§ 70 **Abolition of separate or municipal boards.**—A separate
board of fire, water, light, sewer or cemetery commissioners, or a
municipal board, may be abolished by adopting a proposition therefor at an election. The abolition of such a board shall take effect
immediately upon filing a certificate showing the adoption of the
proposition. Within ten days after such certificate is filed, the
board shall deliver to the clerk of the village its records, books and
papers; and shall also within the same time deliver to the treasurer
all funds, and to the president all other property in its possession
or under its control, belonging to the department.

§ 71. **Books and papers to be open to inspection.**—All books,
papers and records relating to village affairs kept by any board or

officer shall be open to inspection at all reasonable hours by every inhabitant of the village.

§ 79. Transfer of fund and records.—Within ten days after this chapter takes effect, each commissioner or board of commissioners or other village officer heretofore authorized to receive or expend village funds or having such funds under his or its control, shall file with the board of trustees a verified report showing the amount and source of such funds and the object to which the same are applicable. If such funds are under the supervision of a board or officer authorized to contract indebtedness on behalf of the village, such report shall also contain a statement of the amount of such existing indebtedness and the persons to whom and the time when the same is payable. Upon the receipt of such report, the board of trustees may require the treasurer, within ten days after notice therefor, to furnish additional security. Within ten days after the furnishing of such security, approved by the board, or if no such additional security is required, within fifteen days after the filing of the report, all funds belonging to the village shall be paid to the treasurer, and shall be received by him and credited to the proper fund as herein prescribed. All records, books and papers belonging to a board of commissioners, separate from the board of trustees, shall, upon or before the payment of the funds to the treasurer as herein provided, be delivered to the village clerk.

ARTICLE III.

General Duties and Compensation of Officers; Ordinances.

Section 80. President.
81. Treasurer.
82. Clerk.
83. Street commissioner.
84. Board of health.
85. Compensation and duties of village officers not otherwise prescribed.
86. Meetings of the board of trustees.
87. Presiding officer and rules of proceedings.
88. General powers of the board of trustees.
89. Village ordinances.
90. Licensing occupations.
91. Definition of village ordinances.
92. Violation of ordinances.

Section 80. **President.**—The president of a village is its executive officer and the head of its police force. It is his duty to see that the provisions of this chapter, and the resolutions and ordinances of the board of trustees, are enforced, to cause all offenses created thereby to be prosecuted, to institute civil actions in the corporate name of the village for penalties recoverable by the village, to exercise supervision over the conduct of the police and other subordinate officers of the village, and to recommend to the board of trustees such measures as he may think necessary. If the president be absent or unable to perform the duties of his office, the trustees shall appoint one of their number to act as president, who, during the absence or inability of the president, is vested with all the powers and may perform all the duties of the president.

§ 81. **Treasurer.**— The treasurer of a village is its chief fiscal officer. He shall receive all moneys belonging to the village, and keep an accurate account of all receipts and expenditures thereof, showing the funds for which, and the persons from whom, such moneys are received, and the funds from which, and the persons to whom, such moneys are paid. He shall deposit all moneys received by him in the banks designated by the board of trustees, subject to his check, as treasurer. Interest on village money belongs to the village, and must be credited by the treasurer to the proper fund. No money shall be paid from the treasury of the village, except in pursuance of a judgment or order of a court, or an audit and allowance by the board of trustees, and an order designating the fund, signed by the president and countersigned by the clerk, or by an order of a board of commissioners of the village, upon a fund within its jurisdiction. The treasurer shall not draw any money so deposited by him, except in pursuance of such judgment or order. He shall report, in writing, to the board of trustees when requested, the amount of money received by him since his last report, the sources thereof, and the true state of the treasury, which reports shall be filed with the village clerk. He shall, on or before the fifth day of March in each year, file with the village clerk an accurate, detailed and verified statement, showing all moneys paid into the village treasury during the previous fiscal year, the persons by whom, and the funds for which, the same were paid, all expenditures from the treasury during such year, the persons to whom, and the funds from which, such moneys were paid, the balance in the treasury to the credit of each fund at the commencement and at the end of the fiscal year, and all indebtedness of the village outstanding, to whom, so far as practicable, the same is owing, upon what account, and when payable. The treasurer shall make such further reports as may be required by the board of trustees.

§ 82. **Clerk.**— The clerk of each village shall, subject to the direction and control of the board of trustees, have the custody of the corporate seal, and of the books, records and papers of the village, and of all the official reports and communications to the board. He shall act as clerk of the board of trustees, and of each board of village officers, and keep a record of their proceedings; he shall keep an indexed record, in a separate book, of all village ordinances; he shall keep an accurate account of all orders drawn on the treasurer of the village, showing the persons to whom, and the fund from which, the amount of each order is to be paid. He shall, at all reasonable hours, on demand of any person, produce for inspection the books, records and papers of his office, and shall furnish a copy of any portion thereof, certified in the proper form to be read in evidence, upon the payment of his fees therefor, at the rate of six cents per folio.

§ 83. **Street commissioner.**— Under the direction and supervision of the board of trustees, the street commissioner of a village has supervision and charge of the construction, improvement and repair of the public grounds, squares, parks, streets, walks, culverts, wells, and of such other property of the village as the board may determine; and may employ the requisite laborers, and direct them as to the time and manner of the execution of their work. He shall certify to the board of trustees, when required, the names of all persons who have been so employed, the rate of compensation and their term of service.

§ 84. **Board of health.**— The board of health of each village shall have all the powers, and be subject to all the duties, provided by the public health law.

§ 85. **Compensation and duties of village officers not otherwise prescribed.**—The president and trustees, and the fire, water, light, sewer and cemetery commissioners, shall serve without compen-

sation, but the members of the board of trustees shall be entitled
to the compensation fixed by law for inspectors of election when
acting as such, and to the same compensation as town assessors
for each day actually and necessarily spent by them in making the
village assessment.

The board of trustees may fix the compensation and further declare the powers and duties of all other village officers or boards,
and may require any officer or board of the village to furnish reports, estimates or other information relating to any matter within
his or its jurisdiction.

§ 86. Meetings of the board of trustees.—The president and the
trustees of a village shall constitute the board of trustees thereof.
The board shall meet at seven o'clock in the afternoon on the Monday following the annual election, and such meeting is known as the
annual meeting of the board. The board shall hold other regular
meetings at such times and places in the village as it shall, by resolution, provide. Special meetings may be called by the president
or by any two trustees, by causing a written notice, specifying the
time and place thereof, to be served upon each member of the board,
personally, at least one hour, or by leaving a notice at his residence
or place of business with some person of suitable age and discretion, at least twenty-four hours, before the time of meeting.

§ 87. Presiding officer and rules of proceedings.—The president
of the village shall preside at the meetings of the board of trustees,
and shall have a vote upon all matters and questions coming before
the board. A majority of the board shall constitute a quorum for
the transaction of business, but a less number may adjourn and
compel the attendance of absent members. Whenever required
by a member of the board, the vote upon any question shall be taken
by ayes and noes, and the names of the members present and their
votes shall be entered in the minutes. The board may determine
the rules of its procedure, and may compel the attendance of absent
members by the entry of a resolution in the minutes, directing any
peace officer residing within the village, to arrest such absent
member and take him before the board of trustees to answer for
his neglect. A copy of the resolution, certified by the clerk of the
village, shall be sufficient authority to any peace officer residing in
the village, to arrest such absent member and bring him before the
board.

§ 88. General powers of the board of trustees.—The board of
trustees of a village:

1. **Village property and finances.**— Has the management and control of the finances and property of the village, except such as may be under the jurisdiction of the board of health, fire, water, light, sewer or cemetery commissioners, or other boards or officers of the village.

2. **Buildings to be kept in repair and insured.**—Shall keep all buildings and other property of the village in repair, and may cause the same to be insured against loss or damage by fire.

3. **Village lands.**— May purchase, hold and convey real property in the name of the village, but only after the adoption of a proposition therefor at a village election. Every conveyance by the village shall be executed in its corporate name, by the president, in pursuance of a resolution of the board of trustees.

4. **Village buildings.**— May erect and maintain upon village lands, or may rent and furnish, necessary buildings for holding elections, for the use of the village officers, or for other necessary village purposes, and may furnish necessary books, stationery and other supplies for village officers.

5. **Lock-up.**—May erect and maintain a lock-up, or designate a place for the detention of persons arrested under this chapter or under any ordinance of the village; and may contract with a town in which any part of a village is situated for the temporary detention in such lock-up of persons arrested in such town.

6. **Market.**— May purchase or lease lands or buildings for the establishment and maintenance of a market; may lease such market or any part thereof, for such term and at such rent as it may determine; and may prohibit the establishment of a market in the village, except at such place as it may designate.

7. **Fire limits.**— May establish fire limits, by resolution, filed in the office of the village clerk, and posted in three public places in the village.

8. **Official paper.**— May designate a newspaper as the official paper of the village. If but one newspaper is published in the village, it shall be designated as the official paper, if any paper is so designated. If no newspaper is published in the village, any other newspaper published in the same county, having in the opinion of the board, the largest circulation in the village, may be so designated. If no official paper has been designated, the designation of a newspaper for the publication of a notice, resolution, ordinance or other proceeding of the board, shall be deemed a designation thereof as the official paper of the village for the pur-

pose of such publication. The fees of the official paper shall be fixed by the board at a rate not exceeding seventy-five cents per folio.

9. **Village map.**— Shall cause a map of the village to be made and kept on file with the clerk, showing the boundaries of the village and the names and boundaries of all streets and public grounds therein; also the location of all sewers, hydrants, water pipes, and all under-ground pipes and works belonging to the village, and shall, when necessary, cause such map to be revised, corrected and renewed.

10. **Names of streets.**— May give names to the streets and public places, and numbers to the lots or buildings, in the village.

11. **Village attorney.**— May employ an attorney and pay him a reasonable compensation.

12 **Public pound.**— May establish and maintain a public pound and employ a keeper thereof, and fix his compensation, and the fees to be charged by him.

13. **Village clock and scales.**—May establish and maintain a village clock and scales for the public convenience; and fix the fees for the use of such scales.

14. **To act as fence viewers.**—Possesses concurrent jurisdiction with town fence viewers, and has all their powers with respect to division fences within the village.

15. **Drains.**— May construct drains and culverts and regulate water-courses, ponds and watering places within the village.

16. **Water supply.**— May establish, regulate and repair public reservoirs, aqueducts, pumps, wells, fountains, and watering and drinking places.

17. **Lighting streets.**— May provide for the lighting of the streets and the safety of the lamps.

18. **Stands for vehicles.**— May designate stands for hacks, carriages and other vehicles.

19. **When to have powers of other boards.**— Has all the powers and is subject to all the liabilities, and must perform all the duties, of a separate board of fire, water, light, sewer or cemetery commissioners, if the village has no such separate board; and in that case a provision applying to either of such boards applies to the board of trustees

20. **Banks of deposit.**— Shall designate banks for the deposit of all moneys received by the treasurer and may require of any such

bank security for the repayment thereof; and may require a report by the cashier thereof to each regular meeting of the board of the amount on deposit to the credit of the treasurer.

21. Auditing bills.— Shall audit all bills and accounts and all claims for damages against the village, but no bill or account against the village for property purchased, materials furnished, services rendered, or disbursements, shall be audited or paid, nor shall an action be brought thereon unless such bill or account shall be made out in items, and properly dated, with an affidavit attached thereto by the person, or one of the persons, or an officer of a corporation, presenting or claiming the same, that the items of such bill or account are correct, that the services and disbursements charged therein have been in fact rendered or paid, and that no part thereof has been paid or satisfied by the village. The board shall cause to be entered upon its minutes the amount claimed, the amount allowed, and the fund from which each amount allowed shall be paid. No action shall be brought upon any such bill or account within thirty days from the time the same was presented to the board of trustees.

22. Parades of fire department.— May provide for the public inspection and parade of the fire department, at an annual expense, including the hiring of a band, not exceeding two hundred dollars.

§ 89. Village ordinances.— The board of trustees has power to enact, amend and repeal ordinances for the following purposes:

1. Relating to peace and good order generally.—To preserve the public peace and good order; to prevent and suppress vice, immorality, disorderly and gambling houses and houses of ill-fame, riots and tumultuous assemblages, unnecessary crowds upon the streets, or in doorways or stairways adjacent thereto, or loitering about such places, and all disorderly, noisy, riotous or tumultuous conduct within the village, disturbing the peace and quiet of the village or any meeting or assembly therein.

2. Animals at large—To restrain the running at large of horses, cattle, sheep, unmuzzled dogs, fowls or other animals, and may authorize the impounding and sale of the same for the penalty and costs of keeping and proceedings, or the killing of such unmuzzled dogs.

3. Fast driving.—To regulate or prevent fast riding or driving, or the leaving of horses untied or hitched an unreasonable time in the streets or public places, or the driving of animals on the sidewalks.

4. **Amusements.**— To regulate or prevent coasting, ball playing or any act, amusement or practice, endangering property or persons on the streets or public grounds.

5. **Incumbering the streets ; encroachments.**— To regulate or prevent incumbering the streets or public grounds with any material whatever, or any encroachment or projection in, over, or upon any of the streets or public grounds, or any excavations immediately adjacent thereto.

6. **Parades.**—To regulate or prevent all parades, exhibitions, and the parade or playing of bands of music upon the streets or public grounds.

7. **Blowing of steam.**— To regulate or prevent the blowing of steam into, upon or over the streets.

8. **Shade trees.**—To protect and preserve shade trees in the streets and public places, and to prevent the hitching of horses to such trees.

9. **Poles and wires.**—To regulate the erection of telegraph, telephone or electric light poles, or the stringing of wires in, over or upon the streets or public grounds, or upon, over or in front of any building or buildings.

10. **Railroad crossings ; speed.**— To regulate the time during which cars, engines or trains may stand upon the street crossings of railroads; to regulate the speed of locomotives and cars, subject to the provisions of the railroad law, and by a two-thirds vote of all the members of the board, to require railroad companies to erect gates at crossings, to employ competent men to attend the same, and to employ competent flagmen at such crossings.

11. **Sidewalks.**— To compel owners or occupants of lands to clear snow, ice, dirt and other obstructions from the sidewalk in front thereof.

12. **Fireworks and firearms.**— To regulate or prevent the discharge of firearms, rockets, gunpowder or other explosives, or the making of bonfires.

13. **Inflammable materials.**— To regulate the use of candles, kerosene, light, fires or burning materials of any kind in barns, stables or other buildings especially liable to take fire.

14. **Construction of chimneys, etcetera.**—To regulate the use and construction of chimneys, fire-places, stoves and heating apparatus, and the deposit of ashes, and any member of the board or any person authorized by it may enter, when necessary, in the day time any

building within the village, to make an examination with reference to the evasion or violation of such ordinance.

15. **Gunpowder.**— To regulate the storing, sale or transportation of gunpowder or other explosives within the village.

16. **Fire limits.**—To prevent the construction or rebuilding of wooden buildings, or the use in any building within the fire limits of materials liable to take fire. In addition to an action or proceeding to recover the penalty prescribed by the ordinances for a violation of this subdivision, the board of trustees may present a verified petition to a justice of the supreme court, or to a special term of the supreme court of the judicial district, or to the county court or the county judge of a county in which any part of the village is situated, for an order enjoining the violation thereof. Such petition shall state the facts concerning the alleged violation. Upon the presentation of the petition the justice, judge or court shall grant an order requiring such person to appear before him, or before such special term or county court, respectively, on a day specified therein, not more than ten days after the granting thereof, to show cause why such person should not be permanently enjoined from violating such ordinance. A copy of the petition and order shall be served in the manner directed by such order, not less than five days before the return day thereof. On the day specified in such order, the justice, judge or court, before whom the same is returnable, shall hear the proofs of the parties, and may, if deemed necessary and proper, take testimony in relation to the allegations of the petition, or appoint a referee for that purpose. If it appears that such person is violating the ordinance, an order shall be made enjoining him therefrom. If, after the entry of such order in the county clerk's office of a county in which a part of the village is situated, and the service of a copy thereof upon him, or after a substituted service, as the justice, judge or court may direct, such person shall violate such ordinance, such violation shall be deemed a contempt of court, and punishable in the manner provided by the code of civil procedure. Costs upon the application for such injunction may be awarded in favor of and against the parties thereto, in the discretion of the justice, judge or court before whom the petition is heard. If awarded against the village, the costs shall be a village charge.

17. **Swimming and bathing.**— To regulate swimming and bathing in open water, exposed to the public, within or bounding the village.

ply to the board of trustees therefor at a meeting thereof; and the same may be granted or refused by the board. The president may suspend any such license, until the next meeting of the board of trustees, and thereupon the said license may be revoked or continued by the board.

§ 91. Definition of village ordinances.—A village ordinance includes also a rule, by-law, order or regulation of the board of trustees, or of the board of fire, water, light, sewer or cemetery commissioners, approved by the board of trustees, for the violation of which a penalty is imposed; and each provision of this chapter, relating to the enforcement of an ordinance applies to such a rule, by-law, order or regulation.

§ 92. Violation of ordinances.—The board of trustees of a village may enforce obedience to its ordinances by prescribing therein penalties for each violation thereof, not exceeding one hundred dollars for any offense. In addition to the penalty the board may also ordain that a violation thereof shall constitute disorderly conduct, and that the person violating the same shall be a disorderly person; and such violation shall constitute disorderly conduct, and such person shall be a disorderly person. An ordinance of a village shall not declare any conduct to be disorderly conduct, or that the person violating the same shall be a disorderly person, if any statute of the state shall declare such conduct to be disorderly or constitute the person a disorderly person. Every such ordinance shall be void in so far as it violates the provisions of this section.

§ 93. Approved by board of ordinances of separate boards.—An ordinance adopted by the board of fire, water, light, or cemetery commissioners for the violation of which a penalty is imposed, must be approved by the board of trustees. Upon its adoption such an ordinance must be certified to the board of trustees, and upon its approval becomes an ordinance of the village with the same force and effect and enforceable in the same manner as if it had been originally adopted by the board of trustees.

§ 94. When ordinances to take effect.— Every ordinance hereafter adopted or approved by the board of trustees of a village, shall be entered in its minutes, and published in the official paper of the village, and also in each other newspaper actually printed in the village, once each week for two consecutive weeks, and a printed copy thereof posted conspicuously in at least three public places in the village for at least ten days before the same shall take effect, and an affidavit of the publication and posting thereof shall be filed with the clerk. But such an ordinance shall take effect from the date of its service as against a person served personally with a copy thereof, certified by the village clerk under the corporate seal of the village, and showing the date of its passage and entry in the minutes.

ARTICLE IV.
Finances.

Section 100. **Fiscal year.**–The fiscal year begins on the first day of March, and ends on the last day of February. No expenditures shall be made, nor indebtedness incurred, by the village, during the month of March, except for current expenses. The term "assessors," as used in this article, includes the board of trustees of a village which has no separate board of assessors.

§ 101. **Village funds.**—Village funds are classified as follows:

1. The street fund, composed of the poll tax, and all moneys received from taxation or otherwise for the construction, care or maintenance of bridges, streets, crosswalks or sidewalks, the paving and grading of streets, and for the care and maintenance of public parks and squares.

2. The water fund, composed of all money received from taxation or otherwise for supplying the village with water under a contract therefor, or for the purchase, acquisition, construction, care, extension or maintenance of a water-works system, all water rents, all sums received from assessments for fire protection or for the sale of water to be used outside the village, and penalties recovered for violations of the ordinances of the department.

3. The light fund, composed of all moneys received from taxation or otherwise for supplying the village with light under a contract therefor, or for the purchase, acquisition, construction, care, extension or maintenance of a lighting system, light rents and penalties recovered for violations of the ordinances of the department.

4. The sewer fund, composed of all moneys received from taxation or otherwise for the construction, care, extension and maintenance of a sewer or a sewer system, or for the purchase or acquisition of real property therefor.

5. The cemetery fund, composed of all moneys received from taxation or otherwise for the purchase, acquisition, construction, care and maintenance of a cemetery, all moneys received from the sale or use of cemetery lots, and all penalties recovered for violations of the ordinances of the department.

6. The water sinking fund, composed of all sums set apart by the board of water commissioners for that purpose, with all interest or other income thereon.

7. The light sinking fund, composed of all sums set apart by the board of light commissioners for that purpose, with all interest or other income thereon.

8. The general fund, composed of all moneys received from taxa-

tion or otherwise for a purpose not specified in either of the foregoing subdivisions, nor included in any other fund.

9. A special fund may also be created from time to time, composed of a sum set apart as directed by a proposition, or by the board of trustees, for a purpose not otherwise specified in this section. When all charges against such special fund have been paid, the surplus, if any, may be transferred to the general fund.

Expenditures for a purpose specified in either subdivision must be made from the fund therein described. The expense of acquiring real property for the laying out, alteration or widening of a street, or for a public park or square, and the compensation therefor, are a charge upon the general fund.

§ 102. **Annual financial statement.**—The board of trustees shall, after the close of each fiscal year, and at least ten days before the next annual election, make a statement of the total amount of village taxes estimated by them as necessary to be raised during the then next fiscal year, specifying the amount for each fund. The board shall cause the annual report of the treasurer for the last preceding fiscal year and such statement made by them, to be published and posted for at least one week prior to the annual election, in the same manner as the notice of such annual election.

§ 103. **Poll tax.**— Unless a village decides not to impose a poll tax, all men, between the ages of twenty-one and seventy years, residing in the village, are liable to an annual poll tax of one dollar, except exempt firemen, active members of the fire department of the village, honorably discharged soldiers and sailors, who lost an arm or a leg in the service of the United States during the late war, or who are unable to perform manual labor by reason of injury received or disabilities incurred in such service, clergymen and priests of every denomination, paupers, idiots and lunatics. No personal property is exempt from levy and sale in the collection of a poll tax, either upon a village tax warrant, or upon an execution issued upon a judgment for the recovery of such poll tax. A proposition may be adopted at an annual election to the effect that no poll tax be thereafter imposed in the village. Such proposition may be revoked at an annual election, and if revoked, the poll tax shall be imposed as if the proposition for exemption had not been adopted.

§ 104. **Annual assessment-roll.**—The assessors of a village shall, on or before the first Tuesday of June, if a village of the first

or second class, and on or before the first Tuesday of May, if a
village of the third or fourth class, prepare an assessment-roll
of the persons and property taxable within the village in
the same manner and form as is required by law for
the preparation of a town assessment-roll.   They shall also
enter on such roll the names of all persons liable to a poll tax.
The assessors of a village of the third or fourth class, included
wholly within a town, may, and upon the adoption of a proposition therefor at an annual election, shall adopt the assessment-
roll of the town of the last preceding year as the basis of their assessment, so far as practicable.   If such town roll be adopted the
assessors shall copy therefrom a description of all real property
of the village and the value thereof as the same appears thereon;
also all personal property and the value thereof assessed on such
town roll to residents of the village, or to corporations taxable
therefor therein, together with the names of the persons or corporations, respectively, to which such real or personal property is
or should be assessed.   Where the town assessment-roll is adopted
and the valuation of any taxable property can not be ascertained
therefrom, or where the value of such property shall have increased or diminished since the last assessment-roll of the town
was completed, or an error, mistake or omission on the part of
the town assessors shall have been made in the description or valuation of taxable property, the assessors shall ascertain the true
value of the property to be taxed from the best evidence available.

§ 105. **Meeting of assessors to hear complaints.**—The assessors
shall, in a village of the first or second class, at least one week before the first Tuesday in June in each year, and in a village
of the third or fourth class, at least one week before the
first Tuesday in May in each year, cause a notice to be
published in each newspaper published in the village, and
posted in at least five conspicuous public places in the village, that on such first Tuesday in May or June, as the case
may be, at a specified place and during four consecutive hours
to be named, they will meet for the purpose of completing the
assessment-roll, and of hearing and determining complaints in relation thereto, and they may adjourn such meeting from day to
day, not later than Saturday then next succeeding.   Village assessors possess all the powers and are subject to all the duties of
town assessors in hearing and determining complaints as to assessments.   If the village is one in which the assessment-roll is

required to be prepared by copying from the assessment-roll of the town, the assessors at such meeting shall not hear any complaint as to a valuation which has not been changed, except upon proof of a change in the property or in the ownership or valuation since the town assessment was completed.

§ 106. **Completion and verification of assessment-roll.**—When the assessors, or a majority of them, shall have completed the village assessment-roll, they shall severally make, subscribe and attach to such roll, an oath, in substantially the same form as is required of town assessors by the tax law, if such roll was originally prepared by them; or, if such roll was prepared by copying from the assessment-roll of the town, an oath, to the effect that such roll contains, to the best of their knowledge and belief, a true statement, of the property, persons and corporations liable to assessment and taxation within the village, as the same appears upon the assessment-roll of the town in which the village is situated, and, if in making such assessment the valuation of any property has been changed, or any new or additional assessment has been made, that in changing such valuation or in making such new or additional assessment, they have estimated the value of the real estate at the sums which a majority of the assessors have decided to be the full value thereof, and that the personal property so assessed is assessed at the full value thereof, according to their best knowledge and belief. The roll as so completed and verified shall be filed with the village clerk, on or before the second Tuesday in June in villages of the first or second class, and on or before the second Tuesday in May in villages of the third or fourth class.

§ 107. **Failure to hold meeting.**— If the meeting for completing the village assessment-roll and hearing complaints in relation thereto is not held on the first Tuesday in May, or June, as the case may be, each of the assessors shall forfeit to the village ten dollars, and they shall, by resolution, fix another time therefor, and give notice thereof at least ten days prior thereto by publication thereof, in the same manner as for the first meeting, and by posting copies thereof in at least five conspicuous places in the village. The assessors shall meet accordingly at the time and place appointed, shall hear complaints, complete the assessment-roll, and file the same on or before the fourth day after such meeting, in the same manner as near as may be as if their annual meeting had been held as required by law. If the completed assessment-roll shall not be so filed on or before the fourth day after the meeting for completing the same and hearing complaints in relation thereto, in either case, the assessment shall not on that account be invalid, but such roll shall be filed in like manner as soon as may be thereafter and each assessor shall forfeit to the village five dollars for each day of such neglect.

§ 108. **Notice of completion of annual assessment-roll.**—Upon completing and filing the annual assessment-roll, and on or before the second Tuesday of June in villages of the first or second class, and on or before the second Tuesday in May in villages of the third or fourth class, the assessors shall cause notice thereof to be published at least once in the official paper, if any, and copies of such notice posted in not less than five public places in the village, specifying the date of filing, and that the same will remain on file with the clerk, subject to public inspection, for fifteen days after the date of such notice.

§ 109. **Certiorari to review assessment.**— An application for a writ of certiorari to review the assessment-roll may be made within such fifteen days in the manner provided by the tax law.

§ 110. **Annual tax levy.**— Upon the expiration of such fifteen days, the board of trustees shall levy the tax for the current fiscal year, which must include the following items:

1. Such sums as shall have been authorized by the last preceding annual election, or by a special election for which a special tax warrant has not been issued.

2. The total amount of the indebtedness of the village lawfully contracted, which will become due and payable during the current fiscal year.

3. Such sum as the board deems necessary in addition to the poll tax to meet the expenditures from the street fund for the current fiscal year, not exceeding one-half of one per centum of the total valuation of the property assessed upon the annual assessment-roll of the last preceding year.

4. Such additional sums as shall be deemed necessary to meet all other expenditures of the village for the current fiscal year, not exceeding one-half of one per centum of such total valuation.

5. The poll tax.

If by reason of an actual or alleged error or defect in the assessment-roll of the last preceding fiscal year, any taxes authorized and intended to be levied thereby, are not paid, or if a special tax warrant has been returned and taxes levied therein remain unpaid, the amount thereof may be levied upon the same property or to the same person upon the annual assessment-roll of the current year. The tax roll shall be made in duplicate, and upon its completion, the clerk shall endorse upon each duplicate the date thereof. The completed assessment-roll shall be presumptive evidence of the facts therein stated.

§ 111. **Special assessment and levy.**—If the board of trustees is authorized by a special election to levy a special tax, the clerk shall forthwith prepare a copy of the annual assessment-roll, and the same shall be revised and corrected by the board of trustees as shall be just, for the purposes of the assessment of such tax upon the taxable property and persons of the village, and as so corrected and revised shall be filed with the clerk on or before the second Tuesday after such special election. Thereupon the like proceedings shall be taken, as nearly as may be, for completing such assessment-roll, hearing and determining complaints in relation thereto, which must be on a notice of not less than five nor more than ten days, filing the roll when completed, giving notice thereof, and levying the special tax so authorized, as in the case of the annual assessment-roll and the levy of the annual tax.

§ 112. **Lien of tax.**— An annual or special tax is a lien prior and superior to every other lien or claim, except the lien of an existing tax or local assessment, on real property upon which it is levied from the date of the delivery to the collector of the warrant for the collection thereof, until paid or otherwise satisfied or discharged.

§ 113. **Lien of assessment for local improvement.**—An assessment for paving, sewers, fire protection, constructing or repairing sidewalks, sprinkling streets, trimming trees, or keeping sidewalks or streets cleared of weeds, ice, snow or other accumulations, is a lien prior and superior to every other lien or claim, except the lien of an existing tax or local assessment, upon the real property improved or benefited, from the date of the final determination of the amount thereof, until it is paid or otherwise satisfied or discharged. No real property is exempt from assessment for a purpose specified in this section.

§ 114. **Warrant to collector.**—Upon the completion of a tax levy the clerk shall deliver to the collector one of the duplicate rolls, with a warrant thereto annexed signed by the president and attested by the clerk, under the corporate seal of the village, containing a summary statement of the purposes for which the taxes are levied, the amount thereof for each purpose, and the total amount for all purposes, and commanding the collector to collect the taxes therein levied with his fees, and to return said warrant and roll to the clerk within sixty days after the date of the warrant, unless the time shall be extended. The collector shall give a receipt to the clerk for the warrant and assessment-roll delivered to him. The board of trustees may extend the time for the return of the warrant thirty days beyond the first sixty, and such extension shall not affect the validity of the bond given by the collector and his sureties.

§ 115. Collection of taxes by collector.— Upon receiving the assessment-roll and warrant the collector shall cause a notice to be published at least once in the official paper, if any, and also in each other newspaper published in the village, and posted conspicuously in five public places in the village, stating that on six days specified therein, not less than nine nor more than twenty days after the publication and posting thereof, he will attend at a convenient place in the village, specified in the notice, for the purpose of receiving taxes. At least seven days before the first date fixed in such notice, the collector shall serve a copy thereof upon each corporation named in or subject to taxation upon the assessment-roll, and whose principal office is not in the village, by delivering such copy to a person designated by the corporation for that purpose by a written designation filed with the village clerk, or to any person in the village acting as the agent or representative in any capacity of such corporation. If there is no such designated person or agent in the village, service of such notice upon the corporation shall not be required. Any person or corporation paying taxes within twenty days from the date of the notice, shall be charged with one per centum thereon, and thereafter with five per centum, for the fees of the collector. If a notice is not served upon a corporation as herein required, the collector shall only be entitled to one per centum as his fees upon the taxes assessed against it. After the expiration of such twenty days the collector shall proceed to collect the taxes remaining unpaid, and for that purpose he possesses all the powers of a town collector. The laws relating to town collectors shall also, so far as consistent with this chapter, apply to the collection of village taxes.

116. Return of collector; payment of taxes to treasurer.—The collector shall pay all taxes received by him, as soon as practicable

after receipt thereof, to the treasurer, and, upon the expiration of the time fixed therefor, shall deliver the roll and warrant to the clerk and make and file with him a return, in accordance with the directions of the warrant, showing the total amount of tax paid and each tax unpaid, with the receipt of the village treasurer for all taxes paid to him. The clerk shall thereupon deliver to the treasurer a statement showing the unpaid taxes returned by the collector. All taxes so returned unpaid shall be increased five per centum, and, if remaining unpaid for thirty days after such return, shall bear interest at the rate of ten per centum per annum, from the time of their return as unpaid by the collector to the time of their subsequent payment; and such tax and increase may be paid to the treasurer at any time after such return and before a sale for such unpaid tax of any real property upon which the same may be assessed; but if paid after a notice of sale has been given as provided in this article, the expense of such notice shall be added to the amount of the tax. The provisions of this section, so far as practicable, apply to a village in which the taxes are collected by the treasurer.

§ 117. **Collection of taxes by treasurer.**—In a village which has no collector, the tax-roll and warrant shall be delivered to the treasurer of the village, and the provisions of this article relating to the delivery of a tax-roll and warrant, the extension of the time for the collection of taxes, and the return of such tax-roll and warrant, apply to the roll and warrant so delivered to a treasurer, so far as practicable. Upon the delivery of the roll and warrant to the treasurer, he shall publish in each newspaper actually printed in the village, once in each week for four consecutive weeks, and post in five public places in the village, a notice that such tax-roll and warrant have been left with him for the collection of the taxes therein levied, and designating one or more convenient places in the village where he will receive taxes for thirty days after the first publication and posting of said notice, from nine o'clock in the morning until four o'clock in the afternoon, and that for said thirty days taxes may be paid to him without additional charge; and that all such taxes remaining unpaid after the expiration of said thirty days will thereafter bear interest at the rate of twelve per centum per annum, until the return of the tax-roll and warrant. The treasurer shall attend at the time and place specified in said notice, and may receive such taxes. After the expiration

of said thirty days the treasurer shall proceed to collect the taxes remaining unpaid, with interest as herein provided, but without any other fee or charge, and for that purpose be possessed of all the powers of a town collector.

§ 118. **Return and assessment-roll as evidence.**—The return of unpaid taxes by the collector, or treasurer, or a copy thereof certified by the clerk under the corporate seal, shall be presumptive evidence of the facts stated therein. An assessment-roll filed with the clerk, or a copy of the same, or any part thereof, certified by him under the corporate seal, shall be presumptive evidence of the contents thereof, of the regularity of the assessment, and of the right to levy such tax.

§ 119. **When real property to be sold for unpaid tax.**—If a tax assessed upon real property on an annual or special assessment-roll be returned by the collector or treasurer as unpaid, the board of trustees may direct the treasurer to sell an interest in such property for the unpaid tax in the manner herein prescribed. If such sale be directed, the clerk shall deliver to the treasurer a certified copy of the assessment upon such property, and all entries relating thereto contained in the assessment-roll. Upon receiving such statement, the treasurer shall proceed to sell at public auction an estate in such real property for the shortest period not exceeding fifty years, for which any person will take such property, and pay the tax and the percentage and interest then due, together with the expenses of the sale, which shall include giving the notice of sale, and one dollar for the services of the treasurer.

§ 120. **Notice of sale.**—Notice of the sale shall be published in each newspaper published in the village once in each week for at least four consecutive weeks, and posted in at least five conspicuous places in the village, and a copy thereof served on the owners of such real property at least three weeks before the sale. The notice of sale shall contain a brief description of the property and a brief statement of the facts authorizing the sale, and the time and place thereof.

§ 121. **Certificate of sale.**—All such sales shall be for cash, and upon payment by the purchaser, the village treasurer shall deliver to him a certificate of the sale, signed and acknowledged in the same manner as a deed to be recorded, stating the amount paid by the purchaser, the date of sale and payment, and a description of the real property sold. The certificate of sale may be recorded in the

county clerk's office of each county in which any part of the property
is situated, in the same manner and with the same effect as a deed,
and if so recorded within two years after the tax became a lien on
the property, the recording of such certificate shall have the same
effect as the recording of a deed, to give the certificate priority over
every interest therein or lien thereon acquired subsequent to the
lien of the tax; but, unless such certificate is recorded within such
time, it shall be void as to such other interest or lien.

§ 122. Purchaser entitled to possession.—Upon the receipt and
recording of such certificate, the purchaser or other owner of the
certificate shall be entitled to immediate possession and enjoyment
of such real property as against all persons having any title to, interest in, or lien upon the property at the time the tax became a
lien thereon, and against all persons deriving any title to, interest in,
or lien upon, such property, while the tax was a lien thereon, and to
retain possession thereof during the existence of the estate pur
chased, unless such real property is redeemed from such sale.

§ 123. Enforcement of right to possession—The purchaser or
other owner of the certificate may enforce his right to possession by
summary proceedings, in the same manner as a landlord against a
tenant holding over after expiration of term. The purchaser or
other owner of the certificate may, before the expiration of the estate
purchased, remove all buildings and fixtures which he has erected
or placed thereon during its existence, which can be removed without permanent injury to the premises.

§ 124. Village may bid in property; rights of village.—If there be
no other bidder, the treasurer shall bid in the property for the vil
lage for the term of fifty years, and a certificate thereof shall be
issued accordingly. Thereupon the village has all the rights of a
purchaser for such term. Immediately upon the purchase of such
property by the village, the president shall take possession thereof
and hold, manage, lease or otherwise control the same. He may,
in the name of the village, institute and maintain summary proceedings to obtain possession of such property in the same manner
as upon the sale of real property upon execution. The treasurer
shall open an account with such property, and shall charge to the
same the amount of taxes, fees, interest and expenses of the sale,
and shall also add all sums subsequently levied upon the property
by tax or local assessment and remaining unpaid. The president
shall pay to the treasurer during each fiscal year the net amount
received from such property, which amount shall be credited in the

account. Upon payment to the treasurer of the amount of the taxes or assessments charged against such property, together with the interest at the rate of ten per centum per annum from the time of the sale or the return of a subsequent unpaid tax or assessment, after deducting any credits appearing in the account, the president shall on demand execute and deliver to the person making such payment, an assignment of the certificate of sale, or a satisfaction thereof, as may be required. Whenever the amount received from the use of such property equals the taxes, assessments, expenses and interest then due, the right of the village in such property shall cease and determine, and the president shall thereupon execute and deliver to the owner of the property a release and satisfaction of the interest of the village therein. If upon the execution of an assignment of the certificate, or of a release or satisfaction, a surplus derived from such property remains in the treasury, it shall be paid upon the order of the board of trustees to the person entitled thereto, on demand.

§ 125. **Redemption from sale by owner.**—A person who at the time of the sale was the owner of the property, or of a vested interest therein, or a lessee thereof, or his assigns, may redeem from the sale, either by paying to the owner of the certificate of sale other than the village, or by depositing with the treasurer for his benefit, the amount paid by the purchaser on such sale, with interest thereon at the rate of ten per centum per annum from the time of the sale to the time of deposit, and the fees lawfully paid to each county clerk for recording the certificate or any assignment thereof in any county in which the property or any part thereof is situated. If such payment be made to the owner of the certificate he shall thereupon execute and deliver to such person making the payment a written cancellation or receipt of the certificate of sale duly acknowledged in the same manner as a deed to be recorded, and specifying the date of the sale, the amount paid thereon, the purchaser thereat, and the property sold. If such payment be made to the treasurer, he shall deliver to the person making it, a written receipt acknowledged in like manner and containing the like specifications. The recording of such cancellation or receipt in each clerk's office of the county in which any part of such property is situated shall effect a cancellation of such certificate of sale.

§ 126. **Actions to recover unpaid taxes.**—After the lapse of thirty days from the return of the collector, an action may be maintained, as upon contract, by the village, to recover the amount of an unpaid tax, together with five per centum thereof, and interest from the time of such return at the rate of ten per centum per annum. A judgment in such action for any amount, when docketed in the office of the county clerk, shall be a lien upon the real property of the defendant. Supplementary proceedings may also be taken for such tax in accordance with the provisions of the tax law.

§ 127. **Investment of sinking funds.**—If at any time the receipts of the water or light department exceed the amount needed for current expenses, and the payment of principal or interest due or to become due during the next fiscal year, the surplus may be transferred to a fund to be known as the sinking fund of the department, and to be used in the payment of outstanding obligations, or for future expenses of the department if the rents or other income be insufficient for that purpose. A village sinking fund may be invested in

1. The bonds of the United States, the state of New York, or any city of this state, or the bonds, certificates or other obligations issued by the village for the payment of such indebtedness, which may be purchased at any time from such sinking fund at prices not exceeding the par value, and when so purchased the same shall be immediately canceled; or

2. Mortgages on improved land owned by the borrower in a county in which such village or a part thereof is located; but before such a mortgage is accepted the board of trustees must be satisfied that the borrower has a title in fee to such lands, and that the same are free and clear of all incumbrances and are worth twice the amount of the sum loaned, exclusive of buildings.

§ 128. **Borrowing money generally.**—If authorized by an election, money may be borrowed by a village upon its bonds or other obligations, payable in future fiscal years for the purpose of purchasing, constructing and maintaining the following village improvements:

1. A village or town hall.
2. Fire engines and fire alarm system.
3. Laying out, grading or paving streets.
4. Sidewalks.
5. Bridges.
6. Water works.
7. Lighting system.
8. Sewerage.

9. **Parks.**

10. **Cemeteries.**

Money may be borrowed in anticipation of taxes already levied for the current fiscal year, but not in excess thereof, and it must be payable within such year. No contract shall be made involving an expenditure by the village, unless the money therefor is on hand, or a proposition has been adopted authorizing the board of trustees to raise such money.

§ 129. **Bonds or other obligations.**—Bonds or other obligations of the village shall be signed by the president and treasurer, and attested by the clerk under the corporate seal. They shall become due within thirty years from the date of issue, and, unless the whole amount of the indebtedness represented thereby is to be paid within five years from their date, they shall be so issued as to provide for the payment of the indebtedness in equal annual installments, the first of which shall be payable not more than five years from their date. They shall bear interest at a rate not exceeding five per centum per annum, and shall be negotiated for not less than their par value. They shall be sold on sealed proposals or at public auction upon notice published in the official paper, if any, and also in each other newspaper actually printed in the village, and in such other newspapers as the board of trustees may determine, and posted in three public places in the village, at least ten days before the sale, to the person who will take them at the lowest rate of interest. They shall be consecutively numbered from one to the highest number issued, and the clerk shall keep a record of the number of each bond or obligation, its date, amount, rate of interest, when and where payable, and the purchaser thereof or the person to whom they are issued.

§ 130. **Limitation of indebtedness.**—A village shall not incur indebtedness if thereby its total contract indebtedness, exclusive of liabilities for which taxes have already been levied, shall, in addition to obligations issued to provide for the supply of water, exceed ten per centum of the assessed valuation of the real property of such village, subject to taxation, as it appeared on the last preceding village assessment-roll.

§ 131. **Second election upon proposition to raise money.**—If the vote at an election upon a proposition to purchase property or to raise a tax or to incur a debt shall be against such proposition, no proposition embracing the same object shall be again submitted before the next annual election thereafter.

§ 132. **Exemption from taxation of firemen and fire companies.—**
Upon the adoption of a proposition therefor, the members of any
fire, hose, protective or hook and ladder company in any village
may be exempted from taxation to the amount of five hundred dollars on any assessment for village purposes, in addition to the exemptions otherwise allowed by law, and the real and personal
property of any such company may also be exempted from like village taxation.

ARTICLE V.

Streets, Sidewalks and Public Grounds.

Section 140. **Definitions.**—The term "street" as used in this chapter also includes a highway, road, avenue, lane or alley which the public have the right to use; and the term "pavement" includes a macadam, telford, asphalt, brick or other similarly improved roadbed, and is only applied to the portion of the street between the sidewalks or established curb lines.

§ 141. **Separate highway district.**— The streets and public grounds of a village, except as provided in the next section, are under the exclusive control and supervision of the board of trustees. The board of trustees may expend a portion of the street fund upon outside highways connecting with the village streets.

§ 142. **Care of bridges.**— If at the time this chapter takes effect, the board of trustees of a village has the supervision and control of a bridge therein, it shall continue to exercise such control under this chapter. In any other case, every public bridge within a village shall be under the control of the commissioners of highways of the town in which the bridge is wholly or partly situated, or such other officer as may be designated by special law, and the expense of constructing and repairing such bridge and the approaches thereto is a town charge, unless the village assumes the whole or part of such expense.

§ 143. **When village may construct or repair bridges.**—A village may assume the control, care and maintenance of a bridge or bridges wholly within its boundaries, upon the adoption of a proposition therefor, at a village election; or a proposition may be adopted authorizing the board of trustees to enter into an agreement with the commissioners of highways of a town, in which any part of such village is situated, to construct or repair a bridge in any part of the village included in such town, at the joint expense of the village and town, which agreement shall fix the portion to be paid by each.

§ 144. **Dedication of streets.**— An owner of land in a village who has laid out a street thereon may dedicate such street, or any part thereof, or an easement therein, to the village for a public street, or an owner may dedicate for such purpose land not laid out as a street. Upon an offer in writing by the owner to make such a dedication, the board of trustees shall meet to consider the matter; and it may, by resolution, determine to accept a dedication of the whole or any part of the land described in such offer, or of the whole or any part of such street, to be described in such resolution. Upon the adoption of such a resolution the owner may execute and deliver to the village clerk a proper conveyance of the land to be dedicated. The board of trustees may, by resolution, accept the conveyance, and a certified copy of such resolution, together with the conveyance, shall thereupon be recorded in the office of the county clerk. Upon the acceptance of the conveyance the land described therein shall become and be a public street of the village. No street less than two rods in width shall be accepted by dedication. All offers of dedication must be entered at length in the minutes of the board of trustees.

§ 145. **Petition for street improvement.**—Five resident freeholders may present to the board of trustees a petition for laying out, altering, widening, narrowing or discontinuing a street in the village. The petition must be addressed to the board of trustees, and must contain a statement of the following facts:

1. The names and residences of the petitioners.

2. If the petition be for the laying out of a street, the general course thereof, and a description of the land to be taken.

3. If the petition be for the alteration of a street, its name, the proposed alteration, and a description of the land, if any, to be taken.

4. If the petition be for the widening of a street, its name and a description of the land to be taken.

5. If the petition be for the narrowing of a street, its name, its proposed width after such alteration, and the manner in which such narrowing is to be effected.

6. If the petition be for the discontinuance of a street, its name and the part proposed to be discontinued.

7. If the petition be for the laying out, alteration or widening of a street, the names and residences of the owners of all land to be taken.

8. If the petition be for the narrowing or discontinuance of a street, the names and residences of the owners of adjoining lands affected.

§ 146. **Notice of meeting of board to consider petition.**—Upon the presentation of the petition the board shall immediately give notice that it will meet at a specified time and place, not less than ten nor more than twenty days from the date of such notice, to consider the petition. The notice must state the general object of the petition, and if it be for the laying out of a street, a general description of its proposed course, and in any other case, the name of the street proposed to be changed or discontinued.

The notice must be served upon the following persons, unless such service be waived by them in writing:

1. If the petition be for the laying out of a street, upon each owner of land to be taken.

2. If the petition be for the alteration or widening of a street, upon each owner of land, if any, to be taken, and upon each owner of land adjoining the part of the street affected.

3. If the petition be for the narrowing of a street, upon each owner of land adjoining the part of the street affected.

4. If the petition be for the discontinuance of a street, upon each owner of land adjoining the part of the street proposed to be discontinued, and also upon the owner of land otherwise affected by the proposed discontinuance.

If a person other than the owner is in possession of such land, notice must also be served upon him. Such notice shall also be published in each newspaper in the village, and posted in five conspicuous places therein. The notice must be served, posted and published at least ten days before the hearing.

§ 147. **Meeting and determination of board.**—The board shall meet at the time and place specified in the notice to consider the petition and also any objections thereto. A person affected by the proposed improvement, and upon whom notice has not been served, may appear upon the hearing. A voluntary general appearance of such a person is equivalent to personal service of the notice upon him. The board may adjourn the hearing, and must determine the matter within twenty days from the date fixed for such hearing. If the board determine to grant the petition an order must be entered in its minutes containing a description of the land, if any, to be taken.

§ 148. **Effect of determination.**—The determination by the board has the following effect:

1. If the petition for the laying out, alteration or widening of a street be granted, the board of trustees may acquire the land for such improvement by purchase or by proceedings under this article. But no street shall be laid out through a building or any fixtures or erections for the purposes of trade or manufacture, or any yard or enclosure necessary to be used for the enjoyment thereof, without the consent of the owner, except upon the order of a justice of the supreme court residing in the judicial district

in which the village or a part thereof is situated, to be granted upon an application by the board of trustees on a notice to the owner of not less than ten days.

2. If the petition for the narrowing of a street be granted, the board shall enter upon its records a description of the street after such narrowing, and the portion of the former street not included in such description is abandoned.

3. If the petition for the discontinuance of a street be granted, such street or the part thereof so discontinued, is abandoned.

§ 149. Application for commissioners; notice of application.-If a petition for the laying out, alteration or widening of a street be granted, and the board can not agree with an owner upon the purchase-price of land necessary to be acquired, an application may be made by the board to the county court of the county in which such land is situated, for the appointment of three commissioners to determine the compensation to be made to such owner. At least ten days before the making of such application a notice specifying the time and place thereof must be served upon such owner.

§ 150. Appointment of commissioners.—Upon such application the county court must appoint as such commissioners three resident disinterested freeholders of the county in which such land is situated, not residents of the village nor nominated by a person interested in the proceeding. In case of a vacancy another commissioner may be appointed in like manner. The order of appointment must contain the name of each person whose compensation is to be determined by the commissioners.

§ 151. Notice of meeting of commissioners.—The commissioners shall file with the village clerk the constitutional oath of office. They shall appoint a time and place for a hearing and serve a notice thereof upon the board of trustees and upon each person named in the order. Such notice must be served at least ten days before the hearing, which must be held within twenty days after their appointment.

§ 152. Meeting and award of commissioners.-The commissioners shall meet at the time and place appointed and may adjourn from time to time. They shall personally examine the land, compensation for which is to be determined by them, and may take testimony in relation thereto. They shall keep minutes of their proceedings and reduce to writing all evidence taken by them. They shall award to each owner of land named in the order the compensation to which he may be entitled after making allowance for any benefit he may derive from the improvement. After the appointment of the commissioners and before any evidence is taken on the hearing, the board may make an agreement with an owner named in the order for the compensation to be made to him. If such an agreement be made, notice thereof must be served upon the commissioners, and thereupon the proceeding as to such owner is discontinued. The award shall be signed by a majority of the commissioners, and, together with the minutes of their proceedings, the evidence taken by them, and any notice of agreement served upon them, shall be filed in the office of the village clerk.

§ 153. **Appeal from award of commissioners.**—The board of trustees, or an owner to whom an award has been made by the commissioners, may, within twenty days after the filing of the award, appeal therefrom to the county court by which the commissioners were appointed. Such appeal shall be taken by a notice of appeal to be served as follows:

1. If the appeal be taken by the board of trustees, notice thereof must be filed by the village clerk in his office, and addressed to and served upon each owner to whose award objection is made by the board.

2. If the appeal be taken by an owner, the notice of appeal must be addressed to the board of trustees and served upon the village clerk.

The notice must in either case briefly state the grounds upon which the appeal is taken.

§ 154. **Return by clerk.**—Within ten days after such appeal the village clerk shall transmit to the county judge the petition filed with the board for the laying out, alteration or widening of the proposed street, all papers and evidence in the proceeding subsequently filed in his office, and a certified copy of each resolution of the board of trustees relating to the improvement.

§ 155. **Hearing of the appeal.**— The appeal may be brought on by either party by a notice of not less than ten nor more than twenty days. If the appeal is by the board of trustees, it brings up for review all proceedings by or before the commissioners, and the award made by them. If the appeal is by an owner, it brings up for review all proceedings relating to the proposed improvement. If the appeal is by the board of trustees, and two or more owners are made respondents, the county court may affirm or reverse the award of the commissioners as to the whole or any number of such owners; and if the appeal is by an owner, the county court may affirm or reverse the award.

If the award be reversed, the order of reversal must state the reasons therefor, and if upon grounds relating to the amount of the award, or for errors in the proceedings by the commissioners, it must direct a rehearing before the same or other commissioners.

If it appears from the order of the county court that the award is reversed solely upon grounds relating to the amount of compensation, or for errors in the proceedings by the commissioners, no further appeal shall be allowed. The order of the county court upon such appeal, together with the papers transmitted by the village clerk, must be filed by the county judge in the office of such clerk. The order must also be entered in the office of the county clerk.

§ 156. **Compensation of commissioners.**—Each commissioner is entitled to five dollars for each day actually and necessarily spent in such proceeding, together with his necessary traveling and incidental expenses. Such compensation and expenses are a charge against the village.

§ 157. **Costs on appeal.**—Costs on appeal may be allowed as follows:

1. If on appeal by the board of trustees the award of the commissioners be affirmed, the county court may allow to the respondent costs of such appeal, against the village, not exceeding twenty-five dollars.

2. If on such an appeal the award be reversed on the ground that as to a specified owner it is excessive, the court may fix the amount of costs, not exceeding fifty dollars, to be stated in the order, to be paid by the village to such owner, if upon a rehearing the amount awarded to him is not more favorable to the village by the amount of such costs than the first award.

3. If on appeal by an owner the award be affirmed, costs not exceeding twenty-five dollars may be awarded against him, to be recovered by the village.

4. If on such an appeal the award be reversed, the county court may allow to the owner a sum not exceeding twenty-five dollars for the costs of appeal, which shall be a charge against the village.

§ 158. **Payment for property acquired for street improvement.**—Upon the making of an agreement for compensation to an owner under this article, or upon the final order or award fixing the amount of such compensation in proceedings therefor, the board shall immediately pay such amounts and the costs, if any, allowed in such proceedings, if it has funds available for that purpose; if not, money may be borrowed and certificates of indebtedness bearing interest issued therefor, or like certificates may be issued for such amounts, and payable, in either case, not more than one year from the date thereof; and the amount of such certificates shall be included in the next annual tax levy.

§ 159. Changing grade of street or bridge.— If a village has exclusive control and jurisdiction of a street or bridge therein, it may change the grade thereof. If such change of grade shall injuriously affect any building or land adjacent thereto, or the use thereof, the change of grade to the extent of the damage resulting therefrom, shall be deemed the taking of such adjacent property for a public use. A person claiming damages from such change of grade must present to the board of trustees a verified claim therefor, within sixty days after such change of grade is effected. The board may agree with such owner upon the amount of damages to be allowed to him. If no agreement be made, within thirty days after the presentation of the claim, the person presenting it may apply to the supreme court for the appointment of three commissioners to determine the compensation to which he is entitled. Notice of the application must be served upon the board of trustees at least ten days before the hearing thereof. All proceedings subsequent to the appointment of the commissioners shall be taken in accordance with the provisions of the condemnation law, so far as applicable, except that the commissioners in fixing their award may make an allowance for benefits derived by the claimant from such improvement. The amount agreed upon for such damages or the award therefor, together with the costs, if any, allowed to the claimant, shall be a charge against such village. The board may borrow money for the payment thereof, or may issue certificates of indebtedness therefor, in the same manner as in case of damages for laying out a street.

§ 160. Streets on boundary lines —Whenever a street is on a line between two villages, or between a village and a city or town, the highway or street commissioners of such adjoining municipalities shall, on or before the first day of May in each year, meet at a time and place to be determined by them, and divide such street. The officers present at such meeting shall allot a part of the street to each municipality in such manner that the labor and expense of keeping such street in repair may be equal as nearly as practicable.

The officers making such division shall, within ten days thereafter, file in the office of the clerk of each municipality a certificate showing the part of such street allotted to each.

§ 161. **Crosswalks and sidewalks.**—The board of trustees may construct and repair crosswalks upon the streets within the village. It may also construct and repair sidewalks upon such a street wholly at the expense of the village, or of the owners or occupants of the adjoining land, or partly at the expense of each. Upon the adoption of a proposition therefor in a village of the third or fourth class, all sidewalks shall thereafter be constructed and repaired wholly at the expense of the village. If a sidewalk is so required to be constructed or repaired wholly at the expense of the owners or occupants of the adjoining lands, a notice specifying the place and manner, and the time, not less than ten days, in case of a new walk, or not less than twenty-four hours in case of repairs, within which the sidewalk is required to be constructed or repaired, shall be served upon such owners or occupants. If an owner or occupant shall not construct or repair the sidewalk as required by the notice, the board of trustees may cause the same to be so constructed or repaired, and assess the expense thereof upon the adjoining land.

If a sidewalk is to be constructed or repaired at the joint expense of the village and the owner or occupant, the board of trustees may cause the same to be constructed or repaired, and assess upon the adjoining land the proportion of the expense chargeable against the same; or it may direct the owner or occupant to contribute labor or materials therefor.

§ 162. **Credit for flagging sidewalk.** — Whenever the owner or occupant of lands adjoining a street shall, with the consent of the board of trustees, construct a sidewalk of stone, cement, brick or other similar material along the line of such land, of the width of four feet or more, and of the value of at least four dollars per lineal rod. the board of trustees shall credit such owner or occupant on account of his assessment for street taxes in such village, three-fourths of the actual and necessary expense of constructing such sidewalk; or, instead of such credit, may pay to such owner or occupant from the street fund of the current year, one-half of the cost of such sidewalk. If credit is allowed, such owner or occupant shall be exempt from taxation on account of streets in such village until the amount of the exemption equals the credit so allowed.

§ 163. Snow and ice on sidewalks.— The board of trustees may require the owners or occupants of land fronting on sidewalks to keep them clear of snow and ice, and upon default, may cause such sidewalks to be cleared, and assess the expense thereof upon such adjoining land, or may cause the sidewalks on any street or portion thereof to be kept clear of snow and ice, and assess the expense upon the adjoining land.

§ 164. Cleaning streets.—The board of trustees may require the owners of land fronting upon the streets to keep the portion of the street between the land and the center of the street cleared of rubbish or other accumulations thereon, injurious to the use or appearance thereof, and to cause all grass and weeds growing therein to be cut and removed once in each month from May to October, inclusive. If the owner of such adjoining land shall fail to comply with such requirement the board of trustees may cause such work to be done, and assess the expense thereof upon such adjoining land.

§ 165. Sprinkling streets.—The board of trustees may cause a street or a part thereof to be sprinkled, and may assess the expense thereof, in whole or in part, upon the owners or occupants of the adjoining land.

§ 166. Pavements.—The board of trustees may cause a street in the village to be paved, wholly at the expense of the village, or of the owners of the adjoining land, or partly at the expense of each; but such street shall not be paved wholly at the expense of the owners of the adjoining land, unless a petition be presented to the board of trustees signed by the owners of at least two-thirds of the frontage on the street, or portion thereof, proposed to be paved, and a hearing given thereon to all persons interested on a notice of at least ten days. If a pavement is so required to be constructed or repaired wholly at the expense of the owners of the adjoining lands, a notice specifying the place and manner, and the time, not less than thirty days, within which the pavement is required to be constructed or repaired, shall be served upon the owners. If an owner shall not construct or repair the pavement as required by the notice, the board of trustees may cause the same to be so constructed or repaired, and assess the expense thereof upon the adjoining land.

If a pavement is to be constructed or repaired at the joint expense of the village and the owner of the adjoining land, the board of trustees may cause the same to be constructed or repaired, and assess upon the adjoining land the proportion of the expense chargeable against the same; or it may direct the owner to contribute labor or materials therefor.

The total amount expended for street paving in any fiscal year from the moneys raised during such year for street purposes, otherwise than in pursuance of a village election, shall not be more than one-half thereof.   No land owner shall be required to pave or bear the expense of paving any portion of the street not in front of such land, nor beyond the center of the street.   All pavements laid by the owners of adjoining land shall be laid under the supervision and in accordance with the directions of the board of trustees.

§ 167. **Trimming trees.**—The board of trustees may require the owners of land to trim the trees in front thereof, and upon default, may cause such trees to be trimmed, and assess the expense thereof upon the adjoining land.

§ 168. **Local assessments under this article.**— Whenever expenditures are made by the board of trustees for constructing or repairing sidewalks or pavements, trimming trees, sprinkling streets or keeping the sidewalks or streets cleared of weeds, ice, snow or other accumulations thereon, which under this article are assessable upon the land affected or improved thereby, the board shall serve a notice of at least ten days upon the owner or occupant of such property, stating that such expenditure has been made, its purpose and amount, and that at a specified time and place it will meet to make an assessment of the expenditure upon such land.   The board shall meet at the time and place specified.   It shall hear and determine all objections that may be made to such assessment, including the amount thereof, and shall assess upon the land the amount which it may deem just and reasonable, not exceeding, in case of default, the amount stated in the notice.

If the amount so assessed be not paid within twenty days after such assessment, an action to recover the amount may be maintained by the village against the owner or occupant liable therefor, or a special warrant may be issued by the board of trustees for the collection of such assessment, or the amount thereof may be included in the next annual tax levy.

§ 169. **Acquisition of lands for parks and squares.**—The board of trustees may, on behalf of the village, accept by grant or devise a gift of land for a public park or square within the village, or wholly within one mile of the boundaries thereof, or may submit to a village election a proposition to purchase land so located for such purpose at an expense, specified in the proposition, not exceeding one per centum of the value of the taxable property of the village, as appears by the last preceding assessment-roll. Upon the acquisition of land for the purposes of this section, either by gift or purchase, the board may establish and maintain a public park or square thereon.

ARTICLE VI.

The Police Department.

Section 180. Jurisdiction of violations of ordinances.
181. Disposition of penalties; fees of justices.
182. Criminal jurisdiction of police justice.
183. Record of police justice.
184. Compensation of police justice.
185. Accounts, reports and payments of fees and fines by salaried police justice.
186. Civil jurisdiction of police justice.
187. Acting police justice.
188. Village policemen.
189. Powers and duties of policemen.
190. Fees, salaries and expenses of policemen.

Section 180. **Jurisdiction of violations of ordinances.**— Jurisdiction to hear, try and determine charges of violations of village ordinances is hereby conferred upon magistrates as follows:

1. A police justice, or in case of his absence or inability to act, the acting police justice has exclusive jurisdiction, in the first instance.

2. In case of the absence or inability to act of both the police justice and the acting police justice, or if the office of police justice does not exist in the village, a justice of the peace of a town including any part of the village has jurisdiction exclusive of any other justice of the peace.

3. In cases not provided for in the foregoing subdivisions, any justice of the peace has jurisdiction.

§ 181. **Disposition of penalties; fees of justices.**—Every penalty imposed by a justice of the peace for the violation of a village ordinance shall be paid to the village treasurer. In such cases the fees of the justice are a village charge.

§ 182. **Criminal jurisdiction of village police justice.**—The police justice of a village may hold a court of special sessions therein and shall have in the first instance exclusive jurisdiction to hear, try and determine charges of a misdemeanor committed within such village and triable by a court of special sessions. subject to the right of removal, as provided by the code of criminal procedure, to a court having authority to inquire by the intervention of a grand jury into offenses committed' within the county.   Such police justice shall have exclusive jurisdiction to take the examination of a person charged with the commission in such village of a crime not triable by a court of special sessions; and also to hear, try and determine charges against a person of being a vagrant or disorderly person within such village, or of having committed disorderly conduct therein; and to take such proceedings in either of such cases as may be taken by a justice of the peace, with all the powers and subject to all the duties and liabilities of a justice of the peace in respect thereto.   Such police justice shall have all the power and authority, and be subject to all the duties and liabilities, of a justice of the peace in issuing warrants for the arrest of a person charged with the commission of a crime or disorderly conduct, in a county including any portion of such village, but if the offense is charged to have been committed outside of the village, the person arrested by such process shall be taken before another magistrate of the town in which such offense is charged to have been committed, and the papers upon which such process was issued shall be delivered to him, who shall proceed thereon as though such warrant had been issued by him upon such papers.   A person arrested upon a criminal warrant issued by a justice of the peace upon a charge of committing a crime or an offense of a criminal nature within a village, shall be taken before the police justice of such village, and the papers upon which the process was issued delivered to him, who shall proceed thereon as though such warrant had been issued by him upon such papers.   The term "proceeding" as used in this article also includes a special proceeding of a criminal nature.

§ 183. **Records of police justice.**—The board of trustees shall provide the police justice with suitable books in which he shall keep a record of all actions or proceedings for violations of village ordinances and of criminal actions and proceedings, had or tried before him, or in a court of special sessions, held by him, which record in each case shall contain the names of the complainant and defendant, a statement of the nature of the offense charged and, under the proper dates, the proceedings therein, the minutes of all courts of special sessions held by him, and an accurate account of all fines, penalties, fees, expenses and costs imposed, received or ordered paid by him, in all such actions and proceedings.

§ 184. **Compensation of village police justice.**—If the police justice of a village shall not be paid a salary, he shall be entitled to receive for his services the same fees as a justice of the peace for like services, to be paid in like manner, except that his fees in proceedings on account of violations of the village ordinances, shall be paid by the village.

The board of trustees may determine that the police justice shall be paid a salary instead of fees, and may fix the amount thereof, and such salary shall not be increased or diminished during his term of office. Such salary shall be paid in equal monthly installments by the treasurer, except that a ratable proportion shall be deducted from his salary, because of any failure to perform his duties. The amount of such deduction shall be determined by the board of trustees and paid by the treasurer to the acting police justice or other justice who shall have acted during such period. Such police justice and acting police justice shall each report to the board of trustees at the first regular meeting thereof in each month, the time, if any, during the next preceding calendar month that the police justice of such village failed to perform the duties of his office and the time during which the acting police justice or other justice performed such duties.

§ 185. **Accounts, reports and payments of fees and fines by salaried police justice.**—If the police justice of the village is paid by salary, he shall not receive for his own benefit any fees, costs or expenses in any action or proceeding, but shall demand and receive the same fees, costs and expenses therein, as are provided by law to be paid to a justice of the peace of a town, and shall keep an account thereof and of fines and penalties paid to him. All such costs, fees and expenses and all penalties or other money so paid to him in a proceeding for or on account of a violation of an ordinance of the village during any calendar month shall be paid to the village treasurer before the first regular meeting of the board of trustees in the next succeeding month. All other fees, costs, expenses, fines or penalties so collected shall be paid over and accounted for in the same manner as moneys collected by a justice of the peace in like cases. He shall, prior to such meeting in each month, file with the village clerk a complete, detailed and verified statement of all moneys payable to the village treasurer, which were received by him during the last preceding month, with the written receipt of the treasurer therefor attached thereto. No order for the salary of such police justice shall be drawn until such monthly statement and receipt are filed with the clerk. He shall keep an account of all fees in criminal actions and proceedings, which would be payable to him if he were not paid a salary, and which are a town or county charge, and shall present claims for such fees against the town or county to which chargeable. All orders or warrants for such claims shall be made payable to the treasurer of the village, who shall collect the amount thereof.

§ 186. **Civil jurisdiction of police justice.**— The police justice shall have the same jurisdiction as a justice of the peace of a town in civil actions to recover a penalty or forfeiture, payable to the village. The town clerk of each town in which a village or any part thereof is situated, shall furnish to such police justice, jury lists in the same manner as to the justices of the peace of his town.

§ 187. **Acting police justice**— The board of trustees of a village in which the office of police justice is established shall designate a justice of the peace residing in the village, if any, and otherwise, a justice of the peace residing in the town in which the village or a part thereof is situated, as acting police justice of the village. During the absence or inability of the police justice to perform the duties of his office, the acting police justice has all the powers and is subject to all the liabilities of a police justice within the village.

§ 188. **Village policemen.**— The president, each trustee and the street commissioner are ex officio members of the police department, and have all the powers conferred upon policemen by this article. The board of trustees, or if a municipal board continued by section sixty-nine now acts as police commissioners, such board may appoint and fix the terms, not extending beyond the current official year, of one or more village policemen, one of whom may be designated as chief of police.

§ 189. **Powers and duties of policemen.**— The policemen so appointed shall have all the powers and be subject to the duties and liabilities of constables of towns in serving process in any civil action or proceeding to which the village is a party, and in serving warrants, subpoenas or other process in criminal actions or proceedings. for or on account of crimes committed within the village, and in making arrests therefor, or for violations of village ordinances. Except in case of the absence or other disability of a village policeman, such powers shall be exclusive of any constable of a town, in serving all warrants, subpoenas or other process issued by the police justice, acting police justice, or a justice of the peace, for or on account of an offense or a violation of an ordinance committed within the village.

§ 190. **Fees, salaries and expenses of policemen.**— The board of trustees may determine that each village policeman shall be paid a salary instead of fees and may fix the amount thereof. A village policeman shall receive the same fees as constables of towns for similar services, to be paid in like manner, except that his fees for services in proceedings on account of a violation of a village ordinance shall be paid by the village. If a village policeman receives a salary all fees collected or received by him belong to the village and he must account therefor and credit the same upon his salary. A village policeman shall not receive any present or reward for his services other than his fees or salary, except by the consent of the board of trustees. Every village policeman who receives a salary from the village for his services shall keep a book in which shall be entered all services performed by him, which are a town or county charge, and shall present claims therefor against the town or county to which chargeable. All orders or warrants for such claims shall be made payable to the village treasurer, who shall collect the amount thereof.

ARTICLE VII.

The Fire Department.

Section 200. General powers of the board of fire commissioners.
    201. Ordinances.
    202. Organization of companies.
    203. Incorporation of fire department.
    204. Election of company officers and delegates.
    205. Chief engineer and assistant engineers.
    206. Council of fire department.
    207. Meetings of fire department.
    208. Duties of chief engineer and assistants.
    209. General exemptions of firemen.
    210. Annual report of the fire commissioners.

Section 200. **General powers of the board of fire commissioners.** — The board of fire commissioners of a village,

1. Has the care, custody and control of all property belonging to the fire department.

2. May purchase fire engines, hose, hose carts, horses, tools, implements and apparatus suitable and necessary to prevent and extinguish fires within the village, and keep the same in good condition and repair.

3. May erect and maintain suitable and necessary buildings for the fire department.

4. May construct and maintain reservoirs and cisterns and supply them with water for use at fires.

5. May adopt rules for the admission, suspension, removal and discipline of the members, officers and employes of the fire department, may prescribe their powers and duties, and fix their compensation.

6. Has the control and supervision of the members, officers and employes of the department, may direct their conduct at fires, and prescribe methods for extinguishing fires.

7. May appoint persons other than members or officers of the department to take charge of the property of the department, and may fix their compensation.

8. May, in villages of the first or second class, appoint not more than twenty duty or " call men," and fix their duties and compensation.

9. May inquire into the cause and origin of fires occurring in the village, and may take testimony in relation thereto.

§ 201. Ordinances.—The board of fire commissioners may adopt ordinances for the following purposes:

1. To protect and preserve the property and apparatus of the department.

2. To prevent danger from fires and to protect property exposed to destruction or injury by fire.

3. To provide for pulling down, blowing up and the removal of buildings and property to arrest the progress of fires or extinguish the same.

The board may enforce observance of such ordinances by the imposition of penalties.

§ 202. Organization of companies.—The board of fire commissioners may organize and maintain fire, hose, protective, and hook and ladder companies, whenever in its judgment the public interests require, by appointing a sufficient number of suitable persons as members thereof, respectively, not exceeding sixty to each fire company, forty-five to each hook and ladder company, and thirty to each hose company or protective company. Vacancies shall be filled by the board of fire commissioners upon nomination by the company. No new appointment shall be made to a company, unless the number of members thereof shall be less than the number hereby limited. The board of fire commissioners may, by resolution, consent to the incorporation of any of the companies so organized by them, or may consent to the incorporation or the organization without incorporation of as many companies voluntarily organized in said village as may be deemed necessary.

§ 203. Incorporation of fire department.—The members of all the fire, hose, protective and hook and ladder companies of a village, organized and maintained in pursuance of law, constitute a corporation by the name of the "fire department of ——." The term, fire department of a village, as used in this chapter, refers to such a corporation.

§ 204. Election of company officers and delegates.—Each of the several companies whose members constitute the fire department of the village shall hold an annual meeting on the first Tuesday in April in each year. At such meeting the members of each company shall elect by ballot from their number a foreman and an assistant foreman, who must be approved by the board of fire commissioners, two wardens, and three delegates to the general convention of the fire department. The terms of office of the foreman, assistant foreman and wardens shall be one year, respectively, and any vacancies occurring in any of such offices shall be filled by election in like manner.

§ 205. Chief engineer and assistant engineers.—The chief engineer and the first and second assistant engineers of the fire department shall each be a member thereof and an elector of the village. The delegates elected to the general convention of the fire department shall meet at the council room thereof on the Thursday following the first Tuesday in April and nominate a person for each of such offices.

The person acting as secretary of such convention shall forthwith file in the office of the village clerk a certificate of such nominations. The board of fire commissioners at its next meeting shall consider the nominations and appoint such persons as it may approve to the offices for which they were respectively nominated. If a nomination is not approved the board shall appoint a qualified person to such office.

§ 206. Council of fire department.—In a village in which separate fire commissioners are not appointed, the chief engineer, the as-

sistant engineers and the wardens of the several companies constitute the council of the fire department. The council shall meet
on the third Tuesday in April in each year and choose from its own
number a secretary, a treasurer and a collector of the fire department, who shall hold their respective offices for one year unless
sooner removed by the council. A vacancy in the office of secretary, treasurer or collector shall be filled by the council at its next
meeting for the balance of the unexpired term. Two-thirds of the
members of such council constitute a quorum, and may make and
prescribe by-laws for the proper management of the affairs, and the
disposition of the funds of the fire department, may call meetings
of the members, and designate one or more days in each year for
public exercise, inspection and review.

§ 207. **Meetings of fire department.**—The members of the several
companies constituting the fire department shall hold a general
meeting at the council room, or at such other place as the council
may direct, on the first Friday following the first Tuesday in April
of each year, at seven o'clock in the afternoon, to hear the annual
report of the secretary and treasurer, and to transact any other
proper business of the fire department. If a meeting or election of
the fire department shall not be held on the day fixed by this article therefor the corporation shall not on that account be dissolved,
but the meeting or election may be held on a subsequent day in accordance with its by-laws.

§ 208. **Duties of chief engineer and assistants.**—The chief engineer shall be president of the council and of the meetings of the
fire department. He shall, under the direction of a separate board
of fire commissioners, if any, have exclusive control of the members
at all fires, inspections and reviews, the supervision of the engines,
hose and other apparatus owned by the village for the prevention
or extinguishment of fires, of all property owned by the fire department, and of all officers and employes thereof elected or employed by the council or by a separate board of fire commissioners,
if any. He shall, whenever required by the board of fire commissioners, report to the board the condition of the property of the department and such other information respecting the department
as may be required. He shall hold the members, officers and
employes of the department strictly to account for neglect
of duty, and may, in a village in which separate fire commissioners are not appointed, suspend or discharge them at any
time, subject to the approval of two-thirds of the members of the

council at the next meeting. He shall, upon application, and if authorized by the council, or a separate board of fire commissioners, if any, issue through the secretary of the fire department a certificate of the time of service of a member of the fire department, and shall give to each officer of the department immediately after his election a certificate thereof countersigned by the secretary. In case of the inability or absence of the chief engineer, the first assistant engineer, and in case of the absence or inability of both the chief engineer and first assistant, the second assistant engineer, shall perform the duties and have all the powers of the chief engineer.

§ 209. **General exemptions of firemen.**— A full term of service in a fire department is five successive years. A person who has served in a fire department of a village, after becoming eighteen years of age, shall be entitled to a certificate of such service, signed by the president, and under the corporate seal, or by the chief engineer and the secretary of the fire department, under the seal of the department, or by a majority of the members of the board of fire commissioners in a village in which separate fire commissioners are appointed. Such certificate shall be presumptive evidence of the facts stated therein.

A member of a fire department who removes from the village shall be allowed, as part of a full term, the time he has served continuously as fireman therein, if, within three months thereafter, he becomes a member of the fire department of another village or city; and, upon completing a full term, shall be entitled to all the privileges and exemptions thereby secured to firemen.

§ 210. **Annual report of the fire commissioners.**— Between the first and fourth day of March in each year, the board of fire commissioners shall file with the village clerk a report containing a statement of the following facts:

1. The amount of money on hand at the beginning of the preceding fiscal year, and the receipts from all sources during such year.

2. An itemized statement of the amount paid out during such year, and the balance on hand.

3. The outstanding indebtedness of the department, either bonded or otherwise, separately stated.

4. A statement of the principal or interest which will become due during the current fiscal year on bonds or certificates of indebtedness.

5. The improvements made during such preceding year, and the general condition of the property of the fire department.

6. Such other facts as the board deems important for the interest of the village, together with such recommendations concerning the department as may be deemed proper.

ARTICLE VIII.

Water.

§ 220. **Contracts for water supply.**—The board of water commissioners may contract, in the name of the village, with an individual or corporation for supplying water to the village for extinguishing fires or for other public purposes; but such contract shall not be made for a longer period than five years, nor at an expense for each fiscal year exceeding two and a half mills on every dollar of the taxable property of the village as appears on the last preceding village assessment-roll, unless authorized at a village election. The amount of such contract shall be paid in annual instalments, commencing with the date of the contract.

§ 221. **Election for water works.**— A proposition may be submitted at a village election for the establishment of a system of water works for supplying the village and its inhabitants with water, or for the acquisition of an existing private system, at an expense in either case not exceeding the sum stated in the proposition.

§ 222. **Acquisition of existing system.** — If a proposition be adopted for the acquisition of an existing system of water works, the board of water commissioners may purchase the same at a price not exceeding the sum specified therein. If the board can not agree with the owners of the system for its purchase, proceedings may be taken to acquire the same by condemnation. If the value thereof fixed by the commissioners appointed in the condemnation proceedings be greater than the sum specified in the proposition, such proceedings must be discontinued, unless the payment of the additional amount be authorized at a village election If the proceedings be so discontinued the costs and disbursements of the defendants therein are a charge against the village.

§ 223. **Establishment of water works.** — If a proposition to establish a system of water works be adopted, the board of water commissioners shall proceed to construct such system accordingly. It shall prepare a map and plans showing the sources of water supply and a description of the lands, streams, water or water rights to be acquired therefor, and the mode of constructing the proposed water works and the location thereof, including reservoirs, mains, distributing pipes and hydrants. The water commissioners, their agents, servants and employes, may enter upon any lands for the purpose of preparing such map and plans. The map and plans shall be filed with the village clerk, and a certified copy of such map shall also be filed in the county clerk's office of each county in which any of the lands are situated. The board of water commissioners may acquire, in the name of the village, by purchase, if it can agree with the owners, or otherwise by condemnation, any land, streams, water or water rights necessary for such system. The board may amend the map and plans at any time and such amended map shall be filed in the office of the village clerk, and of the county clerk, in like manner as the original. The board may construct such water system by contract or otherwise, and may appoint and at pleasure remove a superintendent to take charge of the system, and may fix his compensation.

§ 224. **Supervision and extension of system.** — A system of water works acquired or established under this article shall be under the control and supervision of the board of water commissioners. The board shall keep it in repair and may, from time to time, extend the mains or distributing pipes within the village, if the expense thereof in any year in a village of the fourth class, shall not exceed five hundred dollars, in a village of the third class, one thousand dollars, in a village of the second class, fifteen hundred dollars, and in a village of the first class, two thousand dollars. If the estimated expense will exceed the above amount, such extension can only be made when authorized by a proposition adopted at an election.

§ 225. **Acquisition of additional water rights.**— A proposition may be submitted at a village election to authorize the board of water commissioners to acquire additional water or water rights, or to construct additional reservoirs, at an expense not exceeding the sum therein stated. If adopted, such improvements shall be made accordingly. For that purpose, the board has the same power and is subject to the same duties and liabilities as in the construction of the original system of water works.

§ 226. **Water pipes in highways outside of village.**—The board of water commissioners of a village may cause water pipes to be laid, relaid or repaired under any public highway in a county in which any part of such village is situated, or in an adjoining county, for the purpose of introducing water into and through the village; and shall cause the surface of such highway to be restored to its usual condition.

§ 227. **Connections with mains.**— Supply pipes connecting with mains and used by private owners or occupants shall be laid and kept in repair at their expense Such pipes can only be connected with the mains by the permission and under the direction of the board of water commissioners. A member of the board or its authorized agent may at any time enter a building or upon premises where water is used from supply pipes, and make necessary examinations.

§ 228. **Ordinances.**—The board of water commissioners may adopt ordinances, not inconsistent with law, for enforcing the collection of water rents and relating to the use of the water, and may enforce observance thereof, by cutting off the supply of water, or by the imposition of penalties.

§ 229. **Establishment of water rents.**— The board of water commissioners shall establish a scale of rents for the use of water, to be called " water rents," and to be paid at such times as the board may prescribe. Such rents shall be a lien on the real property upon which the water is used.

§ 230. **Assessment for fire protection.**— A building and the lot upon which it stands, in or on which water from the water works is not used, situated within five hundred feet of a hydrant, may be assessed by the board of water commissioners for fire protection. Notice of the proposed assessment, and that the board will meet at a time and place specified therein to hear objections thereto, must be served upon the owner or occupant of the building at least ten days before such meeting. The board shall meet at the time and place specified in the notice, and after hearing objections, shall complete such assessment. Upon the completion of the assessment, the board shall make a certificate thereof and deliver the same to the village treasurer. The treasurer may receive such assessments for thirty days without fee; after that time an action may be brought to recover the assessment, or a special warrant may be issued therefor, or the amount may be included in the next annual tax levy.

§ 231. Reservoirs.—In the construction of a storage reservoir connected with the system of water works, all vegetable or other matter subject to decay shall be removed from the banks thereof between its highest and lowest possible flow line, or such space be covered by gravel or stone to prevent such decay.

§ 232. Supplying water outside of corporate limits.—The board of water commissioners may sell to a corporation or individual outside the village the right to make connections with the mains for the purpose of drawing water therefrom, and fix the prices and conditions therefor.

If the mains are or shall be laid in or through another municipal corporation not having a public system of water works, the board of water commissioners may itself lay additional pipes for the purpose of distributing water from such mains, and shall have the same rights in the streets or highways of such other municipal corporation as if the principal system were established therein. The board shall not sell nor permit the use of water under this section if thereby the supply for the village or its inhabitants will be insufficient.

§ 233. Outside extension of mains.— A proposition to extend water mains outside the village may be submitted at an election. Such proposition shall contain a general description of the proposed extension and the estimated expense thereof. If the proposition be adopted, the board of water commissioners shall make the extension accordingly. For that purpose the board shall have the same powers and be subject to the same duties and liabilities as in the construction of the original system of water works.

§ 234. Contracts with other municipalities.— If the mains are or shall be laid into or through a town, another village or a fire district in an unincorporated village, the board of water commissioners may contract with the town board, the board of trustees, or the fire commissioners thereof, respectively, to furnish water for the extinguishment of fires or for sanitary purposes.   Such contract shall not be for a longer period than ten years, nor shall the amount agreed to be paid in any one year exceed two and a half mills for every dollar of the taxable property in such town, village or fire district.   The amount payable each year by such contract shall be raised as a part of the expenses of such town, village or fire district, and paid to the treasurer of the village owning such system of water works.

§ 235. Annual report of water commissioners.— Between the first and fourth day of March in each year the board of water commissioners shall file with the village clerk a report containing a statement of the following facts:

1. The amount of money on hand at the beginning of the preceding fiscal year, and the receipts from all sources during such year.

2. An itemized statement of the amount paid out during such year, and the balance on hand.

3. The outstanding indebtedness of the department, either bonded or otherwise, separately stated.

4. The estimated deficiency in the amount necessary to pay principal or interest or the expenses of the department during the next fiscal year, after applying thereto the probable amount of water rents or other income to be received, and any amount available from the sinking fund.

5. The improvements and extensions made during such preceding year and the general condition of the water works.

6. Such other facts as the board deems important for the information of the village, together with such recommendations concerning the department as may be deemed proper.

ARTICLE IX.

Light.

Section 240. **Contracts for lighting.**—The board of light commissioners may contract, in the name of the village, with an individual or corporation, for lighting the streets, public grounds and public buildings of the village by gas, electricity or other substance; but such contract shall not be made for a longer period than five years, nor at an expense for each fiscal year exceeding two and a half mills on every dollar of taxable property of the village as appears on the last preceding village assessment-roll, unless authorized at a village election. The amount of such contract shall be paid in annual instalments, commencing with the date of the contract.

§ 241. **Election for lighting system.**—A proposition may be submitted at a village election for the establishment of a system for supplying the village and its inhabitants with light by any approved method, or for the acquisition of an existing private system, at an expense in either case not exceeding the sum stated in the proposition.

§ 242. **Acquisition of existing private system.**—If a proposition be adopted for the acquisition of an existing private lighting system, the board of light commissioners may purchase the same at a price not exceeding the sum specified therein. If the board can not agree with the owners of the system for its purchase, proceedings may be taken to acquire the same by condemnation. If the value thereof fixed by the commissioners appointed in the condemnation proceedings be greater than the sum specified in the proposition, such proceedings must be discontinued, unless the payment of the additional amount be authorized at a village election. If the proceedings be so discontinued, the costs and disbursements of the defendants therein are a charge against the village.

§ 243. **Establishment of lighting system.**—If a proposition to establish a lighting system be adopted, the board of light commissioners shall proceed to construct such system accordingly. It shall prepare a map and plans of such system, indicating the streets and localities in the village to be supplied with light thereby, and shall file the same in the office of the village clerk. The board of light commissioners may acquire in the name of the village, by purchase, if it can agree with the owners, or otherwise by condemnation, any land necessary for such system. The board may amend the map and plans at any time and such amended map shall be filed in the office of the village clerk in like manner as the original. The board may construct such lighting system by contract or otherwise.

§ 244. **Supervision and extension of system.**—The lighting system acquired or established under this article shall be under the control and supervision of the board of light commissioners. The board shall keep it in repair and may, from time to time, if it has sufficient funds, extend such system, if the expense thereof in any year will not exceed five hundred dollars. If the estimated expense will exceed five hundred dollars, such extension can only be made when authorized by a proposition adopted at an election.

§ 245. **Ordinances.**—The board of light commissioners may adopt ordinances, not inconsistent with law, for enforcing the collection of light rents and relating to the use of light, and may enforce observance thereto, by cutting off the supply of light or by the imposition of penalties.

§ 246. **Establishment of light rents.**—The board of light commissioners shall establish a scale of rents for the use of light, to be called " light rents," and to be paid at such times as the board may prescribe.

§ 247. **Annual report of light commissioners.**—Between the first and fourth day of March in each year, the board of light commissioners shall file with the village clerk a report containing a statement of the following facts:

1. The amount of money on hand at the beginning of the preceding fiscal year, and the receipts from all sources during such year.

2. An itemized statement of the amount paid out during such year, and the balance on hand.

3. The outstanding indebtedness of the department, either bonded or otherwise, separately stated.

4. The estimated deficiency in the amount necessary to pay the principal or interest or the expenses of the department during the next fiscal year, after applying thereto the probable amount of light rents to be received, and any amount available from the sinking fund.

5. The improvements and extensions made during such preceding year, and the general condition of the lighting system.

6. Such other facts as the board deems important for the information of the village, together with such recommendations concerning the department as may be deemed proper.

ARTICLE X.
Sewers.

Section 260. **Establishment of sewer system.**—The board of sewer commissioners of a village may establish and maintain a sewer system therein. Before taking any proceedings for the construction of a sewer, the board, at the expense of the village, shall cause a map and plan of a permanent sewer system for such village to be made, with specifications of dimensions, connections and outlets or sewage disposal works. It may also include any existing sewer in the village. Such map and plan shall be submitted to the state board of health for its approval, and if approved shall be filed in its office. A copy thereof shall also be filed in the office of the village clerk. The map and plan may be amended, with the approval of the state board of health, and if amended shall be filed in the same office as the original.

§ 261. **Construction of a sewer at expense of village.**—Upon the adoption of a proposition therefor the whole or any part of the sewer system may be constructed at the expense of the village. The proposition shall describe the portion of the system proposed to be so constructed, and shall also contain a statement of the estimated maximum and minimum cost thereof.

§ 262. **Reimbursement for sewers constructed at private expense.**—If the whole of the sewer system be constructed at the expense of the village and a sewer theretofore constructed wholly or partly at private expense be included in the map or plan of the system, the owners of the property upon which such expense was assessed shall be entitled to reimbursement therefor. Claims for such reimbursement may be presented to and audited by the board of sewer commissioners, and the amounts allowed shall be paid in the same manner as other expenditures for the sewer system.

§ 263. **Construction of sewer at joint expense of village and of property benefited.**—Upon the adoption of a proposition therefor, the whole or any part of the sewer system may be constructed at the joint expense of the village and of the property benefited. The proposition shall describe the portion of the system proposed to be so constructed, shall contain a statement of the estimated maximum and minimum cost thereof, and also of the proportion of the expense to be assessed upon the village at large, and the aggregate proportion to be assessed upon the property benefited. If the proposition be adopted such aggregate proportion shall be equitably adjusted with reference to the benefits to be derived therefrom.

§ 264. **Construction of sewers wholly at expense of property benefited.**—The owners of two-thirds of the entire frontage of the portion of a street or streets in which a sewer is proposed to be constructed may present to the board of sewer commissioners a petition for the construction of such a sewer. The board shall cause a notice of at least ten days to be given to each person owning land fronting on such portion of such street or streets, of a time and place where it will meet and hear persons interested in the construction of such sewer. After such hearing the board may grant the petition in whole or in part, and shall construct a sewer as ordered, and assess the entire expense thereof upon the property benefited. Where such petition is for the construction of a sewer through different streets, such sewer shall be deemed one sewer, and such streets, one continuous street, for the purposes of this section. A petition under this section may limit the maximum amount of the expense to be incurred in the construction of such sewer.

§ 265. **Acquisition of property by condemnation.**—If the board of sewer commissioners is unable to agree with the owner for the purchase of real property necessary for the sewer system, it may acquire the same by condemnation.

§ 266. **Contracts for construction of system.** — The board of sewer commissioners of a village authorized to construct the whole or any part of a sewer system shall advertise for proposals for the construction thereof, either under an entire contract, or in parts or sections, as the board may determine. Such advertisement shall be published once in each of two successive weeks in each newspaper published in the village. The board may require a bond or a deposit from the person submitting a proposal, the liability of such bond to accrue, or such deposit to be forfeited to the village, in case such person shall refuse to enter into a contract in accordance with his proposal. The board may accept or reject any proposal, may contract with other than the lowest bidder, or may reject all proposals and advertise again. No contract shall be made by which a greater amount shall be agreed to be paid, than the maximum stated in the proposition or in the petition for the construction of such sewer.

§ 267. **Supervising engineer; inspectors.** — The board of sewer commissioners may employ a supervising engineer to superintend and inspect the construction of any sewer or works connected therewith, and also such inspectors as may be necessary, and fix the compensation of such engineer and inspectors. Such compensation shall be treated as a part of the expense of construction.

§ 268. **Apportionment of local assessment.** — If the whole or any part of the expense of constructing a sewer is to be assessed upon the lands benefited, the board of sewer commissioners shall prepare and file in the office of the village clerk, a map and plan of the proposed area of local assessment. Such expense shall thereupon be apportioned upon the lands within such area in proportion as nearly as may be to the benefit which each lot or parcel will derive therefrom, and the ratio of such benefit shall be established. After making such apportionment the board shall serve upon each land owner a notice thereof and of the filing of such map and plan, and that at a specified time and place a hearing will be had to consider and review the same. Such notice must be served at least six days before the hearing. The board shall meet at the time and place specified and hear objections to such apportionment. It may modify and correct the same, or exclude land from the area of local assessment. The board of sewer commissioners, upon the completion of such apportionment, shall file the same in the office of the village clerk. The apportionment shall be deemed final and conclusive, unless an appeal be taken therefrom within fifteen days after the filing thereof.

§ 269. **Appeal from apportionment.**—A person aggrieved by an apportionment may, within fifteen days after the filing thereof, appeal therefrom to the county court of a county in which any part of the village is situated. Such appeal shall be taken by a notice, stating the grounds thereof, addressed to the board of sewer commissioners, and filed with the village clerk.

§ 270. **Hearing of appeal.**—Either party may bring on the appeal upon a notice of not less than ten nor more than twenty days. All appeals from the same apportionment must be consolidated and heard as one appeal. The county court may affirm or reverse the apportionment. If it be reversed upon the ground that it is erroneous, unequal or inequitable, the court shall by the order of reversal appoint three disinterested freeholders of the village as commissioners to make a new apportionment, and no appeal shall be allowed from such order.

§ 271. **Reapportionment.**—A reapportionment shall be made in the following cases:

1. By the commissioners appointed by the county court, where the original apportionment is reversed on the ground that it is erroneous, unequal or inequitable.

2. By the board of sewer commissioners where the original apportionment is reversed upon any other ground. A reapportionment under this subdivision shall be made in like manner as the original.

§ 272. **Procedure by new commissioners.**—The commissioners appointed by the county court shall give notice of the time and place at which they will meet to make such reapportionment, and shall serve notice thereof at least ten days before such meeting upon each owner of land within the area of local assessment as finally fixed by the board of sewer commissioners. They shall meet at the time and place specified and make such reapportionment in the manner herein prescribed for the board of sewer commissioners. They shall file such reapportionment in the office of the village clerk, and it shall be final and conclusive.

§ 273. **Fees of commissioners.**—Each commissioner appointed by the county court is entitled to five dollars for each day necessarily spent in making such reapportionment, besides his actual necessary expenses. Such fees and expenses are a charge against the village, and must be audited by the board of trustees. The amount thereof shall be added to the portion of the expense of constructing such sewer or sewer system which is to be assessed against property specially benefited.

§ 274 **Expense of construction; how raised.**—The expense of constructing a sewer or a sewer system may be raised in an entire amount or in smaller sums from time to time as the board of sewer commissioners may determine. If any portion of such expense is to be borne by the village, bonds or certificates of indebtedness may be issued therefor. If such expense or any part thereof is to be assessed upon property benefited, the board may assess the same, or the instalment to be raised, on the several benefited lots or parcels, in accordance with the apportionment and ratio established under this article. Notice of such assessment shall be given to the owners, who may pay the amounts assessed within ten days after the service of such notice. At the expiration of such time bonds or certificates of indebtedness may be issued for the aggregate amount of such assessment then remaining unpaid.

§ 275. **Tax for unpaid assessments.**—The board of trustees shall include in the annual tax levy the principal or interest accruing during the same fiscal year upon bonds or certificates of indebtedness issued on account of default in the payment of local assessments under this article, and shall levy the same upon the lots or parcels in default.

Such principal shall be apportioned among the lots or parcels in default so that the tax thereon will be the same as if an equal portion of the assessment were then to be paid. Interest on an unpaid assessment shall be added to such tax at the rate payable by the bond or certificate of indebtedness, which must be computed to the time when the principal or an instalment will become due; or if no principal will become due during the fiscal year, then the interest accruing during that year upon the assessment must be levied upon such lot or parcel.

§ 276. **Contracts with other municipalities.**—The board of sewer commissioners may contract for the connection of the sewers thereof with the sewers of another village, or of a town or city; or jointly with such other village or a town or city may construct, maintain, operate or use sewers, outlets or disposal works. But such contract shall not be made unless a proposition therefor be adopted, stating the maximum expense.

§ 277. **Annual report of sewer commissioners.**—Between the first and fourth day of March in each year, the board of sewer commissioners shall file with the village clerk a report containing a statement of the following facts:

1. The amount of money on hand at the beginning of the preceding fiscal year, and the receipts from all sources during such year.

2. An itemized statement of the amount paid out during such year, and the balance on hand.

3. The outstanding indebtedness of the department, either bonded or otherwise, separately stated.

4. A statement of the principal or interest which will become due during the current fiscal year on bonds or certificates of indebtedness.

5. The improvements and extensions made during such preceding year, and the general condition of the sewer system.

6. Such other facts as the board deems important for the information of the village, together with such recommendations concerning the department as may be deemed proper.

ARTICLE XI.

Cemeteries.

Section 290. The acquisition of lands for cemeteries.
291. Division into lots; conveyances of lots.
292. Ordinances.
293. Interment of strangers.
294. Record of interments.
295. Property in trust.
296. Annual report of cemetery commissioners.

Section 290. The acquisition of lands for cemeteries.—The board of cemetery commissioners of a village may, in behalf of the village, accept by gift, grant or devise thereto, land for a village cemetery within the village, or wholly within three miles of the boundaries thereof; or may require the board of trustees to submit to a village election, a proposition to purchase for such purpose any lands so located, specifying the maximum amount to be paid therefor and the mode of raising such amount. If the proposition be adopted, the board of cemetery commissioners may purchase such lands accordingly, or, if unable to agree with the owners for the purchase thereof, may acquire the title thereto by condemnation; but if the commissioners appointed in the condemnation proceedings shall fix the value of the land at a larger amount than authorized to be paid therefor by such election, the condemnation proceedings shall be abandoned and the costs of the defendant shall be paid by the village unless payment of such larger amount shall be authorized at a village election.

All lands acquired for a village cemetery shall be a part of the territory of the village.

§ 291. Division into lots; conveyances of lots.— The board of cemetery commissioners has the supervision and control of all village cemeteries. It shall cause the same to be divided into lots, and provide for the conveyance thereof to individuals for the sole purpose of interments, and upon the payment of the purchase-price of any lot, shall, in the name of the village, execute, acknowledge and deliver a conveyance to the purchaser thereof. The clerk of the village shall keep a record of the sale of each lot, its number, the date of sale and the name of the purchaser; and shall record each conveyance thereof. No sale, transfer or assignment of such lot or any interest therein subsequent to the sale by the village shall be valid, unless by an instrument in writing signed and duly acknowledged and recorded in the office of the village clerk. The clerk shall be entitled to receive ten cents per folio for the recording of each conveyance.

§ 292. Ordinances.—The board of cemetery commissioners may adopt reasonable ordinances for:

1. The care, management and protection of the cemetery grounds.

2. The use, care and protection of lots therein.

3. The conduct of persons within the cemetery grounds, and the exclusion of improper persons therefrom.

4. Regulating the dividing marks between the various lots and parts of lots, and their size, shape and location.

5. Preventing improper monuments, effigies and structures within the same.

6. Regulating the introduction and growth of plants, trees and shrubs within such grounds.

7. The prevention of the burial in any lot or part of any lot of any person not entitled to burial therein.

The board of cemetery commissioners may fix the penalties, not to exceed twenty dollars, for violations of such ordinances. Such ordinances, when adopted, shall be printed and conspicuously posted in at least five places upon the cemetery grounds.

§ 293. Interment of strangers.—The board of cemetery commissioners shall reserve a portion of the ground in any such cemetery for the interment of strangers and other persons who may die in the village under circumstances which render it unreasonable to require payment for making such interment.

§ 294. Record of interments.— The board of cemetery commissioners shall cause an accurate record to be kept of every interment in such cemetery, specifying the lot in which such interment is made, the time when made, and the name, age and place of birth of the person interred, if these particulars can be conveniently ascertained.

§ 295. Property in trust.— The board of cemetery commissioners of a village may take and hold any property given, bequeathed or devised to it in trust, to apply such property or the income thereof for the improvement or embellishment of such cemetery, or the erection or preservation of a building, structure, fence or walk therein, or for the renewal, erection or preservation of a tomb, monument, stone, fence, railing or other erection or structure, on or around any lot therein or the planting or cultivation of trees, shrubs, flowers or plants in or about a lot therein or for otherwise caring for and maintaining a lot therein, according to the terms of such grant, devise or bequest.

§ 296. Annual report of cemetery commissioners.—Between the first and fourth day of March in each year, the board of cemetery commissioners shall file with the village clerk a report containing a statement of the following facts:

1. The amount of money on hand at the beginning of the preceding fiscal year, and the receipts from all sources during such year.

2. An itemized statement of the amount paid out during such year and the balance on hand.

3. The outstanding indebtedness of the department, either bonded or otherwise, separately stated.

4. The estimated deficiency in the amount necessary to pay principal or interest or the expenses of the department during the next fiscal year, after applying thereto the probable amount available from the cemetery fund.

5. The improvements made during such preceding year and the general condition of the cemetery.

6. The number of interments made since their last annual report.

7. Such other facts as the board deems important for the information of the village, together with such recommendations concerning the department as may be deemed proper.

Section 300. Reincorporation of special village under this chapter. —A village incorporated by special law and subject to its provisions may be reincorporated under this chapter by adopting a proposition therefor. Such a proposition may be submitted at an annual election or at a special election to be called for that purpose.

The board of trustees of such a village may, upon its own motion, and shall, upon the petition of twenty-five electors assessed upon the last assessment-roll of the village, cause to be submitted at a village election a proposition for such reincorporation. The ballots to be used at such an election may be written or printed, and shall contain either the words " For the reincorporation of the village of (naming it) under the village law," or " Against the reincorporation of the village of (naming it) under the village law."

A proposition for the reincorporation of a village under this article shall not be submitted at an election, either annual or special, during the months of February or March.

§ 301. Notice and conduct of election—If the proposition is to be submitted at an annual election notice thereof shall be given by the board of trustees by posting notices in five public places in the village, and publishing the same in each newspaper actually printed therein, if any, at least twenty days before such annual election. If it is to be submitted at a special election notice of such election and of the submission of such proposition thereat shall be given in the same manner and for the same time as for the submission of such a proposition at an annual election. Such a special election shall be held by the same officers and conducted and the result canvassed in the same manner as provided by law for an annual election in such village.

§ 302. Certificate of election.—The officers conducting such election shall make a certificate thereof, showing the whole number of votes cast upon such proposition, and the number in favor of and against it, and within twenty-four hours after the closing of the polls of such election, must file such certificate in the office of the village clerk. If the proposition be adopted the village clerk shall within ten days after the election file a certified copy of such certificate in the office of the clerk of each county in which any part of such village is situated, and also in the office of the secretary of state.

§ 303. **Effect of reincorporation.**—If the proposition be adopted the reincorporation of the village under this chapter shall take effect immediately upon the filing of the certificate of election in the office of the village clerk. From and after such filing such village shall be deemed incorporated under this chapter, and shall possess all the powers, enjoy all the privileges, and be subject to all the liabilities, in all respects and for all purposes, as if it had been originally incorporated thereunder. Such reincorporation shall not affect any action then pending or cause of action existing by or against such village, nor property rights thereof under the provisions of any law to which it was then subject. The officers of the village in office when the reincorporation takes effect shall continue to hold their offices until noon on the Monday following the date when the next annual election in such village may be held under this chapter, at which time their terms of office shall expire.

§ 304. **Determination of number of trustees.**—A special election to determine the number of trustees to be elected in such village at the first annual election after such reincorporation, shall be held in the month of February next preceding, in the manner and upon the notice prescribed by article two of this chapter. If the number of trustees be not determined before such first annual election the village shall elect two trustees. At such first annual election after reincorporation one-half of the trustees shall be elected for one year, and one-half for two years.

ARTICLE XIII.
Miscellaneous Provisions.

Section 310. Enumeration.—An enumeration of the inhabitants of each village shall be taken under the direction of the board of trustees in the month of January, eighteen hundred and ninety-eight, and in the same month in each fourth year thereafter. The enumeration must show the full name of each person, the town in which he resides, and whether he is over or under twenty-one years of age. The persons taking such enumeration shall attach thereto a tabulated statement showing the whole number of inhabitants as appears by the enumeration, the number residing in each town in which any part of the village is situated, the number over and the number under twenty-one years of age. Such enumeration must be signed by the persons taking it and filed with the village clerk on or before the twentieth day of January. The board of trustees must immediately cause a notice to be published in each newspaper published in the village, and posted in at least five conspicuous public places therein, stating that such enumeration has been taken and filed in the office of the village clerk, and that the board will meet at a time and place specified in such notice, which time must not be less than three nor more than six days after the filing of such enumeration, to hear all objections thereto, and to correct and revise the same.

The board of trustees shall meet accordingly, and after hearing all objections, shall finally correct the enumeration and cause it to be filed in the office of the village clerk, on or before the first day of the following February. The village clerk shall, within one week thereafter, transmit to the clerk of each county in which any part of the village is situated, and to the secretary of state, a certificate of the total population of the village, as appears from such enumeration.

§ 311. **Notice; how served.**—Service of a notice under this chapter must be personal, if the person to be served can be found in the village, otherwise the notice may be served personally or by mail by depositing a copy thereof in the post-office of the village, and addressed to such person at his last known place of residence. The provisions of the code of civil procedure, relating to the service of a summons in an action in the supreme court, except as to publication, apply, so far as practicable, to the service of notices under this chapter.

If a person to be served can not with due diligence be found in the village where personal service is required, or his last known place of residence can not be ascertained, the county judge of a county in which any part of the village is situated may, by order, direct the manner of such service, and service shall be made accordingly.

A service on one of two or more joint tenants, or tenants in common, shall be sufficient notice to all for any purpose requiring a notice under this chapter.

§ 312. **Notice; proof of posting.**—Whenever by this chapter or by a rule, by-law or ordinance made in pursuance thereof, a notice or ordinance is authorized or required to be posted, an affidavit thereof by the person posting the same is presumptive evidence of such posting.

§ 313. **Officer not to be interested in contracts.**—An officer shall not be directly or indirectly interested in a contract which he or a board of which he is a member is authorized to make on behalf of the village; nor in furnishing work or materials; nor shall such an officer act as such in any matter or proceeding, involving the acquisition of real property then owned by him, for a public improvement.

§ 314. **Liability on unlawful contracts.**—An officer or person who assumes to create a liability or appropriate money or property of the village without authority of law, or assents thereto, is personally liable for such debt, or to the village for such money or property. Each member of a village board present at a meeting thereof when such unlawful action is taken is deemed to have assented thereto, unless he expressly dissents and requests such dissent to be entered upon the minutes of the meeting. A village is not liable upon a contract made by an officer or a board in the name or on behalf of the village, unless it is authorized by law.

§ 315. Competency of inhabitants as justices or jurors; undertakings not required by village.— In an action brought by or against a village it shall not be an objection against the person acting as justice or juror in such action, that he is a resident of the village or subject to taxation therein. It shall not be necessary for the village to give a bond, undertaking or security to appeal or to obtain a provisional remedy, or to take or prevent any other proceeding; but the village shall be liable to the same extent as if it had given the bond, undertaking or security otherwise required by or in pursuance of law.

§ 316. Board may take testimony.—The board of trustees or the board· of fire, water, light, sewer or cemetery commissioners may take testimony in a proceeding pending before it. The village clerk or any member of the board of trustees may administer oaths and take affidavits upon any claim or account against the village.

§ 317. Woman may institute proceeding.— Where a right is granted by this chapter to institute a proceeding, make an application, present a petition, or take an appeal, such right may be exercised by an adult resident woman who owns property assessed upon the last preceding assessment-roll of the village.

§ 318. Security by contractors.—All contracts under this chapter must be in the name of the village and the contractor must give adequate security to be approved by the officer or board with whom the contract is made.

§ 319. Arrest of disorderly persons.—A disorderly person under this chapter is subject to arrest, with or without process. A member of the police department or a peace officer may arrest a disorderly person without process for a violation of a village ordinance, committed in his presence. An officer making an arrest under this section shall immediately take the person arrested before the police justice of the village or a justice of the peace having jurisdiction, if such magistrate can be found, if not, he may detain the person arrested until such magistrate be found, not exceeding twenty-four hours. Unless the violation complained of is also a crime subject to indictment, the magistrate shall proceed forthwith to hear, try and determine such complaint, or may adjourn the hearing not to exceed five days, and in the meantime commit the offender to the lock-up or place of confinement or county jail until such day, or suffer him to go at large on executing a bond for his appearance on the adjourned day. On conviction the magistrate shall impose the penalty prescribed by the ordinance, and may also require the defendant to pay the costs of the proceeding. Unless the penalty and the costs, if imposed, be paid upon the conviction, the magistrate shall commit the defendant to the county jail of a county in which any part of the village is situated for a term not exceeding twenty days.

§ 320. **Action to recover penalties.**—An action may be maintained by a village to recover a penalty imposed for a violation of an ordinance, and in such action an order of arrest may be issued and executed in the manner prescribed by the code of civil procedure for orders of arrests in justices' courts. In such action it shall be lawful to declare or complain generally for such penalty, stating the section of this chapter, or the ordinance, under which the penalty is claimed, and briefly setting forth the alleged violation. If the defendant in such action has no property out of which the judgment can be collected, the execution shall require him to be imprisoned in the county jail of a county in which any part of the village is situated, for a term not exceeding twenty days.

§ 321. **Discontinuance of action.**— If in an action brought by the village to recover a penalty for the violation of an ordinance, it appears from the complaint, or by the affidavit upon which an order of arrest is granted, that the person committing such violation is a disorderly person under this chapter, the magistrate may, upon the appearance of such person before him, by an order to be entered in his minutes, direct that all subsequent proceedings be taken in the same manner as if such person had been arrested without process as a disorderly person. Such subsequent proceedings shall be taken accordingly, and the action shall be thereupon discontinued.

§ 322. **Actions against the village.**— No action shall be maintained against the village for damages for a personal injury or an injury to property alleged to have been sustained by reason of the negligence of the village or of any officer, agent or employe thereof, unless the same shall be commenced within one year after the cause of action therefor shall have accrued nor unless a written verified statement of the nature of the claim and of the time and place at which such injury is alleged to have been received shall have been filed with the village clerk within six months after the cause of action shall have accrued. An action on such a claim shall not be commenced until the expiration of thirty days after it is presented.

§ 323. **County court always open.**—The county court is always open for the hearing of an application or appeal under this chapter.

§ 324. Location of hospitals and pest-houses.—A building or tent in a village shall not be used, occupied or maintained as a hospital or pest-house for the reception and care of public or private patients without the consent of the board of health of such village.

§ 325. Change of name.—The name of a village may be changed upon the adoption of a proposition therefor at an annual election. The proposition must contain the proposed new name, and be accompanied by the written consent of the postmaster-general of the United States to such change. If the proposition be adopted a certificate thereof, attested by the president and clerk of the village shall, within ten days after the election, be filed in the office of such clerk, in the office of the county clerk of each county in which any part of the village is situated, and also in the office of the secretary of state. The change of name takes effect upon the filing of the certificate in the office of the village clerk.

§ 326. Extension of boundaries.—Territory not in a city or village may be annexed to an adjoining village. A petition for such annexation, describing the territory, stating the number of inhabitants thereof, and signed by a majority of the persons residing therein, if any, qualified to vote for town officers, and also by the owners of a majority in value of the property therein, assessed upon the last preceding town assessment-roll, may be presented to the board of trustees of such village. Each person signing the petition shall state opposite his name the assessed valuation of the property, if any, owned by him in such territory. Such petition must be verified by at least three persons signing the same to the effect that the petitioners constitute a majority of the qualified electors, if any, of such territory, and that the petition represents a majority in value of the property as above described. The petition must also be acknowledged in the same manner as a deed to be recorded.

Such petition must be accompanied by the written consent of a majority of the town board of the town in which such territory is situated, residing outside the village. Upon the presentation of such petition and consent, the board of trustees shall cause a proposition for such annexation to be submitted at a special election. If the proposition be adopted, the petition and consent and the certificate of the election shall be recorded in the village book of records. Such annexation takes effect immediately and a certificate thereof containing a description of the territory annexed shall, within ten days after such election, be filed by the village clerk in the office of the clerk of the town and of the county in which such annexed territory is situated, and also in the office of the secretary of state.

§ 327. Dissolution of villages.—A proposition for the dissolution of a village may be submitted at a special election. If the proposition be adopted, it must be again submitted at the next annual election held not less than six months subsequent to the special election. If the proposition be adopted at such annual election, a certificate thereof shall be filed in the office of the town clerk, and of the county clerk of each county in which any part of the village is situated, and also with the secretary of state. At the expiration of six months from such annual election, the village shall be dissolved. Within that period, the board of trustees must submit at a special election a proposition for the disposition of the village property remaining after the payment of all claims for which the village shall be liable, and also for the raising by tax of any sum that may be necessary to pay and discharge its existing debts and liabilities. Upon the dissolution of the village all its records, books and papers shall be deposited with the town clerk of the town in which the principal portion of such village is situated, and they shall thereupon become a part of the records of such town.

The supervisor of such town shall be the trustee of the property of the village. No suit in which the village is a party, nor any claim for or against the village shall be affected by its dissolution.

§ 328. Expiration of terms of officers.—A police justice or an assessor in office when this chapter takes effect shall continue in office until the expiration of the term for which he was elected or appointed. Except as otherwise provided in this chapter the terms of all other officers shall expire on the Monday following the third Tuesday in March, eighteen hundred and ninety-eight.

ARTICLE XIV.

Effect of Chapter; Repeal.

Section 340. Effect of chapter on special villages.
    341. Effect of revision on general villages.
    342. Repeal.
    343. When to take effect.

Section 340. Effect of chapter on special villages.—A village incorporated under and subject to a special law, and each officer thereof, possesses all the powers and is subject to all the liabilities and responsibilities conferred or imposed upon a village incorporated under this chapter, or upon an officer thereof, not inconsistent with such special law.

§ 341. **Effect of revision on general villages.**— The following villages are subject to the provisions of this chapter, as if incorporated thereunder:

1. Villages incorporated under chapter 426 of the laws of 1847, or the acts amendatory thereof and supplemental thereto, and which have not been reincorporated under a special law.

2. Villages incorporated or reincorporated under chapter 291 of the laws of 1870, or the acts amendatory thereof and supplemental thereto.

3. Villages incorporated by special law and reincorporated under a general law and now subject to its provisions.

§ 342. **Repeal.**—The following acts and parts of acts are hereby repealed:

1. The laws or parts thereof specified in the schedule hereto annexed, and all acts amendatory thereof or supplemental thereto in force when this chapter takes effect, including all such amendatory or supplemental acts passed in 1897.

2. All acts or parts of acts inconsistent with this chapter.

3. All acts or parts of acts relating specially by name or otherwise to villages now subject to a general law.

4. Chapter 113 of the laws of 1883, and the acts amendatory thereof, so far as they relate to the change of grade of streets or bridges by village authorities.

5. Chapter 311 of the laws of 1870, so far as it relates to the division of streets on boundary lines between villages and other municipal corporations.

§ 343. **When to take effect.**— This chapter shall take effect on July 1, 1897.

SCHEDULE OF LAWS REPEALED.

Laws of	Section.	Subject matter.
1847, ch. 151....	All...	Fire companies.
1847, ch. 209....	All...	Cemeteries.
1847, ch. 426....	All...	General village act.
1850, ch. 176....	All...	Amends L. 1847, ch. 426.
1852, ch. 184....	All...	Amends L. 1847, ch. 426.
1861, ch. 178....	All...	Amends L. 1847, ch. 426.
1864, ch. 117....	All...	Amends L. 1847, ch. 426.
1868, ch. 462....	All...	Special elections.
1870, ch. 291....	All...	General village law.
1871, ch. 688....	All...	Amends L. 1870, ch. 291.
1871, ch. 696....	All...	Cemetery commissioners.

Laws of	Section.	Subject matter.
1871, ch. 870....	All...	Amends L. 1870, ch. 291.
1872, ch. 357....	All...	Amends L. 1870, ch. 291.
1872, ch. 696....	All...	Amends L. 1847, ch. 209.
1873, ch. 92.....	All...	Amends L. 1870, ch. 291.
1873, ch. 397....	11...	Firemen's exemption.
1874, ch. 78.....	All...	Amends L. 1870, ch. 291.
1874, ch. 345....	All...	Trustees to publish accounts.
1874, ch. 474....	All...	Amends L. 1870, ch. 291.
1874, ch. 628....	All...	Amends L. 1870, ch. 291.
1875, ch. 149....	All...	Failure to designate terms.
1875, ch. 181....	All...	Water act.
1875, ch. 197....	All...	Amends L. 1874, ch. 345.
1875, ch. 242....	All...	Amends L. 1870, ch. 291, tit. III.
1875, ch. 339....	All...	Amends L. 1870, ch. 291.
1875, ch. 385....	All...	Arrests without warrant.
1875, ch. 514....	All...	Election police justices.
1875, ch. 570....	All...	Amends L. 1870, ch. 291, tit. IV.
1876, ch. 92.....	All.	Failure to designate terms.
1876, ch. 134....	All...	Amends L. 1875, ch. 181.
1876, ch. 308....	All...	Amends L. 1875, ch. 514.
1876, ch. 317....	All...	Amends L. 1870, ch. 291.
1877, ch. 16.....	All...	Amends L. 1870, ch. 291.
1877, ch. 244....	All...	Amends L. 1870, ch. 291, tit. III.
1878, ch. 59.....	All...	Amends L. 1870, ch. 291.
1878, ch. 249....	All...	Amends L. 1870, ch. 291.
1878, ch. 281....	All...	Amends L. 1870, ch. 291.
1878, ch. 396....	All...	Failure to designate terms.
1879, ch. 68.....	All...	Failure to designate terms.
1879, ch. 86.....	All...	Amends L. 1875, ch. 181.
1879, ch. 129....	All...	Amends L. 1870, ch. 291.
1879, ch. 228....	All...	Amends L. 1875, ch. 181, § 5.
1879, ch. 337....	All...	Confirms incorporations.
1880, ch. 64.....	All...	Confirms incorporations.
1880, ch. 78.....	All...	Water contracts; villages in Richmond county.
1880, ch. 144....	All...	Amends L. 1870, ch. 291.
1880, ch. 172....	All...	Amends L. 1847, ch. 426.
1880, ch. 235....	All...	Costs on arrests.
1880, ch. 292....	All...	Amends L. 1870, ch. 291.
1880, ch. 422....	All...	Amends L. 1870, ch. 291.
1880, ch. 496....	All...	Amends L. 1870, ch. 291.

Laws of	Section.	Subject matter.
1881, ch. 17.....	All...	Failure to designate terms.
1881, ch. 175....	All...	Amends L. 1875, ch. 181.
1881, ch. 249....	All...	Amends L. 1870, ch. 291.
1881, ch. 353....	All...	Second election on tax question.
1881, ch. 387....	All...	Amends L. 1870, ch. 291.
1881, ch. 408....	All...	Amends L. 1880, ch. 235.
1881, ch. 615....	All...	Civil jurisdiction police justice.
1881, ch. 690....	All...	Amends L. 1881, ch. 615.
1882, ch. 226....	All...	Renewal of tax warrants.
1882, ch. 305....	All...	Amends L. 1870, ch. 291.
1882, ch. 316....	All...	Amends L. 1870, ch. 291.
1883, ch. 90.....	All...	Amends L. 1870, ch. 291.
1883, ch. 118....	All...	Amends L. 1875, ch. 514.
1883, ch. 153....	All...	Amends L. 1870, ch. 291.
1883, ch. 255.	All...	Amends L. 1875, ch. 181.
1883, ch. 459....	All...	Amends L. 1870, ch. 291, tit. VIII.
1883, ch. 465....	All...	Restraint of peddling.
1884, ch. 129....	All...	Amends L. 1870, ch. 291.
1884, ch. 131....	All...	Amends L. 1870, ch. 291.
1884, ch. 308....	All...	Special village to have power of general.
1884, ch. 423....	All...	Confirms incorporations.
1885, ch. 170....	All...	Amends L. 1875, ch. 181.
1885, ch. 192....	All...	Amends L. 1870, ch. 291.
1885, ch. 211....	All...	Amends L. 1875, ch. 181.
1885, ch. 236....	All...	Amends L. 1870, ch. 291.
1885, ch. 450....	All...	Amends L. 1870, ch. 291, tit. VIII.
1886, ch. 497....	All...	Extension of water mains.
1886, ch. 556....	All...	Amends L. 1870, ch. 291, tit. VIII.
1886, ch. 600....	All...	Amends L. 1870, ch. 291.
1886, ch. 616....	All...	Amends L. 1870, ch. 291.
1887, ch. 68.....	All...	Amends L. 1870, ch. 291.
1887, ch. 244....	All...	Fire departments.
1887, ch. 504....	All...	Power to raise additional money.
1887, ch. 513....	All...	Amends L. 1870, ch. 291.
1887, ch. 514....	All...	Amends L. 1870, ch. 291.
1888, ch. 172....	All...	Amends L. 1870, ch. 291.
1888, ch. 342....	All...	Amends L. 1887, ch. 244.
1888, ch. 452....	All...	Contracts for lighting.
1888, ch. 525....	All...	Acquisition of land for parks.
1889, ch. 174....	All...	Amends L. 1880, ch. 78.

Laws of	Section.	Subject matter.
1889, ch. 186....	All...	Amends L. 1870, ch. 291.
1889, ch. 229....	All...	Amends L. 1870, ch. 291.
1889, ch. 246....	All..:	Amends L. 1870, ch. 291.
1889, ch. 375....	All...	General sewer law.
1889, ch. 440....	All...	Amends L. 1870, ch. 291.
1889, ch. 455....	All...	Amends L. 1875, ch. 181.
1889, ch. 507....	All...	Scale of water rents.
1890, ch. 82.....	All...	Amends L. 1870, ch. 291.
1890, ch. 196....	All...	Amends L. 1870, ch. 291.
1890, ch. 213....	All...	Amends L. 1870, ch. 291.
1890, ch. 235....	All...	Amends L. 1870, ch. 291.
1890, ch. 236....	All...	Amends L. 1870, ch. 291.
1890, ch. 371....	All...	Amends L. 1887, ch. 504.
1890, ch. 527....	All...	Amends L. 1875, ch. 181.
1890, ch. 542....	All...	Amends L. 1870, ch. 291, tit. VIII, § 27, so as to apply to Westchester county.
1891, ch. 74.....	All...	Amends L. 1875, ch. 181.
1891, ch. 116....	All...	Amends L. 1870, ch. 291.
1891, ch. 139....	All...	Amends L. 1870, ch. 291.
1891, ch. 160....	All...	Amends L. 1870, ch. 291.
1891, ch. 201....	All...	Amends L. 1875, ch. 181.
1891, ch. 306....	All...	Amends L. 1889, ch. 375.
1891, ch. 312....	All...	Amends L. 1888, ch. 452.
1891, ch. 316... .	All...	Amends L. 1889, ch. 375.
1892, ch. 194....	All...	Amends L. 1870, ch. 291.
1892, ch. 195....	All...	Amends L. 1875, ch. 181.
1892, ch. 222....	All...	Amends L. 1870, ch. 291.
1892, ch. 349....	All...	Amends L. 1889, ch. 375.
1892, ch. 564....	All...	Amends L. 1889, ch. 375.
1892, ch. 593....	All...	Amends L. 1870, ch. 291.
1892, ch. 640....	All...	Improvement of streets, etc., in certain villages.
1893, ch. 212....	All...	Amends L. 1870, ch. 291.
1893, ch. 400....	All...	Amends L. 1870, ch. 291.
1893, ch. 422....	All...	Amends L. 1889, ch. 375.
1893, ch. 447....	All...	Hospitals or pest-houses in villages.
1893, ch. 464....	All...	Amends L. 1870, ch. 291.
1893, ch. 473....	'All...	Amends L. 1888, ch. 452.
1893, ch. 503....	All...	Amends L. 1870, ch. 291.
1893, ch. 617....	All...	Amends L. 1888, ch. 452.
1893, ch. 618....	All...	Amends L. 1870, ch. 291.

Laws of	Section.	Subject matter.
1893, ch. 624....	All...	Amends L. 1875, ch. 181.
1893, ch. 662....	All...	Amends L. 1889, ch. 507.
1893, ch. 694....	All...	Amends L. 1870, ch. 291.
1894, ch. 284....	All...	Amends L. 1889, ch. 507.
1894, ch. 318....	All...	Amends L. 1875, ch. 181.
1894, ch. 413....	All...	Amends L. 1892, ch. 640.
1894, ch. 673....	All...	Lighting contracts.
1894, ch. 680....	All...	Establishment of electric-light plant.
1895, ch. 113....	All...	Amends L. 1888, ch. 452.
1895, ch. 146....	All...	Amends L. 1870, ch. 291.
1895, ch. 154....	All...	Amends L. 1870, ch. 291.
1895, ch. 187....	All...	Amends L. 1870, ch. 291.
1895, ch. 202....	All...	Amends L. 1889, ch. 375.
1895, ch. 383....	All...	Amends L. 1875, ch. 181.
1895, ch. 430....	All...	Compensation of boards of health.
1895, ch. 437....	All...	Appropriations for fire parades.
1895, ch. 743....	All...	Amends L. 1870, ch. 291.
1895, ch. 879....	All...	Amends L. 1870, ch. 291.
1896, ch. 166....	All...	Amends L. 1888, ch. 452.
1896, ch. 209....	All...	Amends L. 1870, ch. 291.
1896, ch. 243....	All...	Amends L. 1870, ch. 291.
1896, ch. 310....	All...	Amends L. 1875, ch. 181.
1896, ch. 341....	All...	Amends L. 1870, ch. 291.
1896, ch. 329....	All...	Amends L. 1886, ch. 497.
1896, ch. 409....	All...	Amends L. 1889, ch. 375.
1896, ch. 457....	All...	Amends L. 1870, ch. 291.
1896, ch. 458....	All...	Amends L. 1870, ch. 291.
1896, ch. 522....	All...	Amends L. 1870, ch. 291.
1896, ch. 663....	All...	Lighting contracts.
1896, ch. 688....	All...	Amends L. 1870, ch. 291.
1896, ch. 923....	All...	Amends L. 1870, ch. 291.
1896, ch. 978....	All...	Contracts for water.

Code of Criminal Procedure, §§ 75, 76 and 77.

Chap. 415.

AN ACT in relation to labor, constituting chapter thirty-two of the general laws.

Became a law May 13, 1897, with the approval of the Governor. Passed, a majority being present.

The People of the State of New York, represented in Senate and Assembly, do enact as follows:

CHAPTER XXXII OF THE GENERAL LAWS.

THE LABOR LAW.

ARTICLE I.

GENERAL PROVISIONS.

Section 1. **Short title.**— This chapter shall be known as the labor law.

§ 2. **Definitions.**— The term employe, when used in this chapter, means a mechanic, workingman or laborer who works for another for hire.

The person employing any such mechanic, workingman or laborer, whether the owner, proprietor, agent, superintendent, foreman or other subordinate, is designated in this chapter as an employer.

The term "factory," when used in this chapter, shall be construed to include also any mill, workshop or other manufacturing or business establishment where one or more persons are employed at labor.

The term "mercantile establishment," when used in this chapter, means any place where goods, wares or merchandise are offered for sale.

Whenever, in this chapter, authority is conferred upon the factory inspector, it shall also be deemed to include his assistant or a deputy acting under his direction.

§ 3. **Hours to constitute a days work**— Eight hours shall constitute a legal day's work for all classes of employes in this state, except those engaged in farm and domestic labor, unless otherwise provided by law. This section does not prevent an agreement for overwork for extra compensation.

This section applies to work for the state or a municipal corporation, or for contractors therewith.

The wages for such public work shall be not less than the prevailing rate for a legal day's work in the same trade or calling in the locality where the work is performed. Every contract for the construction of a public work, shall contain a provision that the same shall be void and of no effect unless such rate is paid by the contractor to his employés.

§ 4. Violations of preceding section.— Any officer or agent of this state or of a municipal corporation therein, who openly violates or otherwise evades the provisions of this article, relating to the hours of labor of employes, shall be deemed guilty of malfeasance in office, and may be suspended or removed by the authority having the power to appoint such officer or agent, if any, otherwise by the governor. A party contracting with the state or a municipal corporation therein, who fails to comply with, or secretly evades such provisions by exacting and requiring more hours of labor for the compensation agreed to be paid per day than is fixed in this article, shall forfeit such contract, at the option of the state or of such municipal corporation.

§ 5. Hours of labor on street surface and elevated railroads.— Ten consecutive hours' labor, including one-half hour for dinner shall constitute a day's labor in the operation of all street surface and elevated railroads, of whatever motive power, owned or operated by corporations in this state, whose main line of travel or whose routes lie principally within the corporate limits of cities of more than one hundred thousand inhabitants. No employe of any such corporation shall be permitted or allowed to work more than ten consecutive hours, including one-half hour for dinner, in any one day of twenty-four hours.

In cases of accident or unavoidable delay, extra labor may be performed for extra compensation.

§ 6. Hours of labor in brickyards.— Ten hours, exclusive of the necessary time for meals, shall constitute a legal day's work in the making of brick in brickyards owned or operated by corporations. No corporation owning or operating such brickyard shall require employes to work more than ten hours in any one day, or to commence work before seven o'clock in the morning.

But overwork and work prior to seven o'clock in the morning for extra compensation may be performed by agreement between employer and employe.

§ 7. Regulation of hours of labor on steam surface and elevated railroads.— Ten hours labor, performed within twelve consecutive hours, shall constitute a legal day's labor in the operation of steam surface and elevated railroads owned and operated within this state, except where the mileage system of running trains is in operation. But this section does not apply to the performance of extra hours of labor by conductors, engineers, firemen and trainmen in case of accident or delay resulting therefrom. For each hour of labor performed in any one day in excess of such ten hours, by any such employe, he shall be paid in addition at least one-tenth of his daily compensation.

No person or corporation operating a line of railroad of thirty miles in length or over, in whole or in part within this state, shall permit or require a conductor, engineer, fireman or trainman, who has worked in any capacity for twenty-four consecutive hours, to go again on duty or perform any kind of work, until he has had at least eight hours' rest.

§ 8. Payment of wages by receivers.—Upon the appointment of a receiver of a partnership or of a corporation organized under the laws of this state and doing business therein, other than a moneyed corporation, the wages of the employes of such partnership or corporation shall be preferred to every other debt or claim.

§ 9. Cash payment of wages.—Every manufacturing, mining, quarrying, mercantile, railroad, street railway, canal, steamboat, telegraph and telephone company, every express company, and every water company, not municipal, shall pay to each employe engaged in its business the wages earned by him in cash. No such company or corporation shall pay its employes in scrip, commonly known as store money orders.

§ 10. When wages are to be paid.—Every corporation or joint stock association, or person carrying on the business thereof by lease or otherwise, shall pay weekly to each employe the wages earned by him to a day not more than six days prior to the date of such payment.

But every person or corporation operating a steam surface railroad shall, on or before the twentieth day of each month, pay the employes thereof the wages earned by them during the preceding calendar month.

§ 11. **Penalty for violation of preceding sections.**—If a corporation or joint stock association, its lessee or other person carrying on the business thereof, shall fail to pay the wages of an employe as provided in this article, it shall forfeit to the people of the state the sum of fifty dollars for each such failure, to be recovered by the factory inspector in his name of office in a civil action; but an action shall not be maintained therefor, unless the factory inspector shall have given to the employer at least ten days' written notice, that such an action will be brought if the wages due are not sooner paid as provided in this article.

On the trial of such action, such corporation or association shall not be allowed to set up any defense, other than a valid assignment of such wages, a valid set-off against the same, or the absence of such employe from his regular place of labor at the time of payment, or an actual tender to such employe at the time of the payment of the wages so earned by him, or a breach of contract by such employe or a denial of the employment.

§ 12. **Assignment of future wages.**—No assignment of future wages, payable weekly, or monthly in case of a steam surface railroad corporation, shall be valid if made to the corporation or association from which such wages are to become due, or to any person on its behalf, or if made or procured to be made to any person for the purpose of relieving such corporation or association from the obligation to pay weekly, or monthly in case of a steam surface railroad corporation. Charges for groceries, provisions or clothing shall not be a valid off-set for wages in behalf of any such corporation or association.

No such corporation or association shall require any agreement from any employe to accept wages at other periods than as provided in this article as a condition of employment.

§ 13. **Preferences in employment of persons upon public works.**—In the construction of public works by the state or a municipality, or by persons contracting with the state or such municipality, only citizens of the United States shall be employed; and in all cases where laborers are employed on any such public works, preference shall be given citizens of the state of New York. In each contract for the construction of public works, a provision shall be inserted, to the effect that if the provisions of this section are not complied with, the contract shall be void.

§ 14. **Stone used in state or municipal works.**—All stone used in state and municipal works, except paving blocks and crushed

stone, shall be worked, dressed and carved within the state.
There shall be inserted in each contract or specification hereafter
awarded by state, county or municipal authorities, authorizing or
requiring the use of worked, dressed or carved stone, except paving blocks or crushed stone, within the state or such county or
municipality, a clause to the effect that such stone shall be so
worked, dressed or carved within the boundaries of the state as
required by this section. If a contractor of the state or any municipality therein, shall use stone, except paving blocks and crushed
stone, which has been worked, dressed or carved without the state,
the state or such municipality shall revoke the contract of such
contractor and be released from liability thereon.

§ 15. Labels, brands, etc., used by labor organizations.—A union
or association of employes may adopt a device in the form of a
label, brand, mark, name or other character for the purpose of
designating the products of the labor of the members thereof.
Duplicate copies of such device shall be filed in the office of the
secretary of state, who shall, under his hand and seal, deliver to
the union or association filing or registering the same a certified
copy and a certificate of the filing thereof, for which he shall be
entitled to a fee of one dollar. Such certificate shall not be assign-
able by the union or association to whom it is issued.

§ 16. Penalty for illegal use of labels, etc., injunction proceedings.—A person manufacturing, using, displaying or keeping for
sale a counterfeit or colorable imitation of a device so adopted
and filed, or goods bearing the same, shall be subject to a penalty
of two hundred dollars, to be recovered in an action brought in a
court of competent jurisdiction by the person aggrieved; one-half
of which penalty, when recovered, shall be paid to the plaintiff
and one-half to the overseer of the poor of the town or to an officer
having like power of the city, wherein the person aggrieved resides, for the benefit of the poor of such town or city.

After filing copies of such device, such union or association may
commence an action to enjoin the manufacture, use, display or
sale of counterfeit or colorable imitations of such device, or of
goods bearing the same, and the court may restrain such wrongful manufacture, use, display or sale, and every unauthorized use
or display by others of the genuine devices so registered and filed,
if such use or display is not authorized by the owner thereof, and
may award to the plaintiff such damages resulting from such
wrongful manufacture, use, display or sale as may be proved, together with the profits derived therefrom.

§ 17. **Seats for female employes in factories.**—Every person employing females in a factory shall provide and maintain suitable seats for the use of such female employes, and permit the use thereof by such employes to such an extent as may be reasonable for the preservation of their health.

§ 18. **Scaffolding for use of employes.**— A person employing or directing another to perform labor of any kind in the erection, repairing, altering or painting of a house, building or structure shall not furnish or erect, or cause to be furnished or erected for the performance of such labor, scaffolding, hoists, stays, ladders or other mechanical contrivances which are unsafe, unsuitable or improper, and which are not so constructed, placed and operated as to give proper protection to the life and limb of a person so employed or engaged.

Scaffolding or staging swung or suspended from an overhead support, more than twenty feet from the ground or floor, shall have a safety rail of wood, properly bolted, secured and braced, rising at least thirty-four inches above the floor or main portions of such scaffolding or staging and extending along the entire length of the outside and the ends thereof, and properly attached thereto, and such scaffolding or staging shall be so fastened as to prevent the same from swaying from the building or structure.

§ 19. **Inspection of scaffolding, ropes, blocks, pulleys and tackle in cities.**— Whenever complaint is made to the commissioner of police, superintendent or other person in charge of the police force of a city, that the scaffolding or the slings, hangers, blocks, pulleys, stays, braces, ladders, irons or ropes of any swinging or stationary scaffolding used in the construction, alteration, repairing, painting, cleaning or pointing of buildings within the limits of such city, are unsafe or liable to prove dangerous to the life or limb of any person, such police commissioner, superintendent or other person in charge of the police force, shall immediately detail a competent police officer to inspect such scaffolding, or the slings, hangers, blocks, pulleys, stays, braces, ladders, irons or other parts connected therewith. If, after examination, such officer finds such scaffolding or any of such parts to be dangerous to life or limb, he shall prohibit the use thereof, and require the same to be altered and reconstructed so as to avoid such danger.

The officer making the examination shall attach a certificate to the scaffolding, or the slings, hangers, irons, ropes or other parts thereof, examined by him, stating that he has made such exami-

nation, and that he has found it safe or unsafe, as the case may
be. If he declares it unsafe, he shall at once, in writing, notify
the person responsible for its erection of the fact, and warn him
against the use thereof. Such notice may be served personally
upon the person responsible for its erection, or by conspicuously
affixing it to the scaffolding, or the part thereof declared to be unsafe. After such notice has been so served or affixed, the person
responsible therefor shall immediately remove such scaffolding
or part thereof and alter or strengthen it in such a manner as to
render it safe, in the discretion of the officer who has examined it,
or of his superiors.

Any officer detailed to examine or test any scaffolding or part
thereof, as required by this section, shall have free access, at all
reasonable hours, to any building or premises containing them or
where they may be in use.

All swinging and stationary scaffolding shall be so constructed
as to bear four times the maximum weight required to be dependent therefrom or placed thereon, when in use, and not more than
four men shall be allowed upon any swinging scaffolding at one
time.

§ 20. Protection of persons employed on buildings in cities.—
All contractors and owners, when constructing buildings in cities.
where the plans and specifications require the floors to be arched
between the beams thereof, or where the floors or filling in between
the floors are of fire-proof material of brick work, shall complete
the flooring or filling in as the building progresses, to not less
than within three tiers of beams below that on which the iron
work is being erected.

If the plans and specifications of such buildings do not require
filling in between the beams of floors with brick or fire-proof material, all contractors for carpenter work, in the course of construction, shall lay the under flooring thereof on each story, as the
building progresses, to not less than within two stories below
the one to which such building has been erected. Where double
floors are not to be used, such contractor shall keep planked over
the floor two stories below the story where the work is being performed.

If the floor beams are of iron or steel, the contractors for the
iron or steel work of buildings in course of construction, or the
owners of such buildings, shall thoroughly plank over the entire
tier of iron or steel beams on which the structural iron or steel

work is being erected, except such spaces as may be reasonably required for the proper construction of such iron or steel work, and for the raising or lowering of materials to be used in the construction of such building, or such spaces as may be designated by the plans and specifications for stairways and elevator shafts.

The chief officer, in any city, charged with the enforcement of the building laws of such city, is hereby charged with enforcing the provisions of this section.

ARTICLE II.
COMMISSIONER OF LABOR STATISTICS.

Section 30. Commissioner of labor statistics.
　　　31. Duties and powers.
　　　32. Statistics to be furnished upon request.

§ 30. Commissioner of labor statistics.— There shall continue to be a commissioner of labor statistics, who shall be appointed by the governor, by and with the advice and consent of the senate, and shall hold his office for the term of three years, and receive an annual salary of three thousand dollars. He may appoint a deputy commissioner of labor statistics, at an annual salary of two thousand and five hundred dollars, and a chief clerk at an annual salary of two thousand dollars, and such other clerks and assistants as he may deem necessary and fix their salaries.

The term of office of the successor of the commissioner in office when this chapter takes effect is abridged so as to expire on the last day of December preceding the time when such term would otherwise expire, and thereafter the term of office of such commissioner shall begin on the first day of January.

§ 31. Duties and powers.— The commissioner of labor statistics shall collect, assort, systematize and present in annual reports to the legislature, within ten days after the convening thereof in each year, statistical details in relation to all departments of labor in the state, especially in relation to the commercial, industrial, social and sanitary condition of workingmen and to the productive industries of the state. He may subpoena witnesses, take and hear testimony, take or cause to be taken depositions and administer oaths.

§ 32. Statistics to be furnished upon request.— The owner, operator, manager or lessee of any mine, factory, workshop, warehouse, elevator, foundry, machine shop or other manufacturing establishment, or any agent, superintendent, subordinate, or employe thereof, shall, when requested by the commissioner of labor statistics, furnish any information in his possession or under his control which the commissioner is authorized to require, and shall admit him to any place herein named for the purpose of inspection. All statistics furnished to the commissioner of labor statistics, pursuant to this article, may be destroyed by such commissioner after the expiration of two years from the time of the receipt thereof.

A person refusing to admit such commissioner, or a person authorized by him, to any such establishment, or to furnish him any information requested, or who refuses to answer or untruthfully answers questions put to him by such commissioner, in a circular or otherwise, shall forfeit to the people of the state the sum of one hundred dollars for each refusal and answer untruthfully given, to be sued for and recovered by the commissioner in his name of office. The amount so recovered shall be paid into the state treasury.

ARTICLE III.
FREE PUBLIC EMPLOYMENT BUREAUS.

§ 40. **Free public employment bureaus in cities of the first class.**—The commissioner of labor statistics shall organize and establish in all cities of the first class a free public employment bureau, for the purpose of receiving applications of persons seeking employment, and applications of persons seeking to employ labor. No compensation or fee shall be charged or received, directly or indirectly, from persons applying for employment or help through any such bureau. Such commissioner shall appoint for each bureau so organized, and may remove for good and sufficient cause, a superintendent and such clerical assistants as, in his judgment, may be necessary for the proper administration of the affairs thereof. The salaries of such superintendents and clerks shall be fixed by the commissioner. Such salaries and the expenses of such bureaus shall be paid in the same manner as other expenses of the bureau of labor statistics.

§ 41. **Duties of superintendent.**—The superintendent of each free public employment bureau shall receive and record, in a book to be kept for that purpose, the names of all persons applying for employment or for help, designating opposite the name and address of each applicant, the character of employment or help desired.

Each such superintendent shall report, on Thursday of each week, to the commissioner of labor statistics, the names and addresses of all persons applying for employment or help, during the preceding week, the character of the employment or help desired, and the names of the persons receiving employment through his bureau. Such superintendent shall also perform such other duties in the collection of labor statistics, and in the keeping of books and accounts of his bureau, as the commissioner may require, and shall report semi-annually to the commissioner of labor statistics the expense of maintaining his bureau.

§ 42. Applications; list of applicants.— Every application for employment or help made to a free public employment bureau shall be void after thirty days from its receipt, unless renewed by the applicant.

The commissioner of labor statistics shall cause two copies of a list of all applicants for employment or help, and the character of the employment or help desired, received by him from each free public employment bureau, to be mailed on Monday of each week to the superintendent of each·bureau, one of which copies shall be posted by the superintendent, immediately on receipt thereof, in a conspicuous place in his office, subject to the inspection of all persons desiring employment or help, and the other shall be filed in his office for reference.

§ 43. Applicants for help, when to notify superintendent.—If an applicant for help has secured the same, he shall, within ten days thereafter, notify the superintendent of the bureau, to which application therefor was made. Such notice shall contain the name and last preceding address of the employes received through such bureau. If any such applicant neglects to so notify such superintendent, he shall be barred from all future rights and privileges of such employment bureau, at the discretion of the commissioner of labor statistics to whom the superintendent shall report such neglect.

leged violation has occurred of such fact, giving the information
in support of his conclusion. The district attorney shall, at once,
institute the proper proceedings to compel compliance with this
article and secure conviction for such violations.

Upon the conviction of a person or corporation for a violation
of this article, one-half of the fine recovered shall be paid and certified by the district attorney to the commissioner of labor statistics, who shall use such money in investigating and securing information, in regard to violations of this act and in paying the
expenses of such conviction.

§ 55. Articles not to apply to goods manufactured for the use of
the state or a municipal corporation.— Nothing in this article shall
apply to or affect the manufacture in state prisons, reformatories
and penitentiaries, and furnishing of articles for the use of the
offices, departments and institutions of the state or any political
division thereof, as provided by chapter four hundred and twenty-
nine of the laws of eighteen hundred and ninety-six.

ARTICLE V.

FACTORY INSPECTOR, ASSISTANT AND DEPUTIES.

Section 60. Factory inspector and assistant.
61. Deputies and clerks.
62. General powers and duties of factory inspector.
63. Reports.
64. Badges.
65. Payment of salaries and expenses.
66. Sub-office in New York city.
67. Duties of factory inspector relative to apprentices.

§ 60. Factory inspector and assistant.— There shall continue
to be a factory inspector and assistant factory inspector, who shall
be appointed by the governor, by and with the advice and consent
of the senate. The term of office of each shall be three years.
The term of office of the successor of the factory inspector and
assistant factory inspector in office when this chapter takes effect
shall be abridged so as to expire on the last day of December preceding the time when each such term would otherwise expire, and
thereafter each such term shall begin on the first day of January.
There shall be paid to the factory inspector an annual salary of
three thousand dollars, and to the assistant factory inspector an
annual salary of two thousand five hundred dollars.

§ 61. Deputies and clerks.— The factory inspector may appoint, from time to time, not more than thirty-six persons as deputy factory inspectors, not more than ten of whom shall be women, and who may be removed by him at any time.   Each deputy inspector shall receive an annual salary of one thousand two hundred dollars.   The factory inspector may designate six or more of such deputies to inspect the buildings and rooms occupied and used as bakeries and to enforce the provisions of this chapter relating to the manufacture of flour or meal food products.   One of such deputies shall have a knowledge of mining, whose duty it shall be, under the direction of the factory inspector, to inspect mines and quarries and to enforce the provisions of this chapter relating thereto.

The factory inspector may appoint one or more of such deputies to act as clerk in his principal office.

§ 62. General powers and duties of factory inspector.— The factory inspector may divide the state into districts, assign one or more deputy inspectors to each district, and may, in his discretion, transfer them from one district to another.

The factory inspector shall visit and inspect, or cause to be visited and inspected, the factories, during reasonable hours, as often as practicable, and shall cause the provisions of this chapter to be enforced therein and prosecute all persons violating the same.

Any lawful municipal ordinance, by-law or regulation relating to factories or their inspection, in addition to the provisions of this chapter and not in conflict therewith, shall be observed and enforced by the factory inspector.

The factory inspector, assistant and each deputy may administer oaths and take affidavits in matters relating to the enforcement of the provisions of this chapter.

No person shall interfere with, obstruct or hinder, by force or otherwise, the factory inspector, assistant factory inspector or deputies while in the performance of their duties, or refuse to properly answer questions asked by such officers pertaining to the provisions of this chapter.

All notices, orders and directions of assistant or deputy factory inspectors given in accordance with this chapter are subject to the approval of the factory inspector.

§ 63. Reports.— The factory inspector shall report annually to the legislature in the month of January.   The assistant factory inspector and each deputy shall report to the factory inspector, from time to time, as he may require.

§ 64. Badges.— The factory inspector may procure and cause to be used, badges for himself, his assistant and deputies, while in the performance of their duties, the cost of which shall be a charge upon the appropriation made for the use of the department.

§ 65. Payment of salaries and expenses.— All necessary expenses incurred by the factory inspector and his assistant in the discharge of their duties, shall be paid by the state treasurer upon the warrant of the comptroller, issued upon proper vouchers therefor. The reasonable necessary traveling and other expenses of the deputy factory inspectors, while engaged in the performance of their duties, shall be paid in like manner upon vouchers approved by the factory inspector and audited by the comptroller. All such expenses and the salaries of the factory inspector, assistant and deputies shall be payable monthly.

§ 66. Sub-office in New York city.— The factory inspector may establish and maintain a sub-office in the city of New York, if, in his opinion, the duties of his office demand it. He may designate one or more of the deputy factory inspectors to take charge of and manage such office, subject to his direction. The reasonable and necessary expenses of such office shall be paid, as are other expenses of the factory inspector.

§ 67. Duties of factory inspector relative to apprentices.— The factory inspector, his assistant and deputies shall enforce the provisions of the Domestic Relations Law, relative to indentures of apprentices, and prosecute employers for failure to comply with the provisions of such indentures and of such law in relation thereto.

ARTICLE VI.

FACTORIES.

§ 70. Employment of minors.—A child under the age of fourteen years shall not be employed in any factory in this state. A child between the ages of fourteen and sixteen years shall not be so employed, unless a certificate executed by a health officer be filed in the office of the employer.

§ 71. Certificate for employment, how issued.—Such certificate shall be issued by the executive officer of the board, department or commissioner of health of the city, town or village where such child resides, or is to be employed, or by such other officer thereof as may be designated, by resolution, for that purpose, upon the application of the child desiring such employment. At the time of making such application, there shall be filed with such board, department, commissioner or officer, the affidavit of the parent or guardian of such child, or the person standing in parental relation thereto, showing the date and place of birth of such child. Such certificate shall not be issued unless the officer issuing the same is satisfied that such child is fourteen years of age or upwards, and is physically able to perform the work which he intends to do. No fee shall be demanded or received for administering an oath as required by this section.

§ 72. Contents of certificate.—Such certificate shall state the date and place of birth of the child, if known, and describe the color of the hair and eyes, the height and weight and any distinguishing facial marks of such child, and that, in the opinion of the officer issuing such certificate, such child is upwards of fourteen years of age, and is physically able to perform the work which he intends to do.

§ 73. School attendance required.—No such certificate shall be granted unless it appears to the satisfaction of such board, department, commissioner or officer, that the child applying therefor has regularly attended at a school in which reading, spelling, writing, arithmetic, English grammar and geography are taught, or upon equivalent instruction by a competent teacher elsewhere than at a school, for a period equal to one school year, during the year previous to his arriving at the age of fourteen years, or during the year previous to applying for such certificate, and is able to read and write simple sentences in the English language.

The principal or chief executive officer of a school, or teacher elsewhere than at a school, shall furnish, upon demand, to a child who has attended at such school or been instructed by such teacher, or to the factory inspector, his assistant or deputies, a certificate stating the school attendance of such child.

§ 74. Vacation certificates.—A child of fourteen years of age, who can read and write simple sentences in the English language, may be employed in a factory during the vacation of the public schools of the city or school district where such child resides upon complying with all the provisions of the foregoing sections, except that requiring school attendance. The certificate issued to such child shall be designated a " vacation certificate," and no employer shall employ a child to whom such a certificate has been issued, to work in a factory at any time other than the time of the vacation of the public school in the city or school district where such factory is situated.

§ 75. Report of certificates issued.—The board or department of health or health commissioner of a city, village or town, shall transmit, between the first and tenth day of each month, to the office of the factory inspector a list of the names of the children to whom certificates have been issued.

§ 76. Registry of children employed.—Each person owning or operating a factory and employing children therein shall keep, or cause to be kept in the office of such factory, a register, in which shall be recorded the name, birthplace, age and place of residence of all children so employed under the age of sixteen years.

Such register and the certificates filed in such office shall be produced for inspection, upon the demand of the factory inspector, his assistant or deputies.

§ 77. Hours of labor of minors.—A female under the age of twenty-one years or a male under the age of eighteen years shall

not be employed at labor in any factory in this state before six
o'clock in the morning or after nine o'clock in the evening of any
day, or for more than ten hours in any one day or sixty hours in
any one week, except to make a shorter work day on the last day
of the week; or more hours in any one week than will make an
average of ten hours per day for the whole number of days
so worked.   A printed notice stating the number of hours
per day for each day of the week required of such persons, and the
time when such work shall begin and end, shall be kept posted in
a conspicuous place in each room where they are employed.

But such persons may begin their work after the time for
beginning and stop before the time for ending such work, mentioned in such notice, but they shall not be required to perform
any labor in such factory, except as stated therein.   The terms of
such notice shall not be changed after the beginning of labor on
the first day of the week without the consent of the factory inspector.

§ 78. **Change of hours of labor of minors.**—When, in order to
make a shorter work day on the last day of the week, a female
under twenty-one, or a male under eighteen years of age, is to be
required or permitted to work in a factory more than ten hours in
a day, the employer of such persons shall notify the factor inspector, in writing, of such intention, stating the number of hours
of labor per day, which it is proposed to require or permit, and the
time when it is proposed to cease such requirement or permission; a similar notification shall be made when such requirement
or permission has actually ceased.   A record of the names of the
employes thus required or permitted to work overtime, with the
amount of such overtime and the days upon which such work was
performed, shall be kept in the office of such factory, and produced upon the demand of the factory inspector.

§ 79. **Enclosure and operation of elevators and hoisting shafts;
inspection.**—If, in the opinion of the factory inspector, it is necessary to protect the life or limbs of factory employes, the owner,
agent, or lessee of such factory where an elevator, hoisting
shafts, or well hole is used, shall cause, upon written notice
from the factory inspector, the same to be properly and substantially enclosed, secured or guarded, and shall provide such
proper traps or automatic doors so fastened in or at all elevator
ways, except passenger elevators enclosed on all sides, as to form
a substantial surface when closed and so constructed as to open

and close by action of the elevator in its passage either ascending or descending. The factory inspector may inspect the cable, gearing or other apparatus of elevators in factories and require them to be kept in a safe condition.

No child under the age of fifteen years shall be employed or permitted to have the care, custody or management of or to operate an elevator in a factory, nor shall any person under the age of eighteen years be employed or permitted to have the care, custody or management of or to operate an elevator therein, running at a speed of over two hundred feet a minute.

§ 80. **Stairs and doors.**—Proper and substantial hand rails shall be provided on all stairways in factories. The steps of such stairs shall be covered with rubber, securely fastened thereon, if in the opinion of the factory inspector the safety of employes would be promoted thereby. The stairs shall be properly screened at the sides and bottom. All doors leading in or to any such factory shall be so constructed as to open outwardly where practicable, and shall not be locked, bolted or fastened during working hours.

§ 81. **Protection of employes operating machinery.**—The owner or person in charge of a factory where machinery is used, shall provide, in the discretion of the factory inspector, belt-shifters or other mechanical contrivances for the purpose of throwing on or off belts or pulleys. Whenever practicable, all machinery shall be provided with loose pulleys. All vats, pans, saws, planers, cogs, gearing, belting, shafting, set-screws and machinery, of every description, shall be properly guarded. No person shall remove or make ineffective any safeguard around or attached to machinery, vats or pans, while the same are in use, unless for the purpose of immediately making repairs thereto, and all such safeguards so removed shall be promptly replaced. Exhaust fans of sufficient power shall be provided for the purpose of carrying off dust from emery wheels, grindstones and other machinery creating dust. If a machine or any part thereof is in a dangerous condition or is not properly guarded, the use thereof may be prohibited by the factory inspector, and a notice to that effect shall be attached thereto. Such notice shall not be removed until the machine is made safe and the required safeguards are provided, and in the meantime such unsafe or dangerous machinery shall not be used. When, in the opinion of the factory inspector, it is necessary, the halls leading to workrooms shall be properly lighted. No male person under eighteen years of age or woman under twenty-one shall be permitted or directed to clean machinery while in motion.

§ 82. Fire escapes.—Such fire escapes as may be deemed necessary by the factory inspector shall be provided on the outside of every factory in this state consisting of three or more stories in height. Each escape shall connect with each floor above the first, and shall be of sufficient strength, well fastened and secured, and shall have landings or balconies not less than six feet in length and three feet in width, guarded by iron railings not less than three feet in height, embracing at least two windows at each story and connected with the interior by easily accessible and unobstructed openings. The balconies or landings shall be connected by iron stairs, not less than eighteen inches wide, with steps of not less than six inches tread, placed at a proper slant and protected by a well-secured hand-rail on both sides, and shall have a drop ladder not less than twelve inches wide reaching from the lower platform to the ground.

The windows or doors to the landing or balcony of each fire escape shall be of sufficient size and located as far as possible, consistent with accessibility from the stairways and elevator hatchways or openings, and a ladder from such fire escape shall extend to the roof. Stationary stairs or ladders shall be provided on the inside of every factory from the upper story to the roof, as a means of escape in case of fire.

§ 83. Factory inspector may order erection of fire escapes.— Any other plan or style of fire escape shall be sufficient if approved in writing by the factory inspector. If there is no fire escape, or the fire escape in use is not approved by the factory inspector, he may, by a written order served upon the owner, proprietor or lessee of any factory, or the agent or superintendent thereof, or either of them, require one or more fire escapes to be provided therefor, at such locations and of such plan and style as shall be specified in such order.

Within twenty days after the service of such order, the number of fire escapes required therein shall be provided, each of which shall be of the plan and style specified in the order, or of the plan and style described in the preceding section.

§ 84. Walls and ceilings.— The walls and ceilings of each workroom in a factory shall be lime washed or painted, when in the opinion of the factory inspector, it will be conducive to the health or cleanliness of the persons working therein.

§ 85. **Size of rooms.**—No more employes shall be required or permitted to work in a room in a factory between the hours of six o'clock in the morning and six o'clock in the evening than will allow to each of such employes, not less than two hundred and fifty cubic feet of air space; and, unless by a written permit of the factory inspector, not less than four hundred cubic feet for each employe, so employed between the hours of six o'clock in the evening and six o'clock in the morning, provided such room is lighted by electricity at all times during such hours, while persons are employed therein.

§ 86. **Ventilation.**—The owner, agent or lessee of a factory shall provide, in each workroom thereof, proper and sufficient means of ventilation; in case of failure the factory inspector shall order such ventilation to be provided. Such owner, agent or lessee shall provide such ventilation within twenty days after the service upon him of such order, and in case of failure, shall forfeit to the people of the state, ten dollars for each day after the expiration of such twenty days, to be recovered by the factory inspector, in his name of office.

§ 87. **Accidents to be reported.**—The person in charge of any factory, shall report in writing to the factory inspector all accidents or injuries sustained by any person therein, within forty-eight hours after the time of the accident, stating as fully as possible the extent and cause of the injury, and the place where the injured person has been sent, with such other information relative thereto as may be required by the factory inspector who may investigate the cause of such accident, and require such precautions to be taken as will, in his judgment, prevent the recurrence of similar accidents.

§ 88. **Wash-room and water-closets.**—Every factory shall contain a suitable, convenient and separate water-closet or water-closets for each sex, which shall be properly screened, ventilated and kept clean and free from all obscene writing or marking; and also a suitable and convenient wash-room. The water-closets used by women shall have separate approaches. If women or girls are employed, a dressing-room shall be provided for them, when required by the factory inspector.

§ 89. **Time allowed for meals.**—In each factory at least sixty minutes shall be allowed for the noon-day meal, unless the factory inspector shall permit a shorter time. Such permit must be in writing and conspicuously posted in the main entrance of the factory, and may be revoked at any time. Where employes are required or permitted to work overtime for more than one hour after six o'clock in the evening, they shall be allowed at least twenty minutes to obtain a lunch, before beginning to work overtime.

§ 90. **Inspection of factory buildings.**— The factory inspector, or other competent person designated by him, upon request, shall examine any factory outside of the cities of New York and Brooklyn, to determine whether it is in a safe condition. If it appears to him to be unsafe, he shall immediately notify the owner, agent or lessee thereof, specifying the defects, and require such repairs and improvements to be made as he may deem necessary. If the owner, agent or lessee shall fail to comply with such requirement, he shall forfeit to the people of the state the sum of fifty dollars, to be recovered by the factory inspector in his name of office.

ARTICLE VII.
TENEMENT-MADE ARTICLES.

Section 100. Manufacture of articles in tenements.
  101. Register of persons to whom work is given.
  102. Goods unlawfully manufactured to be labeled.
  103. Powers and duties of boards of health relative to tenement-made articles.
  104. Owners of tenements and dwelling-houses not to permit the unlawful use thereof.
  105. Copy of articles to be posted.

§ 100. **Manufacture of articles in tenements.**— No room or apartment in a tenement or dwelling-house shall be used, except by the immediate members of the family living therein, for the manufacture of coats, vests, trousers, knee pants, overalls, cloaks, hats, caps, suspenders, jerseys, blouses, waists, waistbands, underwear, neckwear, furs, fur trimmings, fur garments, shirts, skirts, purses, feathers, artificial flowers, cigarettes or cigars. No person shall be employed to work in a room or apartment of a building in the rear of a tenement or dwelling-house at manufacturing any of such articles, without first obtaining from the factory inspector a written permit stating the maximum number of employes allowed to work therein. Before such permit shall be granted, an inspection of the premises must be made by the factory inspector. Such notice must be framed and posted in a conspicuous place in each room or apartment to which it relates. It may be revoked by the factory inspector if the health of the community or of the employes requires it.

§ 101. **Register of persons to whom work is given.**— Persons contracting for the manufacture of such articles, or giving out material from which they or any part of them are to be manufactured, shall keep a written register of the names and addresses of the persons to whom such work is given to be made, or with whom they have contracted to do the same. Such register shall be subject to inspection by the factory inspector, and a copy thereof shall be furnished on his demand.

§ 102. **Goods unlawfully manufactured to be labeled.**— Such articles manufactured contrary to the provisions of this section shall not be knowingly sold or exposed for sale by any person.

The factory inspector shall conspicuously affix to any such article found to be unlawfully manufactured, a label containing the words "tenement made," printed in small pica capital letters on a tag not less than four inches in length, and an officer finding such article shall notify the person owning or alleging to own such article that he has so labeled it. No person shall remove or deface any tag or label so affixed.

§ 103. **Powers and duties of boards of health relative to tenement-made articles.**— If the factory inspector discovers any of the articles mentioned in this article to be made under unclean or unhealthful conditions, he shall affix to such articles the label prescribed in the preceding section, and immediately report to the local board of health, who shall disinfect such articles, if necessary, and thereupon remove such label. If the factory inspector is convinced that infectious or contagious diseases exist in a workshop, or that articles manufactured or in process of manufacture therein are infected, or that goods used therein are unfit for use, he shall report to the local board of health, and such board shall issue such order as the public health may require. Such board may condemn and destroy all such infected articles or articles manufactured or in the process of manufacture under unclean or unhealthful conditions.

§ 104. **Owners of tenement and dwelling-houses not to permit the unlawful use thereof.**— The owner, lessee or agent of a tenement or dwelling-house shall not permit the use thereof for the manufacture of any of the articles mentioned in this article contrary to its provisions. If a room or apartment in such tenement or dwelling-house be so unlawfully used, the factory inspector shall serve a notice thereof upon such owner, lessee or agent.

Unless such owner, lessee or agent shall cause such unlawful manufacture to be discontinued within thirty days after the service of such notice, or, within fifteen days thereafter, institutes and faithfully prosecutes proceedings for the dispossession of the occupant of a tenement or dwelling-house, who unlawfully manufactures such articles in any room or apartment therein, he shall be deemed guilty of a violation of this article, as if he, himself, was engaged in such unlawful manufacture.

The unlawful manufacture of any of such articles by the occupant of a room or apartment of a tenement or dwelling-house, shall be a cause for dispossessing such occupant by summary proceedings to recover possession of real property, as provided in the Code of Civil Procedure.

§ 105. Copy of article to be posted.—A copy of articles five, six and seven shall be posted in a conspicuous place in each workroom of every factory where persons are employed who are affected by the provisions thereof.

ARTICLE VIII.
BAKERIES AND CONFECTIONERY ESTABLISHMENTS.

Section 110. Hours of labor in bakeries and confectionery establishments.

> 111. Drainage and plumbing of buildings and rooms occupied by bakeries.
>
> 112. Requirements as to rooms, furniture, utensils and manufactured products.
>
> 113. Wash-rooms and closets; sleeping places.
>
> 114. Inspection of bakeries.
>
> 115. Notice requiring alterations.

§ 110. Hours of labor in bakeries and confectionery establishments.—No employe shall be required or permitted to work in a biscuit, bread or cake bakery or confectionery establishment more than sixty hours in any one week, or more than ten hours in any one day, unless for the purpose of making a shorter work day on the last day of the week; nor more hours in any one week than will make an average of ten hours per day for the number of days during such week in which such employe shall work.

§ 111. Drainage and plumbing of buildings and rooms occupied by bakeries.—All buildings or rooms occupied as biscuit, bread, pie or cake bakeries, shall be drained and plumbed in a manner conducive to the proper and healthful sanitary condition thereof, and shall be constructed with air shafts, windows or ventilating pipes, sufficient to insure ventilation. The factory inspector may direct the proper drainage, plumbing and ventilation of such rooms or buildings. No cellar or basement, not now used for a bakery shall hereafter be so occupied or used, unless the proprietor shall comply with the sanitary provisions of this article.

§ 112. Requirements as to rooms, furniture, utensils and manufactured products.—Every room used for the manufacture of flour or meal food products shall be at least eight feet in height and shall have, if deemed necessary by the factory inspector, an impermeable floor constructed of cement, or of tiles laid in cement, or an additional flooring of wood properly saturated with linseed oil. The side walls of such rooms shall be plastered or wainscoted. The factory inspector may require the side walls and ceiling to be whitewashed, at least once in three months. He may also require the wood work of such walls to be painted. The furniture and utensils shall be so arranged as to be readily cleansed and not prevent the proper cleaning of any part of a room. The manufactured flour or meal food products shall be kept in dry and airy rooms so arranged that the floors, shelves and all other facilities for storing the same can be properly cleaned. No domestic animals, except cats, shall be allowed to remain in a room used as a biscuit, bread, pie, or cake bakery or any room in such bakery where flour or meal products are stored.

§ 113. Wash room and closets; sleeping places.— Every such bakery shall be provided with a proper wash-room and water-closet or water-closets apart from the bake-room, or rooms where the manufacture of such food product is conducted, and no water-closet, earth-closet, privy or ash-pit shall be within or connected directly with the bake-room of any bakery, hotel or public restaurant.

No person shall sleep in a room occupied as a bake-room. Sleeping places for the persons employed in the bakery shall be separate from the rooms where flour or meal food products are manufactured or stored. If the sleeping places are on the same floor where such products are manufactured, stored or sold, the factory inspector may inspect and order them put in a proper sanitary condition.

§ 114. Inspection of bakeries.—The factory inspector shall cause all bakeries to be inspected. If it be found upon such inspection that the bakeries so inspected are constructed and conducted in compliance with the provisions of this chapter, the factory inspector shall issue a certificate to the persons owning or conducting such bakeries.

§ 115. Notice requiring alterations.—If, in the opinion of the factory inspector, alterations are required in or upon premises occupied and used as bakeries, in order to comply with the provisions of this article, a written notice shall be served by him upon the owner, agent or lessee of such premises, either personally or by mail, requiring such alterations to be made within sixty days after such service, and such alterations shall be made accordingly.

ARTICLE IX.
MINES AND THEIR INSPECTION.

Section 120. Duties of factory inspector relating to mines; record and report.
121. Outlets of mines.
122. Ventilation and timbering of mines.
123. Riding on loaded cars; storage of inflammable supplies.
124. Inspection of steam boilers and apparatus; steam and water gauges.
125. Use of explosives; blasting.
126. Report of accidents.
127. Notice of dangerous condition.
128. Enforcement of article.
129. Admission of inspectors to mines.

Section 120. Duties of factory inspector relating to mines; record and report.— The factory inspector shall see that every necessary precaution is taken to insure the safety and health of employes employed in the mines and quarries of the state and shall prescribe rules and regulations therefor; keep a record of the names and location of such mines and quarries, and the names of the persons or corporations owning or operating the same; collect data concerning the working thereof; examine carefully into the method of timbering shafts, drifts, inclines, slopes and tunnels, through which employes and other persons pass, in the performance of their daily labor, and see that the persons or corporations owning and operating such mines and quarries comply with the provisions of this chapter; and such information shall be furnished by the person operating such mine or quarry, upon the demand of the factory inspector.

The factory inspector shall keep a record of all mine and quarry examinations, showing the date thereof, and the condition in which the mines and quarries are found, and the manner of working the same. He shall make an annual report to the legislature during the month of January, containing a statement of the number of mines and quarries visited, the number in operation, the number of men employed, and the number and cause of accidents, fatal and nonfatal, that may have occurred in and about the same.

§ 121. **Outlets of mines.**--If, in the opinion of the factory inspector, it is necessary for safety of employes, the owner, operator or superintendent of a mine, operating through either a vertical or oblique shaft, or a horizontal tunnel, shall not employ any person therein unless there are in connection with the subterranean workings thereof not less than two openings or outlets, at least one hundred and fifty feet apart, and connected with each other. Such openings or outlets shall be so constructed as to provide safe and distinct means of ingress and egress from and to the surface, at all times, for the use of the emloyes of such mine.

§ 122. **Ventilation and timbering of mines—** In each mine a ventilating current shall be conducted and circulated along the face of all working places and through the roadways, in sufficient quantities to insure the safety of employes and remove smoke and noxious gases.

Each owner, agent, manager or lessee of a mine shall cause it to be properly timbered, and the roof and sides of each working place therein properly secured. No person shall be required or permitted to work in an unsafe place or under dangerous material, except to make it secure.

§ 123. **Riding on loaded cars ; storage of inflammable supplies.** — No person shall ride or be permitted to ride on any loaded car, cage or bucket into or out of a mine. No powder or oils of any description shall be stored in a mine or quarry, or in or around shafts, engine or boiler-houses, and all supplies of an inflammable and destructive nature shall be stored at a safe distance from the mine openings.

§ 124. **Inspection of steam boilers and apparatus ; steam and water gauges.**—All boilers used in generating steam for mining purposes shall be kept in good order, and the owner, agent, manager or lessee of such mine shall have such boilers inspected by a competent person, approved by the factory inspector, once in six months, and shall file a certificate showing the result thereof in the mine office and a duplicate thereof in the office of the factory inspector. All engines, brakes, cages, buckets, ropes and chains shall be kept in good order and inspected daily by the superintendent of the mine or a person designated by him.

Each boiler or nest of boilers used in mining for generating steam, shall be provided with a proper safety valve and with steam and water gauges, to show, respectively, the pressure of steam and the height of water in the boilers. Every boiler-house in which a boiler or nest of boilers is placed, shall be provided with a steam gauge properly connected with the boilers, and another steam gauge shall be attached to the steam pipe in the engine-house, and so placed that the engineer or fireman can readily ascertain the pressure carried.

§ 125. Use of explosives; blasting.— When high explosives other than gunpowder are used in a mine or quarry, the manner of storing, keeping, moving, charging and firing, or in any manner using such explosives, shall be in accordance with rules prescribed by the factory inspector.

In charging holes for blasting, in slate, rock or ore in any mine or quarry, no iron or steel pointed needle or tamping bar shall be used, unless the end thereof is tipped with at least six inches of copper or other soft material. No person shall be employed to blast unless the mine superintendent or person having charge of such mine, is satisfied that he is qualified, by experience, to perform the work with ordinary safety. When a blast is about to be fired in a mine timely notice thereof shall be given by the person in charge of the work, to all persons who may be in danger therefrom.

§ 126. Report of accidents.—Whenever loss of life or serious accident shall occur in the operation of a mine or quarry, the owner, agent, manager or lessee thereof shall immediately report, in writing, all the facts connected therewith to the factory inspector.

§ 127. Notice of dangerous condition — If the factory inspector, after examination or otherwise, is of the opinion that a mine or anything used in the operation thereof, is unsafe, he shall immediately serve a written notice, specifying the defects, upon the owner, agent, manager or lessee, who shall forthwith remedy the same.

§ 128. Enforcement of article.— The factory inspector may serve a written notice upon the owner, agent, manager or lessee of a mine requiring him to comply with a specified provision of this article. The factory inspector may thereafter begin an action in the supreme court to enforce compliance with such provisions; and upon such notice as the court directs, an order may be granted, restraining the working of such mine during such time as may be therein specified.

§ 129. **Admission of inspectors to mines.**— The owner, agent, manager or lessee of a mine, at any time, either day or night, shall admit to such mine or any building used in the operation thereof, the factory inspector or any person duly authorized by him, for the purpose of making the examinations and inspections necessary for the enforcement of this article, and shall render any necessary assistance for such inspections.

ARTICLE X.
STATE BOARD OF MEDIATION AND ARBITRATION.

Section 140. **Organization of board.**—There shall continue to be a state board of mediation and arbitration, consisting of three competent persons to be known as arbitrators, appointed by the governor, by and with the advice and consent of the senate, each of whom shall hold his office for the term of three years, and receive an annual salary of three thousand dollars. The term of office of the successors of the members of such board in office when this chapter takes effect, shall be abridged so as to expire on the thirty-first day of December preceding the time when each such term would otherwise expire, and thereafter each term shall begin on the first day of January.

One member of such board shall belong to the political party casting the highest, and one to the party casting the next highest number of votes for governor at the last preceding gubernatorial election. The third shall be a member of an incorporated labor organization of this state.

Two members of such board shall constitute a quorum for the transaction of business, and may hold meetings at any time or place within the state. Examinations or investigations ordered by the board may be held and taken by and before any of their number, if so directed, but a decision rendered in such a case shall not be deemed conclusive until approved by the board.

§ 141. **Secretary and his duties.**—The board shall appoint a secretary, whose term of office shall be three years. He shall keep a full and faithful record of the proceedings of the board, and all documents and testimony forwarded by the local boards of arbitration, and shall perform such other duties as the board may prescribe. He may, under the direction of the board, issue subpoenas and administer oaths in all cases before the board, and call for and examine books, papers and documents of any parties to the controversy.

He shall receive an annual salary of two thousand dollars, payable in the same manner as that of the members of the board.

§ 142. **Arbitration by the board.**—A grievance or dispute between an employer and his employes may be submitted to the board of arbitration and mediation for their determination and settlement. Such submission shall be in writing, and contain a statement in detail of the grievance or dispute and the cause thereof, and also an agreement to abide the determination of the board, and during the investigation to continue in business or at work, without a lock-out or strike.

Upon such submission, the board shall examine the matter in controversy. For the purpose of such inquiry they may subpoena witnesses, compel their attendance and take and hear testimony. Witnesses shall be allowed the same fees as in courts of record. The decision of the board must be rendered within ten days after the completion of the investigation.

§ 143. **Mediation in case of strike or lock-out.**—Whenever a strike or lock-out occurs or is seriously threatened, the board shall proceed as soon as practicable to the locality thereof, and endeavor by mediation to effect an amicable settlement of the controversy. It may inquire into the cause thereof, and for that purpose has the same power as in the case of a controversy submitted to it for arbitration.

§ 144. **Decisions of board.**—Within ten days after the completion of every examination or investigation authorized by this article, the board or a majority thereof shall render a decision, stating such details as will clearly show the nature of the controversy and the points disposed of by them, and make a written report of their findings of fact and of their recommendations to each party to the controversy.

Every decision and report shall be filed in the office of the board and a copy thereof served upon each party to the controversy, and in case of a submission to arbitration, a copy shall be filed in the office of the clerk of the county or counties where the controversy arose.

§ 145. Annual report.—The board shall make an annual report to the legislature, and shall include therein such statements and explanations as will disclose the actual work of the board, the facts relating to each controversy considered by them and the decision thereon together with such suggestions as to legislation as may seem to them conducive to harmony in the relations of employers and employes.

§ 146. Submission of controversies to local arbitrators.—A grievance or dispute between an employer and his employes may be submitted to a board of arbitrators, consisting of three persons, for hearing and settlement. When the employes concerned are members in good standing of a labor organization, which is represented by one or more delegates in a central body, one arbitrator may be appointed by such central body and one by the employer. The two so designated shall appoint a third, who shall be chairman of the board.

If the employes concerned in such grievance or dispute are members of good standing of a labor organization which is not represented in a central body, the organization of which they are members may select and designate one arbitrator. If such employes are not members of a labor organization, a majority thereof at a meeting duly called for that purpose, may designate one arbitrator for such board.

§ 147. Consent; oath; powers of arbitrators.—Before entering upon his duties, each arbitrator so selected shall sign a consent to act and take and subscribe an oath to faithfully and impartially discharge his duties as such arbitrator, which consent and oath shall be filed in the clerk's office of the county or counties where the controversy arose. When such board is ready for the transaction of business, it shall select one of its members to act as secretary, and notice of the time and place of hearing shall be given to the parties to the controversy.

The board may, through its chairman subpoena witnesses, compel their attendance and take and hear testimony.

The board may make and enforce rules for its government and the transaction of the business before it, and fix its sessions and adjournments.

§ 148. Decision of arbitrators.—The board shall, within ten days after the close of the hearing, render a written decision signed by them giving such details as clearly show the nature of the controversy and the questions decided by them. Such decision shall be a settlement of the matter submitted to such arbitrators, unless within ten days thereafter an appeal is taken therefrom to the state board of mediation and arbitration.

One copy of the decision shall be filed in the office of the clerk of the county or counties where the controversy arose and one copy shall be transmitted to the secretary of the state board of mediation and arbitration.

§ 149. Appeals.—The state board of mediation and arbitration shall hear, consider and investigate every appeal to it from any such board of local arbitrators and its decisions shall be in writing and a copy thereof filed in the clerk's office of the county or counties where the controversy arose and duplicate copies served upon each party to the controversy. Such decision shall be final and conclusive upon all parties to the arbitration.

ARTICLE XI.

EMPLOYMENT OF WOMEN AND CHILDREN IN MERCANTILE ESTABLISHMENTS.

§ 160. **Application of article.**—The provisions of this article shall apply to all villages and cities which at the last preceding state enumeration had a population of three thousand or more.

§ 161. **Hours of labor of minors.**—No male employe, under sixteen years of age, and no female employe, under twenty-one years of age, shall be required to work in any mercantile establishment more than sixty hours in any one week, nor more than ten hours in any one day, unless for the purpose of making a shorter work day of some one day of the week, nor shall any such employe be required or permitted to work before seven o'clock in the morning or after ten o'clock in the evening of any day. This section does not apply to the employment of such persons on Saturday, provided the total number of hours of labor in a week of any such person does not exceed sixty hours, nor to the employment of such persons between the fifteenth day of December and the following first day of January. Not less than forty-five minutes shall be allowed for the noon-day meal of the employes of any such establishment.

§ 162. **Employment of children.**—A child under the age of fourteen years shall not be employed in any mercantile establishment, except that a child upwards of twelve years of age may be employed therein during the vacation of the public schools of the city or district where such establishment is situated. No child under the age of sixteen years shall be employed in any mercantile establishment, unless such child shall produce a certificate issued as provided in this article, to be filed in the office of such establishment.

§ 163. **Certificate for employment; how issued.**—Such certificate shall be issued by the executive officer of the board, department or commissioner of health of the city, town or village, where such child resides or is to be employed, or by such other officer thereof as may be designated, by resolution for that purpose, upon the application of the child desiring such employment. At the time of making such application there shall be filed with such board, department, commissioner or officer, the affidavit of the parent or guardian of such child or the person standing in parental relation thereto, showing the date and place of birth of such child. Such certificate shall not be issued unless the officer issuing the same, is satisfied that such child is fourteen years of age or upwards, and is physically able to perform the work, which he intends to do. No fee shall be demanded or received for administering an oath as required by this section.

§164. Contents of certificate.—Such certificate shall state the date and place of birth of the child, if known, and describe the color of the hair and eyes, the height and weight and any distinguishing facial marks of such child, and that, in the opinion of the officer issuing such certificate, such child is upwards of fourteen years of age, and is physically able to perform the work which he intends to do.

§ 165. School attendance required.—No such certificate shall be issued unless it appears to the satisfaction of such board, department, commissioner or officer, that the child applying therefor has regularly attended at a school in which reading, spelling, writing, arithmetic, English grammar and geography are taught, or upon equivalent instruction by a competent teacher elsewhere than at a school, for a period equal in length to one school year, during the year previous to his arriving at the age of fourteen years, or during the year previous to applying for such certificate, and is able to read and write simple sentences in the English language.

The principal or other executive officer of a school at which a child has been in attendance, or the teacher who has instructed such child elsewhere than at a school, shall furnish to such child or to the board or department of health, or health officer or commissioner, upon demand, a statement of the school attendance of such child.

§ 166. Employment of children during vacations of public schools.—Children of the age of twelve years or more who can read and write simple sentences in the English language may be employed in mercantile establishments during the vacation of the public schools in the city or school district where such children reside, upon complying with all the provisions of this section, except that requiring school attendance. Certificates, to be designated as "vacation certificates," may be issued to such children in the same form, containing the same statements and issued by the same officers as the other certificates required by this article. Such vacation certificate shall specify the time in which the child may be employed in a mercantile establishment, which in no case shall be other than the time in which the public schools where such children reside, are closed for a vacation.

§ 167. Registry of children employed.— The owner, manager or agent of a mercantile establishment employing children, shall keep, or cause to be kept, in the office of such establishment, a register, in which shall be recorded the name, birthplace, age and place of residence of all children so employed under the age of sixteen years.

Such register and the certificates filed in such office shall be produced for inspection, upon the demand of an officer of the board, department or commissioner of health of the town, village or city where such establishment is situated.

§ 168. Wash-rooms and water-closets.— Suitable and proper wash-rooms and water-closets shall be provided in, adjacent to or connected with mercantile establishments where women and children are employed. Such rooms and closets shall be so located and arranged as to be easily accessible to the employes of such establishments.

Such water-closets shall be properly screened and ventilated, and, at all times, kept in a clean condition. The water-closets assigned to the female employes of such establishments shall be separate from those assigned to the male employes.

If a mercantile establishment has not provided wash-rooms and water-closets, as required by this section, the board or department of health or health commissioners of the town, village or city where such establishment is situated, shall cause to be served upon the owner of the building occupied by such establishment, a written notice of the omission and directing such owner to comply with the provisions of this section respecting such wash-rooms and water-closets.

Such owner shall, within fifteen days after the receipt of such notice, cause such wash-rooms and water-closets to be provided.

§ 169. Lunch-rooms.— If a lunch-room is provided in a mercantile establishment where females are employed, such lunch-room shall not be next to or adjoining the water-closets, unless permission is first obtained from the board or department of health or health commissioners of the town, village or city where such mercantile establishment is situated. Such permission shall be granted unless it appears that proper sanitary conditions do not exist, and it may be revoked at any time by the board or department of health or health commissioner, if it appears that such lunch-room is kept in a manner or in a part of the building injurious to the health of the employes.

§ 170. Seats for women in mercantile establishments.— Chairs stools or other suitable seats shall be maintained in mercantile establishments for the use of female employes therein, to the number of at least one seat for every three females employed, and the use thereof by such employes shall be allowed at such times and to such extent as may be necessary for the preservation of their health. If the duties of the female employes, for the use of whom the seats are furnished, are to be principally performed in front of a counter, table, desk or fixture, such seats shall be placed in front thereof; if such duties are to be principally performed behind such counter, table, desk or fixture, such seats shall be placed behind the same.

§ 171. Employment of women and children in basements.— Women or children shall not be employed or directed to work in the basement of a mercantile establishment, unless permitted by the board or department of health, or health commissioner of the town, village or city where such mercantile establishment is situated. Such permission shall be granted unless it appears that such basement is not sufficiently lighted and ventilated, and is not in good sanitary condition.

§ 172. Enforcement of article.— The board or department of health or health commissioners of a town, village or city affected by this article shall enforce the same and prosecute all violations thereof. Proceedings to prosecute such violations must be begun within thirty days after the alleged offense was committed. All officers and members of such boards or department, all health commissioners, inspectors and other persons appointed or designated by such boards, departments or commissioners may visit and inspect, at reasonable hours and when practicable and necessary, all mercantile establishments within the town, village or city for which they are appointed. No person shall interfere with or prevent any such officer from making such visitations and inspections, nor shall he be obstructed or injured by force or otherwise while in the performance of his duties. All persons connected with any such mercantile establishment shall properly answer all questions asked by such officer or inspector in reference to any of the provisions of this article.

§ 173. Copy of article to be posted.— A copy of this article shall be posted in three conspicuous places in each mercantile establishment affected by its provisions.

ARTICLE XII.

EXAMINATION AND REGISTRATION OF HORSESHOERS.

§ 180. **Application of article.**— This article applies to all cities of the first and second class.

§ 181. **Board of examiners.**— There shall continue to be a board of examiners of horseshoers consisting of one veterinarian, two master horseshoers and two journeyman horseshoers, all of whom shall be citizens and residents of cities of the first or second class. The examiners in office when this chapter takes effect shall continue therein until the thirty-first day of December following the date of the expiration of the terms for which they were respectively appointed, and thereafter their successors shall be appointed by the governor for a term of five years.

§ 182. **Examination of applicants.**— The board of examiners shall, as often as necessary, hold sessions in the cities affected by this article for the purpose of examining applicants, desiring to practice as master or journeyman horseshoers. A person is not qualified to take such examination unless he has served an apprenticeship at horseshoeing for at least three years.

If the person examined is shown to be qualified to practice horseshoeing, the board shall issue to him a certificate stating his name and residence, the time when examined, when and where his apprenticeship was served, and that he is qualified to practice as a master or journeyman horseshoer.

Before he is entitled to be examined, an applicant must file with the board a written application stating his name, place of residence, and when, where and with whom his apprenticeship has been served.

The board shall receive as compensation a fee of five dollars from each person examined.

§ 183. **Registration of horseshoers.**— Each journeyman or master horseshoer shall present such certificate to the clerk of the county where he proposes to practice, and such clerk shall cause his name, residence and place of business to be registered in a book to be

known as the "master and journeyman horseshoers' register."
For each name so registered, the clerk is entitled to a fee of twenty-
five cents. No person shall practice horseshoeing as a master or
journeyman horseshoer in a city of the first or second class unless
he is registered and has a certificate, as provided by this article.

§ 184. **Practice without examination.**— A person who has practiced as a master or journeyman horseshoer outside a city of the
first or second class and within the United States continuously
for a period of three years may present to the board of examiners
his affidavit, stating his name, age, place of residence and when
and where he has practiced as such horseshoer. The board shall
thereupon issue to him a certificate stating the facts set forth in
such affidavit, and that such person is entitled to practice as a
master or journeyman horseshoer, as the case may be.

The person to whom the certificate is issued shall present it to
the county clerk of the county where he intends to practice, and
his name shall be registered, as provided in the preceding section.
Such person may thereafter practice as a master or journeyman
horseshoer in such county without examination.

The board is entitled to a fee of one dollar for each certificate
issued under this section.

ARTICLE XIII.
LAWS REPEALED; WHEN TO TAKE EFFECT.

Section 190. Laws repealed.
     191. When to take effect.

Section 190. **Laws repealed.**—Of the laws enumerated in the
schedule hereto annexed, that portion specified in the third column
thereof is repealed.

§ 191. **When to take effect.**— This chapter shall take effect the
first day of June, eighteen hundred and ninety-seven.

SCHEDULE OF LAWS REPEALED.

Laws of	Sections.	Subject of act.
1870, ch. 385....	All, except § 4.......	Hours of labor regulated.
1871, ch. 934....	3..................	Duties of factory inspector as to apprentices.
1881, ch. 298....	All, except § 2.......	Seats for female employes.

Laws of	Sections.	Subject of act.
1883, ch. 356....	All, except § 3.......	Bureau of labor statistics.
1885, ch. 314....	All.................	Scaffolding for use of employes on buildings.
1885, ch. 376....	All.................	Payment of wages by receiver of corporations.
1886, ch. 151....	All.................	Hours of labor on street, surface and elevated railroads in cities of over 500,000.
1886, ch. 409....	All, except first § 21..	Factory inspector; employment of children and women in factories, tenements, etc.
1886, ch. 410....	All.................	State board of arbitration and mediation. Superseded by L. 1887, ch. 63.
1887, ch. 63.....	All.................	State board of mediation and arbitration.
1887, ch. 462....	All.................	Amends L. 1886, ch. 409.
1887, ch. 529....	All, except § 2.......	Hours of labor of employes of street, surface and elevated railroads in cities of over 100,000.
1888, ch. 437....	All.................	Amends L. 1871, ch. 934, § 3.
1889. ch. 380....	All.................	Preference to citizens of state as laborers on public works.
1889, ch. 381....	All.................	Cash payment of wages by corporation.
1889, ch. 385....	All.................	Registration of labels. etc., by trades unions.
1889, ch. 560....	All.................	Amends L. 1886, ch. 409.

Laws of	Sections.	Subject of act.
1890, ch. 388....	All, except § 2.......	Weekly payment of wages by corporations.
1890, ch. 394....	All, except §§ 8,13,20.	Inspection of mines.
1890, ch. 398....	All.................	Amends L. 1886, ch. 409.
1891, ch. 214....	All.................	Amends L. 1885, ch. 314.
1892, ch. 517....	All, except § 5.......	Examination of scaffoldings.
1892, ch. 667....	All, except § 2.......	Safety of workmen in mines.
1892, ch. 673....	All.................	Amends L. 1886, ch. 409.
1892, ch. 711....	All, except § 4.......	Hours of service on railroads.
1893, ch. 173....	All, except § 6........	Amends L. 1886, ch. 409.
1893, ch. 219....	All.................	Labels, etc., of trades unions.
1893, ch. 339....	All.................	Amends L. 1892, ch. 667.
1893, ch. 691....	All, except § 3.......	Hours of labor in brickyards.
1893, ch. 715....	All.................	Amends L. 1892, ch. 517.
1893, ch. 717....	All.................	Amends L. 1890, ch. 388.
1894, ch. 277....	All.................	Stone used in state or municipal works to be dressed within the state.
1894, ch. 373....	All.................	Badges of factory inspectors.
1894, ch. 622....	All.................	Amends L. 1870, ch. 385, § 2.
1894, ch. 699....	All, except § 8.......	Sale of convict-made goods.
1895, ch. 324....	All.................	Abolishes office of mining inspector.

Laws of	Sections.	Subject of act.
1895, ch. 413....	All.................	Amends L. 1894, ch. 277.
1895, ch. 518....	All, except § 7.......	Manufacture of flour and meal products.
1895, ch. 670....	All.................	Deputy mine inspector.
1895, ch. 765....	All.................	Amends L. 1892, ch. 667, § 1.
1895, ch. 899....	All.................	Payment of wages of employes of co-partnerships by receiver.
1896, ch. 271....	All, except § 6.......	Examination and registration of horseshoers.
1896, ch. 384....	All, except § 11......	Employment of women and children in mercantile establishments.
1896, ch. 672....	All.................	Amends L. 1895, ch. 518.
1896, ch. 789....	All.................	Amends L. 1893, ch. 691, § 2.
1896, ch. 931....	All, except §§ 5, 6....	Labeling and marking convict-made goods.
1896, ch. 936....	All, except § 5.......	Protection of persons employed on buildings in course of construction.
1896, ch. 982....	All, except § 6.......	Free employment bureaus.
1896, ch. 991....	All.................	Amends L. 1886, ch. 409.
1897, ch. 148....	All.................	Amends L. 1896, ch. 271, §§ 3, 4, 6.

Chap. 416.

AN ACT to amend the penal code, relative to violations of provisions of the labor law.

Became a law May 13, 1897, with the approval of the Governor.
Passed, three-fifths being present.

The People of the State of New York, represented in Senate and Assembly, do enact as follows:

Section 1. Sections 384-b and 447-a of the penal code are hereby amended to read as follows:

§ 384-b. Unlawful dealing in convict-made goods.—A person who

1. Sells or exposes for sale convict-made goods, wares or merchandise, without a license therefor, or having such license does not transmit to the secretary of state the statement required by article four of the labor law; or

2. Sells, offers for sale, or has in his possession for sale any such convict-made goods, wares or merchandise without the brand, mark or label required by article four of the labor law; or

3. Removes or defaces or in any way alters such brand, mark or label, is guilty of a misdemeanor, and upon conviction therefor shall be punished by a fine of not more than one thousand nor less than one hundred dollars, or by imprisonment for not less than ten days or by both such fine and imprisonment.

§ 447-a. Negligently furnishing insecure scaffolding.—A person or corporation employing or directing another to do or perform any labor in the erection, repairing, altering or painting, any house, building or structure within this state, who knowingly or negligently furnishes or erects or causes to be furnished or erected for the performance of such labor, unsafe, unsuitable or improper scaffolding, hoists, stays, ladders or other mechanical contrivances; or who hinders or obstructs any officer detailed to inspect the same, destroys or defaces any notice posted thereon, or permits the use thereof after the same has been declared unsafe by such officer contrary to the provisions of article one of the labor law, is guilty of a misdemeanor.

§ 2. The Penal Code is hereby amended by inserting at the end of title twelve the following new section:

§ 447-c. Neglect to complete or plank floors of buildings constructed in cities.—A person, constructing a building in a city, as owner or contractor, who violates the provisions of article one of the labor law, relating to the completing or laying of floors, or the planking of such floors or tiers of beams as the work of construction progresses, is guilty of a misdemeanor, and upon conviction therefor shall be punished by a fine for each offense of not less than twenty-five nor more than two hundred dollars.

§ 3. The Penal Code is hereby amended by inserting at the end of title eleven the following new sections:

§ 384-f. **Failure to furnish statistics to commissioner of labor statistics.**—Any person who refuses, when requested by the commissioner of labor statistics,

1. To admit him or a person authorized by him to a mine, factory, workshop, warehouse, elevator, foundry, machine shop or other manufacturing establishment; or,

2. To furnish him with information relative to his duties which may be in such person's possession or under his control; or,

3. To answer questions put by such commissioner in a circular or otherwise, or shall knowingly answer such questions untruthfully, is guilty of a misdemeanor, and on conviction therefor shall be punished by a fine of not less than fifty nor more than two hundred dollars.

§ 384-g. **Refusal to admit inspector to mines and quarries; failure to comply with requirements of inspector.**— A person,

1. Refusing to admit the factory inspector, or any person authorized by him, to a mine or quarry, for the purpose of examination and inspection.

2. Neglecting or refusing to comply with the provisions of article nine of the labor law upon written notice of the factory inspector, is guilty of a misdemeanor, and upon conviction therefor shall be punished by a fine of not less than fifty dollars, or by imprisonment for not less than thirty days.

§ 384-h. **Hours of labor to be required.**—Any person or corporation,

1. Who, contracting with the state or a municipal corporation, shall require more than eight hours work for a day's labor; or

2. Who shall require more than ten hours labor, including one-half hour for dinner, to be performed within twelve consecutive hours, by the employes of a street surface and elevated railway owned or operated by corporations whose main line of travel or routes lie principally within the corporate limits of cities of more than one hundred thousand inhabitants; or,

3. Who shall require the employes of a corporation owning or operating a brickyard to work more than ten hours in any one day

or to commence work before seven o'clock in the morning, unless by agreement between employer and employe; or,

4. Who shall require the employes of a corporation operating a line of railroad of thirty miles in length or over, in whole or in part within this state to work contrary to the requirements of article one of the labor law, is guilty of a misdemeanor, and on conviction therefor shall be punished by a fine of not less than five hui dred nor more than one thousand dollars for each offense. If any contractor with the state or a municipal corporation shall require more than eight hours for a days labor, upon conviction therefor in addition to such fine, the contract shall be forfeited at the option of the municipal corporation.

§ 384-i. **Payment of wages.**—A corporation or joint stock association or a person carrying on the business thereof, by lease or otherwise, who does not pay the wages of its employes in cash, weekly or monthly as provided in article one of the labor law, is guilty of a misdemeanor, and upon conviction therefor, shall be fined not less than twenty-five nor more than fifty dollars for each offense.

§ 384-j. **Failure to furnish seats for female employes.**—Any person employing females in a factory or mercantile establishment who does not provide and maintain suitable seats for the use of such employes and permit the use thereof by such employes to such an extent as may be reasonable for the preservation of their health, is guilty of a misdemeanor.

§ 384-k. **No fees to be charged for services rendered by free public employment bureaus.**—A person connected with or employed in a free public employment bureau, who shall charge or receive directly or indirectly, any fee or compensation from any person applying to such bureau for help or employment, is guilty of a misdemeanor.

§ 384-l. **Violations of provisions of labor law.**—Any person who violates or does not comply with:

1. The provisions of article six of the labor law, relating to factories and the employment of children therein;

2. The provisions of article seven of the labor law, relating to the manufacture of articles in tenements;

3. The provisions of article eight of the labor law, relating to bakeries and confectionery establishments, the employment of labor and the manufacture of flour or meal food products therein;

4. The provisions of article eleven of the labor law, relating to mercantile establishments, and the employment of women and

children therein is guilty of a misdemeanor, and upon conviction shall be punished for a first offense by a fine of not less than twenty nor more than one hundred dollars; for a second offense by a fine of not less than fifty nor more than two hundred dollars, or by imprisonment for not more than thirty days, or by both such fine and imprisonment; for a third offense by a fine of not less than two hundred and fifty dollars, or by imprisonment for not more than sixty days, or by both such fine and imprisonment.

§ 384-m. Illegal practice of horseshoeing.—A person who presents to a county clerk, for the purpose of registration, a certificate purporting to qualify him to practice horseshoeing in a city of the first or second class, which has been fraudulently obtained, or practices as a horseshoer in any such city without complying with the provisions of article twelve of the labor law, or violates or neglects to comply with any of such provisions, is guilty of a misdemeanor.

§ 4. The following parts of acts are hereby repealed:

Laws of	Chapter.	Section.
1870	385	4.
1871	298	2.
1883	356	3.
1886	409	21, first appearing.
1887	529	2.
1889	381	2.
1890	388	2.
1890	394	8, 20.
1892	517	5.
1892	667	2.
1893	691	3.
1894	699	8.
1895	518	7.
1896	271	6.
1896	384	11.
1896	936	5.
1896	982	6.

Chap. 417.

AN ACT in relation to personal property, constituting chapter forty-seven of the general laws.

Became a law May 13, 1897, with the approval of the Governor. Passed, a majority being present.

The People of the State of New York, represented in Senate and Assembly, do enact as follows:

CHAPTER XLVII OF THE GENERAL LAWS.

THE PERSONAL PROPERTY LAW.

Article I. Future estates; accumulation of income; trust estates. (§§ 1-9.)

II. Agreements not in writing; without consideration; fraudulent. (§§ 20-29.)

III. Laws repealed; when to take effect. (§§ 40-41.)

ARTICLE I.

FUTURE ESTATES; ACCUMULATION OF INCOME; TRUST ESTATES.

Section 1. Short title; definition.

2. Suspension of ownership.

3. Income of trust fund not alienable; merger.

4. Validity of directions for accumulation of income.

5. Anticipation of directed accumulation.

6. Power to bequeath executed by general provisions of will.

7. Disaffirmance of fraudulent acts by executors and others.

8. When trust vests in supreme court.

9. Investment of trust funds.

Section 1. Short title ; definition. — This chapter shall be known as the personal property law. The term " income of personal property," as used in this article, means the income or profits arising from personal property, and includes the interest of money and the produce of stock.

§ 2. Suspension of ownership. — The absolute ownership of personal property shall not be suspended by any limitation or condition, for a longer period than during the continuance and until the termination of not more than two lives in being at the date of the instrument containing such limitation or condition; or, if such instrument be a will, for not more than two lives in being at the death of the testator; in other respects limitations of future or contingent interests in personal property, are subject to the rules prescribed in relation to future estates in real property.

§ 3. **Income of trust fund not alienable ; merger.**— The right of the beneficiary to enforce the performance of a trust to receive the income of personal property, and to apply it to the use of any person, can not be transferred by assignment or otherwise; but the right and interest of the beneficiary of any other trust in personal property may be transferred. Whenever a beneficiary in a trust for the receipt of the income of personal property is entitled to a remainder in the whole or a part of the principal fund so held in trust, subject to his beneficial estate for a life or lives, or a shorter term, he may release his interest in such income, and thereupon the estate of the trustee shall cease in that part of such principal fund to which such beneficiary has become entitled in remainder, and such trust estate merges in such remainder.

§ 4. **Validity of directions for accumulation of income.**— An accumulation of the income of personal property, directed by any instrument sufficient in law to pass such property is valid:

1. If directed to commence from the date of the instrument, or the death of the person executing the same, and to be made for the benefit of one or more minors, then in being, or in being at such death, and to terminate at or before the expiration of their minority.

2. If directed to commence at any period subsequent to the date of the instrument or subsequent to the death of the person executing it, and directed to commence within the time allowed for the suspension of the absolute ownership of personal property, and at some time during the minority of the persons for whose benefit it is intended, and to terminate at or before the expiration of their minority.

All other directions for the accumulation of the income of personal property, not authorized by statute, are void; but a direction for any such accumulation for a longer term than the minority of the persons intended to be benefited thereby, has the same effect as if limited to the minority of such persons, and is void as respects the time beyond such minority.

§ 5. **Anticipation of directed accumulation.**— When a minor, for whose benefit a valid accumulation of the income of personal property has been directed, shall be destitute of other sufficient means of support or education, the supreme court, at special term in any case, or, if such accumulation shall have been directed by a will, the surrogate's court of the county in which such will shall have been admitted to probate, may, on the application of such minor or his guardian cause a suitable sum to be taken from the moneys accumulated or directed to be accumulated, to be applied for the support or education of such minor.

§ 6. **Power to bequeath executed by general provision in will.**— Personal property embraced in a power to bequeath, passes by a will purporting to pass all the personal property of the testator; unless the intent, that the will shall not operate as an execution of the power, appears therein either expressly or by necessary implication.

§ 7. **Disaffirmance of fraudulent acts by executors and others.**— An executor, administrator, receiver, assignee or trustee, may, for the benefit of creditors or others interested in personal property, held in trust, disaffirm, treat as void and resist any act done, or transfer or agreement made in fraud of the rights of any creditor, including himself, interested in such estate, or property, and a person who fraudulently receives, takes or in any manner interferes with the personal property of a deceased person, or an insolvent corporation, association, partnership or individual is liable to such executor, administrator, receiver or trustee for the same or the value thereof, and for all damages caused by such act to the trust estate. A creditor of a deceased insolvent debtor, having a claim against the estate of such debtor, exceeding in amount the sum of one hundred dollars, may, without obtaining a judgment on such claim, in like manner, for the benefit of himself and other creditors interested in said estate, disaffirm, treat as void and resist any act done or conveyance, transfer or agreement made in fraud of creditors or maintain an action to set aside such act, conveyance, transfer or agreement. Such claim, if disputed, may be established in such action. The judgment in such action may provide for the sale of the property involved, when a conveyance or transfer thereof is set aside, and that the proceeds thereof be brought into court or paid into the proper surrogate's court to be administered according to law.

§ 8. **When trust vests in supreme court.**— On the death of a surviving trustee of an express trust, the trust estate does not pass to his next of kin or personal representatives, but, if the trust be unexecuted, it vests in the supreme court and shall be executed by

some person appointed by the court, whom the court may invest
with all or any of the power and duties of the original trustee. The
beneficiary of the trust shall have such notice as the court may
direct of the application for the appointment of such person.

§ 9. **Investment of trust funds.**— An executor, administrator,
guardian, trustee or other person holding trust funds for investment may invest the same in the obligations of a city of this state
issued pursuant to law.

ARTICLE II.

AGREEMENTS NOT IN WRITING; WITHOUT CONSIDERATION; FRAUDULENT.

Section 20. Definitions.

    21. Agreements required to be in writing.

    22. Validity of certain agreements made without con-
        sideration.

    23. Transfers in trust for the transferrer.

    24. Transfers and charges with fraudulent intent.

    25. Sales and charges other than chattel mortgages with-
        out delivery and change of possession.

    26. Fraudulent intent a question of fact.

    27. Transfers or charges without consideration.

    28. Successors to rights of creditors and purchasers.

    29. Bona fide purchasers.

Section 20. **Definitions.**— As used in this article, the term transfer, includes sale, assignment, conveyance, deed and gift, and the
term agreement includes promise and undertaking.

§ 21. **Agreements required to be in writing.**—Every agreement,
promise or undertaking is void, unless it or some note or memorandum thereof be in writing, and subscribed by the party to be
charged therewith, or by his lawful agent, if such agreement,
promise or undertaking;

1. By its terms is not to be performed within one year from the
making thereof;

2. Is a special promise to answer for the debt, default or miscarriage of another person;

3. Is made in consideration of marriage, except mutual promises
to marry;

4. Is a conveyance or assignment of a trust in personal property;

F   ·equent or new promise to pay a debt discharged in

b

6. Is a contract for the sale of any goods, chattels or things in action for the price of fifty dollars or more, and the buyer does not accept and receive part of such goods, or the evidences, or some of them, of such things in action; nor at the time, pay any part of the purchase money.

If goods be sold at public auction, and the auctioneer at the time of the sale, enters in a sale book, a memorandum specifying the nature and price of the property sold, the terms of the sale, the name of the purchaser, and the name of the person on whose account the sale was made, such memorandum is equivalent in effect to a note of the contract or sale, subscribed by the party to be charged therewith.

§ 22. Validity of certain agreements made without consideration.— An agreement for the purchase, sale, transfer or delivery of a certificate or other evidence of debt, issued by the United States or by any state, or a municipal or other corporation, or of any share or interest in the stock of any bank corporation or joint stock association, incorporated or organized under the laws of the United States or of any state, is not void or voidable, for want of consideration, or because of the non-payment of consideration, or because the vendor, at the time of making such contract, is not the owner or possessor of the certificate or certificates or other evidence of debt, share or interest.

§ 23. Transfers in trust for the transferrer.—A transfer of personal property, made in trust for the use of the person making it, is void as against the existing or subsequent creditors of such person.

§ 24. Transfers and charges with fraudulent intent.— Every transfer of any interest in personal property, or the income thereof, and every charge on such property or income, made with the intent to hinder, delay or defraud creditors or other persons of their lawful suits, damages, forfeitures, debts or demands, and every bond or other evidence of debt given, suit commenced, or decree or judgment suffered, with such intent, is void as against every person so hindered, delayed or defrauded.

§ 25. Sales and charges other than chattel mortgages without delivery and change of possession.— Every sale of goods and chattels in the possession or under the control of the vendor, and every assignment of goods and chattels by way of security or on any condition, but not constituting a mortgage nor intended to operate as a mortgage, unless accompanied by an immediate delivery followed by actual and continued change of possession, is presumed to be fraudulent and void as against all persons who are creditors of the vendor or person making the sale or assignment, including all persons who are his creditors at any time while such goods or chattels remain in his possession or under his control or subsequent purchasers of such goods and chattels in good faith; and is conclusive evidence of such fraud, unless it appear, on the part of the person claiming, under the sale or assignment, that it was made in good faith, and without intent to defraud such creditors or purchasers.

But this section does not apply to a contract of bottomry or respondentia, or to an assignment of a vessel of goods at sea or in a foreign port.

§ 26. Fraudulent intent a question of fact.— The question of the existence of fraudulent intent in cases arising under this article, is a question of fact and not of law.

§ 27. Transfers or charges without consideration.—A transfer or charge shall not be adjudged fraudulent as against creditors or purchasers, solely on the ground that it was not founded on a valuable consideration.

§ 28. Successors to rights of creditors and purchasers —A transfer, charge, sale or assignment, or proceeding declared by this article, to be void, as against creditors or purchasers, is equally void as against the heirs, successors, personal representatives or assignees of such creditors or purchasers.

§ 29. Bona fide purchasers.— This article does not affect or impair the title of a purchaser or incumbrancer for a valuable consideration, unless it appear that such purchaser or incumbrancer had previous notice of the fraudulent intent of his immediate vendor, or of the fraud rendering void the title of such vendor.

ARTICLE III.
LAWS REPEALED; WHEN TO TAKE EFFECT.

Section 40. Laws repealed.
    41. When to take effect.

Section 40. Laws repealed.—The laws or parts thereof specified in the schedule hereto annexed, and all acts amendatory thereof are repealed.

§ 41. When to take effect.—This chapter shall take effect on the first day of October, eighteen hundred and ninety-seven.

SCHEDULE OF LAWS REPEALED.

R. S., pt. II, ch. 1, tit. II... § 63.... Powers over trust, of party interested.

R. S., pt. II, ch. 4, tit. IV .. All..... Accumulations of personal property.

R. S., pt. II, ch. 7, tit. II... All..... Fraudulent conveyances of personal property.

R. S., pt. II, ch. 7, tit. III.. All..... General provisions in relation to fraudulent conveyances.

Laws of —	Chapter.	Sections.	Subject matter.
1858....	134.....	All......	Legalizing the sale of stocks on time.
1858....	314.....	1, 2......	When trustees may impeach assignments.
1863....	464.....	All......	Amends R. S., pt. II, ch. 7, tit. II, § 2.
1882....	185.....	All......	Trustees of personal estates.
1882....	324.....	All......	Debts discharged in bankruptcy.
1889....	65.....	All......	Investment of trust funds in bonds or stocks of the cities of the state.
1889....	487.....	All......	Amends L. 1858, ch. 314, § 1.
1891....	173.....	All......	Amends R. S., pt. II, ch. 4, tit. IV, § 5.
1893....	452.....	All......	Amends R. S., pt. II, ch. 1, tit. II, § 63.
1894....	740.....	All......	Amends L. 1858, ch. 314, § 1.

Chap. 418.

AN ACT in relation to liens, constituting chapter forty-nine of the general laws.

Became a law May 13, 1897, with the approval of the Governor. Passed, a majority being present.

The People of the State of New York, represented in Senate and Assembly, do enact as follows:

CHAPTER XLIX OF THE GENERAL LAWS.

THE LIEN LAW.

ARTICLE I.

MECHANICS' LIENS.

Section 1. Short title.—This chapter shall be known as the lien law.

§ 2. Definitions.—The term " lienor," when used in this chapter, means any person having a lien upon property by virtue of its provisions, and includes his successor in interest. The term " real property," when used in this chapter, includes real estate, lands, tenements and hereditaments, corporeal and incorporeal, fixtures, and all bridges and trestle work, and structures connected therewith, erected for the use of railroads, and all oil or gas wells and structures and fixtures connected therewith, and any lease of oil lands or other right to operate for the production of oil or gas upon such lands, and the right or franchise granted by a municipal corporation for the use of the streets or public places thereof, and all structures placed thereon for the use of such right or franchise. The term " owner," when so used, includes the owner in fee of real property, or of a less estate therein, a lessee for a term of years, a vendee in possession under a contract for the purchase of such real property, and all persons having any right, title or interest in such real property, which may be sold under an execution in pursuance of the provisions of statutes relating to the enforcement of liens of judgment, and all persons having any right or franchise granted by a municipal corporation to use the streets and public places thereof, and any right, title or interest in and to such franchise. The purchaser of real property at a statutory or judicial sale shall be deemed the owner thereof, from the time of such sale. If the purchaser at such sale fails to complete the purchase, pursuant to the terms of the sale, all liens created by his consent after such sale shall be a lien on any deposit made by him and not on the real property sold. The term "improvement," when so used, includes the erection, alteration or repair of any structure upon, connected with, or beneath the surface of, any real property and any work done upon such property, or materials furnished for its permanent improvement. The term "public improvement," when so used, means an improvement upon any real property belonging to the state or a municipal corporation. The term "contractor," when so used, means a person who enters into a contract with the owner of real property for the improvement thereof. The term "sub-contractor," when so used, means a person who enters into a contract for the improvement of such real property with a contractor, or with a person who has contracted with or through such contractor, for the performance of his contract or any part thereof. The term "laborer," when so used, means any person who performs labor or services upon such improvement. The term "material man," when so used, means any person, other than a contractor, who furnishes material for such improvement.

§ 3. Mechanics' lien on real property.— A contractor, sub-contractor, laborer or material man, who performs labor or furnishes materials for the improvement of real property with the consent or at the request of the owner thereof, or of his agent, contractor or sub-contractor, shall have a lien for the principal and interest of the value, or the agreed price, of such labor or materials upon the real property improved or to be improved and upon such improvement, from the time of filing a notice of such lien as prescribed in this article.

§ 4. Extent of lien.—Such lien shall extend to the owner's right, title or interest in the real property and improvements, existing at the time of filing the notice of lien. If an owner assigns his interest in such real property by a general assignment for the benefit of creditors, within thirty days prior to such filing, the lien shall extend to the interest thus assigned. If any part of the real property subjected to such lien be removed by the owner or by any other person, at any time before the discharge thereof, such removal shall not affect the rights of the lienor, either in respect to the remaining real property, or the part so removed. If labor is performed for, or materials furnished to, a contractor or sub-contractor for an improvement, the lien shall not be for a sum greater than the sum earned and unpaid on the contract at the time of filing the notice of lien, and any sum subsequently earned thereon. In no case shall the owner be liable to pay by reason of all liens created pursuant to this article a sum greater than the value or agreed price of the labor and materials remaining unpaid, at the time of filing notices of such liens, except as hereinafter provided.

§ 5. **Liens under contracts for public improvements.**—A person performing labor for or furnishing materials to a contractor, his sub-contractor or legal representative, for the construction of a public improvement pursuant to a contract by such contractor with the state or a municipal corporation, shall have a lien for the principal and interest of the value or agreed price of such labor or materials upon the moneys of such corporation applicable to the construction of such improvement, to the extent of the amount due or to become due on such contract, upon filing a notice of lien as prescribed in this article.

§ 6. **Liens for labor on railroads.**—Any person who shall hereafter perform any labor for a railroad corporation shall have a lien for the value of such labor upon the railroad track, rolling-stock and appurtenances of such railroad corporation and upon the land upon which such railroad track and appurtenances are situated, by filing a notice of such lien in the office of the clerk of any county wherein any part of such railroad is situated, to the extent of the right, title and interest of such corporation in such property, existing at the time of such filing. The provisions of this article relating to the contents, filing and entry of a notice of a mechanic's lien, and the priority and duration thereof, shall apply to such liens. A copy of the notice of such lien shall be personally served upon such corporation within ten days after the filing thereof in the manner prescribed by the code of civil procedure for the service of summons in actions in justices' courts against domestic railroad corporations.

§ 7. **Liability of owner for advance payments, collusive mortgages and incumbrances.**— Any payment by the owner to a contractor upon a contract for the improvement of real property, made prior to the time when, by the terms of the contract, such payment becomes due, for the purpose of avoiding the provisions of this article, shall be of no effect as against the lien of a sub-contractor, laborer or material man under such contract, created before such payment actually becomes due. A mortgage, lien or incumbrance made by an owner of real property, for the purpose of avoiding the provisions of this article, with the knowledge or privity of the person in whose favor the mortgage, lien or incumbrance is created, shall be void and of no effect as against a claim on account of the improvement of such real property, existing at the time of the creation of such mortgage, lien or incumbrance.

§ 8. **Terms of contract may be demanded.**— A statement of the terms of a contract pursuant to which an improvement of real property is being made, and of the amount due or to become due thereon, shall be furnished upon demand, by the owner, or his duly authorized agent, to a sub-contractor, laborer or material man performing labor for or furnishing materials to a contractor, his agent or sub-contractor, under such contract. If, upon such demand the owner refuses or neglects to furnish such statement or falsely states the terms of such contract or the amount due or to become due thereon, and a sub-contractor, laborer or material man has not been paid the amount of his claim against a contractor or sub-contractor, under such contract, and a judgment has been obtained and execution issued against such contractor or sub-contractor and returned wholly or partly unsatisfied, the owner shall be liable for the loss sustained by reason of such refusal, neglect or false statement, and the lien of such sub-contractor, laborer or material man, filed as prescribed in this article, against the real property improved for the labor performed or materials furnished after such demand, shall exist to the same extent and be enforced in the same manner as if such labor and materials had been directly performed for and furnished to such owner.

§ 9.— **Contents of notice of lien.**— The notice of lien shall state:

1. The name and residence of the lienor.

2. The name of the owner of the real property against whose interest therein a lien is claimed, and the interest of the owner as far as known to the lienor.

3. The name of the person by whom the lienor was employed, or to whom he furnished or is to furnish materials; or, if the lienor is a contractor or sub-contractor, the person with whom the contract was made.

, 4. The labor performed or to be performed, or materials furnished or to be furnished and the agreed price or value thereof.

5. The amount unpaid to the lienor for such labor or materials.

6. The time when the first and last items of work were performed and materials were furnished.

7. The property subject to the lien, with a description thereof sufficient for identification; and if in a city or village, its location by street and number, if known. A failure to state the name of the true owner or contractor, or a mis-description of the true owner,

shall not affect the validity of the lien. The notice must be verified by the lienor or his agent, to the effect that the statements therein contained are true to his knowledge, except as to the matters therein stated to be alleged on information and belief, and that as to those matters he believes it to be true.

§ 10. **Filing of notice.**—The notice of lien may be filed at any time during the progress of the work and the furnishing of the materials, or within ninety days after the completion of the contract, or the final performance of the work, or the final furnishing of the materials, dating from the last item of work performed or materials furnished. The notice of lien must be filed in the clerk's office of the county where the property is situated. If such property is situated in two or more counties, the notice of lien shall be filed in the office of the clerk of each of such counties. The county clerk of each county shall provide and keep a book to be called the "lien docket," which shall be suitably ruled in columns headed "owners," "lienors," "property," "amount," "time of filing," "proceedings had," in each of which he shall enter the particulars of the notice, properly belonging therein. The date, hour and minute of the filing of each notice of lien shall be entered in the proper column. The names of the owners shall be arranged in such book in alphabetical order. The validity of the lien and the right to file a notice thereof shall not be affected by the death of the owner before notice of the lien is filed.

§ 11. **Service of copy of notice.**—At any time after filing the notice of lien, the lienor may serve a copy of such notice upon the owner, by delivering the same to him personally, or if the owner can not be found, to his agent or attorney, or by leaving it at his last known place of residence in the city or town in which the real property or some part thereof is situated, with a person of suitable age and discretion, or by registered letter addressed to his last known place of residence, or, if such owner has no such residence in such city or town, or can not be found, and he has no agent or attorney, by affixing a copy thereof conspicuously on such property, between the hours of nine o'clock in the forenoon and four o'clock in the afternoon. Until service of the notice has been made, as above provided, an owner, without knowledge of the lien, shall be protected in any payment made in good faith to any contractor or other person claiming a lien.

A failure to serve the notice does not otherwise affect the validity of such lien.

§ 12. **Notice of lien on account of public improvements.**— At any time before the construction of a public improvement is completed and accepted by the municipal corporation, and within thirty days after such completion and acceptance, a person performing work for or furnishing materials to a contractor, his sub-contractor, assignee or legal representative, may file a notice of lien with the head of the department or bureau having charge of such construction and with the financial officer of the municipal corporation, or other officer or person charged with the custody and disbursements of the corporate funds applicable to the contract under which the claim is made. The notice shall state the name and residence of the lienor, the name of the contractor or sub-contractor for whom the labor was performed or materials furnished, the amount claimed to be due or to become due, the date when due, a description of the public improvement upon which the labor was performed and materials expended, the kind of labor performed and materials furnished and give a general description of the contract pursuant to which such public improvement was constructed. If the name of the contractor or sub-contractor is not known to the lienor, it may be so stated in the notice, and a failure to state correctly the name of the contractor or sub-contractor shall not affect the validity of the lien. The financial officer of the municipal corporation or other officer or person with whom the notice is filed shall enter the same in a book provided for that purpose, to be called the "lien book." Such entry shall include the name and residence of the lienor, the name of the contractor or sub-contractor, the amount of the lien and date of filing, and a brief designation of the contract under which the lien arose.

§ 13. **Priority of liens.**— A lien for materials furnished or labor performed in the improvement of real property shall have priority over a conveyance, judgment or other claim against such property not recorded, docketed or filed at the time of filing the notice of such lien ; over advances made upon any mortgage or other incumbrance thereon after such filing ; and over the claim of a creditor who has not furnished materials or performed labor upon such property, if such property has been assigned by the owner by a general assignment for the benefit of creditors, within thirty days before the filing of such notice. Such liens shall also have priority over advances made upon a contract by an owner for an improvement of real property which contains an option to the contractor, his successor or assigns to purchase the property, if such advances were made after the time when the labor began or the first item of material was furnished, as stated in the notice of lien. If several buildings are erected, altered or repaired, or several pieces or parcels of real property are improved, under one contract, and there are conflicting liens thereon, each lienor shall have priority upon the particular building or premises where his labor is performed or his materials are used. Persons standing in equal degrees as co-laborers or material men, shall have priority according to the date of filing their respective liens ; but in all cases laborers for daily or weekly wages shall have preference over all other claimants under this article, without reference to the time when such laborers shall have filed their notices of liens.

§ 14. Assignment of lien.— A lien, filed as prescribed in this article, may be assigned by a written instrument signed and acknowledged by the lienor, at any time before the discharge thereof. Such assignment shall contain the names and places of residence of the assignor and assignee, the amount of the lien and the date of filing the notice of lien, and be filed in the office where the notice of the lien assigned is filed. The facts relating to such an assignment and the names of the assignee shall be entered by the proper officer in the book where the notice of lien is entered and opposite the entry thereof. Unless such assignment is filed, the assignee need not be made a defendant in an action to foreclose a mortgage, lien or other incumbrance. A payment made by the owner of the real property subject to the lien assigned or by his agent or contractor, or by the contractor of a municipal corporation, to the original lienor, on account of such lien, without notice of such assignment and before the same is filed, shall be valid and of full force and effect. Except as prescribed herein, the validity of an assignment of a lien shall not be affected by a failure to file the same.

§ 15. Assignments of contracts and orders to be filed.— No assignment of a contract for the performance of labor or the furnishing of materials for the improvement of real property or of the money or any part thereof due or to become due therefor, nor an order drawn by a contractor or sub-contractor upon the owner of such real property for the payment of such money shall be valid,

until the contract or a statement containing the substance thereof
and such assignment or a copy of each or a copy of such order, be
filed in the office of the county clerk of the county wherein the real
property improved or to be improved is situated, and such contract,
assignment or order shall have effect and be enforceable from the
time of such filing. Such clerk shall enter the facts relating to
such assignment or order in the " lien docket " or in another book
provided by him for such purpose.

§ 16. Duration of lien.—No lien specified in this article shall
be a lien for a longer period than one year after the notice of lien
has been filed, unless within that time an action is commenced
to foreclose the lien, and a notice of the pendency of such action,
whether in a court of record or in a court not of record, is filed with
the county clerk of the county in which the notice of lien is filed,
containing the names of the parties to the action, the object of the
action, a brief description of the real property affected thereby, and
the time of filing the notice of lien; or unless an order be granted
within one year from the filing of such notice by a court of
record, continuing such lien, and such lien shall be redocketed as
of the date of granting such order and a statement made that
such lien is continued by virtue of such order. No lien shall
be continued by such order for more than one year from the
granting thereof, but a new order and entry may be made in each
successive year. If a lienor is made a party defendant in an
action to enforce another lien, and the plaintiff or such defendant
has filed a notice of the pendency of the action within the time
prescribed in this section, the lien of such defendant is thereby
continued. Such action shall be deemed an action to enforce the
lien of such defendant lienor. The failure to file a notice of pendency of action shall not abate the action as to any person liable
for the payment of the debt specified in the notice of lien, and the
action may be prosecuted to judgment against such person.

§ 17. Duration of lien under contract for a public improvement.
— If the lien is for labor done or materials furnished for a public
improvement, it shall not continue for a longer period than three
months from the time of filing the notice of such lien, unless an
action is commenced to foreclose such lien within that time, and
a notice of the pendency of such action is filed with the financial
officer of the municipal corporation, with whom the notice of lien
was filed.

§ 18. **Discharge of lien generally.**— A lien other than a lien for labor performed or materials furnished for a public improvement specified in this article, may be discharged as follows:

1. By the certificate of the lienor, duly acknowledged or proved and filed in the office where the notice of lien is filed, stating that the lien is satisfied and may be discharged.

2. By failure to begin an action to foreclose such lien or to secure an order continuing it, within one year from the time of filing the notice of lien.

3. By order of the court vacating or cancelling such lien of record, for neglect of the lienor to prosecute the same, granted pursuant to the code of civil procedure.

4. Either before or after the beginning of an action by the owner executing an undertaking with two or more sufficient sureties, who shall be freeholders, to the clerk of the county where the premises are situated, in such sums as the court or a judge or justice thereof may direct, not less than the amount claimed in the notice of lien conditioned for the payment of any judgment which may be rendered against the property for the enforcement of the lien. The sureties must together justify in at least double the sum named in the undertaking. A copy of the undertaking, with notice that the sureties will justify before the court, or a judge or justice thereof, at the time and place therein mentioned, must be served upon the lienor or his attorney, not less than five days before such time. Upon the approval of the undertaking by the court, judge or justice an order shall be made discharging such lien. The execution of any such bond or undertaking by any fidelity or surety company authorized by the laws of this state to transact business, shall be equivalent to the execution of said bond or undertaking by two sureties; and such company, if excepted to, shall justify through its officers or attorney in the manner required by law of fidelity and surety companies. Any such company may execute any such bond or undertaking as surety by the hand of its officers, or attorney, duly authorized thereto by resolution of its board of directors, a certified copy of which resolution, under the seal of said company, shall be filed with each bond or undertaking.

§ 19. **Discharge of lien by payment of money into court.**—A lien specified in this article, other than a lien for performing labor or furnishing materials for a public improvement, may be discharged, at any time before an action is commenced to foreclose such lien, by depositing with the county clerk, in whose office the notice of lien is filed, a sum of money equal to the amount claimed in such notice, with interest to the time of such deposit. After such action is commenced the lien may be discharged by a payment into court of such sum of money, as, in the judgment of the court or a judge or justice thereof, after at least five days notice to all the parties to the action, will be sufficient to pay any judgment which may be recovered in such action. Upon any such payment, the county clerk shall forthwith enter upon the lien docket and against the lien for the discharge of which such moneys were paid, the words "discharged by payment." A deposit of money made as prescribed in this section shall be repaid to the party making the deposit, or his successor, upon the discharge of the liens against the property pursuant to law. All deposits of money made as provided in this section shall be considered as paid into court and shall be subject to the provisions of the code of civil procedure relative to the payment of money into court and the surrender of such money by order of the court. An order for the surrender of such moneys may be made by any court of record having jurisdiction of the parties and of the subject matter of the proceeding for the foreclosure of the lien for the discharge of which such moneys were deposited. If no action is brought in a court of record to enforce such lien, such order may be made by any judge of a court of record.

§ 20. **Discharge of lien for public improvement.**—A lien against the amount due or to become due a contractor from a municipal corporation for the construction of a public improvement may be discharged as follows:

1. By filing a certificate of the lienor or his successor in interest, duly acknowledged and proved, stating that the lien is discharged.

2. By lapse of time, when three months have elapsed since filing the notice of lien, and no action has been commenced to enforce the lien.

3. By satisfaction of a judgment rendered in an action to enforce the lien.

4. By the contractor depositing with the financial officer of the municipal corporation, or the officer or person with whom the notice of lien is filed, such a sum of money as is directed by a justice of the supreme court, which shall not be less than the amount claimed by the lienor, with interest thereon for the term of one year from the time of making such deposit, and such additional amount as the

justice deems sufficient to cover all costs and expenses. The amount so deposited shall remain with such financial officer or other officer or person until the lien is discharged as prescribed in subdivisions one, two or three of this section.

§ 21. **Building loan contract..—** A contract for the sale of land with a building loan and any modification thereof, must be in writing, and within ten days after its execution be filed in the office of the clerk of the county in which any part of the land is situated. If not so filed, the interest of each party to such contract in the real property affected thereby, is subject to the lien and claim of a person who shall thereafter file a notice of lien under this chapter. A modification of such contract shall not affect or impair the right or interest of a person, who, previous to the filing of such modification had furnished or contracted to furnish materials, or had performed or contracted to perform labor for the improvement of the real property, but such right or interest shall be determined by the original contract. The county clerk is entitled to a fee of twenty cents for filing such a contract or modification. Such contracts and modifications thereof shall be indexed in a book provided for that purpose, in the alphabetical order of the names of the vendees.

§ 22. **Construction of article.—** This article is to be construed liberally to secure the beneficial interests and purposes thereof. A substantial compliance with its several provisions shall be sufficient for the validity of a lien and to give jurisdiction to the courts to enforce the same.

§ 23. **Enforcement of mechanics' lien.—** The mechanics' liens specified in this article may be enforced against the property specified in the notice of lien and which is subject thereto and against any person liable for the debt upon which the lien is founded. The code of civil procedure regulates and provides for such enforcement.

ARTICLE II.
LIENS ON VESSELS.

Section 30. Liens on vessels.

31. Lien on vessels causing damage.

32. Notice of lien, when to be filed.

33. Duration of lien.

34. Assignment of lien.

35. Enforcement of lien.

Section 30. **Liens on vessels.**— A debt which is not a lien by the maritime law, and which amounts to fifty dollars or upwards, on a sea-going or ocean-bound vessel, or fifteen dollars or upwards on any other vessel shall be a lien upon such vessel, her tackle, apparel and furniture, and shall be preferred to all other liens thereon, except mariners' wages, if such debt is contracted by the master, owner, charterer, builder or consignee of such ship or vessel, or by the agent of either of them, within this state, for either of the following purposes :

1. For work done or material or other articles furnished in this state for or towards the building, repairing, fitting, furnishing or equipping of such vessel.

2. For such provisions and stores, furnished within this state, as are fit and proper for the use of such vessel, at the time when they were furnished.

3. For wharfing and the expense of keeping such vessel in port, and for the expense of employing persons to watch her.

4. For loading or unloading such vessel, or for the advances made to procure necessaries therefor, or for the insurance thereof.

5. For towing or piloting such vessel, or for the insurance or premium of insurance of or on such vessel or her freight ; but no lien exists for a debt contracted for any purpose specified in this subdivision, unless it amounts to the sum of twenty-five dollars or more.

§ 31. **Lien on vessel causing damage.**—When a vessel shall have sustained damage by any other vessel through the negligence or willful misconduct of the person navigating such vessel, to the extent of fifty dollars, the owner of the damaged vessel shall have a lien, unless a lien is given therefor by maritime law, upon the vessel causing the damage, her tackle, apparel and furniture, to the extent of such damage, which shall be deemed a debt for the purposes of this article, and the master, owner, agent or consignee of the damaged vessel may enforce such lien in like manner and with like effect as in case of other liens created by this article; but a notice of the lien must be filed in the office of the clerk of the county in which such damage is sustained, and proceedings to enforce the lien must be commenced within ten days after the damage has been done, or such damage shall cease to be a lien upon such vessel. But if such damage is sustained in either of the counties of New York, Kings or Queens such notice shall be filed in the office of the clerk of the city and county of New York, and if the vessel causing such damage is built, used or fitted for the navigation of any of the canals or lakes of the state, a certified copy of such notice shall be filed in the office of the comptroller as provided in the next section.

§ 32. **Notice of lien, when to be filed.**—Every debt specified in section thirty shall cease to be a lien upon such vessel, unless the lienor shall, within thirty days after it is contracted, file a notice of lien, containing the name of the vessel, the name of the owner, if known, the particulars of the debt and a statement of the amount claimed to be due from such vessel, and verified by the lienor, his legal representative, agent or assignee, to be true and correct. If the debt is based upon a written contract, a copy of such contract shall be attached to such notice. The notice shall be filed in the office of the clerk of the county in which the debt was contracted. But if the debt was contracted in either of the counties of New York, Kings or Queens, such notice shall be filed in the office of the clerk of the city and county of New York. If the vessel is built, used or fitted for the navigation of any of the canals or lakes of the state, the lienor shall immediately after filing the notice in the county clerk's office, file a copy thereof in the office of the comptroller of the state, duly certified by the county clerk in whose office the original notice is filed.

§ 33. **Duration of lien.**—Every lien for a debt shall cease if the vessel navigates the western or northwestern lakes, or either of them, or the Saint Lawrence river, at the expiration of six months after the first of January next succeeding the time when the debt was contracted, and in case of any other vessel, at the expiration of twelve months after the debt was contracted. If, upon the expiration of the time herein limited in either of such cases, such vessel shall be absent from the port at which the debt was contracted, the lien shall continue until the expiration of thirty days after the return of such vessel to such port. If proceedings are instituted for the enforcement of the lien within the time herein limited, such lien shall continue until the termination of such proceedings.

§ 34. **Assignment of lien.**—A lien, a notice of which has been filed pursuant to the provisions of this article, may be assigned by a written instrument duly acknowledged and filed in the same place where the notice of the lien was filed. The assignment shall specify the debt upon which the lien is founded, the date of the filing of the notice thereof and the assignee. Such assignment and the name of the assignee shall be entered by the clerk opposite the original entry of such lien, and after the filing of such assignment, but not otherwise, the assignee may enforce the lien in like manner as the assignor could have done.

§ 35. Enforcement of lien.—If a lien, created by virtue of this article, is founded upon a maritime contract, it can be enforced only by proceedings in the courts of the United States, and in any other case, in the courts of this state, in the manner provided by the code of civil procedure.

ARTICLE III.

LIENS ON MONUMENTS, GRAVESTONES AND CEMETERY STRUCTURES.

Section 40. Liens on monuments, gravestones and cemetery struc-
         tures.
     41. Notice of lien.
     42. Proceedings to enforce liens.
     43. Disposition of proceeds of sale.
     44. Duties of officers of cemetery associations.

Section 40. Liens on monuments, gravestones and cemetery stuc-
tures.—A person furnishing or placing in a cemetery or burial
ground, a monument, gravestone, inclosure or other structure, has
a lien thereon for the agreed price thereof or the part remaining
unpaid, with interest from the time the amount was due, upon filing
with the superintendent or person in charge of such cemetery or
burial ground, a notice of lien as provided in this article.

§ 41. Notice of lien.—Such notice may be filed at any time after
the completion of the work, but must be filed within one year after
the agreed price for furnishing or placing such monument, gravestone, inclosure or other structure becomes due, and shall state that
the lienor has a lien on such monument, gravestone, inclosure or
structure for the purchase price thereof, or some unpaid part of such
purchase price, with interest, specifying the amount agreed to be
paid, and the amount unpaid, with a description of such monument, gravestone, inclosure or other structure, and the location of
the plot upon which it stands, and the names of the persons with
whom the agreement for the purchase and erection of the structure,
or for the performance of such labor was made. The notice shall
be signed and verified by the lienor. The lienor shall, within ten
days after the filing of such notice, serve a copy personally, or by
mail, upon the person with whom the agreement for the purchase
and erection of such monument, gravestone, or other structure, or
for the performance of labor thereon was made, and upon the

owner of the lot upon which such monument, gravestone or other structure is erected, if the name and residence of such owner can, with reasonable diligence be ascertained.

§ 42. **Proceedings to enforce lien.**— After the service of such notice, an action to recover the amount of the debt and to enforce a lien therefor may be maintained by the lienor against the person with whom the agreement was made, for the purchase and erection of such monument, gravestone, inclosure or other structure or for the performance of labor thereon. If such lienor succeeds in establishing his lien, the judgment recovered may authorize him to remove such monument, gravestone, inclosure or other structure from the burial-ground or cemetery and to sell the same at public auction to satisfy the amount of such judgment. Notice of the sale shall be published at least ten days before the time thereof, in a newspaper published in the town or city where such sale is to take place, and if no newspaper is published therein, in a newspaper nearest thereto. Such notice shall state the time and place of the sale, and shall describe the property to be sold. A copy of such notice shall be served personally or by mail at least ten days before such sale upon the persons served with the notice of lien as prescribed in the preceding section.

§ 43. **Disposition of proceeds of sale.**— The lienor shall, out of the proceeds of the sale, pay the expenses thereof, and the expenses of the removal of such monument, gravestone, inclosure or other structure from the cemetery or burial ground, not exceeding fifty dollars, if a monument, and ten dollars, if a gravestone, inclosure or other structure, and retain out of such proceeds, the amount due upon the judgment recovered in the action to enforce the lien, and the residue, if any, shall be forthwith paid to the judgment debtor.

§ 44. **Duties of officers of cemetery associations.**— The superintendent or other person in charge of a cemetery or burial ground shall not permit the removal, alteration or inscription of a monument, gravestone, inclosure or other structure, against which a lien exists, after the notice of such lien has been filed and served as prescribed in this article, except pursuant to the terms of a judgment recovered in an action brought to enforce such lien. No officer of a cemetery association, or other person connected with a cemetery or burial ground, shall hinder or obstruct the removal in a proper manner of any such monument, gravestone, inclosure or other structure pursuant to the terms of such judgment.

ARTICLE IV.

LIENS FOR LABOR ON STONE.

Section 50. **Lien for labor performed in quarrying, dressing and cutting stone.**—A person employed in a quarry, yard or dock at excavating, quarrying, dressing or cutting sandstone, granite, bluestone or marble, may have a lien upon such sandstone, granite, bluestone or marble, for the amount due for the labor expended thereon, upon filing a notice of lien in the office where a chattel mortgage upon such sandstone, granite, bluestone or marble is required to be filed, as provided in this chapter. Such notice must be filed within thirty days after the completion of such labor and must state the amount due therefor, the name and residence of the lienor, and the name of the person for whom the labor was performed, the quantity and a description of the sandstone, granite, bluestone or marble against which the claim is made. Such notice of lien shall be endorsed, filed and entered by the proper officer, in the same manner as chattel mortgages, and the same fees shall be charged therefor. A copy of the notice so filed shall be served upon the owner of such sandstone, granite, bluestone or marble or upon the person in charge of the quarry, yards or docks wherein such services were performed within five days after the filing thereof.

§ 51. **Duration and effect of lien.**— Such lien shall terminate unless an action is brought to enforce the same within three months after the date of filing such notice, as provided in the code of civil procedure for the enforcement of a lien upon a chattel. If the labor on such sandstone, granite, bluestone or marble is performed for a contractor under a contract with the owner of such quarry, yard or dock, the owner shall not be liable to pay by reason of all the liens filed against such quarry, yard or dock a greater sum than the amount unpaid upon such contract at the time of filing such notices, or in case there is no contract, then the aggregate amount unpaid of the value of labor and services performed, pursuant to the preceding section. The lien created by this article shall not attach to any material which shall have become a part of any building or structure, or ceased to be the property of the person for whom such labor was performed.

§ 52. **Discharge of lien.**— Such lien may be discharged by a payment of the amount due thereon, by a failure to bring an action to enforce the same within the time prescribed in the preceding section, by the written consent of the lienor, duly acknowledged and filed with the proper officer to the effect that such lien may be discharged, and by the owner of such sandstone, granite, bluestone or marble filing with such officer an undertaking in an amount equal to twice the sum specified in the notice of lien, executed by one or more sureties who shall justify in such amount and approved by the officer with whom the notice of lien is filed, conditioned for the payment of the sum due such lienor by reason of such lien, and the costs and expenses of enforcing the same.

ARTICLE V.
LIENS FOR SERVICE OF STALLIONS.

Section 60. Lien on mare and foal.

        61. Statement and certificate.

        62. Copy of statement and certificate to be filed.

        63. Penalty.

Section 60. **Lien on mare and foal.**—On complying with the provisions of this article, the owner of a stallion shall have a lien on each mare served together with the foal of such mare from such service, for the amount agreed on at the time of service, or if no agreement was made, for the amount specified in the statement hereinafter required to be filed, if within one year after such service he files a notice of such lien in the same manner and place as chattel mortgages are required by law to be filed. Such notice of lien shall be in writing, specifying the person against whom the claim is made, the amount of the same and a description of the property upon which the lien is claimed, and such lien shall terminate at the end of one year from the date of such filing, unless within that time an action is commenced for the enforcement thereof, as provided in the code of civil procedure for the foreclosure of a lien on chattels.

§ 61. **Statement and certificate.**— A person having the custody or control of a stallion and charging a fee for his services, shall, before advertising or offering such services to the public, file with the clerk of the county in which he resides or in which such stallion is kept for service, a written statement giving the name, age, description and pedigree, if known, and if not, stating that the same is unknown, of such stallion and the terms and conditions on which he will serve. On filing such statement, the county clerk shall record the same in a book provided for that purpose and issue a certificate to such person, that such statement has been so filed and recorded. He shall be entitled to receive ten cents per folio for recording such statement and for such certificate.

§ 62. Copy of statement and certificate to be posted.— The person having the custody and control of such stallion, shall post a written or printed copy of such statement and certificate in a conspicuous place in each locality in which said stallion is kept for service.

§ 63. Penalty.— A person who neglects or refuses to file and post such statement as required in this article, or falsely states the pedigree of such stallion in such statement, forfeits all fees for the services of such stallion and is liable to a person deceived or defrauded thereby for the damages sustained.

ARTICLE VI.
OTHER LIENS ON PERSONAL PROPERTY.

Section 70. Artisans' lien on personal property.

Section 70. Artisans' lien on personal property.— A person who makes, alters, repairs or in any way enhances the value of an article of personal property, at the request or with the consent of the owner, has a lien on such article, while lawfully in possession thereof, for his reasonable charges for the work done and materials furnished, and may retain possession thereof until such charges are paid.

§ 71. Liens of hotel, inn, boarding and lodging house keepers.— A keeper of a hotel, inn, boarding house or lodging house, except an emigrant lodging house, has a lien upon, while in possession, and may detain the baggage and other property brought upon their premises by a guest, boarder or lodger, for the proper charges due from him, on account of his accommodation, board and lodging, and such extras as are furnished at his request. If the keeper of such hotel, inn, boarding or lodging house knew that the property so brought upon his premises was not, when brought, legally in possession of such guest, boarder or lodger, a lien thereon does not exist.

§ 72. Factors' lien on merchandise.—A person, in whose name any merchandise shall be shipped, is deemed the true owner thereof so far as to entitle the consignee of such merchandise to a lien thereon,

1. For any money advanced or negotiable security given by such consignee, to or for the use of the person in whose name such shipment is made; and

2. For any money or negotiable security received by the person in whose name such shipment is made, to or for the use of such consignee.

Such lien does not exist where the consignee has notice, by the bill of lading or otherwise, when or before money is advanced or security is given by him, or when or before such money or security is received by the person in whose name the shipment is made, that such person is not the actual and bona fide owner thereof.

§ 73. Warehouse liens.—A warehouse company, warehouseman or other person lawfully engaged in the business of storing goods, wares and merchandise for hire has a lien on goods deposited and stored with him for his storage charges, and for moneys advanced by him for cartage, labor, weighing and coopering in relation to such goods, or other goods belonging to the same owner; and he may detain such goods until his lien is paid.

§ 74. Lien of bailee of animals.—A person keeping a livery stable, or boarding stable, for animals, or pasturing or boarding one or more animals has a lien dependent upon possession upon each animal kept, pastured or boarded by him under an agreement with the owner thereof, whether such owner be a mortgagor remaining in possession or otherwise, for the sum due him for the care, keeping, boarding or pasture of the animal under the agreement, and may detain the animal accordingly until such sum is paid.

ARTICLE VII.

Section 80. **Sale of personal property to satisfy a lien.**—A lien against personal property, other than a mortgage on chattels, if in the legal possession of the lienor, may be satisfied by the public sale of such property according to the provisions of this article.

§ 81. **Notice to owner.**— Before such sale is held, the lienor shall serve a notice upon the owner of such personal property, personally, if the owner is within the county where such lien arose, and if not, by mailing it to him at his last known place of residence. Such notice shall contain a statement of the following facts:

1. The nature of the debt or the agreement under which the lien arose, with an itemized statement of the claim and the time when due;

2. A brief description of the personal property against which the lien exists;

3. The estimated value of such property;

4. The amount of such lien, at the date of the notice.

It shall also require such owner to pay the amount of such lien on or before a day mentioned therein, not less than ten days from the service thereof, and shall state the time when and place where such property will be sold, if such amount is not paid. If the agreement on which the lien is based, provides for the continuous care of property, the lienor is also entitled to receive all sums which may accrue under the agreement, subsequent to the notice and prior to payment or a sale of the property; and the notice shall contain a statement that such additional sum is demanded. Such notice shall be verified by the lienor to the effect that the lien upon such property is valid, that the debt upon which such lien is founded is due and has not been paid and that the facts stated in such notice are true to the best of his knowledge and belief.

§ 82. **Sale to be advertised.**— Each sale of personal property to satisfy a lien thereon shall be at public auction to the highest bidder, and shall be held in the city or town where the lien was acquired. After the time for the payment of the amount of the lien, specified in the notice required to be served by the preceding section, notice of such sale, describing the property to be sold, and stating the name of the owner and the time and place of such sale, shall be published once a week, for two consecutive weeks, in a newspaper published in the town or city where such sale is to be held, and such sale shall be held not less than fifteen days from the first publication; if there be no newspaper published in such town, such notice shall be posted at least ten days before such sale in not less than six conspicuous places therein.

§ 83. Redemption before sale.— At any time before such property is so sold, the owner thereof may redeem the same by paying to the lienor the amount due on account of the lien, and whatever legitimate expenses have been incurred at the time of such payment in serving the notice and advertising the sale as required in this article. Upon making such payment, the owner of such property is entitled to the possession thereof.

§ 84. Disposition of proceeds.— Of the proceeds of such sale, the lienor shall retain an amount sufficient to satisfy his lien, and the expenses of advertisement and sale. The balance of such proceeds, if any, shall be held by the lienor subject to the demand of the owner, or his assignee or legal representative, and a notice that such balance is so held shall be served personally or by mail upon the owner of the property sold. If such balance is not claimed by the owner or his assignee or legal representative within thirty days from the day of sale, such balance shall be deposited with the treasurer or chamberlain of the city or village, or the supervisor of the town, where such sale was held. There shall be filed with such deposit, the affidavit of the lienor, stating the name and place of residence of the owner of the property sold, if known, the articles sold, the prices obtained therefor, that the notice required by this article was duly served and how served upon such owner, and that such sale was legally and how advertised. There shall also be filed therewith a copy of the notice served upon the owner of the property and of the notice of sale published or posted as required by this article. The officer with whom such balance is deposited shall credit the same to the owner of the property, and pay the same to such owner, his assignee or legal representative, on demand and satisfactory evidence of identity. If such balance remains in the possession of such officer for a period of five years, unclaimed by the person legally entitled thereto, it shall be transferred to the general funds of the town, village or city, and be applied and used as other moneys belonging to such town, village or city.

§ 85. **Remedy not exclusive.**— The provisions of this article do not preclude any other remedy by action or otherwise, now existing, for the enforcement of a lien against personal property, or bar the right to recover so much of the debt as shall not be paid by the proceeds of the sale of the property.

ARTICLE VIII.
CHATTEL MORTGAGES.

Section 90. Chattel mortgage to be filed.

Section 90. **Chattel mortgage to be filed.**—Every mortgage or conveyance intended to operate as a mortgage of goods and chattels, or of any canal boat, steam tug, scow or other craft, or the appurtenances thereto, navigating the canals of the state, which is not accompanied by an immediate delivery, and followed by an actual and continued change of possession of the things mortgaged, is absolutely void as against the creditors of the mortgagor, and as against subsequent purchasers and mortgagees in good faith, unless the mortgage, or a true copy thereof, is filed as directed in this article.

§ 91. **Corporate mortgages against real and personal property.**— Mortgages creating a lien upon real and personal property, executed by a corporation as security for the payment of bonds issued by such corporation, or by any telegraph, telephone or electric light corporation, and recorded as a mortgage of real property in each county where such property is located or through which the line of such telegraph, telephone or electric light corporation runs, need not be filed or refiled as chattel mortgages.

§ 92. Where filed.— An instrument, or a true copy thereof, if intended to operate as a mortgage of a canal boat, steam tug, scow or other craft, or of the appurtenances thereto, navigating the canals of this state, must be filed in the office of the comptroller, and need not be filed elsewhere. Every other chattel mortgage, or an instrument intended to operate as such, or a true copy thereof, must be filed in the town or city where the mortgagor, if a resident of the state, resides at the time of the execution thereof, and if not a resident, in the city or town where the property mortgaged is, at the time of the execution of the mortgage. If there is more than one mortgagor, the mortgage, or a certified copy thereof, must be filed in each city or town within the state where each mortgagor resides at the time of the execution thereof. In the city of New York, such instrument must be filed in the office of the register of the city and county of New York; in the city of Brooklyn, in the office of the register of the county of Kings, and in every other city or town of the state, in the office of the city or town clerk, unless there is a county clerk's office in such city or town, in which case it must be filed therein.

§ 93. Filing and entry.— Such officers shall file every such instrument presented to them for that purpose, and indorse thereon its number and the time of its receipt. They shall enter in a book, provided for that purpose, in separate columns, the names of all the parties to each mortgage so filed, arranged in alphabetical order, under the head of " mortgagors " and " mortgagees," the number of such mortgage or copy, its date, the amount secured thereby, when due, the date of the filing thereof; and, if the mortgage be upon a craft navigating the canals, and filed in the office of the comptroller, the name of the craft shall also be inserted.

§ 94. Fees.—The several clerks and registers are entitled to receive for services hereunder, the following fees: For filing each instrument, or copy, six cents; for entering the same as aforesaid, six cents; for searching for each paper, six cents; and the like fees for certified copies of such instruments or copies as are allowed by law to clerks of counties for copies and certificates of records kept by them. The comptroller is entitled to receive the following fees for services performed under this article, for the use of the state: For filing each instrument or copy and entering the same, twenty-five cents; for searching for each paper, twenty-five cents; and the like fees for certified copies of such instruments or copies, as are allowed by law to be charged by the comptroller for copies and certificates of records kept in his office. No officer is required to file or enter any such paper or furnish a copy thereof, until his lawful fees are paid.

§ 95. Mortgage invalid after one year, unless statement is filed.—A chattel mortgage, except as otherwise provided in this article, shall be invalid as against creditors of the mortgagor, and against subsequent purchasers or mortgagees in good faith, after the expiration of the first or any succeeding term of one year, reckoning from the time of the first filing, unless,

1. Within thirty days next preceding the expiration of each such term, a statement containing a description of such mortgage, the names of the parties, the time when and place where filed, the interest of the mortgagee or of any person who has succeeded to his interest in the property claimed by virtue thereof, or

2. A copy of such mortgage and its endorsements, together with a statement attached thereto or endorsed thereon, showing the interest of the mortgagee or of any person who has succeeded to his interest in the mortgage, is filed in the proper office in the city or town where the mortgagor then resides, if he is then a resident of the town or city where the mortgage or a copy thereof or such statement was last filed; if not such resident, but a resident of the state, a true copy of such mortgage, together with such statement, shall be filed in the proper office of the town or city where he then resides; and if not a resident of the state, then in the proper office of the city or town where the property so mortgaged was at the time of the execution of the mortgage.

§ 96. Duration of lien of mortgage on canal craft.—Every mortgage upon a canal boat or other craft navigating the canals of this state, filed as provided in this article, shall be valid as against the creditors of the mortgagor and against subsequent purchasers or mortgagees in good faith, as long as the debt which the mortgage secures, is enforcible. From the time of filing, every such mortgage shall have preference and priority over all other claims and liens, not existing at the time of such filing.

§ 97. Copies to be evidence of certain facts.—A copy of any such original instrument, or of a copy thereof, including any statement relating thereto, certified by the officer with whom the same is filed, may be received in evidence, but only of the fact that such instrument, or copy, or statement was received and filed according to the endorsement thereon; and the original endorsement upon such instrument or copy may be received in evidence only of the facts stated in such endorsement.

§ 98. Mortgage, how discharged of record.—Upon the payment or satisfaction of a chattel mortgage, the mortgagee, his assignee or legal representative, upon the request of the mortgagor or of any person interested in the mortgaged property, must sign and acknowledge a certificate setting forth such payment or satisfaction.   The officer with whom the mortgage, or a copy thereof is filed, must, on receipt of such certificate, file the same in his office, and write the word "discharged" in the book where the mortgage is entered, opposite the entry thereof, and the mortgage is thereby discharged.

ARTICLE IX.

CONTRACTS FOR THE CONDITIONAL SALE OF GOODS AND CHATTELS.

Section 110. Definitions.

> 111. Conditional sale of railroad equipment and rolling stock.
>
> 112. Conditions and reservations in contracts for the sale of goods and chattels.
>
> 113. Where contract to be filed.
>
> 114. Endorsement, entry, refiling and discharge of conditional contracts.
>
> 115. Preceding sections not to apply to certain articles.
>
> 116. Sale of property retaken by vendor.
>
> 117. Notice of sale.
>
> 118. Disposition of proceeds.

Section 110. **Definitions.**— The term " conditional vendor," when used in this article, means the person contracting to sell goods and chattels upon condition that the ownership thereof is to remain in such person, until such goods and chattels are fully paid for or until the occurrence of any future event or contingency; the term " conditional vendee," when so used, means the person to whom such goods and chattels are so sold.

§ 111. Conditional sale of railroad equipment and rolling stock. — Whenever any railroad equipment and rolling stock is sold, leased or loaned under a contract which provides that the title to such property, notwithstanding the use and possession thereof by the vendee, lessee or bailee, shall remain in the vendor, lessor or bailor, until the terms of the contract as to the payment of installments, amounts or rentals payable, or the performance of other obligations thereunder, are fully complied with and that title to such property shall pass to the vendee, lessee or other bailee on full payment therefor, such contract shall be invalid as

to any subsequent judgment creditor of or purchaser from such
vendee, lessee or bailee for a valuable consideration, without notice, unless

1. Such contract is in writing, duly acknowledged and recorded
in the book in which real estate mortgages are recorded in the
office of the county clerk or register of the county in which is
located the principal office or place of business of such vendee,
lessee or bailee; and unless

2. Each locomotive or car so sold, leased or loaned, has the
name of the vendor, lessor or bailor, or of the assignee of such
vendor, lessor or bailor, plainly marked upon both sides thereof,
followed by the word owner, lessor, bailor or assignee, as the case
may be.

§ 112. Conditions and reservations in contracts for sale of goods
and chattels.— Except as otherwise provided in this article, all
conditions and reservations in a contract for the conditional sale
of goods and chattels, accompanied by immediate delivery and
continued possession of the thing contracted to be sold, to the
effect that the ownership of such goods and chattels is to remain
in the conditional vendor or in a person other than the conditional
vendee, until they are paid for, or until the occurrence of a future
event or contingency shall be void as against subsequent purchasers, pledgees or mortgagees in good faith, and as to them the
sale shall be deemed absolute, unless such contract of sale, containing such conditions and reservations, or a true copy thereof be
filed as directed in this article.

§ 113. Where contract to be filed.— Such contracts shall be filed
in the city or town where the conditional vendee resides, if he resides within the state at the time of the execution thereof; and if
not, in the city or town where such property is at such time. Such
contract shall be filed, in the city of New York, in the office of the
register of the city and county of New York; in the city of Brooklyn, in the office of the register of the county of Kings; in every
other city or town of the state, in the office of the town clerk, unless
there be a county clerk's office in the city or town, when it shall be
filed in such office.

§ 114. Endorsement, entry, refiling and discharge of conditional
contracts.— The provisions of the preceding article relating to
chattel mortgages apply to the endorsement, entry, refiling and
discharge of contracts for the conditional sale of goods and chattels.
The officers with whom such contracts are filed shall enter the future

contingency or event required to occur before the ownership of such goods and chattels shall pass from the vendor to the vendee, and the amount due upon such contract and the time when due. The name of the conditional vendor shall be entered in the column of "mortgagees" and the name of the conditional vendee in the column of "mortgagors." The officers performing services under this article are entitled to receive the same fees as for like services relating to chattel mortgages.

§ 115. Preceding sections not to apply to certain articles.— The preceding sections of this article do not apply to the conditional sale of household goods, pianos, organs, scales, butchers' and meat market tools and fixtures, wood cutting machinery, engines, dynamos, boilers, portable furnaces, boilers for heating purposes, threshing machines, horse powers, mowing machines, reapers, harvesters, grain drills and attachments, dairy sizes of centrifugal cream separators, coaches, hearses, carriages, buggies, phaetons and other vehicles, bicycles, tricycles and other devices for locomotion by human power, if the contract for the sale thereof is executed in duplicate, and one duplicate delivered to the purchaser.

§ 116. Sale of property retaken by vendor.— Whenever articles are sold upon the condition that the title thereto shall remain in the vendor, or in some other person than the vendee, until the payment of the purchase price, or until the occurrence of a future event or contingency, and the same are retaken by the vendor, or his successor in interest, they shall be retained for a period of thirty days from the time of such retaking, and during such period the vendee or his successor in interest, may comply with the terms of such contract, and thereupon receive such property. After the expiration of such period, if such terms are not complied with, the vendor, or his successor in interest, may cause such articles to be sold at public auction.

§ 117. Notice of sale.— Not less than fifteen days before such sale, a printed or written notice shall be served personally upon the vendee, or his successor in interest, if he is within the county where the sale is to be held; and if not within such county, or he can not be found therein, such notice must be mailed to him at his last known place of residence.

Such notice shall state:

1. The terms of the contract.
2. The amount unpaid thereon.
3. The amount of expenses of storage.

4. The time and place of the sale, unless such amounts are sooner paid.

§ 118. **Disposition of proceeds.** — Of the proceeds of such sale, the vendor or his successor in interest may retain the amount due upon his contract, and the expenses of storage and of sale; the balance thereof shall be held by the vendor or his successor in interest, subject to the demand of the vendee or his successor in interest, and a notice that such balance is so held shall be served personally or by mail upon the vendee or his successor in interest. If such balance is not called for within thirty days from the time of sale, it shall be deposited with the treasurer or chamberlain of the city or village, or the supervisor of the town where such sale was held, and there shall be filed therewith a copy of the notice served upon the vendee or his successor in interest and a verified statement of the amount unpaid upon the contract, expenses of storage and of sale and the amount of such balance. The officer with whom such balance was deposited shall credit the vendee or his successor in interest with the amount thereof and pay the same to him on demand after sufficient proof of identity. If such balance remains in possession of such officer for a period of five years, unclaimed by the person legally entitled thereto, it shall be transferred to the funds of the town, village or city, and be applied and used as other moneys belonging to such town, village or city.

ARTICLE X.
LAWS REPEALED; WHEN TO TAKE EFFECT.
Section 120. Laws repealed.

121. When to take effect.

Section 120. **Laws repealed.** — The laws or parts thereof specified in the schedule hereto annexed, and all laws amendatory thereof, are hereby repealed.

§ 121. **When to take effect.** — This chapter shall take effect September first, eighteen hundred and ninety-seven.

SCHEDULE OF LAWS REPEALED.

Laws.	Chapter.	Sections.	Subject.
1830.	179	1, 2	Liens of factors and agents.
1833.	279	All	Chattel mortgages to be filed.
1849.	69	All	Registration of chattel mortgages.
1858.	247	All	Registration of liens and encumbrances upon canal boat.

Laws.	Chapter.	Sections.	Subject.
1860.	446	All..........	Protection of boarding house keepers.
1862.	482	1, 2, 3, 27, 33..	Liens on vessels.
1863.	422	2............	Duration of lien on vessel navigating St. Lawrence river and western and northwestern lakes.
1864.	412	All..........	Registration of mortgages on canal boats.
1868.	779	All..........	Chattel mortgages executed by railroad corporations.
1870.	529	All..........	Liens on railroad bridges and trestle work.
1872.	498	All..........	Liens of livery-stable keepers and agisters.
1872.	669	All..........	Liens on wharves, piers, bulkheads, etc.
1873.	501	All..........	Amends L. 1833, ch. 279, § 3.
1875.	392	1, 2, 5, 6, 7....	Liens for labor on railroads.
1876.	319	All..........	Amends L. 1860, ch. 446.
1878.	315	1, 2, 3, 4, 5, 13, 14, 15......	Liens for public improvements.
1879.	171	All..........	Discharge of chattel mortgages.
1879.	334	1............	Amends L. 1862, ch. 482, § 3.
1879.	336	All..........	Sale of goods to satisfy liens of warehousemen.
1879.	418	All..........	Amends L. 1833, ch. 279, § 3.
1879.	530	All..........	Sale of goods and baggage of guests of hotel, lodging house and boarding house keepers to satisfy liens.
1880.	145	All..........	Amends L. 1872, ch. 498, § 1.
1880.	440	1, 2, 3, 4, 10, 13	Liens on oil and gas wells.
1881.	429	All..........	Adds § 16 to L. 1878, ch. 315.
1883.	383	All..........	Contracts for the lease or conditional sale of railroad equipment and rolling stock.
1883.	421	All..........	Amends L. 1879, ch. 336, § 1.
1884.	315	All..........	Contracts for conditional sale of personal property to be filed.
1885.	216	All..........	Amends L. 1863, ch. 422, § 2.
1885.	273	All..........	Amends L. 1862, ch. 482, § 2.

Laws.	Chapter.	Sections.	Subject.
1885.	342	1, 2, 3, 4, 5, 6, 24, 25......	Mechanics' liens generally.
1885.	488	All.........	Amends L. 1884, ch. 315, § 2.
1885.	526	All.........	Liens of warehousemen.
1886.	88	All.........	Amends L. 1862, ch. 482, § 2.
1886.	382	All.........	Validity of notices filed prior to June 27, 1885.
1887.	458	All.........	Owners of stallions, protection and liabilities of.
1888.	316	All.........	Amends L. 1885, ch. 342, § 1.
1888.	457	All.........	Amends L. 1887, ch. 458, § 3.
1888.	543	All.........	Liens on monuments, gravestones, etc.
1891.	171	All.........	Chattel mortgages executed by telegraph, electric light and telephone companies.
1891.	255	1, 2, 3, 4, 5, 10, 11, 12, 13...	Amends L. 1878, ch. 315.
1892.	91	All.........	Amends L. 1872, ch. 498.
1892.	274	All.........	Amends L. 1864, ch. 412, § 3.
1892.	629	1, 2, 3, 4, 5, 10, 11, 12......	Amends L. 1878, ch. 315.
1893.	300	All.........	Amends L. 1885, ch. 342, § 24.
1893.	405	All.........	Amends L. 1864, ch. 412, § 3.
1894.	253	All.........	Hotelkeepers may detain property of boarders.
1894.	420	All.........	Amends L. 1884, ch. 315, § 7.
1894.	724	All.........	Amends L. 1864, ch. 412, §§ 3, 4.
1895.	161	All.........	Amends L. 1885, ch. 342, § 6.
1895.	354	All.........	Amends L. 1833, ch. 279, § 3.
1895.	523	All.........	Amends L. 1884, ch. 315, § 7.
1895.	529	All.........	Amends L. 1868, ch. 779.
1895.	673	1, 2, 3........	Amends L. 1885, ch. 342, §§ 1, 2, 3.
1895.	884	All.........	Liens of lodging house keepers.
1895.	925	All.........	Amends L. 1884, ch. 315, § 7.
1896.	528	All.........	Amends L. 1833, ch. 279, § 3.
1896.	601	All.........	Amends L. 1884, ch. 315, § 7.
1896.	682	All.........	Amends L. 1878, ch. 315, § 13.
1896.	738	All.........	Liens on stone, etc.
1896.	915	All.........	Amends L. 1885, ch. 342, § 5.

Chap. 419.

AN ACT to amend the code of civil procedure, relating to the enforcement of mechanics' liens on real property and liens on vessels.

Became a law May 13, 1897, with the approval of the Governor.
Passed, a majority being present.

The People of the State of New York, represented in Senate and Assembly, do enact as follows:

Section 1. The code of civil procedure is hereby amended by inserting in chapter twenty-two thereof, a new title to be known as title three, and to read as follows:

TITLE III.

PROCEEDINGS FOR THE ENFORCEMENT OF MECHANICS' LIENS ON REAL PROPERTY.

§ 3398. **Purpose of title; definitions.**—This title is to be construed in connection with article one of the lien law, and provides proceedings for the enforcement of liens for labor performed and materials furnished in the improvement of real property, created by virtue of such article. The terms "real property," "lienor," "owner," "improvement," "public improvement," "contractor," "sub-contractor," "material man" and "laborer," as used in this title, are defined by section two of such law.

§ 3399. **Enforcement of a mechanic's lien on real property.**—A mechanic's lien on real property may be enforced against such property, and against a person liable for the debt upon which the lien is founded, by an action, by the lienor, his assignee or legal representative, in a court which has jurisdiction in an action founded on a contract for a sum of money equivalent to the amount of such debt.

§ 3400. **Enforcement of a lien under contract for a public improvement.**— A lien for labor done or materials furnished for a public improvement may be enforced against the funds of the municipal corporation for which such public improvement is constructed, to the extent prescribed in article one of the lien law, and against the contractor or subcontractor liable for the debt, by a civil action, in the same court and in the same manner as a mechanic's lien on real property.

§ 3401. **Action in a court of record; consolidation.**—The provisions of this code, relating to actions for the foreclosure of a mortgage upon real property, and the sale and the distribution of the proceeds thereof apply to actions in a court of record, to enforce mechanics' liens on real property, except as otherwise provided in this title. If actions are brought by different lienors in a court of record, the court in which the first action was brought, may, upon its own motion, or upon the application of any party in any of such actions, consolidate all of such actions.

§ 3402. **Parties to an action in a court of record.**—In an action in a court of record the following are necessary parties defendant:

1. All lienors having liens against the same property or any part thereof.

2. All other persons having subsequent liens or claims against the property, by judgment, mortgage or otherwise, and

3. All persons appearing by the records in the office of the county clerk or register to be overseers of such property or any part thereof. Every defendant who is a lienor shall, by answer in the action. set forth his lien, or he will be deemed to have waived the same, unless the lien is admitted in the complaint, and not contested by another defendant. Two or more lienors having liens upon the same property or any part thereof, may join as plaintiffs.

§ 3403. **Equities of lienors to be determined.**—The court may adjust and determine the equities of all the parties to the action and the order of priority of different liens, and determine all issues raised by any defense or counter claim in the action.

§ 3404. **Action in a court not of record.**—If an action to enforce a mechanic's lien against real property is brought in a court not of record, it shall be commenced by the personal service upon the owner, anywhere within the state, of a summons and complaint verified in the same manner as a complaint in an action in a court of record. The complaint must set forth substantially the facts contained in the notice of lien, and the substance of the agreement under which the labor was performed or the materials were furnished. The form and contents of the summons shall be the same as provided by this code for the commencement of an action upon a contract in such court. The summons must be returnable not less than twelve nor more than twenty days after the date of the summons, or, if service is made by publication, after the day of the last publication of the summons. Service must be made at least eight days before the return day.

§ 3405. **When personal service can not be made.**—If personal service of the summons can not be made upon a defendant in an action in a court not of record, by reason of his absence from the state, or his concealment therein, such service may be made by leaving a copy thereof at his last place of residence and by publishing a copy of the summons once in each of three successive weeks in a newspaper in the city or county where the property is situated.

§ 3406. **Proceedings on return of summons; judgment by default.**—At the time and place specified in the summons for the return thereof, in a court not of record, issue must be joined, if both parties appear, by the defendant filing with the justice a verified answer, containing a general denial of each allegation of the complaint, or a specific denial of one or more of the material allegations thereof; or any other matter constituting a defense to the lien or to the claim upon which it is founded. If the defendant fail to appear on the return-day, on proof by affidavit of the service of the summons and complaint, judgment may be rendered for the amount claimed, with costs.

§ 3407. **Issue, how tried.**—If issue is joined in such action in a court not of record, it must be tried in the same manner as other issues in such court, and judgment entered thereon, which shall be enforced, if for the plaintiff, in the manner provided in the following section. If for the defendant, in the same manner as in an action on contract in such court.

§ 3408. **Executions.**— Execution may be issued upon a judgment obtained in an action to enforce a mechanic's lien against real property in a court not of record, which shall direct the officer to sell the title and interest of the owner in the premises, upon which the lien set forth in the complaint existed at the time of filing the notice of lien.

§ 3409. **Appeals from judgments in courts not of record.**—An appeal may be taken from such judgment rendered in a court not of record, according to the provisions of this code regulating appeals from judgments in actions on contract in such courts.

§ 3410. **Transcripts of judgment in courts not of record.**— When a judgment is rendered in a court not of record, the justice or judge of the court in which it is tried, or other person authorized to furnish transcripts of judgments therein, shall furnish the successful party a transcript thereof, which he may file with the clerk of the county with whom the notice of lien is filed. The filing of such transcript has the same effect as the filing of a transcript of any other judgment rendered in such courts.

§ 3411. **Costs and disbursements.**— If an action is brought to enforce a mechanic's lien against real property in a court of record, the costs and disbursements shall rest in the discretion of the court, and may be awarded to the prevailing party. The judgment rendered in such an action shall include the amount of such costs and specify to whom and by whom the costs are to be paid. If such action is brought in a court not of record, they shall be the same as allowed in civil actions in such court. The expenses incurred in serving the summons by publication may be added to the amount of costs now allowed in such court.

§ 3412. **Judgment in case of failure to establish lien.**— If the lienor shall fail, for any reason, to establish a valid lien in an action under the provisions of this title, he may recover judgment therein for such sums as are due him, or which he might recover in an action on a contract, against any party to the action.

§ 3413. **Offer to pay into court.**— At any time after an action is brought under the provision of this title, the owner may make and file with the clerk with whom the notice of lien is filed, if in a court of record, and if in a court not of record, with the court, an offer to pay into court the sum of money stated therein, or to execute and deposit securities which he may describe, in discharge of the lien, and serve upon the plaintiff a copy of such offer. If a written acceptance of the offer is filed with such clerk, or court, within ten days after its service, and a copy of the acceptance is served upon the party making the offer, the court, upon proof of such offer and acceptance, may make an order, that on depositing with such clerk, or court, the sum so offered, or the securities described, the lien shall be discharged, and that the money or securities deposited shall take the place of the property upon which the lien existed, and shall be subject to the lien. If the offer is of money only, the court, on application and notice to the plaintiff may make such order, without the acceptance of the offer by the plaintiff. Money or securities deposited upon the acceptance of an offer pursuant to this section shall be held by the clerk or the court until the final determination of the action, including an appeal.

§ 3414. **Preference over contractors.**— When a laborer or a material man shall perform labor or furnish materials for an improvement of real property for which he is entitled to a mechanic's lien, the amount due to him shall be paid out of the proceeds of the sale of such property under any judgment rendered pursuant to this title, in the order of priority of his lien, before any part of such proceeds is paid to a contractor or subcontractor. If several notices of lien are filed for the same claim, as where the contractor has filed a notice of lien for the services of his workmen, and the workmen have also filed notices of lien, the judgment shall provide for but one payment of the claim which shall be paid to the parties entitled thereto in the order of priority. Payment voluntarily made upon any claim filed as a lien shall not impair or diminish the lien of any person except the person to whom the payment was made.

§ 3415. **Judgment may direct delivery of property in lieu of money.**—If the owner has agreed to deliver bills, notes, securities or other obligations or any other species of property, in payment of the debt upon which the lien is based, the judgment may direct that such substitute be delivered or deposited as the court may direct, and the property affected by the lien cannot be sold, by virtue of such judgment, except in default of the owner to so deliver or deposit within the time directed by the court.

§ 3416. **Judgment for deficiency.**—If upon the sale of the property under judgment in a court of record there is a deficiency of proceeds to pay the plaintiff's claim, judgment may be docketed for the deficiency against any person liable therefor, who shall be adjudged to pay the same in like manner and with like effect as in judgments for deficiency in foreclosure cases.

§ 3417. **Discharge of mechanics' lien, by order of court.**—A mechanic's lien on real property may be vacated and cancelled by an order of a court of record. Before such order shall be granted a notice shall be served upon the lienor, either personally or by leaving it at his last-known place of residence, with a person of suitable age, with directions to deliver it to the lienor. Such notice shall require the lienor to commence an action to enforce the lien, within a time specified in the notice, not less than thirty days from the time of service, or show cause at a special term of a court of record, or at a county court, in a county in which the property is situated, at a time and place specified therein, why the notice of lien filed should not be vacated and cancelled of record. Proof of such service and that the lienor has not commenced the action to foreclose such lien, as directed in the notice, shall be made by affidavit, at the time of applying for such order.

§ 3418. **Judgments in actions to foreclose liens on account of public improvements.**— If, in an action to enforce a lien on account of a public improvement, the court finds that the lien is established, it shall render judgment directing the municipal corporation to pay over to the lienors entitled thereto for work done or material furnished for such public improvement, and in such order of priority as the court may determine, to the extent of the sums found due the lienors from the contractors, so much of the funds or money which may be due from the state or municipal corporation to the contractor, as will satisfy such liens, with interest and costs, not exceeding the amount due to the contractor.

§ 3419. **Judgment in actions to foreclose a mechanic's lien on property of a railroad corporation.**— If the lien is for labor done or materials furnished for a railroad corporation, upon its land, or upon or for its track, rolling stock or the appurtenances of its railroad, the judgment shall not direct the sale of any of the real property described in the notice of the lien, but when in such case, a judgment is entered and docketed with the county clerk of the county where the notice of lien is filed, or a transcript thereof is filed and docketed in any other county, it shall be a lien upon the real property of the railroad corporation, against which it is obtained, to the same extent, and enforcible in like manner as other judgments of courts of record against such corporation.

§ 2. The code of civil procedure is hereby amended by inserting in chapter twenty-two, a new title, to be known as title four, and to read as follows:

TITLE IV.

PROCEEDINGS TO ENFORCE LIENS ON VESSELS.

Section * 3420. Enforcement of liens on vessels.
      3421. Application for warrant.
      3422. Undertaking to accompany application.
      3423. Warrant; execution thereof.
     *3423. Order to show cause; contents; service.
      3424. Notice of service to be published and served.
      3425. Proceedings upon return of order to show cause.
      3426. Order of sale.
      3427. Sale and proceeds.
      3428. Notice of the distribution of the proceeds of sale.
      3429. Liens for which no warrants are issued.
      3430. Contested claims.
      3431. Trial of issues and appeal.
      3432. Distribution of proceeds.
      3433. Payment of uncontested claims.
      3434. Court may invest proceeds; distribution of surplus.
      3435. Application for a discharge of warrant.
      3436. Undertaking to accompany application for discharge.
      3437. Discharge of warrant.
      3438. Action on undertaking.
      3439. Costs of proceedings.
      3440. Sheriff must return warrant.
      3441. Discharge of lien before issue of warrant.

---

* So in the original.

*§ 3419. **Enforcement of liens on vessels.**—Liens on vessels, created by virtue of article two of the lien law, and not based upon a maritime contract, may be enforced as prescribed in this title.

§ 3420. **Application for warrant.**—The lienor may make a written application to a justice of the supreme court, at chambers, in the judicial district in which the lienor resides or in a county adjoining such district, for a warrant to enforce a lien on a vessel and to collect the amount thereof.

The application shall specify:

1. By whom and when such debt was contracted and for what vessel; and the name and residence of the owner of the vessel, if known.

2. The items composing the debt and the amount claimed.

3. That the debt is justly due the applicant over and above all payments and just deductions.

4. Any assignment or transfer of the debt which may have taken place since it was contracted.

5. When and where the notice of lien was filed.

The application shall be verified in the same manner as a pleading in a court of record.

§ 3421. **Undertaking to accompany application.**—Such application shall be accompanied by an undertaking in the sum of at least one hundred dollars, to be approved by such justice and filed in the office of the clerk of the county where the notice of lien is filed, with at least one surety, who shall be a resident and freeholder within the state, to the effect that if it is finally adjudged that the applicant was not entitled to the warrant, he will pay all costs which may be awarded against him, not exceeding the amount specified in the undertaking, and any damages sustained by reason of the seizure of the vessel under such warrant, not to exceed fifty dollars.

§ 3422. **Warrant; execution thereof**—Thereupon, such justice shall issue a warrant to the sheriff of the county where such vessel may be, or, generally to the sheriff of any county, specifying the amount of the claim, and the names of the persons making the claim and commanding him to seize and safely keep such ship or vessel, her tackle, apparel and furniture, to satisfy such claim, if established to be a lien upon the vessel according to law, and within ten days after the seizure to make return of his proceedings under the warrant to such justice. The sheriff shall forthwith execute such warrant, and keep the vessel, her tackle, apparel and furni-

---

ture to be disposed of according to law. In his return the sheriff shall state also whether he has seized such vessel by virtue of any other warrant, and if so, in whose behalf and for what sum such warrant was issued and the time of its receipt by him.

§ 3423. Order to show cause; contents; service.—At the time of issuing such warrant the justice shall grant an order to show cause, why the vessel seized by virtue of such warrant should not be sold to satisfy the lien specified in the application. Such order shall be returnable not less than eight days after the service thereof, as required in this section, before the justice and at the time and place mentioned therein. It shall be directed to the master or other person in charge of the vessel seized and to the owner and consignee thereof, if known. A copy of such order and the application for the warrant shall be served personally upon the master or other person in charge of such vessel at the time of the execution of such warrant; and personally upon the owner and consignee of such vessel if a resident of the state, or if not a resident of the state, by mail addressed to such owner or consignee at his last known place of residence, within ten days after the execution of such warrant.

§ 3424. Notice of service to be published and served.—Within three days after the issue of the warrant, the applicant shall cause a notice to be published once in each week for two consecutive weeks, in a newspaper published in the county where the vessel was seized, stating the issuance of the warrant, the date thereof, the amount of the claim specified therein, the name of the applicant, and the time and place of the return of the order to show cause granted as prescribed in this title. If the vessel seized is used to navigate any of the canals or lakes of the state, a copy of such notice shall be served personally, or by mail, within ten days after the first publication, upon all persons who have filed claims or liens against such vessel, by mortgage or otherwise in the office of the comptroller of the state.

§ 3425. Proceedings upon return of order to show cause.— At the time and place mentioned in the order to show cause, the master or other person in charge of such vessel, the owner or consignee thereof or any other person interested therein, may apply and contest the claim of the lienor as contained in the application for a warrant, by filing with the justice an affidavit controverting any material allegation contained in the notice of lien or the application of the lienor. The issue so raised shall be tried as are other

issues in a court of record, without a jury, before the justice granting the order at a time to be fixed by him, or they may be referred
by him to a referee, to be heard and determined.

§ 3426. Order of sale.— An order may be made by the justice
before whom the order to show cause was returnable, for the sale
of the vessel, her tackle, apparel and furniture, in the following
cases:

1. In case the master, owner, consignee or other person interested in the vessel does not appear upon the return day and contest
the claim of the lienor, and proof is made of the service of the order
to show cause and the application and of the publication of the
notice and the service thereof, as required in this title, and due
proof is made of the validity and amount of such claim;

2. In case a trial is had of the issues raised, and it is determined
that the lien is valid and the amount claimed by the lienor or some
part thereof is due.

Such order shall direct the sheriff who seized the vessel to sell
the same and her tackle, apparel and furniture, to satisfy the liens
established on the hearing, and pay the costs and expenses necessarily incurred in the proceedings as prescribed in this title. The
rights of mortgagees whose mortgages have been filed according to
law, prior to the filing of the notice of lien, on account of which
the order of sale is granted, shall not be affected by the sale of such
vessel pursuant to such order.

§ 3427. Sale and proceeds.—Within ten days after the receipt
of the order of sale, the sheriff, unless the order be sooner vacated
or the lien discharged, shall sell the vessel seized, her tackle, apparel and furniture, upon notice, and in the manner prescribed by
law for the sale of personal property upon execution issued out of
a court of record. He shall make a return to the justice granting
the order, of his proceedings thereunder, and shall, after deducting
his fees and expenses in seizing, preserving, watching and selling
the vessel, pay into court the remaining proceeds of the sale.

§ 3428. Notice of the distribution of the proceeds of sale.—The
justice granting the order of sale, upon receiving such proceeds,
shall order a notice to be published once a week for three successive weeks in the same newspaper in which the notice of seizure
was published, requiring all persons having liens upon the vessel
under article two of the lien law, and the master, owner, agent or
consignee thereof, and all other persons interested therein, to appear
before him, or a referee appointed by him, at the time and place

specified in such notice, not less than thirty nor more than forty days from the first publication thereof, to attend a distribution of such proceeds. Such justice may appoint a referee to make such distribution.

§ 3429. **Liens for which no warrants are issued.**—A person who has a lien under article two of the lien law, against the vessel so sold, and has made no application for a warrant thereon, may present to and file with the justice or referee at the time and place specified in the notice of distribution of such proceeds, a verified statement of the facts and allegations required to be stated in the application for a warrant. And thereupon such lien shall be determined, with the same effect as if a warrant had been issued to enforce such lien.

§ 3430. **Contested claims.**—The master, owner, agent or consignee of the vessel, or any person having an interest in the proceeds before final distribution thereof, may contest any claim made against the vessel or its proceeds, by filing with such justice a written answer, verified as a pleading in a court of record, designating the claims contested and controverting any material allegation of the notice of lien, application for a warrant or statement of lien, and setting up any other matter in defense thereto. A copy of such answer shall be served within five days from such filing, upon the person whose claim is contested, or his attorney.

If the answer does not contain any matter of defense to the claim, it may be stricken out on motion of any person who has filed a notice of lien against the vessel.

§ 3431. **Trial of issues and appeal.**—The issues raised by any such answer shall be tried in the same manner as issues are tried in a court of record without a jury, before such justice at a time and place to be fixed by him, or they may be referred by such justice to a referee, to hear and determine. An appeal may be taken from the decision of such justice or referee as in a civil action in a court of record. On such appeal the decision upon the law and the facts, may be reversed, modified or a new trial ordered. Costs, upon appeal, shall be allowed, as in the case of an appeal from a judgment in a court of record, and judgment may be rendered therefor.

§ 3432. **Distribution of proceeds.**—Upon the determination of all the claims presented, the justice or referee shall make an order of distribution of the proceeds. The order shall direct the payment of the claims found to be subsisting liens upon such vessel or proceeds, with all costs, expenses and allowances, in the order of the priority of filing the notices of such liens, as provided in article two of the lien law. Such costs, expenses and allowances shall be in the discretion of the justice, except as otherwise provided in this title.

§ 3433. **Payment of uncontested claims.**— Any uncontested claims, entitled to priority of payment over the claims which are contested, shall, on motion of the parties interested, be paid with costs, in the order of their respective priorities, without awaiting the determination of such contest. If at any time it is made to appear that after the payment of all prior uncontested claims and their respective costs, and after deducting an amount sufficient to pay all prior contested claims and costs, that there remains a surplus of proceeds applicable to the payment of any subsequent uncontested claims such claims may on notice to all the parties interested be paid out of the surplus with costs, without awaiting the determination of such contest.

§ 3434. **Distribution of surplus.**— If upon payment of all claims established as liens against the vessel from the proceeds of its sale, a surplus remains, it may be distributed by the court to the persons entitled thereto, after a hearing and the publication of a notice by the applicants for the same time and in the same manner as the notice of seizure is required by this title to be published. Such notice shall specify the amount of the surplus proceeds, the names of the persons applying therefor, the name of the vessel from the sale of which the same arose, the date of the sale and the time and place when the hearing will be held and the distribution of the surplus made.

§ 3435. **Application for a discharge of warrant.**— The owner, consignee, agent or master of any vessel so seized, or any person interested therein, may at any time before the sale of the vessel under this title, apply in person or by attorney to the justice issuing the warrant, on at least one day's notice to the lienor or his attorney, for an order discharging the same on giving an undertaking therefor. Such notice shall specify the names, places of residence and places of business of the proposed sureties upon such undertaking.

§ 3436. **Undertaking to accompany application for discharge.**— The application shall be accompanied by an undertaking to the lienor executed by at least two sureties in a sum at least twice the amount specified in the warrant, to the effect that the person making the application for the discharge of the vessel will pay

the amount of all claims and demands which shall be established
to be due to the person in whose behalf the warrant was issued,
and to have been a subsisting lien on the vessel at the time of its
issue. The undertaking when found sufficient, must be approved
by the justice to whom the application is made as to the sufficiency
of the sureties, and the lienor may examine the sureties as to their
sufficiency at such time and places as may be fixed by such justice.

§ 3437. Discharge of warrant.— When such undertaking shall
have been executed, approved and delivered to the lienor and the
taxed fees of the sheriff upon the seizure and detention of the
vessel have been paid, the justice shall make an order discharging
the warrant, and no further proceedings against the vessel seized
shall be had under this article founded upon any demand secured
by such undertaking.

§ 3438. Action on undertaking.—The undertaking may be prosecuted by action in any court having jurisdiction thereof, at any
time within three months after its delivery, but not afterward. If,
in such action it is found that any sum is due the plaintiff which
was a subsisting lien upon the vessel at the time the notice of lien
was filed, the plaintiff shall have judgment for the recovery of the
same with the costs and disbursements of the action and the costs
of the proceedings for the seizing of the vessel and shall have execution therefor. If it is found in such action that no such lien
existed, judgment shall be rendered against the plaintiff for the
costs and disbursements of the action and the costs of the proceedings, including the amount paid the sheriff in the discharge of
the vessel from the warrant.

§ 3439. Costs of proceedings.—The costs of the proceedings in
addition to the disbursements shall be: For filing notice of lien, two
dollars. For applying for and procuring a warrant if the lien is
fifty dollars or under, ten dollars; if the lien exceeds fifty dollars
and is not more than two hundred and fifty dollars, twenty dollars;
if the lien exceeds two hundred and fifty dollars, and is not more
than one thousand dollars, thirty dollars; if the lien exceeds one
thousand dollars, forty dollars. For attending proceedings upon
the discharge of the warrant on the execution of an undertaking,
ten dollars.

The sheriff shall be entitled in any such proceedings to
the following fees and expenses: For serving warrant, one
dollar. For return of the same, one dollar. The necessary sums
paid by him for the expense of keeping the vessel in custody, not

exceeding two dollars and fifty cents for each day. The sheriff shall not receive any other or greater sums for any service rendered by him in any proceeding under this title, nor shall he be allowed expense of custody of the vessel upon more than one warrant at the same time. All costs, disbursements and fees shall be verified by affidavit and adjusted by the justices issuing the warrant.

§ 3440. Sheriff must return warrant.—A sheriff to whom a warrant may have been delivered pursuant to the provisions of this title, may be compelled by an order made by the justice issuing it, to return such warrant with his proceedings thereon and pay over moneys in his hands, and to take any necessary steps for the safety of the vessel, pursuant to any order for that purpose. Obedience to such order may be enforced by attachment against the sheriff on the application of any person interested therein.

§ 3441. Discharge of lien before issue of warrant.—When any notice of lien shall have been filed under this article and no warrant has been issued to enforce the same, any person interested in the vessel, may apply to any justice of the supreme court for leave to discharge the lien upon giving an undertaking therefor to the lienor. The application shall be in writing, and shall state the amount of the lien claimed and the grounds of the defense thereto, and the names of the persons proposed as sureties on such undertaking, with their respective residences and places of business. Upon presenting such application with proof that a copy thereof, with at least five days' notice of the time and place of presenting the same, has been served upon the lienor, such justice may, if no just cause be shown in opposition thereto, authorize the execution of such undertaking, which shall be to the same effect as an undertaking required in this article upon the application to discharge a warrant, and an action may be brought thereon in like manner. At the time of the presentation of such application the sureties proposed in such undertaking shall justify before such justice. When such undertaking has been executed and approved by such justice and delivered to the lienor, the justice shall direct the clerk with whom the notice of lien is filed to mark the same as discharged, and it shall cease to be lien upon such vessel.

§ 3. The laws enumerated in the schedule hereto annexed are repealed. Such repeal shall not revive a law repealed by any law hereby repealed, but shall include all laws amendatory of the laws hereby repealed.

§ 4. The repeal of a law or any part of it, specified in the annexed schedule, shall not affect or impair any act done or right accruing, accrued or acquired under or by virtue of the laws so repealed, but the same may be asserted, enforced or prosecuted as fully and to the same extent, as if such laws had not been repealed. And all actions and proceedings commenced under or by virtue of any provision of a law, so repealed, and pending immediately prior to the taking effect of this act, may be prosecuted and defended to final effect in the same manner as they might if such provisions were not repealed.

§ 5. This act shall take effect September first, eighteen hundred and ninety-seven.

SCHEDULE OF LAWS REPEALED.

Laws of	Chapter.	Sections.	Subject.
1862....	482.....	All except §§ 1, 2, 3, 27, 33.	Enforcement of liens on vessels.
1863....	422.....	1..............	Amends L. 1862, ch. 482, § 7.
1875....	392.....	3, 4...........	Enforcement of mechanics' liens on railroad.
1878....	315.....	6, 7, 8, 9, 10, 11, 12.	Enforcement of mechanics' liens on account of public improvement.
1873....	334.....	2..............	Amends L. 1862, ch. 482, § 9.
1880....	440.....	5, 6, 7, 8, 9, 10..	Enforcement of liens on oil wells.
1885....	342.....	All except §§ 1, 2, 3, 4, 5, 6, 24,	Enforcement of mechanics' liens on real property.
1891....	255.....	6, 7, 8, 9.......	Amends L. 1878, ch. 315.
1892....	629.....	6, 7, 8, 9.......	Amends L. 1878, ch. 315.
1895....	673.....	All...........	Amends L. 1885, ch. 342, § 20.

Chap. 420.

AN ACT in relation to partnership, constituting chapter fifty-one of the general laws.

Became a law May 13, 1897, with the approval of the Governor. Passed, three-fifths being present.

The People of the State of New York, represented in Senate and Assembly, do enact as follows:

CHAPTER LI OF THE GENERAL LAWS.

THE PARTNERSHIP LAW.

ARTICLE I.

GENERAL PROVISIONS.

Section 1. **Short title.**— This chapter shall be known as the partnership law.

§ 2. **Partnership defined.**— A partnership, as between the members thereof, is the association, not incorporated, of two or more persons who have agreed to combine their labor, property and skill, or some of them, for the purpose of engaging in any lawful trade or business, and sharing the profits and losses, as such, between them.

§ 3. **General partnership** — A partnership formed otherwise than in the manner prescribed in this chapter for the formation of a limited partnership, is a general partnership.

§ 4. **Limited partnership.**— A limited partnership consists of one or more persons, called general partners, and also one or more persons called special partners.

§ 5. **Authority of general partner.**— Every general partner is agent for the partnership in the transaction of its business, and has authority to do whatever is necessary to carry on such business in the ordinary manner.

§ 6. **Liability of general partner.**— Every general partner is liable to third persons for all the obligations of the partnership, jointly and severally with his general co-partners.

§ 7. **Liability of special partner.**— A special partner, except as declared in this chapter, is liable for the obligations of the limited partnership only to the amount of the capital invested by him therein.

ARTICLE II.
BUSINESS AND PARTNERSHIP NAMES.

Section 20. When business or partnership name may be continued.
21. Certificate to be filed and recorded; clerk's fees.

Section 20. **When partnership or business name may be continued.**— The use of a partnership or a business name may be continued in either of the following cases:

1. Where the business of any firm or partnership in this state, having business relations with foreign countries or which has transacted business in this state for not less than three years, continues to be conducted by some or any of the partners, their assignees or appointees;

2. Where a majority of the members, general or special, of a general or limited partnership formed under the laws of this state, or of the stockholders of any corporation, domestic or foreign, which may theretofore have carried on its business within this state, and where said general or limited partnership or corporation has discontinued or shall be about to discontinue its business within the state, and where a majority of the partners, general or special, in either of such last mentioned co-partnerships or of the survivors thereof shall be members of the new limited co-partnership, or where a majority of the members of such co-partnership theretofore existing or of the surviving members thereof or of the stockholders of such corporation shall consent in writing to the use of such firm or corporate name by the new limited partnership; or

3. Where any resident of this state dies, who at the time of his death and for at least five years immediately prior thereto, conducted and carried on in his sole name, any business in this state, or who at the time of his death, so conducted and carried on any business having relation with other states or foreign countries, the

right to use the name of such person, for the purpose of continuing and carrying on such business, shall survive and pass and be disposed of and accounted for as part of the personal estate of such deceased person, and such business may be continued and carried on under such name by any person who comes into the legal possession thereof.

§ 21. Certificate to be filed and recorded ; clerks's fees.— Whenever a partnership or business name continues to be used as provided by the last preceding section, the person or persons using such name shall sign and acknowledge a certificate, declaring the person or persons intending to deal under such name, with their respective places of residence, and file the same in the clerk's office of the county where the principal place of business is located, and cause a copy of such certificate to be published once in each week for four consecutive weeks in a newspaper of the city or town in which such principal place of business is located, or if none be published in such city or town, in the newspaper nearest thereto. A county clerk with whom any such certificate is filed, shall keep a book in which all such certificates shall be recorded, with their date of record, and also a register in which shall be entered in alphabetical order the name of every such partnership and of the partners thereof, and every such business name of a deceased person and the names of the persons filing certificates therefor. The clerk is entitled to a fee of one dollar for filing and recording such certificate and entering such names, and to an additional fee of ten cents for every name of a partner beyond two, and to a fee of fifty cents for a certified copy of such certificate.

ARTICLE III.
LIMITED PARTNERSHIPS.

Section 30. Formation.
        31. Affidavit to be filed.
        32. Terms of partnership to be published.
        33. Renewal or continuance of partnership.
        34. Effect of false statements or failure to publish terms.
        35. The firm name, list of members to be posted.
        36. Liability of partners.
        37. General powers of partners.
        38. Actions by and against the partnership.
        39. Capital of special partner not to be withdrawn; when he may receive interest.

Section 40. Fraudulent transfers of property by partnership or partner.

41. Dissolution or alterations; by death of partner; when partnership may be continued by survivors.

42. Dissolution by acts of partners.

§ 30. **Formation.**— Two or more persons may form a limited partnership, which shall consist of one or more persons of full age, called general partners, and also of one or more persons of full age, who contribute in actual cash payments, a specified sum as capital, to the common stock, called special partners, for the transaction within this state of any lawful business, except banking and insurance, by making, severally signing and acknowledging, and causing to be filed and recorded in the clerk's office of the county where the principal place of business of such partnership is located, a certificate, in which is stated:

1. The name or firm under which such partnership is to be conducted, and the county wherein the principal place of business is to be located;

2. The general nature of the business intended to be transacted;

3. The names, and whether of full age, of all the general and special partners interested therein, distinguishing which are general and which are special partners, and their respective places of residence :

4. The amount of capital which each special partner has contributed to the common stock;

5. The times at which the partnership is to begin and end.

If the partnership has places of business situated in different counties, a copy of the certificate, and of the acknowledgment thereof, certified by the clerk in whose office it is filed, under his official seal, shall be filed and recorded in like manner, in the office of the clerk of each such county.

§ 31. **Affidavit to be filed.**—At the time of filing such original certificate, an affidavit of one or more of the general partners, stating that the sums specified in the certificate to have been contributed to the common stock by each of the special partners have been actually and in good faith paid in cash, shall also be filed in the same office, and a copy thereof certified by the county clerk, filed in each office in which a copy of the original certificate is filed.

§ 32. **Terms of partnership to be published.**—Immediately after the filing of the certificate, a copy of the same or a notice containing the substance thereof, shall be published once in each week for six successive weeks, in two newspapers of the county in which such original certificate is filed, to be designated by the county clerk, one of which newspapers shall be a newspaper published in the city or town in which the principal place of business is intended to be located, if a newspaper be published therein; or, if no newspaper is published therein, in the newspaper nearest thereto, and proof of such publication by affidavit of the printer or publisher of each of such newspapers must be filed with the original certificate.

§ 33. **Renewal or continuance of partnership.**—Every such partnership may be renewed or continued, beyond the time fixed for its duration, in the manner required for its original formation; and no such partnership shall be deemed to have been originally formed, or so renewed or continued, until a certificate is made, acknowledged, filed and recorded, an affidavit filed, and certificate or notice published as required by law.

§ 34. **Effect of false statements or failure to publish terms.**—If any false statement be made in any such certificate or affidavit, made either upon the formation or renewal or continuance or increase of capital of such partnership, or if any such certificate or notice is not so published, or if such partnership be renewed or continued in any other manner, the persons interested therein shall all be liable as general partners.

§ 35. **The firm name; list of members to be posted.**—The business of the partnership must be conducted under a firm name, which must consist of the name of the general partner, or if there be two or more general partners, of the names of one or more of such partners, with or without the addition of the words " and company." or " and Co." If the name of any special partner be used in such firm name, with his privity, he shall be deemed and be liable as a general partner. The partnership must cause to be placed in a conspicuous place on the outside and in front of the building in which is its principal place of business, a sign on which is printed in legible English, the names in full, of all the members of such partnership, designating which are general and which are special partners. If such sign be not so placed, no action against the partnership shall abate or be dismissed by reason of the failure of the plaintiff to correctly allege in his pleadings, or prove as alleged the number and names of the members of the partnership; but his pleadings may be amended on the trial to conform to the proof in that respect, without costs.

§ 36. **Liability of partners.**— The general partners in such partnership shall be jointly and severally liable as general partners are by law. The special partners shall not be liable for the debts of the partnership beyond the fund contributed by them respectively to the capital of the partnership.

§ 37. **General powers of partners.**— Except as provided in this section, the general partners only may transact the business of the partnership, and they shall be liable to account to each other and to the special partners, for their management of the business, as other partners are by law. Except as provided in this section, a special partner may not sign for the partnership nor bind the same, nor transact any business on account of the partnership, nor be employed for that purpose, as agent, attorney or otherwise. A special partner may, from time to time, examine into the state and progress of the partnership business, and advise as to its management; may loan money to, and advance and pay money for the partnership; and may take and hold the notes, drafts, acceptances and bonds of or belonging to the partnership, as security for the repayment of such money and interest, and may use and lend his name and credit as security for the partnership, in any business thereof, and has the same rights and remedies in these respects as other creditors might have; may lease to the general partner or partners any real or other property for the purposes of the partnership, at such rents and on such terms as may be agreed on; and may negotiate sales, purchases and other business for the partnership, but no business so negotiated is binding on the partnership until approved by a general partner. If a special partner interfere contrary to these provisions, he shall be deemed and be liable as a general partner. If such partnership become insolvent or bankrupt, a special partner shall not. except for claims contracted in pursuance of this section, be allowed to claim as creditor, until the claims of all the other creditors of the partnership are satisfied.

§ 38. **Actions by and against the partnership.**—Actions and special proceedings in relation to the business of the partnership may be brought and conducted by and against the general partners, in the same manner as if there were no special partners.

§ 39. **Capital of special partner not to be withdrawn; when he may receive interest.**—No part of the sum which any special partner contributes to the capital stock, shall be withdrawn by him or paid or transferred to him, in the shape of dividends, profits or otherwise, at any time during the continuance of the partnership; but any such partner may annually receive lawful interest on the sum so contributed by him, if the payment of such interest does not reduce the original amount of such capital; and if, after the payment of such interest, any profits remain to be divided, he may also receive his portion of such profit. But if by the payment of such interest or profits to any special partner, the original capital is reduced, the partner receiving the same must restore the amount necessary to make good his share of capital, with interest, and he becomes liable as a general partner for debts contracted until he returns such amount, to the extent of the amount so withdrawn.

§ 40. **Fraudulent transfers of property by partnership or partner.** —Every sale, assignment or transfer of any of the property or effects of such limited partnership, made by such partnership when insolvent or in contemplation of insolvency, or after or in contemplation of the insolvency of any partner, or of any of the property or effects of a general or special partner, made by any general or special partner, when insolvent or after or in contemplation of the insolvency of such partnership or such partner, with the intent of giving a preference to any creditor of such partnership or insolvent partner over other creditors of the partnership, and every judgment confessed, lien created, or security given, by such partnership or partner, under the like circumstances, and with like intent, is void as against the creditors of the partnership.

Every special partner, who violates this section, or concurs in, or assents to, any such violation by the partnership, or by any individual partner, is liable as a general partner.

§ 41. **Dissolution by alteration ; by death of partner ; when partnership may be continued by survivors.**—Except as provided in this section, every alteration made in the names of the general partners, in the nature of the business, or in the capital, or shares thereof contributed, held or owned, or to be contributed, held or owned, by any of the special partners, and the death of any partner, whether general or special, dissolves the limited partnership, or if such partnership be continued, constitutes such partnership, a general partnership, in respect to all business transacted after such alteration or death, unless the articles of partnership provide that in the event of the death of a partner, the partnership may be continued by the survivors, in which case it shall be so continued with the consent of the personal representatives of the deceased partner, and personal representatives may succeed to the partnership rights of such deceased partner, and continue the business the same as if such partner had remained alive. But any special partner may from time to time increase the amount of capital stock contributed, held or owned by him, or one or more special partners may be added to the partnership, on actually paying in an additional amount of the capital to be agreed on by the general and special partners, and on filing in the office of the clerk with whom the original certificate was filed, an additional certificate of the general partners in the partnership name, verified by the oath of one of them, stating the increase of such capital stock, and by whom, and the names and residences of such additional special partners, and whether of full age, and the amounts contributed by each to the common stock, together with the affidavit of one or more of the general partners stating that the sums specified in such additional certificate have been actually and in good faith paid in cash; and such alteration does not make the partnership general. No additional publication of the terms of the partnership nor of the alteration thereof is required in any of the cases provided for in this section. Any special partner or the legal representatives of any such special partner, deceased, may sell his interest in the partnership, without working a dissolution thereof, or rendering the partnership general, if a notice of such sale be filed within ten days thereafter in the office of the clerk with whom the original certificate of partnership was filed, and the purchaser thereof thereupon becomes a special partner with the same right as an original special partner.

§ 42. **Dissolution by act of partners.**—A limited partnership may be dissolved by the acts of the partners before the time specified for its termination in the certificate of formation, renewal or continuance. But such a dissolution does not take effect, until a notice of the dissolution has been filed with the clerk of the county in which the original certificate is filed and published at least once in each of four successive weeks in a newspaper published in each county where the partnership has a place of business.

ARTICLE IV.

LAWS REPEALED; WHEN TO TAKE EFFECT.

Section 50. Laws repealed.
  51. When to take effect.

§ 50. **Laws repealed.**— The laws or parts thereof specified in the schedule hereto annexed, and all acts amendatory thereof are repealed.

§ 51. **When to take effect.**— This chapter shall take effect on the first day of October, eighteen hundred and ninety-seven.

SCHEDULE OF LAWS REPEALED.

R. S., part II, ch. 4, tit. I. All .. Limited partnerships.

Laws.	Chapter.	Sections.	
1837....	129.....	All.....	Amendatory of R. S., pt. II, ch. 4, tit. I, § 5.
1849....	347.....	All.....	Co-partnership names.
1854....	400.....	All.....	Authorizing use of co-partnership names in certain cases.
1857....	414.....	All.....	Amends R. S., pt. II, ch. 4, tit. I, §§ 3, 17, 23.
1858....	289.....	All.....	Amends R. S., pt. II, ch. 4, tit I, § 12.
1862....	476.....	All.....	Amends R. S., pt. II, ch. 4, tit. I, § 9.
1863....	144.....	All.....	Amends L. 1854, ch. 400.
1866....	70......	All.....	Amends R. S., pt. II, ch. 4, tit. I, § 1.
1866....	661.....	All.....	Amends R. S., pt. II, ch. 4, tit. I, § 13.
1868....	256.....	All.....	Use of partnership names.
1872....	114.....	All.....	Special partners may lease to general partners lands, etc.
1880....	561.....	1, 2, 3, 4.	Use of business names.
1881....	389.....	All.....	Amends L. 1880, ch. 561, § 1.
1881....	425.....	All.....	Amends L. 1850, ch. 256.
1888....	142.....	All.....	Amends L. 1854, ch. 400, § 4.
1893....	263.....	All.....	Amends L. 1868, ch. 256.
1894....	329.....	All.....	Amends L. 1854, ch. 400.
1895....	145.....	All.....	Amends R. S. pt. II, ch. 4, tit. I, § 12.

Chap. 427.

AN ACT to amend the code of criminal procedure, in relation to practice on appeals.

Became a law May 14, 1897, with the approval of the Governor.
Passed, a majority being present.

The People of the State of New York, represented in Senate and Assembly, do enact as follows:

Section 1. Sections three hundred and eight, three hundred and thirteen, three hundred and thirty-two, four hundred and fifty-six, four hundred and fifty-eight, four hundred and sixty, four hundred and eighty-five, five hundred and twenty-one, five hundred and twenty-eight, five hundred and twenty-nine, five hundred and thirty-four, five hundred and forty-three, five hundred and forty-nine, five hundred and fifty-six, five hundred and eighty-five are hereby amended to read as follows:

§ 308. Defendant appearing for arraignment without counsel to be informed of his right to counsel.—If the defendant appear for arraignment without counsel, he must be asked if he desire the aid of counsel, and if he does the court must assign counsel. When services are rendered by counsel in pursuance of such assignment in a case where the offense charged in the indictment is punishable by death or on an appeal from a judgment of death, the court in which the defendant is tried or the action or indictment is otherwise disposed of, or by which the appeal is finally determined, may allow such counsel his personal and incidental expenses upon a verified statement thereof being filed with the clerk of such court, and also reasonable compensation for his services in such court, not exceeding the sum of five hundred dollars, which allowance shall be a charge upon the county in which the indictment in the action is found, to be paid out of the court fund, upon the certificate of the judge or justice presiding at the trial or otherwise disposing of the indictment, or upon the certificate of the appellate court, but no such allowance shall be made unless an affidavit is filed with the clerk of the county by or on behalf of the defendant, showing that he is wholly destitute of means.

§ 313. Indictment, when set aside on motion.—The indictment must be set aside by the court in which the defendant is arraigned, and upon his motion, in either of the following cases, but in no other:

1. When it is not found, indorsed and presented as prescribed in

sections two hundred and sixty-eight and two hundred and seventy-two.

2. When a person has been permitted to be present during the session of the grand jury, while the charge embraced in the indictment was under consideration, except as provided in sections two hundred and sixty-two, two hundred and sixty-three and two hundred and sixty-four.

§ 332. There are three kinds of pleas to an indictment:

1. A plea of guilty.

2. A plea of not guilty.

3. A plea of a former judgment of conviction or acquittal of the crime charged, which may be pleaded either with or without the plea of not guilty.

A conviction shall not be had upon a plea of guilty where the crime charged is or may be punishable by death.

§ 456. Where the defendant is convicted of a crime punishable by death, the stenographer, within ten days after the judgment has been pronounced, shall furnish to the attorney for the defendant, at his request, a copy of the stenographic minutes of the entire proceedings upon the trial. The expense of such copy shall be a county charge, payable to the stenographer out of the court fund upon the certificate of the judge presiding at the trial.

§ 458. Case when necessary, how made and settled.—When a party intends to appeal from a judgment rendered after the trial of an issue of fact he must, except as otherwise prescribed by law, make a case and procure the same to be settled and signed, by the judge or justice, by or before whom the action was tried, as prescribed in the general rules of practice; or, in case of the death or disability of such judge or justice, in such manner as the appellate court directs. The case must contain so much of the evidence, and other proceedings upon the trial, as is material to the questions to be raised thereby, and also the exceptions taken by the party making the case; and in a case where a special question is submitted to the jury, such exceptions taken by any party to the action as shall be necessary to determine whether there should be a new trial, if the judgment be reversed. If it afterwards becomes necessary to separate the exceptions, the separation may be made and the exceptions may be stated with so much of the evidence, and other proceedings, as is material to the questions raised by them, in a case prepared and settled as directed by the general rules of practice, or in the absence of directions therein, by the court, upon motion.

§ 460. **Enlarging the time therefor.**—The time for preparing the case, or the amendments thereto, or for settling the same, may be enlarged by consent of the parties, or by the presiding judge or by a justice of the supreme court, but no other officer. Only one order extending the time shall be granted, except upon notice of at least two days to the adverse party.

§ 485. **The judgment-roll.**—When judgment upon a conviction is rendered, the clerk must enter the same upon the minutes, stating briefly the offense for which the conviction has been had; and must, upon the service upon him of notice of appeal, immediately annex together and file the following papers, which constitute the judgment-roll:

1. A copy of the minutes of a challenge interposed by the defendant to a grand juror, and the proceedings and decision thereon.

2. The indictment and a copy of the minutes of the plea or demurrer.

3. A copy of the minutes of a challenge, which may have been interposed to the panel of the trial jury, or to a juror who participated in the verdict, and the proceedings and decision thereon.

4. A copy of the minutes of the trial.

5. A copy of the minutes of the judgment.

6. A copy of the minutes of any proceedings upon a motion either for a new trial or in arrest of judgment.

7. The case, if there is one.

8. When the judgment is of death, the clerk, upon the settling and filing of the case, must forthwith cause to be prepared and printed, and forwarded to the clerk of the court of appeals, the number of copies of the judgment-roll which are required by the rules of the court of appeals, and three copies shall also be furnished to the defendant's attorney, three to the district-attorney, and one to the governor of the state, and the remainder shall be distributed according to the rules of the court of appeals. The expense of preparing and printing the judgment-roll in such case shall be a county charge payable out of the court fund upon the certificate of the county clerk, approved by the county judge or a justice of the supreme court residing in the county in which the conviction was had.

§ 528. **Stay upon appeal to the court of appeals, et cetera.**—An appeal to the court of appeals, from a judgment of the appellate division of the supreme court, affirming a judgment of conviction, stays the execution of the judgment appealed from, upon filing, with the notice of appeal, a certificate of a judge of the court of appeals, or of a justice of the appellate division of the supreme court, that, in his opinion, there is reasonable doubt whether the judgment should stand, but not otherwise. When the judgment is of death, an appeal to the court of appeals stays the execution, of course, until the determination of the appeal. When the judgment is of death, the court of appeals may order a new trial, if it be satisfied that the verdict was against the weight of evidence or against law, or that justice requires a new trial, whether any exception shall have been taken or not in the court below.

§ 529. **Certificates of stay not to be granted except on notice to the district-attorney.**—The certificate mentioned in the last two sections can not, however, be granted upon an appeal on a conviction of felony, until such notice as the judge may prescribe has been given to the district-attorney of the county where the conviction was had, of the application for the certificate, accompanied by a formal specification in writing of the grounds upon which the appli-cation is based, but the judge may stay the execution of the judg-ment until the determination of such application. When an appli-cation for such certificate shall have been made to and denied by the trial judge or a justice of the supreme court or in case of an appeal to the court of appeals, by a judge of that court or a justice of the appellate division of the supreme court, no other application for such certificate shall be made. If an appeal to the appellate division of the supreme court shall not be brought on for argument by the defendant at the next term of the appellate division begun not less than ten days after the granting of such certificate, or if an appeal to the court of appeals shall not be brought on for argu-ment by the defendant when the court of appeals shall have been in actual session for fifteen days after the granting of such certifi-cate, the district-attorney on two days' notice to the defendant may apply to the judge or justice who granted the certificate, or to any judge or justice of the court in which the appeal is pending, for an order vacating the certificate; and upon the entry of such an order the judgment shall be executed as though a certificate had never been granted to the defendant.

§ 534. **Dismissal for want of return.**— The court may also, upon like motion, dismiss the appeal.

1. If the return be not made, as provided in section five hundred and thirty-two, unless for good cause, the time to make such re-turn be enlarged.

2. If the appeal be not brought on for argument by the appellant as promptly after the return has been made as the circumstances of the case will reasonably admit.

§ 543. **May reverse, affirm or modify the judgment, and order a new trial and on affirmance of capital conviction fix the time for the execution of the sentence.**—Upon hearing the appeal the appellate court may, in cases where an erroneous judgment has been entered upon a lawful verdict, or finding of fact, correct the judgment to conform to the judgment or finding; in all other cases they must either reverse or affirm the judgment appealed from, and in cases of reversal, may, if necessary or proper, order a new trial. If the judgment of death is affirmed, the court of appeals, by an order under its seal, signed by a majority of the judges, shall fix the week during which the original sentence of death shall be executed, and such order shall be sufficient authority to the agent and warden of any state prison for the execution of the prisoner at the time therein specified, and the agent and warden must execute the judgment accordingly.

§ 549. **Jurisdiction of appellate court ceases after judgment remitted.**—After the certificate of the judgment has been remitted, as provided in section five hundred and forty-seven, the appellate court has no further jurisdiction of the appeal, or of the proceedings thereon; and except as provided in section five hundred and forty-three, all orders, which may be necessary to carry the judgment into effect, must be made to the court to which the certificate is remitted, or by any court to which the cause may thereafter be removed.

§ 556. **Nature of bail after conviction and upon appeal.**—After conviction and upon appeal, the defendant may be admitted to bail as follows :

1. If the appeal be from a judgment imposing a fine only, on the undertaking of bail, that he will pay the same, or such part of it as the appellate court may direct, if the judgment be affirmed or modified or the appeal be dismissed, or the certificate of reasonable doubt be vacated as provided in section five hundred and twenty-nine.

2. If judgment of imprisonment have been given, that he will surrender himself in execution of the judgment, upon its being affirmed or modified, or upon the appeal being dismissed, or if the certificate of reasonable doubt be vacated as aforesaid.

§ 585. **Qualifications of bail and how put in.**—The sureties must possess the qualifications, and the bail must be put in, in all re-

when competitive examinations are not practicable in cases relating to the civil service of cities.

Rules and regulations.

§ 5. The civil service commissioners of the state of New York and of the cities of the state are hereby empowered and required to establish rules and regulations to carry this act into effect in their respective jurisdictions, but such rules and regulations shall not go into operation until approved by the governor of the state of New York where the civil service of the state is affected thereby, and by the civil service commissioners of the state where the civil service of cities is affected thereby.

Continuation of existing eligible list.

§ 6. Until eligible lists have been prepared pursuant to this act all existing eligible lists, for appointment or promotion in the civil service of the state or in any of the cities thereof made up or created in any other manner than as in this act provided shall be continued in full force and effect and may be certified to the person or persons

Proviso as to ratings.

holding the power of appointment or promotion, provided, however, that the ratings therein given shall relate exclusively to the merit of the applicants therein named, and shall be revised by the civil service commissioners of the state where the same are applicable to the civil service of the state, and by the civil service commissioners or boards of cities, where the same are applicable to cities, on the basis of the rating for merit as determined in section one of this act, and the fitness of such applicants shall then be determined by examination and their standing ascertained and preference in appointment or promotion given according to the provisions of sections two and three of this act.

Repeal.

§ 7. All acts and parts of acts inconsistent with the provisions of this act are hereby repealed.

Rights of persons not affected.

§ 8. This act shall not be construed to deprive any person of the right to advancement or promotion where such right to advancement or promotion is now or shall hereafter be given by law, nor of the rights heretofore secured both as to appointment and upon discharge from employment, to honorably discharged union soldiers, sailors and marines.

§ 9. This act shall take effect immediately.

Chap. 435.

AN ACT to provide the means, and making appropriations to pay the expenses of superintendence, maintenance and ordinary repairs of the canals for the fiscal year beginning on the first day of October, eighteen hundred and ninety-seven.

Became a law May 15, 1897, with the approval of the Governor.
Passed by a two-thirds vote.

The People of the State of New York, represented in Senate and Assembly, do enact as follows:

Section 1. There shall be imposed for the fiscal year commencing on the first day of October, eighteen hundred and ninety-seven, a state tax of twenty-one one-hundredths of a mill on each dollar of the valuation of the real and personal property in this state, subject to taxation, which tax shall be assessed, levied and collected by the annual assessment and collection of taxes for that year in the manner prescribed by law, and shall be paid by the several county treasurers into the treasury of this state, to be held by the state treasurer for the credit of the canal fund; and for appropriation to the purposes hereinafter designated. *State tax of 21-100 of a mill for canal purposes.*

§ 2. There is hereby appropriated from the proceeds of the tax authorized by the first section of this act, for paying the salaries and expenses of the collectors and compilers of statistics relating to the trade and tonnage of the canals the expenses of the superintendence and ordinary repairs of the canals, the traveling expenses of the state engineer and surveyor, the salaries, traveling expenses, clerk hire and office expenses of the superintendent and assistant superintendents of public works, the clerk hire in the bureau of canal affairs and the incidental expenses of said bureau and of the canal board, for the fiscal year commencing on the first day of October, eighteen hundred and ninety-seven, the sum of nine hundred and twenty-six thousand five hundred dollars, to be distributed, applied, apportioned and disposed of as follows: *Appropriation for salaries and expenses.*

For the salaries, traveling expenses, clerk hire and office expenses of the superintendent and assistant superintendents of public works, fifty thousand dollars, or so much thereof as may be necessary. For the salaries of the section superintendents, thirty thousand dollars, or so much thereof as may be necessary. For the traveling expenses of the state engineer and surveyor, two thousand dollars, and for the traveling expenses of the deputy state engineer and surveyor, one thousand dollars, payable quarterly, in full for all such expenses. For clerk hire in the bureau *Supt. of public works and assistants. Section superintendents. State engineer.*

Bureau of canal affairs. Engineers. of canal affairs, six thousand dollars, or so much thereof as may be necessary. For the salaries and compensation of the engineers employed upon the ordinary repairs of the canals, including the incidental expenses of such engineers, thirty thousand dollars, or so much thereof as may be necessary. For the salaries and

Collectors and compilers. compensation of the collectors and compilers of the statistics relating to the trade and tonnage of the canals, and the inspectors and measurers of boats, including the incidental expenses of such collectors and inspectors, thirty thousand dollars, or so much

Incidental expenses. thereof as may be necessary. For the payment of such incidental and miscellaneous expenses as are necessary to be paid out of the canal fund and charged to the account of the Erie and Champlain canal fund and the canal debt sinking fund, seven thousand five hundred dollars, or so much thereof as may be necessary.

Lock tending and repairs. For the payment of the expenses of lock tending and the ordinary repairs of the canals of the state, seven hundred and seventy thousand dollars, or so much thereof as may be necessary.

Payment in anticipation of tax. § 3. In order that the appropriations made by this act may be made available when needed and before the money can be realized from the tax authorized in the first section hereof, payment may be made from any moneys in the treasury to the credit of the canal fund until the said tax is collected and paid into the state treasury.

§ 4. This act shall take effect immediately.

Chap. 437.

AN ACT to amend chapter five hundred and forty-six of the laws of eighteen hundred and ninety-six, entitled "An act relating to state charities," constituting chapter twenty-six of the general laws.

Became a law May 17, 1897, with the approval of the Governor. Passed, three-fifths being present.

The People of the State of New York, represented in Senate and Assembly, do enact as follows:

Section 1. Section three of chapter five hundred and forty-six of the laws of eighteen hundred and ninety-six, entitled "An act relating to state charities," constituting chapter twenty-six of the general laws, is hereby amended so as to read as follows:

§ 3. **State board of charities.**—There shall continue to be a state board of charities, composed of twelve members, who shall be appointed by the governor, by and with the advice and consent of the senate, one of whom shall be appointed from, and reside in each judicial district of the state, one additional member from the county of Kings, and three additional members from the county of New York, who shall respectively reside in such counties. They shall be known as commissioners of the state board of charities, and hold office for eight years. No commissioner shall qualify or enter upon the duties of his office, or remain therein, while he is a trustee, manager, director or other administrative officer of an institution subject to the visitation and inspection of such board. The commissioners in office at the time this chapter takes effect, shall continue in office for the terms for which they were respectively appointed.

§ 2. This act shall take effect immediately.

Chap. 441.

AN ACT to amend section fifty-two of the banking law, relative to stockholders.

Became a law May 17, 1897, with the approval of the Governor. Passed, three-fifths being present.

The People of the State of New York, represented in Senate and Assembly, do enact as follows:

Section 1. Section fifty-two of chapter six hundred and eighty-nine of the laws of eighteen hundred and ninety-two, entitled "An act in relation to banking corporations," and known as the banking law is hereby amended so as to read as follows:

§ 52. Individual liability of stockholders.—Except as prescribed in the stock corporation law, the stockholders of every such corporation shall be individually responsible, equally and ratably, and not one for another, for all contracts, debts and engagements of such corporation, to the extent of the amount of their stock therein, at the par value thereof, in addition to the amount invested in such shares. In case any such corporation shall have been or shall be dissolved by final order or judgment of a court having jurisdiction, and a permanent receiver or receivers of the said corporation shall have been or shall be appointed, all actions or proceedings to enforce the liability of stockholders under this section shall be taken and prosecuted only in the name and in behalf of such receiver or receivers, unless such receiver or receivers shall refuse to take such action or proceeding upon proper request in that behalf made by any creditor, and in that event such action or proceeding may be taken by any creditor of the corporation. The term "stockholder," when used in this chapter, shall apply not only to such persons as appear by the books of the corporation to be stockholders, but also to every owner of stock, legal or equitable, although the same may be on such books in the name of another person, but not to a person who may hold the stock as collateral for security for the payment of a debt.

§ 2. This act shall take effect immediately.

Chap. 442.

AN ACT supplementary to chapter one hundred and twelve of the laws of eighteen hundred and ninety-six, entitled "An act in relation to the traffic in liquors and for the taxation and regulation of the same and to provide for local option, constituting chapter twenty-nine of the general laws," and to the acts amendatory thereof.

Became a law May 17, 1897, with the approval of the Governor.
Passed, three-fifths being present.

The People of the State of New York, represented in Senate and Assembly, do enact as follows:

Assessment of excise tax. Section 1. On and after the first day of January, eighteen hundred and ninety-eight, the excise taxes assessed under chapter twenty-nine of the general laws, entitled "An act in relation to the traffic in liquors and for the taxation and regulation of the same and to provide for local option, constituting chapter twenty-nine of the general laws," and under the acts amendatory thereof, in cities containing a population of fifteen hundred thousand or more, which are or shall be formed by the consolidation of territory situate in one or more counties, shall continue to be assessed in the several portions of the territory so consolidated to form such city, at the same rate as such taxes are assessed on the thirty-first day of December, eighteen hundred and ninety-seven, in the several portions Payment and collection of same. of the territory so consolidated. Such excise taxes so assessed shall be payable to and collected by the same officers or their successors in office who are charged with the collection thereof on the thirty-first day of December, eighteen hundred and ninety-seven under the provisions of said act. The portion of the taxes belonging to the locality, assessed in such territory so consolidated, shall belong and be paid to the city so formed.

§ 2. This act shall take effect on the first day of January, eighteen hundred and ninety-eight. *When takes effect.*

Chap. 443.

AN ACT to amend chapter nine hundred and eight of the laws of eighteen hundred and ninety-six, entitled "An act in relation to taxation, constituting chapter twenty-four of the general laws," in relation to lands sold or leased by the state.

Became a law May 17, 1897, with the approval of the Governor.
Passed, three-fifths being present.

The People of the State of New York, represented in Senate and Assembly, do enact as follows:

Section 1. Section five of chapter nine hundred and eight of the laws of eighteen hundred and ninety-six, known as "the tax law," is hereby amended so as to read as follows:

§ 5. **Taxation of lands sold or leased by the state.**—All lands which have been sold by the state, although not conveyed, shall be assessed in the same manner as if such purchaser were the actual owner. Where land is leased by the state such leasehold interest, except in cases where by the terms of the lease the state is to pay the taxes imposed upon the property leased, shall be assessed to the lessee or occupant in the tax district where the land is situated.

Chap. 444.

AN ACT to prohibit the assignment and subletting of public contracts.

Became a law May 17, 1897, with the approval of the Governor.
Passed, three-fifths being present.

The People of the State of New York, represented in Senate and Assembly, do enact as follows:

Section 1. A clause shall be inserted in all specifications or contracts hereafter made or awarded by the state, or by any county, or any municipal corporation, or any public department or official thereof, prohibiting any contractor, to whom any contract shall be *Prohibitory clause in contracts, etc.*

let, granted or awarded, as required by law, from assigning, transferring, conveying, subletting or otherwise disposing of the same, or of his right, title or interest therein, or his power to execute such contract to any other person, company or corporation, without the previous consent in writing of the department or official awarding the same.

Revocation of contracts assigned, etc., without consent. § 2. If any contractor, to whom any contract is hereafter let, granted or awarded, as required by law, by the state, or any county, or any municipal corporation in the state, or by any public department or official thereof, shall, without the previous written consent specified in section one of this act, assign, transfer, convey, sublet or otherwise dispose of the same, or his right, title or interest therein, or his power to execute such contract, to any other person, company or other corporation, the state, county, municipal corporation, public department, or official as the case may be, which let, made, granted or awarded said contract shall revoke and annul such contract, **Release of liability to contractor.** and the state, county, municipal corporation, public department or officer, as the case may be, shall be relieved and discharged from any and all liability and obligations growing out of said contract to such contractor, and to the person, company, or corporation to whom he shall assign, transfer, convey, sublet or otherwise **Forfeiture of earnings, etc.** dispose of the same, and said contractor, and his assignee, transferee, or sub-lessee, shall forfeit and lose all monies, theretofore earned under said contract except so much as may be required to **Proviso.** pay his employes; provided that nothing herein contained shall be construed to hinder, prevent or affect an assignment by such contractor for the benefit of his creditors, made pursuant to the statutes of this state.

Repeal. § 3. All acts or parts of acts inconsistent with the provisions of this act are hereby repealed.

§ 4. This act shall take effect immediately.

Chap. 446.

AN ACT to amend chapter five hundred and seventy of the laws of eighteen hundred and ninety-five, entitled "An act for the incorporation of associations for the improvement of the breed of horses, and to regulate the same, and to establish a state racing commission," as amended by chapter three hundred and eighty of the laws of eighteen hundred and ninety-six.

Became a law May 17, 1897, with the approval of the Governor. Passed, three-fifths being present.

The People of the State of New York, represented in Senate and Assembly, do enact as follows:

Section 1. Section three of chapter five hundred and seventy of the laws of eighteen hundred and ninety-five, entitled "An act for the incorporation of associations for the improvement of the breed of horses and to regulate the same, and to establish a state racing commission," is hereby amended to read as follows: *Act amended.*

§ 3. Any corporation formed under the provisions of this act, if so claimed in its certificate of organization, and if it shall comply with all the provisions of this act, and any other corporation entitled to the benefits and privileges of this act, as hereinafter provided, shall have the power and right to hold one or more trotting or running race meetings in each year, and to hold, maintain and conduct trotting or running races at such meetings. At such trotting or running race meetings the corporation, or the owners of horses engaged in such races, or others who are not participants in the race, may contribute purses, prizes, premiums or stakes to be contested for, but no person or persons other than the owner or owners of a horse or horses contesting in a race shall have any pecuniary interest in a purse, prize, premium or stake contested for in such race, or be entitled to or receive any portion thereof after such race is finished, and the whole of such purse, prize, premium or stake shall be allotted in accordance with the terms and conditions of such race. Such meetings shall not be held except during the period extending from the fifteenth day of April to the fifteenth day of November, inclusive, in each year, nor upon any running course for more than forty days, nor upon any trotting course for more than fifteen days, nor upon any steeplechase course for more than five days, within such period. No races are authorized or shall be permitted except during such period nor except between sunrise and sunset. *Right to hold race meetings. Prizes, premiums or stakes. Periods of meetings.*

§ 2. Section eighteen of said act is hereby amended to read as follows:

Penalty for purchase or sale of pools.

§ 18. Any person who, upon any trotting or race course authorized by or entitled to the benefits of this act shall make or record, directly or indirectly, any sale or purchase of any pool or interest therein on the result of any trial or contest of speed or power of endurance of horses, taking place upon such trotting or race course, shall forfeit the value of any pool or interest therein so wagered, received or held by him, to be recovered in a civil action by the person or persons with whom such sale or purchase of said pool or interest therein is made, or by whom any money for the sale or

Proviso.

purchase of said pool or any interest therein is deposited. This penalty is exclusive of all other penalties prescribed by law for the acts in this section specified, except in case of the exchange, delivery or transfer of a record, registry, memorandum, token, paper or document of any kind whatever as evidence of any such sale or purchase of a pool or interest therein, or the subscribing by name, initials, or otherwise, of any record, registry or memorandum in the possession of another person of the sale or purchase of a pool or any interest therein, intended to be retained by such other per-

Right to charge additional entrance fees.

son or any other person as evidence of the sale or purchase of any such pool or interest therein. A corporation or association authorized by or entitled to the benefits of this act, conducting a running or trotting or steeplechase meeting, shall have the right to charge increased or additional entrance fees for admission to any special portion or portions of the grounds of such corporation or association, unless such pool selling or bookmaking as is punishable by fine or imprisonment, or other acts so punishable, be thereon authorized or knowingly permitted.

§ 3. Section twelve of said act, as amended by chapter three hundred and eighty of the laws of eighteen hundred and ninety-six, is hereby amended to read as follows:

Annual tax on gross receipts.

§ 12. A tax of five per centum upon the gross receipts of every corporation, person or persons from every trotting or running race meeting or meetings, held within the state of New York, either under the provisions of this act or otherwise, shall be paid by any person or persons, firm or association or corporation holding such races, or exercising any of the privileges conferred by section three of this act, whether the person or persons holding such races are incorporated or not. Such tax shall be annually paid by said person or persons, association or corporation to the comptroller of the state of New York, within fifteen days after the first day of December in each year. The amount collected by virtue of this section shall be appropriated and distributed as provided by chapter eight hundred and twenty of the laws of eighteen hundred and and ninety-five, and the acts amendatory thereof. Before any such person or persons, firm, association or corporation liable to pay the tax herein imposed shall hold any trotting or running race or exercise any of the privileges conferred by section three of this act or otherwise, they shall pay all taxes due under this act and theretofore assessed thereon and file a statement with the comptroller containing the name of the place and stating the time when such races are to be held, and shall execute to the people of the state a good and sufficient bond to be approved by the comptroller and filed in his office. The amount of such bond shall be determined by the comptroller and shall be conditioned for the payment of the tax imposed by this section. Any person, persons, firm, association or corporation neglecting or refusing to execute such bond, and to file such bond and statement, as herein prescribed, shall be guilty of a misdemeanor. Nothing herein contained shall require such tax to be paid, bond to be executed or statement to be filed by any state, county or other agricultural association organized and in active operation as such prior to the passage of chapter five hundred and seventy of the laws of eighteen hundred and ninety-five, or which is entitled to share in the distribution of moneys for agricultural purposes as provided by chapter eight hundred and twenty of the laws of eighteen hundred and ninety-five or acts amendatory thereof. All the provisions of this act relating to the powers and duties of the comptroller as to the collection of taxes from associations and corporations holding trotting or running races hereunder, and relating to the payment of taxes and the making of reports by such corporations and associations, shall apply to all persons and firms liable to pay a tax upon their gross receipts as provided in this section.

§ 4. This act shall take effect immediately.

Chap. 448.

AN ACT to amend chapter seven hundred and thirty-nine of the laws of eighteen hundred and fifty-seven, entitled "An act to authorize the formation of town insurance companies," and the act amendatory thereof, relating to insurance from loss by lightning.

Became a law May 17, 1897, with the approval of the Governor. Passed, three-fifths being present.

The People of the State of New York, represented in Senate and Assembly, do enact as follows:

Act amended. Section 1. Section four of chapter seven hundred and thirty-nine of the laws of eighteen hundred and fifty-seven, as amended by chapter fifty-four of the laws of eighteen hundred and eighty-four, is hereby amended to read as follows:

Issue of policies for damages from fire or lightning. § 4. The directors of such company may issue policies, signed by their president and secretary, agreeing in the name of such company to pay all damages which may be sustained by fire or lightning for a term not exceeding five years, by the holders of such policies, not exceeding the sum named in such policy and which shall not exceed the sum of seven thousand dollars in any one risk.

§ 2. This act shall take effect immediately.

Chap. 449.

AN ACT to enable the towns and cities of this state to use the Boma automatic ballot machines at all elections therein.

Became a law May 17, 1897, with the approval of the Governor. Passed, three-fifths being present.

The People of the State of New York, represented in Senate and Assembly, do enact as follows:

Adoption of ballot machines authorized. Section 1. The common council of any city, and the town board of any town within this state may adopt the Boma automatic ballot machine for use at all elections, and thereupon it shall be lawful to use such ballot machines for the purpose of voting for all public officers to be elected by the voters of such town or city, or any part thereof, and upon all constitutional amendments or propositions, or questions which may lawfully be submitted to such voters, and for registering and counting the ballots cast at such election.

§ 2. The common council of each city, and the town board of each town adopting said machine, shall provide for each polling place, at each election therein, the necessary ballot machines, in complete working order, with the dials of the counters set at 0, and shall care for said ballot machines, as well as the furniture and equipment of the polling places when not in use at elections. *Equipment of polling place.*

§ 3. The ballot machine and every part of the polling place shall be in plain view of the election officers, including the watchers. The ballot machines shall be placed at least three feet from the wall of the room and at least three feet from the outer guardrail. The inspectors' table shall be at least four feet from the ballot machine. An inner guardrail shall extend from the ballot machine and between the entrance and exit doors thereof to a point at or near the inspectors' table. The outer guardrail shall be so placed as to bar access to within three feet at least of the ballot machine, but with the openings or gateways leading to and from the inspectors' table. Party nominations shall be arranged in columns, or else in horizontal rows, upon the said machines, and at the head of each of said columns, or else at the end of each of said rows, as the case may be, ballot captions shall be placed of cardboard, or heavy paper, not less than four inches long nor less than two and one-half inches wide, which shall have printed thereon, in plain, clear type, as large as the space will reasonably permit, the party or other lawful designation of the nominee, amendments, or other questions or propositions submitted to vote. For each candidate lawfully nominated, and for each constitutional amendment or other proposition lawfully submitted to vote, a push key or lever shall be set as provided in section two of this act, and adjacent thereto or upon said lever shall be attached a printed ballot of cardboard, or heavy paper, not less than two and one-half inches long and not less than one inch wide, upon which shall be printed in plain, clear type, as large as the space will reasonably permit, the name of the office and the name of the candidate or nominee therefor; or a concise statement of the amendment, question or proposition submitted, under successive headings for and against. Should any party fail to make a nomination for any office, the ballot in that party's column or horizontal line upon the keyboard devoted to that office shall be left blank, and the push-knob or lever thereof shall be capped or otherwise arranged so as to be inoperative. Should two or more parties nominate the same person for the same office, or should the same person *Arrangement of polling place.* *Party nominations.* *Push key and ballot.* *Ballots, form of, etc.*

be nominated for the same office by any party and also by independent nomination, his name shall be printed upon the ballot of the party, or in the list of independent nominations, the certificate of which shall first be filed as required by law; provided, however, that such nominee may, within two days after his second nomination, by a written instrument, acknowledged as deeds are required to be acknowledged for record, and filed with the county clerk of the county, require his name to appear in the column or horizontal line of some other party so nominating him, and the county clerk shall prepare his ballot accordingly, and the ballot of the other party or parties which shall have nominated him shall be left blank for that office, and the corresponding push-knob or push-knobs or levers shall be capped or otherwise arranged so as to be inoperative. If two or more officers are to be elected to the same office for different terms, the term for which each is nominated

Party emblems and colors.

shall be designated on the ballot. The ballot captions and ballots of the several political parties or other nominating bodies, and those for and against constitutional amendments or other propositions or questions, shall be distinguished from each other by distinctive colors, and the ballot captions shall contain thereon the party emblems as provided by section fifty-six of chapter eight hundred and ten of the laws of eighteen hundred and ninety-five.

Separate push-knob for straight ticket.

In addition to the push-knob or lever and the ballot for each candidate, such ballot machines may also provide in each column or horizontal line of the party nominations a separate push-knob or lever to vote a ballot printed in plain, large type "straight ticket."

Presidential elections.

In presidential elections such ballot machines may provide in each column or horizontal line of party nominations a separate push-knob or lever to vote a ballot for all the presidential electors nominated by such party.

Providing ballots, etc.

§ 4. The county clerk of the county shall provide at the expense of the county, the requisite number of ballots, ballot captions, counter labels and instruction cards for each polling place, in such town and city for each election to be held thereat, except for town meetings, village elections, and the election of school officers not held at the same time as the general election in which latter case the clerk of such village, town or school district shall provide at the expense of said village, town or school district the requisite number of ballots, ballot captions, counter labels and instruction cards for each polling place. The ballots, ballot captions, counter

When printed and open to inspection.

labels and instruction cards shall be printed and in possession of the clerk charged with the duty of providing them and open to the

public inspection four days before every election, except in case
of a town meeting, village election, or election of school officers
not held at the same time as the general election, in which case
they shall be so printed and open to public inspection two days
before such election.

§ 5. Four sample ballots of each kind shall be provided for each   Sample
polling place, and four instruction cards printed in such other lan-   ballots and
guage or languages as the common council or the town board may   instruction cards.
prescribe, shall be provided for each polling place, together with
four complete sets of ballot captions. The ballot captions and
ballots shall be duplicates of those used upon the machine, and
the instruction cards shall be printed in clear type so as to be
easily read. The instruction cards shall state the prescribed
colors and emblems of the party ballots, and of the ballots of independent nominees, and shall give a summary of the laws punish-
ing violations of the election law and full instructions for the use
of said ballot machines.

§ 6. The county clerk or other officer having charge of the   Correction
printing of the ballots, ballot captions and instruction cards, shall   of error.
on his own motion, correct any error therein upon discovery
thereof, which can be corrected without interfering with their distribution and use at the election.

§ 7. Counter labels shall be of cardboard or heavy paper of the   Counter
same length, width and colors as the ballots, and shall be so   labels.
placed on the machine as that the registering counter for each
push-knob or lever shall show the number of ballots cast for the
candidate whose name is printed upon said counter label.

§ 8. The clerk charged with the duty of providing ballots, ballot   Distribu-
captions, counter labels and instruction cards, shall, on Saturday   tion of
before the election at which they are to be used, deliver to the clerk   ballots, etc.
of each town and city in the county, the ballots, ballot captions,
counter labels and instruction cards required for each polling
place in such town or city.

§ 9. The inspectors of election and poll clerks shall meet at their   Duties of
respective polling places in each election district, thirty minutes   election officers.
before the time of opening of the polls therein. After the election
of one of their number as chairman, they shall post the instruction
cards and sample ballot captions, and shall, if the same has not
already been done, adjust and secure within the frames upon the
keyboard, the ballot captions and ballots in the presence of the
official watchers. The inspectors shall then fully open the doors

of the counting compartment in the presence of the inspectors and watchers, and shall thereupon push the push-knobs or levers on the balloting side of the machine until all the counter dials register at zero. The counting apparatus shall then be locked.

Voting.

§ 10. After the polls shall have been duly opened the voters shall pass through the opening in the outer guardrail singly or in single file to the inspectors' table. If the voter shall be found entitled to vote, one of the inspectors shall admit him to the ballot machine through the entrance.

Disabled voters.

§ 11. Any voter who shall be totally blind or without the use of either hand sufficiently to push the knobs or levers, or who shall be physically unable to enter or leave the ballot machine without assistance, may choose from the inspectors or poll clerks an assistant who shall be admitted to the ballot machine with him, provided he shall have been duly registered as a disabled voter pursuant to section one hundred and five of chapter eight hundred and ten of the laws of eighteen hundred and ninety-five; but intoxication or illiteracy shall not be regarded as a physical disability. The inspector or poll clerk selected by the voter shall not in any manner request nor seek to persuade or induce such voter to vote any particular ballot, or for any particular nominee, amendment, question or proposition, and shall not reveal for whom such disabled voter voted.

Instruction of voter within machine.

§ 12. In case any voter after entering the ballot machine shall ask for further instructions concerning the manner of voting, two inspectors of opposite political parties shall stand outside the machine and give such directions to the voter as they two may agree upon, except that under no circumstances shall either of them give advice as to voting for any particular nominee, amendment, question or proposition.

Time of voting.

§ 13. No voter shall remain within the ballot machine longer than one minute, and if he shall refuse to leave the said machine after the lapse of one minute, he shall be removed by the inspectors.

Proceedings at close of polls.

§ 14. As soon as the polls are closed the ballot machine shall be locked against voting, and the counting compartment opened in the presence of the watchers and all other persons who may be lawfully within the room, or voting place, giving full view to the dial numbers announcing the votes cast for each candidate, and for or against the various constitutional amendments, questions or other propositions.

§ 15. The inspectors shall then add together the votes cast for each candidate upon the straight tickets, if any, and the votes cast for such candidates by reason of the push-knob or lever bearing the name of that candidate, and officially and publicly announce the total vote for each candidate thus ascertained. Before leaving the room or voting place, and before closing and locking the counting compartment, the inspectors shall make and sign written statements of election required by section one hundred and fifteen of chapter eight hundred and ten of the laws of eighteen hundred and ninety-five, except that such statements of the canvass need not contain any ballots, official or defective. The written statement so made, after having been signed by the inspectors, shall be read in the hearing of all persons present and ample opportunity given to compare the results so certified, with the counter dials so exposed to public view. After such comparison and correction, if, any, are made, the inspector shall then close the counting compartment. *Canvass of vote.* *Statements of election.*

§ 16. No ballot clerk shall be elected or appointed in any town or city that shall have adopted the use of the ballot machine. *Ballot clerk.*

§ 17. All provisions of the election law, not inconsistent with this chapter, shall apply with full force to all towns and cities adopting the use of ballot machines. *Election law applicable.*

§ 18. This act shall take effect immediately.

Chap. 450.

AN ACT relating to the use of voting machines.

Became a law May 17, 1897, with the approval of the Governor.
Passed, three-fifths being present.

The People of the State of New York, represented in Senate and Assembly, do enact as follows:

Section 1. Within thirty days after the passage of this act, the governor shall appoint three commissioners, one of whom shall be an expert in patent law, and two of whom shall be mechanical experts. The said commissioners shall hold office for the term of five years, subject to removal, at the pleasure of the governor. *Commissioner to examine machines.*

§ 2. Any person or corporation owning or being interested in any voting machines may call upon the said commissioners to examine the said machine, and make report to the secretary of state upon the capacity of the said machine to register the will of voters, its *Examination and report to secretary of state.*

accuracy and efficiency, and with respect to its mechanical perfections and imperfections. In their report the said commissioners shall certify whether, in their opinion, the said machine can be safely used by the voters at the elections to be held within this state, and whether in their opinion the legislature ought to legalize the adoption thereof. The said commissioners may also certify and report as to the number of voters which said machine can safely and prudently accommodate within the hours specified by law for the holding of an election.

Presentation of report with bill to legislature.

§ 3. Any person or persons who shall hereafter present to the legislature any bill to legalize the adoption of any voting machine may present with said proposed bill a certified copy of the report of said commissioners so filed with the secretary of state upon the machine so proposed to be legalized.

Election districts.

§ 4. In cities or towns using or adopting any voting machine, the officers charged by law with the duty of subdividing said cities or towns into election districts may make such subdivision in accordance with a report of said commissioners as to the number of voters which the machine so reported upon will safely and prudently accommodate in each election district.

Fees and expenses of commissioner.

§ 5. The person or persons applying to the said commissioners for the examination and reports herein provided for, shall pay the fees and expenses of said commissioners in making said examination, not exceeding however, the sum of one hundred fifty dollars to each commissioner as compensation for the examination of and report upon any one machine.

Commissioners not to be interested.

§ 6. No person, while holding the office of commissioner under this act, shall have any pecuniary interest in any voting machine.

§ 7. This act shall take effect immediately.

Chap. 451.

AN ACT to amend chapter four hundred and forty-six of the laws of eighteen hundred and seventy-four, entitled "An act to revise and consolidate the statutes of the state, relating to the care and custody of the insane; the management of the asylums for their treatment and safe keeping, and the duties of the state commissioner in lunacy," relating to the payment of the expenses of an investigation into the sanity of a person in confinement under a criminal charge.

Became a law May 17, 1897, with the approval of the Governor.

Passed, three-fifths being present.

The People of the State of New York, represented in Senate and Assembly, do enact as follows:

Section 1. Section twenty-six of title one of chapter four hundred and forty-six of the laws of eighteen hundred and seventy-four is hereby amended to read as follows : *Act amended.*

§ 26. If any person in confinement under indictment or under sentence of imprisonment, or under a criminal charge, or for want of bail for good behavior, or for keeping the peace, or for appearing as a witness, or in consequence of any summary conviction, or by order of any justice, or under any other than civil process, shall appear to be insane, the county judge of the county where he is confined shall institute a careful investigation, call two legally qualified examiners in lunacy, neither of whom shall be a physician connected with the institution in which such person, so to be examined, is confined, and other credible witnesses, invite the district attorney to aid in the examination, and if he deem it necessary, call a jury, and for that purpose is fully empowered to compel the attendance of witnesses and jurors, and if it be satisfactorily proved that he is insane, said judge may discharge him from imprisonment and order his safe custody and removal to a state asylum, where he shall remain until restored to his right mind, and then the superintendent shall inform the said judge and district attorney, so that the person so confined may, within sixty days thereafter, be remanded to prison and criminal proceedings resumed or otherwise discharged, or if the period of his imprisonment shall have expired, he shall be discharged. When such person is sent to an asylum, the county from which he is sent shall defray all his expenses while there, and of sending him back if returned, but the

Investigation into sanity of criminal prisoners, etc.

county may recover the amount so paid from his own estate, if he have any, or from any relative, town, city or county that would have been bound to provide for and maintain him elsewhere. The fees of the medical examiners called as witnesses, and the other necessary expenses for such investigation shall be audited and allowed at a reasonable sum by said judge, and upon the presentation of the order made by him, such fees and expenses shall be paid by the county treasurer of the county where such person is confined, as a county charge.

Fees and expenses.

§ 2. This act shall take effect immediately.

Chap. 452.

AN ACT to amend section forty-nine of title one of chapter eight of part two of the revised statutes, and the acts amendatory thereof, in relation to the right of remarriage.

Became a law May 17, 1897, with the approval of the Governor. Passed, three-fifths being present.

The People of the State of New York, represented in Senate and Assembly, do enact as follows:

Revised statutes amended.

Section 1. Section forty-nine of title one of chapter eight of part two of the revised statutes, as amended by chapter three hundred and twenty-one of the laws of eighteen hundred and seventy-nine, is hereby amended to read as follows:

Right of remarriage by divorced person.

§ 49. Whenever a marriage has been or shall be dissolved, pursuant to the provisions of this article, the complainant may marry again during the lifetime of the defendant; but no defendant convicted of adultery shall marry again until the death of the complainant, unless the court in which the judgment of divorce was rendered shall in that respect modify such judgment, which modification shall only be made upon satisfactory proof that five years have elapsed since the decree of divorce was rendered, and that the conduct of the defendant since the dissolution of said marriage has been uniformly good.

§ 2. This act shall take effect immediately.

Chap. 454.

AN ACT to amend section ninety of the code of civil procedure, relative to the appointment of certain officers, or persons holding a salaried office, as referee, receiver or commissioner in the county of New York.

Became a law May 17. 1897, with the approval of the Governor.
Passed, three-fifths being present.

The People of the State of New York, represented in Senate and Assembly, do enact as follows:

Section 1. Section ninety of the code of civil procedure is hereby amended so as to read as follows: Amendment.

§ 90. No person holding the office of clerk, deputy clerk, special deputy clerk, or assistant in the clerk's office, of a court of record within the county of New York, shall hereafter be appointed by any court or judge, a referee, receiver or commissioner, except by the written consent of all the parties to the action or special proceeding other than the parties in default for failure to appear to plead. Certain officers in New York not to be receivers, etc.

§ 2. This act shall take effect immediately.

Chap. 459.

AN ACT to provide ways and means for the support of government.

Became a law May 17, 1897, with the approval of the Governor.
Passed by a two-thirds vote.

The People of the State of New York, represented in Senate and Assembly, do enact as follows:

Section 1. There shall be imposed for the fiscal year beginning on the first day of October, eighteen hundred and ninety-seven, on each dollar of real and personal property of this state, subject to taxation, taxes for the purposes hereinafter mentioned, which taxes shall be assessed, levied and collected by the annual assessment and collection of taxes of that year, in the manner prescribed by law, and shall be paid by the several county treasurers into the treasury of this state, to be held by the treasurer, to be applied to the purposes specified, that is to say: For the general fund, and for the payment of those claims and demands which shall constitute State tax levy. General fund.

a lawful charge upon that fund during the fiscal year commencing October first, eighteen hundred and ninety-seven, eighteen one-

Canal fund.

hundredths of a mill; for the canal fund, for the payment of appropriations for those objects and work on the canals of this state, which are not included in the appropriation for the maintenance thereof during said fiscal year, four and one-half one-hundredths of a mill; for the canal fund, for the annual contribution to the canal debt sinking fund, pursuant to chapter seventy-nine, laws of eighteen hundred and ninety-five, thirteen one-hundredths of a

Free school fund.

mill; for the free school fund, for the payment of those claims and demands which shall constitute a lawful charge upon that fund during said fiscal year, ninety-one one-hundredths of a mill.

§ 2. This act shall take effect immediately.

Chap. 460.

AN ACT to appropriate money for the support of the insane, under the provisions of chapter five hundred and forty-five of the laws of eighteen hundred and ninety-six.

Became a law May 17, 1897, with the approval of the Governor. Passed by a two-thirds vote.

The People of the State of New York, represented in Senate and Assembly, do enact as follows:

State tax for care of insane.

Section 1. There shall be imposed for the fiscal year beginning on the first day of October, eighteen hundred and ninety-seven, a tax of one and one-tenth mills on each dollar of real and personal property of the state, to be assessed, levied and collected by the annual assessment and collection of taxes of that year, and paid by the several county treasurers into the treasury of this state, to

Appropriation for state hospitals.

be held by the treasurer for the following purposes: For the maintenance, repairs and enlargement of the state hospitals the sum of four millions five hundred thousand dollars, being on account of the tax to be levied by this act, is hereby appropriated for the purposes defined in and to be expended under the provisions of chapter five hundred and forty-five of the laws of eighteen hundred and ninety-six, and of the money hereby appropriated no money shall be paid out for or on account of the said state hospitals or for other purposes except under the provisions of said act. Any moneys paid in on account of said tax in excess of the amount specifically appropriated shall be available for the foregoing purposes, in excess

of the amounts specifically appropriated by said chapters, is hereby
made available for the foregoing purposes. Such sum or sums as _{Advances in antici-}
may be necessary to provide for additional accommodations for the _{pation of tax.}
insane and for other necessary buildings, repairs and improve-
ments at the state hospitals shall be advanced by the treasurer on
the warrant of the comptroller in anticipation of the collection of
the tax above described, and shall be available upon the passage
of this act for such purposes. Contracts for the erection, repairs _{Contracts.}
or improvements of buildings at the state hospitals, subject to the
provisions of chapter five hundred and forty-five of the laws of
eighteen hundred and ninety-six, relating to estimates, may be let
for the whole or any part of the work to be performed, and in the
discretion of the hospital such contracts may be sublet. All _{Receipts from sale}
moneys received for or on account of the sale of the lands of any _{of land.}
hospital shall be paid to the treasurer of the hospital where such
lands are situated, and shall be available for the use of said hospital, subject to estimates approved by the commission. All goods _{Purchases.}
for the use of the state hospitals shall be bought, as far as practi-
cable, of manufacturers or their immediate agents. Actions at law _{Actions for support of}
for the support of inmates of state hospitals shall be brought in the _{inmates.}
name of the hospital against any relative who may be liable therefor
under the provisions of chapter five hundred and forty-five of the
laws of eighteen hundred and ninety-six. A preliminary deposit _{Deposit with}
or certified check drawn upon some bank authorized to do business _{proposal.}
under the provisions of laws relating to the banking department
shall, in all cases, be required as an evidence of good faith upon all
proposals for buildings, repairs and improvements, to be deposited
with the local hospital treasurer where the work is to be performed
in an amount to be determined by the state architect   The comp- _{Deposits of funds in}
troller shall deposit in banks in the cities of New York and Brook- _{New York and}
lyn sufficient sums of money to meet any drafts that may be made _{Brooklyn}
for expenditures for or on account of the Manhattan and Long Is-
land state hospitals. All plans and specifications for the erection, _{Plans and specifica-}
repairs and improvements of state hospital buildings shall be pre- _{tions.}
pared by the state architect, and he may employ such experts, engineers and assistants as may be necessary for the proper conduct
of such work, whose compensation shall be fixed by said architect,
with the approval of the commission, and shall be paid by the
hospital treasurer where the work is to be performed out of any
moneys alloted by the commission for that purpose. The comp- _{Advertise-ment for}
troller and the commission shall determine to what extent and for _{proposals.}

what length of time advertisements are to be inserted in newspapers for proposals for the erection, repairs or improvements of Mainte-nance of criminals. state hospital buildings. The maintenance of any inmate of a state hospital committed upon a court order arising out of any criminal action or proceeding shall be paid by the county from which such inmate was committed, and in the event that any such inmate is transferred to the Matteawan State Hospital or transferred from said hospital to one of the state hospitals, such transAward of contracts. portation shall be paid by said county. All contracts shall be awarded to the lowest responsible bidder, subject to the provisions relating to estimates in chapter five hundred and forty-five of the Receiving of gifts prohibited. laws of eighteen hundred and ninety-six. Officers, managers or employes of state hospitals are especially prohibited from receiving any gifts for or on account of said officers or for or on account of said hospital, its managers or employes from any person, firm or corporation dealing in goods or supplies suitable or necessary for Residence of officers and em-ployes. the use of said hospitals. With the approval of the commission, officers or employes of state hospitals may be permitted to live outside of said hospital and shall receive such sum in lieu of the quarSettle-ment of claims. ters or supplies furnished by the hospital as may be equitable. Out of the moneys hereby appropriated such sum or sums as may be necessary may be paid for the settlement by the commission of any legal or equitable claim against any of the state hospitals, or against officers or employes of the same, as provided by section forty-six of chapter five hundred and forty-five of the laws of eighInsurance. teen hundred and ninety-six. The state commission in lunacy is hereby authorized to secure a blanket policy of insurance which shall cover any of the buildings, property or fixtures of the state Attorneys. hospitals for the insane. The commission shall appoint an attorney for each state hospital, who shall conduct all of the legal business required to be done for or on account of said hospital, at a stated sum to be fixed by the commission, and which shall be a charge upon the maintenance account, and paid as other expenses of the Legislation as to aliens and non-residents. hospitals are now paid. The commission is hereby authorized to secure legislation from congress to more effectually provide for the removal of alien and nonresident insane, and is authorized to expend from the moneys hereby appropriated such sum or sums as Rate for support of inmates by relatives. may be necessary for the purpose. The commission is hereby authorized to fix a rate to be paid for the support of inmates of state hospitals by relatives liable for such support, or by those not liable for such support who may be willing to assume the cost of support of such inmates, but said rate shall be sufficient to cover a proper proportion of the cost of maintenance and of necessary repairs and improvements. The commission is directed, to the fullest extent, Buildings deemed practicable, to provide additional buildings for the removal moval of insane. of the insane from Hart's Island and Blackwell's Island departments of the Manhattan State Hospital and from the Flatbush department of the Long Island State Hospital. All contracts for the erection, repairs or improvements to hospitals shall contain a clause Clause in contracts, that the contract shall only be deemed executory to the extent of the moneys available, and no liability shall be incurred by the state beyond the moneys available for the purpose. Any moneys Pathological institute. necessary for the support of the Pathological Institute provided by tute. section sixteen of chapter five hundred and forty-five of the laws of eighteen hundred and ninety-six shall be paid out of the moneys hereby appropriated. The term " commission " when used in this Term commission chapter shall be deemed to mean the "State Commission in defined. Lunacy."

§ 2. This act shall take effect immediately.

Chap. 463.

AN ACT to amend chapter one hundred and twelve of the laws of eighteen hundred and fifty-four, entitled "An act for the incorporation of private and family cemeteries," relative to the removal of remains from family cemeteries.

Became a law May 17, 1897, with the approval of the Governor.
Passed, three-fifths being present.

The People of the State of New York, represented in Senate and Assembly, do enact as follows:

Section 1. Section eleven of chapter one hundred and twelve of the laws of eighteen hundred and fifty-four, entitled " An act for the incorporation of private and family cemeteries," as added by chapter fifty-nine of the laws of eighteen hundred and ninety-three, is hereby amended to read as follows :

§ 11. **Removal of remains to other cemeteries.**—The supervisor of any town containing a private cemetery may remove any dead bodies or human remains interred in such cemetery to any other cemetery within such town, if the owners of such cemeteries and the persons residing within the state who are next of kin of such deceased persons consent to such removal. The owners of such cemeteries may remove the remains of deceased persons interred therein to any cemetery within such town, or to some cemetery designated by the persons who are next of kin of such deceased persons. Notice of such removal shall be mailed or served personally upon the next of kin of such deceased persons, if known to such owners, within ten days of such removal.

§ 2. This act shall take effect immediately.

Chap. 464.

AN ACT to release to Thomas E. Pressenger, right, title and interest of the people of the state of New York, in and to certain real estate in the city of Brooklyn, county of Kings and state of New York.

Became a law May 17, 1897, with the approval of the Governor.
Passed by a two-thirds vote.

The People of the State of New York, represented in Senate and Assembly, do enact as follows:

Interest of
state
released.

Section 1. All the estate, right, title and interest of the people of the state of New York in and to all that certain piece or parcel of land, situate in the city of Brooklyn, county of Kings and state of New York and known and designated as lot number fifty-five on map of one hundred and seventy-four lots at East New York, belonging to William Alexander, surveyed by Martin G. Johnson, filed in the register's office of the county of Kings, March, eighteen hundred and fifty-nine; is hereby released to Thomas E. Pressenger.

Proviso.

§ 2. Nothing herein contained shall be construed to impair, release or discharge any right, claim or interest of any heir-at-law, devisee or grantee, purchaser or creditor of judgments, mortgages or otherwise in and to said premises or any part thereof.

§ 3. This act shall take effect immediately.

Chap. 465.

AN ACT to release to Marie Sophie Layer, Adele Layer and Amelia Herrscher, all the right, title and interest in and to the real and personal property and estate of Charles Alfred Granvilliers.

Became a law May 17, 1897, with the approval of the Governor.
Passed by a two-thirds vote.

The People of the State of New York, represented in Senate and Assembly, do enact as follows:

Section 1. All the right, title and interest of the people of the state Interest of state of New York of, in and to the real and personal property and estate released. whereof Charles Alfred Granvilliers, late of the city of New York, died possessed, is hereby released to Marie Sophie Layer, Adele Layer and Amelia Herrscher, born Layer, all of Colmar, Province of Alsace, Germany, or to the lawful heirs of the said Marie Sophie Layer, Adele Layer and Amelia Herrscher, born Layer, aforesaid.

§ 2. Nothing herein contained shall affect the right of any creditor Proviso. of said Charles Alfred Granvilliers.

§ 3. This act shall take effect immediately.

Chap. 466.

AN ACT to amend the consolidated school law, and the acts amendatory thereof, relative to clerk of the board of education.

Became a law May 17, 1897, with the approval of the Governor.
Passed, a majority being present.

The People of the State of New York, represented in Senate and Assembly, do enact as follows:

Section 1. Section seven of article one, title eight, of chapter School law amended. five hundred and fifty-six of the laws of eighteen hundred and ninety-four, entitled "An act to revise, amend and consolidate the general acts relating to public instruction," and known as the consolidated school law, as amended by chapter two hundred and forty-six of the laws of eighteen hundred and ninety-six, is hereby amended so as to read as follows:

§ 7. The said boards of education are hereby severally created Boards of education. bodies corporate, and each shall, at its first meeting, and at each annual meeting thereafter, elect one of their members president.

Clerk of
board.

In every union free school district other than those whose limits correspond with those of an incorporate city or village the board of education shall have power to appoint one of their number, or a qualified voter in said district, and a person other than a trustee, or a teacher employed in said district, as clerk of the board of education of such district. Such clerk shall also act as clerk of said district, and shall perform all the clerical and other duties pertaining to his office, and for his services he shall be entitled to receive such compensation as shall be fixed at an annual meeting of the qualified voters of such district. In case no provision is made at an annual meeting of the inhabitants for the compensation of a clerk, then and in that case the board of education shall

Treasurer
and col-
lector.

have power to fix the same. Said board of education shall also have power to appoint one of the taxable inhabitants of their district treasurer, and fix his compensation, and another collector of the moneys to be raised within the same for school purposes, who shall severally hold such appointments during the pleasure of the board. Such treasurer and collector shall each, and within ten days after notice in writing of his appointment, duly served upon him, and before entering upon the duties of his office, execute and deliver to the said board of education a bond, with such sufficient penalty and sureties as the board may require, conditioned for the faithful discharge of the duties of his office, and in case such bond shall not be given within the time specified, such office shall thereby become vacant, and said board shall thereupon, by appointment,

Vacancy in
office of
clerk.

supply such vacancy. And said board of education shall also have power to supply, by appointment any vacancy in the office of such clerk, occasioned by death, resignation, removal from the district or otherwise.

§ 2. Section fourteen of article three, title eight, of said act, as amended by chapter one hundred and ninety-six of the laws of eighteen hundred and ninety-six, is hereby amended so as to read as follows:

Election of
boards of
education
in districts
over 300.

§ 14. In union free school districts other than those whose limits correspond with those of an incorporated village or city, in which the number of children of school age exceeds three hundred, as shown by the last annual report of the board of education to the school commissioner, the qualified voters of any such district may by a vote of a majority of those present and voting, at any annual meeting, or at any duly called special meeting, to be ascertained by taking and recording the ayes and noes, determine that the election of the members of the board of education shall be held on the Wednesday next following the day designated by law for holding the annual meeting of said district. Until such determination shall be changed, such election shall be held on the Wednesday next following the day on which such annual meeting of such district shall be held, in each year, between the hours of twelve o'clock noon, and four o'clock in the afternoon at the principal schoolhouse in the district, or at such other suitable place as the trustees may designate. When the place of holding such election is other than at the principal schoolhouse, the trustees shall give notice thereof by the publication of such notice, at least one week before the time of holding such election, in some newspaper published in the district, or by posting the same in three conspicuous places in the district. The trustees may, by resolution, extend the time of holding the election from four o'clock until sunset. The board of education, or such of them as may be present, shall act as inspectors of election if a majority of such board shall not be present at the time of opening the polls, those members of the board in attendance may appoint any of the legal voters of the district present, to act as inspectors in place of the absent trustees; and if none of the board of education shall be present at the time of opening the polls, the legal voters present may choose three of their number to act as inspectors. The clerk of the board of education, shall attend at the election and record in a book, to be provided for that purpose, the name of each elector as he or she deposits his or her ballot. If the clerk of the board of education shall be absent, or shall be unable or refuse to act, the board of education or inspectors of election shall appoint some person who is a legal voter in the district to act in his place. Any clerk or acting clerk who shall neglect or refuse to record the name of a person whose ballot is received by the inspectors, shall be liable to a fine of twenty-five dollars, to be sued for by the supervisor of the town. If any person offering to vote at any such election shall be challenged as unqualified by any legal voter, the chairman of the inspectors shall require the person so offering to vote to make the following declaration: " I do declare and affirm that I am and have been for the thirty days last passed an actual resident of this school district, and that I am legally qualified to vote at this election." And every person making such declaration shall be permitted to vote; but if any person shall refuse to make such declaration his or her ballot shall not be re-

[margin notes:] Time of holding election. Notice of election. Extension of time. Inspectors of election. Record of vote. Penalty for refusal to record names. Challenge.

ceived by the inspectors. Any person who upon being so challenged shall wilfully make a false declaration of his or her right to vote **Penalty for illegal voting, etc.** at such election, is guilty of a misdemeanor. Any person who shall vote at such election, not being duly qualified, shall, though not challenged, forfeit the sum of ten dollars, to be sued for by the supervisor of the town for the benefit of the school or schools of **Ballot box and ballots.** the district. The board of education shall, at the expense of the district, provide a suitable box in which the ballots shall be deposited as they are received. Such ballots shall contain the names of the persons voted for, and shall designate the office for which each one is voted. The ballots may be either written or printed, **Canvass and declaration of result.** or partly written and partly printed. The inspectors immediately after the close of the polls shall proceed to canvass the votes. They shall first count the ballots to determine if they tally with the number of names recorded by the clerk, and if they exceed that number, enough ballots shall be withdrawn to make them correspond. Such inspectors shall count the votes and announce the result. The person or persons having a majority of the votes respectively for the several offices shall be elected, and the clerk shall record the result of such ballot and election as announced by **Special election.** the inspectors. Whenever the time for holding such election as aforesaid shall pass without such election being held in any such district, a special election shall be called by the board of education, but if no such election be called by said board within twenty days after such times shall have passed, the school commissioner or the state superintendent of public instruction may order any inhabitant of said district to give notice of such election in the manner prescribed by section ten of this title; and the officers elected at such special election shall hold their respective offices only until the next annual election, and until their successors are elected and **Election disputes, settlement of.** shall have qualified, as in this act provided. All disputes concerning the validity of any such election or of any votes cast thereat, or of any of the acts of the inspectors or clerks, shall be referred to the superintendent of public instruction, whose decision in the matters shall be final. Such superintendent may, in his discretion **Limitation of provisions.** order a new election in any district. The foregoing provisions shall not apply to union free school districts in cities, nor to union free school districts whose boundaries correspond with those of an incorporated village, nor to any school district organized under a special act of the legislature, in which the time, manner and form of the election of district officers shall be different from that prescribed for the election of officers in union free school districts, organized under the general law, nor to any of the union free school districts in the counties of Suffolk, Chenango, Warren, Erie and Saint Lawrence.   In Richmond county, whenever any district Election in Richmond shall have determined to hold its annual election on Wednesday county. following the date of its annual school meeting, the same shall be held between the hours of four o'clock and nine o'clock in the evening.

§ 3. This act shall take effect immediately.

Chap. 469.

AN ACT to amend the code of civil procedure in relation to costs against executors and administrators.

Became a law May 17, 1897, with the approval of the Governor. Passed, three-fifths being present.

The People of the State of New York, represented in Senate and Assembly, do enact as follows:

Section 1. Section eighteen hundred and thirty-six of the code of civil procedure is hereby amended to read as follows:

§ 1836. **Costs, when awarded, et cetera.**— Where it appears in a case specified in the last section that the plaintiff's demand was presented within the time limited by a notice published as prescribed by law, requiring creditors to present their claims and that the payment thereof was unreasonably resisted or neglected, or that the defendant did not file the consent provided in section eighteen hundred and twenty-two at least ten days before the expiration of six months from the rejection thereof the court may award costs against the executor or administrator to be collected either out of his individual property or out of the property of the decedent as the court directs, having reference to the facts which appear upon the trial.   Where the action is brought in the supreme court, the facts must be certified by the judge or referee before whom the trial took place.

§ 2. This act shall take effect immediately.

Chap. 470.

AN ACT to amend the code of civil procedure, in relation to amendments of pleadings, of course.

Became a law May 17, 1897, with the approval of the Governor.
Passed, three-fifths being present.

The People of the State of New York, represented in Senate and Assembly, do enact as follows:

Amendment.

Section 1. Section five hundred and forty-two of the code of civil procedure is hereby amended so as to read as follows:

Amendment of pleadings, of course.

§ 542. Within twenty days after a pleading, or the answer, demurrer or reply thereto, is served, or at any time before the period for answering it expires, the pleading may be once amended by the party, of course, without costs and without prejudice to the proceedings already had. But if it is made to appear to the court that the pleading was amended for the purpose of delay, and that the adverse party will thereby lose the benefit of a term, for which the cause is or may be noticed, the amended pleading may be stricken out, or the pleading may be restored to its original form, and such terms imposed as the court deems just.

§ 2. This act shall take effect September first, eighteen hundred and ninety-seven.

Chap. 474.

AN ACT to amend section two hundred and fifty of the code of civil procedure, relative to the publication of reports.

Became a law May 17, 1897, with the approval of the Governor.
Passed, three-fifths being present.

The People of the State of New York, represented in Senate and Assembly, do enact as follows:

Amendment.

Section 1. Section two hundred and fifty of the code of civil procedure is hereby amended so as to read as follows:

Supreme court report.

§ 250. The supreme court reporter must cause the reports, published as prescribed in the last section, to be kept constantly for sale to persons within the state, at a price not exceeding two dollars, for a bound volume of not less than seven hundred pages. He may also cause advance sheets to be published at not to exceed fifty cents a volume. He must cause a copy of each volume of the reports as soon as printed to be delivered to each judge of the court of appeals, and each justice of the supreme court during his term of office.

§ 2. This act shall take effect immediately.

Chap. 475.

AN ACT to amend section three hundred and sixty of the code of civil procedure, relative to the appointment of an interpreter.

Accepted by the city.

**Became a law May 17, 1897, with the approval of the Governor.
Passed, three-fifths being present.**

The People of the State of New York, represented in Senate and Assembly, do enact as follows:

Section 1. Section three hundred and sixty of the code of civil procedure is hereby amended so as to read as follows:

§ 360. Interpreters for county court and surrogate's court in Kings county.— The surrogate and the county judges of Kings county must each from time to time appoint, and may at pleasure remove, an interpreter to be attached respectively to the surrogate's court and the county court of said county. Each interpreter shall receive a salary of twelve hundred dollars per annum, to be paid by the comptroller of the city of Brooklyn in monthly installments. Each interpreter so appointed shall, before entering upon his duties, file in the office of the clerk of the county of Kings the constitutional oath of office in which there shall also be incorporated, language to the effect that he will fully and correctly interpret and translate each question propounded through him to a witness, and each answer thereto in said courts. The said county judges of Kings county shall also appoint and at pleasure remove an interpreter of the Slavonic languages, who shall receive the compensation above provided, to be paid in the same manner and who shall take and file the constitutional oath of office above provided, such compensation to be taken out of the amount appropriated for the support of the said county court.

§ 2. This act shall take effect immediately.

Chap. 476.

AN ACT to amend section twenty-four hundred and thirty-four of the code of civil procedure, relating to proceedings supplementary to an execution against property.

Became a law May 17, 1897, with the approval of the Governor. Passed, three-fifths being present.

The People of the State of New York, represented in Senate and Assembly, do enact as follows:

Amendment.

Section 1. Section twenty-four hundred and thirty-four of the code of civil procedure is hereby amended so as to read as follows:

Proceedings supplementary to execution against property.

§ 2434. Either special proceedings may be instituted before a judge of the court, out of which, or the county judge, the special county judge, or the special surrogate, of the county to which the execution was issued; or where it was issued to the city and county of New York, from a court other than the city court of that city, before a justice of the supreme court for that city and county. Where the execution was issued out of a court other than the supreme court, and it is shown by affidavit, that each of the judges, before whom the special proceedings might be instituted, as prescribed by this section, is absent from the county, or, for any reason, unable or disqualified to act, the special proceedings may be instituted before a justice of the supreme court. In that case, if he does not reside within the judicial district embracing the county to which the execution was issued, the order made or warrants issued by him must be returnable to a justice of the supreme court, residing in that district, or the county judge, or the special judge, or special surrogate, of that or an adjoining county, as directed in the order or warrant. Where the judgment upon which the execution was issued was recovered in a district court of the city of New York, either special proceeding shall be instituted before a justice of the city court of the city of New York.

§ 2. This act shall take effect immediately.

Chap. 477.

AN ACT to amend the membership corporation law, relating to the taxation of lot owners by cemetery corporations.

Became a law May 17, 1897, with the approval of the Governor.
Passed, three-fifths being present.

The People of the State of New York, represented in Senate and Assembly, do enact as follows:

Section 1. Section fifty-two or article three of chapter five hundred and fifty-nine of the laws of eighteen hundred and ninety-five, entitled " An act relating to membership corporations, constituting chapter forty-three of the general law," is hereby amended to read as follows:

§ 52. **Taxation of lot owners by corporation.**—If the funds of a cemetery corporation, applicable to the improvement of its cemetery wholly outside of a city of the first or second class, or applicable to the construction of a receiving vault therein for the common use of lot owners, be insufficient for such purposes, the directors of the corporation, not oftener than once in any year and for such purposes only, may levy a tax of two dollars on the owners of each lot, or, with the written consent of two-thirds of the lot owners, or with the concurrent vote of a majority of the lot owners, at an annual meeting, or at a special meeting duly called for such purpose, may levy a tax on the lot owners at a rate not exceeding five dollars for each lot of average value proportionately to the prices at which the lots were respectively sold by the corporation. Notice of such tax shall be served on the lot owners or where two or more persons are owners of the same lot, on one of them, either personally, or by leaving it at his residence with a person of mature age and discretion, or by mail, if he resides in a city, town or village where the office of the corporation is not located. If such tax remain unpaid for more than thirty days after the service of such notice, the president and secretary of the corporation may issue a warrant to the treasurer of the corporation, requiring him to collect such tax in the same manner as school collectors are required to collect school taxes; and such treasurer shall have the same power and be subject to the same liabilities in executing such warrant as a collector of school taxes has or is subject to by law in executing a warrant for the collection of school taxes.

§ 2. This act shall take effect immediately.

Chap. 481.

AN ACT to amend the town law and the acts amendatory thereof, relating to the holding of biennial town meetings.

Became a law May 17, 1897, with the approval of the Governor.
Passed, three-fifths being present.

The People of the State of New York, represented in Senate and Assembly, do enact as follows:

Section 1. Section ten of chapter five hundred and sixty-nine of the laws of eighteen hundred and ninety, entitled "An act in relation to towns, constituting chapter twenty of the general laws," and known as the town law, as amended by chapter eighty-two of the laws of eighteen hundred and ninety-three, is hereby amended to read as follows:

§ 10. Time and place of biennial town meeting.—The electors of a town, shall biennially, on the second Tuesday of February, assemble and hold town meetings at such place in the towns as the electors thereof at their biennial town meeting shall, from time to time appoint. If no place shall have been fixed for such meeting, the same shall be held at the place of the last town meeting in the town or election district, when town meetings of a town are held in election districts. The board of supervisors of any county may, by resolution, adopted at an annual meeting of such board, fix a time when the biennial town meetings in such county shall be held, which shall be on some day between the first day of February and the first day of May, inclusive, and such time, when so fixed, shall not be changed for the period of three years. The biennial town meetings in the towns in each county containing more than three hundred thousand and less than six hundred thousand inhabitants, according to the then last preceding state or federal enumeration, shall be held on the second Tuesday of March, eighteen hundred and ninety-nine, and biennially thereafter on the second Tuesday of March until otherwise directed by the board of supervisors of such county.

§ 2. Section eleven of said act, as amended by chapter twenty-three of the laws of eighteen hundred and ninety-three, is hereby amended to read as follows:

§ 11. Changing place of biennial town meeting.— The electors of a town may upon the application of fifteen electors therein, to be filed with the town clerk twenty days before a biennial town meeting, is to be held, determine at such meeting, by ballot, where future town meetings shall be held. Where town meetings in any town are held in separate election districts, the electors of each district, may, at a biennial town meeting, determine the resolution where its future town meetings shall be held. If any place so designated shall thereafter and before the close of the next biennial town meeting, be destroyed, or for any reason become unfit for use, or can not for any reason be used for such purpose, the town board shall forthwith designate some other suitable place for holding such town meeting in said town or election district, as the case may be.

§ 3. Sections twelve and thirteen of said act, as amended by chapter three hundred and forty-four of the laws of eighteen hundred and ninety-three, are hereby amended to read as follows:

§ 12. **Election of officers.**— There shall be elected at the biennial town meeting in each town by ballot, one supervisor, one town clerk, two justices of the peace, three assessors, one collector, one or two overseers of the poor, except in the counties of Richmond and Kings, one, two or three commissioners of highways, not more than five constables, and two inspectors of election for each election district in the town; if there shall be any vacancies in the office of justice of the peace, of any town at the time of holding its biennial town meeting, persons shall then also be chosen to fill such vacancies, who shall hold their offices for the residue of the unexpired term for which they are respectively elected.

§ 13. **Term of office.**—Supervisors, town clerks, assessors, commissioners of highways, collectors, overseers of the poor, inspectors of election and constables, when elected, shall hold their respective offices for two years But whenever there is or shall be a change in the time of holding town meetings in any town, persons elected to such offices at the next biennial town meeting after such change shall take effect, shall enter upon the discharge of their duties at the expiration of the term of their predecessors, and serve until the next biennial town meeting thereafter or until their successors are elected and have qualified.

§ 4. Section fourteen of said act is hereby amended to read as follows:

§ 14. **Justices of the peace.**—There shall be four justices of the peace in each town, divided into two classes, two of whom shall be elected biennially. Such justices shall hold office for a term of four years commencing on the first day of January succeeding their election.

§ 5. Sections fifteen and sixteen of said act are hereby repealed.

§ 6. Section seventeen of the town law, as amended by chapter two hundred and thirty-nine of the laws of eighteen hundred and ninety-five, is hereby renumbered section fifteen and amended to read as follows :

§ 15. Commissioners of highways.— The electors of each town may, at their biennial town meetings, determine by ballot whether there shall be elected in their town one or three commissioners of highways. Whenever any town shall have determined upon having three commissioners of highways and shall desire to have but one, the electors thereof may do so by a vote by ballot taken at a biennial town meeting, and when such proposition shall have been adopted no other commissioner shall be elected or appointed until the term or terms of those in office at the time of adopting the proposition shall expire or become vacant; and they may act until their terms shall severally expire or become vacant as fully as if three continued in office. When there shall be but one commissioner of highways in any town, he shall possess all the powers and discharge all the duties of commissioners of highways as prescribed by law.

§ 7. Section eighteen of said act, as amended by chapter one hundred and seven of the laws of eighteen hundred and ninety-four, is hereby renumbered section sixteen and amended to read as follows :

§ 16. Overseers of the poor.— The electors of each town may, at their biennial town meeting, determine by resolution whether they will elect one or two overseers of the poor, and the number so determined upon shall be thereafter biennially elected for a term of two years. Whenever any town shall have determined upon having two overseers of the poor, the electors thereof may determine by a resolution at a biennial town meeting, to thereafter have but one, and if they so determine thereafter no other overseer shall be elected or appointed, until the term of the overseer continuing in office at the time of adopting the resolution shall expire or become vacant, and the overseer in office may continue to act until his term shall expire or become vacant. The electors of any town may, at any biennial or regularly called special town meeting on the application of at least twenty-five resident taxpayers whose names appear upon the then last preceding town assessment-roll, adopt by ballot a resolution that there shall be appointed in and for such town one overseer of the poor. If a majority of the ballots so cast shall be in favor of appointing an overseer of the poor, no overseer of the poor shall thereafter be elected in such town except as hereinafter provided, and the overseers of the poor of such town elected at the town meeting at which such resolution is adopted or who shall then be in office shall continue to hold office for the terms for which they were respectively chosen; and within thirty days before the expiration of the term of office of such elected overseer whose term expires latest, the town board of such town shall meet and appoint one overseer of the poor for such town, who shall hold office for one year from the first day of May next after his appointment; and annually in the month of April in each year thereafter an overseer of the poor shall be appointed by the town board of such town for the term of one year from the first day of May next following such month of April. Each overseer of the poor so appointed shall execute and file with the town clerk an official undertaking in such form and for such sum as the town board may by resolution require and approve. An overseer of the poor, so appointed, shall not hold any other town office during the term for which he is so appointed, and if he shall accept an election or appointment to any other town office he shall immediately cease to be an overseer of the poor. If a vacancy shall occur in the office of an overseer of the poor, so appointed, such vacancy shall be filled by the town board, by appointment, for the balance of the unexpired term. The compensation of an overseer of the poor so appointed, shall be fixed by the town board of such town, but shall not exceed, in any one year, the sum of one thousand dollars, and shall be a town charge. At any subsequent town meeting after the expiration of three years from the adoption of a resolution by any town to appoint an overseer of the poor, the electors of the town may determine by ballot to thereafter elect one or more overseers of the poor, and if they determine so to elect, then at the next biennial town meeting thereafter one or more overseers of the poor shall be elected in pursuance of the laws regulating the election of overseers of the poor, and the term or terms of the overseer or overseers first so elected shall commence upon the expiration of the term of office of the overseer of the poor last theretofore appointed in pursuance of law, and shall expire as though each such term commenced at the time of election; and their successors shall thereafter be elected in pursuance of law.

§ 8. Section nineteen of said act, as amended by chapter three hundred and forty-eight of the laws of eighteen hundred and ninety-four, is hereby renumbered section seventeen and amended to read as follows:

§ 17. Inspectors for towns.— The presiding officer of each biennial town meeting shall, immediately after the votes are canvassed, appoint by writing, two additional inspectors of election for each election district, to be associated with the two inspectors who shall have been elected, and which inspectors, so to be appointed, shall be those two persons in each election district who shall have received the highest number of votes next to the two persons who shall have been elected inspectors, and which inspectors, so to be appointed, shall belong to and be of the same political faith and opinion on state and national issues as one or the other of the two political parties which, at the last preceding general election for state officers, shall have cast the greatest and next to the greatest number of votes in said town, but they shall not belong to the same political party nor be of the same political faith and opinion on state and national issues as the inspectors who shall have been elected. If the two inspectors elected belong to different political parties, the inspectors appointed shall be the two candidates for inspectors not elected and receiving the highest and next to the highest number of votes respectively, and belonging to different political parties. No ballot shall be counted upon which more than two names for inspector for any one election district shall appear. The various election inspectors elected, or elected and appointed, for towns, under the provision of existing laws, shall continue to serve as such inspectors until January first, eighteen hundred and ninety-five. On or before the second Tuesday in September next the several election inspectors in the various towns, appointed under the provisions of existing laws, shall each appoint one additional election inspector, who shall serve with the other three election inspectors during their term of office; such appointment shall be made in writing, and filed in the office of the town clerk. Such additional inspector shall belong to and be of the same political faith on state and national issues as the political party which, at the last preceding town meeting, shall have cast next to the highest number of votes, and when possible shall be one of the persons who, at the said town meeting, received next to the highest number of votes for election inspector. The additional inspector so appointed shall be subject to the provisions of existing laws, and of this act.

§ 9. Section twenty of said act is hereby renumbered section eighteen, and amended to read as follows:

§ 18. Ballots for full term and vacancies.— When the electors of any town are entitled to vote for a justice of the peace, to fill a vacancy caused otherwise than by expiration of term, each elector may designate upon his ballot the person intended for a full term and for a vacancy, and if there are two vacancies, they may be designated as the longer and the shorter vacancy; and if three vacancies, the longer, shorter and shortest vacancy, and each person having the greatest number of votes with reference to each designation, shall be deemed duly elected for the term or vacancy designated. If ballots are voted without designation, the first name on the ballot shall be deemed as intended for the full term of the office voted for, the second name for the longer vacancy, the third name for the shorter vacancy and the fourth name for the shortest vacancy. The provisions of this section shall apply to new towns erected; and officers to be elected in such towns, except for a full term, shall be deemed elected to fill vacancies.

§ 10. Sections twenty-one, twenty-two and twenty-three of said act are hereby renumbered sections nineteen, twenty and twenty-one, respectively.

§ 11. Section twenty-four of the town law is hereby renumbered section twenty-two and is amended to read as follows:

§ 22. Powers of biennial town meetings.—The electors of each town may, at their biennial town meeting:

1. Determine what number of constables, not exceeding five and pound-masters shall be chosen in their town for the then ensuing two years;

2. Elect such town officers as may be required to be chosen;

3. Direct the prosecution or defense of all actions and proceedings in which their town is interested, and the raising of such sum therefor as they may deem necessary;

4. Take measures and give directions for the exercise of their corporate powers;

5. Make provisions and allow rewards for the destruction of noxious weeds and animals, as they may deem necessary, and raise money therefor;

6. Establish and maintain pounds at such places within their town as may be convenient;

7. Direct public nuisances in their town, affecting the security of life and health, to be changed, abated or removed and raise a sum of money sufficient to pay the expense thereof.

8. Make from time to time such prudential rules and regulations, as they may think proper, for the better improving of all lands owned by their town, in its corporate capacity, whether common or otherwise; for maintaining and amending partition or other fences around or within the same, and directing the time and manner of using such land.

9. Make like rules and regulations for ascertaining the sufficiency of all fences in such town and for impounding animals, impose such penalties on persons offending against any rule or regulation established by their town, excepting such as relate to the keeping and maintaining of fences, as they may think proper, not exceeding ten dollars for each offense, and apply the same, when recovered, in such manner as they may think most conducive to the interests of their town;

10. In towns bound to support their own poor, direct such sums to be raised, as they may deem necessary for such purpose, and to defray any charges that may exist against the overseers of the poor in their town;

11. Determine any other question lawfully submitted to them;

Every order or direction, and all rules and regulations made by any town meeting, shall remain in force until the same shall be altered or repealed at some subsequent town meeting.

§ 12. Section twenty-five of said act as amended by chapter two hundred and eighty of the laws of eighteen hundred and ninety-four is hereby renumbered section twenty-three.

§ 13. Section twenty-six of said act is hereby renumbered section twenty-four and amended to read as follows:

§ 24. **Notices of town meetings.**—No previous notice need be given of the biennial town meetings; but the town clerk shall, at least ten days before the holding of any special town meeting cause notice thereof under his hand, to be posted conspicuously in at least four of the most public places in the town; which notices shall specify the time, place and purposes of the meeting.

§ 14. Sections twenty-seven, twenty-eight, twenty-nine, thirty, thirty-one, thirty-two, thirty-three, thirty-four, thirty-five, thirty-six and thirty-seven of said act are hereby renumbered sections twenty-five, twenty-six, twenty-seven, twenty-eight, twenty-nine, thirty, thirty-one, thirty-two, thirty-three, thirty-four and thirty-five respectively.

§ 15. Section thirty-eight of said act as amended by chapter two hundred and sixty-two of the laws of eighteen hundred and ninety-five is renumbered section thirty-four, and amended to read as follows:

§ 36. **Balloting; electors in incorporated village when not to vote on highway questions.**—When the electors vote by ballot, all the officers voted for shall be named in one ballot, which shall contain written or printed, or partly written or partly printed, the names of the persons voted for, and the offices to which such persons are intending to be elected, and shall be delivered to the presiding officers so folded as to conceal the contents, and shall be deposited by such officers in a box to be constructed, kept and disposed of, as near as may be, in the manner prescribed in the general election law. When any town shall have within its limits an incorporated village, constituting a separate road district, exempt from the supervision and control of the commissioners of highways of the town, and from payment of any tax for the salary or fees of said commissioners, and from payment of any tax for the opening, erection, maintenance and repair of any highway or bridge of said town, without the limits of said village, no residents of such village shall vote at any biennial or special election in such town for any commissioner of highways for said town, nor for or against any appropriation for the opening, laying out, maintenance, erection or repair of any highway or bridge in said town, without the limits of said village. At the biennial elections in such towns, the names of candidates for the office of highway commissioner shall be printed on a different ballot from the one containing the names of candidates for other town offices. Such ballots shall be indorsed " commissioner of highways," and shall be deposited, when voted, in a separate ballot box, which also shall be marked " commissioner of highways." Such ballots and ballot box shall be furnished by the officers now charged by law with that duty at town elections. A poll list shall be kept by the clerk of the meeting on which shall be entered the name of each person voting by ballot.

§ 16. Sections thirty-nine, forty, forty-one, forty-two and forty-three of said act are hereby renumbered sections thirty-seven, thirty-eight, thirty-nine, forty and forty-one respectively.

§ 17. Section sixty-five of said act is hereby amended to read as follows:

§ 65. Filling of vacancies.—When a vacancy shall occur or exist in any town office, the town board or a majority of them may, by an instrument under their hands and seals, appoint a suitable person to fill the vacancy, and the person appointed, except justices of the peace, shall hold the office until the next biennial town meeting. A person so appointed to the office of justice of the peace shall hold the office until the next biennial town meeting, unless the appointment shall be made to fill the vacancy of an officer whose term will expire on the thirty-first day of December next thereafter, in which case the term of office of the person so appointed shall expire on the thirty-first day of December next succeeding his appointment. The board making the appointment shall cause the same to be forthwith filed in the office of the town clerk, who shall forthwith give notice to the person appointed. A copy of the appointment of a justice of the peace shall also be filed in the office of the county clerk before the person appointed shall be authorized to act.

§ 18. Subdivision four of section eighty of said act is hereby amended to read as follows :

4. On the Tuesday preceding the biennial town meeting and on the corresponding date in each alternate year account with the justices of the peace and town clerk of the town for the disbursement of all moneys received by him.

§ 19. Sections one hundred and sixty, one hundred and sixty-one and one hundred and sixty-two of said act are amended to read, respectively, as follows :

§ 160. Constitution and regular meetings of the town board—The supervisor, town clerk and the justices of the peace, or any two of such justices shall constitute the town board in each town, and shall hold at least two meetings annually at the office of the town clerk, one on the Tuesday preceding the biennial town meeting and on the corresponding date in each alternate year, and the other on the Thursday next preceding the annual meeting of the board of supervisors.

§ 161. Meeting of town board for receiving accounts of town officers.—At the meeting of the town board held on the Tuesday preceding the biennial town meeting and on the corresponding date in each alternate year, all town officers who receive or disburse any moneys of the town, shall account with the board for all such moneys received and disbursed by them by virtue of their office, but no member of the board shall sit as a member of the board when any account in which he is interested is being audited by the board. The board shall make a statement of such accounts, and append thereto a certificate, signed by at least a majority of them, showing the state of the accounts of each officer at the date of the certificate, which statement and certificate shall be filed with the town clerk of the town, and be open to public inspection during the office hours of such town clerk.

§ 162. **Meeting of town board for auditing accounts.**—The meeting of the town board held on the Thursday preceding the annual meeting of the board of supervisors, shall be for the purpose of auditing accounts and allowing or rejecting all charges, claims and demands against the town. If any account is wholly rejected, the board shall make a certificate to that effect, signed by at least a majority of them, and file the same in the office of the town clerk. If the account is allowed, wholly or in part, the board shall make a certificate to that effect, signed by at least a majority of them, and if allowed only in part, they shall state in the certificate the items or parts of items allowed, and the items or parts of items rejected, and shall cause a duplicate of every certificate allowing an account, wholly or in part to be made. One of which duplicates shall be delivered to the town clerk of the town, to be kept on file for the inspection of any of the inhabitants of the town; and the other shall be delivered to the supervisor of the town, to be by him laid before the board of supervisors of his county at their annual meeting. The board of supervisors shall cause to be levied and raised upon the town the amount specified in the certificate, in the same manner as they are directed to levy and raise other town charges.

§ 20. Sections one hundred and seventy-two and one hundred and seventy-three of said act are hereby amended to read as follows:

§ 172. **Electing town auditors.**—The electors in each of the towns may, on the application of twenty freeholders residing therein, at any biennial town meeting, determine by ballot whether there shall be elected, at the next succeeding biennial town meeting, held in the town, a board of town auditors, in and for the town, independent of the town board in the manner, and under the restrictions hereinafter prescribed.

§ 173. **Board to be elected.**—If a majority of the ballots so cast, shall be in favor of electing a board of town auditors there shall be elected at the next succeeding biennial town meeting, and at every biennial town meeting held thereafter, until otherwise determined three town auditors, who shall form the board of town auditors of the town whose term of office shall be two years.

§ 21. There shall be elected at the town meeting in each town, in the spring of eighteen hundred and ninety-eight, one supervisor, one town clerk, one highway commissioner, one assessor, one collector, one or two overseers of the poor, not more than five constables and two inspectors of election for each election district, all of whom shall hold office for a term of one year. At the town meeting to be held in the spring of eighteen hundred and ninety-nine, all of such officers shall be elected in the manner and for the terms prescribed in this act. There shall be elected at the town meeting to be held in the spring of eighteen hundred and ninety-eight, one justice of the peace for a term of four years, beginning on the first day of January, eighteen hundred and ninety-nine. At the town meeting to be held in the spring of eighteen hundred and ninety-nine, there shall be elected two justices of the peace for a term of four years beginning on the first day of January, nineteen hundred; and at the biennial town meetings thereafter held there shall be elected two justices of the peace for a like term, beginning on the succeeding first day of January. At the town meeting to be held in the spring of eighteen hundred and ninety-nine, there shall be elected two assessors, one for a full term of two years and another for a term of one year, beginning at the expiration of the term of office of the assessor whose term will expire in the spring of nineteen hundred. At every biennial town meeting thereafter held, three assessors shall be elected for a term of two years. If in any town there are three commissioners of highways, there shall be elected at the town meeting to be held in the spring of eighteen hundred and ninety-nine, two commissioners of highways, one for a term of two years and one for a term of one year, beginning at the expiration of the term of office of the commissioner whose term will expire in the spring of nineteen hundred. At every biennial town meeting thereafter held in any such town, three commissioners of highways shall be elected for a term of two years. The provisions of this act shall not affect or abridge the term of office of any town officer elected prior to the passage of this act.

§ 22. This act shall take effect immediately.

Chap. 483.

AN ACT entitled An act to amend chapter five hundred and thirty-three of the laws of eighteen hundred and eighty, entitled "An act to regulate the passage of lumber, logs and other timber, upon the rivers of this state, recognized by law or common use as public highways, for the purpose of floating or running lumber, logs and other timber, over or upon the same to market or places of manufacture," as amended by chapters sixteen and seventy-four of the laws of eighteen hundred and eighty-one, as amended by chapter three hundred and eighty-five of the laws of eighteen hundred and ninety-one, as amended by chapter six hundred and eighty-three of the laws of eighteen hundred and ninety-six.

Became a law May 17, 1897, with the approval of the Governor.
Passed, three-fifths being present.

The People of the State of New York, represented in Senate and Assembly, do enact as follows:

Section 1. Section three of chapter five hundred and thirty-three *Act amended.* of the laws of eighteen hundred and eighty, is hereby amended to read as follows:

§ 3. Persons desirous of floating or running lumber, logs or *Construction of booms or other works.* other timber down the rivers mentioned in the first section of this act may construct a chute or apron in connection with any dam across said rivers, and may reconstruct any booms or other works already constructed in, over or across said rivers in such manner as to allow lumber, logs or other timber to pass by the same, and may remove obstructions in said rivers and construct such other piers, booms or other works as may be necessary for the passage of lumber, logs or other timber over and through the channels of said rivers, doing no injury or damage to the owner or occupant of such boom, dam or other works, or to the owner or occupant of any land on which such piers, booms, dams or other works may be constructed, or lands flooded thereby, and paying to such owner *Payment of damages.* or occupant such damages as he or they may sustain by reason of the construction of such piers, booms or other works, or the flooding of lands thereby, and paying also all damages and loss that may be occasioned or done to any and all property, public or private, in or upon said river or its banks, by reason of the floating of logs or lumber, or by reason of the removal of obstructions in the floatable channel of said river, and in case the amount *Commissioners of appraisal.* of such damage can not be amicably arranged by the parties interested, the same shall be appraised by three commissioners,

.o be appointed by the supreme court of the judicial district wherein the property is situated, on the application of any person interested in the appraisal of such damage, on three days notice, in writing, to the opposite parties of the time

Works subject to provisions. and place of making such application. Such booms and other works which shall be so constructed as aforesaid, and the owners and occupants thereof shall hereafter be subject to the provisions

Application of act. of section two of this act. This act shall apply to all statutes of this state declaring streams and rivers public highways for the floating of logs, unless otherwise provided, and shall be deemed to be supplemental thereto, so far as there is or may be any failure in any of such acts to provide for full and complete compensation to the riparian owner or those having vested rights upon such streams or rivers for any and all damages occasioned by making such streams or rivers public highways for the purpose of floating logs, the intent of this statute being to provide compensation to the riparian owner in all cases where rivers and streams have been declared to be public highways for the purpose of floating logs where no compensation has been provided therein to the riparian owners, and to those having vested rights upon said streams and rivers.

§ 2. This act shall take effect immediately.

Chap. 484.

AN ACT to amend chapter ten hundred and twenty-seven of the laws of eighteen hundred and ninety-five, entitled "An act in relation to the issue of mileage books by railroad corporations," and the act amendatory thereof.

Became a law May 17, 1897, with the approval of the Governor.
Passed, three-fifths being present.

The People of the State of New York, represented in Senate and Assembly, do enact as follows:

Amendment. Section 1. Section one of chapter ten hundred and twenty-seven of the laws of eighteen hundred and ninety-five, entitled "An act in relation to the issue of mileage books by railroad corporations," as amended by chapter eight hundred and thirty-five of the laws of eighteen hundred and ninety-six, is hereby amended to read as follows:

Issue of mileage books. § 1. Every railroad corporation operating a railroad in this state, the line or lines of which are more than one hundred miles in length, and which is authorized by law to charge a maximum fare of more than two cents per mile, and not more than three cents per mile, and which does charge a maximum fare of more than two cents per mile, shall issue mileage books having one thousand coupons attached thereto, entitling the holder thereof, upon complying with the conditions hereof, to travel one thousand miles on the line or lines of such railroad, for which the corporation may charge a sum not to exceed two cents per mile. Such mileage books shall be kept for sale by such corporation at every ticket office of such corporation in an incorporated village or city and shall be issued immediately upon application therefor. The holder of any such mileage book or any member of his family or firm, or any salesman of his firm to whom such book is delivered by him shall be entitled, upon surrendering, at any ticket office on the line or lines of such railroad coupons equal in number to the number of miles which he or such member of his family or firm, or such salesman of such firm wishes to travel on the line or lines of such railroad, to a mileage exchange ticket therefor. Such mileage exchange ticket shall entitle the holder thereof without producing the mileage book upon which such exchange ticket was issued, to the same rights and privileges in respect to the transportation of person and property to which the highest class ticket issued by such corporation would entitle him. Such mileage books shall be good until all coupons attached thereto have been used. Any railroad corporation which shall refuse to issue a mileage book as provided by this section, or, in violation hereof, to accept such mileage book for transportation, shall forfeit fifty dollars, to be recovered by the party to whom such refusal is made; but no action can be maintained therefor unless commenced within one year after the cause of action accrues.

Mileage exchange tickets.

Penalty for violations.

§ 2. This act shall take effect immediately.

Chap. 486.

AN ACT to amend the transportation corporations law, by requiring the inspection of meters used by natural gas corporations.

Became a law May 17, 1897, with the approval of the Governor. Passed, three-fifths being present.

The People of the State of New York, represented in Senate and Assembly, do enact as follows:

Section 1. Section sixty-two of chapter five hundred and sixty-six of the laws of eighteen hundred and ninety, entitled "An act in relation to transportation corporations, constituting chapter forty of the general laws," as amended by chapter nine hundred and seventy-two of the laws of eighteen hundred and ninety-five, is hereby amended to read as follows:

§ 62. **Inspector of gas meters.**— The governor shall nominate and by and with the consent of the senate appoint an inspector of gas meters, who shall have an office in the city of New York, whose duty it shall be, when required, to inspect, examine, prove and ascertain the accuracy of any and all gas meters used or intended to be used for measuring or ascertaining the quantity of illuminating gas furnished by any gaslight corporation in this state or corporation engaged in supplying natural gas to consumers, to or for the use of any person or persons, and, when found to be or made correct, to seal, stamp or mark all such meters, and each of them, with some suitable device, which device shall be recorded in the office of the secretary of state. Such inspector shall hold his office for the term of five years and until the appointment of his successor, but may be removed by the governor for sufficient cause. He shall receive an annual salary of five thousand dollars, to be paid in the first instance out of the state treasury on the warrant of the comptroller, which shall be charged to and paid into the state treasury by the several gas corporations in this state, in amounts proportionate to the amount of the capital stock of such corporations respectively, to be ascertained and assessed by the comptroller of the state. If any such corporation shall refuse or neglect to pay into the state treasury the amount or portion of such salary required of them respectively, for the space of thirty days after written notice given it by the comptroller to make such payment, then the comptroller may maintain an action, in his name of office, against any such delinquent corporation for its portion or amount of such salary, with interest thereon at the rate of ten per centum per annum from the time when such notice was given and the costs of the action.

§ 2. This act shall take effect immediately.

Chap. 488.

AN ACT for the relief of James O. Hale.

Became a law May 17, 1897, with the approval of the Governor.
Passed, three-fifths being present.

The People of the State of New York, represented in Senate and Assembly, do enact as follows:

Section 1. The adjutant-general is hereby authorized to receive proofs, in pursuance of sections one hundred and twenty-nine, one hundred and thirty and one hundred and thirty-one of the military code, as to injuries received by James C. Hale a former member of the national guard, at Buffalo creek, in the year eighteen hundred and seventy-seven, and to grant to said James C. Hale, or to his widow or minor children, a pension on account of such injuries, notwithstanding any settlement heretofore made with the state by the said James C. Hale, or any previous application for a pension in respect thereof or any action had thereon. *(margin: Adjutant-general may receive proofs and grant pension.)*

§ 2. The adjutant-general may, in the consideration of this claim, take into account any money heretofore paid by the state to the said James C. Hale, as a remuneration or pension for injuries received by him at Buffalo creek, in the year eighteen hundred and seventy-seven. *(margin: May take into consideration money paid.)*

§ 3. This act shall take effect immediately.

Chap. 489.

AN ACT to amend the tax law, in relation to receipts for taxes.

Became a law May 17, 1897, with the approval of the Governor.
Passed, three-fifths being present.

The People of the State of New York, represented in Senate and Assembly, do enact as follows:

Section 1. Section ninety-four of chapter nine hundred and eight of the laws of eighteen hundred and ninety-six, entitled " An act in relation to taxation, constituting chapter twenty-four of the general laws," is hereby amended to read as follows :

§ 94. **Receipts for taxes.**— The collector shall deliver a receipt to each person paying a tax, specifying the date of such payment, the name of such person, the description of the property as shown on the assessment-roll, the name of the person to whom the same

in relation to transportation corporations, constituting chapter forty of the general laws," as amended by chapter nine hundred and seventy-two of the laws of eighteen hundred and ninety-five, is hereby amended to read as follows:

§ 62. Inspector of gas meters.— The governor shall nominate and by and with the consent of the senate appoint an inspector of gas meters, who shall have an office in the city of New York, whose duty it shall be, when required, to inspect, examine, prove and ascertain the accuracy of any and all gas meters used or intended to be used for measuring or ascertaining the quantity of illuminating gas furnished by any gaslight corporation in this state or corporation engaged in supplying natural gas to consumers, to or for the use of any person or persons, and, when found to be or made correct, to seal, stamp or mark all such meters, and each of them, with some suitable device, which device shall be recorded in the office of the secretary of state. Such inspector shall hold his office for the term of five years and until the appointment of his successor, but may be removed by the governor for sufficient cause. He shall receive an annual salary of five thousand dollars, to be paid in the first instance out of the state treasury on the warrant of the comptroller, which shall be charged to and paid into the state treasury by the several gas corporations in this state, in amounts proportionate to the amount of the capital stock of such corporations respectively, to be ascertained and assessed by the comptroller of the state. If any such corporation shall refuse or neglect to pay into the state treasury the amount or portion of such salary required of them respectively, for the space of thirty days after written notice given it by the comptroller to make such payment, then the comptroller may maintain an action, in his name of office, against any such delinquent corporation for its portion or amount of such salary, with interest thereon at the rate of ten per centum per annum from the time when such notice was given and the costs of the action.

§ 2. This act shall take effect immediately.

Chap. 488.

AN ACT for the relief of James C. Hale.

Became a law May 17, 1897, with the approval of the Governor.
Passed, three-fifths being present.

*The People of the State of New York, represented in Senate and
Assembly, do enact as follows:*

Section 1. The adjutant-general is hereby authorized to receive Adjutant-general
proofs, in pursuance of sections one hundred and twenty-nine, one may receive
hundred and thirty and one hundred and thirty-one of the military proofs and grant pension.
code, as to injuries received by James C. Hale a former member of
the national guard, at Buffalo creek, in the year eighteen hundred
and seventy-seven, and to grant to said James C. Hale, or to his
widow or minor children, a pension on account of such injuries,
notwithstanding any settlement heretofore made with the state by
the said James C. Hale, or any previous application for a pension
in respect thereof or any action had thereon.

§ 2. The adjutant-general may, in the consideration of this claim, May take into consideration money paid.
take into account any money heretofore paid by the state to the
said James C. Hale, as a remuneration or pension for injuries received by him at Buffalo creek, in the year eighteen hundred and
seventy-seven.

§ 3. This act shall take effect immediately.

Chap. 489.

AN ACT to amend the tax law, in relation to receipts for taxes.

Became a law May 17, 1897, with the approval of the Governor.
Passed, three-fifths being present.

*The People of the State of New York, represented in Senate and
Assembly, do enact as follows:*

Section 1. Section ninety-four of chapter nine hundred and eight
of the laws of eighteen hundred and ninety-six, entitled "An act
in relation to taxation, constituting chapter twenty-four of the
general laws," is hereby amended to read as follows :

§ 94. **Receipts for taxes.**— The collector shall deliver a receipt
to each person paying a tax, specifying the date of such payment,
the name of such person, the description of the property as shown
on the assessment-roll, the name of the person to whom the same

is assessed, the amount of such tax, and the date of the delivery to him of the assessment-roll on account of which such tax was paid. For the purpose of giving such receipt, each collector shall have a book of blank receipts, so arranged that when a receipt is torn therefrom a corresponding stub will remain. The state board of tax commissioners shall prescribe the form of such receipts, stubs and books and they shall be furnished to the collector by the board of supervisors, at the expense of the county. At the time of giving such a receipt, the collector shall make the same entries on the corresponding stub as are required to be made on the receipt. Such book shall be subject to public inspection and shall be filed by the collector with his return, together with the assessment-roll in the office of the county treasurer.

§ 2. Said chapter is hereby amended by adding thereto a new section following section ninety-four to be known as section ninety-five, and to read as follows :

§ 95. Article, how applicable.—This article shall apply to all the cities or towns of the state, ir so far as the matters herein provided for do not conflict with the special and local laws of such cities or towns.

§ 3. This act shall take effect immediately.

Chap. 490.

AN ACT to amend the tax law, in relation to description in conveyance made by county treasurers.

Became a law May 17, 1897, with the approval of the Governor. Passed, three-fifths being present.

The People of the State of New York, represented in Senate and Assembly, do enact as follows:

Section 1. Section one hundred and fifty-three of chapter nine hundred and eight of the laws of eighteen hundred and ninety-six, entitled "An act in relation to taxation, constituting chapter twenty-four of the general laws," known as the tax law, is hereby amended to read as follows:

§ 153. Conveyance by county treasurer.— If such real estate, or any portion thereof, be not redeemed as herein provided, the county treasurer shall execute to the purchaser a conveyance of the real estate so sold, the description of which real estate shall include a specific statement of whose title or interest is thereby conveyed, so far as appears on the record, which conveyance shall vest in the grantee an absolute estate in fee, subject, however, to all claims the county or state may have thereon for taxes or liens or incumbrance. The county treasurer shall receive from the purchaser fifty cents for preparing such conveyance, and ten cents additional for each piece or parcel of land described therein, exceeding the first. All purchases made for the county shall be included in one conveyance for which the county treasurer shall receive ten dollars. Every such conveyance shall be executed by the treasurer of the county, under his hand and seal, and executed and acknowledged as other conveyances of real estate. Every certificate of conveyance executed by the county treasurer under this act may be recorded in the same manner and with like effect as a conveyance of real estate properly acknowledged or proven. The money received by the county treasurer on every such sale shall be applied by him, after deducting the expenses thereof, in like manner as if the same had been paid to him by the collectors of the several towns.

§ 2. This act shall take effect immediately.

Chap. 492.

AN ACT to amend section twenty-eight hundred and thirty-eight of the code of civil procedure, relative to the application for ancillary letters to foreign guardian.

Became a law May 17, 1897, with the approval of the Governor. Passed, a majority being present.

The People of the State of New York, represented in Senate and Assembly, do enact as follows:

Section 1. Section twenty-eight hundred and thirty-eight of the code of civil procedure is hereby amended as follows: _{Code amended.}

§ 2838. Where an infant, who resides without the state and within the United States, is entitled to property within the state, or to maintain an action in any court thereof, a general guardian of his property, who has been appointed by a court of competent jurisdiction, within the state or territory where the ward resides, and has there given security, in at least twice the value of the personal property, and of the rents and profits of the real property, of the ward, may present, to the surrogate's court having jurisdiction, a written petition, duly verified, setting forth the facts, and praying for ancillary letters of guardianship accordingly. The petition must be accompanied with exemplified copies of the records and other papers, showing that he has been so appointed, and has given the security required in this section, which must be authenticated in the mode prescribed in article seventh of title third of this chapter, for the authentication of records and papers, upon an application for ancillary letters testamentary, or ancillary letters of administration.

Application where infant resides in foreign country. 2. Where an infant who resides without the state and within a foreign country is entitled to personal property within the state, or to maintain an action, or special proceeding in any court thereof respecting such personal property, a general guardian of his property, authorized to act as such within the foreign country where the ward resides, may apply to the surrogate's court of the county where such personal property or any part thereof is situated, for ancillary letters of guardianship on the personal estate of such infant, and the person so authorized must present to the surrogate's court having jurisdiction a written petition duly verified, setting forth the facts and praying for ancillary letters of guardianship on the personal estate of such infant. The petition must be accompanied with the exemplified copies of the records and other papers showing the appointment of such foreign guardian, or where such foreign guardian has not been appointed by any court, with other proof of his authority to act as such guardian within such foreign country, and also with proof that pursuant to the laws of such foreign country, such foreign guardian is entitled to the possession of the ward's personal estate. Exemplified copies of the records, where used pursuant to this subdivision, must be authenticated by the seal of the court, or officer, by which or by whom such foreign guardian was appointed, or the officer having the custody of the seal or of the record thereof, and the signature of a judge of such court, or the signature of such officer and of the clerk of such court or officer, if any; and must be further authenticated by the certificate, under the principal seal of the department of foreign affairs, or the department of justice of such country, attested by the signature or seal of a United States consul.

When takes effect. § 2. This act shall take effect September first, eighteen hundred and ninety-seven.

Chap. 493.

AN ACT to amend chapter six hundred and ninety of the laws of eighteen hundred and ninety-two, entitled "An act in relation to insurance corporations, constituting chapter thirty-eight of the general laws," relating to reports of corporations.

Became a law May 17, 1897, with the approval of the Governor. Passed, a majority being present.

The People of the State of New York, represented in Senate and Assembly, do enact as follows:

Section 1. Section forty-four of chapter six hundred and ninety of the laws of eighteen hundred and ninety-two, entitled "An act in relation to insurance corporations, constituting chapter thirty-eight of the general laws," is hereby amended so as to read as follows:

§ 44. Reports of corporations.—Every corporation engaged wholly or in part in the transaction of the business of insurance in this state, whether heretofore or hereafter incorporated by a general or special law, except corporations formed under articles sixth, seventh, eighth and ninth of this chapter, shall annually, on the first day of January, or within two months thereafter if a corporation under article two of this chapter, and within one month thereafter, if a corporation under articles three and four of this chapter, file in the office of the superintendent of insurance a statement verified by the oath of at least two of the principal officers of such corporation, showing its condition on the thirty-first day of December then next preceding, which shall be in such form and shall contain such matters as the superintendent shall prescribe. If a foreign corporation incorporated under the laws of a state or country outside of the United States, such oath may be made by the manager thereof within the United States. The superintendent may also address any inquiry to any such insurance corporation or its officers in relation to its doings or condition, or any other matter connected with its transactions. Every corporation so addressed shall promptly and truthfully reply in writing to any such inquiries, and such reply shall be verified if required by the superintendent, by such officer of the corporation as he shall designate.

§ 2. This act shall take effect immediately.

ARTICLE V.

SUGAR BEET CULTURE.

Section 71. Commissioners of agriculture to apportion moneys appropriated for promotion of sugar beet culture.—Money appropriated for the promotion of sugar beet culture by scientific and practical experiment shall be apportioned by the commissioners of agriculture to the persons, firms, associations or corporations entitled thereto, according to the provisions of this article.

§ 72. Persons, et cetera, to whom moneys may be distributed.— Any person, firm, association or corporation, engaged in the manufacture of sugar from beets grown in the state of New York, upon registration in the office of the commissioner of agriculture, and filing a certificate therein, stating the name of such person, firm, association or corporation, the location of the factory, and the capacity thereof, and the time when the manufacture of sugar began or is to begin, shall be entitled to a distributive share of the amount appropriated for the promotion and encouragement of sugar beet culture, as provided in this article. No such person, firm, association or corporation shall receive any portion of the moneys so appropriated, unless all the beets used in the manufacture of such sugar are grown within the state of New York, and unless the grower received therefor a net sum of not less than five dollars per ton, and provided such beets are not grown by the manufacturer of such sugar. No money shall be distributed to such manufacturers, unless the sugar manufactured by them shall contain at least ninety per centum of crystalized sugar. The commissioner of agriculture may expend such sum or sums as he may deem necessary or expedient, not exceeding ten per centum of the amount appropriated for the purposes of this article, in practical and scientific experiments in growing sugar beets in one or more sections of this state, for the purpose of determining the adaptability of the soil thereof for the production of sugar beets.

§ 73. Statements; inspections, branding of packages.–The quantity and quality of sugar upon which said money is to be paid shall be determined by the commissioner of agriculture of this state, with whom all claimants shall, from time to time, file verified statements showing the quantity and quality of sugar manufactured by them, the price paid the producer for beets and upon which said money is claimed. The said commissioner shall, without unnecessary delay, visit or cause to be visited by such persons as he shall designate in writing, the factory where said sugar has been produced or manufactured, and take such evidence by the sworn testimony of the officers or employes of such factory or others, as to the amount and quality of sugar so manufactured, and the price paid for beets as to him or the person so designated by him shall appear satisfactory and conclusive. The sugar so manufactured shall be placed by the manufacturer in original packages, which shall be examined and branded by the said commissioner or person by him designated, with a suitable brand, showing the quantity and the quality of sugar contained in each of said packages, of which an accurate account shall be kept by said inspector, and filed in the office of the commissioner of agriculture of this state.

§ 74. Inspectors, to be appointed by commissioner.—It shall be the duty of the commissioner of agriculture to appoint a resident inspector in each town or city where one or more manufactories of sugar may be located in this state, the aggregate output of which factories shall exceed two thousand pounds of sugar per day, and such examiner shall make such examinations, take such evidence and make such records and reports as is specified in section two of this act. The compensation or fee for such service of said inspector shall not exceed the sum of twenty-five cents for each package so branded, nor the sum of five dollars per day for any one day's service, and such resident inspector shall be required to give a good and sufficient bond in the sum of not less than two thousand dollars to the state of New York, contingent on the faithful performance of his duties, said bond to be approved by the said commissioner of agriculture. Said fees or compensation, together with the cost of said brand and any and all analysis that the said commissioner of agriculture or other authorized inspector shall require to be made, shall be borne and paid by the claimant of said money.

§ 75. **Weighman, powers and duties.**—It shall be the duty of the commissioner of agriculture to appoint at each sugar manufactory in this state where the output of such manufactory shall exceed two thousand pounds of sugar per day, a person who shall weigh all beets received by the person or persons, corporation or association operating said manufactory. Such person shall be known as the weighman, and he shall keep accurate record of all duties performed by him. He shall discharge all duties pertaining to his position in an impartial manner, and shall furnish the commissioner of agriculture with a good and sufficient bond in the sum of two thousand dollars for the faithful discharge of his duties as prescribed by this act. The commissioner of agriculture may appoint such person or persons to assist said weighman as the service to be performed may require. Each person so appointed shall give bond as provided by this section. The weighman shall take into his possession, promptly on receipt of beets at such manufactory, such samples of beets as he deems fair and equitable, from which to remove dirt or other dockage. He shall then promptly weigh all beets from which samples have been taken and keep an accurate record of all weights, and all of such records shall show the names of both the seller and the buyer. The weights furnished by said weighman shall be accepted by both the seller and the buyer, and upon such weights so furnished settlement between the seller and the buyer shall be made. The compensation or fee allowed such weighman shall not exceed the sum of five dollars per day for time actually employed and for his assistants a sum not to exceed three dollars per day for the time actually employed. All expenses arising from the duties of said weighman or his assistants, as prescribed by this act, shall be paid by the person or persons, corporation or association operating such manufactory where such expense is incurred.

§ 76. **Distribution of moneys by commissioner of agriculture.**—On or before the first day of February in each year, the commissioner of agriculture shall prepare a detailed statement of the quantity of sugar manufactured by each person, firm or association or corporation entitled to receive a portion of the moneys appropriated for the promotion and encouragement of sugar beet culture. He shall apportion to each such person, firm, association or corporation the moneys so appropriated according to the amount of sugar of the grade described in this article manufactured by each of them, during the preceding year. Not more than one cent a pound shall be paid in any one year on account of the sugar so manufactured. Such commissioner of agriculture shall certify to the comptroller the amount apportioned to each manufacturer of sugar according to the provisions of this article; and the comptroller shall draw his warrant upon the state treasurer for the amount so certified, payable to the party or parties to whom such apportionment was made.

§ 2. Articles five and six of said act are hereby made articles six and seven.

§ 3. The sum of twenty-five thousand dollars, or so much thereof as may be necessary, is hereby appropriated out of any moneys in the treasury not otherwise appropriated, to be paid in the manner prescribed in this act for the purpose of making effectual the provisions thereof.

§ 4. This act shall take effect immediately.

Chap. 503.

AN ACT to amend the insurance law, relative to mailing notices.

Became a law May 18, 1897, with the approval of the Governor.

Passed, three-fifths being present.

The People of the State of New York, represented in Senate and Assembly, do enact as follows:

Section 1. Section two hundred and thirty-eight of chapter six hundred and ninety of the laws of eighteen hundred and ninety-two, entitled "An act in relation to insurance corporations, constituting chapter thirty-eight of the general laws," and known as the insurance law, is hereby amended so as to read as follows:

§ 238. Rights of members; exemptions; notices of assessment.— Membership in any such society, order or association shall give to the member the right at any time, upon the consent of such society, order or association, in the manner and form prescribed by its by-laws, to make a change in its payee or payees, beneficiary or beneficiaries, without requiring the consent of such payees or beneficiaries. All money or other benefit, charity, relief or aid to be paid, provided or rendered by any such society, order or association, whether voluntary or incorporated under this article or any other law, shall be exempt from execution, and shall not be liable to be seized, taken or appropriated by any legal or equitable process, to pay any debt or liability of a member, beneficiary, or beneficiaries of a member. All notices of assessment made upon its lodges, councils, branches or members, or any of them by any such society, order or association, shall truly state the cause and purpose of the assessment, and what portion or amount thereof, if any, is to be used for the payment of other than beneficiary claims. An affidavit made by any officer of such society, order or association that such notice was mailed, stating the date of mailing, shall be presumptive evidence thereof.

§ 2. This act shall take effect immediately.

Chap. 504.

AN ACT to amend the railroad law, relative to additional corporate powers.

Became a law May 18, 1897, with the approval of the Governor.
Passed, three-fifths being present.

The People of the State of New York, represented in Senate and Assembly, do enact as follows:

Section 1. Section eighteen of chapter five hundred and sixty-five of the laws of eighteen hundred and ninety, entitled "An act in relation to railroads, constituting chapter thirty-nine of the general laws," is hereby amended so as to read as follows:

§ 18. Additional corporate powers of such road.—The corporation specified in the preceding section shall have the following additional powers:

1. To expend money in making preliminary examinations and surveys for its proposed railroad, telegraph lines, and lines of steamboats and sailing vessels, and in acquiring from foreign countries, nations or governments, the grants, concessions and privileges herein authorized.

2. To take and receive from foreign countries, nations and governments, such grants, concessions or privileges, for the construction, acquisition, maintenance and operation of railroads, telegraph lines and vessels, as may be consistent with the purposes of the corporation, and as may be granted and conceded to it, and to hold the same under such restrictions and with such duties and liabilities as may be fixed by the laws of such foreign country, nation or government, or as may be annexed to such grants or concessions.

3. To construct, acquire, maintain and operate the lines of railroad, telegraph and shipping provided for by its certificate of incorporation, and to take and hold by purchase or by voluntary

grant such real estate and other property in foreign countries as may be necessary and convenient for the construction, maintenance and accommodation of such lines, and to sell, convey, mortgage or lease such real estate or other property; and to acquire by purchase or otherwise any railroad or lines of telegraph constructed or in process of construction in any foreign country, and any grants, concessions, franchises, rights, privileges and immunities relating thereto, and to issue therefor the capital stock of the company or any part thereof at such valuation or valuations and on such terms as may be agreed upon, and to mortgage or sell and convey such railroad or lines of telegraph constructed or in process of construction in any foreign country, and any grants, concessions, franchises, rights, privileges and immunities relating thereto, or any part of its property to any person or corporation created by this or any other state or foreign government, subject to the laws of the country or countries where such property may be, and the power of sale hereby granted shall be exercised only by a majority of the entire board of directors of the corporation, with the written concurrence of the holders of two-thirds in amount of its capital stock.

4. To take and convey persons and property on its transportation lines by the power or force of steam or of animals, or by mechanical or other power, and receive compensation therefor subject to the laws of the place or country where the same are situated.

5. To acquire and use such real estate and other property in this state as may be necessary in the conduct of its business, but the value of such real estate held at any one time shall not exceed the sum of one million dollars.

§ 2. This act shall take effect immediately.

Chap. 506.

AN ACT to amend the penal code, relative to the sale of passenger tickets.

Became a law May 18, 1897, with the approval of the Governor. Passed, three-fifths being present.

The People of the State of New York, represented in Senate and Assembly, do enact as follows:

Section 1. The penal code is hereby amended by inserting therein a new section, to be known as section six hundred and fifteen, to read as follows:

§ 615. **Sale of passage tickets on vessels and railroads forbidden except by agents specially authorized.**—No person shall issue or

sell, or offer to sell, any passage ticket, or an instrument giving
or purporting to give any right, either absolutely or upon any condition or contingency to a passage or conveyance upon any vessel
or railway train, or a berth or state-room in any vessel, unless he
is an authorized agent of the owners or consignees of such vessel,
or of the company running such train, except as allowed by sections
six hundred and sixteen and six hundred and twenty-two; and no
person is deemed an authorized agent of such owners, consignees
or company, within the meaning of the chapter, unless he has
received authority in writing therefor, specifying the name of the
company, line, vessel or railway for which he is authorized to act
as agent, and the city, town or village together with the street
and street number, in which his office is kept, for the sale of
tickets.

§ 2. Section six hundred and sixteen of the penal code is hereby
amended so as to read as follows:

§ 616. **Sales by authorized agents restricted.** –No person, except
as allowed in section six hundred and twenty-two, shall ask, take
or receive any money or valuable thing as a consideration for any
passage or conveyance upon any vessel or railway train, or for the
procurement of any ticket or instrument giving or purporting to
give a right, either absolutely or upon a condition or contingency,
to a passage or conveyance upon a vessel or railway train, or a berth
or state-room on a vessel, unless he is an authorized agent within
the provisions of the last section; nor shall any person, as such
agent, sell or offer to sell, any such ticket, instrument, berth or
state-room, or ask, take or receive any consideration for any such
passage, conveyance, berth or state-room, excepting at the office
designated in his appointment, nor until he has been authorized
to act as such agent according to the provisions of the last section,
nor for a sum exceeding the price charged at the time of such sale
by the company, owners or consignees of the vessel or railway
mentioned in the ticket.   Nothing in this section or chapter contained shall prevent the properly authorized agent of any transportation company from purchasing from the properly authorized
agent of any other transportation company a ticket for a passenger to whom he may sell a ticket to travel over any part of
the line for which he is the properly authorized agent, so as
to enable such passenger to travel to the place or junction from
which his ticket shall read.   Every person who shall have
purchased a passage ticket from an authorized agent of a railroad

company, which shall not have been used, or shall have been used only in part, may, within thirty days after the date of the sale of said ticket, present the same, unused or partly used, for redemption, at the general office of the railroad company which issued said ticket, or at the ticket office where said ticket was sold, or at the ticket office at the point to which the ticket has been used. If said ticket, wholly unused, shall be presented for redemption at the ticket office where sold, the same shall be then and there redeemed by the agent in charge of said ticket office at the price paid for said ticket. If said ticket, partly used, shall be presented for redemption at the ticket office where sold, or at the ticket office at the point to which used, the ticket agent at either of said offices, upon the delivery of said ticket, shall issue to the holder thereof a receipt, properly describing said ticket and setting forth the date of the receipt of said ticket, and the name of the person from whom received, and shall thereupon forthwith transmit said ticket for redemption to the general office. It shall be the duty of every railroad company to redeem tickets presented for redemption, as in this section provided for, promptly and within not to exceed thirty days from the date of presentation at the general office or from the date of the aforesaid receipt. A wholly unused ticket shall be redeemed at the price paid therefor. A partly used ticket shall be redeemed at a rate which shall be equal to the difference between the price paid for the whole ticket and the cost of a ticket of the same class between the points for which said ticket was actually used. Mileage books shall be redeemed within thirty days after the date of the expiration thereof in the same manner. Every railroad company which shall wrongfully refuse redemption, as in this section provided for, shall forfeit to the aggrieved party fifty dollars, which sum may be recovered, together with the amount of redemption money to which the party is entitled, in an action in any court of competent jurisdiction, together with costs; but no such action can be maintained unless commenced within one year after the cause of action accrued.

§ 3. This act shall take effect September first, eighteen hundred and ninety seven.

Chap. 507.

AN ACT to amend chapter two hundred and twenty-five of the laws of eighteen hundred and ninety-six, entitled "An act in relation to the poor, constituting chapter twenty-seven of the general laws."

Became a law May 18, 1897, with the approval of the Governor.
Passed, three-fifths being present.

The People of the State of New York, represented in Senate and Assembly, do enact as follows:

Poor law amended.

Section 1. Section three of chapter two hundred and twenty-five of the laws of eighteen hundred and ninety-six, entitled "An act in relation to the poor, constituting chapter twenty-seven of the general laws," is hereby amended by inserting at the end of the section the following paragraph:

Limitations of expenditures by superintendent of poor.

"Expenditures by the superintendent of the poor in the administration of his department are subject to the following limitations: The board of supervisors, at its annual meeting, may fix the maximum sum which may be expended by the superintendent, at his discretion, during the next ensuing year, and may provide that expenditures in excess of that sum shall be made only with the written approval of the chairman of the board of supervisors, or of a committee of the board, composed of not exceeding three members. If such limitation is fixed and such provision made, the county treasurer shall not pay any draft or order of the superintendent in excess of the sum so fixed by the board, unless it is accompanied with the written approval of such chairman or committee."

§ 2. This act shall take effect immediately.

Chap. 511.

AN ACT to amend the public buildings law, in relation to the completion of the capitol.

**Became a law May 18, 1897, with the approval of the Governor.
Passed, three-fifths being present.**

The People of the State of New York, represented in Senate and Assembly, do enact as follows:

Section 1. Article one of the public buildings law is hereby amended by adding at the end thereof a new section to be known as section twelve and to read as follows:

§ 12. Lighting system for the capitol.—The superintendent of public works, in connection with the completion of the capitol, may establish a lighting system therein.

§ 2. This act shall take effect immediately.

Chap. 512.

AN ACT to amend the consolidated school law.

**Became a law May 18, 1897, with the approval of the Governor.
Passed, a majority being present.**

The People of the State of New York, represented in Senate and Assembly, do enact as follows:

Section 1. Subdivision four of section thirteen of title five of the consolidated school law, relating to the condemnation of schoolhouses by the school commissioner, is hereby amended so as to read as follows: *School law amended.*

4. By an order under his hand, reciting the reason or reasons, to condemn a schoolhouse, if he deems it wholly unfit for use and not worth repairing, and to deliver the order to the trustees, or to one of them, and transmit a copy to the superintendent of public instruction. Such order, if no time for its taking effect be stated in it, shall take effect immediately. He shall also state what sum, will, in his opinion, be necessary to erect a schoolhouse capable of accommodating the children of the district. Immediately upon the receipt of said order, the trustee or trustees of such district shall call a special meeting of the inhabitants of said district, for the purpose of considering the question of building a schoolhouse therein. Such meeting shall *Condemnation of schoolhouses by commissioner.*

have power to determine the size of said schoolhouse, the material to be used in its erection, and to vote a tax to build the same. But such meeting shall have no power to reduce the estimate made by the commissioner aforesaid by more than twenty-five per centum of such estimate. And where no tax for building such house shall have been voted by such district within thirty days from the time of holding the first meeting to consider the question, then it shall be the duty of the trustee or trustees of such district to contract for the building of a schoolhouse capable of accommodating the children of the district, and to levy a tax to pay for the same, which tax shall not exceed the sum estimated as necessary by the commissioner aforesaid, and which shall not be less than such estimated sum by more than twenty-five per centum thereof. But such estimated sum may be increased by a vote of the inhabitants at any school meeting subsequently called and held according to law.

§ 2. Section six of title six of the consolidated school law, relating to the alteration of school districts, is hereby amended so as to read as follows:

Alteration of school districts.

§ 6. Any school commissioner may also, with the written consent of the trustees of all the districts to be affected thereby, dissolve one or more school districts adjoining any union free school district other than one whose limits correspond with any city or incorporated village, and annex the territory of such districts so dissolved to such union free school district. He may alter the boundaries of any union free school district whose limits do not correspond with those of any city or incorporated village, in like manner as alterations of common school districts may be made as herein provided; but no school district shall be divided, which has any bonded indebtedness outstanding.

§ 3. Title six of the consolidated school law is hereby amended by adding thereto a new section, to be known as section fourteen, to read as follows:

Rights, etc., extended to districts organized under special acts.

§ 14. All the rights, powers and duties conferred upon school commissioners by titles five and six of this act, including the sole authority to examine and license, under the rules prescribed by the superintendent of public instruction, all persons proposing to teach common schools, not possessing the qualifications mentioned in subdivision five of section thirteen of title five, shall extend to all districts organized under special acts, and all parts of such special acts inconsistent therewith are hereby repealed.

§ 4. Section seventy-four of title seven of the consolidated school law, relating to the payment of unpaid school taxes by the county treasurer, is hereby amended so as to read as follows:

§ 74. Out of any moneys in the county treasury, raised for con-tingent expenses, or for the purpose of paying the amount of the taxes so returned unpaid, the treasurer shall pay to the collector the amount of the taxes so returned as unpaid, with one per centum of the amount in addition thereto, for the compensation of such collector, and if there are no moneys in the treasury applicable to such purpose, the board of supervisors, at the time of levying said unpaid taxes, as provided in the next section, shall pay to the collector of the school district the amount thereof, with said addition thereto, by voucher or draft on the county treasurer, in the same manner as other county charges are paid, and the collector shall be again charged therewith by the trustees. *Payment of unpaid school taxes by county treasurer.*

§ 5. Section four of title ten of the consolidated school law, relating to the closing of schools during institute week, is hereby amended so as to read as follows:

§ 4. All schools in school districts and parts of school districts within any school commissioner district wherein an institute is held, not included within the boundaries of an incorporated city, except as hereinafter provided, shall be closed during the time such institute shall be in session. The closing of a school within the school commissioner district wherein an institute shall be held, at which a teacher has attended, shall not work a forfeiture of the contract under which such teacher was employed. In all districts having a population of more than five thousand, and employing a superintendent whose time is exclusively devoted to the supervision of the schools therein, the schools may be closed or not at the option of the boards of education in such districts. The trustees of every school district are hereby directed to give the teacher or teachers employed by them, the whole of the time spent by them in attending at an institute or institutes held as hereinbefore stated, without deducting anything from the wages of such teacher or teachers for the time so spent. All teachers under a contract to teach in any commissioner district shall attend such institute so held for that district, and shall receive wages for such attendance. *Closing of school during institute week.*

§ 6. This act shall take effect immediately.

Chap. 513.

AN ACT to provide for the establishment of a fish hatchery for the propagation of food or commercial fishes.

Became a law May 18, 1897, with the approval of the Governor. Passed, three-fifths being present.

The People of the State of New York, represented in Senate and Assembly, do enact as follows:

Establishment of fish hatchery.

Section 1. The commissioners of fisheries, game and forests are hereby authorized and directed to erect and maintain a fish hatchery at or near one of the inland lakes of the state, for the purpose of the artificial propagation and distribution of food or commercial fishes, the site to be selected by the said commissioners.

Acquisition of land.

§ 2. The necessary land on which is to be erected the hatchery mentioned in the first section of this act may be obtained by purchase or otherwise by said commissioners of fisheries, game and forests, taking deed or deeds therefor in the name of the people of the state of New York.

Appropriation.

§ 3. The sum of six thousand dollars is hereby appropriated for the purpose of carrying out the provisions of this act, payable out of any funds in the treasury not otherwise appropriated, to be expended by the commissioners of fisheries, game and forests, in the same manner that the other expenditures by said commissioners are now authorized by law.

§ 4. This act shall take effect immediately.

Chap. 514.

AN ACT to appropriate moneys for the completion and improvement of the state armory at Binghamton.

Became a law May 18, 1897, with the approval of the Governor. Passed, three-fifths being present.

The People of the State of New York, represented in Senate and Assembly, do enact as follows:

Appropriation.

Section 1. The sum of six thousand dollars, or so much thereof as may be necessary, is hereby appropriated out of any moneys in the treasury not otherwise appropriated, for the completion and improvement of the state armory at Binghamton; said amount to be paid by the treasurer upon the warrant of the comptroller on bills for said completion and improvements approved by the adjutant-general.

§ 2. This act shall take effect immediately.

Chap. 515.

AN ACT authorizing the superintendent of public works to fill an excavation in lands belonging to the state, and making an appropriation therefor.

**Became a law May 18, 1897, with the approval of the Governor.
Passed, three-fifths being present.**

The People of the State of New York, represented in Senate and Assembly, do enact as follows:

Section 1. The superintendent of public works is hereby author- Filling th ized to fill a certain pond-hole or excavation on lands belonging of lands to the state, and situate between the Seneca turnpike and the lands ized. of the West shore railroad, and immediately east of the Oneida creek in the town of Vernon, Oneida county.

§ 2. The sum of one thousand dollars, or so much thereof as Appropria- may be necessary, is hereby appropriated out of any money in tion. the treasury not otherwise appropriated, to carry into effect the provisions of section one of this act, payable on the warrant of the comptroller upon the requisition of the superintendent of public works, as he may desire the same in the progress of such work.

§ 3. The work herein authorized shall be performed in accord- Plans, eto. ance with plans, specifications and estimates to be furnished and approved by the state engineer and surveyor.

§ 4. This act shall take effect immediately.

Chap. 536.

AN ACT to amend the code of criminal procedure, in relation to appeals from courts of special sessions.

**Became a law May 18, 1897, with the approval of the Governor.
Passed, three-fifths being present.**

The People of the State of New York, represented in Senate and Assembly, do enact as follows:

Section 1. Sections seven hundred and fifty-two, seven hundred and fifty-four, and seven hundred and fifty nine of the code of criminal procedure are hereby amended to read respectively as follows:

§ 752. **How allowed.**—If, in the opinion of the judge, it is proper that the question arising on the appeal should be decided by the county court, he must indorse on the affidavit an allowance of the appeal to that court; and the defendant, or his attorney, must within five days thereafter, serve a copy of the affidavit upon which the appeal is granted, together with a notice that the same has been allowed, upon the district attorney of the county in which the appeal is to be heard.

§ 754. **Undertaking, when and with whom filed.**—The undertaking upon the appeal must be immediately filed with the clerk of the county court, and the said clerk of the county court shall within five days thereafter, give notice to the district attorney of the county that such bond has been filed, which notice shall give the name of the defendant and his sureties, the offense for which the defendant was charged and the amount of the bail given.

§ 2. This act shall take effect September first, eighteen hundred and ninety-seven.

Chap. 538.

AN ACT providing for the sale of land of cemetery associations or cemetery corporations.

Became a law May 18, 1897, with the approval of the Governor.
Passed, three-fifths being present.

The People of the State of New York, represented in Senate and Assembly, do enact as follows:

Sale of cemetery land.

Section 1. It shall be lawful for any cemetery association, duly incorporated under the act authorizing the incorporation of rural cemetery associations, to dispose of its land from which all bodies have been removed with the consent of the former owners of the

Proof to supreme court.

lots in which such bodies had been interred, upon proving to the satisfaction of the supreme court of the district where its land is located, that all bodies have been removed from said lots with the consent of the former owners thereof, and properly and decently interred in some other cemetery; that all said lots and parts of lots have been reconveyed to said cemetery association and are not used for burial purposes; that burials have been prohibited in said cemetery; that all parties interested in said cemetery as trustees or creditors consent thereof, and that its debts and liabilities have been paid. The supreme court may, in its discretion, appoint a

Order of court.

referee to take proof of the facts above stated. Upon being satisfied that such cemetery association has complied with the requirements above stated, the court may make an order authorizing it to sell and dispose of its said land.

§ 2. This act shall take effect immediately.

Chap. 542.

AN ACT in relation to the armory of the Thirty-fourth Separate Company at Geneva, New York, to provide for the erection of an addition thereto and alterations therein and for the purpose of preserving the property of the state and making an appropriation therefor.

Became a law May 18, 1897, with the approval of the Governor.
Passed, three-fifths being present.

The People of the State of New York, represented in Senate and Assembly, do enact as follows:

Section 1. The sum of seven thousand dollars or as much thereof as may be necessary is hereby appropriated out of any moneys in the treasury not otherwise appropriated, for the purpose of erecting an addition to the armory of the Thirty-fourth Separate Company at Geneva, New York, and for making such alterations and improvements as may be necessary for the better preservation of the property of the state therein. The said sum of seven thousand dollars or so much thereof as may be necessary shall be payable by the treasurer upon the warrant of the comptroller, to the order of the adjutant-general, the inspector-general and the chief of ordnance, and shall be expended by them upon plans to be approved by them; and they are hereby appointed commissioners for such purposes. *Appropriation for improvement of armory.*

§ 2. This act shall take effect immediately.

Chap. 543.

AN ACT making an appropriation for completing and furnishing the state normal and training school building at Jamaica.

Became a law May 18, 1897, with the approval of the Governor.
Passed, three-fifths being present.

The People of the State of New York, represented in Senate and Assembly, do enact as follows:

Section 1. The sum of twenty-five thousand dollars is hereby appropriated out of any money in the treasury not otherwise appropriated, for the purpose of and to provide for heating, ventilating, lighting, equipping, furnishing, and grading grounds of the State Normal school at Jamaica.

§ 2. This act shall take effect immediately.

Chap. 546.

AN ACT to amend section fifty-six, subdivision thirty-seven, of the code of criminal precedure, in relation to the manner in which an accused shall elect to be tried in a court of special sessions.

Became a law May 18, 1897, with the approval of the Governor.
Passed, a majority being present.

The People of the State of New York, represented in Senate and Assembly, do enact as follows:

Code amended.

Section 1. Section fifty-six, subdivision thirty-seven, of the code of criminal procedure, is hereby amended so as to read as follows:

Jurisdiction of court of special sessions.

§ 56. Subdivision 37.—When a complaint is made to or a warrant is issued by a committing magistrate for any misdemeanor not included in the foregoing subdivisions of this section, if the accused shall elect to be tried by a court of special sessions, as provided by section two hundred and eleven. But this subdivision shall not apply to any misdemeanor which is or may be punishable by a fine exceeding fifty dollars, or by imprisonment exceeding six months.

§ 2. This act shall take effect October first, eighteen hundred and ninety-seven.

Chap. 547.

AN ACT to amend section six hundred and thirteen of the code of criminal procedure of the state of New York, relative to subpoenas.

Became a law May 18, 1897, with the approval of the Governor.
Passed, a majority being present.

The People of the State of New York, represented in Senate and Assembly, do enact as follows:

Code amended.

Section 1. Section six hundred and thirteen of the code of criminal procedure of the state of New York, is hereby amended to read as follows:

Requirements in subpoena to produce chattels, books, etc.

§ 613. If chattels, books, papers or documents be required, a direction to the following effect must be contained in the subpoena: "And you are required also to bring with you the following," (describing intelligibly the chattels, books, papers or documents required.)

§ 2. This act shall take effect September first, eighteen hundred and ninety-seven.

Chap. 548.

AN ACT to amend the penal code by adding a section to be known as section one hundred and eighty-three-a, relative to murder in the first degree.

Became a law May 18, 1897, with the approval of the Governor.
Passed, a majority being present.

The People of the State of New York, represented in Senate and Assembly, do enact as follows:

Section 1. The penal code is hereby amended by adding thereto the following section, to be known as section one hundred and eighty-three-a:

§ 183a. **Murder in the first degree** — A person who wilfully, by loosening, removing or displacing a rail, or by any other interference, wrecks, destroys or so injures any car, tender, locomotive or railway train, or part thereof, while moving upon any railway in this state, whether operated by steam, electricity or other motive power, as to thereby cause the death of a human being, is guilty of murder in the first degree, and punishable accordingly.

§ 2. This act shall take effect immediately.

Chap. 549.

AN ACT to amend section four hundred and eighty-nine of the penal code, relating to the punishment of arson.

Became a law May 18, 1897, with the approval of the Governor.
Passed, a majority being present.

The People of the State of New York, represented in Senate and Assembly, do enact as follows:

Section 1. Section four hundred and eighty-nine of the penal code is hereby amended so as to read as follows:

§ 489. **Arson, how punished.**— Arson is punishable as follows:

1. In the first degree, by imprisonment for a term not exceeding forty years.

2. In the second degree, by imprisonment for a term not exceeding twenty-five years.

3. In the third degree, by imprisonment for a term not exceeding fifteen years.

§ 2. The penalties above prescribed shall, however, only apply to offenses committed after the taking effect of this act. Nothing

herein contained shall in any manner affect or impair any liability
or punishment incurred prior to the time this act takes effect, under
or by virtue of the then existing provisions of the section hereby
amended, and all offenses of arson committed before that time shall
be punishable according to such previously existing provisions, as
fully, and in the same manner, as though this act had not been
passed.

§ 3. This act shall take effect September first, eighteen hundred
and ninety-seven.

Chap. 550.

AN ACT conferring jurisdiction upon and authorizing the board
of claims to hear, audit and determine the claim of John J.
Corkery against the state of New York, and to make an award
therefor.

**Became a law May 18, 1897, with the approval of the Governor.
Passed, three-fifths being present.**

*The People of the State of New York, represented in Senate and
Assembly, do enact as follows:*

Jurisdiction to hear claims.

Section 1. Jurisdiction is hereby conferred upon the board of
claims, to hear, audit and determine the claim of John J. Corkery
against the state of New York, for personal injuries received by
him in the year eighteen hundred and seventy-eight, at the city of
Auburn, New York, while tending target for rifle practice for the
Forty-ninth regiment of the national guard of the state of New
York, wherein and whereby the said John J. Corkery lost his right
eye, and partially lost the sight of the left eye, and for loss of time,
and for expenses incurred by him in endeavoring to preserve sight
in the left eye, and to make an award therefor not exceeding six
thousand dollars, as if such claim had accrued within two years
from the time of such hearing.

Appeals from award.

§ 2. Either party may take an appeal to the third appellate
division of the supreme court from any award made under authority of this act, provided such appeal be taken by service of a notice
of appeal within thirty days after service of a copy of the award.

§ 3. This act shall take effect immediately.

Chap. 551.

AN ACT legalizing town and village elections held since January first, eighteen hundred and ninety-seven.

Became a law May 18, 1897, with the approval of the Governor.
Passed, a majority being present.

The People of the State of New York, represented in Senate and Assembly, do enact as follows:

Section 1. The town and village elections held since January first, eighteen hundred and ninety-seven, and the election of officers thereat, are hereby legalized and confirmed and shall be of the same force and effect as though certificates of nomination of candidates voted for thereat had been regularly filed as required by law, and the official acts of persons elected as town or village officers at such elections performed since their election are also legalized, ratified and confirmed and shall be of the same force and effect as though the certificates of nomination which made them candidates at such elections had been regularly filed as required by law. Elections legalized.

§ 2. This act shall take effect immediately.

Chap. 554.

AN ACT to amend chapter three hundred and thirty-eight of the laws of eighteen hundred and ninety-three, entitled "An act in relation to agriculture, constituting articles one, two, three, four and five of chapter thirty-three of the general laws," and the penal code, relative to violations of the agricultural law.

Became a law May 18, 1897, with the approval of the Governor.
Passed, three-fifths being present.

The People of the State of New York, represented in Senate and Assembly, do enact as follows:

Section 1. Section thirty-seven of chapter three hundred and thirty-eight of the laws of eighteen hundred and ninety-three, entitled "An act in relation to agriculture, constituting articles one, two, three, four and five of chapter thirty-three of the general laws," is hereby amended so as to read as follows: Agricultural law amended.

§ 37. Every person violating any of the provisions of this article shall forfeit to the people of the state of New York the sum of not exceeding one hundred dollars for every Violations of law.

such violation. When such violation consists of the man-ufacture or production of any prohibited article, each day during which or any part of which such manufacture or pro-duction is carried on or continued, shall be deemed a separate vio-lation of the provisions of this article. When the violation con-sists of the sale, or the offering or exposing for sale or exchange of any prohibited article or substance, the sale of each one of several packages shall constitute a separate violation, and each day on which any such article or substance is offered or exposed for sale or exchange, shall constitute a separate violation of this article. When the use of any such article or substance is prohibited, each day during which or any part of which said article or substance is so used or furnished for use, shall constitute a separate violation, and the furnishing of the same for use to each person to whom the

Penalties. same may be furnished shall constitute a separate violation. Who-ever by himself or another violates any of the provisions of article two of said chapter, shall be guilty of a misdemeanor, and upon conviction shall be punished by a fine of not less than twenty-five dollars, nor more than two hundred dollars, or by imprisonment of not less than one month nor more than six months or by both such fine and imprisonment, for the first offense; and by six months imprisonment for the second offense; and any person who violates any of the provisions of article three of said chapter, is guilty of a misdemeanor, and shall be punished by a fine of not less than fifty dollars, nor more than one hundred dollars; and in addition thereto shall forfeit to the people of the state of New York, the sum of one hundred dollars for every such violation.

§ 2. Section four hundred and eight-a of the penal code is hereby amended so as to read as follows:

Penal code amended. § 408a. **Violations of the agricultural law.**—Any person who disregards, disobeys or violates any proclamation, notice, order or regulation, lawfully issued or prescribed by the commissioner of agriculture, for the suppression or prevention of the spread of infectious or contagious diseases among domestic animals, or who violates any of the provisions of sections eighty and eighty-two of article five of the agricultural law, is guilty of a misdemeanor

§ 3. This act shall take effect immediately.

Chap. 558.

AN ACT for the improvement of the Cayuga and Seneca canal
and making an appropriation therefor.

Became a law May 19, 1897, with the approval of the Governor.
Passed, three-fifths being present.

*The People of the State of New York, represented in Senate and
Assembly, do enact as follows:*

Section 1. The superintendent of public works is hereby author- Improve-
ized and directed to improve the channel of the Cayuga and Seneca ment Of
canal by dredging and excavating from the terminus of said canal
at Seneca Lake at Geneva, New York, to a point at the intersection
of said canal with the outlet of Seneca lake.

§ 2. The work shall be done in accordance with plans and specifi- Plans, etc.
cations furnished by the state engineer and surveyor.

§ 3. The sum of ten thousand dollars, or so much thereof as is Appropri-
necessary, is hereby appropriated out of any moneys in the treasury ation.
of the state not otherwise appropriated, to carry into effect the
provisions of this act.

§ 4. This act shall take effect immediately.

Chap. 559.

AN ACT making an appropriation to provide means for drainage
of lands in the town of Wheatfield, in the county of Niagara,
by deepening and improving Cayuga creek and its tributaries.

Became a law May 19, 1897, with the approval of the Governor.
Passed, three-fifths being present.

*The People of the State of New York, represented in Senate and
Assembly, do enact as follows:*

Section 1. The sum of five thousand dollars, or so much thereof Appropri-
as may be necessary, is hereby appropriated for the purpose of ation.
clearing out, deepening and improving the channel of Cayuga
creek and the tributaries thereto, and providing means for drainage where necessary in the town of Wheatfield, in the county of
Niagara, in order to drain land in said town overflooded by back
water at spring, summer and fall flood, occasioned by the erection of
a state dam for canal purposes across Tonawanda creek, and by the
construction of state ditches.

How payable, etc.

§ 2. The money hereby appropriated for purposes aforesaid shall be payable by the state treasurer on the warrant of the comptroller, to the superintendent of public works, to be expended by him for

Plans.

the purposes mentioned in section one of this act. All work called for by this act shall be done in accordance with plans, specifications and estimates prepared and approved by the state engineer and surveyor.

§ 3. This act shall take effect immediately.

Chap. 560.

AN ACT to provide for the removal of a portion of the dock or pier in the Hudson river at Piermont, and making an appropriation therefor.

Became a law May 19, 1897, with the approval of the Governor. Passed, three-fifths being present.

The People of the State of New York, represented in Senate and Assembly, do enact as follows:

Removal of portion of dock.

Section 1. The superintendent of public works is hereby authorized and directed to remove a portion of the dock or pier in the Hudson river, at or near Piermont, in the county of Rockland, built upon land granted by this state to Eleazer Lord, by patent dated the fourteenth day of January, eighteen hundred and fifty-three, which land is therein described as follows: Beginning at a point at the junction of the north and south, or cross dock with the south line of the location pier of the New York and Erie railroad, and running thence east along said pier twenty-five hundred feet to a point in Hudson's river; thence south four hundred and fifty feet; thence west twenty-five hundred feet to the cross dock aforesaid; and thence north along the same four hundred and fifty feet to the place of beginning. The portion of such dock or pier to be removed under this act shall be not less than one thousand nor more than twelve hundred feet in length, extending into the river, and between such points as may be determined by the superintendent of public works.

Acquisition of dock or land.

§ 2. The superintendent of public works may acquire in the name of the state by purchase, if he can agree with the owners, or otherwise by condemnation, such portion of the dock or pier or the land on which it stands as may be necessary to enable him to comply with the provisions of this act.

§ 3. The sum of five thousand dollars, or so much thereof as may be necessary, is hereby appropriated for the purposes of this act out of any moneys in the treasury not otherwise appropriated, to be paid to the superintendent of public works on the warrant of the comptroller. Appropriation.

§ 4. This act shall take effect immediately.

Chap. 561.

AN ACT to provide for continuing and completing the repairs to the breakwater and piers protecting the entrance of the canal feeder at Owasco lake outlet, removing bars therefrom and repairing dam and gates at dam number one of said outlet, and constructing a wall of rubble masonry along the Owasco highway or road at the foot of Owasco lake, and making an appropriation therefor.

Became a law May 19, 1897, with the approval of the Governor.
Passed, three-fifths being present.

The People of the State of New York, represented in Senate and Assembly, do enact as follows:

Section 1. The superintendent of public works is hereby authorized and directed to continue and complete the repairs now in process of construction and under contract to the breakwater and piers protecting the entrance of the canal feeder at Owasco lake outlet, removing bars therefrom and repairing dam and gates at dam number one on said outlet, and constructing a wall of rubble masonry along the Owasco highway or road at the foot of Owasco lake. Completion of repairs.

§ 2. The sum of eighteen thousand dollars or as much thereof as may be necessary is hereby appropriated for the purposes specified in this act, out of any moneys in the treasury not otherwise appropriated, to be paid by the treasurer upon the warrant of the comptroller to the order of the superintendent of public works, payable out of the canal fund. Appropriation.

§ 3. All work done under this act shall be based upon plans, specifications and estimates furnished and approved by the state engineer and surveyor. Plans.

§ 4. This act shall take effect immediately.

Chap. 562.

AN ACT providing for an additional appropriation for the construction of a lift bridge, or hoist bridge, over the Erie canal, in the village of Canajoharie.

Became a law May 19, 1897, with the approval of the Governor.

Passed, three-fifths being present.

The People of the State of New York, represented in Senate and Assembly, do enact as follows:

Additional appropriation.

Section 1. The additional sum of five thousand dollars, or so much thereof as may be necessary, is hereby appropriated for the construction and maintenance, over the Erie canal, in the village of Canajoharie, in the county of Montgomery, of a lift or hoist bridge, and the necessary machinery to operate such bridge, as provided by chapter five hundred and ninety-two of the laws of eighteen hundred and ninety-four.

Payment thereof.

§ 2. That the additional sum of five thousand dollars, or so much thereof as may be necessary, hereby appropriated for the purpose specified in the preceding section of this act, shall be payable by the treasurer, on the warrant of the comptroller, to the order of the superintendent of public works.

§ 3. This act shall take effect immediately.

Chap. 563.

AN ACT providing for the construction of a lift or hoist bridge over the Erie canal on Whitesboro street in the city of Utica, and making an appropriation therefor, and authorizing the city of Utica to raise money for the construction thereof.

Accepted by the city.

Became a law May 19, 1897, with the approval of the Governor.

Passed, three-fifths being present.

The People of the State of New York, represented in Senate and Assembly, do enact as follows:

Construction of bridge.

Section 1. Whenever the city of Utica shall, by its proper authorities, deposit in some bank of deposit, which shall be approved of by the superintendent of public works, the sum of ten thousand dollars to be expended in the manner hereinafter described, which money shall be made payable to the order of the superintendent of public works for the purpose hereinafter mentioned, the superintendent of public works is authorized to construct a suitable lift or hoist bridge with the necessary abutments and appurtenances thereto, over the Erie canal in the city of Utica on Whitesboro street. The plans for said bridge shall be prepared by the state Plans. engineer and surveyor, and the said bridge, when completed, shall be operated under the direction of the superintendent of public works. The sum of ten thousand dollars, or so much thereof as may Appropri-ation. be necessary, is hereby appropriated out of any money in the treasury not otherwise appropriated, for the purpose of carrying into effect the provisions of this act, and the said treasurer is hereby directed to pay the above amount, or such part thereof as may be necessary upon the warrant of the comptroller to the order of the superintendent of public works for the purpose defined by this act. Any deficiency arising from the construction of said bridge or the abutments or appurtenances thereof, in excess of the sum of ten thousand dollars herein appropriated by the state, shall be paid by the superintendent of public works out of any moneys in the state treasury not otherwise appropriated, but such deficiency shall not exceed five thousand dollars. But no work shall Contracts for work. be done or money expended under the provisions of this act until the same shall be let by contract to the lowest bidder or bidders offering to do the same, after due advertisement thereof. The Expense of operating entire expense of operating said bridge shall be paid by said city bridge. of Utica, and not by the state.

§ 2. It shall be lawful for the common council of the city of Issue and sale of city Utica, and it shall have the power to borrow the sum of ten thou- bonds. sand dollars upon the corporate bonds of the city of Utica at a rate of interest not exceeding five per centum per annum for the purpose of paying such additional expense, if any, necessary for constructing said bridge over the Erie canal, on Whitesboro street in Utica. Said bonds hereby authorized to be issued shall not be sold for less than par value, and said money to be used for the construction of said bridge and for no other purpose.

§ 3. The said bonds, principal and interest, shall be payable in When pay-able, etc. ten annual installments of not more than one thousand dollars each, payable on the first day of November of each and every year until the whole thereof shall be paid, and said common council shall levy and collect as part of, and in addition to the annual city tax Tax for principal authorized by the city charter, such sums as may be necessary to and interest. pay both principal and interest of the bonds which shall fall due on each of said years aforesaid. The money so collected shall be applied to the payment of said bonds and the interest thereon.

§ 4. This act shall take effect immediately.

Chap. 564.

AN ACT making an appropriation for the better equipment, improvement and betterment of the Rome State Custodial Asylum, and to erect additional buildings therefor.

Became a law May 19, 1897, with the approval of the Governor.
Passed, three-fifths being present.

The People of the State of New York, represented in Senate and Assembly, do enact as follows:

Appropri-
ation for
improve-
ments.

Section 1. The sum of one hundred and one thousand three hundred dollars, or as much thereof as may be necessary, is hereby appropriated out of any money in the treasury not otherwise appropriated, for the Rome State Custodial Asylum, to be expended under the direction of the board of managers of said asylum as follows: For an administration building and proper equipment thereof, twenty-five thousand dollars; for a kitchen building with associate dining-rooms for inmates, dining-rooms for attendants and employes, a bakery, bread and flour room, pantry, refrigerator, store-rooms, scullery and sleeping apartments for twenty-five people. fifty-five thousand dollars; to complete steam-heating and ventilation, fourteen thousand dollars; for painting, repairing and betterments to buildings, two thousand five hundred dollars; for farm stock and utensils, fifteen hundred dollars; for medical and surgical appliances, three hundred dollars; for furniture for wards and buildings, one thousand dollars; for musical instruments and music, five hundred dollars; for fire apparatus, five hundred dollars; for machinery for carpenter and machine shops and for mechanical purposes, one thousand dollars.

Payment
thereof.

§ 2. Said sum shall be paid by the treasurer of the state to the treasurer of said asylum upon a warrant of the comptroller after contracts or estimates for said sums have been submitted and duly approved by the comptroller.

§ 3. This act shall take effect immediately.

Chap. 565.

AN ACT providing for the construction of a lift or hoist bridge over the Erie canal on Broad street in the city of Utica, and making an appropriation therefor, and authorizing the city of Utica to raise money for the construction thereof.

Accepted by the city.

Became a law May 19, 1897, with the approval of the Governor.

Passed, three-fifths being present.

The People of the State of New York, represented in Senate and Assembly, do enact as follows:

Section 1. Whenever the city of Utica shall, by its proper authori- Construc-
ties, deposit in some bank of deposit, which shall be approved of by bridge.
the superintendent of public works, the sum of five thousand dollars to expend in the manner hereinafter described, which money
shall be made payable to the order of the superintendent of public
works for the purpose hereinafter mentioned, the superintendent of
public works is authorized to construct a suitable lift or hoist bridge,
with the necessary abutments and appurtenances thereto, over the
Erie canal in the city of Utica on Broad street. The plans for said Plans.
bridge shall be prepared by the state engineer and surveyor and the
said bridge, when completed, shall be operated under the direction
of the superintendent of public works. The sum of twenty thou- Appropri-
sand dollars, or so much thereof as may be necessary, is hereby ation.
appropriated out of any money in the treasury not otherwise appropriated for the purpose of carrying into effect the provisions of this
act and the said treasurer is hereby directed to pay the above
amount or such part thereof as may be necessary, upon the warrant
of the comptroller to the order of the superintendent of public
works for the purpose defined by this act. No part of the money
deposited by the city of Utica shall be expended until the aforesaid
sum of twenty thousand dollars herein appropriated shall be all
expended for the purpose aforesaid. Any deficiency arising from
the construction of said bridge or the abutments or appurtenances
thereof in excess of the sum of the twenty thousand dollars herein
appropriated shall be paid by the superintendent of public works
from the said money deposited by the city of Utica, but said defici
ency shall not exceed the sum of such deposit and the surplus
thereof, if any there be, shall be repaid by said superintendent of
public works to said city of Utica upon demand, after the completion of said work, and applied by said city towards the payment

and redemption of bonds of said city hereinafter authorized to be

Contracts for work. issued by said city. But no work shall be done or money expended under the provisions of this act until the same shall be let by contract to the lowest bidder or bidders offering to do the same, after

Expense of operating bridge. due advertisement thereof. The entire expense of operating said bridge shall be paid by said city of Utica and not by the state.

Issue and sale of city bonds. § 2. It shall be lawful for the common council of the city of Utica, and it shall have the power to borrow the sum of five thousand dollars upon the corporate bonds of the city of Utica at a rate of interest not exceeding five per centum per annum for the purpose of paying such additional expense, if any, necessary for constructing said bridge over the Erie canal on Broad street in Utica, as shall be in excess of the sum appropriated as provided in section one of this act. Said bonds hereby authorized to be issued shall not be sold for less than par value and said money to be used for the construction of said bridge and for no other purposes.

When payable, etc. § 3. The said bonds, principal and interest shall be payable in five annual installments of not more than one thousand each, payable on the first day of November of each and every year until

Tax for interest and principal. the whole thereof shall be paid, and said common council shall levy and collect as part of, and in addition to the annual city tax authorized by the city charter, such sums as may be necessary to pay both principal and interest of the bonds which shall fall due on each of said years aforesaid. The money so collected shall be applied to the payment of said bonds and the interest thereon.

§ 4. This act shall take effect immediately.

Chap. 566.

AN ACT to provide for the extraordinary repairs and improvement of existing mechanical and other structures and work on and connected with the canals of this state, and for introducing electrical communication between the offices of the superintendents thereof, and the several subordinate employes on the canals under their charge.

Became a law May 19, 1897, with the approval of the Governor. Passed by a two-thirds vote.

The People of the State of New York, represented in Senate and Assembly, do enact as follows:

State tax. Section 1. There shall be imposed for the fiscal year commencing on the first day of October, eighteen hundred and ninety-seven, a state tax of nine and one-half one-hundredths of a mill on each dollar of the valuation of the real and personal property in this state subject to taxation, which tax shall be assessed, levied and collected by the annual assessment, and collection of taxes for that year in the manner prescribed by law, and shall be paid by the several county treasurers into the treasury of the state, to be held by the state treasurer for appropriation to the purposes hereinafter designated.

§ 2. Of the proceeds of the tax authorized by section one of this act, the sum of four hundred and ten thousand dollars is hereby appropriated for the extraordinary repairs and improvement of the existing mechanical and other constructions and works on and connected with the canals of this state, and to facilitate the control and management of the canals by the introduction of electric communication between the superintendents thereof and their several employes. *Appropriation of proceeds.*

§ 3. Of the moneys directed to be appropriated by section two of this act the sum of three hundred and sixty thousand dollars is hereby appropriated to be expended by the superintendent of public works of this state in the extraordinary repairs and improvement of the mechanical and other constructions and works on and connected with the canals of this state, on plans prepared by the state engineer and surveyor, and approved by the superintendent of public works. *For extraordinary repairs. etc.*

§ 4. Of the moneys directed to be appropriated by section two of this act the sum of fifty thousand dollars is hereby appropriated to be used by the superintendent of public works in the installation of electric communication between the offices of superintendents of the canals and the several locks and other important structures thereon to facilitate the control and management of the same and to facilitate communication with the lock tenders, patrolmen, bank-watchers, captains of state scows and other employes. *Electrical communication.*

§ 5. The comptroller is hereby authorized to borrow on the credit of this state, by the issue of emergency bonds, therefor the said sum of four hundred and ten thousand dollars provided by section two of this act, so that the same may be made available for the purposes therein named before the collection of the tax hereby authorized, and the said bonds shall be paid from the avails of said tax when collected, prior to the fifteenth day of May, eighteen hundred and ninety-eight. *Issue of emergency bonds.*

§ 6. This act shall take effect immediately.

Chap. 567.

AN ACT to authorize the superintendent of public works to purchase the Fort Miller bridge, crossing the Hudson river near the state dam at Northumberland, New York.

Became a law May 19, 1897, with the approval of the Governor.
Passed, three-fifths being present.

The People of the State of New York, represented in Senate and Assembly, do enact as follows:

Purchase of bridge.

Section 1. The superintendent of public works is hereby authorized to purchase of the president, directors and company of the Fort Miller Bridge company its bridge crossing the Hudson river, near the state dam at Northumberland, New York, together with the approaches thereto, and all the rights therein, owned by said company, including its franchises, at a price to be agreed upon between said superintendent of public works and said company, not to exceed the sum of ten thousand dollars ; being the same bridge now used by the state of New York as a part of its canal system, and for which, it now pays to said company an annual rental of one thousand dollars. The sum so agreed upon between said superintendent of public works and the said company may be paid by the treasurer on the warrant of the comptroller to the superintendent of public works for the purposes aforesaid, out of any moneys in the treasury not otherwise appropriated.

§ 2. This act shall take effect immediately.

Chap. 568.

AN ACT to provide for the construction of a bridge over the Erie canal at Hamilton street, in the city of Buffalo, and making an appropriation therefor.

Became a law May 19, 1897, with the approval of the Governor.
Passed, three-fifths being present.

The People of the State of New York, represented in Senate and Assembly, do enact as follows:

Appropriation.

Section 1. The sum of ten thousand dollars, or so much thereof as may be necessary, is hereby appropriated, out of any money in the treasury not otherwise appropriated, for the construction of a bridge over the Erie canal, at the crossing of Hamilton street, in the city of Buffalo, and for the removal of the bridge at that point.

Such money shall be expended and such bridge shall be con- Plans, etc. structed under the direction and supervision of the superintendent of public works, upon plans and specifications approved by the state engineer and surveyor. Such money shall be payable by the treasurer, on the warrant of the comptroller, on the order of the superintendent of public works.

§ 2. This act shall take effect immediately.

Chap. 569.

AN ACT making an appropriation for carrying on the improvement of the Erie canal, the Champlain canal and the Oswego canal, required by chapter seventy-nine of the laws of eighteen hundred and ninety-five and chapter seven hundred and ninety-four of the laws of eighteen hundred and ninety-six.

Became a law May 19, 1897, with the approval of the Governor. Passed, three-fifths being present.

The People of the State of New York, represented in Senate and Assembly, do enact as follows:

Section 1. The sum of five million dollars is hereby appropriated, Appropriation. payable out of the moneys realized from the sale of bonds provided by section one of chapter seventy-nine of the laws of eighteen hundred and ninety-five and chapter seven hundred and ninety-four of the laws of eighteen hundred and ninety-six, which said sum of five million dollars, or so much thereof as may be necessary, is to be expended in the work of improving the Erie canal, the Champlain canal and the Oswego canal, required to be performed by said chapters seventy-nine of the laws of eighteen hundred and ninety-five and seven hundred and ninety-four of the laws of eighteen hundred and ninety-six. Said sum of five million Payment thereof. dollars is to be paid by the treasurer on the warrant of the comptroller, to the order of the superintendent of public works when certified by said superintendent of public works, to be needed from time to time in the promotion of said work of improvement.

§ 2. This act shall take effect immediately.

Chap. 570.

AN ACT to provide for the construction of a foot-bridge over the Champlain canal, in the town of Waterford, Saratoga county, and making an appropriation therefor.

Became a law May 19, 1897, with the approval of the Governor.
Passed, three-fifths being present.

The People of the State of New York, represented in Senate and Assembly, do enact as follows:

Construction of bridge.

Section 1. The superintendent of public works is hereby authorized to construct, or cause to be constructed, an iron foot-bridge over the Champlain canal, in the town of Waterford, Saratoga county, at a point where Sixth street in said town crosses the Champlain canal, in such manner as shall not interfere with the navigation of the canal; the cost of said bridge not to exceed the sum of two thousand dollars to be paid from the moneys

Appropriation.

in the treasury not otherwise appropriated. And the sum of two thousand dollars is hereby appropriated, or so much thereof as is

Plans.

necessary for this purpose; and said bridge to be erected upon plans and specifications to be approved by the state engineer and surveyor.

§ 2. This act shall take effect immediately.

Chap. 571.

AN ACT to provide for the construction of a swing or hoist-bridge over the Erie canal at Salina street, in the city of Syracuse, and making an appropriation therefor.

Became a law May 19, 1897, with the approval of the Governor.
Passed, three-fifths being present.

The People of the State of New York, represented in Senate and Assembly, do enact as follows:

Construction of bridge

Section 1. Whenever there shall be deposited in some bank of deposit, which shall be approved by the superintendent of public works, the sum of eighteen thousand dollars by the city of Syracuse, or by property owners of said city, payable to the order of said superintendent of public works, the superintendent of public works is hereby authorized to provide for the construction of a swing or hoist-bridge with two roadways each twenty-two feet in the clear, and two sidewalks eight feet in the clear, over the Erie canal in the city of Syracuse at Salina street, for the necessary machinery to operate such bridge, upon plans and specifications to be drawn up and prepared by the state engineer and surveyor immediately after the passage of this act, said plans and specifications to be approved by the mayor and common council of said city, and to cost not exceeding thirty-six thousand dollars. Said bridge shall be operated under the direction of the superintendent of public works at the expense of the city of Syracuse. Plans. Expense of operating bridge.

§ 2. Upon the completion and approval of such plans and specifications the superintendent of public works is authorized to proceed as soon as practicable with the construction of such bridge, the approaches thereto and the machinery therefor, in accordance with such plans and specifications; but before any money appropriated for the above mentioned work shall be expended, except for plans and specifications, the said work shall be let by contract to the lowest responsible bidder after duly advertising therefor, as public works are usually let by contract. Commencement of work. Contracts.

§ 3. The sum of eighteen thousand dollars is hereby appropriated for the purpose of this act, payable by the treasurer on the warrant of the comptroller to the order of the superintendent of public works. Appropriation.

§ 4. This act shall take effect immediately.

Chap. 572.

AN ACT to reappropriate certain unexpended balances of former appropriations.

Became a law May 19, 1897, with the approval of the Governor. Passed, three-fifths being present.

The People of the State of New York, represented in Senate and Assembly, do enact as follows:

Section 1. The following unexpended balances of former appropriations are hereby reappropriated to the objects and purposes of the original appropriations as designated herein, namely: The sum of seven thousand six hundred and thirty-one dollars and five cents, being the unexpended balance of the appropriation for defraying the cost of electrical experiments, pursuant to chapter one hundred and nineteen of the laws of eighteen hundred and ninety-three. The sum of eight thousand nine hundred and forty dollars and seventy-five cents, being the unexpended balance of the appro- Reappropriation. Electrical experiments. Bridges at Utica.

priation for bridges at Genesee street, Utica, pursuant to chapter one hundred and seventy of the laws of eighteen hundred and ninety-five. The sum of one thousand one hundred and forty dollars and sixty-eight cents, being the unexpended balance of the appropriation for building a bridge between Carthage and West Carthage, pursuant to chapter one hundred and two of the laws of eighteen hundred and ninety-five. The sum of three thousand four hundred and thirty-three dollars and fifty cents, being the unexpended balance of the appropriation for repairing and strengthening berme bank and breakwater at foot of Seneca lake, pursuant to chapter one hundred and forty-two of the laws of eighteen hundred and ninety-five. The sum of five thousand one hundred and seventy-two dollars and seven cents, being the unexpended balance of the appropriation for dredging lower Black Rock harbor, pursuant to chapter three hundred and twenty of the laws of eighteen hundred and ninety-five. The sum of eight thousand two hundred and ninety-two dollars and thirty-six cents, being the unexpended balance of the appropriation for rebuilding the apron of Braddock's dam on the Oswego river, pursuant to chapter three hundred and sixty-eight of the laws of eighteen hundred and ninety-five. The sum of six thousand eight hundred and fifty-six dollars and forty-five cents, being the unexpended balance of the appropriation for improving Cayuga and Seneca canal, pursuant to chapter five hundred and twelve of the laws of eighteen hundred and ninety-five. The sum of twenty-four thousand two hundred and fifty dollars, being the unexpended balance of the appropriation for constructing bridge at Exchange street, Rochester, pursuant to chapter five hundred and fourteen of the laws of eighteen hundred and ninety-five. The sum of thirteen thousand one hundred and forty-nine dollars and forty-eight cents, being the unexpended balance of the appropriation for repairing Rexford Flats dam, pursuant to chapter five hundred and sixty of the laws of eighteen hundred and ninety-five. The sum of two thousand seven hundred and fifty-six dollars and forty-three cents, being the unexpended balance of the appropriation for repairing state dams on Beaver river and Fulton chain of lakes, pursuant to chapter nine hundred and thirty-two of the laws of eighteen hundred and ninety-five. The sum of one thousand and seventy-one dollars and fifty-four cents, being the unexpended balance of the appropriation for repairs of bridge on Cattaraugus Indian reservation, pursuant to chapter nine hundred and thirty-two of the laws of eighteen hundred and ninety-five.

(marginal notes)
Bridge at Carthage.
Seneca lake breakwater, etc.
Black Rock harbor.
Braddock's dam.
Cayuga and Seneca canal.
Bridge at Rochester.
Rexford Flats dam.
State dams.
Bridge at Indian reservation.

The sum of four thousand nine hundred and forty-six dollars and Bridge at Little Falls. fifty cents, being the unexpended balance of the appropriation for bridge at German street, Little Falls, pursuant to chapter six hundred and eighty of the laws of eighteen hundred and ninety-five. The sum of one thousand and seventy-two dollars and eighteen Canaseraga creek culvert. cents, being the unexpended balance of the appropriation for repairing and enlarging Canaseraga creek culvert, pursuant to chapter nine hundred and sixty-nine of the laws of eighteen hundred and ninety-five. The sum of four thousand seven hundred and fifty- Flow ground at Stillwater. seven dollars and seventeen cents, being the unexpended balance of the appropriation for bridges over Twitchell creek, pursuant to chapter two hundred and twenty-four of the laws of eighteen hundred and ninety-three, being the sum reappropriated by chapter two hundred and nineteen of the laws of eighteen hundred and ninety-five, is hereby reappropriated for the purpose of cleaning the flow ground at Stillwater, pursuant to chapter one hundred and nineteen of the laws of eighteen hundred and ninety-three. The Bridge at DeWitt. sum of thirty-eight hundred and forty-seven dollars and fifty-four cents, being the unexpended balance of the appropriation for constructing a bridge over the Erie canal at Nichols street in the town of DeWitt, pursuant to chapter ninety-four of the laws of eighteen hundred and ninety-three, being the sum reappropriated by chapter two hundred and nineteen of the laws of eighteen hundred and ninety-five, is hereby reappropriated for the purpose of construct ing said bridge as provided in said act.

§ 2. This act shall take effect immediately.

Chap. 573.

AN ACT making an appropriation for the purchase of materials for the erection of buildings at the Elmira state reformatory.

Became a law May 19, 1897, with the approval of the Governor.
Passed, three-fifths being present.

The People of the State of New York, represented in Senate and Assembly, do enact as follows:

Section 1. The sum of twenty-five thousand dollars, or so much Appropriation. thereof as may be necessary, is hereby appropriated out of any moneys in the treasury not otherwise appropriated, to be paid by the state treasurer on the warrant of the comptroller to the order of the board of managers of the Elmira state reformatory to be used by said managers in purchasing materials for the erection of buildings at said reformatory to take the place of the buildings destroyed by fire in December, eighteen hundred and ninety-six.

§ 2. This act shall take effect immediately.

Chap. 574.

AN ACT making an appropriation for the Craig colony for epileptics.

Became a law May 10, 1897, with the approval of the Governor. Passed, three-fifths being present.

The People of the State of New York, represented in Senate and Assembly, do enact as follows:

Appropriation for improvements.

Section 1. The following sums are hereby appropriated to the uses and purposes of the Craig colony for epileptics, from any moneys in the treasury not otherwise appropriated: For dormitory buildings, forty thousand dollars; for an administrative building, thirty thousand dollars; for furnishing, twelve thousand dollars; for extension of water and sewerage systems, five thousand dollars; for six tenant houses, five thousand dollars; for a slaughter house, one thousand dollars; for a piggery, one thousand two hundred dollars; for a hennery, one thousand two hundred dollars; for a granary, two thousand dollars; for a blacksmith shop, one thousand dollars; for two horse stables, three thousand dollars; for plumbing and heating west group, five thousand two hundred dollars; for plumbing, heating and ventilating hospital building, five thousand dollars; for nursery, forcing beds, roadways, walks and grading grounds, two thousand five hundred dollars; for industries, including a two-story brick building, five thousand dollars; for laundry machinery, seven hundred and fifty dollars; for general repairs and improvements, including sheds for cattle and sheep, fencing, moving buildings, painting barns and outhouses, increasing storage capacity for coal, improving creek water supply, and increasing spring water supply, six thousand seven hundred and fifty dollars.

§ 2. This act shall take effect immediately.

Chap. 575.

AN ACT making an appropriation for the construction of a bridge over the side-cut of the Champlain canal at the foot of Fourth street in the town of Waterford.

Became a law May 19, 1897, with the approval of the Governor.
Passed, three-fifths being present.

The People of the State of New York, represented in Senate and Assembly, do enact as follows:

Section 1. The superintendent of public works is hereby directed to cause a bridge to be built in the year eighteen hundred and ninety-seven over the side-cut of the Champlain canal at the foot of Fourth street, in the town of Waterford, to take the place of the present bridge, and the state treasurer is hereby directed to pay the amount herein appropriated, upon the warrant of the comptroller to the order of the superintendent of public works, for the purpose aforesaid. The sum of four thousand dollars, or so much thereof as may be necessary, is hereby appropriated from any money in the treasury not otherwise appropriated for the purpose of carrying into effect the provision of this act. All the work called for in this act shall be done in accordance with the plans, specifications and estimates prepared and approved by the state engineer and surveyor. Construction of bridge.
Appropriation.
Plans.

§ 2. This act shall take effect immediately.

Chap. 576.

AN ACT authorizing and empowering the superintendent of public works to construct a life or hoist-bridge and foot-bridge over the Erie canal in the village of Fort Plain.

Became a law May 19, 1897, with the approval of the Governor.
Passed, three-fifths being present.

The People of the State of New York, represented in Senate and Assembly, do enact as follows:

Section 1. The superintendent of public works is hereby authorized to construct or cause to be constructed and maintained, at the expense of the state, over the Erie canal, in the village of Fort Plain, in the county of Montgomery, a lift or hoist bridge, together with a bridge for foot passengers, at the junction of River street and Canal street, which said lift or hoist bridge, if constructed, shall Construction of bridge.

be operated at the expense of the town of Minden under the direction of the superintendent of public works, provided, however, that the owners of land at the point where said bridge shall be built, shall release to the state all claims for damages arising or growing

Appropriation. out of the building of said bridges. The sum of fourteen thousand dollars, or so much thereof as may be necessary, is hereby appropriated out of any money in the treasury not otherwise appropriated, to be paid upon the warrant of the comptroller to the order of the superintendent of public works for the purpose of constructing the aforesaid bridges and for necessary excavations on either

Plans. side of said Erie canal for proper abutments. The work to be done in accordance with plans and specifications to be furnished by the state engineer and surveyor.

§ 2. This act shall take effect immediately.

Chap. 577.

AN ACT to provide for the payment of certain local assessments against state property in the city of Rochester, in the county of Monroe, and making an appropriation therefor.

Became a law May 19, 1897, with the approval of the Governor. Passed, three-fifths being present.

The People of the State of New York, represented in Senate and Assembly, do enact as follows:

Appropriation. Section 1. The sum of twenty-two thousand dollars, or so much thereof as may be necessary, the amount justly due to be determined by the comptroller, is hereby appropriated out of any unexpended balance in the treasury not otherwise appropriated, for the purpose of paying all local assessments against the state lands situate in the city of Rochester except for assessments for the construction of the west side sewer, now due and payable, which assessments are hereby chargeable to the state of New York, and which payments shall be made by the treasurer upon the warrant of the comptroller.

§ 2. This act shall take effect immediately.

Chap. 578.

AN ACT to provide for strengthening the berme bank of the Glens Falls feeder of the Champlain canal east of the guard lock at Glens Falls, New York.

Became a law May 19, 1897, with the approval of the Governor.
Passed, three-fifths being present.

The People of the State of New York, represented in Senate and Assembly, do enact as follows:

§ 1. The superintendent of public works is hereby authorized to strengthen the berme bank of the Glens Falls feeder of the Champlain canal, at Glens Falls, by extending easterly the new wall at the foot of the guard lock. Strengthening of bank.

§ 2. The work herein authorized shall be done in accordance with plans and specifications furnished by the state engineer and surveyor. Plans.

§ 3. The sum of twenty-eight hundred and eighty-seven dollars and ninety-three cents (being the unexpended balance of the appropriation made under chapter two hundred and eighty-four of the laws of eighteen hundred and ninety-five for making repairs and improvements to the Glens Falls feeder of the Champlain canal), or so much thereof as shall be necessary therefor, is hereby appropriated for the purpose designated in section one, to be paid by the treasurer on the warrant of the comptroller to the order of the superintendent of public works. Appropriation.

§ 4. This act shall take effect immediately.

Chap. 580.

AN ACT conferring jurisdiction upon the board of claims to hear, audit and determine the claim of the mayor, aldermen and commonalty of the city of New York against the state, for water furnished to Sing Sing prison between certain dates, and to make an award thereon, and conferring upon both parties the right to take an appeal from any award made under the authority of this act.

Accepted by the city.

Became a law May 19, 1897, with the approval of the Governor.
Passed, three-fifths being present.

The People of the State of New York, represented in Senate and Assembly, do enact as follows:

Section 1. Jurisdiction is hereby conferred upon the board of claims to hear, audit and determine the claim of the mayor, alder- Jurisdiction to hear claim.

men and commonalty of the city of New York against the state
for water furnished to the Sing Sing prison from and including the
first day of January, eighteen hundred and ninety-two, to and including the thirty-first day of December, eighteen hundred and
ninety-six, pursuant to the provisions of chapter two hundred and
eighty-two of the laws of eighteen hundred and sixty-one, entitled
"An act to supply Sing Sing prison with Croton water, and
for the sale of certain lands of the state," as amended by chapter one hundred and ninety-eight of the laws of eighteen hundred
and sixty-two, and to award thereon such sums as in the judgment
of said board shall be just and equitable.

Jurisdic-
tion ex-
tended.

§ 2. In hearing, auditing or determining the aforesaid claim or
making an award thereon the jurisdiction of the said board of
claims shall not be limited to such claim as may have accrued
within two years prior to the time when such claim is filed with
said board, but said jurisdiction is hereby extended over the whole
of the aforesaid claim set forth in section one of this act provided
such claim be filed with the said board of claims prior to January
first, eighteen hundred and ninety-eight.

Appeals
from
award.

§ 3. Either party may take an appeal to the appellate division
of the supreme court of the third department from any award made
under the authority of this act, provided such appeal be taken by
service of a notice of appeal within thirty days from the service of
a copy of the award.

§ 4. This act shall take effect immediately.

Chap. 584.

AN ACT to amend the penal code, in relation to offenses against
the navigation law.

Became a law May 19, 1897, with the approval of the Governor.
Passed, three-fifths being present.

*The People of the State of New York, represented in Senate and
Assembly, do enact as follows:*

Section 1. The penal code is hereby amended by inserting therein
a new section, to be known as section three hundred and fifty-nine-a
and to read as follows:

§ 359a. Offenses against the navigation law.—Any person having
the charge, command or control of a steamboat or vessel who,

1. Permits a line used for the purpose of landing or receiving
passengers, to be attached in any way to the machinery of any

steamboat, or permits a small boat used for the purpose of landing or receiving passengers to be hauled by means of such machinery; or,

2. Carries or permits a steamboat to carry a greater number of passengers than is stated in the certificate of such steamboat issued under the navigation law; or,

3. Wilfully violates any of the provisions of section eleven of the navigation law, relating to the sailing rules; or,

4. Neglects to carry and show on a vessel the lights required by section twelve of the navigation law; or,

5. Neglects to carry on a vessel the life boats and life preservers required by sections fourteen and fifteen of the navigation law; or,

6. Neglects to carry on a vessel the steam fire pump required by section thirteen of the navigation law; or,

7. Intentionally loads or obstructs or causes to be loaded or obstructed in any way the safety valve of the boiler of any steamboat or naphtha launch, or employs any other means or device whereby the boiler of such vessel may be subjected to a greater pressure than is allowed by the inspectors' certificate, or intentionally deranges or hinders the operation of any machinery or device employed to denote the stage of the water or steam in any boiler or to give warning of approaching danger, or intentionally permits the water to fall below the prescribed low water limit of the boiler; or,

8. Acts or permits another person to act as officer of a vessel without having the license required by section seventeen of the navigation law, except as permitted by the provisions of section thirty of the navigation law; or,

9. Uses or permits to be used in lamps, lanterns or other lights, on a vessel, any oil which will not stand a fire test of at least three hundred degrees Fahrenheit; or,

10. After employing a steam vessel for towing, receives any commission or compensation for orders given to the owner, captain or agent of any vessel for towage; or interferes with or hinders any such owner, captain or agent, while in the prosecution of his business; or,

11. Neglects to cause the dampers in the pipes or chimneys of a steamboat to be closed, or to otherwise prevent the escape of sparks and coals therefrom while passing near any of the villages or cities situated on the Hudson river, or while landing or receiving passengers or freight, or while lying at the docks or wharves thereof,

Is guilty of a misdemeanor.

§ 2. The penal code is hereby amended by inserting therein a new section, to be known as section three hundred and fifty-nine-b, and to read as follows:

§ 359b. A person who violates any other provision of the navigation law for which no other punishment is prescribed is guilty of a misdemeanor.

§ 3. This act shall take effect immediately.

Chap. 589

AN ACT to amend chapter three hundred and thirty-eight of the laws of eighteen hundred and ninety-three, entitled "An act in relation to agriculture, constituting articles one, two, three, four and five of chapter thirty-three of the general laws," as amended by chapter two hundred and twenty-one of the laws of eighteen hundred and ninety-six, relative to the apportionment of moneys appropriated for the promotion of agriculture.

Became a law May 19, 1897, with the approval of the Governor. Passed, three-fifths being present.

The People of the State of New York, represented in Senate and Assembly, do enact as follows:

Section 1. Section eighty-eight of article five of chapter three hundred and thirty-eight of the laws of eighteen hundred and ninety-three, as amended by chapter two hundred and twenty-one of the laws of eighteen hundred and ninety-six, is hereby amended to read as follows:

§ 88. Receipts and apportionment of moneys for the promotion of agriculture.— Of all moneys appropriated for the promotion of agriculture in any one year, twenty thousand dollars thereof shall be distributed in premiums by the New York State Agricultural Society; two thousand dollars thereof shall be paid to each of the agricultural societies, agricultural clubs, or agricultural expositions which shall have held annual agricultural fairs or meetings during each of the three years next preceding such appropriation, and which shall have paid at each of such annual fairs or meetings during such three years the sum of three thousand dollars as premiums for agricultural interests, exclusive of the premiums paid for trials or tests of speed, skill or endurance of man or beast, under the conditions and in the manner provided by section eighty-nine of this chapter. Seventy per centum of the balance of the amount so appropriated shall be apportioned and distributed among the various county agricultural societies and the American Institute in the city of New York; and thirty per centum thereof among the various town and other agricultural societies, agricultural clubs or agricultural expositions entitled by this section to receive thirty per centum of the moneys received by the comptroller from the tax collected from the racing associations, corporations or clubs of the state. Such apportionment and distribution shall be made by the commissioner of agriculture in the following manner. One-half of the seventy per centum to be apportioned to such county agricultural societies and the American Institute in the city of New York shall be apportioned and distributed equally and the remainder in proportion to the actual premiums paid during the previous year by such societies and institute, exclusive of premiums paid for trials or tests of speed, skill or endurance of man or beast. If there is no county agricultural society in any county, or if the county agricultural society is not in active operation as such, then the town society or societies in such county, or other agricultural societies in such county, except the New York State Agricultural Society, that would otherwise be entitled to share under the thirty per centum distribution referred to in this section, shall share jointly in the distribution of such money on the same basis as they would if they were a county agricultural society, provided such societies sustain a public fair with premium list, which premium list and reports of such societies shall be forwarded and made to the commissioner of agriculture. Of the thirty per centum to be distributed among the various town and other agricultural societies, clubs or expositions one-third thereof shall be apportioned and distributed equally and the remainder in proportion to the premiums awarded and paid by said society, club or exposition for exhibits made at the annual fair upon the awards or premiums of which they seek a portion of the money to be distributed, exclusive of premiums paid for trials or tests of speed, skill or endurance of man or beast. No proportion of such amount shall be paid to any such society, club or exposition in which the actual amount paid by it as such premiums in the year preceding such apportionment, is less than five hundred dollars. All revenues which have been or shall be received by the comptroller, and not distributed as heretofore provided, and all moneys received by him from the tax collected

from racing associations pursuant to chapter one hundred and
ninety-seven of the laws of eighteen hundred and ninety-four, and
chapter five hundred and seventy of the laws of eighteen hundred
and ninety-five, and all acts amendatory thereto, or hereafter otherwise collected from racing associations, corporations or clubs, shall
constitute a fund,which shall be annually disbursed on behalf of the
state for prizes for improving the breed of cattle, sheep and horses
at the various fairs throughout the state as hereinafter prescribed.
Thirty per centum of the funds so collected shall be disbursed by
the commissioner of agriculture among the agricultural societies,
agricultural clubs or agricultural expositions of the state,
which had not previous to May twenty-ninth, eighteen hundred and ninety-five, received appropriations from the state, as follows: One-third shall be apportioned and distributed equally and the
remainder in proportion to the premiums awarded and paid by said
society, club or exposition for exhibits made at the annual fairs upon
the awards or premiums of which they seek a portion of the money
to be distributed, such sums shall only be paid to such societies
which have received appropriations from the state previous to the
passage of this act, and are now duly organized under the laws of
the state of New York, and in active operation in counties having
a population according to the census of eighteen hundred and
ninety-two of over three hundred and twenty-five thousand inhabitants, or which shall have held fairs, annually, during each of the
three years prior to May twenty-ninth, eighteen hundred and ninety-
five, and which shall have paid, at their annual meetings or fairs
during such three years, not less than one thousand dollars in the
aggregate as premiums for agricultural, mechanical and domestic
products, exclusive of the premiums paid for trials or tests of speed,
skill or endurance of man or beast, and which shall have filed their
report with the commissioner of agriculture, on or before July first.
eighteen hundred and ninety-five, as heretofore provided in chapter
eight hundred and twenty of the laws of eighteen hundred and
ninety-five. Seventy per centum of such funds shall be disbursed
by the commissioner of agriculture among the various county agricultural societies throughout the state, and the American Institute.
in the city of New York, as follows: One-half shall be apportioned
and distributed equally, and the remainder in proportion to the premiums awarded and paid by said society, club or exposition, for
exhibits made at the annual fair upon the awards or premiums of

which they seek a portion of the money to be distributed, exclusive of premiums paid for trials or tests of speed, skill or endurance of man or beast. If there is no county agricultural society in any county, or if the county agricultural society is not in active operation as such, then the town society or societies in such county, or other agricultural societies in such county, except the New York State Agricultural Society, that would otherwise be entitled to share under the thirty per centum distribution referred to in this section, shall share jointly in the distribution of such money on the same basis as they would if they were a county agricultural society, provided such societies sustain a public fair, with premium lists and reports of such societies shall be forwarded and made to the commissioner of agriculture. All agricultural societies, agricultural clubs or agricultural expositions entitled to receive any portion of the moneys appropriated by the state must hereafter, on or before the fifteenth day of December, in each year, file a statement, duly verified by the secretary and treasurer, showing the amount of premiums paid at the last annual fair, exclusive of premiums paid for trials or tests of speed, skill or endurance of man or beast, which statement shall be filed in the office of the commissioner of agriculture, otherwise such society, club or exposition shall forfeit its right to participate in the distribution of such moneys for premiums paid for such year. No proportion of such moneys shall be paid to any such society, club or exposition in which the actual amount paid by it as such premiums in the year preceding such apportionment, is less than five hundred dollars. Any town or other agricultural society in a county in which there is no county agricultural society in active operation and which, according to the terms of this section receives any portion of the seventy per centum of such funds apportioned to county agricultural societies, shall not receive any portion of the thirty per centum of such funds. Any such society, club or exposition, receiving the sum of two thousand dollars under the provisions of section eighty-nine of this act, shall not receive any other portion of the money appropriated for the promotion of agriculture. Any such agricultural society, agricultural club, agricultural exposition, or agricultural fair association, organized under the laws of the State of New York, which shall fail or neglect to hold annual fairs and file their annual reports, as provided by this law, with the commissioner of agriculture for two consecutive years, shall forfeit all of their chartered rights including any privileges or moneys they might thereafter otherwise be entitled to under this act.

§ 2. The sum of fifty thousand dollars of the amount collected and due from racing associations in pursuance of chapter four hundred and seventy-nine of the laws of eighteen hundred and eighty-seven, as amended by chapter one hundred and ninety-seven of the laws of eighteen hundred and ninety-four, and chapter five hundred and seventy of the laws of eighteen hundred and ninety-five and all acts amendatory thereof or supplementary thereto is hereby appropriated out of any moneys in the treasury so collected at the time of the distribution thereof as provided herein. Such sum shall be distributed in the manner provided by section eighty-eight of the agricultural law, as amended, and in the proportion provided therein for the distribution of such moneys, and shall be payable by the treasurer on the warrant of the comptroller on the order of the commissioner of agriculture.

§ 3. All acts and parts of acts inconsistent with the provisions of this act are hereby repealed.

§ 4. This act shall take effect immediately.

Chap. 591.

AN ACT to amend chapter five hundred and fifty-nine of the laws of eighteen hundred and ninety-three, the title to which was amended by chapter four hundred and fifty-seven of the laws of eighteen hundred and ninety-four, to read "An act in relation to the militia, constituting chapter sixteen of the general laws," relative to the composition of a battalion.

Became a law May 19, 1897, with the approval of the Governor.
Passed, three-fifths being present.

The People of the State of New York, represented in Senate and Assembly, do enact as follows:

Section 1. Section fourteen of chapter five hundred and fifty-nine of the laws of eighteen hundred and ninety-three as amended by chapter nine hundred and twenty-four of the laws of eighteen hundred and ninety-five, is hereby amended to read as follows:

§ 14. Composition of a battalion.—Each battalion, not a part of a regiment, shall consist of not more than six nor less than four companies or batteries, one major, and a battalion staff of one adjutant, one quartermaster, one commissary of subsistence, and one inspector of rifle practice of the grade of first lieutenant, one assistant surgeon and one chaplain of the grade of captain, one sergeant-major and other non-commissioned staff officers as provided for a regiment; and whenever any regiment shall fall below the number of eight companies, or batteries, it may be reorganized as a battalion, and the commander-in-chief may, in his discretion, retain or command the field officers of the regiment so reduced to a battalion. A squadron of cavalry, equivalent to a battalion, shall consist of not less than two nor more than four troops and it shall be allowed in addition to the above officers and non-commissioned staff officers, one assistant surgeon of the grade of first lieutenant, one veterinary surgeon, and in lieu of a drum-major, one signal sergeant.

§ 2. Section fifteen of chapter five hundred and fifty-nine of the laws of eighteen hundred and ninety-three as amended by chapter eight hundred and fifty-three of the laws of eighteen hundred and ninety-six is hereby amended so as to read as follows:

§ 15. Company, troop and battery organization.—To each company, troop or battery there shall be one captain, one first lieutenant, and one second lieutenant, and one first sergeant and one quartermaster sergeant, four sergeants, eight corporals, two musicians and thirty-one privates as a minimum, and eighty-four privates as a maximum.   To each separate troop of cavalry and each battery of light artillery there shall be one captain, two first lieutenants, two second lieutenants, one first sergeant, one quartermaster sergeant, one commissary sergeant, one veterinary surgeon, one guidon sergeant, four sergeants, eight corporals, four artificers, two trumpeters and forty-eight privates as a minimum and eighty-four privates as a maximum. To any battery of light artillery, or separate troop, battery or company, the commander-in-chief may appoint and commission an assistant surgeon of the grade of first lieutenant, and to each separate company one additional second lieutenant. No musician shall be allowed to a company attached to a regiment or battalion not a part of a regiment in which field music is organized pursuant to section twenty of this act.

§ 3. Section thirty-four of chapter five hundred and ninety-five of the laws of eighteen hundred and ninety-three is hereby amended so as to read as follows:

§ 34. Duties of inspector-general.—The inspector-general shall personally, or through his assistants at general headquarters, or the division or brigade inspectors, inspect as often as may be deemed necessary by the commander-in-chief, every branch connected with the military service, including armories, arsenals, storehouses, camps, and military property, and report to the general headquarters the condition, discipline, drill and instruction of the national guard, the condition of military property belonging to the state and all matters pertaining to his department.

§ 4. Section thirty-eight of chapter five hundred and ninety-five of the laws of eighteen hundred and ninety-three is hereby amended so as to read as follows :

§ 38. Bureau of records of war of rebellion.— The adjutant-general shall establish and maintain as part of his office, a bureau of records of the war of the rebellion, in which all records in his office relating to such war, and the records and relics of the bureau of military statistics shall be united and kept. He shall be the custodian of all such records, relics, colors, standards and battle-flags of New York volunteers, now the property of the state or in its possession, or which the state may hereafter acquire or become possessed of. The chief of this bureau shall hold office for six years. The legislature shall make suitable appropriations annually to enable the adjutant-general to carry out this section and the next three following.

§ 5. Section one hundred and twenty-five of chapter five hundred and fifty-nine of the laws of eighteen hundred and ninety-three as amended by chapter eight hundred and fifty-three of the laws of eighteen hundred and ninety-six, is hereby amended so as to read as follows :

§ 125. Allowance for headquarters.—On the certificate of the adjutant-general, the comptroller shall, annually, draw his warrant upon the treasurer for the following sums, namely: Twelve hundred dollars for each division and for each brigade headquarters; fifteen hundred dollars for each regimental headquarters; five hundred dollars for each battalion and squadron; two hundred and fifty dollars for each separate troop of cavalry, battery of light artillery and signal corps. For brigade headquarters in brigades covering a territory of more than ten counties, five hundred dollars additional shall be allowed. The funds thus allowed shall only be expended by the respective commanding officers on the approval of the adjutant-general.

§ 6. Section one hundred and twenty-six of chapter five hundred and fifty-nine of the laws of eighteen hundred and ninety-three as amended by chapter eight hundred and fifty-three of the laws of eighteen hundred and ninety-six is hereby amended so as to read as follows :

§ 126. **Allowances for military organizations:—Military fund.**— On the certificate of the adjutant-general, the comptroller shall likewise annually draw his warrant upon the treasurer in favor of each county treasurer specified in such certificates, for the organization of the national guard mentioned therein as follows : Fifteen hundred dollars for each battery of light artillery and each troop, seven hundred and fifty dollars for each signal corps, to be expended for mounted drills and parades, including the annual inspection and muster required by this chapter; two hundred and fifty dollars for each separate company; and for each regiment, battalion not a part of a regiment, separate troop, separate battery, separate company and signal corps for the purpose of defraying other necessary military expenses, a sum equal to eight dollars for each of its enlisted men present for duty, based upon the percentage present for duty for the year at the five compulsory parades required in this chapter, and which percentage shall be certified to by the inspector-general, which sums, together with the fines and penalties collected from delinquent officers and enlisted men, shall constitute the military fund of such regiment, battalion not a part of a regiment, separate troop, separate battery, separate company or signal corps.

§ 7. Article two of said act, as amended by chapter eight hundred and fifty-three of the laws of eighteen hundred and ninety-six, is hereby amended by adding thereto a new section, to read as follows:

§ 20. **Field music.**—The commander-in-chief may upon the application of the commanding officer of a regiment or battalion not a part of a regiment organize the musicians of such regiment or battalion into a separate body, to be known as the " field music," such organization to be composed of the present enlisted musicians, and such others as may hereafter be enlisted or transferred as musicians, on a basis of not more than four men for each company attached to such regiment or battalion. The commanding officer of an organization to which such field music is attached may appoint and warrant from the members thereof one sergeant and one corporal. The field music, when organized, shall be in addition to the strength provided by section fifteen of this act.

§ 5. This act shall take effect immediately.

Chap. 592.

AN ACT in relation to navigation, constituting chapter thirty of
the general laws.

Became a law May 19, 1897, with the approval of the Governor.
Passed, three-fifths being present.

*The People of the State of New York, represented in Senate and
Assembly, do enact as follows:*

CHAPTER XXX OF THE GENERAL LAWS.

THE NAVIGATION LAW.

ARTICLE I.

GENERAL PROVISIONS.

Section 1. Short title ; extent of application.— This chapter shall be known as the navigation law, and shall be applicable to all steam vessels navigating the waters within the jurisdiction of this state, excepting vessels which are subject to inspection under the laws of the United States.

§ 2. Definitions.— As used in this chapter, the term master includes every person having for the time, the charge, control or direction of a steamboat or vessel; and the term steamboat or steam vessel, includes every vessel propelled in whole or in part by steam.

§ 3. Duty of superintendent of public works.— The superintendent of public works shall superintend the administration of the provisions of this article, appoint the inspectors provided for in this act and exercise supervision over them in the performance of their duties.

§ 4. Inspectors; appointment; qualifications; terms of office and compensation.—Within thirty days after the passage of this chapter, and thereafter, from time to time, the superintendent of public works shall appoint two inspectors of steam vessels, one of whom shall have a practical knowledge of the management of steam vessels by an experience of at least five years as a licensed master and pilot of steam vessels, and the other of the construction and use of boilers, engines and their appurtenances, and who shall be otherwise properly qualified to perform the duties prescribed by this article, each of whom shall hold office during the term of office of the superintendent appointing them. Each inspector shall receive an annual salary of three thousand dollars, to be paid monthly by the state treasurer, on the warrant of the comptroller. Each inspector shall receive his actual and necessary traveling expenses upon a verified statement of such expenses duly audited by the superintendent of public works. If

the office of inspector becomes vacant, the superintendent shall fill
such vacancy by the appointment of a person to serve for the remainder of such unexpired term. The superintendent of public
works may remove such inspectors at any time.

§ 5. Duties of inspectors.— The inspectors shall annually or
oftener, if they have good cause to believe it reasonable, inspect
every steam vessel engaged in carrying passengers for hire or
towing for hire, examine carefully her hull, boats and other equipments, examine her engine and boiler, ascertain how long it will be
safe to use the same, determine the pressure of steam to be allowed
and so regulate the fusible plugs, safety valves and steam cocks as
to insure safety, and they may require such changes, repairs and
improvements to be adopted and used as they may deem expedient
for the contemplated route. They shall also fix the number of
passengers that may be transported. The inspectors shall also,
whenever they or either of them deem it expedient, visit any vessel
licensed under this article, and examine into her condition for the
purpose of ascertaining whether or not any party thereon, having
a certificate from said inspectors, has conformed to and obeyed the
conditions of such certificates, and the provisions of this act: and
the owner, master, pilot, captain or engineer of such vessel shall
answer all reasonable questions, and give all the information in his
or their power, in regard to said vessel, her machinery and the
manner of managing the same. In case of damage by fire or by
explosion, or by means of an electrical apparatus, the inspectors may
investigate the cause thereof, and if found by them to have been
occasioned by a violation of any of the provisions of this chapter,
or of the orders, regulations and requirements of said inspectors,
they shall so certify to the district attorney of the county where
such violation occurred, together with the names of the persons
guilty thereof and of the witnesses.

§ 6. Inspection and test of boilers.— The inspectors shall also
test the boilers of all steam vessels before the same shall be used,
and at least once in every year thereafter. In subjecting to the
hydrostatic test, boilers called and usually known under the designation of high pressure boilers, the hydrostatic pressure applied
must be in proportion of one hundred and fifty pounds to the
square inch to one hundred pounds to the square inch of
the steam pressure allowed. And in subjecting to the hydrostatic test, that class of boilers usually designated and known
as low pressure boilers, the inspectors shall allow as the

working power of each new boiler, a pressure of only three-fourths the number of pounds to the square inch, to which it shall have been subjected by the hydrostatic test, and found to be sufficient therefor; but should said inspectors be of the opinion that such boiler, by reason of its construction or material will not safely allow so high a working pressure they may, for reasons specifically stated in their certificate, fix the working pressure of such boiler at less than three-fourths of said test pressure; and no boiler or pipe, or any of the connections therewith, shall be approved which is made, in whole or in part of bad material, or is unsafe in its form, or dangerous from defective workmanship, age, use or other cause. In addition to the hydrostatic test as herein provided, the inspectors may cause a hammer test to be made and an internal examination of such boiler or boilers so tested, whenever deemed necessary. Any boiler having been in use ten years or more may be drilled at the bottom of shell or boiler, and also at such other points as the inspectors may direct, to determine the thickness of such material at those points, and the general condition of such boiler or boilers at the time of inspection and the steam pressure allowed shall be determined by such ascertained thickness and general condition of the boiler. They shall also see that all connections to the said boiler or engines are of suitable material, size and construction; and that the boiler, machinery and appurtenances are such as may be employed with safety in the service to be performed. They shall also satisfy themselves that the safety valves are of suitable dimensions, and that the weights of the same are properly adjusted, so as to allow no greater pressure than the maximum amount prescribed by them; and that there is a sufficient number of gauge-cocks properly attached to the boiler, so as to indicate the quantity of water therein; and suitable steam-gauges to correctly show the amount of steam carried; and as to any other matter connected with such steam vessel or the machinery thereof, that to said inspectors shall appear necessary to the safety of her passengers and crew. And they shall make such inspection, examination and test of naphtha launches and electric launches, and their apparatus and machinery, as will enable them to determine whether they can be safely used in navigation.

§ 7. Certificate of inspection, etc.— The inspectors, if satisfied that such vessel is in all respects safe and conforms to the requirements of this chapter, shall make and subscribe duplicate certificates, setting forth the age of the vessel and date of inspection, the name of the vessel, the name of the owner, the master, the number of licensed officers and crew deemed necessary to manage the vessel with safety, the number of boats and life preservers required, and the number of passengers that she can safely carry, and if a steam vessel, the age of the boiler, and the pressure of steam she is authorized to carry. One of said certificates shall be kept posted in some conspicuous place on the vessel to be designated by the inspectors in the certificate and the other copy shall be kept by the inspectors and by them recorded in a book to be kept for that purpose. If the inspectors refuse to grant a certificate of approval, they shall make a statement in writing, giving their reasons for such refusal, and deliver the same to the owner or master of the vessel.

§ 8. **Number of passengers carried.**— No greater number of passengers shall be transported upon any licensed steam vessel than the number allowed in the certificate of such vessel, under a penalty of ten dollars, to be paid by the master for each passenger in excess of the allowed number, unless special permission is first obtained from the inspectors under such precautions as they deem expedient.

§ 9. **Construction of steamboats.**— All steamboats, to which this article is applicable, shall hereafter be so constructed that the woodwork about the boilers, chimneys, fire-boxes, cook-houses, stove and steam-pipes, exposed to ignition, shall be so shielded by some incombustible material, that the air may circulate freely between such material and woodwork, or other ignitible substances, and before granting a certificate of inspection, the inspectors shall require that all other necessary provisions be made throughout such vessel, as they may judge expedient to guard against loss or damage by fire.

§ 10. **Stairways and gangways.**— Every vessel engaged in carrying passengers, shall be provided with permanent stairways and other sufficient means convenient for passing from one deck to the other, with gangways large enough to allow persons freely to pass, which shall be open, fore and aft of the length of the vessel, and to and along the guards; and whoever obstructs such gangways by freight or otherwise shall forfeit fifty dollars to the people of the state for every such violation.

§ 11. **Sailing rules.**— From and after the passage of this chapter, the following rules shall be observed in navigating all steam vessels, when under steam, and all boats propelled by machinery on the waters within the jurisdiction of the state, excepting the waters which are under the jurisdiction of the United States.

1. When two steamboats are meeting, end on, or nearly end on, so as to involve risk of collision, each shall alter her course to starboard, so that each may pass on the port side of the other.

2. When two steam vessels are crossing so as to involve risk of collision, the vessel which has the other on her own starboard side shall keep out of the way of the other.

3. When a steam vessel and a sailing vessel are proceeding in such directions as to involve risk of collision, the steam vessel shall keep out of the way of the sailing vessel.

4. When, by any of these rules, one of two vessels is to keep out of the way, the other shall keep her course and speed.

5. Every vessel under steam, when approaching another steamboat or small boat or vessel of any kind, so as to involve the risk of collision, shall slacken her speed, or if necessary, shall stop and reverse her engine, and every vessel under steam shall, when in a fog, go at a moderate speed.

6. Any steam vessel overtaking another steam vessel shall keep out of the way of the last-mentioned steam vessel.

7. When two steam vessels are going in the same direction the stern steam vessel wishing to pass the other shall signal the forward steam vessel of her intention to pass on the port side by two distinct whistles, and to pass on her starboard side, by one distinct whistle, which shall be answered by the forward steam vessel with the same number of whistles, and the forward steam vessel shall keep on her course as if no signal had been given.

8. Steamboats approaching each other shall, at not less than three hundred yards distance between each other, give a signal with one loud, distinct whistle.

9. When two steamboats are approaching each other, and if the course of such steamboats is so far on the starboard side of each as not to be considered by the pilots as meeting end on, or nearly so, or if the steamboats are approaching each other, in such manner that passing to the right as in rule one is deemed unsafe by the pilot of either steamboat, the pilot so first deciding shall give two short and distinct blasts on his steam whistle, which the pilot of the other steamboat shall answer promptly by two blasts of his steam whistle, and they shall pass to the left (on the starboard) side of each other.

10. When two steamboats are approaching each other and the pilot of either steamboat fails to understand the course or intention of the other, wLether from the signals being given or answered erroneously or from other cause, the pilot so in doubt shall immediately signify the same by giving several short and rapid blasts of the steam whistle, and if the boats shall have approached within five hundred yards of each other, both shall be immediately slowed to a speed barely sufficient for steerageway until the proper signals are given, answered and understood, or until the boats have passed each other.

11. When a steamboat is running in a fog or thick weather it shall be the duty of the pilot to cause a long blast of the steam whistle to be sounded at intervals not exceeding one minute.

12. Signals of distress shall be four distinct blasts of the whistle, and shall be recognized by the master of any steamboat hearing the same, and he shall render such assistance as is in his power.

13. Any steamboat landing at a wharf shall have the right of the wharf for a period of five minutes; if detained at the wharf for a longer period than five minutes, the steamboat at the wharf shall allow another steamboat to land alongside and discharge her passengers and freight over her decks for at least ten minutes, and thereafter until such first steamboat shall leave said wharf.

14. In construing these provisions, due regard must be had to all the dangers of navigation, and to any special circumstances which may exist, rendering a departure therefrom necessary in order to avoid immediate danger.

15. Every steam vessel which is under sail and not under steam is to be considered a sailing vessel, and every vessel under steam, whether under sail or not, is to be considered a steam vessel.

16. Nothing in this article shall be construed to extend to any boat or lighter not being masted, or if masted and not decked, employed in the harbor of any town or city.

17. All steamboats licensed under the provisions of this article shall conform to and obey such other rules and regulations as the inspectors may prescribe, not inconsistent herewith.

18. The inspectors provided for in this chapter are authorized to make further rules and regulations, applying generally to all steamboats, especially to one or more of them; and on framing rules for the government of managers and employes of boats, the said inspectors shall, as far as practicable, be governed by the

general rules and regulations prescribed by the United States board of supervising inspectors of steam vessels.

19. Every steam vessel carrying passengers for hire on the waters within the jurisdiction of this state, shall have two copies of this section framed, one to be placed in the pilot-house for the government of the pilot, and the other to be hung in a conspicuous place on the steamboat, for the inspection of the passengers.

§ 12. **Lights on vessels.**— The master of every steamboat or vessel propelled by machinery when navigating between sunset and sunrise, shall cause the same to carry the following lights:

1. At the foremast head, a bright white light, of such a character as to be visible on a dark night, with a clear atmosphere, at a distance of at least two miles, and so constructed as to show a uniform and unbroken light over an arc of the horizon of twenty points of the compass, and to be so fixed as to throw the light ten points on each side of the vessel, namely, from right ahead to two points abaft the beam on either side.

2. On the starboard side a green light, of such a character as to be visible on a dark night, with a clear atmosphere, at a distance of at least two miles; and be so constructed as to show a uniform and unbroken light over an arc of the horizon of ten points of the compass, and so fixed as to throw the light from right ahead to two points abaft the beam on the starboard side.

3. On the port side, a red light, of such a character as to be visible on a dark night, with a clear atmosphere, at a distance of at least two miles, and so constructed as to show a uniform and unbroken light over an arc of the horizon of ten points of the compass, and so fixed as to throw the light from right ahead to two points abaft the beam on the port side.

The green and red lights shall be fitted with inboard screens, projecting at least three feet forward from the lights, so as to prevent them from being seen across the bow.

4. The master of every vessel other than a steamboat anchored in the night time shall cause her peak to be lowered and a good and sufficient light to be thrown from her taffrail in some part of her rigging and at least twenty feet above her deck. In the case of small vessels, the inspectors may make specific rules for lights different from the foregoing.

§ 13. **Steam fire pump.**— Every steam vessel permitted by her certificate to carry one hundred passengers or upwards, shall be

provided with a good double acting steam fire pump or other equivalent apparatus for throwing water, the same to be at all times
during the navigation of such vessel, kept ready for immediate
use, having at least one hundred feet of hose of suitable size and
of sufficient strength to stand a pressure of at least seventy-five
pounds to the square inch.

§ 14. Life boats.— Every ferry boat propelled by steam or electricity shall be provided with at least one substantial boat, fifteen
feet or more in length, and properly supplied with oars, and kept
tight and in good condition at all times, and so attached to such
ferry boat that it may in case of need be launched into the water
for immediate use. Every steamboat or vessel propelled by
machinery and carrying passengers shall be provided, if of the
measurement of two hundred and fifty and less than five hundred
tons burden, with at least two substantial row-boats, with life
lines attached and properly supplied with oars, and kept tight and
in good condition at all times, and so attached as to be capable of
being launched into the water for immediate use in case of need:
and if of the measurement of five hundred tons or more, with at
least one first class life-boat and one row-boat twenty-five feet long
by seven wide, capable of carrying or supporting fifty persons each.
and at least one row-boat of the usual size and construction, all
to be properly supplied with oars, and kept tight and in good condition at all times, and so attached as to be capable of being
launched into the water for immediate use in case of need. Every
such vessel may also be required to carry such other boats, as the
inspectors, on account of the route, or the number of passengers.
deem requisite, and the master of such vessel shall exercise and
discipline his crew in the launching, use and management of the
boats until they become skillful boatmen.

§ 15. Life preservers, etc.— Every steam vessel or vessel propelled by machinery used in the transportation of passengers for
hire, shall have a life preserver or life float for each passenger she
is allowed to carry and for each member of her crew. At least one
half thereof shall be life preservers, and shall be made of good
sound cork blocks, adjustable to the body of a person, with belts
and shoulder straps properly attached, and shall be so constructed
as to place the cork underneath the shoulders and around the body
of the person wearing it; each such life preserver to contain at least
six pounds of good cork having a buoyancy of at least four pounds
to each pound of cork, and the other half or part thereof may be

life floats, to be constructed of dry pine plank, four feet long, two inches thick and twelve inches wide, with lines properly attached in such manner as to be convenient for use; and it shall be the duty of the inspectors to satisfactorily ascertain that every life preserver and such life floats are as herein required. Such life preservers and life floats shall be kept in convenient, accessible places in such vessel in readiness for immediate use in case of accident, and the places where the same are to be kept shall be designated in the inspectors' certificate, and also pointed out by printed notices posted in such places as the inspectors direct. Every such vessel shall carry in convenient places, at least ten buckets filled with water, with dip lines attached, and three axes in good condition; but the inspectors may, if they deem it necessary or proper, require a larger, or in case of very small vessels, permit a smaller number of buckets and axes.

§ 16. **Interference with safety valve.**— Whoever intentionally loads or obstructs, or causes to be loaded or obstructed, in any way, the safety valve of the boiler, or employs any other means or device whereby the boiler may be subjected to a greater pressure than the amount allowed by the inspectors' certificate, or intentionally deranges or hinders the operation of any machinery or device employed to denote the stage of the water or steam in any boiler, or to give warning of approaching danger, or intentionally permits the water to fall below the prescribed low water limit of the boiler, shall forfeit to the people of the state the sum of five hundred dollars for each violation.

§ 17. **Licenses.**— Every person employed as master, pilot or engineer on board of a steam vessel or a vessel propelled by machinery, carrying passengers for hire or towing for hire, shall be examined by the inspectors as to his qualifications, and if satisfied therewith they shall grant him a license for the term of one year for such boat, boats or class of boats as said inspectors may specify in such license. In a proper case, the license may permit and specify that the master may act as pilot, and in case of small vessels also as engineer and pilot. The license shall be framed under glass, and posted in some conspicuous place on the vessel on which he may act. Whoever acts as master, pilot or engineer, without having first received such license, or upon a boat or class of boats not specified in his license, shall be liable to a penalty of fifty dollars for each day that he so acts, except as in this article otherwise specified, and such license may be revoked by the inspectors for intemperance, incompetency or willful violation of duty.

§ 18. **Lamps.**— No licensed vessel carrying passengers for hire shall be allowed to use in lamps, lanterns or other lights on such vessel, any oil which will not stand a fire test of at least three hundred degrees Fahrenheit.

§ 19. **Names of vessels to be painted on stern**— Every vessel subject to the provisions of this chapter, shall have her name and the port to which she belongs painted on her stern on a black background in white, yellow or gilt letters, of not less than three inches in length. If any vessel, which is subject to the provisions of this chapter, shall be found without having her name, and the name of the port to which she belongs so painted, the owner or owners shall be liable to a penalty of fifty dollars to the people of the state. The inspectors may, however, in the case of small vessels, permit such name to be placed elsewhere and in letters of less length, the permission, the place of name and length of letters to be stated in a certificate to be given to the master, who shall exhibit the same whenever requested.

§ 20. **Method of landing passengers.**— Small boats containing passengers may be landed from or drawn to a steamboat by means of a line hauled in by hand, but in no case shall the line be attached to or hauled in by the machinery of any vessel. No passenger shall be put or suffered to go into any such small boat for the purpose of being landed until such small boat shall be completely afloat and wholly disengaged from the vessel, except held by a painter. A good and sufficient pair of oars suitable for the purpose shall be kept in such small boat. In landing or receiving any passenger in the night time, there shall be a signal from the small boat at the shore by means of a horn or trumpet, to enable those having charge on board the vessel to determine when the small boat, having landed or received her passengers, is ready to leave the shore.

§ 21. **Engine stopped.**— While landing or receiving passengers the engine of the vessel shall not be put in motion except:

1. To give sufficient force to carry the small boat to the shore, or

2. To keep the vessel in proper direction and to prevent her from drifting or being driven on shore; but in no case shall it be put in motion while passengers are being transferred from such vessel into a small boat for the purpose of being landed.

§ 22. **Loose hay, etc., not to be carried** — No loose hay, loose cotton or loose hemp, camphene, nitro-glycerine, naphtha, benzine, benzole, coal oil, crude petroleum, or other like explosive burning fluids or dangerous articles, shall be carried as freight or used in stoves on any steamer licensed to carry passengers under this chapter; except that refined petroleum which will not ignite at a temperature of less than one hundred and ten degrees Fahrenheit may be carried on the main deck of any vessel, provided the barrels or cases containing such oil are fully covered with a tarpaulin. But nothing in this section provided shall be construed to prevent any vessel of twenty tons burden or under which uses refined petroleum for fuel from carrying sufficient refined petroleum, which will not ignite at a temperature of less than one hundred and ten degrees Fahrenheit, with which to replenish the fires and properly equip such vessel for use; said petroleum to be carried in metal cans or tanks which shall be properly protected by a covering of wood or other substance which would equally protect from accident and be approved by said inspectors, and to be conveyed from said cans or tanks to the said fires through metal pipes.

§ 23. Racing.— No master, engineer or other person having charge of the boiler or apparatus for the generation of steam of any steamboat shall create, or allow to be created, an undue or unsafe quantity of steam in order to increase the speed of such steamboat or to excel another boat in speed. Any person violating the provisions of this section shall forfeit to the people of the state the sum of five hundred dollars for every such violation.

§ 24. Penalties.— Every master of a steamboat or vessel who shall violate any of the preceding sections of this article shall, for every such violation, forfeit to the people of the state the sum of two hundred and fifty dollars, unless a different penalty is prescribed.

§ 25. Liability of owner.— The owner of every steamboat or vessel shall be responsible for the good conduct of the master employed by him, and if any penalty incurred by such master is not paid by him and can not be collected from him by due course of law, it may be recovered of the owner or owners, jointly or severally, of the steamboat or vessel in whose employ he was at the time of the incurring of such penalty, in the same manner as if such owner or owners were sureties of such master.

§ 26. Copy posted.— The master of every licensed vessel shall keep a copy of the preceding sections of this article posted in a conspicuous place on such vessel for the inspection of all persons on board thereof. Every master violating the provisions of this section shall forfeit to the people of the state twenty-five dollars, and the additional sum of twenty-five dollars for each month while such violation continues.

§ 27. Annual report.— The inspectors shall on or before the first day of January in each year, make a verified report to the super-intendent of public works, containing a detailed statement of the names and number of vessels examined and licensed, the names and number of vessels to which licenses were refused and stating the reasons for the refusal, the names and number of persons examined and licensed, the names of and number to whom licenses were refused and stating the reasons therefor, and may include in such report any other information the inspectors deem desirable.

§ 28. Persons employing steamboats, to receive no compensa-tion.— No person employing steamboats for towing shall receive any commission or compensation for any orders given to the own-ers, captain or agent of such steamboat for such towage and no person shall interfere with or hinder such owner, captain or agent while in the prosecution of his business. The provisions of this section shall not apply to the towage of canal-boats, or to the waters of Lake Champlain, or repeal, amend or affect any existing law or regulations in regard to pilotage or quarantine in the port of New York. Any person violating the provisions of this section shall forfeit to the people of the state the sum of fifty dollars for the first offense, and fifty dollars for the second offense, and there-after for each and every offense the sum of not less than one hun-dred dollars.

§ 29. What vessels must comply with this article.— All steam vessels, naphtha and electric launches, carrying passengers for hire, or towing for hire must comply with all the terms and pro-visions of the preceding sections, and with all orders, regulations and requirements of the inspectors, except that any such vessel not propelled by steam, or when not under steam, is exempt from the provisions in regard to the blowing of whistles. If any such vessel is navigated without complying therewith, except as herein stated, or without the requisite certificates of the inspectors, the owners and master shall forfeit to the people of the state the penal-ties prescribed in this article, and the vessel so navigated shall also be liable therefor, and may be attached and proceeded against in any court having jurisdiction. But if any such vessel is deprived of the services of any licensed officer, without the consent, fault or collusion of the master, owner, or any person interested in the vessel, the deficiency may be temporarily supplied, until a licensed officer can be obtained.   If the owner or master of any vessel shall at least twenty days before the expiration of his certificate, notify the inspectors of such expiration and request a new inspection and certificate, the certificate then expiring shall continue in force until an inspection is made and such owners and masters are not liable for any of the penalties provided in this article on account of navigating said vessel, without such new certificate.

ARTICLE II.

HUDSON RIVER NAVIGATION.

Section 35. Obstructions.
     36. Steamboats not to tow mud-scows.
     37. Escape of sparks.
     38. Rafts.
     39. Wharfage.
     40. Lights upon swing-bridges.

Section 35. Obstructions.— No person shall make use of any net or weir, or set, drive or place any hedge, stake, stone, post, pole, anchor or other fixture in the Hudson river, out of the channel thereof, between the city of New York and the state dam at Fort Edward, other than such as are permitted by law to be used or placed to catch fish.   No person shall by means of or from any steamboat, scow or vessel, or in any other manner whatever, cast, throw, dump, or deposit into the Hudson river any food, or contrivance or device, used to keep, carry or preserve food; or any solid substance or material, except dirt accumulated from the use of the boat by human beings; or place, construct or build any contrivance, substance or thing whatever within such waters which shall or may tend to decrease the depth of such waters or interfere with, imperil or jeopardize the free and safe navigation thereof.   This section shall not be construed to prevent the hauling of fire from the furnace-grate of a steamboat having state-rooms above the main deck, or dumping the ashes which may accumulate thereon during a trip except between the city of New York and Stony Point, and between Tivoli and the state dam above Troy; or depositing materials to build wharves or piers, or to fill land under water granted by the state to any person, if a permanent and substantial bulkhead be first properly and securely built, inclosing the whole area of any such pier or wharf; or the setting of shad poles in shad season or the use of any other device or contrivance for fishing in any season of the year authorized by law, except below the northerly line established by the harbor commissioners of the city of New York. Any person violating any of the provisions of this section shall forfeit to the people of the state the sum of fifty dollars for each violation.

§ 36. **Steamboats not to tow mud-scows.**— No steamboat or tug shall tow a mud-scow carrying mud, earth, soil, ashes, refuse, stone, rock or other solid substance or material which is to be dumped or deposited in the Hudson river in violation of the provisions of this article. The masters of such steamboat or tug and the contractor using the same shall, jointly and severally, forfeit the sum of two hundred dollars to the people of the state for every violation of the provisions of this section.

§ 37. **Escape of sparks.**— The master, engineer and fireman of steamboats navigating the Hudson river shall cause the dampers in the pipes or chimneys thereof to be closed, or otherwise prevent the escape of sparks and coals from such chimneys or pipes while passing near the cities and villages along the Hudson river, or landing passengers or freight or lying at the docks or wharfs thereof. Such person or persons and the owner or owners of such steamboats shall be, jointly and severally, liable for all damages by fire occasioned by the violation of any provision of this section, and shall forfeit to the city or village adjacent to where such violation occurred the sum of one hundred dollars.

§ 38. **Rafts.**— All rafts of timber or lumber floating on the Hudson river at night shall show two red lights, one on each end of such raft, at a height of not less than ten feet from the upper logs or plank. Every person violating any provision of this section shall forfeit to the people of the state the sum of fifty dollars for every such violation.

§ 39. **Wharfage.**— Wharfage or dockage may be charged to and received from every steamboat or vessel using or making fast to any wharf or pier along the Hudson river, except at the city of Yonkers, between the north shore of Harlem river and the southerly limits of the city of Albany, erected by virtue of any water grant from the state, at the following rates for every day or part of a day's use of the same. For every steamboat or vessel of two hundred tons burden or under, one-half cent per ton. For every steamboat or vessel of over two hundred tons, one cent for each additional ton not exceeding two hundred, and one-quarter of a cent for every additional ton over four hundred. For every steamboat or vessel making fast to another lying at any such wharf or pier, one-half of the above rates, except that all steamboats or vessels landing or receiving passengers or light freight at any such wharf or pier may be charged for each landing a sum not to exceed fifty cents. The wharfage provided by this section shall be a lien on the vessel liable therefor.

§ 40. **Lights upon swing-bridges.**— Every corporation, company or individual, owning, maintaining or operating a swing-bridge across the Hudson river shall, during the season of navigation between sundown and sunrise keep and maintain the following lights: Upon every swing-bridge with water on each side of pivot pier, eight lights, located as follows: One red light on or over the north and one on or over the south end of the east rest piers; one red light on or over the north and one on or over the south end of the west rest pier, and a green light on each corner of the bridge when open. If there is a waterway on only one side of the pivot pier, five lights, located as follows: One red light on or over the north and one on or over the south end of the rest pier nearest the channel, and a green light upon each end of the bridge when open upon the corners nearest the channel. Such lights shall be of the usual brilliancy of lights used for such purposes and known as signal lanterns.

ARTICLE III.

OTHER WATERS OF THE STATE.

Section 50. Buoys.
     51. Removal of gravel prohibited.
     52. Deposit of dead animals in Lake George prohibited.
     53. Deposit of dead animals, etc., in the Saint Lawrence prohibited.
     54. Prevention of ice gorges in Saint Lawrence river.
     55. Deposits in Racket river, Oswegatchie river and east branch of the Saint Regis river prohibited.

Section 50. **Buoys.**— No person shall moor or fasten a vessel, scow or raft to any buoy placed by the United States in the Niagara river; and if such buoy shall be removed or destroyed by any person by accident or otherwise, such person shall immediately notify the collector of the port next entered thereafter of such removal or destruction. Every person violating any provision of this section shall forfeit to the collector of the port of Buffalo, the sum of one

hundred dollars for every such violation, to be used by such collector in maintaining and restoring such buoys.

§ 51. **Removal of gravel prohibited.**— No person shall take or
carry away by means of a vessel or otherwise, any gravel, sand or
stones from the beach or shore of Long Island sound between Old
Field Point and Mount Misery Point, in the town of Brookhaven,
Suffolk county; or from the beaches or shores separating such
sound from Setauket or Port Jefferson harbors in such town; or
from the outer bar or other bars or flats adjoining the channel or
entrance to Smithtown harbor in such sound; or land or go upon
any such beach, shore, bar or flat with intent to remove, take or
carry away or assist in removing, taking or carrying away any such
gravel, sand or stones, or have on board his boat or vessel or on
any boat or vessel in his possession any such gravel, sand or stones,
taken therefrom with intent to carry the same away. Every person violating any provision of this section shall forfeit to the town
where the violation occurred the sum of two hundred dollars for
every such violation.

§ 52. **Deposit of dead animals in Lake George prohibited.**— No
person or persons shall drain, deposit or cast any dead animal,
carrion, offal, excrement, garbage or other putrid or offensive matter in the waters of Lake George or Schroon lake in this state; or
moor or store logs or rafts in any bay or inlet to such lakes. This
section shall not be construed to prevent the deposit of the usual
waste or drainage from factories, or the storage of logs or rafts by
adjacent owners in front of their own uplands, or the rafting or
floating of logs through Schroon lake in the usual manner, or the
erection of booms prior to the twentieth day of June in each year
to secure and prevent the separation of logs in such lake for such
time as is required to float them through the outlet in such manner
as not to interfere with its navigation by any party employing
steamboats to carry freight or passengers. Every person violating
any provision of this section shall forfeit to the town where the
violation occurred the sum of one hundred dollars for every such
violation.

§ 53. **Deposit of dead animals, etc., in the Saint Lawrence, prohibited.**— No person shall throw or cast any dead animal, carrion
or offal, or other putrid or offensive matter in the waters of the
Saint Lawrence river within the jurisdiction of this state; or any
debris, coal ashes, or other material, when such debris, coal ashes
or other material shall diminish the natural depth of such navi-

gable waters to less than twelve feet from low-water mark within
one hundred feet of any dock, wharf or land, unless the owner or
owners thereof consider such debris, coal ashes or other material
necessary to fill in and improve such dock, wharf or water front.
Every person violating any provision of this section shall forfeit
to the people of the state the sum of fifty dollars for every such
violation and shall be liable to the owner and occupant of any
premises injuriously affected by such violation for all damages
sustained thereby.

§ 54. Prevention of ice gorges in Saint Lawrence river.— No person shall cut, loosen or detach from any bay, estuary, inlet or main
or island shore of the Saint Lawrence river within the jurisdiction
of this state, any field or large body of ice for the purpose or with
the intent of using the same as a bridge between any islands of
such river or between any island and the main shore, whereby the
full, free and natural flow of the waters of such river shall be
impeded, interfered with or threatened. The sheriff of Saint Lawrence county is hereby authorized to appoint one or more deputies
of said sheriff, as shall to him seem necessary, to patrol said river,
within said county, at such time or times as to him shall seem
proper, and to arrest any person or persons there found engaged in
performing or attempting to perform, any of the acts hereby forbidden; and the fees, charges and expenses of such deputy or
deputies, for such service, shall be a county charge against such
county, to be audited and allowed by the board of supervisors of
said county and paid out of its treasury. Any person injured or
liable to suffer injury from an ice gorge in such river may remove
such ice gorge as far as it may interfere with or impede the full,
free and natural flow of the waters of such river. This section
shall not prevent the placing of an ice bridge from the south shore
of Long Sault island to the American shore across the south channel of such river if such bridge shall not cause floating or anchor
ice to jam or gorge at or above the point where it may be placed
and shall not otherwise interfere with the full, free and natural
flow of the water. If such bridge shall cause the ice to gorge or
jam or shall interfere with the full, free and natural flow of the
waters of such river, the party placing it must remove it on the
application of any person injured or liable to be injured thereby.
If such party refuses, the bridge may be removed and the party
responsible therefor shall bear the charge and expense of such

removal. This section shall not exempt parties constructing ice bridges in such river from their common-law liability.

§ 55. **Deposits in Racket river, Oswegatchie river and east branch of the Saint Regis river, prohibited.**—No corporation, company, person or persons shall deposit or put into the Racket, Oswegatchie or east branch of the Saint Regis rivers, in this state, any buttings, edgings, slabs, or other debris except sawdust and planer shavings from any mills engaged in the manufacture of shingles, wood or lumber upon or adjacent to such rivers to be floated down the same. Every person violating any provision of this section shall forfeit for every such violation the sum of fifty dollars, to be sued for and recovered by any person aggrieved thereby for his own use and benefit.

ARTICLE IV.

PORT OF ALBANY.

Section 60. **Harbor master.**—There shall continue to be a harbor master for the port of Albany, who shall be appointed by the governor, by and with the advice and consent of the senate. Such port shall comprehend within its limits all that portion of the Hudson river situate in front of the city of Albany, and extending northerly two miles above and southerly two miles below the boundaries of such city, together with all the wharves, slips and basins connected with such river within the above prescribed tide-water limits.

§ 61. **Powers and duties.**—Such harbor master shall regulate and station all steamboats, vessels, wharves and piers within such port and remove such steamboats and vessels as are not employed in receiving and discharging their cargoes and prevent them from obstructing for an unreasonable time the passage or entrance into the basin of the city of Albany. He may determine how far and in what instances masters having charge of steamboats or vessels should accommodate each other in their respective situations, and may, if no one has charge of the same, remove any steamboat or vessel lying within such port, at the expense of the master or owner thereof. If any master or person having control of any vessel within the limits of such port shall neglect or refuse to obey the directions of such harbor master in any matters within his authority, or if any person shall resist or oppose him in the execution of his duties, he shall forfeit to the city of Albany the sum of fifty dollars for every such neglect or refusal or for any such resistance or opposition, and all money so collected shall be·applied to the support of the poor of said city and county.

§ 62. **Rate of speed ; anchors.**— No steamboat or vessel shall navigate the Hudson river opposite the docks, piers or wharves in the city of Albany at a greater rate of speed than six miles an hour, and all vessels shall rig in their jibboom on coming to the wharves, and all steamboats and vessels shall take their anchors upon deck to prevent injury therefrom to other steamboats and vessels.

§ 63. **Fees.**— The master, owner or consignee of every steamboat or vessel entering the port of Albany or loading, unloading or making fast to any wharf therein, shall, within forty-eight hours after the arrival thereof, pay to the harbor master for his services the sum of one and one-half cents per ton per annum, which shall be computed from the registered tonnage of such steamboat or vessel. If such fee is not paid within such time and after due demand, the master, owner or consignee, upon whom such demand is made, shall pay double the amount of such fees to be sued for and recovered, together with costs by the harbor master. The harbor master may employ assistance to collect such fees, and in case of his sickness, inability or absence, he may, by and with the assent of the mayor of the city of Albany, appoint some proper person to act in his stead and perform the duties of his office during such sickness, inability or absence. This section shall not apply to boats navigating the state canals which enter tide water for the purpose of being towed out of such port, unless receiving or discharging cargoes, or portions thereof, in tide water within the limits of such port, or unless navigating the canals of private companies or corporations.

§ 64. **Fees for settling disputes.**— If such harbor master is called upon to decide any dispute relating to berths between the masters of steamboats or vessels, the party against whom the decision is rendered shall pay to the harbor master the sum of two dollars. If both parties are in fault, each shall pay the sum of one dollar.

§ 65. **Annual report.**— The harbor master shall keep an exact

account of all moneys received by him and shall make report of
the same to the legislature annually on or before the first day of
February.

ARTICLE V.

§ 70. **Dams and bridges.**— No dam shall be erected on any river
or stream in this state, recognized by law or use as a public highway for the purpose of floating and running lumber, logs or other
timber, over or upon the same, unless there be built in such dam an
apron, at least fifteen feet in width, in the middle of the current
of such river or stream, of a proper slope for the safe passage of
lumber, logs and other timber. No bridge shall be built over any
such river or stream in such a manner as to obstruct or prevent the
free and uninterrupted passage of lumber, logs and other timber
down and along such river or stream.

§ 71. **Booms, etc., to be opened on notice ; penalty for failure.**—
Every person who shall build any boom or other obstruction in
the waters of any river or stream, for the purpose of stopping or
securing lumber, logs or other timber, shall within ten days after
the receipt of a written notice from any person who shall have
lumber, logs or other timber to transport on such river or stream,
open such boom or remove such obstruction or part thereof so as
to permit the assorting and passage of such lumber, logs and other
timber through and down such river or stream. Every person who
willfully obstructs, by booms or otherwise, the channel of any river
or stream so as to hinder or delay the free passage of lumber, logs
or timber over or through the same, shall be liable to a penalty of
fifty dollars for each day of the continuance of such obstruction, to
be recovered by the person aggrieved thereby, and in addition to
such penalty, shall be liable for all damages caused by such
obstruction.

§ 72. **Shutes and aprons in connection with dams, etc., damages to be paid.**— Any person desiring to float or run lumber, logs or timber down a river or stream, recognized by law or use as a public highway. may construct a shute or apron in connection with any dam across such river or stream, and may reconstruct any booms or other works already constructed in, over or across such river or stream, in such manner as to allow lumber, logs or other timber to pass the same, and may remove obstructions in such river or stream and construct such other piers, booms or other works as may be necessary for the passage of lumber, logs or other timber over and through the channels of such river or stream. In such constructions no injury or damage shall be done to the owner or occupant of any such booms, dams or other works, or to the owner or occupant of any land on which such piers, booms or other works are constructed, or lands flooded thereby. Every such person shall pay to the owner or occupant of such lands all damages he may sustain by reason of the construction of such piers, booms, or other works, or the flooding of lands thereby. In case the amount of such damages can not be agreed upon by the parties interested, the same shall be appraised by three commissioners to be appointed by the county judge of the county in which the owner or occupant claiming damages shall reside, on the application of any person interested in the appraisal of such damages, on three days' notice in writing to the opposite parties of the time and place of making such application. Any person making claim for damages under this article, shall apply within one year after the occurrence of the same, or be debarred from recovering the same. This article shall apply to all booms or other works heretofore or hereafter constructed, but shall not be constructed so as to impair or abridge any private or individual rights, except so far as may be necessary for the improvement of rivers and streams, for floating or running lumber, logs or other timber down the same.

§ 73. **Marks on logs and timber to be recorded.**— Every person who shall run any logs or timber down any river or stream recognized by law or use as a public highway, shall select some mark different from any mark previously recorded, and shall put the same on each log or stick of timber in some conspicuous place, and shall cause such mark to be recorded in the county clerk's office of each county in or through which such river or stream runs. The county clerk shall be entitled to the sum of fifty cents for recording such mark, to be paid by the person having the same recorded, and a copy of said entry, certified by the clerk, shall be presumptive evidence that the logs or timber so marked are the property of the person by whom such mark was selected and recorded.

§ 74. Persons prohibited from landing logs, etc.— No person shall stop, take up or draw to, or lodge on the shore of any river or stream used for floating logs, timber or lumber, or on any island therein, any lumber, logs, timber, boards or planks floating in such river or stream, without the consent of the owner thereof. Any person violating the provisions of this section shall for each violation forfeit to the person aggrieved thereby the sum of ten dollars, and in addition thereto shall be liable to the owner of such logs, timber or lumber for all damages sustained thereby.

§ 75. Undertakings of persons floating lumber and logs.— Every person intending to float or run lumber, logs or other timber upon any river or stream recognized by law or use as a public highway, shall execute a bond to the people of the state with sufficient sureties in the sum of five thousand dollars as an indemnity against all loss and damage that may be caused to any property, by reason of the use of such river or stream as provided in this article, and such bond may be sued upon by any person suffering such loss or damage. Such bond shall be approved by the county judges of the counties through which such river or stream flows and shall be filed in one of the offices of the clerks of such counties, and certified copies thereof in the other of such offices. No person shall float or run any lumber, logs or timber upon such streams until such bond shall have been executed, approved and filed.

§ 76. Application of article.— This article shall not apply to the Hudson river, the Alleghany river and its tributaries, nor the Delaware river and its tributaries, nor the waters located in Franklin county, nor the Beaver river and its tributaries, nor the Oswegatchie and its tributaries, nor the Grass river and its tributaries, nor the Racquette river and its tributaries, nor the West Canada creek and its tributaries, nor the Black river and its tributaries above its junction with the Moose river, nor the waters located in Lewis county used for floating or driving logs or lumber; nor be construed to repeal any existing law now applicable to any creek or river in this state.

ARTICLE VI.

LAWS REPEALED; WHEN TO TAKE EFFECT.

Section 80. Laws repealed.
      81. When to take effect.

Section 80. Laws repealed.— The laws or parts thereof specified in the schedule hereto annexed, and all acts amendatory thereof are repealed.

§ 81. When to take effect.— This chapter shall take effect immediately.

SCHEDULE OF LAWS REPEALED.

R. S., pt. 1, ch. 20, tit. 10 . . . . All. Inland navigation.

Laws.	Chapter.	Sections.	
1837	153	All	Lights on vessels navigating Niagara and Saint Lawrence river and Lake Ontario.
1837	356	All	Harbor master for port of Albany.
1839	112	All	Protection of cities of Hudson and Poughkeepsie from fire by steamboats.
1839	175	All	Speed of steamboats.
1839	349	All	Damages for collision.
1841	65	All	Lights on rafts.
1844	248	All	Speed of steamboats on Hudson river.
1849	411	All	Life boats.
1860	103	10, 12 . . .	Sale of passenger tickets.
1865	569	All	Rate of wharfage along Hudson river.
1866	374	All	Amendatory of L. 1837, ch. 356.
1871	253	All	Protection of harbors in Suffolk county.
1871	277	All	Protection of buoys in Niagara river.
1876	376	All	Dumping of garbage in Hudson river prohibited.
1879	204	1, 3, 4 . . .	Prevention of ice gorges in Saint Lawrence river.
1880	215	All	Amends L. 1876, ch. 376.

Chap. 593.

AN ACT to enable certain aliens to take, hold and convey real estate.

Became a law May 19, 1897, with the approval of the Governor. Passed, three-fifths being present.

The People of the State of New York, represented in Senate and Assembly, do enact as follows:

Certain aliens may take and hold real estate.

Section 1. Any citizen of a state or nation which, by its laws, confers similar privileges on citizens of the United States, may take, acquire, hold and convey lands or real estate within this state, in the same manner and with like effect as if such person were, at the time, a citizen of the United States; provided, however, that nothing in this act contained shall affect the rights of this state in any case in which proceedings for escheat have been or may be instituted before the passage of this act.

§ 2. This act shall take effect immediately.

Chap. 594.

AN ACT authorizing the commissioners of the land office to convey a tract of land situated on the Long Island state hospital
farm to school district number five in the town of Smithtown,
county of Suffolk.

Became a law May 19, 1897, with the approval of the Governor.
Passed, three-fifths being present.

*The People of the State of New York, represented in Senate and
Assembly, do enact as follows:*

Section 1. The commissioners of the land office shall, upon an ^{Convey-}
application being filed with them by the trustee of school district ^{land auth-}
number five of the town of Smithtown, county of Suffolk, convey
to such school district one acre of land lying north of the highway
which runs through such farm. But such conveyance shall not be
made unless the application shall contain a description by metes
and bounds of the land to be conveyed, and also have indorsed Consent required.
upon it the consent of a majority of the members of the state
commission in lunacy and also of the managers of the Long Island
State hospital.

§ 2. This act shall take effect immediately.

Chap. 595.

AN ACT to provide for securing a revenue to the state from surplus waters arising from enlargements or improvements of the
canals.

Became a law May 19, 1897, with the approval of the Governor.
Passed, three-fifths being present.

*The People of the State of New York, represented in Senate and
Assembly, do enact as follows:*

Section 1. The superintendent of public works, with the approval Lease of surplus
of the canal board, is hereby authorized, upon such terms as he shall canal waters.
deem advantageous to the state, to make a lease of any of the surplus waters of the canals of this state arising from enlargement or
improvements of the same, actually made, or in progress, which
waters shall not be necessary for the navigation or operation of
such canals, or may be withdrawn for use for power and returned
without detriment thereto, and which have not heretofore been

leased. Such lease or leases shall provide that it or they may be terminated in whole or in part whenever the superintendent of public works shall deem the whole, or any part of such waters de-sirable for the purposes of the canals. All connections for with-drawing the waters and for the return of the same shall be made in accordance with plans to be approved by the state engineer and surveyor and under the supervision of said superintendent of public works. The power conferred by this act is in addition to any power in the premises now given by statute.

§ 2. This act shall take effect immediately.

Connections for withdrawing waters.

Chap. 596.

AN ACT to authorize the acquisition of turnpikes and plankroads by counties adjoining cities of more than eight hundred thousand and less than fifteen hundred thousand inhabitants, and by vil-lages in such counties.

Became a law May 19, 1897, with the approval of the Governor. Passed, three-fifths being present.

The People of the State of New York, represented in Senate and Assembly, do enact as follows:

Acquisition of roads by county.

Section 1. If in any county adjoining a city having at any time by the then last preceding state or federal enumeration a popula-tion of more than eight hundred thousand and less than fifteen hundred thousand inhabitants, a turnpike or plankroad shall have been laid out, maintained or operated by an incorporated turnpike or plankroad company from any point in such county to or into any such city, and a street surface railroad corporation shall have acquired or succeeded to the rights or to any of the rights of such turnpike or plankroad company, then and in such case the board of supervisors of such county, in the name and in behalf of such county, is authorized to acquire by purchase or condemnation so much of such turnpike or plankroad as shall be situated in such county, for the purpose of laying out, maintaining, improving and repairing such portion of such turnpike or plankroad as a public highway and as a county road, subject to the retention of the fee thereof by such turnpike, plankroad or street surface railroad cor-poration, and subject also to all then existing rights, franchises and privileges of any such turnpike, plankroad or street surface rail-road corporation to construct, maintain and operate a street sur-

Subject to certain conditions.

face railroad upon and along such portion of such turnpike or plankroad substantially as then located, with such switches, crossovers, sidings and turnouts as may from time to time be necessary to the reasonable and convenient operation of such railroad except as may be otherwise agreed between such board of supervisors and any such corporation. And such board of supervisors in the name and in behalf of such county may make further agreements as to the terms and conditions upon which such street surface railroad shall thereafter be operated by any such corporation; and the acquisition by any such county by condemnation of any right, title or interest in and to such turnpike or plankroad shall be subject to such agreements, if any be so made. *Agreements with railroad companies.*

§ 2. The board of supervisors of any such county may thereafter *Improvements of road, etc.* adopt and incorporate into the county road system of the said county and improve the roadbed and sidewalks or any portion thereof of such turnpike or plankroad although the same or any part thereof be within the corporate limits of one or more incorporated villages, and for that purpose may issue the bonds of the *Issue of bonds.* said county for the payment of the expenses of the acquisition, repair and improvement of the said road in the same manner as now provided by the general law in relation to county roads, and *Apportionment of expense.* shall apportion the expense thereof among the several towns and city or cities of said county, or charge the same wholly to one or more of said towns as to said board may seem equitable and just.

§ 3. If the board of supervisors of any such county shall by reso- *Acquisition of roads by villages.* lution determine not to acquire such portion of any such turnpike or plankroad as shall be located in any incorporated village in such county, or shall not within six months from the passage of this act acquire, by purchase, such portion of such turnpike or plankroad as shall be situated in any such village, or shall not within such six months commence proceedings to acquire such portion thereof by condemnation, then the board of trustees of any such incorporated village is authorized in the name and in behalf of such village to acquire by purchase or condemnation for the purposes of a public highway the same right, title and interest in and to such portion of such turnpike or plankroad as may be situated in such village, and to make the same agreements relating to such *Agreements.* portion thereof as by the first section of this act the board of supervisors of such county is authorized to acquire and make as to such portion of such turnpike or plankroad as is situated in the county. In case of such acquisition by any such village, the expense and cost of acquiring, maintaining and improving such portion of any such turnpike or plankroad as shall be so acquired shall be borne entirely by the village acquiring, maintaining and improving the same, and such village may issue its bonds to pay for the expense and cost thereof.

§ 4. This act shall take effect immediately.

Chap. 598.

AN ACT to amend the code of civil procedure, relating to the probate of wills and the extent to which such probate should be conclusive as to personalty.

Became a law May 19, 1897, with the approval of the Governor. Passed, three-fifths being present.

The People of the State of New York, represented in Senate and Assembly, do enact as follows:

Section 1. Section twenty-six hundred and twenty-six of the code of civil procedure is hereby amended so as to read as follows :

§ 2626. **Probate; how far conclusive as to personalty.**—A decree admitting to probate a will of personal property, made as prescribed in this article, is conclusive, as an adjudication, upon all the questions determined by the surrogate pursuant to this article, until it is reversed upon appeal, or revoked by the surrogate, except in an action brought under section twenty-six hundred and fifty-three-a of this act to determine the validity or invalidity of such will; and except that a determination, made under section twenty-six hundred and twenty-four of this act, is conclusive only upon the petitioner, and each party who was duly cited or appeared, and every person claiming from, through, or under either of them.

Chap. 602.

AN ACT to amend section fifteen hundred and eighty-one of the code of civil procedure, in relation to the disposition of the shares of infants.

Became a law May 20, 1897, with the approval of the Governor.
Passed, a majority being present.

The People of the State of New York, represented in Senate and Assembly, do enact as follows:

Section 1. Section fifteen hundred and eighty-one of the code of civil procedure is hereby amended so as to read as follows:

§ 1581. **Shares of infants.**—Where a party entitled to receive a portion of the proceeds is an infant, the court may direct it to be invested in permanent securities in the name and for the benefit of the infant, or it may direct it to be paid over to the general guardian of the said infant when the guardian shall have executed to such infant a bond with two sureties which shall be approved by the court; or, if any of the moneys arising from the proceeds of such sale shall have been paid to the county treasurer, and on due proof that such money has remained uninvested in permanent securities for the space of three months, may direct the same to be paid to the general guardian of such infant upon his giving an undertaking in an amount and with securities satisfactory to the court for the faithful execution of his trust. In the case of an infant residing without the state, and having in the state or country where he or she resides a general guardian, or person duly appointed under the laws of such state or country, to the control and entitled, by the laws of such state or country, to the custody of the money of such infant, the court, upon satisfactory proof of such facts and of the sufficiency of the bond or security given by such general guardian or person in such state or country by the certificate of a judge of a court of record of such state or country, or otherwise, may direct that the portion of such infant arising upon such sale shall be paid over to such general guardian or person.

§ 2. This act shall take effect September first, eighteen hundred and ninety-seven.

Chap. 603.

AN ACT to amend the code of civil procedure, relative to the authentication of foreign wills and letters testamentary as evidence in the courts of this state.

Became a law May 19, 1897, with the approval of the Governor.
Passed, a majority being present.

The People of the State of New York, represented in Senate and Assembly, do enact as follows:

Code amended.

Section 1. Section two thousand seven hundred and four of the code of civil procedure is hereby amended so as to read as follows:

Authentication of wills, etc., proved in other states, etc.

§ 2704. To entitle a copy of a will admitted to probate or letters testamentary or of letters of administration, granted in any other state or in any territory of the United States, and of the proofs or of any statement of the substance of the proofs of any such will, or of the record of any such will, letters, proofs or statement, to be recorded or used in this state as provided in this article, such copy must be authenticated by the seal of the court or officer by which or whom such will was admitted to probate or such letters were granted, or having the custody of the same or of the record thereof, and the signature of a judge of such court, or the signature of such officer and of the clerk of such court or officer if any; and must be further authenticated by a certificate under the great or principal seal of such state or territory, and the signature of the officer who has the custody of such seal, to the effect that the court or officer by which or whom such will was admitted to probate or such letters were granted, was duly authorized by the laws of such state or territory to admit such will to probate, or to grant such letters; that the will, or letters, or records, the accompanying copy of which is so authenticated, is or are kept pursuant to those laws, by such court or by the officer who authenticated such copy; that the seal of such court or officer affixed to such copy is genuine, and that the officer making such certificate under such seal of such state or territory verily believes that each of the signatures attesting such copy is genuine; and to entitle any certificate concerning proofs accompanying the copy of the will or of the record so authenticated, to be recorded or used in this state, as provided in this article, such certificate must be under the seal of the court or officer by which or whom such will was admitted to probate, or having the custody of such will or record, and the signature of a judge or the clerk of such

court, or the signature of such officer, authenticated by a certificate
under such great or principal seal of such state or territory, and the
signature of the officer having the custody thereof, to the effect
that the seal of the court or officer affixed to such certificate concerning proofs is genuine, and that such officer making such certificate under such seal of such state or territory, verily believes
that the signature to such certificate concerning proofs is genuine.
To entitle a copy of a will admitted to probate or of letters testamentary or of letters of administration granted in a foreign country, and of the proofs or of any statement of the substance of the
proofs of any such will or of the record of any such will, letters,
proofs or statement to be recorded or used in this state as provided
in this article, such copy must be authenticated by the seal of the
court or officer by which or by whom such will so admitted to probate or such letters were granted or having the custody of the same
or of the record thereof and the signature of a judge of such court
or the signature of such officer and of the clerk of such court or
officer, if any; and must be further authenticated by a certificate
under the principal seal of the department of foreign affairs or the
department of justice of such foreign country and the signature of
the officer who has the custody of such seal to the effect that the
seal or officer by which or by whom such will was admitted to
probate or such letters were granted was duly authorized by the
laws of such foreign country to admit such will to probate or to
grant such letters; that the will, letters or records, the accompanying copy of which is so authenticated, is or are kept pursuant to
those laws by such court or by the officer who authenticated such
copy and that the seal of such court or officer affixed to such copy
is genuine, and that the officer making such certificate under such
seal of the department of foreign affairs or of the department of
justice of such foreign country verily believes that each of the
signatures attesting such copy is genuine and the seal of such department of foreign affairs or department of justice of such foreign
country and the signature of the officer having the custody of such
seal shall be attested by a United States consul and to entitle any
certificate concerning proofs accompanying the copy of the will,
or of the record so authenticated, to be recorded or used in this
state as provided in this article, such certificate concerning proofs
must be similarly authenticated and attested.

§ 2. This act shall take effect September first, eighteen hundred
and ninety-seven.

Chap. 604.

AN ACT to amend the code of civil procedure, relative to the justice's court of the city of Troy.

Became a law May 19, 1897, with the approval of the Governor. Passed, a majority being present.

The People of the State of New York, represented in Senate and Assembly, do enact as follows:

Code amended.

Section 1. The code of civil procedure is hereby amended by adding thereto the following section to be known as section thirty-two hundred and twenty-five-a.

Application of provisions to justices' court of Troy.

§ 3225a. The provisions of sections twenty-nine hundred and ninety to thirty hundred and nine of this act, both inclusive, apply to the justices' court of the city of Troy, except that the city clerk of the city of Troy shall fulfil all the duties therein required of the town clerk.

When takes effect.

§ 2. This act shall take effect September first, eighteen hundred and ninety-seven.

Chap. 605.

AN ACT to amend section twenty-seven hundred and three of the code of civil procedure relative to recording wills probated in other states or territories of the United States.

Became a law May 19, 1897, with the approval of the Governor. Passed, a majority being present.

The People of the State of New York, represented in Senate and Assembly, do enact as follows:

Section 1. Section twenty-seven hundred and three of the code of civil procedure is hereby amended to read as follows:

§ 2703. **Recording will proved in other States.** — Where real property situated within this state, or an interest therein, is devised, or made subject to a power of disposition, by a will, duly executed in conformity with the laws of this state, of a person who was, at the time of his death, a resident elsewhere within the United States, and such will has been admitted to probate within any state or territory of the United States and is filed or recorded in the proper office as prescribed by the laws of that state or territory, a copy of such will or of the record thereof and of the proofs or of the record thereof, or, if the proofs are not on file or recorded in such office, of any statement, on file or recorded in such office, of the substance of the proofs, authenticated as prescribed in this article, or if no proofs and no statement of the substance of the proofs be on file or recorded in such office, a copy of such will, or of the record thereof, authenticated as prescribed in this article, accompanied by a certificate that no proofs or statement of the substance of proofs of such will, are or is on file, or recorded in such office, made and likewise authenticated as prescribed in this article, may be recorded in the office of the surrogate of any county of this state where such real property is situated; and such record in the office of such surrogate, or an exemplified copy thereof, shall be presumptive evidence of such will, and of the execution thereof, in any action or special proceeding relating to such real property.

§ 2. This act shall take effect September first, eighteen hundred and ninety-seven.

Chap. 606.

AN ACT to amend section eight hundred and ninety-five of the code of civil procedure relating to depositions taken without the state.

Became a law May 19, 1897, with the approval of the Governor. Passed, a majority being present.

The People of the State of New York, represented in Senate and Assembly, do enact as follows:

Section 1. Section eight hundred and ninety-five of the code of civil procedure is hereby amended to read as follows:

§ 895. **Depositions where adverse party is an infant or committee.**— The last two sections are not applicable, where the adverse party is an infant, or the committee of a person judicially declared to be incapable of managing his affairs, by reason of lunacy, idiocy or habitual drunkenness. Nor can the applicant be examined in his own behalf, as prescribed in those sections, except by consent of the parties.

§ 2. This act shall take effect immediately.

Chap. 608.

AN ACT to amend chapter nine hundred and nine of the laws of eighteen hundred and ninety-six, entitled "An act in relation to the elections, constituting chapter six of the general laws."

Became a law May 19, 1897, with the approval of the Governor. Passed, a majority being present.

The People of the State of New York, represented in Senate and Assembly, do enact as follows:

Section 1. Section sixty-one of article three of chapter nine hundred and nine of the laws of eighteen hundred and ninety-six, entitled "An act in relation to the elections, constituting chapter six of the general laws," is hereby amended so as to read as follows:

§ 61. **Publication of nominations.**—At least six days before an election to fill any public office the county clerk of each county, except New York and Kings, the board of police commissioners of the city of New York, shall cause to be published in not less than two or more than four newspapers within such county or city respectively, and in any county having one hundred thousand or more inhabitants, adjoining a city having a population of one million or more, in not less than six nor more than ten newspapers, a list of all nominations of candidates for offices to be filled at such election, certified to such clerk or board by the secretary of state. or filed in the office of such clerk or board, and in the city of Brooklyn the board of elections of the city of Brooklyn shall cause such publication to be made in the newspapers designated as corporation newspapers of said city. Such publication shall contain the name and residence, and if in a city, the street number of the residence and place of business, if any, and the party or other designation of each candidate, and a fac simile of the emblems or devices selected and designated as prescribed by the fifty-sixth and fifty-seventh sections of this act, to represent and distinguish the candidates of the several political parties or independent bodies. The city clerk of each city, except New York and Brooklyn, and the boards named in such cities, shall at least six days before an election of city officers thereof, held at a different time from a general election, cause like publication to be made as to candidates for offices to be filled at such city election in at least two newspapers published in such city. One of such publications shall be made in a newspaper which advocates the principles of the political party that, at the last preceding election for governor, cast the largest number of votes in the state for such office; and another of such publications shall be made in a newspaper which advocates the principles of the political party that at the last preceding election for governor cast the next largest number of votes in the state for such office. The clerk or board, in selecting the papers for such publications, shall select those which, according to the best information he can obtain, have a large circulation within such county or city. In making additional publications, the clerk or board shall keep in view the object of giving information, so far as possible, to the voters of all political parties. The clerk or board shall make such publication twice in each newspaper so selected in a county or city in which daily newspapers are published; but if there be no daily newspaper published within the county, one publication only shall be made in each of such newspapers. Should the county clerk find it impracticable to make the publication six days before election day in counties where no daily newspaper is printed, he shall make the same at the earliest possible day thereafter, and before the election.

Chap. 609.

AN ACT to amend the election law, being chapter nine hundred and nine of the laws of eighteen hundred and ninety-six.

Became a law May 19, 1897, with the approval of the Governor.
Passed, a majority being present.

The People of the State of New York, represented in Senate and Assembly, do enact as follows:

Section 1. Section eighty of the election law is hereby amended so as to read as follows:

§ 80. Official ballots for elections.— Official ballots shall be provided at public expense at each polling place for every election at which public officers are to be elected directly by the people, except an election of school district officers or school officers of a city or village at which no other public officer is to be elected, and except an election of officers of a fire district outside of cities and incorporated villages, at which excepted elections any form of ballots which may be adopted and used by the meeting at which such election shall be had shall be legal.

§ 2. This act shall take effect immediately.

Chap. 610.

AN ACT to authorize and direct the comptroller of this state to hear and determine the application of James D. Casey for the redemption of lot one hundred and eighty-one, in town lot sixty-three, on the south side of Buffalo street, in the city of Rochester, Monroe county, New York, from the sale thereof by the comptroller, in the year eighteen hundred and ninety, for unpaid taxes.

Became a law May 19, 1897, with the approval of the Governor.
Passed, three-fifths being present.

The People of the State of New York, represented in Senate and Assembly, do enact as follows:

Jurisdiction to hear applica- tion.

Section 1. Jurisdiction is hereby conferred upon the comptroller of the state to hear and determine the application of James D. Casey for the redemption of lot one hundred and eighty-one, in town lot sixty-three, on the south side of Buffalo street, in the city of Rochester, Monroe county, New York, from the sale thereof for unpaid taxes made by the comptroller in the year eighteen hundred and ninety. The said James D. Casey claiming to be the owner of said land and to have been in the occupation thereof at the time of such sale and ever since, and that no notice to redeem has ever been served on him as prescribed by law; the said comptroller is hereby authorized and directed to act upon such application in the same manner, and with the same effect, as if the application had been made within the time allowed by law for the redemption thereof.

Chap. 611.

AN ACT to amend section two hundred and eleven of the code of criminal procedure, in relation to the jurisdiction of magistrates and their duties in certain cases.

Became a law May 19, 1897, with the approval of the Governor.
Passed, a majority being present.

The People of the State of New York, represented in Senate and Assembly, do enact as follows:

Section 1. Section two hundred and eleven of the code of criminal procedure is hereby amended so as to read as follows:

§ 211. **Defendant to choose how he shall be tried.**— If the crime with which the defendant is charged be one triable, as provided in subdivision thirty-seven of section fifty-six, by a court of special

sessions of the county in which the same was committed, the magistrate, before holding the defendant to answer, must inform him of
his right to be tried by a court of special sessions, and must ask
him how he will be tried. If the defendant shall not require to be
tried by a court of special sessions, he can only be held to answer
to a court having authority to inquire by the intervention of a
grand jury in offenses triable in the county.

§ 2. This act shall take effect October first, eighteen hundred and
ninety-seven.

Chap. 612.

AN ACT in relation to negotiable instruments, constituting chapter fifty of the general laws.

Became a law May 19, 1897, with the approval of the Governor.
Passed, a majority being present.

*The People of the State of New York, represented in Senate and
Assembly, do enact as follows:*

CHAPTER L OF THE GENERAL LAWS.

THE NEGOTIABLE INSTRUMENTS LAW.

ARTICLE I.

General Provisions.

Section 1. Short title.

    2. Definitions and meaning of terms.

    3. Person primarily liable on instrument.

    4. Reasonable time, what constitutes.

    5. Time how computed; when last day falls on holiday.

    6. Application of chapter.

    7. Rule of law merchant; when governs.

Section 1. Short title.—This act shall be known as the negotiable instruments law.

§ 2. Definitions and meaning of terms.—In this act, unless the context otherwise requires:

"Acceptance" means an acceptance completed by delivery or notification.

"Action" includes counter-claim and set-off.

"Bank" includes any person or association of persons carrying on the business of banking, whether incorporated or not.

"Bearer" means the person in possession of a bill or note which is payable to bearer.

"Bill" means bill of exchange, and "note" means negotiable promissory note.

"Delivery" means transfer of possession, actual or constructive, from one person to another.

"Holder" means the payee or indorsee of a bill or note, who is in possession of it, or the bearer thereof.

"Indorsement" means an indorsement completed by delivery.

"Instrument" means negotiable instrument.

"Issue" means the first delivery of the instrument, complete in form to a person who takes it as a holder.

"Person" includes a body of persons, whether incorporated or not.

"Value" means valuable consideration.

"Written" includes printed, and "writing" includes print.

§ 3. Person primarily liable on instrument.—The person "primarily" liable on an instrument is the person who by the terms of the instrument is absolutely required to pay the same. All other parties are "secondarily" liable.

§ 4. Reasonable time, what constitutes.—In determining what is a "reasonable time" or an "unreasonable time" regard is to be had to the nature of the instrument, the usage of trade or business (if any) with respect to such instruments, and the facts of the particular case.

§ 5. Time, how computed; when last day falls on holiday.—Where the day, or the last day, for doing any act herein required or permitted to be done falls on Sunday or on a holiday, the act may be done on the next succeeding secular or business day.

§ 6. Application of chapter.—The provisions of this act do not apply to negotiable instruments made and delivered prior to the passage hereof.

§ 7. Law merchant; when governs.—In any case not provided for in this act the rules of the law merchant shall govern.

ARTICLE II.
FORM AND INTERPRETATION.

Section 20. Form of negotiable instrument.— An instrument to be negotiable must conform to the following requirements:

1. It must be in writing and signed by the maker or drawer.

2. Must contain an unconditional promise or order to pay a sum certain in money;

3. Must be payable on demand, or at a fixed or determinable future time;

4. Must be payable to order or to bearer; and

5. Where the instrument is addressed to a drawee, he must be named or otherwise indicated therein with reasonable certainty.

§ 21. Certainty as to sum; what constitutes.— The sum payable is a sum certain within the meaning of this act although it is to be paid:

1. With interest; or

2. By stated installments; or

3. By stated installments, with a provision that upon default in payment of any installment or of interest, the whole shall become due; or

4. With exchange, whether at a fixed rate or at the current rate; or

5. With costs of collection or an attorney's fee, in case payment shall not be made at maturity.

§ 22. When promise is unconditional.— An unqualified order or promise to pay is unconditional within the meaning of this act, though coupled with:

1. An indication of a particular fund out of which reimbursement is to be made, or a particular account to be debited with the amount; or

2. A statement of the transaction which gives rise to the instrument.

But an order or promises to pay out of a particular fund is not unconditional.

§ 23. Determinable future time; what constitutes.— An instrument is payable at a determinable future time, within the meaning of this act, which is expressed to be payable:

1. At a fixed period after date or sight; or

2. On or before a fixed or determinable future time specified therein; or

3. On or at a fixed period after the occurrence of a specified event, which is certain to happen, though the time of happening be uncertain.

An instrument payable upon a contingency is not negotiable, and the happening of the event does not cure the defect.

§ 24. Additional provisions not affecting negotiability.—An instrument which contains an order or promise to do any act in addition to the payment of money is not negotiable. But the negotiable character of an instrument otherwise negotiable is not affected by a provision which:

1. Authorizes the sale of collateral securities in case the instrument be not paid at maturity; or

2. Authorizes a confession of judgment if the instrument be not paid at maturity; or

3. Waives the benefit of any law intended for the advantage or protection of the obligor; or

4. Gives the holder an election to require something to be done in lieu of payment of money.

But nothing in this section shall validate any provision or stipulation otherwise illegal.

§ 25. Omissions; seal; particular money.—The validity and negotiable character of an instrument are not affected by the fact that:

1. It is not dated; or

2. Does not specify the value given, or that any value has been given therefor; or

3. Does not specify the place where it is drawn or the place where it is payable; or

4. Bears a seal; or

5. Designates a particular kind of current money in which payment is to be made.

But nothing in this section shall alter or repeal any statute requiring in certain cases the nature of the consideration to be stated in the instrument.

§ 26. When payable on demand.—An instrument is payable on demand:

1. Where it is expressed to be payable on demand, or at sight, or on presentation; or

2. In which no time for payment is expressed.

Where an instrument is issued, accepted or indorsed when overdue, it is, as regards the person so issuing, accepting or indorsing it, payable on demand.

§ 27. When payable to order.—The instrument is payable to order where it is drawn payable to the order of a specified person or to him or his order. It may be drawn payable to the order of:

1. A payee who is not maker. drawer or drawee; or
2. The drawee or maker; or
3. The drawee; or
4. Two or more payees jointly; or
5. One or some of several payees; or
6. The holder of an office for the time being.

Where the instrument is payable to order the payee must be named or otherwise indicated therein with reasonable certainty.

§ 28. When payable to bearer.— The instrument is payable to bearer:

1. When it is expressed to be so payable; or
2. When it is payable to a person named therein or bearer; or
3. When it is payable to the order of a fictitious or non-existing person, and such fact was known to the person making it so payable; or
4. When the name of the payee does not purport to be the name of any person; or
5. When the only or last indorsement is an indorsement in blank.

§ 29. Terms when sufficient.— The instrument need not follow the language of this act, but any terms are sufficient which clearly indicate an intention to conform to the requirements hereof.

§ 30. Date, presumption, as to.—Where the instrument or an acceptance or any indorsement thereon is dated, such date is deemed prima facie to be the true date of the making, drawing, acceptance or indorsement as the case may be.

§ 31. Ante-dated and post-dated.—The instrument is not invalid for the reason only that it is ante-dated or post-dated, provided this is not done for an illegal or fraudulent purpose. The person to whom an instrument so dated is delivered acquires the title thereto as of the date of delivery.

§ 32. When date may be inserted.—Where an instrument expressed to be payable at a fixed period after date is issued undated, or where the acceptance of an instrument payable at a fixed period after sight is undated, any holder may insert therein the true date of issue or acceptance, and the instrument shall be payable accordingly. The insertion of a wrong date does not avoid the instrument in the hands of a subsequent holder in due course; but as to him, the date so inserted is to be regarded as the true date.

§ 33. Blanks; when may be filled.—Where the instrument is wanting in any material particular, the person in possession thereof has a prima facie authority to complete it by filling up the blanks therein. And a signature on a blank paper delivered by the person making the signature in order that the paper may be converted into a negotiable instrument operates as a prima facie authority to fill it up as such for any amount. In order, however, that any such instrument when completed, may be enforced against any person who became a party thereto prior to its completion, it must be filled up strictly in accordance with the authority given and within a reasonable time. But if any such instrument, after completion, is negotiable to a holder in due course, it is valid and effectual for all purposes in his hands, and he may enforce it as if it had been filled up strictly in accordance with the authority given and within a reasonable time.

§ 34. Incomplete instrument not delivered.—Where an incomplete instrument has not been delivered it will not, if completed and negotiated, without authority, be a valid contract in the hands of any holder, as against any person whose signature was placed thereon before delivery.

§ 35. Delivery; when effectual; when presumed.—Every contract on a negotiable instrument is incomplete and revocable until delivery of the instrument for the purpose of giving effect thereto. As between immediate parties, and as regards a remote party other than a holder in due course, the delivery, in order to be effectual, must be made either by or under the authority of the party making, drawing, accepting or indorsing, as the case may be; and in such case the delivery may be shown to have been conditional, or for a special purpose only, and not for the purpose of transferring the property in the instrument. But where the instrument is in the hands of a holder in due course, a valid delivery thereof by all parties prior to him so as to make them liable to him is conclusively presumed. And where the instrument is no longer in the possession of a party whose signature appears thereon, a valid and intentional delivery by him is presumed until the contrary is proved.

§ 36. Construction where instrument is ambiguous.—Where the language of the instrument is ambiguous, or there are omissions therein, the following rules of construction apply:

1. Where the sum payable is expressed in words and also in figures and there is a discrepancy between the two, the sum de-

noted by the words is the sum payable; but if the words are ambiguous or uncertain, references may be had to the figures to fix the amount;

2. Where the instrument provides for the payment of interest, without specifying the date from which interest is to run, the interest runs from the date of the instrument, and if the instrument is undated, from the issue thereof;

3. Where the instrument is not dated, it will be considered to be dated as of the time it was issued;

4. Where there is a conflict between the written and printed provisions of the instrument, the written provisions prevail;

5. Where the instrument is so ambiguous that there is doubt whether it is a bill or note, the holder may treat it as either at his election;

6. Where a signature is so placed upon the instrument that it is not clear in what capacity the person making the same intended to sign, he is to be deemed an indorser;

7. Where an instrument containing the words "I promise to pay" is signed by two or more persons, they are deemed to be jointly and severally liable thereon.

§ 37. Liability of person signing in trade or assumed name.— No person is liable on the instrument whose signature does not appear thereon, except as herein otherwise expressly provided. But one who signs in a trade or assumed name will be liable to the same extent as if he had signed in his own name.

§ 38. Signature by agent; authority; how shown.— The signature of any party may be made by a duly authorized agent. No particular form of appointment is necessary for this purpose; and the authority of the agent may be established as in other cases of agency.

§ 39. Liability of person signing as agent, etc.— Where the instrument contains or a person adds to his signature words indicating that he signs for or on behalf of a principal, or in a representative capacity, he is not liable on the instrument if he was duly authorized; but the mere addition of words describing him as an agent, or as filling a representative character, without disclosing his principal, does not exempt him from personal liability.

§ 40. Signature by procuration; effect of.— A signature by "procuration" operates as notice that the agent has but a limited authority to sign, and the principal is bound only in case the agent in so signing acted within the actual limits of his authority.

§ 41. Effect of indorsement by infant or corporation.— The indorsement or assignment of the instrument by a corporation or by an infant passes the property therein, notwithstanding that from want of capacity the corporation or infant may incur no liability thereon.

§ 42. Forged signature; effect of.— Where a signature is forged or made without authority of the person whose signature it purports to be, it is wholly inoperative, and no right to retain the instrument, or to give a discharge therefor, or to enforce payment thereof against any party thereto, can be acquired through or under such signature, unless the party, against whom it is sought to enforce such right, is precluded from setting up the forgery or want of authority.

ARTICLE III.

CONSIDERATION OF NEGOTIABLE INSTRUMENTS.

Section 50. Presumption of consideration.—Every negotiable instrument is deemed prima facie to have been issued for a valuable consideration; and every person whose signature appears thereon to have become a party thereto for value.

§ 51. Consideration, what constitutes.—Value is any consideration sufficient to support a simple contract. An antecedent or preexisting debt constitutes value; and is deemed such whether the instrument is payable on demand or at a future time.

§ 52. What constitutes holder for value.—Where value has at any time been given for the instrument, the holder is deemed a holder for value in respect to all parties who became such prior to that time.

§ 53. When lien on instrument constitutes holder on value.— Where the holder has a lien on the instrument, arising either from contract or by implication of law, he is deemed a holder for value to the extent of his lien.

§ 54. Effect of want of consideration.— Absence or failure of consideration is matter of defense as against any person not a holder in due course; and partial failure of consideration is a defense pro tanto whether the failure is an ascertained and liquidated amount or otherwise.

§ 55. Liability of accommodation indorser.—An accommodation party is one who has signed the instrument as maker, drawer, acceptor or indorser, without receiving value therefor, and for the purpose of lending his name to some other person. Such a person is liable on the instrument to a holder for value, notwithstanding such holder at the time of taking the instrument knew him to be only an accommodation party.

ARTICLE IV.

NEGOTIATION.

Section 60. What constitutes negotiation.—An instrument is negotiated when it is transferred from one person to another in such manner as to constitute the transferee the holder thereof. If payable to bearer it is negotiated by delivery; if payable to order it is negotiated by the indorsement of the holder completed by delivery.

§ 61. Indorsement; how made.—The indorsement must be written on the instrument itself or úpon a paper attached thereto. The signature of the indorser, without additional words, is a sufficient indorsement.

§ 62. Indorsement must be of entire instrument.—The indorsement must be an indorsement of the entire instrument. An indorsement, which purports to transfer to the indorsee a part only of the amount payable, or which purports to transfer the instrument to two or more indorsees severally, does not operate as a negotiation of the instrument. But where the instrument has been paid in part, it may be indorsed as to the residue.

§ 63. Kinds of indorsement.—An indorsement may be either special or in blank; and it may also be either restrictive or qualified, or conditional.

§ 64. Special indorsement; indorsement in blank.—A special indorsement specifies the person to whom, or to whose order the instrument is to be payable; and the indorsement of such indorsee is necessary to the further negotiation of the instrument. An indorsement in blank specifies no indorsee, and an instrument so indorsed is payable to bearer, and may be negotiated by delivery.

§ 65. Blank indorsement; how changed to special indorsement.— The holder may convert a blank indorsement into a special indorsement by writing over the signature of the indorser in blank any contract consistent with the character of the indorsement.

§ 66. When indorsement restrictive.—An indorsement is restrictive, which either:

1. Prohibits the further negotiation of the instrument; or

2. Constitutes the indorsee the agent of the indorser; or

3. Vests the title in the indorsee in trust for or to the use of some other person.

But the mere absence of words implying power to negotiate does not make an indorsement restrictive.

§ 67. Effect of restricting indorsement; rights of indorsee.—A restrictive indorsement confers upon the indorsee the right:

1. To receive payment of the instrument;

2. To bring any action thereon that the indorser could bring;

3. To transfer his rights as such indorsee, where the form of the indorsement authorizes him to do so.

But all subsequent indorsees acquire only the title of the first indorsee under the restrictive indorsement.

§ 68. Qualified indorsement constitutes the indorser a mere assignor of the title to the instrument. It may be made by adding to the indorser's signature the words "without recourse" or any words of similar import. Such an indorsement does not impair the negotiable character of the instrument.

§ 69. Conditional indorsement.—Where an indorsement is conditional, a party required to pay the instrument may disregard the condition, and make payment to the indorsee or his transferee, whether the condition has been fulfilled or not. But any person to whom an instrument so indorsed is negotiated, will hold the same, or the proceeds thereof, subject to the rights of the person indorsing conditionally.

§ 70. Indorsement of instrument payable to bearer.—Where an instrument, payable to bearer, is indorsed specially, it may nevertheless be further negotiated by delivery; but the person indorsing specially is liable as indorser to only such holders as make title through his indorsement.

§ 71. Indorsement where payable to two or more persons.—Where an instrument is payable to the order of two or more payees or indorsees who are not partners, all must indorse, unless the one indorsing has authority to indorse for the others.

§ 72. Effect of instrument drawn or indorsed to a person as cashier.— Where an instrument is drawn or indorsed to a person as "cashier" or other fiscal officer of a bank or corporation, it is deemed prima facie to be payable to the bank or corporation of which he is such officer; and may be negotiated by either the indorsement of the bank or corporation, or the indorsement of the officer.

§ 73. Indorsement where name is misspelled, et cetera.—Where the name of a payee or indorsee is wrongly designated or misspelled, he may indorse the instrument as therein described, adding, if he think fit, his proper signature.

§ 74. Indorsement in representative capacity.— Where any person is under obligation to indorse in a representative capacity, he may indorse in such terms as to negative personal liability.

§ 75. Time of indorsement; presumption.— Except where an indorsement bears date after the maturity of the instrument, every negotiation is deemed prima facie to have been effected before the instrument was overdue.

§ 76. Place of indorsement; presumption.— Except where the contrary appears every indorsement is presumed prima facie to have been made at the place where the instrument is dated.

§ 77. Continuation of negotiable character.— An instrument negotiable in its origin continues to be negotiable until it has been restrictively indorsed or discharged by payment or otherwise.

§ 78. Striking out indorsement.— The holder may at any time strike out any indorsement which is not necessary to his title. The indorser whose indorsement is struck out, and all indorsers subsequent to him, are thereby relieved from liability on the instrument.

§ 79. Transfer without indorsement; effect of.— Where the holder of an instrument payable to his order transfers it for value without indorsing it, the transfer vests in the transferee such title as the transferer had therein, and the transferee acquires, in addition, the right to have the indorsement of the transferer. But for the purpose of determining whether the transferee is a holder in due course, the negotiation takes effect as of the time when the indorsement is actually made.

§ 80. When said party may negotiate instrument.— Where an instrument is negotiated back to a prior party, such party may, subject to the provisions of this act, reissue and further negotiate the same. But he is not entitled to enforce payment thereof against any intervening party to whom he was personally liable.

ARTICLE V.

RIGHTS OF HOLDER.

Section 90. Right of holder to sue; payment.
91. What constitutes a holder in due course.
92. When person not deemed holder in due course.
93. Notice before full amount paid.
94. When title defective.
95. What constitutes notice of defect.
96. Rights of holder in due course.
97. When subject to original defenses.
98. Who deemed holder in due course.

Section 90. Right of holder to sue; payment.—The holder of a negotiable instrument may sue thereon in his own name; and payment to him in due course discharges the instrument.

§ 91. What constitutes a holder in due course.—A holder in due course is a holder who has taken the instrument under the following conditions:

1. That it is complete and regular upon its face;

2. That he became the holder of it before it was overdue, and without notice that it had been previously dishonored, if such was the fact;

3. That he took it in good faith and for value;

4. That at the time it was negotiated to him he had no notice of any infirmity in the instrument or defect in the title of the person negotiating it.

§ 92. When person not deemed holder in due course.—Where an instrument payable on demand is negotiated an unreasonable length of time after its issue, the holder is not deemed a holder in due course.

§ 93. Notice before full amount paid.—Where the transferee receives notice of any infirmity in the instrument or defect in the title of the person negotiating the same before he has paid the full amount agreed to be paid therefor, he will be deemed a holder in due course only to the extent of the amount theretofore paid by him.

§ 94. When title defective.—The title of a person who negotiates an instrument is defective within the meaning of this act when he obtained the instrument, or any signature thereto, by fraud, duress, or force and fear, or other unlawful means, or for an illegal consideration, or when he negotiates it in breach of faith, or under such circumstances as amount to a fraud.

§ 95. What constitutes notice of defect.—To constitute notice of an infirmity in the instrument or defect in the title of the person negotiating the same, the person to whom it is negotiated must have had actual knowledge of the infirmity or defect, or knowledge of such facts that his action in taking the instrument amounted to bad faith.

§ 96. Rights of holder in due course.—A holder in due course holds the instrument free from any defect of title of prior parties and free from defenses available to prior parties among themselves, and may enforce payment of the instrument for the full amount thereof against all parties liable thereon.

§ 97. When subject to original defenses.—In the hands of any holder other than a holder in due course, a negotiable instrument is subject to the same defenses as if it were non-negotiable. But a holder who derives his title through a holder in due course, and who is not himself a party to any fraud or illegality affecting the instrument, has all the rights of such former holder in respect of all parties prior to the latter.

§ 98. Who deemed holder in due course.—Every holder is deemed prima facie to be a holder in due course; but when it is shown that the title of any person who has negotiated the instrument was defective, the burden is on the holder to prove that he or some person under whom he claims acquired the title as a holder in due course. But the last-mentioned rule does not apply in favor of a party who became bound on the instrument prior to the acquisition of such defective title.

ARTICLE VI.

Liabilities of Parties.

Section 110. Liability of maker.
    111. Liability of drawer.
    112. Liability of acceptor.
    113. When person deemed indorser.
    114. Liability of irregular indorser.
    115. Warranty; where negotiation by delivery, et cetera.
    116. Liability of general indorsers.
    117. Liability of indorser where paper negotiable by delivery.
    118. Order in which indorsers are liable.
    119. Liability of agent or broker.

§ 110. Liability of maker.—The maker of a negotiable instrument by making it engages that he will pay it according to its tenor; and admits the existence of the payee and his then capacity to indorse.

§ 111. Liability of drawer.—The drawer by drawing the instrument admits the existence of the payee and his then capacity to indorse; and engages that on due presentment the instrument will be accepted and paid, or both, according to its tenor, and that if it be dishonored, and the necessary proceedings on dishonor be duly taken, he will pay the amount thereof to the holder, or to any subsequent indorser who may be compelled to pay it. But the drawer may insert in the instrument an express stipulation negativing or limiting his own liability to the holder.

§ 112. Liability of acceptor.—The acceptor by accepting the instrument engages that he will pay it according to the tenor of his acceptance; and admits:

1. The existence of the drawer, the genuineness of his signature, and his capacity and authority to draw the instrument; and

2. The existence of the payee and his then capacity to indorse.

§ 113. When person deemed indorser.—A person placing his signature upon an instrument otherwise than as maker, drawer or acceptor is deemed to be an indorser, unless he clearly indicates by appropriate words his intention to be bound in some other capacity.

§ 114. Liability of irregular indorser.—Where a person, not otherwise a party to an instrument, places thereon his signature in blank before delivery, he is liable as indorser in accordance with the following rules:

1. If the instrument is payable to the order of a third person, he is liable to the payee and to all subsequent parties.

2. If the instrument is payable to the order of the maker or drawer, or is payable to bearer, he is liable to all parties subsequent to the maker or drawer.

3. If he signs for the accommodation of the payee, he is liable to all parties subsequent to the payee.

§ 115. Warranty where negotiation by delivery, et cetera.—Every person negotiating an instrument by delivery or by a qualified indorsement, warrants:

1. That the instrument is genuine and in all respects what it purports to be;

2. That he has a good title to it;

3. That all prior parties had capacity to contract;

4. That he has no knowledge of any fact which would impair the validity of the instrument or render it valueless.

But when the negotiation is by delivery only, the warranty extends in favor of no holder other than the immediate transferee. The provisions of subdivision three of this section do not apply to persons negotiating public or corporate securities, other than bills and notes.

§ 116. Liability of general indorser.—Every indorser who indorses without qualification, warrants to all subsequent holders in due course:

1. The matter and things mentioned in subdivisions one, two and three of the next preceding section; and,

2. That the instrument is at the time of his indorsement valid and subsisting.

And, in addition, he engages that on due presentment, it shall be accepted or paid, or both, as the case may be, according to its tenor, and that if it be dishonored, and the necessary proceedings on dishonor be duly taken, he will pay the amount thereof to the holder, or to any subsequent indorser who may be compelled to pay it.

§ 117. Liability of indorser where paper negotiable by delivery.— Where a person places his indorsement on an instrument negotiable by delivery he incurs all the liabilities of an indorser.

§ 118. Order in which indorsers are liable.—As respects one another, indorsers are liable prima facie in the order in which they indorse; but evidence is admissible to show that as between or among themselves they have agreed otherwise. Joint payees or joint indorsees who indorse are deemed to indorse jointly and severally.

§ 119. Liability of agent or broker.—Where a broker or other agent negotiates an instrument without indorsement, he incurs all the liabilities prescribed by section sixty-five of this act, unless he discloses the name of his principal, and the fact that he is acting only as agent.

ARTICLE VII.

PRESENTMENT FOR PAYMENT.

Section 130. Effect of want of demand on principal debtor.—Presentment for payment is not necessary in order to charge the person primarily on the instrument; but if the instrument is, by its terms, payable at a special place, and he is able and willing to pay it there at maturity, such ability and willingness are equivalent to a tender of payment upon his part. But except as herein otherwise provided, presentment for payment is necessary in order to charge the drawer and indorsers.

§ 131. Presentment where instrument is not payable on demand.— Where the instrument is not payable on demand, presentment must be made on the day it falls due. Where it is payable on demand, presentment must be made within a reasonable time after its issue, except that in the case of a bill of exchange, presentment for payment will be sufficient if made within a reasonable time after the last negotiation thereof.

§ 132. What constitutes a sufficient presentment.— Presentment for payment, to be sufficient, must be made:

1. By the holder, or by some person authorized to receive payment on his behalf;

2. At a reasonable hour on a business day;

3. At a proper place as herein defined;

4. To the person primarily liable on the instrument, or if he is absent or inaccessible, to any person found at the place where the presentment is made.

§ 133. Place of presentment.— Presentment for payment is made at the proper place:

1. Where a place of payment is specified in the instrument and it is there presented;

2. Where no place of payment is specified, but the address of the person to make payment is given in the instrument and it is there presented;

3. Where no place of payment is specified and no address is given and the instrument is presented at the usual place of business or residence of the person to make payment;

4. In any case if presented to the person to make payment wherever he can be found, or if presented at his last known place of business or residence.

§ 134. Instrument must be exhibited.— The instrument must be exhibited to the person from whom payment is demanded, and when it is paid must be delivered up to the party paying it.

§ 135. Presentment where instrument payable at bank.— Where the instrument is payable at a bank, presentment for payment must be made during banking hours, unless the person to make payment has no funds there to meet it at any time during the day, in which case presentment at any hour before the bank is closed on that day is sufficient.

§ 136. Presentment where principal debtor is dead.— Where the person primarily liable on the instrument is dead, and no place of payment is specified, presentment for payment must be made to his personal representative, if such there be, and if with the exercise of reasonable diligence, he can be found.

§ 137. Presentment to persons liable as partners.— Where the persons primarily liable on the instrument are liable as partners, and no place of payment is specified, presentment for payment may be made to any one of them, even though there has been a dissolution of the firm.

§ 138. Presentment to joint debtors.—Where there are several persons not partners, primarily liable on the instrument, and no place of payment is specified, presentment must be made to them all.

§ 139. When presentment not required to charge the drawer.— Presentment for payment is not required in order to charge the drawer where he has no right to expect or require that the drawee or acceptor will pay the instrument.

§ 140. When presentment not required to charge the indorser.— Presentment for payment is not required in order to charge an indorser where the instrument was made or accepted for his accommodation, and he has no reason to expect that the instrument will be paid if presented.

§ 141. When delay in making presentment is excused.— Delay in making presentment for payment is excused when the delay is caused by circumstances beyond the control of the holder and not imputable to his default, misconduct or negligence. When the cause of delay ceases to operate, presentment must be made with reasonable diligence.

§ 142. When presentment may be dispensed with.— Presentment for payment is dispensed with:

1. Where after the exercise of reasonable diligence presentment
as required by this act can not be made;

2. Where the drawee is a fictitious person;

3. By waiver of presentment express or implied.

§ 143. When instrument dishonored by non-payment.— The instrument is dishonored by non-payment when:

1. It is duly presented for payment and payment is refused or
can not be obtained; or

2. Presentment is excused and the instrument is overdue and
unpaid.

§ 144. Liability of person secondarily liable, when instrument
dishonored.— Subject to the provisions of this act, when the
instrument is dishonored by non-payment, an immediate right
of recourse to all parties secondarily liable thereon, accrues to
the holder.

§ 145. Time of maturity.— Every negotiable instrument is payable at the time fixed therein without grace. When the day of
maturity falls upon Sunday, or a holiday, the instrument is payable on the next succeeding business day. Instruments falling
due on Saturday are to be presented for payment on the next
succeeding business day, except that instruments payable on
demand may, at the option of the holder be presented for payment before twelve o'clock noon on Saturday when that entire
day is not a holiday.

§ 146. Time; how computed.— Where the instrument is payable at a fixed period after date, after sight, or after the happening of a specified event, the time of payment is determined by
excluding the day from which the time is to begin to run, and by
including the date of payment.

§ 147. Rule where instrument payable at bank.— Where the
instrument is made payable at a bank it is equivalent to an order
to the bank to pay the same for the account of the principal
debtor thereon.

§ 148. What constitutes payment in due course.— Payment is
made in due course when it is made at or after the maturity of
the instrument to the holder thereof in good faith and without
notice that his title is defective.

ARTICLE VIII.

NOTICE OF DISHONOR.

Section 160. To whom notice of dishonor must be given.—Except as herein otherwise provided, when a negotiable instrument has been dishonored by non-acceptance or non-payment, notice of dishonor must be given to the drawer and to each indorser, and any drawer or indorser to whom such notice is not given is discharged.

§ 161. By whom given.—The notice may be given by or on behalf of the holder, or by or on behalf of any party to the instrument who might be compelled to pay it to the holder, and who, upon taking it up would have a right to reimbursement from the party to whom the notice is given.

§ 162. Notice given by agent.—Notice of dishonor may be given by an agent either in his own name or in the name of any party entitled to give notice, whether that party be his principal or not.

§ 163. Effect of notice given on behalf of holder.—Where notice is given by or on behalf of the holder, it enures for the benefit of all subsequent holders and all prior parties who have a right of recourse against the party to whom it is given.

§ 164. Effect where notice is given by party entitled thereto.—Where notice is given by or on behalf of a party entitled to give notice, it enures for the benefit of the holder and all parties subsequent to the party to whom notice is given.

§ 165. When agent may give notice.—Where the instrument has been dishonored in the hands of an agent, he may either himself give notice to the parties liable thereon, or he may give notice to his principal. If he give notice to his principal, he must do so within the same time as if he were the holder, and the principal upon the receipt of such notice has himself the same time for giving notice as if the agent had been an independent holder.

§ 166. When notice sufficient.—A written notice need not be signed and an insufficient written notice may be supplemented and validated by verbal communication.   misdescription of the instrument does not vitiate the notice unless the party to whom the notice is given is in fact misled thereby.

§ 167. Form of notice.—The notice may be in writing or merely oral and may be given in any terms which sufficiently identify the instrument, and indicate that it has been dishonored by non-acceptance or non-payment. It may in all cases be given by delivering it personally or through the mails.

§ 168. To whom notice may be given.—Notice of dishonor may be given either to the party himself or to his agent in that behalf.

§ 169. Notice where party is dead.—When any party is dead, and his death is known to the party giving notice, the notice must be given to a personal representative, if there be one, and if with reasonable diligence, he can be found. If there be no personal representative, notice may be sent to the last residence or last place of business of the deceased.

§ 170. Notice to partners.—Where the parties to be notified are partners notice to any one partner is notice to the firm even though there has been a dissolution.

§ 171. Notice to persons jointly liable.—Notice to joint parties who are not partners must be given to each of them, unless one of them has authority to receive such notice for the others.

§ 172. Notice to bankrupt.—Where a party has been adjudged a bankrupt or an insolvent, or has made an assignment for the benefit of creditors, notice may be given either to the party himself or to his trustee or assignee.

§ 173. Time within which notice must be given.—Notice may be given as soon as the instrument is dishonored; and unless delay is excused as hereinafter provided, must be given within the times fixed by this act.

§ 174. Where parties reside in same place.—Where the person giving and the person to receive notice reside in the same place, notice must be given within the following times:

1. If given at the place of business of the person to receive notice, it must be given before the close of business hours on the day following;

2. If given at his residence, it must be given before the usual hours of rest on the day following;

3. If sent by mail, it must be deposited in the post-office in time to reach him in usual course on the day following.

§ 175. Where parties reside in different places.—Where the person giving and the person to receive notice reside in different places, the notice must be given within the following times:

1. If sent by mail, it must be deposited in the post-office in time to go by mail the day following the day of dishonor, or if there be no mail at a convenient hour on that day, by the next mail thereafter.

2. If given otherwise than through the post-office, then within the time that notice would have been received in due course of mail, if it had been deposited in the post-office within the time specified in the last subdivision.

§ 176. When sender deemed to have given due notice.—Where notice of dishonor is duly addressed and deposited in the post-office, the sender is deemed to have given due notice, notwithstanding any miscarriage in the mails.

§ 177. Deposit in post-office; what constitutes.—Notice is deemed to have been deposited in the post-office when deposited in any branch post-office or in any letter box under the control of the post-office department.

§ 178. Notice to subsequent party; time of.—Where a party receives notice of dishonor, he has, after the receipt of such notice, the same time for giving notice to antecedent parties that the holder has after the dishonor.

§ 179. Where notice must be sent.—Where a party has added an address to his signature, notice of dishonor must be sent to that address; but if he has not given such address, then the notice must be sent as follows:

1. Either to the post-office nearest to his place of residence, or to the post-office where he is accustomed to receive his letters; or

2. If he live in one place, and have his place of business in another, notice may be sent to either place; or

3. If he is sojourning in another place, notice may be sent to the place where he is so sojourning.

But where the notice is actually received by the party within the time specified in this act, it will be sufficient, though not sent in accordance with the requirements of this section.

§ 180. Waiver of notice.—Notice of dishonor may be waived, either before the time of giving notice has arrived, or after the omission to give due notice, and the waiver may be express or implied.

§ 181. Whom affected by waiver.—Where the waiver is embodied in the instrument itself, it is binding upon all parties; but where it is written above the signature of an indorser, it binds him only.

§ 182. Waiver of protest.—A waiver of protest, whether in the case of a foreign bill of exchange or other negotiable instrument, is deemed to be a waiver not only of a formal protest, but also of presentment and notice of dishonor.

§ 183. When notice is dispensed with.—Notice of dishonor is dispensed with when, after the exercise of reasonable diligence, it can not be given to or does not reach the parties sought to be charged.

§ 184. Delay in giving notice; how excused.—Delay in giving notice of dishonor is excused when the delay is caused by circumstances beyond the control of the holder and not imputable to his default, misconduct or negligence. When the cause of delay ceases to operate, notice must be given with reasonable diligence.

§ 185. When notice need not be given to drawer.—Notice of dishonor is not required to be given to the drawer in either of the following cases:

1. Where the drawer and drawee are the same person;

2. Where the drawee is a fictitious person or a person not having capacity to contract;

3. Where the drawer is the person to whom the instrument is presented for payment;

4. Where the drawer has no right to expect or require that the drawee or acceptor will honor the instrument;

5. Where the drawer has countermanded payment.

§ 186. When notice need not be given to indorser.—Notice of dishonor is not required to be given to an indorser in either of the following cases:

1. Where the drawee is a fictitious person or a person not having capacity to contract, and the indorser was aware of the fact at the time he indorsed the instrument;

2. Where the indorser is the person to whom the instrument is presented for payment;

3. Where the instrument was made or accepted for his accommodation.

§ 187. Notice of non-payment where acceptance refused.—Where due notice of dishonor by non-acceptance has been given, notice of a subsequent dishonor by non-payment is not necessary, unless in the meantime the instrument has been accepted.

§ 188. Effect of omission to give notice of non-acceptance.—An omission to give notice of dishonor by non-acceptance does not prejudice the rights of a holder in due course subsequent to the omission.

§ 189. When protest need not be made; when must be made.— Where any negotiable instrument has been dishonored it may be protested for non-acceptance or non-payment, as the case may be; but protest is not required, except in the case of foreign bills of exchange.

ARTICLE IX.
DISCHARGE OF NEGOTIABLE INSTRUMENTS.

§ 200. Instrument; how discharged.—A negotiable instrument is discharged:

1. By payment in due course by or on behalf of the principal debtor;

2. By payment in due course by the party accommodated, where the instrument is made or accepted for accommodation;

3. By the intentional cancellation thereof by the holder;

4. By any other act which will discharge a simple contract for the payment of money;

5. When the principal debtor becomes the holder of the instrument at or after maturity in his own right.

§ 201. When persons secondarily liable on, discharged.—A person secondarily liable on the instrument is discharged:

1. By any act which discharges the instrument;

2. By the intentional cancellation of his signature by the holder;

3. By the discharge of a prior party;

4. By a valid tender of payment made by a prior party.

5. By a release of the principal debtor, unless the holder's right of recourse against the party secondarily liable is expressly reserved;

6. By any agreement binding upon the holder to extend the time of payment or to postpone the holder's right to enforce the instrument, unless the right of recourse against such party is expressly reserved;

§ 202. Right of party who discharges instrument.—Where the instrument is paid by a party secondarily liable thereon, it is not discharged; but the party so paying it is remitted to his former rights as regards all prior parties, and he may strike out his own and all subsequent indorsements, and again negotiate the instrument, except:

1. Where it is payable to the order of a third person, and has been paid by the drawer; and

2. Where it was made or accepted for accommodation, and has been paid by the party accommodated.

§ 203. Renunciation by holder.— The holder may expressly renounce his rights against any party to the instrument, before, at or after its maturity. An absolute and unconditional renunciation of his rights against the principal debtor made at or after the maturity of the instrument, discharges the instrument. But a renunciation does not affect the rights of a holder in due course without notice. A renunciation must be in writing, unless the instrument is delivered up to the person primarily liable thereon.

§ 204. Cancellation; unintentional; burden of proof.—A cancellation made unintentionally, or under a mistake, or without the authority of the holder, is inoperative; but where an instrument or any signature thereon appears to have been canceled the burden of proof lies on the party who alleges that the cancellation was made unintentionally, or under a mistake or without authority.

§ 205. Alteration of instrument; effect of.— Where a negotiable instrument is materially altered without the assent of all parties liable thereon, it is avoided, except as against a party who has himself made, authorized or assented to the alteration and subsequent indorsers. But when an instrument has been materially altered and is in the hands of a holder in due course, not a party to the alteration, he may enforce payment thereof according to its original tenor.

§ 206. What constitutes a material alteration.— Any alteration which changes:

1. The date;
2. The sum payable, either for principal or interest;
3. The time or place of payment;
4. The number or the relations of the parties;
5. The medium or currency in which payment is to be made; ·

Or which adds a place of payment where no place of payment is specified, or any other change or addition which alters the effect of the instrument in any respect, is a material alteration.

ARTICLE X.

BILLS OF EXCHANGE; FORM AND INTERPRETATION.

Section 210. Bill of exchange defined.
211. Bill not an assignment of funds in hands of drawee.
212. Bill addressed to more than one drawee.
213. Inland and foreign bills of exchange.
214. When bill may be treated as promissory note.
215. Drawee in case of need.

Section 210. Bill of exchange defined.—A bill of exchange is an unconditional order in writing addressed by one person to another, signed by the person giving it, requiring the person to whom it is addressed to pay on demand or at a fixed determinable future time a sum certain in money to order or to bearer.

§ 211. Bill not an assignment of funds in hands of drawee.—A bill of itself does not operate as an assignment of the funds in the hands of the drawee available for the payment thereof and the drawee is not liable on the bill unless and until he accepts the same.

§ 212. Bill addressed to more than one drawee.—A bill may be addressed to two or more drawees jointly, whether they are partners or not; but not to two or more drawees in the alternative or in succession.

§ 213. Inland and foreign bills of exchange.—An inland bill of exchange is a bill which is, or on its face purports to be, both drawn and payable within this state. Any other bill is a foreign bill. Unless the contrary appears on the face of the bill, the holder may treat it as an inland bill.

§ 214. When bill may be treated as promissory note.—Where in a bill drawer and drawee are the same person, or where the drawee is a fictitious person, or a person not having capacity to contract, the holder may treat the instrument, at his option, either as a bill of exchange or a promissory note.

§ 215. Drawee in case of need.—The drawer of a bill and any indorser may insert thereon the name of a person to whom the holder may resort in case of need, that is to say, in case the bill is dishonored by non-acceptance or non-payment. Such person is called the referee in case of need. It is in the option of the holder to resort to the referee in case of need or not as he may see fit.

ARTICLE XI.

ACCEPTANCE OF BILLS OF EXCHANGE.

Section 220. Acceptance, how made, et cetera.

221. Holder entitled to acceptance on face of bill.

222. Acceptance by separate instrument.

223. Promise to accept; when equivalent to acceptance.

224. Time allowed drawee to accept.

225. Liability of drawee retaining or destroying bill.

226. Acceptance of incomplete bill.

227. Kinds of acceptances.

228. What constitutes a general acceptance.

229. Qualified acceptance.

230. Rights of parties as to qualified acceptance.

Section 220. Acceptance: how made, et cetera.—The acceptance of a bill is the signification by the drawee of his assent to the order of the drawer. The acceptance must be in writing and signed by the drawer. It must not express that the drawee will perform his promise by any other means than the payment of money.

§ 221. Holder entitled to acceptance on face of bill.—The holder of a bill presenting the same for acceptance may require that the acceptance be written on the bill and if such request is refused, may treat the bill as dishonored.

§ 222. Acceptance by separate instrument.—Where an acceptance is written on a paper other than the bill itself, it does not bind the acceptor except in favor of a person to whom it is shown and who, on the faith thereof, receives the bill for value.

§ 223. Promise to accept; when equivalent to acceptance.—An unconditional promise in writing to accept a bill before it is drawn is deemed an actual acceptance in favor of every person who, upon the faith thereof, receives the bill for value.

§ 224. Time allowed drawee to accept.—The drawee is allowed twenty-four hours after presentment in which to decide whether or not he will accept the bill; but the acceptance if given dates as of the day of presentation.

§ 225. Liability of drawee retaining or destroying bill.—Where a drawee to whom a bill is delivered for acceptance destroys the same, or refuses within twenty-four hours after such delivery, or within such other period as the holder may allow, to return the bill accepted or non-accepted to the holder, he will be deemed to have accepted the same.

§ 226. Acceptance of incomplete bill.—A bill may be accepted before it has been signed by the drawer, or while otherwise incomplete, or when it is overdue, or after it has been dishonored by a previous refusal to accept, or by non-payment. But when a bill payable after sight is dishonored by non-acceptance and the drawee subsequently accepts it, the holder, in the absence of any different agreement, is entitled to have the bill accepted as of the date of the first presentment.

§ 227. Kinds of acceptances.—An acceptance is either general or qualified. A general acceptance assents without qualification to the order of the drawer. A qualified acceptance in express terms varies the effect of the bill as drawn.

§ 228. What constitutes a general acceptancy.—An acceptance to pay at a particular place is a general acceptance unless it expressly states that the bill is to be paid there only and not elsewhere.

§ 229. Qualified acceptance.—An acceptance is qualified, which is:

1. Conditional, that is to say, which makes payment by the acceptor dependent on the fulfillment of a condition therein stated;

2. Partial, that is to say, an acceptance to pay part only of the amount for which the bill is drawn;

3. Local, that is to say, an acceptance to pay only at a particular place;

4. Qualified as to time;

5. The acceptance of some one or more of the drawees, but not of all.

§ 230. Rights of parties as to qualified acceptance.—The holder may refuse to take a qualified acceptance, and if he does not obtain an unqualified acceptance, he may treat the bill as dishonored by non-acceptance. Where a qualified acceptance is taken, the drawer and indorsers are discharged from liability on the bill, unless they have expressly or impliedly authorized the holder to take a qualified acceptance, or subsequently assent thereto. When the drawer or an indorser receives notice of a qualified acceptance, he must within a reasonable time express his dissent to the holder, or he will be deemed to have assented thereto.

ARTICLE XII.

PRESENTMENT OF BILLS OF EXCHANGE FOR ACCEPTANCE.

Section 240. When presentment for acceptance must be made.
241. When failure to present releases drawer and indorser.
242. Presentment; how made.
243. On what days presentment may be made.
244. Presentment; where time is insufficient.
245. When presentment is excused.
246. When dishonored by non-acceptance.
247. Duty of holder where bill not accepted.
248. Rights of holder where bill not accepted.

Section 240. When presentment for acceptance must be made.—Presentment for acceptance must be made:

1. Where the bill is payable after sight, or in any other case where presentment for acceptance is necessary in order to fix the maturity of the instrument; or

2. Where the bill expressly stipulates that it shall be presented for acceptance; or

3. Where the bill is drawn payable elsewhere than at the residence or place of business of the drawee.

In no other case is presentment for acceptance necessary in order to render any party to the bill liable.

§ 241. When failure to present releases drawer and indorser.— Except as herein otherwise provided, the holder of a bill which is required by the next preceding section to be presented for acceptance must either present it for acceptance or negotiate it within a reasonable time. If he fails to do so, the drawer and all indorsers are discharged.

§ 242. Presentment; how made.—Presentment for acceptance must be made by or on behalf of the holder at a reasonable hour, on a business day, and before the bill is overdue, to the drawer or some person authorized to accept or refuse acceptance on his behalf; and

1. Where a bill is addressed to two or more drawees who are not partners, presentment must be made to them all, unless one has authority to accept or refuse acceptance for all, in which case presentment may be made to him only;

2. Where the drawee is dead, presentment may be made to his personal representative;

3. Where the drawee has been adjudged a bankrupt or an insolvent, or has made an assignment for the benefit of creditors, presentment may be made to him or to his trustee or assignee.

§ 243. On what days presentment may be made.—A bill may be presented for acceptance on any day on which negotiable instruments may be presented for payment under the provisions of sections seventy-two and eighty-five of this act. When Saturday is not otherwise a holiday, presentment for acceptance may be made before twelve o'clock noon on that day.

§ 244. Presentment where time is insufficient.—Where the holder of a bill drawn payable elsewhere than at the place of business or the residence of the drawee has not time with the exercise of reasonable diligence to present the bill for acceptance before presenting it for payment on the day that it falls due, the delay caused by presenting the bill for acceptance before presenting it for payment is excused and does not discharge the drawers and indorsers.

§ 245. Where presentment is excused.—Presentment for acceptance is excused and a bill may be treated as dishonored by non-acceptance in either of the following cases:

1. Where the drawee is dead, or has absconded, or is a fictitious person or a person not having capacity to contract by bill;

2. Where after the exercise of reasonable diligence, presentment can not be made;

3. Where although presentment has been irregular, acceptance has been refused on some other ground.

§ 246. When dishonored by non-acceptance.—A bill is dishonored by non-acceptance:

1. When it is duly presented for acceptance, and such an acceptance as is prescribed by this act is refused or can not be obtained; or

2. When presentment for acceptance is excused and the bill is not accepted.

§ 247. Duty of holder where bill not accepted.—Where a bill is duly presented for acceptance and is not accepted within the prescribed time, the person presenting it must treat the bill as dishonored by non-acceptance or he loses the right of recourse against the drawer and indorsers.

§ 248. Rights of holder where bill not accepted.—When a bill is dishonored by non-acceptance, an immediate right of recourse against the drawers and indorsers accrues to the holder and no presentment for payment is necessary.

ARTICLE XIII.
PROTEST OF BILLS OF EXCHANGE.

Section 260. In what cases protest necessary.
      261. Protest; how made.
      262. Protest; by whom made.
      263. Protest; when to be made.
      264. Protest; where made.
      265. Protest both for non-acceptance and non-payment.
      266. Protest before maturity where acceptor insolvent.
      267. When protest dispensed with.
      268. Protest; where bill is lost, et cetera.

Section 260. In what cases protest necessary.— Where a foreign bill appearing on its face to be such is dishonored by non-acceptance, it must be duly protested for non-acceptance, and where such a bill which has not previously been dishonored by non-acceptance is dishonored by non-payment, it must be duly protested for non-payment. If it is not so protested, the drawer and indorsers are discharged. Where a bill does not appear on its face to be a foreign bill, protest thereof in case of dishonor is unnecessary.

§ 261. Protest; how made.— The protest must be annexed to

the bill, or must contain a copy thereof, and must be under the hand and seal of the notary making it, and must specify:

1. The time and place of presentment;

2. The fact that presentment was made and the manner thereof;

3. The cause or reason for protesting the bill;

4. The demand made and the answer given, if any, or the fact that the drawee or acceptor could not be found.

§ 262. Protest; by whom made.— Protest may be made by:

1. A notary public; or

2. By any respectable resident of the place where the bill is dishonored, in the presence of two or more credible witnesses.

§ 263. Protest; when to be made.— When a bill is protested, such protest must be made on the day of its dishonor, unless delay is excused as herein provided. When a bill has been duly noted, the protest may be subsequently extended as of the date of the noting.

§ 264. Protest; where made.— A bill must be protested at the place where it is dishonored, except that when a bill drawn payable at the place of business or residence of some person other than the drawee, has been dishonored by non-acceptance, it must be protested for non-payment at the place where it is expressed to be payable, and no further presentment for payment to, or demand on, the drawee is necessary.

§ 265. Protest both for non-acceptance and non-payment.— A bill which has been protested for non-acceptance may be subsequently protested for non-payment.

§ 266. Protest before maturity where acceptor insolvent.— Where the acceptor has been adjudged a bankrupt or an insolvent or has made an assignment for the benefit of creditors, before the bill matures, the holder may cause the bill to be protested for better security against the drawer and indorsers.

§ 267. When protest is dispensed with.— Protest is dispensed with by any circumstances which would dispense with notice of dishonor. Delay in noting or protesting is excused when delay is caused by circumstances beyond the control of the holder and not imputable to his default, misconduct, or negligence. When the cause of delay ceases to operate, the bill must be noted or protested with reasonable diligence.

§ 268. Protest where bill is lost, et cetera.—Where a bill is lost or destroyed or is wrongly detained from the person entitled to hold it, protest may be made on a copy or written particulars thereof.

ARTICLE XIV.

ACCEPTANCE OF BILLS OF EXCHANGE FOR HONOR.

Section 280.—When bill may be accepted for honor.—Where a bill of exchange has been protested for dishonor by non-acceptance or protested for better security and is not overdue, any person not being a party already liable thereon, may, with the consent of the holder, intervene and accept the bill supra protest for the honor of any party liable thereon or for the honor of the person whose account the bill is drawn. The acceptance for honor may be for part only of the sum for which the bill is drawn; and where there has been an acceptance for honor for one party, there may be a further acceptance by a different person for the honor of another party.

§ 281. Acceptance for honor; how made.—An acceptance for honor supra protest must be in writing and indicate that it is an acceptance for honor, and must be signed by the acceptor for honor.

§ 282. When deemed to be an acceptance for honor of the drawer. —Where an acceptance for honor does not expressly state for whose honor it is made, it is deemed to be an acceptance for the honor of the drawer.

§ 283. Liability of acceptor for honor.—The acceptor for honor is liable to the holder and to all parties to the bill subsequent to the party for whose honor he has accepted.

§ 284. Agreement of acceptor for honor.—The acceptor for honor by such acceptance engages that he will on due presentment pay the bill according to the terms of his acceptance, provided it shall not have been paid by the drawee, and provided also, that it shall have been duly presented for payment and protested for non-payment and notice of dishonor given to him.

§ 285. Maturity of bill payable after sight; accepted for honor.—Where a bill payable after sight is accepted for honor, its maturity is calculated from the date of the noting for non-acceptance and not from the date of the acceptance for honor.

§ 286. Protest of bill accepted for honor, et cetera.—Where a dishonored bill has been accepted for honor supra protest or contains a reference in case of need, it must be protested for non-payment before it is presented for payment to the acceptor for honor or referee in case of need.

§ 287. Presentment for payment to acceptor for honor; how made.—Presentment for payment to the acceptor for honor must be made as follows:

1. If it is to be presented in the place where the protest for non-payment was made, it must be presented not later than the day following its maturity;

2. If it is to be presented in some other place than the place where it was protested, then it must be forwarded within the time specified in section one hundred and four.

§ 288. When delay in making presentment is excused.—The provisions of section eighty-one apply where there is delay in making presentment to the acceptor for honor or referee in case of need.

§ 289. Dishonor of bill by acceptor for honor.—When the bill is dishonored by the acceptor for honor it must be protested for non-payment by him.

ARTICLE XV.

PAYMENT OF BILLS OF EXCHANGE FOR HONOR.

Section 300. Who may make payment for honor.

301. Payment for honor; how made.

302. Declaration before payment for honor.

303. Preference of parties offering to pay for honor.

304. Effect on subsequent parties where bill is paid for honor.

305. Where holder refuses to receive payment supra protest.

306. Rights of payer for honor.

Section 300. Who may make payment for honor.—Where a bill has been protested for non-payment, any person may intervene and pay it supra protest for the honor of any person liable thereon or for the honor of the person for whose account it was drawn.

§ 301. Payment for honor how made.— The payment for honor supra protest in order to operate as such and not as a mere voluntary payment must be attested by a notarial act of honor which may be appended to the protest or form an extension to it.

§ 302. Declaration before payment for honor.—The notarial act of honor must be founded on a declaration made by the payer for honor or by his agent in that behalf declaring his intention to pay the bill for honor and for whose honor he pays.

§ 303. Preference of parties offering to pay for honor.—Where two or more persons offer to pay a bill for the honor of different parties, the person whose payment will discharge most parties to the bill is to be given the preference.

§ 304. Effect on subsequent parties where bill is paid for honor.— Where a bill has been paid for honor all parties subsequent to the party for whose honor it is paid are discharged, but the payor for honor is subrogated for, and succeeds to, both the rights and duties of the holder as regards the party for whose honor he pays and all parties liable to the latter.

§ 305. Where holder refuses to receive payment supra protest.— Where the holder of a bill refuses to receive payment supra protest, he loses his right of recourse against any party who would have been discharged by such payment.

§ 306. Rights of payer for honor.—The payer for honor on paying to the holder the amount of the bill and the notarial expenses incidental to its dishonor, is entitled to receive both the bill itself and the protest.

ARTICLE XVI.
BILLS IN A SET.

Section 310. Bills in sets constitute one bill.
     311. Rights of holders where different parts are negotiated.
     312. Liability of holder who indorses two or more parts of a set to different persons.
     313. Acceptance of bills drawn in sets.
     314. Payment by acceptor of bills drawn in sets.
     315. Effect of discharging one of a set.

Section 310. Bills in sets constitute one bill.—Where a bill is drawn in a set, each part of the set being numbered and containing a reference to the other parts, the whole of the parts constitute one bill.

§ 311. Rights of holders where different parts are negotiated.— Where two or more parts of a set are negotiated to different holders in due course, the holder whose title first accrues is as between such holders the true owner of the bill.   But nothing in this section affects the rights of a person who in due course accepts or pays the part first presented to him.

§ 312. Liability of holder who indorses two or more parts of a set to different persons.—Where the holder of a set indorses two or more parts to different persons he is liable on every such part, and every indorser subsequent to him is liable on the part he has himself indorsed, as if such parts were separate bills.

§ 313. Acceptance of bills drawn in sets.—The acceptance may be written on any part and it must be written on one part only. If the drawee accepts more than one part, and such accepted parts are negotiated to different holders in due course, he is liable on every such part as if it were a separate bill.

§ 314. Payment by acceptor of bills drawn in sets.—When the acceptor of a bill drawn in a set pays it without requiring the part bearing his acceptance to be delivered up to him, and that part at maturity is outstanding in the hands of a holder in due course, he is liable to the holder thereon.

§ 315. Effect of discharging one of a set.—Except as herein otherwise provided where any one part of a bill drawn in a set is discharged by payment or otherwise the whole bill is discharged.

ARTICLE XVII.

PROMISSORY NOTES AND CHECKS.

Section   320. Promissory note defined.

321. Check defined.

322. Within what time a check must be presented.

323. Certification of check; effect of.

324. Effect where holder of check procures it to be certified.

325. When check operates as an assignment.

Section 320. Promissory note defined.—A negotiable promissory note within the meaning of this act is an unconditional promise in writing made by one person to another signed by the maker engaging to pay on demand or at a fixed or determinable future time, a sum certain in money to order or to bearer. Where a note is drawn to the maker's own order, it is not complete until indorsed by him.

§ 321. Check defined.—A check is a bill of exchange drawn on a bank payable on demand. Except as herein otherwise provided, the provisions of this act applicable to a bill of exchange payable on demand apply to a check.

§ 322. Within what time a check must be presented.—A check must be presented for payment within a reasonable time after its issue or the drawer will be discharged from liability thereon to the extent of the loss caused by the delay.

§ 323. Certification of check; effect of.—Where a check is certified by the bank on which it is drawn the certificate is equivalent to an acceptance.

§ 324. Effect where the holder of check procures it to be certified.—Where the holder of a check procures it to be accepted or certified the drawer and all indorsers are discharged from liability thereon.

§ 325. When check operates as an assignment.—A check of itself does not operate as an assignment of any part of the funds to the credit of the drawer with the bank, and the bank is not liable to the holder, unless and until it accepts or certifies the check.

ARTICLE XVIII.

NOTES GIVEN FOR A PATENT RIGHTS AND FOR A SPECULATIVE
CONSIDERATION.

Section 330. Negotiable instruments given for patent rights.

331. Negotiable instruments given for a speculative consideration.

332. How negotiable bonds are made non-negotiable.

Section 330. Negotiable instruments given for patent rights.—A promissory note or other negotiable instrument, the consideration of which consists wholly or partly of the right to make, use or sell any invention claimed or represented by the vendor at the time of sale to be patented, must contain the words "given for a patent right" prominently and legibly written or printed on the face of such note or instrument above the signature thereto; and such note or instrument in the hands of any purchaser or holder is subject to the same defenses as in the hands of the original holder; but this section does not apply to a negotiable instrument given solely for the purchase price or the use of a patented article.

§ 331. Negotiable instrument for a speculative consideration.— If the consideration of a promissory note or other negotiable instrument consists in whole or in part of the purchase price of any farm product, at a price greater by at least four times than the fair market value of the same product at the time, in the locality, or of the membership and rights in an association, company or combination to produce or sell any farm product at a fictitious rate, or of a contract or bond to purchase or sell any farm product at a price greater by four times than the market value of the same product at the time in the locality, the words, "given for a speculative consideration," or other words clearly showing the nature of the consideration must be prominently and legibly written or printed on the face of such note or instrument above the signature thereof; and such note or instrument, in the hands of any purchaser or holder, is subject to the same defenses as in the hands of the original owner or holder.

§ 332. How negotiable bonds are made non-negotiable.—The owner or holder of any corporate or municipal bond or obligation (except such as are designated to circulate as money, payable to bearer), heretofore or hereafter issued in and payable in this state, but not registered in pursuance of any state law, may make such bond or obligation, or the interest coupon accompanying the same, non-negotiable, by subscribing his name to a statement indorsed thereon, that such bond, obligation or coupon is his property; and thereon the principal sum therein mentioned is payable only to such owner or holder, or his legal representatives or assigns, unless such bond, obligation or coupon be transferred by indorsement in blank, or payable to bearer, or to order, with the addition of the assignor's place of residence.

ARTICLE XIX.
Laws Repealed; When to Take Effect.

Section 340. Laws repealed.

341. When to take effect.

Section 340. Laws repealed.—The laws or parts thereof specified in the schedule hereto annexed are hereby repealed.

§ 341. When to take effect.—This chapter shall take effect on the first day of October, eighteen hundred and ninety-seven.

SCHEDULE OF LAWS REPEALED.

Revised Statutes.			Sections.	Subject matter.
R. S., pt. II, ch. 4, tit. II........			All........	Bills and notes.

Laws of—	Chap.	Sections.	Subject matter.
1835....	141.....	All.....	Notice of protest; how given.
1857....	416.....	All.....	Commercial paper.
1865....	309.....	All.....	Protest of foreign bills, etc.
1870....	438.....	All.....	Negotiability of corporate bonds; how limited.
1871....	84.....	All.....	Negotiable bonds; how made non-negotiable.
1873....	595.....	All.....	Negotiable bonds; how made negotiable.
1877....	65.....	1, 3.....	Negotiable instruments given for patent rights.
1887....	461.....	All.....	Effect of holidays upon payment of commercial paper.
1888....	229.....	All.....	One hundredth anniversary of the inauguration of George Washington.
1891....	262.....	1.....	Negotiable instruments given for a speculative consideration.
1894....	607.....	All.....	Days of grace abolished.

Chap. 613.

AN ACT to amend the penal code, relative to violation of the negotiable instruments law.

Became a law May 19, 1897, with the approval of the Governor.
Passed, a majority being present.

The People of the State of New York, represented in Senate and Assembly, do enact as follows:

Section 1. The penal code is hereby amended by inserting at the end of title twelve the following new sections:

§ 384m. **Notes given for patent rights.**—A person who takes, sells or transfers a promissory note or other negotiable instrument, knowing the consideration of such note or instrument to consist in whole or in part, of the right to make, use or sell any patent invention or inventions, or any invention claimed or represented to be patented, without having the words "given for a patent right" written or printed legibly and prominently on the face of such note or instrument above the signature thereto, is guilty of a misdemeanor.

§ 384n. **Notes given for a speculative consideration.**—A person who takes, sells or transfers a promissory note or other negotiable instrument, knowing the consideration of such note or instrument to consist in whole or in part of the purchase price of any farm product at a price greater by four or more times than the fair market value of the same product at the time in the locality, or in which the consideration shall be in whole or in part, membership of and rights in an association, company or combination to produce or sell any farm product at a fictitious rate, or of a contract or bond to purchase or sell any farm product at such rate, without having the words "given for a speculative consideration," or other words clearly showing the nature of the consideration prominently and legibly written or printed on the face of such note or instrument above the signature thereof is guilty of a misdemeanor

§ 2. Section two of chapter sixty-five of the laws of eighteen hundred and seventy-seven, and section two of chapter two hundred and sixty-two of the laws of eighteen hundred and ninety-one are hereby repealed.

§ 3. This act shall take effect the first day of October, eighteen hundred and ninety-seven.

Chap. 614.

AN ACT to amend the statutory construction law, in relation to public holidays.

Became a law May 19, 1897, with the approval of the Governor.

Passed, a majority being present.

The People of the State of New York, represented in Senate and Assembly, do enact as follows:

Section 1. Section twenty-four of chapter six hundred and seventy-seven of the laws of eighteen hundred and ninety-two, entitled "An act relating to the construction of statutes, constituting chapter one of the general laws," is hereby amended to read as follows:

§ 24. **Public Holidays; half holidays.**— The term holiday includes the following days in each year: the first day of January, known as New Year's day; the twelfth day of February, known as

Lincoln's birthday; the twenty-second day of February, known as Washington's birthday; the thirtieth day of May, known as Memorial day; the fourth day of July, known as Independence day; the first Monday of September, known as Labor day, and the twenty-fifth day of December, known as Christmas day, and if either of such days is Sunday, the next day thereafter; each general election day and each day appointed by the president of the United States or by the governor of this state as a day of general thanksgiving, general fasting and prayer, or other general religious observances. The term, half-holiday, includes the period from noon to midnight of each Saturday which is not a holiday. The days and half days aforesaid shall be considered as the first day of the week, commonly called Sunday, and as public holidays or half-holidays, for all purposes whatsoever as regards the transaction of business in the public offices of this state, or counties of this state. On all other days and half days, excepting Sundays, such offices shall be kept open for the transaction of business.

§ 2. Chapter twenty-seven of the laws of eighteen hundred and seventy-five, chapter thirty of the laws of eighteen hundred and eighty-one, chapter two hundred and eighty-nine of the laws of eighteen hundred and eighty-seven and chapter six hundred and three of the laws of eighteen hundred and ninety-five, are hereby repealed.

§ 3. This act shall take effect October first, eighteen hundred and ninety-seven.

Chap. 619.

AN ACT to amend section seven hundred and fifty-nine of the code of criminal procedure, relative to the argument of appeals.

Became a law May 19, 1897, with the approval of the Governor.
Passed, a majority being present.

The People of the State of New York, represented in Senate and Assembly, do enact as follows:

Section 1. Section seven hundred and fifty-nine of the code of criminal procedure, is hereby amended so as to read as follows:

§ 759. Appeal, by whom and how brought to argument.— When the return is made the appeal may be brought to argument by the defendant, on any day in term, upon a notice of not less than five days before the term to the district attorney of the county, and must be so brought to argument within one year after the return has been filed in the office of the county clerk.

§ 2. This act shall take effect September first, eighteen hundred and ninety-seven.

Chap. 620.

AN ACT to exempt the real estate of the Montefiore home for chronic invalids from taxation, assessments and water rates.

Accepted by the city.

Became a law May 19, 1897, with the approval of the Governor.
Passed, three-fifths being present.

The People of the State of New York, represented in Senate and Assembly, do enact as follows:

Section 1. The real estate now owned or which may be here- Exemption after acquired by the Montefiore home for chronic invalids, a of real estate from corporation created by and under the laws of the state of New York taxation, etc. for charitable and benevolent purposes, shall so long as said property shall be held or used exclusively for the charitable and benevolent purposes of said corporation be exempt from any and all taxes, assessments and water rates heretofore or hereafter imposed, assessed or levied ; and the officer, officers and official bodies having charge of such taxes, assessments and water rates, are hereby required and directed to cancel and discharge any and all of such taxes, assessments and water rates from the records of any department wherein they now or hereafter may exist.

§ 2. This act shall take effect immediately.

Chap. 621.

AN ACT to amend sections five and eighty of chapter seven hundred and twenty-three of the laws of eighteen hundred and ninety-five, entitled "An act in relation to religious corporations, constituting chapter forty-two of the general laws," as amended by chapters three hundred and thirty-six and three hundred and thirty-seven of the laws of eighteen hundred and ninety-six, and further to amend the said act by adding an additional article thereto.

Became a law May 19, 1897, with the approval of the Governor.
Passed, a majority being present.

The People of the State of New York, represented in Senate and Assembly, do enact as follows:

Section 1. Section five of chapter seven hundred and twenty-three of the laws of eighteen hundred and ninety-five, known as the "religious corporations law," as amended by chapters three hundred and thirty-six and three hundred and thirty-seven of the laws of eighteen hundred and ninety-six, is hereby amended so as to read as follows:

§ 5. General powers and duties of trustees of religious corporations.— The trustees of every religious corporation shall have the custody and control of all the temporalities and property, real or personal, belonging to the corporation and of the revenues therefrom, and shall administer the same in accordance with the discipline, rules and usages of the corporation and of the ecclesiastical governing body, if any, to which the corporation is subject, and with the provisions of law relating thereto, for the support and maintenance of the corporation, or, providing the members of the corporation at a meeting thereof shall so authorize, of some religious, charitable, benevolent or educational object conducted by said corporation or in connection with it, or with the denomination, if any, with which it is connected; and they shall not use such property or revenues for any other purpose or divert the same from such uses. By-laws may be adopted or amended, by a two-thirds vote of the qualified voters present and voting at the meeting for incorporation or at any subsequent meeting, after written notice, embodying such by-laws or amendment, has been openly given at a previous meeting, and also in the notices of the meeting at which such proposed by-laws or amendment is to be acted upon. By-laws thus adopted or amended shall control the action of the trustees. But this section does not give to the trustees of an incorporated church, any control over the calling, settlement, dismissal or removal of its minister, or the fixing of his salary; or any power to fix or change the times, nature or order of the public or social worship of such church.

§ 2. Section eighty of said act is hereby amended so as to read as follows:

§ 80. **Application of this article.**—This article is not applicable to a Baptist church, a Congregational or Independent church, a Protestant Episcopal church, a Roman Catholic church or a Christian Orthodox Catholic church of the Eastern Confession. No provision of this article is applicable to a Reformed church in America, a true Reformed Dutch church in the United States of America, a Presbyterian church in connection with the Presbyterian church in the United States of America, a Reformed Presbyterian church, or to an Evangelical Lutheran church, incorporated after October first, eighteen hundred and ninety-five, except as declared to be su applicable by the next preceding article of this chapter; this article is applicable to an Evangelical Lutheran church incorporated before October first, eighteen hundred and ninety-five, if the trustees thereof were then elective as such and so long as they continue to be elective as such. The next preceding article of this chapter is applicable to an Evangelical Lutheran church incorporated before October first, eighteen hundred and ninety-five, if its trustees were not then elective as such and so long as its trustees continue not to be elective as such. This article is applicable to churches of all other denominations.

§ 3. The said chapter seven hundred and twenty-three of the laws of eighteen hundred and ninety-five, as amended by the said laws of eighteen hundred and ninety-six, is hereby amended by adding thereto, immediately after section seventy-seven, a new article, in the words and figures following:

ARTICLE VI.

SPECIAL PROVISIONS FOR THE INCORPORATION AND GOVERNMENT OF CON-
GREGATIONAL AND INDEPENDENT CHURCHES.

Section 78.   Notice of meeting for incorporation.

   78a.   The meeting for incorporation.

   78b.   The certificate of incorporation.

   78c.   Time, place and notice of corporate meetings.

§ 78. Notice of meeting for incorporation.—Notice of a meeting
for the purpose of incorporating an unincorporated Congregational
or Independent church shall be given as follows: The
notice shall be in writing, and shall state, in substance,
that a meeting of such unincorporated church will be held
at its usual place of worship at a specified day and hour,
for the purpose of incorporating such church, electing trustees
thereof, and selecting a corporate name therefor. The notice must
be signed by at least six persons of full age, who have statedly
worshipped with such church and have regularly contributed to its
support, according to its usages, for at least one year or since it
was formed. A copy of such notice shall be publicly read at a
regular meeting of such unincorporated church for public worship,
on the two successive Sundays immediately preceding the meeting,
by the minister of such church, or a deacon thereof or by any person
qualified to sign such notice.

§ 78a. The meeting for incorporation.—At the meeting for incorporation, held in pursuance of such notice, the qualified voters,
until otherwise decided as hereinafter provided, shall be all persons of full age who have statedly worshipped with such church
and have regularly contributed to its support, according to its
usages, for at least one year or since it was formed. At such
meeting the presence of a majority of such qualified voters, at least
six in number, shall be necessary to constitute a quorum, and all
matters or questions shall be decided by a majority of the qualified
voters voting thereon. The meeting shall be called to order by
one of the signers of the call. There shall be elected at such meeting, from the qualified voters then present, a presiding officer, a
clerk to keep the record of proceedings of the meeting and two
inspectors of election to receive the ballots cast. The presiding
officer and the inspectors shall decide the result of the ballots cast

on any matter, and shall be the judges of the qualifications of the voters. If the meeting shall decide that such unincorporated church shall become incorporated, the meeting shall also decide upon the name of the proposed corporation, the number of the trustees thereof, which shall be three, six or nine, and the date, not more than fifteen months thereafter, on which the first annual election of the trustees thereof shall be held; and it may, by a two-thirds vote, decide that all members of the unincorporated church, of full age, in good and regular standing, who have stately worshipped with such church but who have not contributed to the financial support thereof, shall also be qualified voters at such meeting, and that such church members, who, for one year next preceding any subsequent corporate meeting, shall have stately worshipped with such church and have been members thereof in good and regular standing, but have not regularly contributed to the financial support thereof, shall be qualified voters at such corporate meetings. Such meeting shall thereupon elect by ballot from the persons qualified to vote thereat one-third of the number of trustees so decided on, who shall hold office until the first annual election of trustees thereafter, and one-third of such number of trustees who shall hold office until the second annual election of trustees thereafter, one-third of such number of trustees who shall hold office until the third annual election of trustees thereafter, or until the respective successors of such trustees shall be elected. Such meeting shall also elect by ballot a clerk of the corporation, who shall hold his office until the close of the next annual meeting.

§ 78b. The certificate of incorporation.— If the meeting shall decide that such unincorporated church shall become incorporated, the presiding officer of such meeting and the two inspectors of election shall execute a certificate setting forth the name of the proposed corporation, the number of the trustees thereof, the names of the persons elected as trustees, the terms of office for which they were respectively elected and the county and town, city or village in which its principal place of worship is or is intended to be located. On the filing and recording of such certificate, after it shall have been acknowledged or proved as hereinbefore provided, the persons qualified to vote at such meeting and those persons who shall thereafter, from time to time, be qualified voters at the corporate meetings thereof, shall be a corporation by the name stated in such certificate, and the persons therein stated to be elected trustees of such church shall be the trustees thereof for the terms for which they were respectively elected and until their respective successors shall be elected.

§ 78c. Time, place and notice of corporate meetings.— The annual corporate meeting of every church incorporated under this article shall be held at the time and place fixed by its by-laws, or if no time and place be so fixed, then at a time and place to be first fixed by its trustees, but to be changed only by a by-law adopted at an annual meeting. A special corporate meeting of any such church may be called by the board of trustees thereof, on its own motion, and shall be called on the written request of at least ten qualified voters of such church. The trustees shall cause notice of the time and place of its annual corporate meeting, and of the names of any trustees whose successors are to be elected thereat, and if a special meeting, of the business to be transacted thereat, to be publicly read by the minister of such church or any trustees thereof at a regular meeting of the church for public worship, on the two successive Sundays immediately preceding such meeting.

§ 78d. Organization and conduct of corporate meetings; qualification of voters.— At every corporate meeting of a church incorporated under this article all persons of full age who, for one year next preceding such meeting, have statedly worshipped with such church and have regularly contributed to its financial support, according to its usages, and no others, shall be qualified voters; but, if so decided, by a two-thirds vote at the original meeting or at any annual corporate meeting thereof, after notice of intention so to do has been given with every notice of such meeting, all members of such church of full age and in good and regular standing, by admission into full communion or membership therewith, who have statedly worshipped with such church, for one year next preceding the meeting at which they vote, may also be admitted as qualified voters at corporate meetings. At such corporate meetings, the presence of at least six persons qualified to vote thereat shall be necessary to constitute a quorum; and all matters or questions shall be decided by a majority of the qualified voters voting thereon, except that by-laws can be adopted or amended only by a two-thirds vote. The clerk of the corporation shall call the meeting to order; and under his supervision the qualified voters then present shall choose a presiding officer and two inspectors of election to receive the ballots cast. The presiding officer and the inspectors of election shall declare the result of the ballots cast on any

matter and shall be the judges of the qualifications of voters. At
each annual corporate meeting, successors to those trustees whose
terms of office then expire shall be elected by ballot from the qualified voters, for a term of three years thereafter, and until their successors shall be elected. A clerk of the corporation shall be elected
by ballot, who shall hold office until the close of the next annual
meeting, and until his successor shall be elected.

§ 78e. Changing date of annual corporate meetings.—An annual
corporate meeting of any church incorporated under this article
may change the date of its subsequent annual meetings. If the
date fixed for the annual meeting shall be less than six months.
after the annual meeting at which such change is made, the next
annual meeting shall be held one year from the date so fixed. For
the purpose of determining the terms of office of trustees, the time
between the annual meeting at which such change is made and the
next annual meeting thereafter shall be reckoned as one year.

§ 78f. Changing number of trustees.— Any such incorporated
church may, at an annual corporate meeting, change the number
of its trustees to three, six or nine, classifying them so that the
terms of one-third expire each year, provided that notice of such
intended change be included in the notice of such annual corporate
meeting. No such change shall affect the terms of the trustees
then in office; and if the change reduces the number of trustees,
elections shall not be held to fill the vacancies caused by the expiration of the terms of trustees, until the number of trustees equals
the number to which the trustees were reduced. Whenever the
number of trustees in office is less than the number so determined
on, sufficient additional trustees shall be elected to make the number of trustees equal to the number so determined on. The trustees
so elected, up to and including one-third of the number so determined on, shall be elected for three years, the remainder up to and
including one-third of the number so determined on for two years,
and the remainder for one year.

§ 78g. Meetings of trustees.— Meetings of the trustees of any
such incorporated church shall be called by giving at least twenty-
four hours' notice thereof personally or by mail to all the trustees;
and such notice may be given by two of the trustees; but by the
unanimous consent of the trustees, a meeting may be held without
previous notice thereof. A majority of the whole number of trustees shall constitute a quorum for the transaction of business, at
any meeting lawfully convened.

§ 78h. The creation and filling of vacancies among trustees of such churches.—If any trustee of any such incorporated church declines to act, resigns or dies, or ceases to be a qualified voter at a corporate meeting thereof, his office shall be vacant; and such vacancy may be filled by the remaining trustees until the next annual corporate meeting of such church; at which meeting the vacancy shall be filled for the unexpired term.

§ 78i. Limitation of powers of trustees.— The trustees of any such incorporated church shall have no power to call, settle or remove a minister or to fix his salary, nor without the consent of a corporate meeting, to incur debts, beyond what is necessary for the administration of the temporal affairs of the church and for the care of the property of the corporation; or to fix or change the time, nature or order of the public or social worship of such church.

§ 78j. Election and salary of ministers.— The ministers of any such church shall be called, settled or removed and their salaries fixed, only by the vote of a majority of the members of such corporation duly qualified to vote at elections present and voting at a meeting of such corporation specially called for that purpose, in the manner hereinbefore provided for the call of special meetings; and any such corporation may, by its by-laws, make the call, settlement or removal of its ministers dependent upon a concurrent vote of the unincorporated church connected with such corporation; and in that case the concurrence of a majority of the members of such unincorporated church, present and voting at a meeting thereof, called for that purpose, shall be necessary to the call, settlement or removal of such ministers.

§ 78k. Transfer of property to other corporations.—Any incorporated Congregational church, created by or existing under the laws of the state of New York, having its principal office or place of worship in the state of New York, or whose last place of worship was within the state of New York, is hereby authorized and empowered, by the concurrent vote of two-thirds of its qualified voters present and voting therefor, at a meeting regularly called for that purpose, and of two-thirds of all its trustees, to direct the transfer and conveyance of any of its property, real or personal, which it now has or may hereafter acquire, to any religious, charitable or missionary corporation connected with the Congregational denomination and incorporated by or organized under any law or laws of the state of New York, either solely, or among other purposes, to establish or maintain, or to assist in establishing or maintaining churches, schools or mission stations, or to erect or assist in the erection of such buildings as may be necessary for any of such purposes, with or without the payment of any money or other consideration therefor; and upon such concurrent votes being given, the trustees shall execute such transfer or conveyance; and upon the same being made, the title to and the ownership and right of possession of the property so transferred and conveyed shall be vested in and conveyed to such grantee; provided, however, that nothing herein contained shall impair or affect in any way any existing claim upon or lien against any property so transferred or conveyed, or any action at law or legal proceeding; and such transfer shall be subject, in respect to the amount of property the said grantee may take and hold, to the restrictions and limitations of all laws then in force.

§ 4. The heading in said act "Article VI," immediately preceding the words " Special provisions for incorporation of churches of other denominations," is hereby amended to read as follows: "Article VII."

§ 5. The heading in said act "Article VII," immediately preceding the words " Special provisions for the incorporation and government of two or more unincorporated churches as a union church," is hereby amended so as to read as follows:

ARTICLE VIII.

§ 6. The heading in said act "Article VIII," immediately preceding the words " Laws repealed; when to take effect," is hereby amended so as to read as follows:

ARTICLE IX.

§ 7. The index to chapter seven hundred and twenty-three of the laws of eighteen hundred and ninety-five, entitled "An act in relation to religious corporations, constituting chapter forty-two of the general laws," preceding article one of said act, as amended by chapter three hundred and thirty-six of the laws of eighteen hundred and ninety-six, is hereby amended by inserting after article five as follows:

VI. Special provisions for the incorporation and government of Congregational and Independent churches; also by striking out the figures " VI " and inserting in place thereof the figures " VII; "

also by striking out the figures "VII" and inserting in place thereof the figures "VIII;" also by striking out the figures "VIII" and inserting in place thereof the figures "IX."

§ 8. This act shall take effect immediately.

Chap. 622.

AN ACT to authorize the records of the New York state weather bureau to be received and read in evidence in any court of the state.

Became a law May 19, 1897, with the approval of the Governor. Passed, a majority being present.

The People of the State of New York, represented in Senate and Assembly, do enact as follows:

Records of observations evidence. Section 1. Any record of the observations in regard to the conditions of the weather, or in regard to the amount and conditions of the precipitation, taken under the direction of the New York state weather bureau, or any copy thereof, when certified in the form of and pursuant to law by the officer in charge thereof at the place where such record is duly filed, that the same is a true copy of such record, may be read in evidence in any court of this state, and shall be prima facie evidence of the facts and circumstances therein stated.

§ 2. This act shall take effect immediately.

Chap. 623.

AN ACT to amend section one hundred and seven of chapter four hundred and twenty-nine of the laws of eighteen hundred and ninety-six, entitled "An act to amend title two of chapter three of part four of the revised statutes relating to state prisons, and for other purposes connected therewith, as amended and superseded by chapter three hundred and eighty-two of the laws of eighteen hundred and eighty-nine, to conform the same to the provisions of the revised constitution."

Became a law May 19, 1897, with the approval of the Governor. Passed, a majority being present.

The People of the State of New York, represented in Senate and Assembly, do enact as follows:

Act amended.   Section 1. Section one hundred and seven of chapter four hundred and twenty-nine of the laws of eighteen hundred and ninety-

six, entitled, " An act to amend title two of chapter three of part
four of the revised statutes relating to state prisons, and for other
purposes connected therewith as amended and superseded by chapter three hundred and eighty-two of the laws of eighteen hundred
and eighty-nine, to conform the same to the provisions of the revised
constitution," is hereby amended so as to read as follows:

§ 107. The comptroller, the state commission of prisons and the Board of classification.
superintendent of state prisons and the lunacy commission are tion.
hereby constituted a board to be known as the board of classification. Said board shall fix and determine the prices at which all Fixing of prices.
labor performed, and all articles manufactured and furnished to
the state, or the political divisions thereof, or to the public institutions thereof, shall be furnished, which prices shall be uniform
to all, except that the prices for goods or labor furnished by the
penitentiaries to or for the county in which they are located, or the
political divisions thereof, shall be fixed by the board of supervisors
of such counties, except New York and Kings counties, in which
the prices shall be fixed by the commissioners of charities and correction, respectively. The prices shall be as near the usual market
price for such labor and supplies as possible. The state commis- Form for requisition.
sion of prisons shall devise and furnish to all such institutions a tion.
proper form for such requisition and the comptroller shall devise
and furnish a proper system of accounts to be kept for all such
transactions. It shall also be the duty of the board of classifica- Classification of buildings, etc.
tion to classify the buildings, offices and institutions owned or man-
aged and controlled by the state, and it shall fix and determine
the styles, patterns, designs and qualities of the articles to be manufactured for such buildings, offices and public institutions in the
penal institutions in this state. So far as practicable, all supplies Supplies for buildings, etc.
used in such buildings, offices and public institutions shall be uni- ings, etc.
form for each class, and of the styles, patterns, designs and qualities
that can be manufactured in the penal institutions in this state.

§ 2. This act shall take effect immediately.

Chap. 624.

AN ACT to amend chapter four hundred and sixty-six of the laws of eighteen hundred and seventy-seven, entitled "An act in relation to assignments of estates of debtors for the benefit of creditors," as amended by chapter three hundred and twenty-eight of the laws of eighteen hundred and eighty-four, as amended by chapter two hundred and eighty-three of the laws of eighteen hundred and eighty-six.

Became a law May 19, 1897, with the approval of the Governor. Passed, three-fifths being present.

The People of the State of New York, represented in Senate and Assembly, do enact as follows:

Act amended.

Section 1. Section twenty-nine of chapter four hundred and sixty-six of the laws of eighteen hundred and seventy-seven, entitled "An act in relation to assignments of the estates of debtors for the benefit of creditors," as amended by chapter three hundred and twenty-eight of the laws of eighteen hundred and eighty-four, as amended by chapter two hundred and eighty-three of the laws of eighteen hundred and eighty-six, is hereby amended so as to read as follows:

Preference of wages and salaries.

§ 29. In all distribution of assets under all assignments made in pursuance of this act, the wages or salaries actually owing to the employes of the assignor or assignors at the time of the execution of the assignment for services rendered within one year prior to the execution of such assignment, shall be preferred before any other debt; and should the assets of the assignor or assignors not be sufficient to pay in full all the claims preferred, pursuant to this section they shall be applied to the payment of the same pro rata to the amount of each such claim.

§ 2. This act shall take effect immediately.

Chap. 625.

AN ACT to legalize the election and official acts of persons heretofore elected as officers of fire districts outside of cities and incorporated villages.

Became a law May 19, 1897, with the approval of the Governor.
Passed, a majority being present.

The People of the State of New York, represented in Senate and Assembly, do enact as follows:

Section 1. The election and all official acts of all persons heretofore elected or designated as officers of any of the fire districts established outside of a city or an incorporated village in this state, in so far as such elections or designations may have been or may be affected, impaired or questioned by the reasons of such elections or designations having been had and made by ballots other than official ballots, or for any omission of any of the requirements of the election law of this state, are hereby legalized, ratified and confirmed, and the same shall have all the force, effect and validity as if the said election law had been fully and in all respects complied with. *Election and official acts legalized.*

§ 2. Nothing in this act shall affect any suit or proceeding now pending. *Proviso.*

§ 3. This act shall take effect immediately.

Chap. 628.

AN ACT to amend the fisheries, game and forest law, relating to the close season of black bass or Oswego bass.

Became a law May 21, 1897, with the approval of the Governor.
Passed, three-fifths being present.

The People of the State of New York, represented in Senate and Assembly, do enact as follows:

Section 1. Section one hundred and ten of chapter four hundred and eighty-eight of the laws of eighteen hundred and ninety-two, the title to which was amended by chapter three hundred and ninety-five of the laws of eighteen hundred and ninety-five to read " An act relating to game, fish and wild animals and to the forest preserve and Adirondack park, constituting chapter thirty-one of the general laws and to be known as the fisheries, game

and forest law," as amended by chapter five hundred and thirty-
one of the laws of eighteen hundred and ninety-six is hereby
amended to read as follows:

§ 110. Black bass, Oswego bass, pickerel pike or wall-eyed pike;
close season.—Black bass or Oswego bass, shall not be fished for,
caught, killed or possessed except from the fifteenth day of
June to the thirty-first day of December, both inclusive, and shall
not be fished for, caught or killed in the Schoharie river or in Foxes
creek within three years from the thirty-first day of May, eighteen
hundred and ninety-six, except in the month of August. Pickerel,
pike, or wall-eyed pike shall not be fished for, caught or killed or
possessed except from the first day of May to the thirty-
first day of January, both inclusive, except as provided
in section one hundred and forty-one. Provided, however,
that the commissioners of fisheries, game and forest shall
have power to permit the taking or destruction of pickerel
at any time in the waters inhabited by trout. The provisions of this section shall not apply to the Saint Lawrence
between Tibbett's Point lighthouse and the city of Ogdensburg.
Whoever shall violate or attempt to violate the provisions of this
section shall be deemed guilty of a misdemeanor and in addition
thereto shall be liable to a penalty of twenty-five dollars for each
fish so caught killed or possessed. Every person fishing in the
Schoharie river or in Foxes creek, or having fish in his possession
caught in either of said waters, shall, whenever requested by any
fish and game protector, or by any sheriff, deputy sheriff, constable,
game constable or police constable, permit such officer to inspect
and examine the fish taken by him or in his possession or control
or in the boat, basket, creel, lock-up, or other thing occupied or
possessed by him, and in case of his refusal to permit such inspection or examination he shall be liable to a penalty of twenty-five
dollars for each such refusal, and such officer making such request
shall have power, and he is hereby authorized, without a search-
warrant to at once proceed and make such inspection and examination of said fish, boat, basket, creel, lock-up, or other thing in his
possession or control, and to use such force as may be necessary for
such purpose. Such refusal, if in the open season in said waters,
shall be presumptive evidence that such person so refusing had
intentionally taken from said waters, in said open season, and kept
and not returned thereto, one black bass less than eight inches in

length, in violation of this article, and if the closed season in said waters, that he has taken one black bass from said waters during such closed season, in violation of the provisions of this section.

§ 2. This act shall take effect immediately.

Chap. 661.

AN ACT to amend section two hundred and fifty-four of the code of civil procedure, relating to the salary of stenographers in the supreme court, county of Kings.

Became a law May 22, 1897, with the approval of the Governor.
Passed, three-fifths being present.

The People of the State of New York, represented in Senate and Assembly, do enact as follows:

Section 1. Section two hundred and fifty-four of the code of civil procedure is hereby amended so as to read as follows:

§ 254. The justices of the supreme court, residing in the county of Kings, or a majority of them, may appoint and may at pleasure remove, nine stenographers who shall severally attend, as directed by the respective justices appointing them, the terms of the appellate division and trial and special terms of the supreme court, in the county of Kings and shall each receive an annual salary of three thousand dollars and the expense thereof shall be raised with the annual tax levy as a county charge.

§ 2. This act shall take effect immediately.

Chap. 682.

AN ACT for licensing and regulating bonds of auctioneers in cities of one million and over.

Accepted by the cities.
Became a law May 22, 1897, with the approval of the Governor.
Passed, three-fifths being present.

The People of the State of New York, represented in Senate and Assembly, do enact as follows:

Section 1. No person, persons, corporation or association shall hereafter carry on the business of auctioneer in cities of one million inhabitants and over, without having first obtained from the mayor of said city a license authorizing such person, persons, corporation or association to carry on the business of auctioneer.

Mayor to grant.

§ 2. The mayor of said city shall, under his hand and seal of his office grant to such citizen or citizens a license to carry on the business of auctioneer on payment of the sum of two hundred and fifty dollars per annum.

Proceeds.

§ 3. The moneys collected shall be paid over to the city treasury.

Auctioneer's bond.

§ 4. All auctioneers in cities of one million inhabitants and over, shall, before the license to them issued shall become operative, file with the comptroller or city treasurer of the city in which they shall be licensed, a bond with two real estate sureties or one surety company as provided by law, in the penal sum of two thousand dollars. Such bond, if sufficient, shall be approved by said comptroller or city treasurer.

Liability of sureties.

§ 5. The sureties upon a bond as provided in section one hereof, shall be liable for breach of contract or of duty towards the person or persons consigning goods for sale, as well as for the other acts, omissions and matters now provided by law.

Precedence of bonds on recovery of judgment.

§ 6. On recovery of judgment for any violation of this or other provisions regulating the duties, rights and requirements of auctioneers, the bonds herein provided for shall for the purposes of execution or proceedings upon or collection of such judgments take precedence of all mortgages, liens, conveyances or other encumbrances, affecting or relating to the property of the sureties upon such bonds.

Repeal.

§ 7. All acts or parts of acts inconsistent with the above provisions are hereby repealed.

§ 8. This act shall take effect immediately.

Chap. 688.

AN ACT to amend the railroad law, relating to the rate of fare on street surface railroads.

Became a law May 22, 1897, with the approval of the Governor. Passed, a majority being present.

The People of the State of New York, represented in Senate and Assembly, do enact as follows:

Section 1. Section one hundred and one of chapter five hundred and sixty-five of the laws of eighteen hundred and ninety, entitled " An act in relation to railroads constituting chapter thirty-nine of the general laws," as amended by chapter six hundred and seventy six of the laws of eighteen hundred and ninety-two, is hereby amended to read as follows:

§ 101. **Rate of fare.**— No corporation constructing and operating a railroad under the provisions of this article, or of chapter two hundred and fifty-two of the laws of eighteen hundred and eighty-four, shall charge any passenger more than five cents for one continuous ride from any point on its road, or on any road, line or branch operated by it, or under its control, to any other point thereof, or any connecting branch thereof, within the limits of any incorporated city or village. Not more than one fare shall be charged within the limits of any such city or village, for passage over the main line of road and any branch or extension thereof if the right to construct such branch or extension shall have been acquired under the provisions of such chapter or of this article; except that in any city of the third class, or incorporated village, it shall be lawful for such corporation to charge and collect as a maximum rate of fare for each passenger, ten cents, where such passenger is carried in a car which overcomes an elevation of at least four hundred and fifty feet within a distance of one and a half miles. This section shall not apply to any part of any road constructed prior to May six, eighteen hundred and eighty-four, and then in operation, unless the corporation owning the same shall have acquired the right to extend such road, or to construct branches thereof under such chapter, or shall acquire such right under the provisions of this article, in which event its rate of fare shall not exceed its authorized rate prior to such extension. The legislature expressly reserves the right to regulate and reduce the rate of fare on any railroad constructed and operated wholly or in part under such chapter or under the provisions of this article.

§ 2. This act shall take effect immediately.

Chap. 689.

AN ACT to provide for the administration of the State Veterinary College, established by chapter one hundred and fifty-three of the laws of eighteen hundred and ninety-four.

Became a law May 22, 1897, with the approval of the Governor.
Passed, three-fifths being present.

The People of the State of New York, represented in Senate and Assembly, do enact as follows:

Section 1. The State Veterinary College, established by chapter one hundred and fifty-three of the laws of eighteen hundred and ninety-four, shall be known as the New York State Veterinary

Corporate name.

College. The object of said veterinary college shall be: To con-

duct investigations as to the nature, prevention and cure of all
diseases of animals, including such as are communicable to man
and such as cause epizootics among live stock; to investigate the
economical questions which will contribute to the more profitable
breeding, rearing and utilization of animals; to produce reliable
standard preparations of toxins, antitoxins and other products
to be used in the diagnosis, prevention and cure of diseases and
in the conducting of sanitary work by approved modern methods;
and to give instruction in the normal structure and function of
the animal body, in the pathology, prevention and treatment of
animal diseases, and in all matters pertaining to sanitary science
as applied to live stock and correlatively to the human family.

All buildings, furniture, apparatus and other property heretofore
or hereafter erected or furnished by the state for such veterinary
college shall be and remain the property of the state. The Cornell
University shall have the custody and control of said property,
and shall, with whatever state moneys may be received for the
purpose, administer the said veterinary college, with authority
to appoint investigators, teachers and other officers, to lay out
lines of investigation, to prescribe the requirements for admission and the course of study and with such other power and
authority as may be necessary and proper for the due administration of such veterinary college. Said university shall receive
no income, profit or compensation therefor, but all moneys received from state appropriations for the said veterinary college
or derived from other sources in the course of the administration
thereof, shall be kept by said university in a separate fund from
the moneys of the university, and shall be used exclusively for
said New York State Veterinary College. Such moneys as may
be appropriated to be paid to the Cornell University by the state
in any year, to be expended by said university in the administration of said veterinary college, shall be payable to the treasurer
of Cornell University in three equal payments to be made on the
first day of October, the first day of January, and the first day of
April in such year, and within thirty days after the expiration of
the period for which each installment is received the said university shall furnish the comptroller of the state of New York satisfactory vouchers for the expenditure of such installment. The
said university shall expend such moneys and use such property
of the state in administering said veterinary college, and shall

report to the governor during the month of January in each year, Report to governor. a detailed statement of such expenditures and of the general operations of the said veterinary college. No tuition fee shall be Tuition fee. required of a student pursuing the regular veterinary course, who, for a year or more immediately preceding his admission to said veterinary college shall have been a resident of this state. The tuition fees charged to other students and all other fees and charges in said veterinary college shall be fixed by Cornell University, and the moneys so received shall be expended for the current expenses of the said veterinary college.

§ 2. This act shall take effect immediately.

Chap. 690.

AN ACT to amend chapter five hundred and fifty-nine of the laws of eighteen hundred and ninety-three, entitled "An act in relation to the militia, constituting chapter sixteen of the general laws."

Became a law May 22, 1897, with the approval of the Governor.
Passed, three-fifths being present.

The People of the State of New York, represented in Senate and Assembly, do enact as follows:

Section 1. Section one hundred and sixty-two of the military code is hereby amended to read as follows:

§ 162. When sheriffs or mayors may call on commanding officers for aid.—In case of any breach of the peace, tumult, or resistance to process of this state, or immediate danger thereof, any sheriff of any county, or the mayor of any city, may call for aid upon the commanding officer of the national guard, stationed therein or adjacent thereto. The commanding officer upon whom such call is made, shall order out, in aid of the civil authorities, the military force or any part thereof under his command, and shall immediately report what he has done and all circumstances of the case to the commander-in-chief, but no company which may be enlisted or enrolled at any college or university under the provisions of this act, shall be ordered to do duty outside of the county where such college or university is located, except by the commander-in-chief.

§ 2. This act shall take effect immediately.

Chap. 699.

AN ACT to amend the game law, and the act amendatory thereof, relative to the protection of fish, birds and wild animals.

Became a law May 22, 1897, with the approval of the Governor.
Passed, three-fifths being present.

The People of the State of New York, represented in Senate and Assembly, do enact as follows:

Section 1. Section seventy-eight of chapter four hundred and eighty-eight of the laws of eighteen hundred and ninety-two, the title to which was amended by chapter three hundred and ninety-five of the laws of eighteen hundred and ninety-five, to read "An act relating to game, fish and wild animals, and to the forest preserve and Adirondack park, constituting chapter thirty-one of the general laws, and to be known as the fisheries, game and forest law," as amended by chapter nine hundred and seventy-four of the laws of eighteen hundred and ninety-five, is hereby amended to read as follows:

§ 78. **Certain wild birds protected—** Wild birds shall not be killed or caught at any time or possessed living or dead. This provision does not affect any birds the killing of which is prohibited between certain dates by the provisions of this act, nor does it protect the English sparrow, crow, hawk, crane, raven, crow-blackbird, common blackbird and kingfisher; and it does not apply to any person holding a certificate under the provisions of this act. Whoever shall violate or attempt to violate the provisions of this section shall be deemed guilty of misdemeanor and in addition thereto shall be liable to a penalty of twenty-five dollars for each bird killed, trapped or possessed contrary to the provisions of this section.

§ 2. This act shall take effect immediately.

Chap. 700.

AN ACT to amend the fisheries, game and forest law, and the acts amendatory thereof, in relation to the prevention of fires.

Became a law May 22, 1897, with the approval of the Governor.
Passed, three-fifths being present.

The People of the State of New York, represented in Senate and Assembly, do enact as follows:

Section 1. Chapter four hundred and eighty-eight of the laws of eighteen hundred and ninety-two, the title to which was amended by chapter three hundred and ninety-five of the laws of eighteen hundred and ninety-five to read "An act relating to game, fish and wild animals and to the forest preserve and Adirondack park, constituting chapter thirty-one of the general laws and to be known as the fisheries, game and forest law," as amended by chapter three hundred and ninety-five of the laws of eighteen hundred and ninety-five by the addition of two articles numbered twelve and thirteen respectively, containing section two hundred and eighty-one, which said section was amended by chapter six hundred and fifty-five of the laws of eighteen hundred and ninety-six, and is hereby amended to read as follows:

§ 281. **Fallow fires.**—It shall be unlawful for any person to light fires for the purpose of clearing land, burning fallows, stumps, logs or fallen timber, in the towns hereinafter specified in this section, between April first and June tenth, and between September first and November tenth; but from June tenth to September first such fires may be started upon giving three days' notice to a fire warden or district fire warden and securing his written permission. During the period last mentioned, if the place where a fire is to be lighted is near any woodlands or forest which might possibly be endangered by lighting such fire, it shall be the duty of the town fire warden or district fire warden to be present personally when the fire is lighted, and the fire warden or district fire warden thus in attendance shall not permit the starting of any fallow fires, or brush fires, or fires for clearing land, during a dangerous wind, nor until the person desirous of starting such fires shall have employed at his own expense a sufficient number of persons to watch and prevent any possible spreading of the flames, and who shall remain on watch until the fire is out and completely extinguished. The services of a fire warden or district fire warden at such times shall be a town charge, the same as when employed in extinguishing a forest fire; and one-half of the expense thus incurred by the town may be refunded by the comptroller of the state as hereinbefore provided in case of forest fires.   Any person violating the requirements of this section by lighting fallow fires or fires for clearing land otherwise than as herein provided, shall be guilty of a misdemeanor, and in addition thereto shall be liable to a fine of not less than fifty dollars nor more than three hundred dollars, one-half of which amount shall be paid to the person or persons furnishing the evidence necessary to conviction.   The provisions of this section shall apply to Hamilton county, and to the towns of Minerva, Newcomb, North Hudson, Schroon, Keene, Jay, Lewis, North Elba, Saint Armand, and Wilmington, of Essex county; to the towns of Waverly, Harrietstown, Brandon, Santa Clara, Brighton, Belmont, Franklin, Duane and Altamont, of Franklin county; to the towns of Hopkinton, Colton, Clifton, Fine, Edwards, Pitcairn, Clara, Russell, and Parishville, of Saint Lawrence county; to the towns of Diana, Croghan, Watson, Creig, and Lyonsdale, of Lewis county; to the towns of Wilmurt, Ohio, Salisbury, Remson, and Russia, of Herkimer county; to the town of Forestport in Oneida county; to the towns of Stratford, Caroga, Bleecker, and Mayfield, of Fulton county; to the towns of Day, Edinburgh, Hadley, and Corinth, of Saratoga county; to the towns of Johnsburgh, Thurman, and Stony Creek, of Warren county; to the towns of Putnam, Dresden, and Fort Ann, of Washington county; to the towns of Altona, Dannemora, Ellenburgh, Saranac, and Black Brook, of Clinton county; to the towns of Denning, Hardenburgh, Shandaken, Olive, Rochester, Wawarsing, and Woodstock, of Ulster county; to the towns of Neversink and Rockland, of Sullivan county; to the towns of Andes, Colchester, Hancock, and Middletown, of Delaware county; and to the towns of Hunter, Jewett, Lexington, and Windham, of Greene county.

§ 2. This act shall take effect immediately.

Chap. 701.

AN ACT to amend the code of civil procedure, relating to an action establishing the validity of the probate of a last will and testament.

Became a law May 22, 1897, with the approval of the Governor.
Passed, three-fifths being present.

The People of the State of New York, represented in Senate and Assembly, do enact as follows:

Section 1. Section twenty-six hundred and fifty-three-a of the code of civil procedure is hereby amended so as to read as follows:

§ 2653a. **Determining validity of a will.**— Any person interested as devisee, legatee or otherwise, in a will or codicil admitted to probate in this state, as provided by the code of civil procedure, or any person interested as heir-at-law, next of kin or otherwise, in any estate, any portion of which is disposed of, or affected, or any portion of which is attempted to be disposed of, or affected, by a will or codicil admitted to probate in this state, as provided by the code of civil procedure, within two years prior to the passage of this act, or any heir-at-law or next of kin of the testator making such will, may cause the validity or invalidity of the probate thereof to be determined in an action in the supreme court for the county in which such probate was had. All the devisees, legatees and heirs of the testator and other interested persons, including the executor or administrator, must be parties to the action. Upon the completion of service of all parties, the plaintiff shall forthwith file the summons and complaint in the office of the clerk of the court in which said action is begun and the clerk thereof shall forthwith certify to the clerk of the surrogate's court in which the will has been admitted to probate, the fact that an action to determine the validity of the probate of such will has been commenced, and on receipt of such certificate by the surrogate's court, the surrogate shall forthwith transmit to the court in which such action has been begun a copy of the will, testimony and all papers relating thereto, and a copy of the decree of probate, attaching the same together, and certifying the same under the seal of the court. The issue of the pleadings in such action shall be confined to the question of whether the writing produced is or is not the last will and codicil of the testator, or either. It shall be tried by a jury and a verdict thereon shall be conclusive as to the real or personal property, unless a new trial be granted or the judgment thereon be reversed or vacated. On the trial of such issue the decree of the surrogate admitting the will or codicil to probate shall be prima facie evidence of the due attestation, execution and validity of such will or codicil. A certified copy of the testimony of such of the witnesses examined upon the probate, as are out of the jurisdiction of the court, dead, or have become incompetent since the probate, shall be admitted in evidence on the trial. The party sustaining the will shall be entitled to open and close the evidence and argument. He shall offer the will in probate and rest. The other party shall then offer his evidence. The party sustaining the will shall then offer his other evidence and rebutting testimony may be offered as in other cases. If all the defendants make default in pleading, or if the answers served in said action raise no issues, then the plaintiff may enter judgment as provided in article two of chapter eleven of the code of civil procedure in the case of similar defaults in other actions. If the judgment to be entered in an action brought under this section is that the writing produced is the last will and codicil, or either of the testator, said judgment shall also provide that all parties to said action, and all persons claiming under them subsequently to the commencement of the said action, be enjoined from bringing or maintaining any action or proceeding, or from interposing or maintaining a defense in any action or proceeding based upon a claim that such writing is not the last will or codicil, or either, of the testator. Any judgment heretofore entered under this section determining that the writing produced is the last will and codicil, or either, of the testator, shall, upon application of any party to said action, or any person claiming through or under them, and upon notice to such persons as the court at special term shall direct, be amended by such court so as to enjoin all parties to said action, and all persons claiming under the parties to said action subsequently to the commencement thereof, from bringing or maintaining any action or proceeding impeaching the validity of the probate of the said will and codicil, or either of them, or based upon a claim that such writing is not the last will and codicil, or either, of the testator, and from setting up or maintaining such impeachment or claim by way of answer in any action or proceeding. When final judgment shall have been entered in such action, a copy thereof shall be certified and transmitted to the clerk of the surrogate's court in which such will was admitted to probate. The action brought as herein provided shall be commenced within two years after the will or codicil has been admitted to probate, but persons within the age of minority, of unsound mind, imprisoned, or absent from the state, may bring such action two years after such disability has been removed.

§ 2. This act shall take effect immediately.

Chap. 704.

AN ACT providing for the surveying and mapping of certain oyster lands under waters of Long Island sound.

Became a law May 22, 1897, with the approval of the Governor
Passed, three-fifths being present.

The People of the State of New York, represented in Senate and Assembly, do enact as follows:

Section 1. The state engineer and surveyor is hereby authorized Survey and directed to cause a survey and map of newly discovered beds bed, and map of of oysters of natural growth under the water of Long Island sound, located between Mount Sinai and Orient point on Long Island, and shall also cause to be erected substantial monuments and signals for the purpose of accurately locating same. Said surveying, mapping and erection of monuments and signals shall be done according to the general direction of the state shell fish commissioner. The sum of five thousand dollars is hereby appropriated Appropriation. for carrying out the provisions of this act, to be paid out of any funds in the treasury not otherwise appropriated.

§ 2. This act shall take effect immediately.

Chap. 706.

AN ACT to amend the game law and the act amendatory thereof, relative to regulations for dredging and raking for oysters and clams.

Became a law May 22, 1897, with the approval of the Governor.
Passed, three-fifths being present.

The People of the State of New York, represented in Senate and Assembly, do enact as follows:

Section 1. Section one hundred and ninety-one of chapter four hundred and eighty-eight of the laws of eighteen hundred and ninety-two, the title to which was amended by chapter three hundred and ninety-five of the laws of eighteen hundred and ninety-five to read "An act relating to game, fish and wild animals and to the forest preserve and Adirondack park, constituting chapter thirty-one of the general laws and to be known as the fisheries, game and forest law," as amended by chapter nine hundred and seventy-four of the laws of eighteen hundred and ninety-five is hereby amended so as to read as follows:

§ 191. Dredging and raking for oysters and clams regulated.— No dredge, operated by steam power, or weighing over fifty pounds, shall be used on beds of natural growth in dredging for shellfish. No rake, tongs, dredge or other device shall be used for taking hard or round clams, with spaces or openings, between the teeth or prongs of less than one inch in width. Whoever violates or attempts to violate the provisions of this section shall be guilty of a misdemeanor, and in addition thereto shall be liable to a penalty of one hundred dollars for each violation thereof.

§ 2. This act shall take effect immediately.

Chap. 707.

AN ACT providing for an addition to the New York State School for the Blind, and making an appropriation therefor.

Became a law May 22, 1897, with the approval of the Governor. Passed, three-fifths being present.

The People of the State of New York, represented in Senate and Assembly, do enact as follows:

Erection of building.

Section 1. A building to be used as a boys' industrial department, including piano tuning, shall be erected at the New York State School for the Blind at Batavia, by the board of managers of said institution, pursuant to plans and specifications to be furnished by the state architect and approved by the state board of charities, and the work of construction to be performed under the supervision of the state board of charities, at a cost not exceeding eight thousand dollars for the completion of said building and

Appropriation.

fifteen hundred dollars for heating and plumbing, the sum of two thousand five hundred dollars appropriated by chapter nine hundred and fifty of the laws of eighteen hundred and ninety-six for refitting building for school work-shops is hereby reappropriated towards the construction of said building, and the sum of seven thousand dollars is hereby appropriated therefor from any moneys in the treasury not otherwise appropriated.

§ 2. The moneys appropriated by section one of this act shall Payment of appropriation. be paid upon the warrants of the comptroller drawn upon the treasurer from time to time as required by said board of trustees for the payment of sums due in the progress of said work, the accounts for which shall be verified by the officers of said board of trustees and approved and indorsed by an authorized member of the state board of charities. No contract made under this act shall take Contracts. effect until approved by said state board of charities, and certified copies thereof shall be filed with the comptroller before payments thereon.

§ 3. This act shall take effect immediately.

Chap. 725.

AN ACT conferring jurisdiction upon the court of claims to hear, audit and determine the claim of Charles W. Little against the state of New York.

Became a law May 22, 1897, with the approval of the Governor.
Passed, three-fifths being present.

The People of the State of New York, represented in Senate and Assembly, do enact as follows:

Section 1. Jurisdiction is hereby conferred upon the court of Jurisdiction to hear claim. claims to hear, audit and determine the alleged claim of Charles W. Little, doing business at Albany, New York, under the firm name of W. C. Little and Company, against the state of New York for damages claimed to have been sustained by said Little through an alleged breach on the part of the state, of a contract made in its behalf on the sixteenth day of December, eighteen hundred and ninety-five, by state officers, with said Little, for printing and delivering the slips of the session laws for the legislative session of eighteen hundred and ninety-six, as ordered by the secretary of state, and printing, publishing and delivering to the secretary of state twenty-five hundred copies of the laws of eighteen hundred and ninety-six, and furnishing the edition to the public as required by the terms of said contract.

§ 2. If the facts proved before said court shall establish a legal Determination and award of damages. or valid claim against the state for the damages alleged to have been sustained by said Little as aforesaid, the said court shall determine the amount of said damages and award such sum therefor as may be just and equitable, not to exceed the sum of ten thousand dollars.

§ 3. Either party may take an appeal to the appellate division of the supreme court in the third department from any award made under authority of this act, or from any judgment of affirmance or reversal thereof in the appellate division to the court of appeals, provided such appeal be taken by service of a notice of appeal within thirty days after service of a copy of the award or of the judgment of the appellate division.

§ 4. This act shall take effect immediately.

Chap. 726.

AN ACT to amend section fifteen hundred and thirty-eight of the code of civil procedure, relating to actions for partition.

Became a law May 22, 1897, with the approval of the Governor. Passed, a majority being present.

The People of the State of New York, represented in Senate and Assembly, do enact as follows:

Section 1. Section fifteen hundred and thirty-eight of the code of civil procedure is hereby amended so as to read as follows:

§ 1538. **Who must be parties.**—Every person having an undivided share, in possession, or otherwise, in the property, as tenant in fee, for life, by the curtesy, or for years; every person entitled to the reversion, remainder or inheritance of an undivided share, after the determination of a particular estate therein; every person who, by any contingency contained in a devise or grant, or otherwise, is or may become entitled to a beneficial interest in an undivided share thereof; every person having an inchoate right of dower in an undivided share in the property; and every person having a right of dower in the property, or any part thereof, which has not been admeasured, must be made a party to an action for a partition. But no person, other than a joint tenant, or a tenant in common of the property, shall be a plaintiff in the action. Whenever an action for the partition of real property shall be brought before the expiration of three years from the time when letters of administration or letters testamentary, as the case may be, shall have been issued upon the estate of the decedent from whom the plaintiff's title is derived, the executors, or administrators, as the case may be, if any, of the estate of said decedent, shall be made parties defendant. In case no executor or administrator of such decedent shall have been appointed at the time said action is begun, that fact shall be alleged in the complaint. The executors or administrators, if any, as the case may be, of a deceased person, who, if living, should be a party to such action, shall be made parties defendant therein, and in case no executor or administrator of such deceased person shall have been appointed, that fact shall be alleged in the complaint. Where the interlocutory judgment directs a sale of the premises sought to be partitioned; or of some part thereof, the premises so sold pursuant to such interlocutory judgment, shall be free from the lien of every debt of such decedent or decedents, except debts which were a lien upon the premises before the death of such decedent or decedents. When the action is brought before three years have elapsed from the granting of such letters of administration or letters testamentary, as the case may be, upon the estate of the decedent from whom the plaintiff derived his title, the final judgment shall direct that the proceeds of the sale remaining after the payment of the costs, referee's fees, expenses of sale, taxes, assessments, water rates, and liens established before the death of the decedent, including any sum allowed to a widow in satisfaction of her right of dower, therein directed to be paid, be forthwith paid into court by the referee making such sale by depositing the same with the county treasurer of the county, in which the trial of the action is placed, to the credit of the parties entitled thereto, to await the further order in the premises. Where the action is brought before three years have elapsed from the granting of letters of administration or letters testamentary, as the case may be, upon the estate of a deceased person, who, if living, should be a party to the action, the final judgment shall direct that the share of the proceeds of such sale, which would have been his, if living, be paid into court by such referee, by depositing the same with such county treasurer, to await the further order in the premises. Upon the certificate of the surrogate of the county of which the decedent was, at the time of his death, a resident, showing that three years have elapsed since the issuing of letters testamentary or letters of administration, as the case may be, upon the estate of said decedent, and that no proceedings for the mortgage, lease or sale of the real property of said decedent for the payment of his debts or funeral expenses, or both, is pending, and upon the certificate of the county clerk of the county where the real prop-

erty sold under the interlocutory judgment is located, showing
that no notice provided for in section twenty-seven hundred and
fifty-one of the code of civil procedure has been filed in his office,
the court wherein the final judgment was made shall, upon the
application of any party to said action, make an order directing the
county treasurer to pay to said party from said deposit, the amount
to which he is entitled under the said final judgment, with the
accumulation thereon, if any, less the fees of said county
treasurer. Any party to such action may, at any time after final
judgment, upon notice to the executors or administrators of the
decedent from whom the party applying derived his share or
interest, apply to the court in which said action is pending for
leave to withdraw the deposit or share of the deposit, adjudged
in the final judgment to belong to him; and, upon said application, the court may, in its discretion, make an order directing the
county treasurer to pay over to said party the deposit, or the
share of the deposit, adjudged in the final judgment to belong
to him, but said order shall not be made until said party so applying shall have-furnished a bond to the people of the state of New
York in the penalty of twice the amount of the deposit sought
to be withdrawn, with two or more good and sufficient sureties,
approved by the judge or justice of the court making such order,
and filed, with such approval, in the office of the clerk of the
county in which such action is pending, to the effect that the
said party so withdrawing said deposit will pay any and all claims,
not exceeding the amount of said deposit, when thereunto required
by order of the court or by order of the surrogate or of the surrogate's court in a proceeding to mortgage, lease or sell the real
property of such decedent. But where final judgment shall be
rendered in any action for partition after three years have elapsed
from the granting of letters of administration or letters testamentary, as the case may be, upon the estate of the decedent from
whom the plaintiff derived title, upon producing to the court the
certificate of the surrogate of the county of which the decedent
was at the time of his death a resident, showing that three years
have elapsed since the issuing of letters of administration or letters
testamentary as the case may be upon the estate of said decedent
and that no proceeding for the mortgage, lease or sale of the real
property of the decedent for the payment of his debts or funeral
expenses or both is pending and upon the certificate of the clerk
of the county where the real property sold under the interlocutory

judgment is located showing that no notice provided for in section twenty-seven hundred and fifty-one of the code of civil procedure has been filed in his office, the court rendering the final judgment shall direct the payment of the different shares to the several parties entitled thereto; except that the share of a deceased person who, if living, should be a party to the action when the action was commenced before three years have elapsed from the granting of letters of administration or letters testamentary on his estate shall be paid into court as above provided.

§ 2. This act shall take effect September first, eighteen hundred and ninety-seven.

Chap. 730.

AN ACT conferring jurisdiction upon the board of claims to hear, audit and determine the claim of Michael T. Horner against the state, and to make an award therefor.

Became a law May 22, 1897, with the approval of the Governor.
Passed, three-fifths being present.

The People of the State of New York, represented in Senate and Assembly, do enact as follows:

Section 1. Jurisdiction is hereby conferred upon the board of claims to hear, audit and determine the alleged claim of Michael T. Horner against the state, for money alleged to have been paid by him to the state in excess of what is alleged to have been due under a certain contract, for stove hollow-ware and enamelled stoveware and plumbers' iron castings supplies, to be manufactured by the convicts in Auburn state prison, alleged to have been made between him and the agent and warden of Auburn state prison in the year eighteen hundred and ninety-three, and to award thereon such sum as the said board shall deem just and reasonable, although such claim may have accrued more than two years prior to the time when it is filed; provided, however, that such claim shall be filed with said board within one year after the passage of this act.

§ 2. Either party may take an appeal from any award made under authority of this act, to the third appellate division of the supreme court, provided such appeal be taken by service of a notice of appeal within thirty days after service of a copy of the award.

§ 3. This act shall take effect immediately.

Chap. 732.

AN ACT to amend chapter five hundred and eighty-four of the laws of eighteen hundred and ninety-six, entitled " An act providing for the erection of an armory and the acquisition of a site therefor, in the city of Buffalo, for the seventy-fourth regiment, national guard of the state of New York, and making an appropriation for commencing the erection of such armory."

Became a law May 22, 1897, with the approval of the Governor.

Passed, three-fifths being present.

The People of the State of New York, represented in Senate and Assembly, do enact as follows:

Act amended.

Section 1. Section three of chapter five hundred and eighty-four of the laws of eighteen hundred and ninety-six, entitled "An act providing for the erection of an armory and the acquisition of a site therefor, in the city of Buffalo, for the seventy-fourth regiment, national guard of the state of New York, and making an appropriation for commencing the erection of such armory," is hereby amended so as to read as follows:

Issue of county bonds.

§ 3. The treasurer of the county of Erie, whenever a written notice shall be served upon him by the adjutant-general, the inspector-general and the chief of ordnance of the state of New York, who are hereby made and constituted a commission for the purposes of this act, stating that the title to such land has been acquired, as provided in this act, shall execute in behalf of and in the name of the county of Erie interest bearing bonds in the amount, or aggregating the amount, named in such notice, and shall, after ten days' notice, specifying the time and place where bids will be received therefor, sell the same to the highest bidder, at a price not less than the par value thereof, such notice to be published for five days in the official paper of the county of Erie. The aforesaid bonds shall bear interest at the rate of not to exceed four per centum per annum, payable semi-annually; both principal and interest to be made payable at the office of the county treasurer of Erie county, at the city of Buffalo, New York; one-third of said bonds shall be made payable in five years, one-third thereof in ten years and one-third thereof in fifteen years from the date of their issue; or at such other periods as said treasurer may decide

Tax for interest and principal.

is for the best interests of said county; and the amount thereof and the semi-annual interest, as it shall respectively become due thereon, shall be raised in the several tax budgets of said county for the years when said bonds and semi-annual interest shall become due and shall be applied to the payment of such bonds. The proceeds of the sale of such bonds shall be retained by said county treasurer and shall by him be paid out for the costs and expenses of acquiring said title and for grading, filling, excavating, draining, paving, fencing, making sewer and water connections and laying sidewalks about said land, upon the written requisition of the aforesaid commission.

§ 2. This act shall take effect immediately.

Chap. 742.

AN ACT authorizing the state commissioner of excise to treat that portion of the city of Rome not included within the corporation tax district limits of said city as a separate town.

Accepted by the city.

Became a law May 22, 1897, with the approval of the Governor. Passed, three-fifths being present.

The People of the State of New York, represented in Senate and Assembly, do enact as follows:

Section 1. The state commissioner of excise shall, on or before the first day of May, eighteen hundred and ninety-seven, cause an enumeration to be made of the inhabitants of the city of Rome residing without the limits of the tax corporation district " for the purpose of fixing the excise taxes to be assessed in said territory under the provision of section eleven of the liquor tax law," and thereafter, said territory shall be treated as a separate town by said state commissioner of excise under the provisions of chapter one hundred and twelve of the laws of eighteen hundred and ninety-six for such purpose, and the excise taxes assessed therein shall be collected and distributed as now provided by law." *Enumeration of inhabitants. Separate town for excise purposes.*

§ 2. This act shall take effect immediately.

Chap. 754.

AN ACT to amend railroad law, and the act amendatory thereof, relative to grade crossings.

Became a law May 22, 1897, with the approval of the Governor.
Passed, three-fifths being present.

The People of the State of New York, represented in Senate and Assembly, do enact as follows:

Railroad law amended. Section 1. Article two of chapter five hundred and sixty-five of the laws of eighteen hundred and ninety, entitled "An act in relation to railroads, constituting chapter thirty-nine of the general laws," known as the railroad law, as amended by chapter six hundred and seventy-six of the laws of eighteen hundred and ninety-two, is hereby amended by adding thereto the following sections:

Grade crossings of steam railroads. § 60. All steam surface railroads, hereafter built except additional switches and sidings, must be so constructed as to avoid all public crossings at grade, whenever practicable so to do. When-

Application to railroad commissioners. ever application is made to the board of railroad commissioners, under section fifty-nine of the railroad law, there shall be filed with said board a map showing the streets, avenues and highways proposed to be crossed by the new construction, and the said board shall determine whether such crossings shall be under or over the proposed railroad, except where said board shall determine such

Hearing upon manner of crossing. method of crossing to be impracticable. Whenever an application is made under this section to determine the manner of crossing, the said board shall designate a time and place when and where a hearing will be given to such railroad company, and shall notify the municipal corporation having jurisdiction over such streets, avenues or highways proposed to be crossed by the new railroad. The said board shall also give public notice of such hearing in at least two newspapers, published in the locality affected by the application, and all persons owning land in the vicinity of the pro-

Decision of board. posed crossings shall have the right to be heard. The decision of the said board rendered in any proceedings under this section shall be communicated, within twenty days after final hearing, to all parties to whom notice of the hearing in said proceedings was given, or who appeared at said hearing by counsel or in person.

New streets, etc., across railroads. § 61. When a new street, avenue or highway, or new portion of a street, avenue or highway shall hereafter be constructed across a steam surface railroad, such street, avenue or highway, or portion of such street, avenue or highway, shall pass over or under such railroad or at grade as the board of railroad commissioners shall direct. Notice of intention to lay out such street, avenue or high- way, or new portion of a street, avenue or highway, across a steam surface railroad, shall be given to such railroad company by the municipal corporation at least fifteen days prior to the making of the order laying out such street, avenue or highway by service personally on the president or vice-president of the railroad corporation, or any general officer thereof. Such notice shall designate the time and place and when and where a hearing will be given to such railroad company, and such railroad company shall have the right to be heard before the authorities of such municipal corporation upon the question of the necessity of such street, avenue or highway. If the municipal corporation determines such street, avenue or highway to be necessary, it shall then apply to the board of railroad commissioners before any further proceedings are taken, to determine whether such street, avenue or highway shall pass over or under such railroad, or at grade, whereupon the said board of railroad commissioners shall appoint a time and place for hearing such application, and shall give such notice thereof, as they judge reasonable, not, however, less than ten days, to the railroad company whose railroad is to be crossed by such new street, avenue or highway, or new portion of a street, avenue or highway, to the municipal corporation and to the owners of land adjoining the railroad and that part of the street, avenue or highway to be opened or extended. The said board of railroad commissioners shall determine whether such street, avenue or highway, or new portion of a street, avenue or highway, shall be constructed over or under such railroad or at grade; and if said board determine that such street, avenue or highway shall be carried across such railroad above grade, then said board shall determine the height, the length and the material of the bridge or structure by means of which such street, avenue or highway shall be carried across such railroad, and the length, character and grades of the approaches thereto; and if said board shall determine that such street, avenue or highway shall be constructed or extended below the grade, said board shall determine the manner and method in which the same shall be so carried under, and the grade or grades thereof and if said board shall determine that said street, avenue or highway shall be constructed or extended at grade, said board shall determine the manner and method in which the same shall be carried over said

Decision of board. railroad at grade and what safeguards shall be maintained. The decision of the said board as to the manner and method of carrying such new street, avenue or highway, or new portion of a street, avenue or highway, across such railroad, shall be final, subject, however, to the right of appeal hereinafter given. The decision of said board rendered in any proceeding under this section shall be communicated within twenty days after final hearing to all parties to whom notice of the hearing in such proceeding was given or who appeared at such hearing by counsel or in person.

Changes in existing crossings. § 62. The mayor and common council of any city, the president and trustees of any village, the town board of any town within which a street, avenue or highway crosses or is crossed by a steam surface railroad at grade, or any steam surface railroad company, whose road crosses or is crossed by a street, avenue or highway at grade, may bring their petition, in writing, to the board of railroad commissioners, therein alleging that public safety requires an alteration in the manner of such crossing, its approaches, the method of crossing, the location of the highway or crossing, the closing and discontinuance of a highway crossing and the diversion of the travel thereon to another not at grade, and praying that the same may be ordered; whereupon the said board of railroad commissioners shall appoint a time and place for hearing the petition, and shall give such personal notice thereof as they shall judge reasonable, of not less than ten days, however, to said petitioner, the railroad company, the municipality in which such crossing is situated, and to the owners of the lands adjoining such crossing and adjoining that part of the highway to be changed in grade or location, and shall cause notice of said hearing to be advertised in at least two newspapers published in the locality affected by the application; and after such notice of hearing the said board of railroad commissioners shall determine what alterations or changes, if any, shall be made. The decision of said board of railroad commissioners rendered in any proceeding under this section, shall be communicated within twenty days after final hearing to all parties to whom notice of the hearing in said proceeding was given, or who appeared at said hearing by counsel or in person. Any person aggrieved by such decision, or by a decision made pursuant to sections sixty and sixty-one hereof, and who was a party to said proceeding, may appeal therefrom to the appellate division of the supreme court in the department in which such grade crossing is situated and to the court of appeals, in the same manner and with like effect

margin notes: Petition to railroad commission. Hearing upon petition. Decision of board. Appeals from decision.

as is provided in the case of appeals from an order of the supreme court.

§ 63. The municipal corporation in which the highway crossing is located, may, with the approval of the railroad company acquire by purchase any lands, rights or easements necessary or required for the purpose of carrying out the provisions of section sixty, sixty-one and sixty-two of this act, but if unable to do so shall acquire such lands, rights or easements by condemnation under the condemnation law. The railroad company shall have notice of any such proceedings and the right to be heard therein. *Acquisition of lands by municipal corporations.*

§ 64. When a highway crosses a railroad by an overhead bridge, the frame work of the bridge and its abutments shall be maintained and kept in repair by the railroad company, and the roadway thereover and the approaches thereto shall be maintained and kept in repair by the municipality in which the same are situated. When a highway passes under a railroad, the bridge and its abutments shall be maintained and kept in repair by the railroad company, and the subway and its approaches shall be maintained and kept in repair by the municipality in which the same are situated. *Repair and maintenance of bridges and subways.*

§ 65. Whenever, under the provisions of section sixty of this act, new railroads are constructed across existing highways, the expense of crossing above or below the grade of the highway shall be paid entirely by the railroad corporations. Whenever under the provisions of section sixty-one of this act a new street, avenue or highway is constructed across an existing railroad, the railroad corporation shall pay one-half and the municipal corporation wherein such street, avenue or highway is located, shall pay the remaining one-half of the expense of making such crossing above or below grade; and whenever a change is made in an existing crossing in accordance with the provisions of section sixty-two of this act, fifty per centum of the expense thereof shall be borne by the railroad corporation, twenty-five per centum by the municipal corporation, and twenty-five per centum by the state. Whenever, in carrying out the provisions of sections sixty-one or sixty-two of this act, two or more lines of steam surface railroad, owned and operated by different corporations, cross a highway at a point where a change in grade is made, each corporation shall pay such proportion of fifty per centum of the expense thereof as shall be determined by the board of railroad commissioners. In carrying out the provisions of sections sixty, sixty-one and sixty-two of this act the work shall be done by the railroad corporation or corporations affected there- *Expenses of crossings, how paid.*

by, subject to the supervision of and approval of the board of railroad commissioners, and in all cases, except where the entire expense is paid by the railroad corporation, the expense of construction shall be paid primarily by the railroad company, and the expense of acquiring additional lands, rights or easements, shall be paid primarily by the municipal corporation wherein such high-

Plans and estimates of changes. way crossings are located. Plans and specifications of all changes proposed under sections sixty-one and sixty-two of this act, and an estimate of the expense thereof shall be submitted to the board of railroad commissioners for their approval before the letting of any

Submission of proposals for work. contract. In case the work is done by contract the proposals of contractors shall be submitted to the board of railroad commissioners, and if the board shall determine that the bids are excessive it shall have the power to require the submission of new proposals.

Supervision of work by railroad commissioners. The board of railroad commissioners may employ temporarily such experts and engineers as may be necessary to properly supervise any work that may be undertaken under sections sixty, sixty-one or sixty-two of this act, the expense thereof to be paid by the comptroller upon the requisition and certificate of the said board, said expense to be included in the cost of the particular change in grade on account of which it is incurred and finally apportioned in the

Accounting upon completion of work. manner provided in this section. Upon the completion of the work and its approval by the board of railroad commissioners, an accounting shall be had between the railroad corporation and the municipal corporation, of the amounts expended by each with interest, and if it shall appear that the railroad corporation or the municipal corporation have expended more than their proportion of the expense of the crossing as herein provided, a settlement shall be forthwith made in accordance with the provisions of this section. All items of expenditure shall be verified under oath, and,

Disputes. in case of a dispute between the railroad corporation and the municipal corporation as to the amount expended, any judge of the supreme court in the judicial district in which the municipality is situated, may appoint a referee to take testimony as to the amount expended, and the confirmation of the report of the referee shall

Failure or refusal to make payments. be final. In the event of the failure or refusal of the railroad corporation to pay its proportion of the expense, the same, with interest from the date of such accounting, may be levied and assessed upon the railroad corporation and collected in the same manner that taxes and assessments are now collected by the municipal corporation within which the work is done; and in the event of the failure or refusal of the municipal corporation to pay its proportion of the expense, suit may be instituted by the railroad corporation for the collection of the same with interest from the date of such accounting, or the railroad corporation may offset such amount with interest against any taxes levied or assessed against it or its property by such municipal corporation. The legislature shall annually appropriate out of any moneys not otherwise appropriated, the sum of one hundred thousand dollars for the purpose of paying the state's proportion of the expense of a change in an existing grade crossing. If, in any year, any less sum than one hundred thousand dollars is expended by the state for the purpose aforesaid the balance remaining unexpended shall be applied to reduce the amount appropriated by the state in the next succeeding year, except that no such deduction shall be made in case there are outstanding and unadjusted obligations on account of a change in an existing grade crossing for a proportion of which the state is liable under the provisions of this section. In the event of the appropriation made by the state in any one year being insufficient to pay the state's proportion of the expense of any change that may be ordered the first payment from the appropriation of the succeeding year shall be on account of said change, and no payment shall be made on account of any subsequent change that may be ordered, nor shall any subsequent change be ordered until the obligation of the state on account of the first-named change in grade has been fully discharged, unless the same shall be provided for by an additional appropriation to be made by the legislature. The state's proportion of the expense of changing any existing grade crossing shall be paid by the state treasurer on the warrant of the comptroller, to which shall be appended the certificate of the board of railroad commissioners to the effect that the work has been properly performed and a statement showing the situation of the crossing that has been changed, the total cost and the proportionate expense thereof, and the money shall be paid in whole or in part to the railroad corporation or to the municipal corporation, as the board of railroad commissioners may direct, subject, however, to the rights of the respective parties as they appear from the accounting to be had as hereinbefore provided for.

Appropriations by state.

State's proportion, how paid.

§ 66. The railroad commissioners may, in the absence of any application therefor, when, in their opinion, public safety requires an alteration in an existing grade crossing, institute proceedings

Powers of railroad commissioners as to change of existing crossings.

on their own motion for an alteration in such grade crossing, upon such notice as they shall deem reasonable, of not less than ten days, however, to the railroad company, the municipal corporation and the person or persons interested, and proceedings shall be conducted as provided in section sixty-two of this act. The changes in existing grade crossings authorized or required by the board of railroad commissioners in any one year shall be so distributed and apportioned over and among the railroads and the municipalities of the state as to produce such equality of burden upon them for their proportionate part of the expenses as herein provided for as the nature and circumstances of the cases before them will permit.

Compliance with provisions of act.

§ 67. It shall be the duty of the corporation, municipality or person or persons to whom the decisions or recommendations of the board of railroad commissioners are directed, as provided in sections sixty, sixty-one, sixty-two and sixty-six of this act to comply with such decisions and recommendations, and in case of their failure so to do, the board shall present the facts in the case to the attorney-general, who shall thereupon take proceedings to compel obedience to the decisions and recommendations of the board of railroad commissioners. The supreme court at a special term shall have the power in all cases of such decisions and recommendations by the board of railroad commissioners to compel compliance therewith by mandamus, subject to appeal to the appellate division of the supreme court and the court of appeals, in the same manner, and with like effect, as is provided in case of appeals from any order of the supreme court.

Mandamus to compel same.

Crossings by street surface railroads.

§ 68. All street surface railroads hereafter constructed across a steam railroad shall be above, below or at grade of such steam railroad as the board of railroad commissioners shall determine, and such board shall in such determination fix the proportion of expense of such crossing to be paid by the street surface railroad.

Application of provisions.

§ 69. The provisions of this act shall also apply to all existing or future steam surface railroads, on which, after the passage of this act, electricity or some other agency than steam shall be substituted as a motive power.

Exceptions.

§ 2. None of the provisions of this act shall apply to crossings in the city of Buffalo under the jurisdiction of the grade crossing commissioners of that city, nor shall they apply to the University avenue or Brown street crossing, in the city of Rochester.

§ 3. All acts and parts of acts inconsistent with this act are Repeal. hereby repealed.

§ 4. This act shall take effect the first day of July, eighteen hundred and ninety-seven. When takes effect.

Chap. 755.

AN ACT to release to James McGee and Mary McEvoy all the right, title and interest of the people of the state of New York of, in and to certain real estate situate in the city of Rochester, county of Monroe, and state of New York.

Became a law May 22, 1897, with the approval of the Governor. Passed by a two-thirds vote.

The People of the State of New York, represented in Senate and Assembly, do enact as follows:

Section 1. All the right, title and interest which the people of Interest of state the state of New York acquired by escheat of, in and to the several released. pieces or parcels of land hereinafter particularly described, and of which James McGee, late of the city of Rochester, Monroe county, New York, died seized and intestate, is hereby granted, conveyed and released to James McGee and Mary McEvoy, both of Dundrum, in the county of Down, Ireland, and to their heirs and assigns forever, equally, share and share alike.

Parcel number one.—All that tract or parcel of land situate in Description of the city of Rochester, county of Monroe and state of New York, property. known as lots numbers one hundred and thirty-eight and one hundred and thirty-nine, as laid down on a map of the south part of the Champeny tract; said lots being each thirty-three feet wide in front on the east side of Lawrence street, the same width in rear and one hundred feet deep, being the same premises conveyed to the said James McGee by Hiram Sibley and wife, by deed recorded in Monroe county clerk's office in liber one hundred and thirty of deeds, at page twenty-six.

Parcel number two.—Also all that other certain tract or parcel of land situate in the city of Rochester, county of Monroe and state of New York, bounded and described as follows: Beginning in the north line of East avenue one hundred and seventeen feet east of the east line of Union street; thence running easterly on said East avenue twenty-five feet; thence northerly, parallel with Union street, to the south line of lands now or formerly owned by Hugh Mulholland; thence westerly, and parallel with East avenue, twenty-five feet; thence southerly to the place of beginning; being the same premises conveyed by Hiram Sibley and wife to said James McGee by deed recorded in Monroe county clerk's office in liber one hundred and nineteen of deed at page four hundred and twenty-five.

Parcel number three.—Also that certain other tract or parcel of land situate in the city of Rochester, county of Monroe and state of New York, known as lot number twenty, in the Champeny tract, being sixty-six feet wide in front and rear, and about one hundred and sixty feet deep, lying on the west side of Alexander street, as laid down on a map of the south part of said tract, on file in Monroe county clerk's office, being the same premises conveyed to said James McGee by Hiram Sibley and wife, by deed recorded in Monroe county clerk's office in liber one hundred and fifty-two of deeds at page eighty-four.

Parcel number four.—Also all that certain other tract or parcel of land situate in the city of Rochester, county of Monroe and state of New York, known as parts of lots numbers eighteen and nineteen, in the Champeny tract, and being about forty feet wide in front on the south side of Charlotte street, the same width in rear and one hundred and thirty-two feet deep, and forty feet distant west from the west side of Alexander street, and the west lot east of and adjoining lands now or formerly owned by Michael Connors, being the same premises conveyed to said James McGee by Hiram Sibley and wife, by deed recorded in Monroe county clerk's office in liber one hundred and eighty-five of deeds at page one hundred and thirty-two.

Parcel number five.— Also all that certain other tract or parcel of land situate in the city of Rochester, county of Monroe and state of New York, bounded and described as follows: Beginning at a point in the east line of Union street two hundred feet northerly from the north line of East avenue and six feet northerly from the southwesterly corner of lot number twelve, as designated on the map of the subdivision of the south part of the Champeny tract lithographed from the survey of J. M. Bruff, surveyor, and filed in Monroe county clerk's office in the great book of maps, running thence easterly on a line at right angles with the east line of Union street one hundred and eighty feet to the east line of said lot number twelve; thence northerly along said east line, and parallel with the east line of Union street sixty feet to the northeast corner of said lot number twelve; thence west-

erly along the north line of said lot number twelve one hundred
and eighty feet to the place of beginning, excepting and reserv-
ing the right and privilege of putting and maintaining an inch and
a half pipe in the well near the south line of the premises herein
conveyed, by digging down on the premises adjoining and on the
south of the premises herein conveyed, and inserting such pipe
through the wall of said well, and the privilege of obtaining water
from such well through said pipe for family use, as specified and
granted in a deed of said adjoining premises executed by Hugh
Mulholland and wife to Marie J. Hough, April twenty-eighth, eighteen hundred and sixty-four, being the same premises conveyed
by Hugh Mulholland and wife to said James McGee by deed recorded in Monroe county clerk's office in liber one hundred and
eighty-five of deeds as page one hundred and fifty-six.

Parcel number six.— Also all that certain other tract or parcel
of land situate in the city of Rochester, formerly in the town of
Brighton, county of Monroe and state of New York, described as
follows: Commencing in the center of Schancks avenue at the
northeasterly corner of Henry street; thence running southerly
in the center of Henry street to the southeasterly corner of Henry
street, to the center of Van Buren avenue; thence westerly in the
center of said Van Buren avenue to the easterly of Bernard Klem's
farm; thence running westerly along the said Klem's easterly line
to the center of said Schancks avenue, and thence running easterly
in the center of said avenue to the place of beginning; intending
to convey lots numbers fifteen, sixteen, seventeen and eighteen, on
Schancks avenue, and lots numbers thirty-two, thirty-three, thirty-
four and thirty-five, on Van Buren avenue, as laid down on a map
made by James Edmunds, surveyor, and filed in Monroe county
clerk's office, containing eight and sixty-three one-hundredths acres
of land, being the same premises conveyed to said James McGee
by Kendrick V. B. Schanck and wife by deed recorded in Monroe
county clerk's office in liber three hundred and sixty-three of deeds
at page two hundred and thirty-one.

Parcel number seven.— Also all those certain other tracts or
parcels of land known and distinguished as lots numbers twelve,
fourteen, sixteen and eighteen, as the same are severally defined
upon a map of Robert Lineys; subdivision of lot twenty-six, part of
town lots forty-three, forty-four and fifty-one, filed in Monroe
county clerk's office in liber seven of maps, at page seventy-nine.
Said map being made by I. H. Quinby, surveyor, the premises

intended to be conveyed are situate in the east Gunther street and said lots twelve, fourteen and sixteen are each forty feet in front, the same width in rear, and run back from said street each one hundred and thirty-eight and twenty-five one hundredths feet, said lot eighteen, fronts twenty-two feet on said street, is ninety-two feet in the rear, more or less, and one hundred and thirty-eight and one-quarter feet in depth on its south line and one hundred and fifty-five and one-quarter feet on its north line, being part of the premises conveyed to Robert Liney by deed dated the thirteenth day of January, eighteen hundred and fifty-four, and recorded in Monroe county clerk's office in liber one hundred and sixteen of deeds, at page forty-three, and said subdivision being made for said Robert Liney according to said map, and being the same premises conveyed to said James McGee by said Robert Liney by deed recorded in Monroe county clerk's office in liber four hundred and fifty-nine of deeds, at page four hundred and five.

Parcel number eight.— All that certain other tract or parcel of land situate in the city of Rochester, county of Monroe, and state of New York, being a part of lands lately or formerly owned by Davis S. Bates, deceased, and laid down on a map of the Bates farm recorded in Monroe county clerk's office in liber fifty-eight of deeds, at page three hundred and ninety-two, as lots number fifty-eight, containing one acre and four-hundredths of an acre, be the same more or less, being the same premises conveyed to said James McGee by Thomas Raines, referee, by deed recorded in Monroe county clerk's office in liber three hundred and seventy of deeds, at page two hundred and sixty-six.

Parcel number nine.— Also all that certain other tract or parcel of land situate in the city of Rochester, county of Monroe, and state of New York, known as lots numbers one hundred and thirty and one hundred and thirty-one, in the Champeny tract, so called, as laid down on the lithographic map of said tract on file in Monroe county clerk's office. Said lots fronting on Lawrence street thirty-three feet each, and running back ninety-eight feet, and being the same premises conveyed to the said James McGee by Peter Babst and wife by deed recorded in Monroe county clerk's office in liber two hundred and seven of deeds, at page eighty-one.

Parcel number ten.— Also that certain other tract or parcel of land situate in the city of Rochester, county of Monroe, and state of New York, known as lot number thirteen, on a map of the Champeny farm made by James M. Bruff, surveyor, bounded and described as follows: Commencing on the east side of Union street two hundred and sixty-four feet from the corner of Charlotte street; thence southerly on Union street sixty-six feet; thence easterly along the south line of said lot number thirteen to the west line of lot number four, about one hundred and seventy-six feet; thence northerly along said west line to the north line of said lot number thirteen; thence westerly to the place of beginning, intending to convey hereby all of said premises now or lately occupied by Eliza A. Benton, on North Union street, which, as is supposed, will overrun the area of the premises above specifically described and being the same premises conveyed to the said James McGee by Patrick Cooper, by deed recorded in Monroe county clerk's office in liber four hundred and six of deeds, at page seventy-eight.

§ 2. Nothing in this act contained shall be construed to impair or affect, in any way, the dower right or thirds of Ellen McGee, the widow of said James McGee, deceased, in the real estate described in the first section of this act, or to impair or affect the rights in said real estate of any heir-at-law, devisee, grantee or creditor by judgment, mortgage or otherwise in and to said premises or any part thereof, or any action or suit now pending. *Rights, etc., not affected.*

§ 3. This act shall take effect immediately.

Chap. 756.

AN ACT to amend section six of chapter five hundred and forty-seven of the laws of eighteen hundred and ninety-six, entitled " An act relating to real property, constituting chapter forty-six of the general laws."

Became a law May 22, 1897, with the approval of the Governor.
Passed, three-fifths being present.

The People of the State of New York, represented in Senate and Assembly, do enact as follows:

Section 1. Section six of chapter five hundred and forty-seven of the laws of eighteen hundred and ninety-six, entitled "An act relating to real property, constituting chapter forty-six of the general laws," is hereby amended so as to read as follows :

§ 6. Effect of woman's marriage with alien on rights of herself and her descendants.—Any woman born a citizen of the United States, who shall have married or shall marry an alien, and the foreign-born children and descendants of any such woman, shall, notwithstanding her or their residence or birth in a foreign country, be entitled to take, hold, convey and devise real property situated within this state in like manner, and with like effect, as if such woman and such foreign-born children and descendants were citizens of the United States; and the title to any such real property shall not be impaired or affected by reason of such marriage, or residence, or foreign birth; provided that the title to such real property shall have been or shall be derived from or through a citizen of the United States.

§ 2. This act shall take effect immediately.

Chap. 757.

AN ACT conferring jurisdiction upon the court of claims to hear, audit and determine the claim of Sarah E. Lembeck, as executrix of the estate of Henry F. Lembeck, deceased, against the state, arising from damages caused by the overflow of water from Mill creek in the town of Watkins.

Became a law May 22, 1897, with the approval of the Governor. Passed, three-fifths being present.

The People of the State of New York, represented in Senate and Assembly, do enact as follows:

Jurisdiction to hear claim.

Section 1. Jurisdiction is hereby conferred upon the court of claims to hear, audit and determine the claim, if any, of Sarah E. Lembeck, as executrix and trustee under the last will and testament of Henry F. Lembeck, deceased, late of Watkins, New York, against the state for alleged damages to the property belonging to the estate of the said Henry F. Lembeck, caused by the overflow of water from Mill creek, in said village, and for moneys paid, laid out and expended in piling, planking and otherwise improving the bank of said creek. If any legal claim is found to exist, such damages and compensation shall be awarded as the court of claims shall deem just and reasonable, not exceeding in the aggregate the sum of two thousand five hundred dollars.

Appeal from award.

§ 2. Either party may take an appeal to the appellate division of the supreme court for the third judicial department from any award made under authority of this act, if the sum in controversy exceeds five hundred dollars, provided such appeal be taken by the service of a notice of appeal within thirty days after the service of a copy of the award.

§ 3. This act shall take effect immediately.

Chap. 763.

AN ACT to amend chapter seven hundred and forty-two of the laws of eighteen hundred and ninety-four, entitled "An act to incorporate the Equitable Security company."

Became a law May 22, 1897, with the approval of the Governor.
Passed, a majority being present.

The People of the State of New York, represented in Senate and Assembly, do enact as follows:

Section 1. Section two of chapter seven hundred and forty-two of _{charter amended} the laws of eighteen hundred and ninety-four, entitled "An act to incorporate the Equitable Securities company," is hereby amended so as to read as follows:

§ 2. The amount of capital stock of said company shall be two Capital stock. million, one hundred thousand dollars divided into twenty-one thousand shares of one hundred dollars each and one-half of said stock may be preferred stock entitled to such preference or preferences as shall be provided in the by-laws of the company to be adopted as hereinafter provided. Such stock or any part thereof may be issued in exchange for the stock of the said Equitable Mortgage Company upon such terms as may be provided for in the original by-laws, to be adopted as hereinafter provided. The Increase or reduction preferred and common stock of said company may be increased or of same. reduced in all respects in the manner provided by sections forty-five and forty-six of chapter six hundred and eighty-eight of the laws of eighteen hundred and ninety-two, being part of an act entitled "An act to amend the stock corporation law," provided that such increase or reduction need not be in like proportion as respects the preferred and common stock; provided, however, that in increasing or reducing said stock in different proportions, it shall be necessary to obtain the votes of the stockholders owning at least a majority of each class of stock respectively; and provided always that when the capital stock is in any manner reduced the debts and liabilities of the corporation shall not exceed the amount of its reduced capital and other assets, and provided further that the capital stock shall not be reduced to an amount less than eight hundred and fifty thousand dollars.

§ 2. This act shall take effect immediately.

Chap. 764.

AN ACT to provide for acquiring the site of the battle of Stony
Point, in Rockland county, and making an appropriation
therefor.

Became a law May 22, 1897, with the approval of the Governor.

Passed, three-fifths being present.

*The People of the State of New York, represented in Senate and
Assembly, do enact as follows:*

Acquisition of title.

Section 1. The commissioners of the land office may, on the rec-
ommendation of the "trustees of scenic and historic places and
objects," a corporation duly incorporated by chapter one hundred and sixty-six of the laws of eighteen hundred and ninety-
five, by agreement with the owner or owners, upon such price
and terms as they may deem just, not exceeding the sum of one
thousand dollars, acquire title, on behalf, and in the name of,
the peopel of the state, to the following described land commemor-
ative of the battle of Stony Point, viz.: All that plot and parcel
of land in the town of Stony Point, county of Rockland, known as
the "Stony Point peninsula," which is bounded on the west by
the easterly side of lands of the New York, West Shore and Buffalo
Railroad company, and on all other sides by the Hudson river;
containing about thirty-six acres of land.

Control and jurisdiction of trustees.

§ 2. After title to said lands shall have been acquired as aforesaid, said trustees shall have control and jurisdiction thereof for
the purposes mentioned in said chapter one hundred and sixty-six
of the laws of eighteen hundred and ninety-five.

Payment by comptroller.

§ 3. Upon the requisition of said commissioners of the land office,
and upon a voucher or vouchers certified by said commisisoners, or
by such officer or officers thereof as they may designate for that
purpose, in form to be approved by the comptroller, the comptroller
shall pay the sum or sums that may be necessary to pay for the
lands authorized to be acquired by the authority of this act.

Appropriation.

§ 4. The sum of twenty-five thousand dollars, or so much thereof
as may be necessary, payable by the treasurer out of any moneys in
the treasury not otherwise appropriated, is hereby appropriated,
subject to the audit of the comptroller, to carry out the provisions
of this act, and the same shall be payable by the comptroller on the
requisition of said commissioners of the land office.

§ 5. This act shall take effect immediately.

Chap. 766.

AN ACT to abolish fine and imprisonment for nonpayment of taxes.

Became a law May 22, 1897, with the approval of the Governor.
Passed, three-fifths being present.

The People of the State of New York, represented in Senate and Assembly, do enact as follows:

Section 1. After the passage of this act a neglect or a refusal to pay any tax shall not be punishable as a contempt, and fine and imprisonment for any such nonpayment is hereby abolished.

§ 2. This act shall not apply to proceedings supplementary to execution upon judgment recovered for taxes.

§ 3. This act shall take effect immediately.

Chap. 767.

AN ACT providing for horticultural investigations, experiments, instruction and information, and for the dissemination of horticultural knowledge in the second judicial department, at the agricultural station at Geneva, in the county of Ontario, and making an appropriation therefor.

Became a law May 22, 1897, with the approval of the Governor
Passed, three-fifths being present.

The People of the State of New York, represented in Senate and Assembly, do enact as follows:

Section 1. The sum of eight thousand dollars, or so much thereof as may be necessary, is hereby appropriated out of any moneys in the treasury not otherwise appropriated, for the purpose of conducting horticultural investigations, experiments, instruction and information, and to disseminate horticultural knowledge in the second judicial department, to be paid to the New York State Agricultural Experiment Station at Geneva, county of Ontario, as provided for in and pursuant to section eighty-five of the agricultural law. Such money hereby appropriated shall be paid by the treasurer on the warrant of the comptroller, upon vouchers approved by the commissioner of agriculture. *[margin: Appropriation for experiments.]*

§ 2. This act shall take effect immediately.

Chap. 768.

AN ACT to amend chapter three hundred and thirty-eight of the laws of eighteen hundred and ninety-three, entitled " An act in relation to agriculture, constituting articles one, two, three, four and five of chapter thirty-three of the general laws."

Became a law May 22, 1897, with the approval of the Governor.

Passed, three-fifths being present.

The People of the State of New York, represented in Senate and Assembly, do enact as follows:

Section 1. Section twenty-six of chapter three hundred and thirty-eight of the laws of eighteen hundred and ninety-three, entitled "An act in relation to agriculture, constituting articles one, two, three, four and five of chapter thirty-three of the general laws," is hereby amended so as to read as follows:

§ 26. **Manufacture and sale of imitation butter prohibited.**—No person by himself, his agents or employes, shall produce or manufacture out of or from any animal fats or animal or vegetable oils not produced from unadulterated milk or cream from the same, the article known as oleomargarine or any article or product in imitation or semblance of natural butter produced from pure, unadulterated milk or cream of the same; or mix, compound with or add to milk, cream or butter any acids or other deleterious substance or any animal fats or animal or vegetable oils not produced from milk or cream, so as to produce any article or substance or any human food in imitation or in semblance of natural butter, nor sell, keep for sale or offer for sale any article, substance, or compound made, manufactured or produced in violation of the provisions of this section, whether such article, substance or compound shall be made or produced in this state or elsewhere. Any dealer in any article or product, the manufacture or sale of which is prohibited by this act, who shall keep, store or display such article or product, with other merchandise or stock in his place of business, shall be deemed to have the same in his possession for sale.

§ 2. This act shall take effect immediately.

Chap. 770.

AN ACT to provide for the completion of the armory in the city of Buffalo, for the Seventy-fourth regiment, national guard of the state of New York, and making an appropriation therefor.

Became a law May 24, 1897, with the approval of the Governor. Passed, three-fifths being present.

The People of the State of New York, represented in Senate and Assembly, do enact as follows:

Section 1. The sum of three hundred and seventy-five thousand dollars is hereby appropriated out of any moneys in the treasury not otherwise appropriated, for the completion of the armory in the city of Buffalo for the seventy-fourth regiment of the national guard of the state of New York, the erection and construction of which was authorized and provided for by chapter five hundred and eighty-four of the laws of eighteen hundred and ninety-six. Such completion shall be in accordance with the provisions of such act and with the plans and specifications adopted and approved by the adjutant-general, the inspector-general and the chief of ordnance of the state of New York, who were by such act constituted a commission for the erection and construction of such armory. The amount so appropriated shall be paid by the state treasurer upon the warrant of the comptroller, drawn upon the written requisition of such commission and shall be expended in accordance with the provisions of such act. *(marginal: Appropriation for armory. Plans. Payment of appropriation.)*

§ 2. Of the amount hereby appropriated, the sum of seventy-five thousand dollars shall be paid by the treasurer upon the warrant of the comptroller during the year eighteen hundred and ninety-seven; and one hundred and fifty thousand dollars, together with any unexpended balance of the amount hereby made available during the year eighteen hundred and ninety-seven, shall be paid in like manner during the year eighteen hundred and ninety-eight; and one hundred and fifty thousand dollars, or so much thereof as may be necessary for the completion of such armory, together with any unexpended balance of the amounts hereby made available during the years of eighteen hundred and ninety-seven and eighteen hundred and ninety-eight, shall be paid in like manner during the year eighteen hundred and ninety-nine. *(marginal: Appropriation, when available.)*

§ 3. This act shall take effect immediately.

Chap. 771.

AN ACT for the construction of a state armory in the city of
Schenectady, and making an appropriation therefor.

Became a law May 24, 1897, with the approval of the Governor.
Passed by a two-thirds vote.

*The People of the State of New York, represented in Senate and
Assembly, do enact as follows:*

Appropriation for armory.

Section 1. The treasurer shall pay on the warrant of the comptroller, the sum of sixty thousand dollars, or so much thereof, as
may be necessary, thirty thousand dollars of which shall become available in the year eighteen hundred and ninety-seven
and thirty thousand dollars in the year eighteen hundred and
ninety-eight, which such sum is hereby appropriated for the erection of an armory in the city of Schenectady, for the use of the
Thirty-sixth and Thirty-seventh separate companies of the national

Commission to expend same.

guard of the state of New York, to be expended under the direction
of the adjutant-general, the inspector-general and the chief of ordnance, who are hereby appointed a commission for this purpose.

Conditions of expenditure.

But no part of this appropriation shall be expended by said commissioners, except for plans and expenses of the commissioners, until
said plans and specifications of the building shall have been submitted to the comptroller and until he shall have been satisfied that
the buildings, including the necessary sewerage and the necessary
expenses of the commission and for superintendence and completion of the work, can and will be completed within the limits of
the sums and the material herein specified and appropriated.

Plans.

§ 2. Plans and specifications of said armory shall be prepared in
detail and shall receive the approval of the said commissioners,

Contracts for work.

and all work upon said armory, except the interior furnishing and
finishing, shall be done upon contract executed by and between the
contractor or contractors and said commissioners, which shall be
awarded to the lowest responsible bidder or bidders, after due
publication and advertisement, based upon said plans and specifications. Provided, however, that the said commissioners shall
have the right to reject any and all bids.

Removal of present armory.

§ 3. In the erection of said armory, the said commissioners shall
have the right and authority to remove and take down the present
armory building, and to use all such material thereof as may be
available in the erection of the armory hereby provided for, and to

dispose of all such material as shall not be available therefor, by Use or sale of materials. public sale, after due publication and advertisement of such sale and use the proceeds of such sale in the erection and construction of the building herein provided for.   Such material to be used and the proceeds of the sale above provided for, to be expended in addition to the amount above appropriated.

§ 4. The contractor or contractors for the building of said armory Contractor's bond. shall, before commencing the same, make and execute to the state, a bond in such form as the said commissioners shall prescribe, in the penalty of double the amount to be expended under said contract, with two or more sureties to be approved by the comptroller, for the faithful performance of such work.

§ 5. A room in said armory shall be set apart for the use of the Room for Grand Army post. post of the Grand Army of the Republic, located at the city of Schenectady.

§ 6. This act shall take effect immediately.

Chap. 774.

AN ACT conferring jurisdiction upon the court of claims to hear and determine the claim of the E. S. Higgins Carpet company against the state, and to make an award therefor.

Became a law May 24, 1897, with the approval of the Governor.
Passed, three-fifths being present.

The People of the State of New York, represented in Senate and Assembly, do enact as follows:

Section 1. Jurisdiction is hereby conferred upon the court of Jurisdiction to hear claim claims to hear and determine the alleged claim of E. S. Higgins Carpet company against the state, for thirteen hundred and fifty dollars paid to the comptroller of the state May nineteenth, eighteen hundred and ninety-three, and seven hundred and fifty dollars paid to the comptroller of the state January tenth, eighteen hundred and ninety-four, being a total of twenty-one hundred dollars, alleged to have been erroneously paid for the years eighteen hundred and ninety-two and eighteen hundred and ninety-three, under an alleged misapprehension of the provisions of chapter five hundred and forty-two of the laws of eighteen hundred and eighty, and the acts amendatory, and to award such damages to said E. S. Higgins Carpet company therefor as such court deem just and reasonable if the state would have been liable therefor, with interest thereon, as if it were a natural person, and if the claim therefor shall be filed within one year after the passage of this act. Either party may appeal to the appellate division of the supreme court of the third department from any award made under the authority of this act, provided such appeal be taken by the service of a notice of appeal and exceptions within thirty days after the service of a copy of the award.

§ 2. This act shall take effect immediately.

Chap. 778.

AN ACT authorizing the building and completing of retaining walls and approaches to Ship street bridge, crossing the Champlain canal in the city of Cohoes, and making an appropriation therefor.

Became a law May 24, 1897, with the approval of the Governor.
Passed, three-fifths being present.

The People of the State of New York, represented in Senate and Assembly, do enact as follows:

Section 1. The superintendent of public works is hereby authorized to build and complete the retaining walls on the west side of the Champlain canal, at the westerly end of Ship street bridge in the city of Cohoes, and to build and complete the retaining walls on the east side of the Champlain canal, at the easterly end of Ship street bridge in said city, and to build and complete the approaches to said Ship street bridge.

§ 2. The work herein authorized shall be based upon plans and specifications furnished and approved by the state engineer and surveyor.

§ 3. The sum of six thousand dollars, or so much thereof as shall be necessary, is hereby appropriated out of any money in the treasury not otherwise appropriated, for the purposes specified in this act, to be paid by the treasurer on the warrant of the comptroller, to the order of the superintendent of public works.

§ 4. This act shall take effect immediately.

Chap. 779.

AN ACT authorizing and directing the board of commissioners of the land office of the state of New York, to convey to the city of Buffalo, for park purposes, a strip of land on the south side of Scajaquada creek, in said city, known as portion of the land of the Buffalo state hospital

Accepted by the city.

Became a law May 24, 1897, with the approval of the Governor.

Passed, three-fifths being present.

The People of the State of New York, represented in Senate and Assembly, do enact as follows:

Section 1. In consideration of the payment of the sum of money as hereinafter provided, the board of commissioners of the land office are hereby authorized and directed to execute letters-patent, granting and conveying to the city of Buffalo, for park purposes, the strip of land hereinafter described. _{Convey-ance authorized.}

§ 2. The strip of land so to be granted and conveyed is described as follows: Beginning at a point in the northerly line of the state hospital grounds at the distance of six hundred and twenty-four and three-tenths feet westerly from the westerly line of Elmwood avenue measured along the northerly line of said state hospital grounds; thence westerly seven hundred and fifty feet; thence on a curve to the left with a radius of twenty-eight hundred and fifteen feet, fifteen hundred and fifty-five and eighty-two one-hundredths feet to the northwesterly corner of the state hospital grounds; thence easterly along the present northerly line of said hospital grounds to the place of beginning, containing ten and eighty one-hundredths acres, be the same more or less. _{Designation of land.}

§ 3. The said strip of land so granted and conveyed to the city shall be used only for the purpose of maintaining thereon, without expense to the state, a boulevard, speedway or drive, and for the improvement and embellishment of so much of said strip as shall not be embraced within such boulevard, speedway or drive. _{Use and improvement of land.}

§ 4. The compensation to be paid by said city of Buffalo for said tract or parcel of land shall be determined by the said board of land commissioners, and shall be such a sum as in the judgment of said board shall be a just and fair compensation therefor, due regard being had to the purposes for which it shall be used by said city of Buffalo. _{Compensation for land.}

Disposition
of money
paid.

§ 5. In case the said city of Buffalo shall determine to take said land at the valuation placed upon it by said board of land commissioners, the money so paid by said city of Buffalo shall be paid to the state treasurer, to be held by him as a special deposit; said money to serve as a fund for the purchase of such additional lands as may be found necessary for the use of the Buffalo state hospital.

§ 6. This act shall take effect immediately.

Chap. 781.

AN ACT to amend section seven hundred and fifty-one of the code of criminal procedure, in relation to appeals from courts of special sessions.

Became a law May 24, 1897, with the approval of the Governor.
Passed, three-fifths being present.

The People of the State of New York, represented in Senate and Assembly, do enact as follows:

Amendment.

Section 1. Section seven hundred and fifty-one of the code of criminal procedure, is hereby amended to read as follows:

Appeal
from court
of special
sessions.

§ 751. For the purpose of appealing, the defendant, or some one on his behalf, must within sixty days after the judgment, or within sixty days after the commitment where the appeal is from the latter, make an affidavit showing the alleged errors in the proceedings or conviction or commitment complained of, and must within that time present it to the county judge or a justice of the supreme court, or in the city and county of New York, to the recorder or a judge authorized to hold a court of general sessions in that city or in the city of Albany, to the recorder, and apply thereon for the allowance of the appeal.

§ 2. This act shall take effect immediately.

Chap. 782.

AN ACT to amend the highway law, in relation to highway districts.

Became a law May 24, 1897, with the approval of the Governor.
Passed, three-fifths being present.

The People of the State of New York, represented in Senate and Assembly, do enact as follows:

Highway
law
amended.

Section 1. Subdivision three of section four of chapter five hundred and sixty-eight of the laws of eighteen hundred and ninety, known as the highway law, is hereby amended to read as follows:

3. From time to time, not oftener than once a year, divide the Division of town into highway districts. town into so many highway districts as they shall judge convenient, by writing, under their hands, to be filed with the town clerk, and by him to be entered in the town book, at least ten days before an annual town meeting. A territory not exceeding one square mile, containing a population of not less than one hundred and fifty, and not including a part of a city or village, may be established as a separate highway district in the following manner: Separate districts for certain territory. A verified petition of two-thirds of the electors of such territory representing two-thirds of the taxable property therein and describing the territory, may be presented to the highway commissioner at least twenty days before the annual town meeting. The petition shall state the population of the proposed district, and the taxable persons and property as appears by the last preceding assessment-roll of the town. A farm or lot shall not be divided in the formation of such district. Within ten days after the presentation of such a petition, the highway commissioner shall establish the district in the manner above required for other highway districts. The highway district so established shall not be abolished, except upon the petition or written consent of two-thirds of the electors representing two-thirds of the taxable property of the district. The highway commissioner may extend the highway district, so established, not more than half a mile in any direction, and if it is so extended an order shall be entered accordingly.

§ 2. This act shall take effect immediately.

Chap. 785.

AN ACT to amend chapter nine hundred and eight of the laws of eighteen hundred and ninety-six, entitled "An act in relation to taxation, constituting chapter twenty-four of the general laws," in relation to exempting laundry corporations from taxation on their capital stock.

Became a law May 24, 1897, with the approval of the Governor.
Passed, three-fifths being present.

The People of the State of New York, represented in Senate and Assembly, do enact as follows: .

Section 1. Section one hundred and eighty-three of article nine of chapter nine hundred and eight of the laws of eighteen hundred and ninety-six, entitled " An act in relation to taxation, constituting chapter twenty-four of the general laws," is hereby amended to read as follows:

§ 183. **Certain corporations exempt from tax on capital stock.**— Banks, savings banks, institutions for savings, insurance or surety corporations, laundry corporations, manufacturing corporations to the extent only of the capital actually employed in this state in manufacturing, and in the sale of the product of such manufacturing, mining corporations wholly engaged in mining ores within this state, agricultural and horticultural societies or associations, and corporations, joint-stock companies or associations operating elevated railways or surface railroads not operated by steam, or formed for supplying water or gas for electric or steam heating, lighting or power purposes, and liable to a tax under sections one hundred and eighty-five and one hundred and eighty-six of this chapter, shall be exempt from the payment of the taxes prescribed by section one hundred and eighty-two of this chapter. This exemption shall not be construed to include title guaranty or trust companies.

§ 2. This act shall take effect immediately.

Chap. 786.

AN ACT to provide for the improvement of the state dam at Waterloo, and for the completion of the state ditch between the villages of Waterloo and Seneca Falls, and making an appropriation therefor.

Became a law May 24, 1897, with the approval of the Governor. Passed, three-fifths being present.

The People of the State of New York, represented in Senate and Assembly, do enact as follows:

Appropriation for improvement of state dam and ditch. Section 1. The sum of fifteen thousand dollars, or so much thereof as may be necessary, is hereby appropriated out of any moneys in the treasury not otherwise appropriated, for the purpose of rebuilding or reconstructing the south wing of the state dam at Waterloo, and for completing the construction of the state ditch between the villages of Waterloo and Seneca Falls. The money hereby appropriated shall be expended under the supervision of the superintendent of public works, upon plans and specifications provided by the state engineer and surveyor.

§ 2. This act shall take effect immediately.

Chap. 790.*

AN ACT making appropriations for certain expenses of government and supplying deficiencies in former appropriations.

Became a law May 24, 1897, with the approval of the Governor. Passed by a two-thirds vote.

The People of the State of New York, represented in Senate and Assembly, do enact as follows:

Section 1. The treasurer shall pay on the warrant of the comp- Payments by treas- urer.
troller, from the several funds specified, to the persons and for
the objects indicated in this act, the amounts named or such parts
of those amounts as shall be sufficient to accomplish, in full, the
purposes designated by the appropriations, but no warrants shall Audit of accounts.
be issued, except in cases of salaries, until the amounts claimed
shall have been audited and allowed by the comptroller, who is
hereby authorized to determine the same. The persons demanding Verified state- ments.
payment shall present to him a detailed statement, in items, verified by affidavit; and if the account shall be for services it must
show when, where and under what authority they were rendered;
if for expenditures, when, where and under what authority they
were made; if for articles furnished, when and where they were
furnished, to whom they were delivered, and under what authority; and if the demand be for traveling expenses, the account
must also specify the distance traveled, the place of starting and
destination, the duty or business and the date and items of expendi-
ture. On all accounts for transportation, furniture, blank and Certified bill to be furnished.
other books furnished for the use of officers, binding, blanks,
printing, stationery and postage, a bill duly certified must be furnished; but whenever an appropriation shall have been provided
otherwise, the sum herein directed to be paid shall not be considered as an addition to such other appropriation unless it shall be
expressly so declared in this act.

GENERAL FUND.

For the clergymen officiating as chaplain of the assembly, during Chaplain of assem- bly.
the session of eighteen hundred and ninety-seven, for compensation,

---

* Items of appropriation contained in this act, as passed by the legislature, and objected to by the governor, with the statement of his objections thereto, are not included in this publication, which contains only so
much of the act as actually became a law, under section nine of article
four of the constitution.

to be paid to the clerk of the assembly for distribution by him to
those clergymen, at the rate of five dollars a day for every day
of attendance, five hundred dollars.

Chaplain
of senate.
    For the clergymen officiating as chaplain of the senate during
the session of eighteen hundred and ninety-seven, for compensation, to be paid to the clerk of the senate, for distribution by him
to those clergymen, at the rate of five dollars a day for every day
of attendance, five hundred dollars.

DEPARTMENTS.

EXECUTIVE DEPARTMENT.

Reim-
bursement
of contin-
gent fund.
    For the governor to reimburse the executive contingent fund
for moneys advanced for witness' fees and other expenses in the
matter of the "Sheriff Tamsen" investigation, not provided for
in chapter nine hundred and fifty, laws of eighteen hundred and
ninety-six, the sum of six hundred and fifty-four dollars and eighty-
five cents.

FOR THE COMPTROLLER.

Surro-
gate's fees.
    For fees of surrogates in furnishing to the secretary of state
copies of letters of administration, copies of wills, probated in
other states and subsequently filed in this state, as provided by
section twenty-five hundred and three of the code of civil procedure, two hundred dollars, or so much thereof as may be necessary.

Assess-
ments on
state
property.
    The sum of four thousand six hundred and sixty-nine dollars
and twenty-five cents, being the unexpended balance of appropriation of ten thousand dollars, made by chapter three hundred and
fifty-eight. laws of eighteen hundred and ninety-four, and chapter
nine hundred and thirty-two, laws of eighteen hundred and ninety-
five for the comptroller to pay assessments for local improvements on property owned by the state, is hereby reappropriated
for the same purpose, and all fees, interest and expenses of sale
or collection incurred by local authority, officer or agent, in making any assessment, levy or collection or sale upon or of state property, or property held in trust for the state, for street or other municipal improvements in any municipal corporation of the state,
shall be rejected by the comptroller.

Mainte-
nance of
convicts in
peniten-
tiaries.
    For deficiency in appropriation for the maintenance of convicts
sentenced to penitentiaries, in pursuance of chapter one hundred
and fifty-eight of the laws of eighteen hundred and fifty-six, chapter five hundred and eighty-four of the laws of eighteen hundred
and sixty-five, chapter six hundred and sixty-seven of the laws of

eighteen hundred and sixty-six, chapter five hundred and seventy-four of the laws of eighteen hundred and sixty-nine, chapter two hundred and forty-seven of the laws of eighteen hundred and seventy-four, chapter five hundred and seventy-one of the laws of eighteen hundred and seventy-five, chapter four hundred and ninety of the laws of eighteen hundred and eighty-five, chapter one hundred and fifteen of the laws of eighteen hundred and ninety-one, and chapter five hundred and eighty-seven of the laws of eighteen hundred and ninety-two, and chapter three hundred and seventy-two of the laws of eighteen hundred and ninety-five, one hundred and eleven thousand dollars, or so much thereof as may be necessary.

For the comptroller, for the payment of compensation and ex- *Payment of counsel.* penses of counsel employed by the comptroller in legal actions or proceedings, eight thousand dollars, or so much thereof as may be necessary.

For compensation of justices of the supreme court whose terms *Justices of supreme court.* of office have been abridged pursuant to section twelve, article six of the constitution, and who have served as such ten years, forty-three thousand two hundred dollars.

For Robert Earl, associate justice of the court of appeals, whose *Robert Earl.* term of office is abridged under the provisions of section twelve, article six, of the constitution, who has served as such associate judge ten years, twelve thousand dollars, or so much thereof as may be necessary.

For Joseph F. Barnard, late a justice of the supreme court in *Joseph F. Barnard.* the second judicial district, not residing in the county of Kings, whose term of office was abridged under the provisions of section twelve of article six of the constitution, and who served as such justice for ten years, for additional compensation, pursuant to chapter seven hundred and sixty-five of the laws of eighteen hundred and sixty-eight, as amended by chapter one hundred and fourteen of the laws of eighteen hundred and ninety-four, the sum of twenty-five hundred dollars, to be paid only from moneys which shall have been or shall be paid into the treasury for taxes levied for the purpose of said acts and in pursuance thereof.

For the comptroller, one thousand dollars, for the deputy comp- *Expenses and disbursements of comptroller and deputies.* troller, one thousand dollars, and for the second deputy comptroller, seven hundred and fifty dollars, in full of all expenses and disbursements incurred by them respectively in attendance and conducting examinations and investigations for the purposes of taxation under the corporation and inheritance tax laws, and of all expenses and disbursements incurred by them respectively in the visitations of the prisons, reformatories and other public institutions of the state, whose accounts are audited by the comptroller, and for all other expenses and disbursements incurred by them respectively while in the discharge of their official duties.

Advances to county treasurers. For deficiency in appropriation for advances to county treasurers, on account of taxes on property of non-residents, which may be returned to the comptroller's office, and for adjusting accounts of state taxes with counties, ten thousand dollars.

Examinations of public institutions. For the expenses of examinations and investigations of public institutions, made pursuant to law, the sum of four thousand dollars, or so much thereof as may be necessary, to be paid upon vouchers audited by the comptroller.

Expenses for monthly estimates by institutions. For the comptroller, for compensation of employes, and for expenses in enforcing the provisions of the general appropriation act of eighteen hundred and ninety-four, providing for the monthly estimate of expenditures, and the rendering of accounts of state, charitable and reformatory institutions other than the state prisons and state hospitals for the insane, the sum of fifteen thousand dollars, or so much thereof as may be necessary.

Tax clerks and examinations. For the comptroller, for compensation of persons employed by the comptroller in the collection of corporation and inheritance taxes, and for expenses incurred therefor, and for expenses of examinations and investigations for the purposes of taxation, under chapter nine hundred and eight, laws of eighteen hundred and ninety-six, and the acts amendatory thereof, twenty thousand dollars.

Postage and expressage for public offices. For deficiency in appropriation for postage or expressage on official letters, documents and all other matter sent by mail or express by the governor, secretary of state, comptroller, treasurer, attorney-general, state engineer and surveyor, superintendent of public instruction, regents of the university, adjutant-general, clerk of the court of appeals, state board of charities, state board of health, civil service commission and bureau of labor statistics for the year ending September thirtieth, eighteen hundred and ninety-seven, two thousand dollars, or so much thereof as may be necessary.

County treasurer's accounts. For the comptroller, the sum of eight thousand dollars, or so much thereof as may be necessary, to defray the expenses of making an examination of the accounts of the several county treasurers of the state, as required by chapter six hundred and fifty-one of the **Court funds.** laws of eighteen hundred and ninety-two, and for the expenses and disbursements incurred by him in the supervision and administration of funds paid into court as may be necessary and required by said act.

For the comptroller, for the payment of judgments against the people of the state of New York, for costs in certain actions pursuant to section thirty-two hundred and forty-one of the code of civil procedure, three thousand dollars, or so much thereof as may be necessary. Judgments against state.

To the comptroller, the sum of eight hundred and six and sixty-two one hundredths dollars, for the purpose of paying an assessment made by the city of Watertown for certain paving in front of the state arsenal on Arsenal street in said city. Assessment of property at Watertown.

To the comptroller, for the purpose of paying the salaries of confidential clerks to certain justices of the supreme court of the fifth judicial district, resident in the city of Syracuse, the sum of twenty-four hundred dollars, or so much thereof as may be necessary, payable upon the certificates of such justices. Salaries of justices' clerks.

For deficiency in appropriation, for supplying other states with reports of the court of appeals and the supreme court, pursuant to section twenty-seven of the executive law, as amended by chapter two hundred and forty-eight of the laws of eighteen hundred and ninety-three, five hundred dollars, or so much thereof as may be necessary. Court reports.

For deficiency in appropriation (for the justices of the supreme court, for salaries and expenses for the fiscal year ending September thirtieth, eighteen hundred and ninety-seven), for expenses of justices of the appellate division of the supreme court, pursuant to chapter three hundred and ninety of the laws of eighteen hundred and ninety-six, twenty thousand dollars, or so much thereof as may be necessary. Salaries, etc., of justices of supreme court.

For expenses of the appellate division of the supreme court, pursuant to chapter three hundred and seventy-six, laws of eighteen hundred and ninety-five, and chapter nine hundred and forty-six, laws of eighteen hundred and ninety-five, twenty thousand dollars, or so much thereof as may be necessary. Expenses of appellate division.

The sum of sixteen hundred dollars, or so much thereof as may be necessary, is hereby appropriated for the care, maintenance, repairs and improvements of the Saratoga monument and the grounds connected therewith, to be expended under the supervision of the comptroller, pursuant to the provisions of chapter five hundred and fifty-five of the laws of eighteen hundred and ninety-five. Saratoga monument.

Transportation of books, etc.

For deficiency in appropriation for expenses of transportation of the session laws, journals and documents of the legislature, reports, books and packages, by express or freight, for public officers, and for boxes therefor, three thousand dollars, or so much thereof as may be necessary.

Comptroller's certificates, redemption of.

For the comptroller for the redemption of certificate number two, due January thirtieth, eighteen hundred and ninety-eight, issued for the purchase of land for the Adirondack park, under chapter five hundred and sixty-one of the laws of eighteen hundred and ninety-five, fifty-five thousand dollars, and for one year's interest, at three per centum, on certificates numbers two to ten, issued for the same purpose, fourteen thousand eight hundred and fifty dollars.

Legislative printing.

For deficiency in appropriation for the legislative printing of the state, including binding, mapping, lithographing and engraving, one hundred and fifty thousand dollars, or so much thereof as may be necessary.

Experts to examine books of racing associations.

The sum of two thousand one hundred eleven dollars and fifty cents is hereby appropriated for the payment of the salaries and expenses of experts appointed by the comptroller for the year eighteen hundred and ninety-six, pursuant to the provisions of chapter three hundred and eighty of the laws of eighteen hundred and ninety-six, to examine the books of the incorporated racing associations of the state, and to make such investigations as were necessary to ascertain the amount of tax payable by such associations; and there is also appropriated for the salaries and expenses of experts, for the year eighteen hundred and ninety-seven, the sum of three thousand two hundred dollars, or so much thereof as may be necessary, the amounts herein appropriated to be paid from the funds collected from the said associations.

Revolutionary war records.

For the comptroller, for the completion of the work in the examination, arrangement, compilation, printing and binding of the records of the revolutionary war, in the comptroller's office, two thousand dollars, or so much thereof as may be necessary.

Legislative expenses.

For deficiency in appropriation for postage, expenses of committees, compensations of witnesses, legislative manual, Croswell's manual, clerks' manual, indexing the bills, journals and documents of the senate and assembly, and other contingent expenses of the legislature, thirty thousand dollars, or so much thereof as may be necessary.

For the comptroller, for recopying, binding and repairing tax ^{Repairing bo ks and records.} books, sales books, tax diaries, redemption diaries and other books and records of the land bureau in the comptroller's office, three thousand dollars, or so much thereof as may be necessary.

For deficiency in appropriation for printing of constitutional ^{Printing for constitutional convention.} convention of eighteen hundred and ninety-four, under contract made by the secretary of state and comptroller pursuant to chapter eight of the laws of eighteen hundred and ninety-three, particularly for payment of certificate of indebtedness of the state of New York, and for bills audited by the comptroller pursuant to chapter two hundred and twenty-eight of the laws of eighteen hundred and ninety-four, the sum of thirty-eight thousand dollars, or so much thereof as may be necessary, to be paid upon the audit of the comptroller.

SECRETARY OF STATE.

*   *   *   *   *   *   *   *

For the secretary of state for the purpose of complying with ^{Election law and registration books.} the provisions of section nineteen and subdivision one of section thirty-six of the election law; for the purpose of complying with the provisions of chapter two hundred and eighteen of the laws of eighteen hundred and ninety-five; for the purchase of law books and for the compilation and printing of the proceedings of ^{Electoral college proceedings.} the electoral college, the sum of twenty-eight thousand dollars, or so much thereof as may be necessary.

For deficiency in appropriation for clerk hire in the office of the ^{Clerk hire.} secretary of state, one thousand five hundred dollars, or so much thereof as may be necessary.

For the secretary of state, to furnish session laws and records ^{Law books for town.} for the town clerk's office in the town of Ashford, Cattaraugus county, destroyed by fire September sixteenth, eighteen hundred and ninety-six, the sum of one hundred dollars, or so much thereof as may be necessary.

For the secretary of state, to furnish session laws for the town clerk's office in the town of Fowler, Saint Lawrence county, the session laws having been destroyed by fire, the sum of one hundred dollars, or so much thereof as may be necessary.

COMMISSIONERS OF QUARANTINE.

For the board of commissioners of quarantine, the sum of two ^{Dock at health officers' station.} thousand one hundred and sixty-eight dollars and nine cents, being the unexpended balance of appropriation made by chapter seven hundred and sixty-eight of the laws of eighteen hundred and ninety-four for the board of commissioners of quarantine, created by chapter two hundred and seventy of the laws of eighteen hundred and eighty-eight, for extension of dock at health officers' station; and the sum of seven hundred and forty-four dollars and twenty-four cents, being the amount refunded to the treasury of a balance of an appropriation under chapter three hundred and forty-one of the laws of eighteen hundred and eighty-eight for crematory at Swinburne island, are hereby reappropriated for the commissioners of quarantine for dredging slips and repairing docks at the headquarters of the health officer.

Dredging and dock repairs.

For the board of commissioners created by chapter two hundred and seventy of the laws of eighteen hundred and eighty-eight, the following sums, namely: for care, maintenance and repairs to the quarantine establishment, including the completion of the renovating work commenced last year, and ventilating the dormitories and repairing roofs, the sum of twenty-five thousand dollars; for building or repairing landings or docks on Swinburne island, the sum of thirty-five hundred dollars.

Maintenance and repairs of establishment.

ATTORNEY-GENERAL.

For the attorney-general, the sum of six thousand five hundred and thirty-one dollars and seventy-four cents to reimburse James Shanahan, late superintendent of public works, for moneys due and paid by him upon a judgment recovered against him as superintendent of public works, in an action brought in the supreme court by David Wright and entered in Cayuga county July eighteenth, eighteen hundred and ninety-five, together with costs taxed thereon, June eleventh, eighteen hundred and ninety-six and interest thereon, all of which is included in the above judgment.

Reimbursement of James Shanahan.

For the attorney-general for payment of attorneys and counsel designated or employed by the governor or attorney-general, for the transaction of legal business in pursuance of the provisions of chapter eight hundred and twenty-one of the laws of eighteen hundred and ninety-five, twenty thousand dollars, but no warrants shall be issued for such payments until the amounts claimed shall be certified, audited and allowed by the governor and attorney-general.

Payment of attorney and counsel.

For the attorney-general, the sum of nine thousand dollars, or so much thereof as may be necessary, to pay counsel and commissioners employed by him in pursuance of law.

Id.

STATE ENGINEER AND SURVEYOR.

For the state engineer and surveyor, for surveys and maps for the use of the attorney-general in cases before the board of claims arising on account of the canals in the state, the sum of seven thousand dollars, or so much thereof as may be necessary, payable from the canal fund. Surveys and maps before board of claims.

For the state engineer and surveyor, to enable him to continue the surveying, platting and monumenting of the state lands now under lease or to be leased in the future of the oyster industry, the sum of two thousand dollars. Monumenting oyster lands.

For the state engineer and surveyor for traveling expenses and disbursements and for expenses incurred by his department, in making examinations, surveys and maps and for restoring and placing monuments on the boundary lines of the state, pursuant to chapter four hundred and twenty-one, laws of eighteen hundred and eighty-seven, the sum of six thousand eight hundred dollars, payable from the general fund. Traveling expenses. Monuments on state boundary lines.

For the state engineer and surveyor for copying and preserving old maps, survey notes and miscellaneous records of his office, relating to lands and land patents of colonial and early state times, the sum of one thousand dollars, or so much thereof as may be necessary. Preservation of records.

INSURANCE DEPARTMENT.

For the examination of insurance companies by direction of the superintendent of insurance, to be used in his discretion, and to be collected from and be refunded to the treasury by the companies so examined as provided by law, twenty thousand dollars, or so much thereof as may be necessary. Examinations.

For the payment of the expense of the actuarial work imposed upon the superintendent of insurance by chapter three hundred and ninety-nine of the laws of eighteen hundred and ninety-two, three thousand dollars, or so much thereof as may be necessary, to be refunded to the treasury as provided by law. Actuarial work.

For the superintendent of insurance, to enable him to carry into effect the provisions of section eighty-four of chapter six hundred and ninety of the laws of eighteen hundred and ninety-two, known as the insurance law; for expenses of computation, compilation and publication of new valuation tables; for valuation and other incidental expenses connected therewith, rendered necessary by said section, eight thousand dollars, or so much thereof as may be New valuation tables.

necessary payable out of the surplus in the treasury, arising from
taxes, license fees and other moneys collected from the insurance
companies, agents and other persons and paid into the treasury over
and above the appropriations for maintaining said department.

Counsel.   For the payment of counsel designated by attorney-general to
represent the state in proceedings instituted against certain Lloyds
associations, three thousand dollars, or so much thereof as may be
necessary.

Purchase   For the purchase of a safe in which to keep securities deposited
of safe and
furniture.   in the department and the building of necessary galleries in the
office for keeping of records in a suitable manner and for the purchasing of necessary furniture, et cetera, for New York office, five
thousand dollars, or so much thereof as may be necessary.

RAILROAD COMMISSION.

Electrical   For the board of railroad commissioners, for an electrical expert
expert and
books.   and for the purchase of necessary law and statistical books, the
sum of three thousand dollars, this amount to be paid by the comptroller upon the requisition of the board of railroad commissioners,
and to be refunded to the treasury by the several corporations
owning or operating railroads in this state, in such manner and
proportion as is prescribed by law.

COURT OF CLAIMS.

Contingent   The unexpended balance heretofore appropriated for the pay-
fund.   ment of the expenses of the clerk, stenographer and messenger of
the board of claims while attending sessions of the board at places
other than at Albany, is hereby reappropriated into the contingent
fund of the court of claims.

DEPARTMENT OF AGRICULTURE.

Commis-   For the commissioner of agriculture, for the expenses and for the
sioner of
agricul-   continuance and extension of the work of his department, pursuant
ture.   to chapter three hundred thirty-eight, laws of eighteen hundred
ninety-three, to the close of the fiscal year, the sum of twenty thousand dollars; the assistant commissioners of agriculture shall receive such salaries as shall be fixed by the commissioner of agriculture, and all necessary expenses incurred in the performance
of their duties.

Promotion   For the promotion of agriculture, the sum of ten thousand dol-
of agricul-
ture.   lars, to be distributed by the commissioner of agriculture as provided in section eighty-eight of the agricultual law.

For the maintenance of farmers' institutes, held under the Farmers' institutes. auspices of the commissioner of agriculture, to be paid upon the order of said commissioner, and certified in sums as needed and for which vouchers for expenditures, duly audited and verified by him, shall be rendered, the sum of fifteen thousand dollars.

For the New York State Agricultural society, for the interest of State Agricultural Society. the state and the promotion of agriculture therein, to be expended under the direction of the commissioner of agriculture, the sum of ten thousand dollars, for the purpose of constructing on the grounds of the society additions to the horticultural and dairy buildings, and for such other improvements and expenditures for improving said grounds and property as may be found necessary by the society for the promotion of agriculture in this state.

For the state weather bureau, to be expended under the direction State weather bureau. of the commissioner of agriculture, the sum of four thousand five hundred dollars, or so much thereof as may be necessary, for the prosecution of its work to the close of the next fiscal year, pursuant to the provisions of the agricultural law.

NATIONAL GUARD.

For the adjutant-general, for repairs, improvements and better- Armories, state camp and rifle ranges. ments of the state arsenals, armories, camp grounds and the rifle ranges at Creedmoor and throughout the state, the sum of twenty thousand dollars, or so much thereof as may be necessary.

For the adjutant-general, for the payment of pensions to members Pensions. of the national guard and naval militia and pay and care for the same when injured or disabled in service, pursuant to sections one hundred and twenty-nine and one hundred and thirty-two, chapter five hundred and fifty-nine, of the laws of eighteen hundred and ninety-three and the acts amendatory thereof, and for payment of expenses and examinations of claims for pensions, under said acts, the sum of six thousand dollars, or so much thereof as may be necessary.

For the adjutant-general, for services and necessary traveling War claims, prosecution of. expenses in prosecuting the war claims of the state against the United States, under his direction, eight thousand dollars, or so much thereof as may be necessary, to be approved by the governor as commander-in-chief.

For the adjutant-general, for the uniforming and equipping of the Uniforms and equipment. national guard and naval militia and furnishing the necessary cooking implements and stores and other necessaries for the national guard for field service, and for replacing uniforms, blankets, overcoats and trousers worn out in service, and to complete the medical outfit and hospital corps supplies of the national guard and naval militia, the sum of thirty thousand dollars.

Armory at Ogdensburg. For the erection of a state armory in the city of Ogdensburg, the sum of forty thousand dollars, being the unexpended appropriation made by chapter five hundred and eighty of the laws of eighteen hundred and ninety-six, and also the additional sum of seventeen thousand dollars, all such money to be expended under and in pursuance of said chapter, for the purposes, and subject to the conditions, specified therein.

Rifle range, Kingston. For the adjutant-general, for the completion of the rifle range and plumbing of the state armory in the city of Kingston, the sum of four thousand five hundred dollars, or so much thereof as may be necessary.

Armory at Malone. For the adjutant-general, for the completion of the state armory in the village of Malone, three thousand dollars, or so much thereof as may be necessary.

Armory at Oneonta. For the adjutant-general, for the improvement and betterment of the state armory of the Third separate company at Oneonta, the sum of two thousand five hundred dollars, or so much thereof as may be necessary.

War records, completion, etc., of. For the adjutant-general, to enable him to comply with sections thirty-eight, thirty-nine and forty, chapter sixteen, of the general laws of the state, and to complete the personal records of the regiments, companies, troops, batteries and marines of this state which served in the late war for the Union, and for printing and binding the same in book form, under the direction of the adjutant-general, the sum of twenty thousand dollars, or so much thereof as may be necessary.

Acquisition of land for armory at Olean. For the acquisition of a piece of land, about one hundred feet square, on the northwest corner of North and Barry streets in the city of Olean, for the use of the state armory in such city, the sum of four thousand dollars, or so much thereof as may be necessary; and the adjutant general, inspector-general and chief of ordnance, who are appointed a commission for the purposes hereof, are hereby authorized to acquire such lands for and in the name of the state by purchase or condemnation, the title to which shall be approved by the attorney-general.

Boat-house, etc., for naval militia at Rochester. For the adjutant-general, for the Second Separate Naval division, Rochester, New York, for deficiency in appropriation for the completion of the boat-house and necessary accessories thereto, and for repairing launch 'boiler, and for the boat carriage and bab-bit fittings thereto, the sum of nine hundred dollars; for water service, heating, dredging and equipment of said boat-house, with its approaches, for the use of the naval militia located in the city of Rochester, Monroe county, the sum of two thousand dollars, or so much thereof as may be necessary, is hereby appropriated out of any moneys in the treasury, not otherwise appropriated, to be expended under the direction of the adjutant-general, the inspector-general and the chief of ordnance of the state, who are commissioners for the completion of the said boat-house with its approaches.

The sum of fifteen thousand dollars, or so much thereof as may Armory at Newburgh. be necessary, is hereby appropriated to defray the expenses of repairs and betterments of the state armory at Newburgh, said amount to be paid by the treasurer, upon the warrant of the comptroller, out of any moneys in the treasury not otherwise appropriated, on bills for said repairs and betterments approved by the adjutant-general.

For the betterment of the road leading from the state camp to Roads at state camp. Roa Hook dock, and for the construction of a military road to connect the state camp with the river road near Highland station, five thousand dollars, or so much thereof as may be necessary, to be expended under the order and direction of the adjutant-general.

BANKING DEPARTMENT.

For the superintendent of banks, for rent of office for examiners Office for examiners. in the city of New York, one thousand dollars, to be assessed and collected and refunded to the treasury, as provided for in the banking law.

For the superintendent of banks, two thousand dollars, for pay- Salary of superintendent. ment of increase of salary of said superintendent of banks, from the first day of October, eighteen hundred and ninety-seven, to the first day of October, eighteen hundred and ninety-eight, to be assessed and collected and refunded as provided in the banking law.

For the superintendent of banks, one thousand dollars, for pay- Id. ment of increase of salary of said superintendent dating from the first day of April, eighteen hundred and ninety-seven, to the first day of October, of the same year, to be assessed and collected and refunded as provided in the banking law.

BUREAU OF LABOR STATISTICS.

For the bureau of labor statistics, for deficiency in the annual Deficiencies in appropriation for the year eighteen hundred and ninety-seven, the appropriation.

sum of five thousand dollars; and for a deficiency in the appropriation for the free employment bureau in New York city for the year
eighteen hundred and ninety-seven, the sum of one thousand and
five hundred dollars; and for deficiency in the annual appropriation for the year eighteen hundred and ninety-eight, the sum of
four thousand dollars; and for the salary of deputy commissioner
of labor statistics, the sum of twenty-five hundred dollars.

STATE BOARD CHARITIES.

Inspection department and office expenses. For the state board of charities, for carrying on the work of the
inspection department and for deficiency in appropriation for office
and contingent expenses and clerk hire, three thousand dollars.

FISH, GAME AND FOREST COMMISSION.

Claims by fire wardens. For the commissioners of fisheries, game and forest, for paying
claims against the state incurred by fire wardens in the several
counties of the forest preserve in fighting forest fires, two thousand
dollars, or so much thereof as may be necessary.

Purchase of lands in Adirondack park. The sum of four thousand sixty-nine dollars and forty-five cents,
being the sum paid into the state treasury from proceeds of lands
sold and leased and interest on deposits by the fisheries, game and
forest commission, pursuant to chapter three hundred and thirty-
two, laws of eighteen hundred and ninety-three hereby appropriated for the purchase of lands within the Adirondack park, as
provided by section one hundred and twenty-three, article eight of
said act.

Hatcheries, etc. For construction and maintenance of hatcheries and hatching
stations and the collection and distribution of fish and fish fry,
seven thousand five hundred dollars.

Weirs, etc., at inlets of Cayuga lake. For the commissioners of fisheries, game and forests, the sum of
five hundred dollars, or so much thereof as may be necessary, is
hereby appropriated, to be expended by said commissioners or under
their direction, for the erection and maintenance of weirs or traps at
the inlets of Cayuga lake to exterminate from said lake, lampreys,
suckers and other deleterious fish and for the scientific study by the
biological department of the Cornell university, of the nature and
habits of the various fishes of said lake.

Bill-fish. For the extermination of bill-fish in Chautauqua lake, five hundred dollars.

SOLDIERS AND SAILORS' HOME.

For the Soldiers and Sailors' home at Bath, for the payment of _{Indebtedness, repairs, etc.} the present outstanding indebtedness, the sum of eight thousand eight hundred and twelve dollars and forty-one cents, or so much thereof as may be necessary; for deficiency in maintenance, the sum of seven thousand dollars; for repairs to buildings and the construction of the new house for the farmer, the sum of fifteen thousand dollars.

STATE MUSEUM.

For the state museum, for deficiency in appropriation for eighteen hundred and ninety-six and eighteen hundred and ninety-seven, for the maintenance of the state museums, eight hundred dollars.

CIVIL SERVICE COMMISSION.

For the civil service commission, for deficiency in appropriation for the expenses of examination, three thousand dollars.

MISCELLANEOUS REPORTER.

For the miscellaneous reporter, for deficiency in former appropriations for assistance, clerk hire, obtaining copies of opinions and office expenses, the sum of five thousand five hundred dollars, to be paid by the state treasurer, on the certificate of the reporter and audit and certificate of the comptroller.

SUPERINTENDENT OF PUBLIC INSTRUCTION.

For the state superintendent of public instruction, for the purpose of providing facilities for instruction in natural history, geography and kindred subjects by means of pictorial representations and lectures to the free common schools of each city and village of the state having a superintendent of free common schools, in accordance with the provisions of chapter three hundred and sixty-two of the laws of eighteen hundred and ninety-five, the sum of fifteen thousand dollars, or so much thereof as may be necessary, payable by the treasurer on the warrant of the comptroller, upon vouchers approved by the superintendent of public instruction, and audited by the comptroller.

For the superintendent of public instruction, for printing from the plates from which the official edition was printed, at an expense not exceeding one dollar per volume, three thousand extra copies in quarto form of the annual report of the state botanist for the

year eighteen hundred and ninety-four, as transmitted to the legislature in January, eighteen hundred and ninety-five, to be distributed as follows: One thousand copies to the state superintendent of public instruction, to be by him distributed to public libraries
and school district libraries under his charge; eighteen hundred
copies to the members of the legislature; and two hundred copies
to the state officers, the sum of three thousand dollars, or so much
thereof as may be necessary, payable by the treasurer on the warrant of the comptroller, upon vouchers approved by the superintendent of public instruction and audited by the comptroller.

Normal
schools.

For repairs, renewals, betterments of buildings, equipment, fixtures, furniture and such additional accommodations in the normal schools of the state as may be necessary, including the equipment and heating of the new normal school at Jamaica, the sum
of eighty-six thousand nine hundred and seventy-nine dollars, or
so much thereof as may be necessary, to be apportioned by the
state superintendent of public instruction, and to be expended by
the local boards of managers, and payable upon bills audited by
the comptroller upon vouchers approved by said superintendent.

Indian
school-
houses.

For the erection, repairs, improvements and furnishing of schoolhouses upon the various Indian reservations in the state, and for
supplies for schools therein, the sum of fifteen hundred dollars, to
be expended under the direction of the state superintendent of
public instruction, and payable upon bills audited by the comptroller upon vouchers approved by said superintendent.

Code of
public in-
struction.

The sum of nineteen thousand three hundred and fifty-nine dollars and seventy cents, being the unexpended balance of moneys
appropriated by chapter nine hundred and eighty-seven of the
laws of eighteen hundred and ninety-five for the preparation and
publication of the code of public instruction, and its distribution
to the several school districts of the state, is hereby reappropriated
for the completion of such work.

Educa-
tional
report,
compila-
tion, etc.,
of.

The sum of three thousand six hundred and twenty-five dollars
and thirty-nine cents, being the unexpended balance of moneys
appropriated by chapter nine hundred and thirty-two of the laws
of eighteen hundred and ninety-five, for the compilation under the
direction of the state superintendent of public instruction, of the
reports of the superintendents of other states, foreign countries,
and leading cities, and the publication and distribution of the
same among educational and state officers and members of the
legislature, is hereby reappropriated for the same purpose.

For the construction, equipment and furnishing of a new school-house and repairing present school building upon the Saint Regis Indian Reservation, the sum of fifteen hundred dollars, or so much thereof as may be necessary, and to be expended under the direction of the state superintendent of public instruction. School-house, St. Regis Reservation.

For the superintendent of public instruction, for payment of insurance upon the Plattsburgh normal school, the sum of one thousand four hundred and sixty-eight dollars, or so much thereof as may be necessary. Plattsburgh normal school.

SUPERINTENDENT OF PUBLIC WORKS.

The sum of three thousand dollars, or so much thereof as may be necessary, is hereby appropriated to repair and preserve the highways on the Allegany Indian Reservation in the county of Cattaraugus, said moneys to be expended under the direction of the superintendent of public works. Highways on Indian Reservations.

The sum of one thousand dollars, or so much thereof as may be necessary, is hereby appropriated to repair and preserve the highways on the Cattaraugus Indian Reservation, in the township of Perrysburgh, Cattaraugus county, to be expended under the direction of the superintendent of public works.

For the superintendent of public works, for the purpose of dredging and removing obstructions in Findley's lake, in the county of Chautauqua, the sum of one thousand dollars. Findley's lake.

For the purpose of making and improving the state roads through the Saint Regis Indian Reservation in the county of Franklin, three thousand dollars, or so much thereof as may be necessary; said work to be executed and said moneys to be expended under the direction of the superintendent of public works. State roads, Franklin county.

For the superintendent of public works, for completing the work of constructing embankments upon and along the Chemung river in the city of Elmira, for the purpose of preventing overflows and freshets from the Chemung river, the sum of four thousand dollars, or so much thereof as may be necessary. Embankment at Elmira.

For the superintendent of public works, the unexpended balance, nine hundred and forty-seven dollars, of chapter three hundred and sixty-four of the laws of eighteen hundred and ninety-six, is hereby reappropriated for the purpose of rebuilding the walls of the weigh-lock outlet at Waterford, Saratoga county. Weigh-lock walls, Waterford.

Channels of canal at Waterloo. For the superintendent of public works, for deficiency in appropriation, pursuant to chapter five hundred and twelve, of the laws of eighteen hundred and ninety-five, for improving the channel of the Seneca river and Old Bear race at Waterloo, known as South Channels of Cayuga and Seneca canal, the sum of one hundred and ninety-one dollars, or so much thereof as may be necessary, payable from the canal fund.

State ditch, Cowaselon swamp. For the superintendent of public works, the sum of two thousand five hundred dollars, or so much thereof as may be necessary, payable from the canal fund, is hereby appropriated for the payment of the balance now due the contractor for deepening, clearing out and improving the state ditch through Cowaselon swamp, under chapter three hundred sixty-six, laws of eighteen hundred and ninety-five, with interest upon the same from the twentieth day of October, eighteen hundred and ninety-six until the twelfth day after the comptroller is authorized to issue his warrant for the payment thereof, under the provisions of this act, or until payment, if payment be sooner made. The sum herein appropriated shall be paid by the treasurer on the warrant of the comptroller, upon a certificate of the state engineer and surveyor.

Bridge at Rochester. For the superintendent of public works, for deficiency in appropriation, pursuant to chapter three hundred sixty-six, of the laws of eighteen hundred and ninety-three, chapter five hundred and sixty of the laws of eighteen hundred and ninety-six, for the erection of a lift-bridge over Erie canal at Emerson street at Rochester, the sum of one hundred and seven dollars and forty-seven cents, payable from the canal fund.

North Branch reservoir. For the superintendent of public works, for deficiency in appropriation, pursuant to chapter one hundred and forty-eight of the laws of eighteen hundred and ninety-five, for repairs on the North Branch reservoir, in town of Wilmurt, county of Herkimer, twenty-two hundred and fifty-six dollars and fifty-eight cents, payable from the canal fund.

Highways, Onondaga Reservation. For repairs of highways on the Onondaga Indian Reservation, to be expended under the direction of the superintendent of public works, on the roads known as the "Quarry," "Cardiff," "South Hollow," "William Hill" and "Albert Everingham" roads, the sum of two thousand dollars, or so much thereof as may be necessary.

Bridges, Tona-wr e' For improvement of state roads and bridges on Tonawanda In- Reservation in Genessee county, one thousand dollars, to be ex- l under the direction of the superintendent of public works.

For the superintendent of public works, for the completion and construction of a bridge over the canal feeder at Medina, as provided for in chapter seven hundred and ninety-one of the laws of eighteen hundred and ninety-six, the sum of two thousand five hundred dollars. *Bridge at Medina.*

For the superintendent of public works, the sum of six thousand dollars, or so much thereof as may be necessary, is hereby appropriated for the purpose of constructing a bridge over the Allegheny river between the towns of Carrollton and Allegheny situate in Cattaraugus county. *Bridge over Allegheny river.*

For the superintendent of public works, for the operation, maintenance and repair of the drawbridge, known as Drake's drawbridge, spanning the Wappinger creek near the village of New Hamburg in the county of Dutchess, for the year ending March first, eighteen hundred and ninety-eight, as provided by chapter two hundred and thirty-nine of the laws of eighteen hundred and ninety-two, as amended by chapter four hundred and one of the laws of eighteen hundred and ninety-three, the sum of seven hundred dollars. *Drake's drawbridge.*

For the superintendent of public works and state engineer and surveyor, for continuance of the work of deepening and widening of the channel from Shinnecock bay to Great South bay, the sum of five thousand dollars. *Channel from Shinnecock bay.*

For the superintendent of public works, for removing obstructions caused by the pile foundations remaining from the old Chemung canal dam, in the city of Corning, and the repair and enlargement of the stone slope wall, on the south side of the river i said city, heretofore built and maintained by the state, the sum of five thousand dollars. Should there be left of said sum of five thousand dollars, a sum sufficient to warrant the state engineer in so doing, he is hereby authorized and empowered to expend the same in repairing and extending the docking built by the state, on the north side of the Chemung river in the town of Corning, adjacent to the lands of William Gorten and James Flynn. *Old Chemung canal dam, Elmira.* *Docking on Chemung river.*

The sum of three thousand eight hundred and sixty-eight dollars and eighty-nine cents, being the unexpended balance of the appropriation for the superintendent of public works for contingent office expenses, pursuant to chapter nine hundred and thirty-two, laws of eighteen hundred and ninety-five, is hereby appropriated for the object and purposes of the original appropriation. *Office expenses, superintendent public works.*

For the superintendent of public works, the sum of two thousand five hundred dollars, payable in monthly installments, in lieu of and *Traveling expenses.*

in full of traveling expenses and disbursements incurred by
him.

State dam, Carthage.   For the superintendent of public works, for the repair of the state
dam in the village of Carthage, county of Jefferson, the sum of two
thousand dollars, or so much thereof as may be necessary.

Highway, Cattaraugus Reservation.   For superintendent of public works, the sum of eight hundred
dollars, or so much thereof as may be necessary, for repairing and
graveling the public highway across the Cattaraugus Indian Reservation in Erie county, leading from Lawton station to the Thomas
asylum.

*   *   -   -   -   -   -

SUPERINTENDENT OF PUBLIC BUILDINGS.

*   *   *   *   *   *   *   *

Geological hall.   For new pumps in engine room, for new piping and repairs to
main drain, for new roof, for rebuilding chimneys and repairs to
heating apparatus at the geological hall, the sum of eight thousand dollars.

Repairs, alterations, etc.   For the superintendent of public buildings, for repairs and alterations, and for building partitions, cases, shelves, pigeon holes and
desks and for supplies and for panelling, cutting doorways, laying
floors, the sum of seven thousand three hundred and eighty-eight
dollars.

STATUTORY REVISION.

Prosecution of work.   For the commissioners of statutory revision, for the prosecution
of their work during the year eighteen hundred and ninety-seven
and to the close of the annual session of the legislature of eighteen
hundred and ninety-eight, twenty-two thousand dollars, or so much
thereof as may be necessary, to pay for their services, personal and
incidental expenses, clerk hire and printing, as shall be certified to
be just and reasonable by the governor, the payment of each commissioner for services not to exceed at the rate of two hundred
and fifty dollars per month.

STATE GEOLOGIST.

Paleontology of state.   For Charles Van Benthuysen and Sons, for completing the printing of balance of two thousand copies of text and plates of volume
eight, part two, paleontology of the state of New York, as follows:
For paper and printing two thousand impressions each of forty-six
plates, and for paper and printing ninety-six pages of text and
explanations, the sum of three thousand seven hundred and twenty-nine dollars and three cents, to be paid upon the certificate of the

state geologist and the audit of the comptroller; the printed sheets and plates with explanations when completed, to be delivered to the state library, to be put with the sheets of text and plates already delivered.

BOARD OF TAX COMMISSIONERS.

For the state board of tax commissioners, for deficiency in appropriation for services, clerk hire, traveling and other expenses of the tax commissioners incurred pursuant to chapter nine hundred and eight of the laws of eighteen hundred and ninety-six, the sum of five thousand dollars, or so much thereof as may be necessary.

Clerk hire, and expenses.

COMMISSIONER OF EXCISE.

For the state commissioner of excise, for payment of compensation of four additional bookkeepers and clerks, legal expenses incurred in cases prosecuted for payment of additional liquor tax, increase of salary special deputy commissioner of excise of Erie county, increase of expenses of commissioner and deputy-commissioner, printing additional liquor tax certificates under subdivisions three, five and six, and for other necessary additional printing, expenses of procuring records of enumeration from the United States census bureau and records of incorporation from county clerk's offices of the state of New York, expenses of enumeration of villages not incorporated and villages not separately enumerated, assorting, indexing and putting up old excise records, sixteen thousand one hundred dollars.

Office expenses, etc.
Printing.
Enumeration expenses.

For state commissioner of excise, for payment of refunds upon surrender of liquor tax certificates, to be paid by the state treasurer from excise moneys in his hands, eighty-five thousand dollars.

Payment of refunds.

FACTORY INSPECTOR.

For the factory inspector, to pay the salaries of seven deputies and expenses, as authorized by chapters nine hundred and ninety-one and six hundred and seventy-two of the laws of eighteen hundred and ninety-six, the sum of twelve thousand six hundred dollars.

Salaries and expenses of deputies.

SUPERINTENDENT OF THE STATE LAND SURVEY.

For the state land survey, to meet the expenses of work of immediate necessity (in accordance with the requisitions made under authority of law by the state comptroller, and other state officers)

Expenses of work.

and for the location of the boundaries of counties, townships and allotments adjacent thereto, in accordance with the provisions of chapter five hundred and eighty-nine of the laws of eighteen hundred and ninety-five, ten thousand dollars.

STATE HISTORIAN.

Office expenses.

For the state historian, for copyist, indexer, typewriter and for extra clerical service, and for printing, stationery, maps and supplies, the sum of one thousand seven hundred dollars, or so much thereof as may be necessary.

Salary.

For the state historian, for deficiency in salary, from May to October, one thousand eight hundred and seventy-eight dollars and sixty cents.

LIBRARIES.

Supreme court library, Brooklyn.

For the library of the supreme court in the second judicial district in Brooklyn, for the purchase of books to be paid on bills therefor audited by a majority of the trustees having charge of said library, the sum of three thousand dollars.

*   *   *   *   *   *   *   *

State library and regents office.

For the care and cleaning of the rooms of the state library, regents office, examinations, extension, public libraries and duplicate departments and other rooms occupied by the university of the state, in the basement and on the first, third, fourth and fifth floors of the capitol, and for janitors, watchmen, porters, running two elevators, labor of cleaning and handling books, for necessary repairs, fittings and supplies connected with the janitorial department, to be paid on vouchers duly authenticated by the regents of the university, as for their other expenses, the sum of fifteen thousand dollars.

Public library money.

For deficiency caused by increase in the number of public libraries in conforming to the law, entitling them to share in the apportionment of public library money by the regents of the university for the benefit of free libraries and for books to be lent in accordance with sections fourteen, forty-seven and fifty of chapter three hundred and seventy-eight of the laws of eighteen hundred and ninety-two, fifteen thousand eight hundred and ninety-four and sixty-four one-hundredths dollars.

State medical library.

For books, serials, binding and other necessary expenses of maintaining the state medical library pursuant to chapter three hundred and seventy-seven of the laws of eighteen hundred and ninety-one, the sum of one thousand dollars.

For deficiencies in the general examination appropriation caused Regents examinations. by increase in number of schools and students, the sum of ten thousand dollars payable to the regents of the university on the audit of the comptroller.

For the court of appeals library, situated at Syracuse, Onondaga Court of appeals library, Syracuse. county, for the purchase of books and other supplies for said library, the sum of three thousand dollars, to be paid on bills therefor audited by a majority of the trustees having charge of said library.

*   *   *   *   *   *   *   *

For the supreme court law library of the eighth judicial district Supreme court library, Buffalo. in the city of Buffalo, for the purchase of law books, reports, et cetera, the sum of three thousand dollars, to be paid on bills therefor audited by a majority of the trustees having charge of said library.

For the court of appeals library, situated in the city of Rochester, Court of appeals library, Rochester. Monroe county, for the purchase of books and supplies for said library, the sum of three thousand dollars, out of which said sum there shall be paid not to exceed the sum of fifteen hundred dollars for a working library for the appellate division of the supreme court, fourth judicial department.

*   *   *   *   *

STATE PRISONS.

For providing current literature for the several state prisons the Literature. sum of two thousand dollars, to be expended under the direction of the superintendent of state prisons.

For securing additional instruction in the several state prisons, Instruction. two thousand four hundred dollars, or so much thereof as may be necessary, to be expended under the direction of the superintendent of state prisons.

For the superintendent of state prisons, for traveling expenses Superintendent state prisons. for the superintendent and his clerks, the sum of five hundred dollars.

For the superintendent of state prisons, for additional clerk hire Clerk hire. in his office, the sum of one thousand dollars, payable from the capital funds of the state prisons.

MATTEAWAN STATE HOSPITAL FOR INSANE CRIMINALS.

For the Matteawan State Hospital, to be expended under the Improvements at hospital. direction of the superintendent of state prisons, for: Painting in-

terior walls and interior and exterior woodwork, three thousand
five hundred dollars; mortuary, one thousand dollars; books and
cases and surgical instruments, eight hundred dollars; raising laundry and tailor shop, three thousand dollars; electric wiring, two
thousand five hundred dollars; spray baths, one thousand dollars;
additional room for employes, one thousand four hundred dollars;
replacing old furniture and wooden bedsteads, eight hundred dollars; furniture for additional patients, twelve hundred dollars;
roadways, five hundred dollars; for deficiency in maintenance,
thirty-two thousand dollars.

STATE INDUSTRIAL SCHOOL.

Mainte-
nance and
repairs.

For the state industrial school at Rochester, the sum of thirteen
hundred twenty dollars and sixty-five cents, the balance remaining
unexpended in the treasury of eight thousand dollars appropriated by chapter nine hundred thirty-two of the laws of eighteen
hundred ninety-five, is hereby reappropriated for completing the
work of changing the old chapel into officers' quarters and for
furnishing rooms; for deficiency for the fiscal year ending September thirty, eighteen hundred and ninety-seven, created by chapter
five hundred and thirty, laws of eighteen hundred ninety-six, the
sum of fifteen thousand dollars, being the difference between the
cost of hard and soft coal for the year; for renewing and repairing
roofs, two thousand dollars; for renewing and repairing floors and
ceilings, three thousand dollars; for military equipment already
purchased and to be purchased, three thousand dollars; for additional tools for trade schools, instruments for band, and additional
desks for school rooms and books for the library, two thousand dollars; for cement walks connecting main building with shop buildings
and with drill hall and with hospital and with guardhouse and
closets and primary department, two thousand dollars.

SYRACUSE STATE INSTITUTION FOR FEEBLE-MINDED CHILDREN.

Improve-
ments and
repairs.

For the Syracuse state institution for feeble-minded children, to
be expended under the direction of the local board of managers,
for excavation for and the construction of an underground tunnel
or conduit for the steam and other pipes, between the boiler house,
girls' building and hospital, and for covering to the steam pipes,
three thousand eight hundred and seventy-five dollars; for completing the stone wall fence at the front of the institution grounds
on Delaware street and Grand avenue, two thousand dollars;

and for the erection of a hennery at the Fairmount farm, the unexpended balance of one hundred sixty-seven dollars and sixty-three cents, appropriated for a new corridor, by chapter three hundred and fifty-eight, laws of eighteen hundred and ninety-four, and an unexpended balance of six hundred and fifty-eight dollars and forty-five cents, appropriated for a new corridor, by chapter nine hundred and fifty, laws of eighteen hundred and ninety-six, are hereby reappropriated.

NEW YORK STATE SCHOOL FOR THE BLIND.

For the New York state school for the blind, at Batavia, for five typewriting machines, five hundred dollars; for an embossing machine, five hundred dollars; for six sewing machines, two hundred and forty dollars; for removing boiler-house and paving space in boys' court, two hundred and fifty dollars; for general repairs, two thousand dollars; for repainting woodwork, one thousand dollars; for furniture for dormitories, five hundred dollars; for books for library, apparatus, et cetera, seven hundred dollars; for completion of bay windows, eight hundred dollars; for balance due on repairs to hospital, seven hundred dollars; for cold storage room, six hundred and fifty dollars; for indebtedness to Weaver and Wilson, one hundred and ten dollars, being a total of eight thousand dollars, for which six thousand four hundred and thirteen dollars and ninety-one cents is hereby appropriated, and the remainder by reappropriations of the following unexpended balances of sums appropriated to said institution by chapter nine hundred and fifty of the laws of eighteen hundred and ninety-six; for pianos and musical instruments, four hundred and forty-six dollars and sixty-six cents; for repairs to organ, fifty-nine dollars and thirteen cents; for bedsteads and wire mattresses, four hundred and seventy-three dollars and seventy-five cents; for kitchen boiler, eighty-five dollars and thirty-five cents; bathing facilities, two hundred and thirty-four dollars and fifty-five cents; for relaying floors, one hundred and forty-two dollars and sixty-six cents; repairs to steam pipes, one hundred and forty-three dollars and ninety-nine cents.

Improvements and repairs.

*   •   *   •   •   ‿   ‿   ‿

FOR THE STATE CUSTODIAL ASYLUM FOR FEEBLE-MINDED WOMEN.

For the board of managers of the State Custodial Asylum, at Newark, for site for and moving power-house plant, building necessary conduit, carriage of steam and establishing plant for electric

Improvements and repairs.

light, twenty thousand dollars; for grading and improving grounds, removing and rebuilding greenhouses and laying walks, the sum of two thousand five hundred dollars; for ventilation, contingent and extraordinary repairs, the sum of two thousand five hundred dollars; for rebuilding icehouse, the sum of six hundred dollars; for removing and repairing the cottage now occupied by the gardener, the sum of one thousand dollars; the sum of sixteen hundred and ninety-nine dollars and seventy-two cents, being the balance of three thousand dollars appropriated by chapter seven hundred and twenty-six of the laws of eighteen hundred and ninety-three, for completing the sewerage system for said asylum, is hereby reappropriated for the purpose specified, payable upon vouchers to be approved by the comptroller.

HOUSES OF REFUGE FOR WOMEN.

Hudson.   For the House of Refuge for Women at Hudson, for extending electric-light plant to buildings not now wired, two thousand dollars, or so much thereof as may be necessary.

Albion.   For the Western House of Refuge for Women, at Albion, one thousand dollars, for the equipment of cottages numbers three and four; two hundred dollars for constructing a pigpen and henhouse; one thousand dollars for extraordinary repairs and general equipment; and seven thousand five hundred dollars for sewerage and drainage ordered by the state board of health.

NORTHERN NEW YORK INSTITUTION FOR DEAF MUTES.

    *   *   *   *   *   *   *   *

Improvements.   An aditional sum of five thousand nine hundred and fifty-one dollars and eighty-one cents, or so much thereof as may be necessary, is hereby appropriated, out of any moneys in the treasury not otherwise appropriated, to be paid by the treasurer on the warrant of the comptroller, for lighting, heating, plumbing and furnishing the kindergarten building above mentioned, and for providing the same with fire-escapes and for introducing and completing a new system of water closets in the main building of said institution.

MISCELLANEOUS.

Board of electrical control.   For the board of electrical control in and for the city of New York, for the services and expenses of the commissioners thereof, for the fiscal year ending September thirtieth, eighteen hundred and ninety-seven, forty-five thousand dollars, which amounts to

gether with such reasonable compensation for services and expenses of clerks in the office of the comptroller as may be certified by him, not exceeding the sum of two thousand dollars, which is hereby appropriated for the expense of the levy and collection thereof, shall be refunded to the treasury of the state by the ^{Refunding} several companies operating electrical conductors in said city, which are or shall be required to place and operate any of their conductors underground, pursuant to the provisions of chapter four hundred and ninety-nine of the laws of eighteen hundred and eighty-five, and the acts amendatory thereof, which said company shall furnish to the comptroller the data and necessary information required to make assessments pursuant to sections seven and eight of chapter four hundred and ninety-nine, as amended, and said commissioners shall furnish to the comptroller a list of such companies. The employes of the said board of electrical control shall be subject to municipal civil service examination. The assessments of the amounts to be paid to the said board of electrical control shall be made according to law upon the several corporations and companies liable therefor by the comptroller, at such time or times, at his office in the city of Albany, as he shall designate, when they may be heard thereon, of which the comptroller shall give such corporations or companies at least one week's prior notice, to each, a written or printed copy of such notice in the usual way, by mail, directed to them at their respective places of business, postage thereon prepaid.

Refunding of amount.

Civil service assessment, how made.

For the health officers for the port of New York, for the expenses of maintenance and repairs on Fire island, and for the salaries of the superintendent, watchman and other employes during the year eighteen hundred and ninety-seven, the sum of five thousand dollars.

Fire island.

To O. P. Clarke for salary as custodian of the Grant Cottage situated on Mount McGregor, Saratoga county, for the years eighteen hundred and ninety-six and eighteen hundred and ninety-seven, two thousand dollars, pursuant to the provisions of chapter six hundred and sixty-seven of the laws of eighteen hundred and ninety-six.

O. P. Clarke.

＊　　＊　　＊　　＊　　＊　　＊　　＊　　＊

For M. D. Makepeace, for services rendered by him as architect, preparing drawings and specifications and superintending the erection of a kitchen building and other improvements at Auburn state prison, the sum of six hundred dollars, payable upon the audit of the comptroller.

M. D. Makepeace.

Clerks in office of capitol commissioner.

For the payment of the necessary force of clerks, draughtsmen and inspectors in the office of the capitol commissioner, for their services in the repairs, improvements and erection of state buildings other than the new capitol, the sum of thirty-five thousand dollars.

Henry F. Glisan.

For Henry F. Glisan, for balance due him for services as stenographer to the special railroad committee appointed to investigate surface and elevated railroads, pursuant to a resolution of the assembly, session of eighteen hundred and ninety-five, the sum of two thousand seven hundred and fifty-five dollars and seventy cents, which has been audited and allowed by the comptroller.

C. V. C. Van Deusen.

For Clarance V. C. Van Deusen, for services and expenses in assisting in the drafting of chapter nine hundred and nine of the laws of eighteen hundred and ninety-six, known as the election law, constituting chapter six of the general laws, and the amendments thereto in the year eighteen hundred and ninety-seven, the sum of one thousand dollars.

Robert C. Chapin.

For Robert C. Chapin, the sum of one thousand four hundred and twenty-two dollars and eighty cents, being the amount which has been audited and allowed by the comptroller, for his services in reporting the investigation of the management of the New York and Brooklyn bridge, for the senate committee on the affairs of cities.

Deaf-Mute Journal.

For supplying the Deaf-Mute Journal for the indigent deaf and dumb of this state, the sum of six hundred and fifty dollars.

Albany Home School for Deaf.

For the support and instruction of eight pupils at the Albany Home School for the Deaf during the balance of the year eighteen hundred and ninety-seven and until October first, eighteen hundred and ninety-eight, at an annual compensation of two hundred and sixty dollars each per year, twenty-four hundred and fifty-five dollars; a proportionate amount for a shorter period of time than one year, or for a smaller number of pupils, shall be allowed and paid by the comptroller upon certificates verified by oath of the president and secretary of such institution and upon approval of the superintendent of public instruction.

*   *   *   *   *   *   *   *

S. N. Gallup.

For Silas N. Gallup, for his traveling and other expenses as trustee of the New York State Custodial Asylum for Feeble-Minded Women during the years eighteen hundred and ninety-two, eighteen hundred and ninety-three and eighteen hundred and ninety-four, two hundred and seventy-five dollars and fifty-six cents.

*   *   *   *   *   *   *   *

To William J. Youngs, for services and disbursements as counsel W. J. Youngs. to the special committee on the investigation of the question of highway improvement, appointed by resolution of the assembly, adopted on the twenty-first day of February, eighteen hundred and ninety-five, the sum of one thousand five hundred dollars.

For Lafayette B. Gleason, in full for services as counsel to the L. B. Gleason. special committee appointed by resolution of the assembly adopted on the fourth day of April, eighteen hundred and ninety-five, and for his expenses and disbursements, the sum of two thousand five hundred dollars.

For William M. Walsh, for repairs and for plumbing, and for a W. M. Walsh. new system of closets and drainage in the geological hall, the sum of four thousand five hundred and eighty dollars.

The sum of twenty-five thousand dollars, or so much thereof State hall. as may be necessary, is hereby appropriated out of any moneys in the treasury not otherwise appropriated for repairing the interior and exterior of the state hall, to be expended under the direction of the comptroller, superintendent of the banking department, and the state engineer and surveyor.

For the commissioners of the state reservation at Niagara, for Niagara reservation. grading, planting and other improvements in the reservation, the sum of fifteen thousand dollars.

For the New York State Agricultural Experiment Station at Agricultural experiment station, Geneva. Geneva.—For the expenses of bulletins and of enforcing the provisions of the law in relation to commercial fertilizers as shall be authorized by the board of control, pursuant to chapter four hundred and thirty-seven, laws of eighteen hundred and ninety, the sum of ten thousand dollars, or so much thereof as may be necessary.

For deficiency in expenses of the state capitol celebration, under Capitol celebration. chapter seven hundred and forty-three of the laws of eighteen hundred and ninety-six, three thousand dollars.

For furniture, carpets, and repairs to furniture of committee Senate committee rooms, furniture, etc., for. rooms and cartage and supplies for senate committees on finance, codes, cities, banks, taxation and retrenchment, forest, fish and game, canals, railroads, lieutenant-governor's room, and desks, chairs and tables for senate reporters' room, as follows: To John G. Myers, the sum of three thousand three hundred and fifty-four dollars and fifty-four cents; to James Farrell, the sum of ten dollars; to H. C. Burch, the sum of seventy-nine dollars and eighty cents; to Van Husen Charles company, the sum of one hundred and five dollars and eighty cents; to the Hayden furniture company, the sum of five hundred and eighty-seven dollars and fifty-two cents.

County treasurer, Albany county.
For the county treasurer of Albany county, the sum of nine hundred and twenty dollars, for the expense incurred by the county of Albany in investigating and prosecuting the charge of bribery against Eugene F. Vacheron, a member of assembly in and for the third district of Queens county for the year eighteen hundred and ninety-five, which charge after a trial by a jury resulted in an acquital.

Advances to clerks of senate and assembly.
For advances by the comptroller to the clerks of the senate and assembly to pay the expenses of receiving reports and printed documents from the several state departments, addressing and forwarding same to members of senate and assembly, forty-five hundred dollars, or so much thereof as may be necessary. Such reports and documents shall be delivered by the printer to the document departments of the senate and assembly in the proportion to which such departments are respectively entitled.

File boards, stationery, etc.
For the clerks of the senate and assembly, for the use of the senate and assembly for file boards, stationery, printing, for revising the clerk's manual and books and copies of codes for the use of the senate and assembly judiciary and codes committees, twelve thousand nine hundred and ninety-five dollars and fifty cents.

*   *   *   *   *   *   *   *   *

Index to session laws.
For the clerk of the assembly, three thousand dollars, for the work of preparing and compiling a general index to the session laws.

Robert C. Chapin.
For Robert C. Chapin, the sum of three thousand four hundred and ninety-seven dollars, being the amount which has been audited and allowed by the comptroller, for his services in reporting the proceedings of the special committee of the assembly appointed pursuant to the resolution adopted March sixth, eighteen hundred and ninety-five, to investigate the condition of female labor in New York city.

Clerical services for senate committees
For extra clerical service, to the committee on finance of the senate for the year eighteen hundred and ninety-six, and for the ways and means committee and committee on finance for the year eighteen hundred and ninety-seven, the sum of twenty-five hundred dollars, payable by the comptroller to the party who performed the service, upon the audit of the chairman of the finance committee of the senate, and the audit of the chairman of the ways and means committee of the assembly.

To Charles Z. Lincoln, in lieu of and in full of all expenses as a Charles Z. Lincoln. commissioner of statutory revision for the year beginning May first, eighteen hundred and ninety-seven, the sum of fifteen hundred dollars, payable in equal monthly installments.

To Abram Hurd, for services and disbursements as bridge Abram Hurd. tender of the state bridge at Stony Point, Rockland county, the sum of two hundred and thirty-eight dollars and ninety-five cents, or so much thereof as may be necessary, payable upon the audit of the comptroller.

* * * * * * * *

For the employment of clergymen at the Willard state hospital, Willard hospital. the sum of one thousand dollars is hereby appropriated, to be paid under the direction of the board of trustees.

For the payment of expenses incurred in the appraisal of glan- Glandered horses. dered horses and for compensation to owners of glandered horses destroyed pursuant to the provisions of section sixty-three of chapter six hundred and seventy-four of the laws of eighteen hundred and ninety-four, the sum of five thousand dollars.

The sum of six thousand dollars is hereby appropriated to be Pasteur institute. paid to the Pasteur Institute of the city of New York, as a full equivalent for services, as provided in chapter seven hundred and seventy of the laws of eighteen hundred and ninety-five.

For James B. Lyon, for printing ten thousand copies of the J. B. Lyon. consolidated school law containing the amendment of eighteen hundred and ninety-six, the sum of seven hundred dollars, payable on the audit of the comptroller.

For repairs of closets and drains, and other incidental expenses State hall. in connection with the sewerage system of the state hall, three thousand and twenty-two dollars and fifty cents, said amount to be paid after due audit by the comptroller.

For Jennie L. Dexter, the sum of one hundred dollars, for assist- J. L. Dexter. ing in preparing the index to the assembly journal of eighteen hundred and ninety-six.

To Miss Lizzie Kingsbury, for taking charge of the senate direct- Lizzie Kingsbury. ory of eighteen hundred and ninety-seven, the sum of three hundred dollars.

For Curtis D. Cooper, for services as lock-tender on the Oswego Curtis D. Cooper. canal, during the years of eighteen hundred and ninety-three, eighteen hundred and ninety-four and eighteen hundred and ninety-five, and the month of May, eighteen hundred and ninety-six, at the rate of ten dollars per month, the sum of two hundred and fifty dollars.

John S
Parsons.

For John S. Parsons, for services rendered as deputy compiler of the constitutional convention, state of New York, from March fifteenth, eighteen hundred and ninety-four, to May eighth, eighteen hundred and ninety-five, fifty-four days, at seven dollars per day, the sum of three hundred and seventy-eight dollars.

John S.
Casey.

To John S. Casey, for clerical services of the senate for the sessions of the senate of eighteen hundred and ninety-six and eighteen hundred and ninety-seven, two hundred and forty dollars.

May E.
Helmer.

To May E. Helmer, as stenographer for the finance committee for the session of eighteen hundred and ninety-seven, the sum of six hundred and fifty dollars.

Stenographers
for judges
of court of
appeals.

For services of stenographers for judges of the court of appeals, under chapter three hundred and sixty-nine of the laws of eighteen hundred and eighty-one, as amended by chapter three hundred and thirty-three of the laws of eighteen hundred and eighty-four, the sum of one thousand dollars, or so much thereof as may be necessary.

Bridge at
Glendale.

The sum of one thousand dollars is hereby appropriated out of any money in the treasury not otherwise appropriated, being an additional amount to the sum mentioned in chapter eight hundred of the laws of eighteen hundred and ninety-six, for the construction of a steel bridge over Black river, at Glendale, in the county of Lewis.

* * * ▼ * * * *

Washington head-
quarters.

For maintenance and expenses in regard to Washington headquarters, at Newburgh, Orange county, sixteen hundred dollars.

C. J. Bode
and S. S.
Pickford.

To Christian J. Bode and S. Sherman Pickford, for services and disbursements as counsel to the special investigating committee in the matter of the investigation of the civil service of the state of New York, one thousand one hundred and ten dollars.

PAYABLE FROM THE FREE SCHOOL FUND.

Indian
schools.

For deficiency in the appropriation for maintenance and support of Indian schools, in accordance with the provisions of chapter seventy-one of the laws of eighteen hundred and fifty-six, one thousand dollars.

Summer
institutes.

For the maintenance of summer institutes, in accordance with the provisions of chapter one hundred and fifty-six of the laws of eighteen hundred and ninety-six, the sum of six thousand dollars, or so much thereof as may be necessary.

Teachers'
classes in
schools.

For the purpose of complying with the provisions of chapter ten hundred and thirty-one of the laws of eighteen hundred and ninety-five as amended by chapter six hundred and forty-six of the laws of eighteen hundred and ninety-six, the sum of forty thousand dollars, or so much thereof as may be necessary.

PAYABLE FROM THE MILITARY RECORD FUND.

For the adjutant-general, for deficiency in appropriation for the present fiscal year of the bureau of military records, five hundred dollars, or so much thereof as may be necessary. *Bureau of military records.*

No manager, trustee or other officer of any state, charitable or other institution receiving moneys under this act from the state treasury for maintenance and support shall be individually interested in any purchase, sale or contract made by any officer for any of said institutions. *Managers, etc., not to be interested.*

All institutions receiving moneys under this act from the state treasury for maintenance, in whole or in part, shall deposit all their funds in some responsible bank, banks or banking-house, in pursuance of the provisions of chapter three hundred and twenty-six of the laws of eighteen hundred and eighty-eight, and the comptroller, in addition to the liability of said bank, shall require for all such funds so deposited the bond of said bank, with such good and sufficient sureties, to be approved by him as to form and amount as he shall deem necessary, and all state institutions and departments, except charitable institutions, reformatories, houses of refuge and state industrial schools, shall pay into the treasury, quarterly, all receipts and earnings other than receipts from the state treasury. *Deposit of funds in bank.* *Quarterly reports.*

All charitable institutions, reformatories, houses of refuge and the state industrial school, receiving moneys under this act, shall file with the comptroller on or before the twentieth of October of each year, a certified inventory of all articles of maintenance on hand at the close of the preceding year, naming in such inventory the kind and amount of such articles of maintenance. *Annual inventory to be filed.*

The comptroller is hereby authorized and empowered to devise a form of accounts to be observed in every state charitable institution, reformatory. houses of refuge, state industrial school, or department receiving moneys under this act, which shall be accepted and followed by such institutions and departments after thirty days' notice thereof has been submitted to them by the comptroller, and such form of accounts shall include such a uniform method of bookkeeping, filing and rendering of accounts as may insure a uniform mention of purchase of like articles, *Form of accounts.*

whether by weight, measure or otherwise, as the interest of the public service requires. Such form shall also include a uniform rate of allowance in reporting in such institutions and departments, the amount in value of all produce and other articles of maintenance raised upon lands of the state, and which may enter into the maintenance of such institutions or departments.

Duty of clerk or bookkeeper of institutions. It shall be the duty of the clerk or bookkeeper in each state charitable institution, reformatory, houses of refuge, state industrial schools or any state department receiving moneys under this act, to receive and examine all articles purchased by the proper officer or received for the maintenance thereof, to compare them with the bill therefor, to ascertain whether they correspond in weight, quantity and quality, and to inspect the supplies thus received; and the said clerk or bookkeeper shall also enter each bill of goods thus received in the book of the institution or department in which he is employed at the time of the receipt of the articles; and if any discrepancy is found between such bill and the articles received, he shall make a note thereof, whether it be in weight, quality or quantity, and no goods or other articles of purchase, or farm or garden production of lands of the institution, shall be received unless an entry thereof be made in the book of accounts of the institution, with the proper bill, invoice or mention, according to the form of accounts and record prescribed by the comptroller.

Accounts for repairs. In accounts for repairs or new work provided for in this act the name of each workman, the number of days he is employed, and the rate and amount of wages paid to him shall be given. If contracts are made for repairs or new work, or for supplies, a duplicate thereof, with specifications, shall be filed with the comptroller.

Chap. 791.*

AN ACT making appropriations for certain expenses of government and supplying deficiencies in former appropriations.

Became a law May 24, 1897, with the approval of the Governor.
Passed by a two-thirds vote.

The People of the State of New York, represented in Senate and Assembly, do enact as follows:

Section 1. The treasurer shall pay on the warrant of the comptroller, from the several funds specified, to the persons and for the objects indicated in this act, the amounts named or such parts of those amounts as shall be sufficient to accomplish, in full, the purposes designated by the appropriations, but no warrants shall be issued, except in cases of salaries, until the amounts claimed shall have been audited and allowed by the comptroller, who is hereby authorized to determine the same. The persons demanding payment shall present to him a detailed statement, in items, verified by affidavit; and if the account shall be for services it must show when, where and under what authority they were rendered; if for expenditures, when, where and under what authority they were made; if for articles furnished, when and where they were furnished, to whom they were delivered, and under what authority; and if the demand be for traveling expenses, the account must also specify the distance traveled, the place of starting and destination, the duty or business and the date and items of expenditure. On all accounts for transportation, furniture, blank and other books furnished for the use of officers, binding, blanks, printing, stationery and postage, a bill duly certified must be furnished; but whenever an appropriation shall have been provided otherwise, the sum herein directed to be paid shall not be considered as an addition to such other appropriation unless it shall be expressly so declared in this act.

For compensation of clerks of judges of the court of appeals, and for expenses incurred pursuant to chapter two hundred and twenty-one of the laws of eighteen hundred and ninety-seven, the sum of five thousand dollars, or so much thereof as may be necessary.

Marginal notes: Payments by treasurer. Audit of accounts. Verified statements. Certified bill to be furnished. Clerks of judges of court of appeals.

---

* Items of appropriation contained in this act, as passed by the legislature, and objected to by the governor, with the statement of his objections thereto, are not included in this publication, which contains only so much of the act as actually became a law, under section nine of article four of the constitution.

Deputy clerk of appellate division, second department. For deficiency in appropriation for salary of the deputy clerk of the appellate division of the supreme court, in the second judicial department, fifteen hundred dollars, or so much thereof as may be necessary, to be refunded to the treasury pursuant to chapter ninety-nine of the laws of eighteen hundred and ninety-six, as amended by chapter two hundred and twenty-three of the laws of eighteen hundred and ninety-seven.

Confidential clerks to certain justices of supreme court. For deficiency in appropriation for confidential clerks to the justices of the supreme court in the fifth judicial district, four thousand eight hundred dollars, or so much thereof as may be necessary, to be refunded to the treasury pursuant to chapter eight hundred and ninety-three of the laws of eighteen hundred and ninety-six, as amended by chapter one hundred and forty-five of the laws of eighteen hundred and ninety-seven.

Rifle range, Rochester. For the adjutant-general, for the completion of the rifle range in the state armory in the city of Rochester, for wiring and rewiring the same, for alterations for the purpose of constructing and equipping an electric fan and for furniture for the use of the said armory, the sum of one thousand dollars, or so much thereof as may be necessary.

*   *   *   *   *   *   *   *

Rush F. Simms. For Rush F. Simms, for balance due him for his services as messenger in the legislative railroad investigating committee of the session of eighteen hundred and ninety-five, the sum of two hundred and seventy-four dollars.

Bridge at Rochester. For the superintendent of public works, for the purpose of completing the bridge over the Erie canal at Exchange street, in the city of Rochester, heretofore authorized to be constructed pursuant to chapter five hundred and fourteen of the laws of eighteen hundred and ninety-five, the sum of fifteen thousand dollars, or so much thereof as may be necessary.

Assessments on state property. For the payment of assessments on state property located in the tenth, fifteenth and twentieth wards of the city of Rochester, and the town of Gates, Monroe county, being for the construction of the west-side sewer, authorized by chapter six hundred and three of the laws of eighteen hundred and ninety-two, as amended by chapter four hundred and thirty-eight of the laws of eighteen hundred and ninety-five, the sum of twenty-one thousand nine hundred and eighty-six dollars and sixty-seven cents, or so much thereof as may be necessary, to be paid after due audit by the comptroller, and in pursuance of section twenty of chapter three hundred and seventeen of the laws of eighteen hundred and ninety-four.

*   *   *   *   *   *   *   *   *   *

For the secretary of state, for revising and indexing the six
volumes of the record of debates and proceedings of the New York
state constitutional convention of eighteen hundred and ninety-six,
under the contract therefor, the sum of six thousand dollars, or
so much thereof as may be necessary.

Indexing
constitu-
tional con-
vention
debates,
etc.

For Hugo Hirsch, for his services as counsel for the assembly
cities committee, appointed pursuant to resolution of the assembly,
on the sixteenth day of May, eighteen hundred and ninety-five,
to investigate the department of charities and correction in the
county of Kings, for his costs, fees and disbursements, employment of detectives, experts, et cetera, including services of associate counsel, James Taylor and John H. Kemble, appointed by
said committee, in examining the accounts and workings of said
departments of charities and correction, for the fiscal years of
eighteen hundred and eighty-nine and eighteen hundred and
ninety, up to and including the fiscal years eighteen hundred and
ninety-four and eighteen hundred and ninety-five, entailing employment of counsel and associate counsel during a period extending over nearly five months, from the tenth day of June, eighteen
hundred and ninety-five, to the end of October, eighteen hundred
and ninety-five, and for his other necessary expenses connected
with said investigation, the sum of twenty thousand dollars.

Hugo
Hirsch.

For Byron Traver, the sum of two thousand dollars, for his legal
services in defending the action brought by Patrick J. Andrews,
member of assembly of the twenty-sixth district, New York county,
against the committee on privileges and elections of the assembly,
where the committee was sought to be restrained from opening
the ballot-boxes and counting the ballots in the contested election
case of Frank A. Sovak against said Patrick J. Andrews, and
also for his services as counsel for the committee in the contested
election cases of Frank A. Sovak against Patrick J. Andrews and of
Otto Kempner against Jeremiah J. Sullivan, sitting member from
the tenth district, county of New York.

Byron
Traver.

For repairs, coal and supplies for the old senate house in the
city of Kingston, the sum of three hundred and five dollars.

Senate
house.

For Jeremiah J. Sullivan, for his legal and other expenses incurred in the matter of the contest for membership in the assembly
for eighteen hundred and ninety-seven, for the tenth district of

Jeremiah
J. Sullivan.

New York, Otto Kempner, contestant, against Jeremiah J. Sullivan, sitting member, for his costs, fees and disbursements, in the matter of such contest, the sum of five thousand dollars.

State treasurer.

For deficiency in appropriation for clerk hire in the office of state treasurer, one thousand five hundred and fifty dollars.

Examiners of fire-arms.

For the board of examiners of improved firearms for the use of the military of this state, for expenses and disbursements, the sum of one thousand and fifty dollars, or so much thereof as may be necessary, in pursuance of chapter six hundred of the laws of eighteen hundred and ninety-five, and chapter one hundred and ninety-seven of the laws of eighteen hundred and ninety-six.

Craig colony.

For the Craig colony for epileptics, for deficiency in appropriation, twenty thousand dollars.

Adjutant-general.

For the adjutant-general, for the purchase of Farrows' military encyclopedia for distribution to the officers and men of the national guard, the sum of two thousand dollars, or so much thereof as may be necessary.

Monuments commissioners.

For the board of Gettysburg and Chattanooga monuments commissioners, the sum of nine thousand seven hundred and sixty-six dollars, for the payment of necessary engineers, surveyors, agents and employes for the battle fields of Gettysburg and Chattanooga, and for such other expenses that may be required for the work of said commission, including actual and necessary traveling and other contingent expenses, incurred by said commissioners in the discharge of their duties, and for compensation of their services as provided for in section six of chapter three hundred and seventy-one of the laws of eighteen hundred and ninety-four, under the provisions of chapter three hundred and sixty-nine of the laws of eighteen hundred and ninety-seven.

Officers and members of legislature.

For the comptroller for deficiency in appropriation for compensation and mileage of officers and members of the legislature, for the fiscal year ending September thirtieth, eighteen hundred and ninety-seven, the sum of thirty thousand dollars, or so much thereof as may be necessary.

*   *   *   *   *   *   *   *   *   *

Engraving, etc., of canal bonds.

From the canal fund, for deficiency in appropriation for miscellaneous expenses, under chapter nine hundred and forty-six of the laws of eighteen hundred and ninety-six, on account of advertising, engraving and printing bonds for canal improvement, the sum of twenty-five hundred dollars, or so much thereof as may be necessary.

For J. Blanche Wood, for services as stenographer and type- _{J. Blanche Wood.} writer to the committee of insurance, railroads and printing for the session of eighteen hundred and ninety-seven, the sum of four hundred dollars.

*   *   *   *   *   *   *   *   *

For Eugene J. Wells, for extra clerical service in office of finan- _{Eugene J. Wells.} cial clerk of the assembly, the sum of two hundred and fifty dollars.

For Cornelius Coughlin, for his legal costs and expenses neces- _{Cornelius Coughlin.} sarily incurred by him in the matter of election contest for his seat in the assembly of eighteen hundred and ninety-six, as member of assembly for the first assembly district of Erie county, state of New York, and for his other necessary expenses in such contest, the sum of fifteen hundred dollars, or so much thereof as may be necessary.

For L. G. DeCant, for the payment of the balance due for ser- _{L. G. DeCant.} vices, expenses and disbursements incurred in the matter of the prosecution of charges against the superintendent of state prisons, during the year eighteen hundred and ninety-six, the sum of five hundred and thirty-nine dollars and thirty-four cents, said accounts having been duly certified by the governor and attorney-general.

For building a sidewalk on the west side of Irving bridge in the _{Sidewalk in Irving.} village of Irving, county of Chautauqua, the sum of seven hundred and fifty dollars, or so much thereof as may be necessary, to be expended under the supervision of the superintendent of public works.

For the purchase of typewriters, furniture, stationery and sup- _{Supplies, etc., for legislative committees.} plies belonging thereto, for the use of the senate and assembly committees, the sum of four hundred and sixty-four dollars and ninety cents, or so much thereof as may be necessary, payable upon the audit of the chairman of the finance committee of the senate and the chairman of the ways and means committee of the assembly.

For the secretary of state, for supplying to each election district _{Election law.} for the use of election boards and to the other officers mentioned in section nineteen of the election law of eighteen hundred and ninety-six, one copy each of said laws, together with one copy of the amendments to the said law, passed in eighteen hundred and ninety-seven, the sum of five thousand dollars.

For the making of abstracts of patents and maps of lands in the _{Abstracts of patents and maps.} Onondaga salt springs, the work to be done under the supervision of the secretary of state, to be paid upon his certificate, the sum of twenty-five hundred dollars, or so much thereof as may be necessary.

E. N. Mc-Gonigal. For E. N. McGonigal, for the balance in full for services as assistant in the compiling department of the constitutional convention, from January first, eighteen hundred and ninety-five to June fifteenth, eighteen hundred and ninety-five, the sum of five hundred and sixty-two dollars.

Repairs at Clear Creek bridge. For the superintendent of public works, for the repair of abutments and filling of a washout at the Clear Creek bridge on the road leading from Versailles to Irving on the Cattaraugus Indian Reservation, Erie county, the sum of three hundred dollars, or so much thereof as may be necessary.

Victor J. Dowling. For Victor J. Dowling for legal services in the matter of the contest for membership in the assembly of eighteen hundred and ninety-seven, for the twenty-sixth assembly district of New York, Frank A. Sovak, contestant, versus Patrick J. Andrews, sitting member, for his costs, fees and disbursements in the matter of the above contest, the sum of five thousand dollars.

Indian museum. For additions to the Indian museum, in accordance with chapter five hundred and eighty-six of the laws of eighteen hundred and ninety-six, providing that the curator shall serve without salary, the sum of two thousand dollars.

Expenses of Tennessee exhibition commissioners. For the board of commissioners to represent the state of New York at the Tennessee centennial and international exhibition to be held at Nashville, in addition to the sum already appropriated, pursuant to chapter seven of the laws of eighteen hundred and ninety-seven, the sum of three thousand dollars, or so much thereof as may be necessary.

Clerks to president of senate and speaker. For services of the clerk to the president of the senate, and for services of the clerk to the speaker of the assembly, one thousand dollars each, for the year eighteen hundred and ninety-seven.

Contingent expenses for clerk of assembly. For additional contingent expenses for the clerk of the assembly, for the year eighteen hundred and ninety-seven, the sum of three thousand dollars.

J. P. Martin and Thomas Burns. For John P. Martin and Thomas Burns, being the balance remaining unpaid for services and expenses for reporting the investigation of the charges against the superintendent of state prisons, the sum of three hundred and forty-seven dollars and twenty-eight cents, or so much thereof as may be necessary, payable upon the audit of the comptroller.

German Looking Glass Plate company. For the German Looking Glass Plate company, of West Virginia, the sum of eleven hundred and eleven dollars and sixty-three cents, being balance of a rebate granted on account of taxes collected from said company for the year eighteen hundred and ninety-one, which could not have been lawfully demanded, and is hereby refunded said company, which amount shall be payment in full of all claims against the state.

For the state reformatory for women at Bedford, Westchester *State reformatory for women, Bedford.* county, the sum of ten thousand dollars, or so much thereof as may be necessary, for the completion of the present contract and the payment of any extras which may be allowed and certified to by the state architect, not to exceed three thousand dollars; the sum of twelve thousand dollars for the construction and completion of the drainage and sewerage system, in accordance with the plans heretofore agreed upon by the board of managers and the department of public works of New York city; the sum of eight thousand dollars for a complete electric light and power plant for buildings and grounds, including dynamos, engine and wiring and fixtures; the sum of three thousand five hundred dollars for steam mains placed in conduits, for conduits, and for all needed piping to connect boiler-house with the several buildings; the sum of two thousand dollars for sewer pump, for addition to the powerhouse, and for additional boilers and engine; the sum of ten thousand dollars for building reservoir, for putting in water mains, for constructing stand pipe, and for placing fire hydrants and completing system of water-works connecting with each building; the sum of fifteen hundred dollars for frame barn and other necessary out buildings, making a total of forty-seven thousand dollars.

All of the foregoing work to be done under the direction of the *Plans and contracts.* state architect, upon his plans and specifications, except as above provided, after the due letting of contracts, which contracts shall each contain a condition that the contract price shall provide for the full completion of the objects mentioned in the respective items appropriating money therefor.

For the preparation of supplementary indices of assembly bills, *Indexes.* journals and documents, the sum of seven hundred and fifty dollars, to be paid by the comptroller on the certificate of the speaker of the assembly.

To pay for work performed for finishing and furnishing additional committee rooms for the use of senate committee on finance, *Improvements in capitol.* cities and codes in the fourth story of the tower; finishing the third story of the tower for telegraph, telephone and press association offices and a restaurant; making alterations, addition and betterments in the state library; installing a system of heating and ventilation in the senate chamber, assembly chamber and senate committee rooms, the sum of ninety-nine thousand seven hundred and fifty-nine dollars and eighty-nine cents.

Secretary of state. For the secretary of state, the sum of one hundred dollars, to replace volumes of session laws, town of Springwater, Livingston county, destroyed by fire.

Shinnecock and Peconic Bays canal. For the superintendent of public works and state engineer and surveyor, for repairing and maintaining the gates and piling on the Shinnecock and Peconic Bays canal, the sum of five thousand dollars, or so much thereof as may be necessary.

Attorneygeneral. For the attorney-general, the sum of eight hundred dollars, or so much thereof as may be necessary, to pay costs of suits now owing or which may accrue before October first, eighteen hundred and ninety-seven.

Id. For the attorney-general, the sum of one thousand five hundred dollars, or so much thereof as may be necessary, for carpets and furniture for the attorney-general's department.

Lands for hatchery. For the commissioners of fisheries, game and forestry, five hundred dollars, for the purchase of additional land for hatchery purposes.

Comptroller. For the comptroller, for the purchase of one thousand copies of "New York in the revolution," as compiled by the comptroller; eight hundred copies for the use of the legislature and two hundred copies for the comptroller, one thousand dollars.

* * * * * * * * * *

C. W. Francis. To Clarence W. Francis, the sum of two thousand dollars, for rent and expenses in maintaining the office of the attorney-general in the city of New York.

American Steel Barge company. For the comptroller, for the payment of the claim of the American Steel Barge company, for taxes erroneously paid to the comptroller under the corporation tax laws, the sum of twelve thousand eight hundred and thirteen dollars and fifty-three cents.

General Electric company. For the comptroller, for the payment of the claim of the General Electric company, for taxes erroneously paid to the comptroller under the corporation tax laws, the sum of eighteen thousand six hundred and seventy-two dollars and fifty-four cents.

Newton creek, Horseheads. For the superintendent of public works for continuing the work of improving the channel of Newtown creek, now commenced, pursuant to the provisions of chapter nine hundred and forty-nine of the laws of eighteen hundred and ninety-six, in the town of Horseheads, county of Chemung, the sum of seven thousand five

hundred dollars. The work to be done and moneys expended upon
plans and specifications prepared and furnished by the state engineer and surveyor, and all of said work, so far as practicable, to
be done by contract and let to the lowest bidder or bidders.

For the superintendent of public buildings, for removing old
stairway, putting in floor, cutting doorways, painting, refinishing
and furnishing rooms under the executive chamber for the state
prison department, and for fitting up storeroom underneath same
for the executive department, and for putting in water-closet, cutting doorways, painting, decorating and furnishing, and for all
necessary repairs and equipments for new room for the insurance
department, formerly occupied by the state prison department, the
sum of five thousand dollars. *Improvements in capitol.*

*　*　*　*　*　*　*　*　*　*

For the superintendent of public works, for payment of salaries
and expenses of inspectors of hulls and boilers, as provided in the
navigation law, nine thousand dollars. *Inspectors of hulls and boilers.*

For the comptroller, for compensation to owners of glandered
horses destroyed pursuant to the provisions of section sixty-three
of chapter six hundred and seventy-four of the laws of eighteen
hundred and ninety-four, the sum of one thousand five hundred
dollars. *Glandered horses.*

For the commissioners of fisheries, game and forest, to carry
out the provisions of chapter two hundred and fifty-nine of the
laws of eighteen hundred and ninety-seven, the sum of seven hun-
dred and fifty dollars, to be paid out on the certificate of said board. *Acquisition of lands in Ulster county.*

*　*　*　*　*

No manager, trustee or other officer of any state, charitable or
other institution receiving moneys under this act from the state
treasury for maintenance and support shall be individually interested in any purchase, sale or contract made by any officer for
any of said institutions. *Managers, etc., not to be interested.*

All institutions receiving moneys under this act from the state
treasury for maintenance, in whole or in part, shall deposit all their
funds in some responsible bank, banks or banking-house, in pursuance of the provisions of chapter three hundred and twenty-six of
the laws of eighteen hundred and eighty, and the comptroller, in
addition to the liability of said bank, shall require for all such
funds so deposited the bond of said bank, with such good and sufficient sureties, to be approved by him as to form and amount as he
shall deem necessary, and all state institutions and departments *Deposit of funds in bank.*

Quarterly reports.

except charitable institutions, reformatories, houses of refuge and state industrial schools, shall pay into the treasury, quarterly, all receipts and earnings other than receipts from the state treasury.

Annual inventory to be filed.

All charitable institutions, reformatories, houses of refuge and the State Industrial School, receiving moneys under this act, shall file with the comptroller on or before the twentieth of October of each year, a certified inventory of all articles of maintenance on hand at the close of the preceding year, naming in such inventory the kind and amount of such articles of maintenance.

Form of accounts.

The comptroller is hereby authorized and empowered to devise a form of accounts to be observed in every state charitable institution, reformatory, houses of refuge, state industrial school, or department receiving moneys under this act, which shall be accepted and followed by such institutions and departments after thirty days' notice thereof has been submitted to them by the comptroller. and such form of accounts shall include such a uniform method of bookkeeping, filing and rendering of accounts as may insure a uniform mention of purchase of like articles, whether by weight, measure or otherwise, as the interest of the public service requires. Such form shall also include a uniform rate of allowance in reporting in such institutions and departments, the amount in value of all produce and other articles of maintenance raised upon lands of state, and which may enter into the maintenance of such institutions or departments.

Duty of clerk or book-keeper of institutions.

It shall be the duty of the clerk or bookkeeper in each state charitable institution, reformatory, houses of refuge, state industrial schools or any state department receiving moneys under this act, to receive and examine all articles purchased by the proper officer or received or the maintenance thereof, to compare them with the bill therefor, to ascertain whether they correspond in weight, quantity and quality, and to inspect the supplies thus received; and the said clerk or bookkeeper shall also enter each bill of goods thus received in the book of the institution or department in which he is employed at the time of the receipt of the articles; and if any discrepancy is found between such bill and the articles received, he shall make a note thereof, whether it be in weight, quality or quantity, and no goods or other articles of purchase, or farm or garden production of lands of the institution, shall be received unless an entry thereof be made in the book of accounts of the institution, with the proper bill, invoice or mention, according to the form of accounts and record prescribed by the comptroller.

In accounts for repairs or new work provided for in this act the _{Accounts for repairs.} name of each workman, the number of days he is employed, and the rate and amount of wages paid to him shall be given. If contracts are made for repairs or new work, or for supplies, a duplicate thereof, with specifications, shall be filed with the comptroller.

Chap. 794.

AN ACT to authorize the comptroller of the state to hear and determine the application of William Harris, for cancellation of the tax sales of lot number forty-eight, township three, Totten and Crossfield's purchase, Hamilton county, for unpaid taxes.

Became a law May 24, 1897, with the approval of the Governor.
Passed, three-fifths being present.

The People of the State of New York, represented in Senate and Assembly, do enact as follows:

Section 1. Jurisdiction is hereby conferred upon the comptrol- _{Jurisdiction to hear application.} ler of the state to hear and determine the application of William Harris, for cancellation of the tax sales of lot number forty-eight, township three, Totten and Crossfield's purchase, Hamilton county, for unpaid taxes. Said Harris claiming to be the owner thereof, and the said comptroller is hereby authorized to act upon said application in the same manner and with the same effect as if the application were made by the purchaser at the tax sale.

§ 2. Such application shall be heard and granted only upon _{Conditions.} the ground that the land was legally exempt from taxation at the time of the levy of the taxes for which the sales were made, and that the people of the state had no legal title thereto at the time of the sales.

§ 3. Prior to the hearing on said application, the said William _{Notice of hearing.} Harris shall cause to be served upon the attorney general of the state, a notice of said hearing; said notice shall be served at least fourteen days before the date of the hearing.

§ 4. This act shall take effect immediately.

Chap. 796.

AN ACT conferring jurisdiction upon the board of claims to hear, audit and determine the alleged claim of Peter Harris against the state, and to make an award thereon.

Became a law May 24, 1897, with the approval of the Governor.

Passed, three-fifths being present.

The People of the State of New York, represented in Senate and Assembly, do enact as follows:

Jurisdic-
tion to hear
claim.

Section 1. Jurisdiction is hereby conferred upon, and authority is granted to the board of claims, to hear, audit and determine the amount of the alleged claim of Peter Harris, the assignee or transferee, and successor in interest of Jere W. Finch, and of his rights, interests, and alleged claim against this state, for repayment of the purchase money paid into the state treasury on or about February second, eighteen hundred and eighty-two, by said Jere W. Finch, upon his purchase from the state and the conveyance to him by the certificate of sale of the state engineer and surveyor of certain lands, namely, "Hamilton county, Palmer's purchase; general allotment lot eight subdivisions four, five, six, seven, eight, nine, ten," by reason of the failure of the title of the people of this state thereto; the title of the people thereto having been acquired by purchase by the comptroller upon the comptroller's state tax sales for unpaid taxes returned from Hamilton county, held in the years eighteen hundred and seventy-one, eighteen hundred and seventy-seven, and eighteen hundred and eighty-one; and the said tax sales and the taxes for which said sales were had for the sale of said lands, and the state's title obtained thereby, having been cancelled by the comptroller upon the application of said Peter Harris on or about March twenty-ninth, eighteen hundred and ninety-two. And the board of claims is authorized and empowered to make an award to the said Peter Harris for the amount found due him for principal and interest for his said alleged claim against the state, and as payable in cases of failure of the title of the people of this state to lands granted under its authority, provided by law.

Appeal
from
award.

§ 2. Either party may appeal from the award made in said case to the appellate division of the supreme court, third judicial department, in the same manner and as in the cases provided by law for appeals from awards of said board.

§ 3. This act shall take effect immediately.

Chap. 797.

AN ACT authorizing the Chenango County Patrons Fire Relief association to include within its membership persons other than patrons of husbandry.

Became a law May 24, 1897, with the approval of the Governor. Passed, three-fifths being present.

The People of the State of New York, represented in Senate and Assembly, do enact as follows:

Section 1. The Chenango County Patrons Fire Relief association is hereby authorized to include within its membership persons other than Patrons of Husbandry as now required by its certificate of incorporation, and to issue insurance to such persons as provided by its certificate of incorporation, and its by-laws, rules and regulations, notwithstanding any provision in its certificate of incorporation which restricts the members of such association to the Patrons of Husbandry and limits and restricts the insurance of such association to such Patrons of Husbandry.

§ 2. This act shall take effect immediately.

CONCURRENT RESOLUTIONS

SENATE AND ASSEMBLY.

CONCURRENT RESOLUTION

Proposing an amendment to section twenty-six, article three, of the constitution.

Section 1. Resolved (if the Senate concur), That section twenty-six, article third, of the constitution be amended so as to read as follows:

§ 26. There shall be in each county, except in a county wholly included in a city, a board of supervisors, to be composed of such members and elected in such manner and for such period as is or may be provided by law. In a city which includes an entire county, or two or more entire counties, the powers and duties of a board of supervisors may be devolved upon the municipal assembly, common council, board of aldermen or other legislative body of the city.

<table>
<tr><td>STATE OF NEW YORK,
IN ASSEMBLY, March 23, 1897.
This bill was duly passed, a majority of all the members elected to the assembly voting in favor thereof, three-fifths being present.
By order of the assembly,
JAMES M. E. O'GRADY,
Speaker.</td><td>STATE OF NEW YORK,
IN SENATE, March 25, 897.
This bill was duly passed, a majority of all the senators elected voting in favor thereof, three-fifths being present.
By order of the senate.
TIMOTHY L. WOODRUFF,
President.</td></tr>
</table>

CONCURRENT RESOLUTION

Proposing an amendment to section ten, article eight, of the constitution.

Section 1. Resolved (if the Senate concur), That section ten, article eight, of the constitution be amended so as to read as follows:

§ 10. **Counties, cities and towns not to give or loan money or credit ; limitation of indebtedness.**— No county, city, town or village shall hereafter give any money or property, or loan its money or credit to or in aid of any individual, association or corporation, or become directly or indirectly the owner of stock in, or bonds of, any association or corporation; nor shall any such county, city, town or village be allowed to incur any indebtedness except for county, city, town or village purposes. This section shall not prevent such county, city, town or village from making such provision for the aid or support of its poor as may be authorized by law. No county or city shall be allowed to become indebted for any purpose or in any manner to an amount which, including existing indebtedness, shall exceed ten per centum of the assessed valuation of the real estate of such county or city subject to taxation, as it appeared by the assessment-rolls of said county or city on the last assessment for state or county taxes prior to the incurring of such indebtedness; and all indebtedness in excess of such limitation, except such as may now exist, shall be absolutely void, except as herein otherwise provided. No county or city whose present indebtedness exceeds ten per centum of the assessed valuation of its real estate subject to taxation, shall be allowed to become indebted in any further amount until such indebtedness shall be reduced within such limit. This section shall not be construed to prevent the issuing of certificates of indebtedness or revenue bonds issued in anticipation of the collection of taxes for amounts actually contained, or to be contained in the taxes for the year when such certificates or revenue bonds are issued and payable out of such taxes. Nor shall this section be construed to prevent the issue of bonds to provide for the supply of water; but the term of the bonds issued to provide the supply of water shall not exceed twenty years, and a sinking fund shall be created on the issuing of the said bonds for their redemption, by raising annually a sum which will produce an amount equal to the sum of the principal and interest of said bonds at their maturity. All certificates of indebtedness or revenue bonds issued in anticipation of the collection of taxes, which are not retired within five years after their date of issue, and bonds issued to provide for the supply of water, and any debt hereafter incurred by any portion or part of a city, if there shall be any such debt, shall be included in ascertaining the power of the city to become otherwise indebted. Whenever the boundaries of any city are the same as those of a county, or when any city shall include within its boundaries more than one county, the power of any county wholly included within such city to become indebted shall cease, but the debt of the county heretofore existing shall not, for the purposes of this section, be reckoned as a part of the city debt. The amount hereafter to be raised by tax for county or city purposes, in any county containing a city of over one hundred thousand inhabitants, or any such city of this state, in addition to providing for the principal and interest of existing debt, shall not in the aggregate exceed in any one year two per centum of the assessed valuation of the real and personal estate of such county or city, to be ascertained as prescribed in this section in respect to county or city debt.

STATE OF NEW YORK,
IN ASSEMBLY, *March* 23, 1897.
This bill was duly passed, a majority of all the members elected to the assembly voting in favor thereof, three fifths being present
By order of the assembly
JAMES M. E. O'GRADY,
Speaker.

STATE OF NEW YORK,
IN SENATE, *March* 25, 1897.
This bill was duly passed, a majority of all the senators elected voting in favor thereof, three-fifths being present.
By order of the Senate.
TIMOTHY L. WOODRUFF,
President.

ALBANY, N. Y., *January* 21, 1897.

To the Secretary of State:

This is to certify that at a joint assembly of the Senate and Assembly of the State of New York, held in the Assembly Chamber, in the city of Albany, on Wednesday, the 20th day of January, one thousand eight hundred and ninety-seven, in pursuance of law, Chester S. Lord, of the city of Brooklyn, county of Kings, was declared duly elected as a Regent of the University of the State of New York, to fill the vacancy caused by the death of the Honorable William L. Bostwick.

In witness whereof, we have placed our hands and the seals of the Senate and Assembly of the State of New York, this 21st day of Janaury, one thousand eight hundred and ninety-seven.

TIMOTHY L. WOODRUFF,
President of the Senate.

(Seal.)   JOHN S. KENYON,
Clerk of the Senate.

JAMES M. E. O'GRADY,
Speaker of the Assembly.

(Seal.)   A. E. BAXTER,
Clerk of the Assembly.

Endorsed: Filed Jan. 28, 1897.

ANDREW DAVIDSON,
Deputy Secretary of State.

•

NEW TOWNS ERECTED OR TOWN BOUNDARIES ALTERED AND ESTABLISHED BY BOARDS OF SUPERVISORS.

AN ACT to divide the town of Wilmurt, Herkimer county, and to erect a new town therein to be named Webb, pursuant to chapter 686 of the Laws of 1892, being chapter 18 of the General Laws.

Passed January 25, 1896, by the board of supervisors of Herkimer county, at its annual session, at Herkimer, two-thirds of all the members elected thereto voting in the affirmative, twenty members voting therefor.

The Board of Supervisors of Herkimer county, in pursuance of the statutes for such cases made and provided do enact as follows:

Section 1. The town of Wilmurt shall be and it is hereby divided by and following the line of division:

Beginning on a point on the county line between the counties of Herkimer and Hamilton, where the south line of lot No. 76 of the Moose River tract intersects and crosses said dividing line between the said counties of Herkimer and Hamilton; thence southwesterly along the south boundary of lots Nos. 88, 100, 112, 124, 136 of township No. 3, Moose River tract, to the southeast corner of lot No. 10, Township No. 2, Moose river tract; thence southwesterly along south boundaries of lots Nos. 10, 22, 84, 46, 58, 70, 82, 94, 106, 118, 130 and 142; thence along the south boundaries of lots Nos. 10, 23, 36, 49, 62, 75, 88, 101, 114, 127, 139, 149, 157, 163 and 167, township No. 1, Moose River Tract, to the patent line of Adgate's eastern tract; thence northwesterly along the westerly boundary of township 1, Moose River tract and the northeast boundaries of Adgate's eastern tract, Deaveroux lot and on the last-mentioned line and course to the westerly line of the county of Herkimer.

Section 2. All that part of the present town of Wilmurt lying and being northerly of said line shall be and constitute a new and separate town which is hereby named and distinguished as the town of Webb.

Section 3. All the remaining part of said town of Wilmurt shall remain and continue to be the town of Wilmurt and known and distinguished as the town of Wilmurt, and from and after the passage of this act all laws now in force applicable to the town of Wilmurt shall apply to the town of Wilmurt.

4. The first town meeting in the town of Webb hereby 'll be held in said town on the 11th day of February,

1896, at the boat shop occupied by Riley Parsons in said town, and thereafter the annual town meetings of said town shall be held on the same day as the annual town meetings of the other towns of the county of Herkimer are held, and Riley Parsons, David Charbonneau and George Goodsell are hereby appointed to preside at such first town meeting, so to be held in said new town of Webb, who shall appoint a clerk, open and keep the polls for the election of town officers for said town, and shall have and exercise all the powers conferred by law upon justices of the peace when presiding at town meetings.

Section 5. This act shall take effect immediately.

———

STATE OF NEW YORK, ⎱ *ss.:*
County of Herkimer, ⎰

We, Rufus H. Smith, chairman, and W. D. Newell, clerk of the board of supervisors of Herkimer county, N. Y., do hereby certify and attest that the foregoing resolution and act was duly passed at a regular annual session of said board duly held at Herkimer on the 25th day of January, 1896, two-thirds of all the members elected to said board being present and voting in favor thereof, and the vote of said members was as follows: Ayes:

William Tibbitts, Danube.
J. W. Ford, Fairfield.
G. I. Seaman, Frankfort.
Henry Spohn, German Flatts.
A. T. Smith, Herkimer.
T. P. Parker, Litchfield.
Frank Senioe, Little Falls town.
F. W. Smith, Little Falls city, 1st district.
R. I. Davis, Little Falls city, 2d district.
Wheeler Knapp, Manheim.
B. K. Brown, Newport.
C. B. Gray, Norway.
E. E. Kelly, Ohio.
Milo Moore, Russia.
George A. Marsh, Salisbury.
R. H. Smith, Schuyler.
O. H. Young, Stark.
George H. Casler, Warren.

J. A. Harvey, Wilmurt.

Frank L. Brace, Winfield.

In witness whereof, we have set hereto our hands and affixed the official seal of said board this 25th day of January, 1896.

Seal.   RUFUS H. SMITH,
                                                    Chairman.

W. D. NEWELL,
        Clerk.

HERKIMER COUNTY, *ss.:*

I, W. D. Newell, clerk of the board of supervisors of Herkimer county, hereby certify that I have compared the above act with the original on file in my office, and the same is a correct and true copy thereof, and of the whole thereof.

Seal.   W. D. NEWELL,
                                                    Clerk.

Endorsed: Filed Feby. 17, 1896.

ANDREW DAVIDSON,
        Deputy Secretary of State.

AN ACT to change, establish and define the northern boundary line of the town of Lake Pleasant and the southern boundary line of the town of Long Lake, in the county of Hamilton, and to legalize certain acts of the assessors of the town of Lake Pleasant.

Whereas, Chapter two hundred of the laws of eighteen hundred and sixty, entitled " An act changing the boundaries of certain towns in the county of Hamilton, and for other purposes," fixed the boundary line between the towns of Long Lake and Lake Pleasant at the south line of township number six of Totten and Crossfield's purchase, and

Whereas, An act passed by the board of supervisors of the county of Hamilton, on November fifteenth, eighteen hundred and sixty-one, entitled "An act to change the boundary lines between the towns of Arietta, Long Lake and Morehouse, in the county of Hamilton " (being chapter four hundred and ninety-one of the laws of eighteen hundred and sixty-two), so changed the southern boundary line of said town of Long Lake as to leave certain lots and parts of lots in said township six still in said town of Long Lake although separated from the remainder of said town of Long Lake by a distance of nearly two miles, and

Whereas, Since said act of November fifteenth, eighteen hundred and sixty-one, the town of Lake Pleasant has assumed and has exercised jurisdiction over said lots and parts of lots and said town of Long Lake has made no claim thereto, and

Whereas, Pursuant to the provisions of chapter six hundred and eighty-six of the laws of eighteen hundred and ninety-two, (known as the " County Law "), notice has been given of an intention to apply to the board of supervisors of said county to establish and define the boundary line of said towns, which said notice has been duly published and served and due proof thereof has been furnished to this board, and

Whereas, Application has also been made to this board, subscribed by at least twelve freeholders of the town of Long Lake and also subscribed by at least twelve freeholders of the town of Lake Pleasant, to change the boundary line of said towns as they now exist, and reference being made to the map of the Adirondack forest, compiled by authority of the fisheries, game and forest commission, and on file in the state department at Albany, for a description of lands showing the proposed alteration; and said application and notice having been duly posted and published and due proof thereof having been furnished this board as provided by said " County Law."

Therefore, The Board of Supervisors of the county of Hamilton, do enact as follows:

Section 1. The northern boundary of the town of Lake Pleasant is hereby changed, established and defined as follows: Commencing on the northeasterly line of township number six, of Totten and Crossfield's purchase, at the point where the old or former line (prior to eighteen hundred and sixty), between the towns of Arietta and Lake Pleasant intersects said northeasterly line, and running from said point of intersection a southeasterly course on said northeasterly line of township number six and townships number seven and eight of said purchase, to the northwesterly corner of the town of Wells — said line being also the southwesterly line of townships number thirty-two, thirty-three and thirty-four of said purchase, thereby taking from the town of Long Lake as now appears all that part of township number six of Totten and Crossfield's purchase lying east of the easterly line of the town of Arietta, and annexing the same to the town of Lake Pleasant.

§ 2. The southern boundary of the town of Long Lake shall be (as now appears on said map of the Adirondack forest) as follows: Commencing on the east line of the county of Hamilton,

at the point where the county line intersects the north line of the
third tier of lots (from the south) of township number twenty of
Totten and Crossfield's purchase, and running from said point
of intersection a southwesterly course along said north line of said
third tier of lots, to the northeasterly line of township number
nineteen; thence a northwesterly course to the most northerly corner of township number nineteen; thence southwesterly along
the northwesterly line of townships number nineteen and thirty-
four, to the most northerly corner of township number six, being
the south bounds of said town to this point, as fixed by act of
the legislature (chapter two hundred, laws of eighteen hundred
and sixty); thence continuing the same course along the northwesterly side of township number six, to township number
five; thence northwesterly to the most northerly corner of the
same; thence southwesterly, along the northwesterly side of
township number five to the northeasterly side of lot
number eight of John Brown's tract near the most easterly
corner thereof; thence northwesterly along the line of
said lot number eight, John Brown's tract, to the point where
the same intersects the west line of the county of Hamilton —
the courses from the northerly corner of township number six,
being the same in part and in reverse order as fixed by act of the
board of supervisors of the county of Hamilton, passed November
fifteenth, eighteen hundred and sixty-one, and published as chapter four hundred and ninety-one, laws of eighteen hundred and
sixty-two.

§ 3. The acts of the assessors of the town of Lake Pleasant for
the year eighteen hundred and ninety-six (in assessing the lands,
lots and parts of lots, contained in the territory annexed to the said
town of Lake Pleasant by section one of this act, are hereby ratified, legalized and confirmed.

§ 4. This act shall take effect immediately.

———

STATE OF NEW YORK: ⎫
OFFICE OF THE CLERK OF THE BOARD ⎬ ss.:
    OF SUPERVISORS OF   ⎪
THE COUNTY OF HAMILTON.   ⎭

I, Thomas J. Hanley, clerk of the board of supervisors of the
county of Hamilton, do hereby certify, that I have compared the
foregoing copy of an act duly passed by said board of supervisors,
on the 13th day of November, 1896, all the supervisors being present, with the original act now on file in my office, and that the
same is a true and correct copy of such act and of the whole thereof.

I further certify, that such act was passed by the following vote, to wit: — Ayes, 8; Noes, None.

> In testimony whereof, I have hereunto set my hand and affixed the official seal of the board of supervisors of said county, this 17th day of November, 1896.

(Seal.) T. J. HANLEY,

Clerk.

Endorsed: Filed Nov. 20, 1896.

ANDREW DAVIDSON,
Deputy Secretary of State.

AN ACT to alter the boundaries of the towns of Clare and Clifton in the county of St. Lawrence, pursuant to the County Law.

Passed by the board of supervisors of St. Lawrence county on the 2d day of December, 1896, 29 of the members elected thereto voting in favor thereof, and 3 against, the number voting in favor being two-thirds of all the members elected thereto.

The Board of Supervisors of St. Lawrence county, do enact as follows:

Section 1. All that part of the town of Clifton in the county of St. Lawrence, heretofore known as the Township of Clifton and bounded as follows, namely. Beginning at the southeasterly corner of the town of Clare, where said corner strikes the westerly line of the township of Granshue, and running thence southerly along the westerly bounds of the said township of Granshue and the westerly bounds of the township of Harewood, five hundred and sixty-two chains to the southeasterly corner of the said township of Clinton; thence westerly along the northerly line of the township of Chaumont, five hundred and fifty chains to the southwesterly corner of the said township of Clifton; thence northerly along the eastern boundary of the township of Sarahsburgh and the easterly boundary of the town of Russell, five hundred and sixty chains to the southwesterly corner of the town of Clare; thence easterly along the southern boundary of said town of Clare and the northern boundary of said township of Clifton, five hundred fifty-three chains to the place of beginning, is hereby taken from the said town of Clifton and added to the said town of Clare, and shall be and hereafter become a part and parcel of the said town of Clare.

§ 2. The remaining part of the present town of Clifton not included within the boundaries mentioned in section one of this act, shall be and remain and constitute the town of Clifton.

§ 3. Nothing in this act contained shall affect the rights or abridge the term of office of any town officer in the said town of Clifton.

§ 4. This act shall take effect on the first day of February, 1897.

The foregoing has been compared with the original act passed by the board of supervisors of St. Lawrence county on the second day of December, 1896, and is a correct copy of the same and of the whole thereof.

In witness whereof, we have hereunto affixed the seal of the board of supervisors of St. Lawrence county. Witness, Geo. W. Hurlbut, chairman, Chas. M. Hale, clerk of said board, this second day of December, 1896.

(Seal.)   GEORGE W. HURLBUT,

Chairman.

CHAS. M. HALE,

Clerk.

Endorsed: Filed Dec. 14, 1896.

ANDREW DAVIDSON,

Deputy Secretary of State.

NAMES CHANGED.

UNDER AND PURSUANT TO TITLE X, CHAPTER XVII OF THE CODE OF CIVIL PROCEDURE.

STATE OF NEW YORK:

STEUBEN COUNTY CLERK'S OFFICE, }
BATH, N. Y., *December* 17, 1896. }

Hon. JOHN PALMER, *Secretary of State:*

Sir.— I have the honor to report the following:

On the 24th day of September, 1896, Frank H. Robinson, county judge of the county of Steuben, made an order permitting and authorizing Jesse H. Townsend of the village of Bath, Steuben Co., N. Y., to assume the name of Jesse H. Niles on the 20th day of November, 1896.

Respectfully yours,

J. A. CONROY,
Deputy Clerk.

Endorsed: Filed Dec. 18, 1896.

ANDREW DAVIDSON,
Deputy Secretary of State.

———

ONONDAGA COUNTY, }
OFFICE OF THE COUNTY CLERK, }

SYRACUSE, N. Y., *December* 31, 1896.

Hon. JOHN PALMER, *Secretary of State, Albany, N. Y.:*

Dear Sir.— In accordance with section 2417 of the Code of Civil Procedure, I herewith send you the names of all persons who have changed their names in Onondaga county during the preceding year.

Former name, Abraham Tekulsky; present name, Abraham Teclar; date, May 18, 1896.

Former name, Zelia Wright; present name, Zelena Wright; date November 28, 1896.

Respectfully yours,

GEO. J. YAECKEL,
Onondaga County Clerk.

Endorsed: Filed Jan. 2, 1897.

J. B. H. MONGIN,
Second Deputy Secretary of State.

STATE OF NEW YORK,   }
COLUMBIA COUNTY CLERK'S OFFICE, } *ss.:*

To Hon. JOHN PALMER, *Secretary of State:*

Pursuant to statute in such case made and provided, I, Isaac P. Rockefeller, clerk of Columbia county, do hereby certify that the following changes of names were made by the Supreme Court during the year ending December 31, 1896, by orders filed and entered in my office, viz.:

The Second Reformed Church of Claverack to The Reformed Church of Mellenville, from June 17, 1896. Order entered May 5, 1896.

Burnham Industrial Farm to the Berkshire Industrial Farm, from and after Oct. 15, 1896. Order entered August 25th, 1896.

> In witness whereof, I have hereunto set my hand and affixed my official seal at the city of Hudson, N. Y., this 31 day of December, 1896.

(Seal.)   ISAAC P. ROCKEFELLER,
Clerk of Columbia County.

Endorsed: Filed Jan. 2, 1897.

J. B. H. MONGIN,
Second Deputy Secretary of State.

BROOKLYN, N. Y., Dec. 31, 1896.

Hon. JOHN PALMER, *Secretary of State:*

Dear Sir.— The following are the change of names filed in the Kings county clerk's office for 1896:

Aass, Gustav, changed to Gustav Ooss.

Aranoosky, Loui, changed to Louis Aaron.

Bergster, Per August, changed to August Stone.

Bulcroft, Sidney, changed to Sidney Bancroft.

Boyan, Michael W., changed to William Boyan.

Cestaro, Michael A., changed to Michael A. Cestar.

Dreschler, Carl Louis Hugo, changed to Hugo Louis Beil.

Donovan, Joseph J., changed to Joseph J. Donnelly.

Denton, Charles Tweed, changed to Charles Tweed Holliday.

Gladstone, Percy Bartlett, changed to Percy Bartlett Canning.

Hoyle, Agnes Jenny, changed to Agnes Jenny Bailey.

Heidenheimer, Leopold, changed to Leopold Heidenheim.

Heidenheimer, Jacob, changed to Jacob Heidenheim.

Juffs, Henry F., changed to Henry F. Jeffs.

Klyachko, Benzion, changed to Benzion Glasgow.

Liebnitz, Frank Rudolph, changed to Rudolph Townsend.

Louis, Richard, changed to Richard Lewis.

Littman, Adolph, changed to Alfred Little.

Muir, Alexander Francis, changed to Frank Muir Stoops.

Meyers, Heimsn, changed to Herman Meyersohn.

Olson, Carl, changed to Carl Olven.

Rasmussen, Carl August, changed to Carl A. Nielsen.

Rovensky, Harris M., changed to Harris M. Rovenger.

Rublinsky, Louis, changed to Louis Rublin.

Schleglmunig, Oscar Eugene Otto, changed to Oscar Eugene Otto Schlegel.

Scaramellino, Guiseppe, changed to Joseph Palma.

Sauloveizig, Louis, changed to Louis Saul.

Sauloveizig, Coleman, changed to Coleman Saul.

Sauloveizig, Hyman Herman, changed to Hyman Heman Saul.

Simons, Samuel C., changed to Samuel C. Seaman.

Seeth, Jurgen, changed to George Seeth.

Soloweitschyk, Julius, changed to Julius Solow.

Schaffer, Lewis, changed to Tuigi Cieuffe.

Skalnik, Morris, changed to Morris Scalenick.

Tenny, John, changed to John Kenney.

Tarnowsky, Bernhard, changed to Bernhard Stehlin.

West End Baptist Church, changed to Fourth Avenue Baptist Church.

Weimann, Willy E. A., changed to Willy E. A. Wyman.

Winklar, Charles, changed to Charles Missenharter, Jr.

Yours respectfully,

JACOB WORTH,

Clerk.

Endorsed: Filed Jan. 2, 1897.

J. B. H. Mongin,

Second Deputy Secretary of State.

RICHMOND, N. Y., *December* 31, 1896.

STATE OF NEW YORK, ⎰ *ss.:*
COUNTY OF RICHMOND, ⎱

Pursuant to the statute in such case made and provided, I, John H. Elsworth, clerk of the county of Richmond, aforesaid, do hereby certify that the following changes of names have been made by the courts of said county during the year, 1896, to-wit:

Hattie Woodbridge Bagley to Henriette Woodbridge Bagley, to take effect June 3, 1896.

Order made by Supreme Court, and entered May 7, 1896.

In testimony whereof, I have hereunto set my hand and affixed my official seal, this 31st day of December, 1896.

(Seal.)   JOHN H. ELSWORTH,
                                         Clerk.

Endorsed: Filed Jan. 5, 1897.

ANDREW DAVIDSON,
Deputy Secretary of State.

———

AUBURN, N. Y., *December* 31, 1896.

Hon. JOHN PALMER, *Albany, N. Y.:*

Dear Sir.— I have the honor to report, that no papers have been filed in this office, changing the name of any person, during the year ending December 31, 1896.

·Respectfully,

(Seal.)   CHAS. G. ADAMS,
                                 Cayuga County Clerk.

Endorsed: Filed Jan. 7, 1897.

ANDREW DAVIDSON,
Deputy Secretary of State.

STATE OF NEW YORK, } ss.:
CITY COURT OF NEW YORK, }

Pursuant to section 2418 of the Code, I, John B. McGoldrick, clerk of the City Court of New York, do hereby certify that the names of the following persons have been changed by the said court during the year 1896:

Murray Pakulski to William P. Murray.
  Order entered January 3d, 1896.
Leon J. Bernstein to Leon J. Barwood.
  Order entered January 3d, 1896.
Abraham Isaac Wartovsky to Abraham Isaac Ward.
  Order entered January 10th, 1896.
Isaac Samuels to Samuel P. Sammis.
  Order entered January 10th, 1896.
Joseph Janusz Wyganowski to Joseph Janusz Vygan.
  Order entered January 13th, 1896.
David Orentlicher to David Orently.
  Order entered January 21st, 1896.
Solomon Schlomowitz to Solomon White.
  Order entered January 22d, 1896.
Jacob Wrosnofsky to Jacob Ross.
  Order entered January 30th, 1896.
Moses Wineston to Moses Wolf Wineston.
  Order entered February 6th, 1896.
Hugo Lilienthal to Harry Brunelle.
  Order entered February 7th, 1896.
Abraham Obersitzko to Abraham Lippmann.
  Order entered February 13th, 1896.
Harry (alias) Hirsch Jakubowic to Harry Unger.
  Order entered February 15th, 1896.
Margaret Atcheson to Margaret Harding.
  Order entered February 19th, 1896.
Arthur De Lancy Green to Arthur De Lancy Neal.
  Order entered February 20th, 1896.
Celie Hecht to Celie Allovon.
  Order entered February 29th, 1896.
Madeline Hecht to Madeline Allovon.
  Order entered February 29th, 1896.
Christian Schmitt to Christian Smith.
  Order entered March 2d, 1896.
Naphtali Klan to Nathan Klan.
  Order entered March 4th, 1896.
Phillip Bauerfaind to Phillip Brown.
  Order entered March 10th. 1896.

Paul Strochio to Paul Couilloud.
        Order entered March 17th, 1896.
Isidore H. Fischer to Joseph H. Fischer.
        Order entered March 18th, 1896.
Emma Greiner to Emma Morrison.
        Order entered March 20th, 1896.
Clara Lorraine Sands Connor to Clara Lorrane Sands.
        Order entered March 23d, 1896.
Helen Francis Sands Connor to Helen Francis Sands.
        Order entered March 23d, 1896.
Elizabeth Ramsay Sands Connor to Elizabeth Ramsay Sands.
        Order entered March 23d, 1896.
Morris Schlimowitz to Morris Salem.
        Order entered March 27th, 1896.
Ida Amalia Anderson to Ida Amalia Okerlind.
        Order entered April 1st, 1896.
Harry Litvinoff to Abraham Litvin.
        Order entered April 20th, 1896.
Charles Hickey to Charles Hickey Wilson.
        Order entered April 27th, 1896.
Julius Persky to Julius Pearson.
        Order entered May 11th, 1896.
Elias Parker Pakulskifor to Edward Elias Parker.
        Order entered May 15th, 1896.
Vincinzo Chaffalo to James Smith.
        Order entered May 18th, 1896.
Owen Scovill Gladstone to Owen Scovill Canning.
        Order entered May 18th, 1896.
Herman Herskovitz to Herman Herst.
        Order entered May 23d, 1896.
Herman Herskovitz, Jr., to Herman Herst, Jr.,
        Order entered May 23d, 1896.
Barnet Rosenhouse to Barnet House.
        Order entered June 5th, 1896.
David Spolansky to Alfred Pionier.
        Order entered June 8th, 1896.
Samuel Brodsky to Samuel Broads.
        Order entered June 8th, 1896.
Lizzie Benorah Hagelman to Lizzie Benorah Blackburn.
        Order entered June 22d, 1896.
Frederich Theodor Roper to Frederich Theodore Ralf.
        Order entered June 23d, 1896.
Fabiano Budrovich to Frank B. Brown.
        Order entered June 26th, 1896.
Abraham Schumerwitz to Albert Simpson.
        Order entered July 7th, 1896.

Michael Wyekruzer to Michael Porter.
> Order entered July 24th, 1896.

Fritz Margulis to Pincus Margulies.
> Order entered July 30th, 1896.

Raphael Bunimovitz to Raphael B. Arkin.
> Order entered July 30th, 1896.

Albert Michnewitsch to Henry Newman.
> Order entered August 5th, 1896.

Maurice Horoginski to Maurice Herbert.
> Order entered August 13th, 1896.

Henry Wasserdruttirnger to Henry Waterman.
> Order entered August 19th, 1896.

Samuel Jaretsky to Samuel Jay.
> Order entered August 20th, 1896.

Louis Cohen to Louis Balsam.
> Order entered August 29th, 1896.

Francisco Baro to Joseph Altimira.
> Order entered September 11th, 1896.

Abraham Wishinsky to Abraham Wilson.
> Order entered September 12th, 1896.

David Brenner to Victor David Brenner.
> Order entered September 12th, 1896.

Jacob Strashunski to Jacob Strauss.
> Order entered September 15th, 1896.

Jake Frank to Jacques Frank.
> Order entered September 18th, 1896.

Johan Charles Henckendorff to Charles Staff.
> Order entered September 23d, 1896.

John J. Fillweber to John Baab.
> Order entered September 23d, 1896.

Henry W. Rupprecht to Henry W. Ruppert.
> Order entered September 23d, 1896.

Jesse Paulmier Whiton to Jesse Paulmier Whiton-Stuart.
> Order entered September 23d, 1896.

Louise Clifford Evans to Phyllis Carey Evans.
> Order entered September 24th, 1896.

Morris Rosenthal to Morris Rose.
> Order entered October 3d, 1896.

Jacob Strashunski to Jacob Strauss.
> Order entered October 3d, 1896.

Louis Alfred Steckler to Alfred Steckler, Jr.
> Order entered October 5th, 1896.

Eugene Pearkowsky to Eugene Boyd.
> Order entered October 8th, 1896.

Julius D. Butinsky to Julius D. Booth.
> Order entered October 9th, 1896.

Albert Ressler to Albert Russell.
    Order entered October 12th, 1896.
Otto Fasoli to Otto Fredericks.
    Order entered October 26th, 1896.
Alexander A. Olarovsky to Alexander A. Austin.
    Order entered October 27th, 1896.
Desiderius David Deutsch to Desiderius Davy Memeth.
    Order entered October 29th, 1896.
Theodore K. Wood to George H. Cassidy.
    Order entered November 24th, 1896.
Joe Klonitzky to Joe Colvin.
    Order entered November 24th, 1896.
Louis Cohen to Alexander L. Cazdan.
    Order entered November 25th, 1896.
Aaron Janowsky to Aaron Janes.
    Order entered November 25th, 1896.
Laura Lichtenstein to Laura Morgan.
    Order entered November 30th, 1896.
Theodore K. Wood to George H. Cassidy.
    Order entered December 2d, 1896.
Samuel Mulwitzky to Samuel Miller.
    Order entered December 7th, 1896.
Bernhard Kamanetelzky to Jessie K. Bernhard.
    Order entered December 8th, 1896.
Charles Percy Deady to Howard Percy Deady.
    Order entered December 17th 1896.
Leon Boukosky to Leon Sultan.
    Order entered December 18th, 1896.
Elias Silverman to Emil Silverman.
    Order entered December 28th, 1896.

    Witness my hand, and the seal of said court this 31st day of
    December, 1896.
(Seal.)   JNO. B. McGOLDRICK,
                    Clerk of the City Court of New York.

Endorsed: Filed Jan. 2, 1897.

                    J. B. H. MONGIN,
                    Second Deputy Secretary of State.

STATE OF NEW YORK,   } *ss.:*
CITY AND COUNTY OF NEW YORK, }

Pursuant to section 2418 of the Code of Civil Procedure, I, Henry D. Purroy, clerk of the city and county of New York, and clerk of the Supreme Court, do report and hereby certify, that the names of the following persons and corporations have been changed by the said court during the year 1896:

Arthur Eisig to Arthur Essing. Order entered January 8, 1896. To take effect February 6, 1896.

Morris Tuch to Morris Schoenfeld. Order entered March 3, 1896. To take effect March 31, 1896.

Marcus Teitz to Marcus T. Goldsmith. Order entered March 5, 1896. To take effect March 25, 1896.

Isidor Brown to Harry Brown. Ordered entered March 18, 1896. To take effect April 13, 1896.

Julius Solow to Julius Soloweitschyk. Order entered March 23, 1896. To take effect April 25, 1896.

George Silva to George de Silva. Order entered April 2, 1896. To take effect May 1, 1896.

Joseph E. Lord to Joseph Edwin Potter Lord. Order entered April 14, 1896. To take effect July 1, 1896.

Israel Wilensky to Israel Willis. Order entered May 7, 1896. To take effect June 27, 1896.

Joseph Yesky to Joseph Yeska. Order entered May 9, 1896. To take effect June 25, 1896.

Munro Bannister Smith to Munro Bannister Smith Munro. Order entered May 20, 1896. To take effect June 8, 1896.

Andrew Demartini to Andrew Cuneo. Order entered May 21, 1896. To take effect June 16, 1896.

Lee Cooke to Justus Lee Cooke. Order entered May 21, 1896. To take effect June 22, 1896.

Julian A. Moses to Julian Florian. Order entered June 1, 1896. To take effect June 30, 1896.

Florian Moses to Walter Florian. Order entered June 1, 1896. To take effect June 30, 1896.

Martin Mosesman to Fred Mann. Order entered June 25, 1896. To take effect August 1, 1896.

Solomon Thomashewsky to Solomon Thomas. Order entered July 29, 1896. To take effect August 31, 1896.

Joseph Schaffer to Joseph Schiffer. Order entered July 29, 1896. To take effect August 20, 1896.

George Bilmoser to George Stops. Order entered August 31, 1896. To take effect October 1, 1896.

Albert Gerard Thies to Albert Gerard Thiers. Order entered October 3, 1896. To take effect November 4, 1896.

Martha Louise Thies to Martha Louise·Thiers. Order entered October 3, 1896. To take effect November 4, 1896.

Gerard Thies to Gerard Thiers. Order entered October 3, 1896. To take effect November 4, 1896.

Squire Wilbert Smith to Squire Wilbert Stone. Order entered October 14, 1896. To take effect October 12, 1896.

Elizabeth Mary Greenbaum to Elizabeth Mary Wilson Greenbowe. Order entered October 22, 1896. To take effect November 25, 1896.

Edwin Greenbaum to Edwin Willson Greenbowe. Order entered October 22, 1896. To take effect November 25, 1896.

Grace May Greenbaum to Grace May Greenbowe. Order entered October 22, 1896. To take effect November 25, 1896.

Lillie Victoria Greenbaum to Lillian Victoria Greenbowe. Order entered October 22, 1896. To take effect November 25, 1896.

Vitaliano Moreschi to Amedo Aspasia. Order entered December 11, 1896. To take effect January 8, 1897.

Anna Quirsfeld to Anna Q. Smythe. Order entered December 15, 1896. To take effect January 15, 1897.

Julius Pitzulirties to Julius Russ. Order entered December 17, 1896. To take effect January 20, 1897.

Joseph McDermott to Joseph Meagher. Order entered December 18, 1896. To take effect January 20, 1897.

Peter Cooper Savings and Loan Society to Investors' Savings and Loan Society. Order entered January 9, 1896. To take effect February 11, 1896.

Baby Sewing Machine Company to The Modern Sewing Machine Company. Order entered February 13, 1896. To take effect March 12, 1896.

The Hygeia Sparkling Distilled Water Company to the Hygeia Distilled Water Company. Order entered February 25, 1896. To take effect March 28, 1896.

Buttrick-Godfrey Company to Buttrick-West Company. Order entered April 6, 1896. To take effect May 6, 1896.

The Church of Christ Scientist, of New York City, to First Church of Christ, Scientist, of New York City. Order entered March 5, 1896. To take effect April 7, 1896.

Deutscher Rechts Schutz Verein to The Legal Aid Society. Order entered April 21, 1896. To take effect June 1, 1896.

Aberthaw Construction Company of New York to Manhattan Concrete Company. Order entered April 25, 1896. To take effect May 18, 1896.

The Smith & Oettinger Company to The Oettinger Company. Order entered April 25, 1896. To take effect May 25, 1896.

The Daily News Savings and Building-Loan Association to The Franklin Society for Home-Building and Savings. Order entered May 14, 1896. To take effect June 20, 1896.

The New Manhattan Athletic Club to Knickerbocker Athletic Club. Order entered June 1, 1896. To take effect July 1, 1896.

Chevra Bnai Rachmunim Anschei Sochatzower to Warsaw Soch atzow Congregation. Order entered June 4, 1896. To take effect July 15, 1896.

The Chasmar Press to Chasmar-Winchell Press. Order entered June 17, 1896. To take effect July 18, 1896.

United States Mercantile Reporting Company to The Howard Mercantile Agency. Order entered July 11, 1896. To take effect August 10, 1896.

Knickerbocker Chemical Company to Knickerbocker Fire Extinguisher Company. Order entered July 29, 1896. To take effect September 10, 1896.

The Bond Record Publishing Company to The Bond Record Company. Order entered August 13, 1896. To take effect September 14, 1896.

Washington Heights Library to Washington Heights Free Library. Order entered August 25, 1896. To take effect October 1, 1896.

Clark and Geiger Photo Engraving Co. to Payne Engraving Company. Order entered August 29, 1896. To take effect October 10, 1896.

Holy Trinity Church, Harlem, to Holy Trinity Church, New York. Order entered October 19, 1896. To take effect November 20, 1896.

A. Ward Phelps Company to Globe Lithograph Company. Order entered October 31, 1896. To take effect December 10, 1896.

In testimony whereof I have hereunto signed my name and affixed the seal of said court this 31st day of December, 1896.

(Seal.)   HENRY D. PURROY,

                                                    Clerk.

Endorsed: Filed Jan. 4 1897.

ANDREW DAVIDSON,

Deputy Secretary of State.

SUPPLEMENTAL REPORT.

STATE OF NEW YORK,   } *ss.:*
CITY AND COUNTY OF NEW YORK, }

Pursuant to section 2417, Code of Civil Procedure, I, Henry D. Purroy, clerk of the city and county of New York, do report and certify that the name Isaac Irving Brokaw was changed to Irving Brokaw; to take effect March 15, 1895, by order of the Court of Common Pleas for the city and county of New York, and entered February 4, 1895.

In attestation whereof I have hereunto subscribed my name, and affixed my official seal this 21st day of April, 1897.

(Seal.)   HENRY D. PURROY,

Clerk.

Endorsed: Filed Apr. 22, 1897.

ANDREW DAVIDSON,
Deputy Secretary of State.

TABLE

GENERAL LAWS AND SECTIONS OF THE CODES

AMENDED OR REPEALED BY THE LAWS OF 1897.

PREPARED BY THE COMMISSION OF STATUTORY REVISION.

I. GENERAL LAWS AMENDED.

Revised Statutes.

Part.	Chapter.	Title.	Section.	SUBJECT OF SECTION.	Chapter.	Page.
2	8	1	49	Right of marriage by divorced person......	452	594
3	8	16	11	Payment of assessments for drainage of wet lands	249	115
4	3	2	67	State lands around Clinton prison..........	216	89
4	3	2	107	Fixing prices of prison-made goods	623	770

Laws.

Laws of.	Chapter.	Title.	Section.	SUBJECT OF SECTION.	Chapter.	Page.
1847..	183	......	3	Cemeteries, powers of boards of supervisors relative to.........	129	48
1854..	112	......	11	Removal of remains from private cemeteries	463	599
1855..	421	......	1	Liability of steamboat proprietors.........	305	175
1857..	739	......	4	Policies issued by town fire insurance companies...........................	448	586
1864..	88	......	2, 5	Missionary Society of Most Holy Redeemer.	192	79
1866..	466	......	3	Normal schools, boards of managers	224	102
1870..	291	......	33	Villages, extension of boundaries	332	255
1874..	446	1	26	Sanity of criminals, investigation..........	451	593
1877..	466	......	29	Preference of wages of employes of assignors.	{ 266 624	139 772
1880..	583	......	3	Floating timber.	483	631
1885..	848	.. ...	7	Compensation of stenographers to grand juries	25	10
1888..	107	......	2	Free Sons of Israel	264	139
1889..	332	......	......	See R. S. pt. IV, ch. 3, tit. 2................	......	.....

Gᴇɴᴇʀᴀʟ Lᴀᴡꜱ Aᴍᴇɴᴅᴇᴅ, Eᴛᴏ.— (*Continued*).

* Sections 15 and 16 of the town law were repealed, and §§ 17–48, inclusive, of such law were renumbered and made §§ 15–41, inclusive. The amendments above referred to are to the sections as renumbered.

Gᴇɴᴇʀᴀʟ Lᴀᴡs Aᴍᴇɴᴅᴇᴅ, Eᴛᴄ.— *(Continued)*.

Laws of.	Chapter.	Title.	Section.	SUBJECT OF SECTION.	Chapter.	Page.
				Legislative law :		
1892..	682	......	46, subd. 3	Distribution of session laws.....	19	ᵕ
				Executive law :		
1892..	683	......	26, subd.12	Fees for filing certificates of incorporation..	411	336
1892..	683	......	31	Second deputy comptroller	217	90
				Salt springs law :		
1892..	684	......	....	Superseded and amended..................	261	123
				General municipal law :		
1892..	685	......	7	Funded and bonded indebtedness	54	25
				County law :		
1893..	686	......	37	Fire districts	329	250
1893..	686	......	54	Clerks of boards of supervisors	406	331
1892..	686	......	121	Tax for sheep killed..	171	67
1892..	686	......	203	Assistant district attorney in Erie, Monroe and Rensselaer..........................	409	334
1892..	686	......	222, subd.49	Salary of county judge and surrogate in Suffolk county......................	232	106
1893..	686	......	228	Salaries and expenses of county judges and surrogates.	407	332
				Banking law :		
1892..	689	......	8	Salary of superintendent of banks........	184	48
1892..	689	......	52	Individual liability of stockholders.	441	579
1892..	689	......	116, subd. 5	Investment of savings bank deposits.......	386	317
				Insurance law :		
1892..	690	.....	16	Investment of capital of insurance companies..........................	218	91
1892..	690	......	44	Reports of insurance companies..........	498	629
1892..	690	......	92	No forfeiture of policy without notice......	218	92
1892..	690	......	178	Credit guaranty companies..............	387	318
1892..	690	......	212	Exemption of policies from execution......	345	261
1892..	690	......	258	Mailing notices of assessment.	503	635
1892..	690	......	268	Assessments by town and county co-operative insurance companies	29	12
				Public buildings law :		
1893..	227	.....	6–11	Completion of capitol	78	29
1893..	227	.....	12	Added. Lighting system for capitol.......	511	641
				Agricultural law :		
1893..	338	......	26	Manufacture and sale of imitation butter...	768	810
1893..	338	......	37	Violation of agricultural law.	554	651
1893..	338	......	71–76	Art. IV inserted, and articles V and VI made articles VI and VII. Beet sugar...	500	631
1893..	338	......	88	Apportionment of moneys to agricultural societies	589	674
				Military code :		
1893..	559	.....	14	Composition of battalion..................	591	678
1893..	559	.....	15	Company, troop and battery......	591	679
1893..	559	.....	20	Added. Field music	591	681
1893..	559	.....	34	Duties of inspector-general..............	591	679
1893..	559	.....	38	Bureau of records	591	680
1893..	559	.....	125, 126	Allowances for militia..................	591	680
1893..	559	.....	162	Sheriffs and mayors, when may call for aid.	690	779
				Public health law :		
1893..	661	......	20	Local boards of health..................	282	148
1893..	661	......	22	Vital statistics.	138	51
1893..	661	......	29	Jurisdiction of local boards of health.......	169	66
1893..	661	......	187	Sale of domestic remedies...............	297	173
1894..	468	......	1	New York State Woman's Relief Corps Home	47	28

Laws of.	Chapter.	Title.	Section.	SUBJECT OF SECTION.	Chapter.	Page.
				Consolidated school law :		
1894..	556	5	13, subd. 4	Condemnation of schoolhouses	512	641
1894..	556	6	6	Alteration of school districts	512	642
1894..	556	6	14	Added. Titles 5 and 6 extended	512	642
1894..	556	7	74	Unpaid school taxes	512	642
1894..	556	8	7	Clerk of board of education................	466	601
1894..	556	8	13	Tax for text-books........................	195	83
1894..	556	8	14	Election of boards of education	466	602
1894..	556	10	4	Schools closed during institute week........	512	642
1894..	556	15	14, 15	Contracts between common school districts..	294	173
1894..	556	15	51	Separate neighborhoods in school districts ..	298	169
1894..	556	15	52–54	Added. Neighborhood school meetings, etc.	298	170
1894..	743	.....	2	Equitable Security Company....	768	807
1895..	369	.....	16, 23	Commissioners of jurors in certain counties.	21	7
1895..	884	......	17, 18	Added. Drainage of agricultural lands ...	168	65
				Membership corporations law :		
1895..	559	......	31	Certificates of incorporation................	205	87
1895..	559	......	52	Taxation of lot owners.	477	609
1895..	559	......	123	Added. Transfer of funds of unincorporated associations..................	327	248
1895..	570	......	3, 12, 18	Racing associations	446	583
				Religious corporations law :		
1895..	723	......	5	Powers of trustees	{ 144 / 621	54 / 762
1895..	723	......	15	Property of extinct churches............	238	111
1895..	723	......	78–78k	Added, articles VI, VII and VIII are made articles VII, VIIIand IX. Incorporation of congregational and independent churches.	621	762
1895..	723	......	80	Application of article 5	621	762
1895..	723	......	94	Added. President of meetings....	144	55
1895..	1027	......	1	Issue of mileage books...................	484	629
1895..	1081	......	1	Establishment of teachers' training classes..	495	631
1896..	99	......	1	Clerks and attendants of Appellate Division in second department...................	228	109
				Liquor tax law :		
1896..	112	......	All except 4, 5,7,12, 14, 20, 26, 33, 38, 39	General amendments	312	207
				Poor law :		
1896..	225	......	8	Expenditures of superintendents of the poor.	507	640
1896..	225	......	18	Temporary or out-door relief.	48	24
1896..	225	......	26	Books of accounts of overseers of the poor..	222	100
1896..	225	......	57	Added. Settlement of poor person, how lost.	203	85
1896..	271	......	3, 4, 6	Horseshoers, examination, etc.............	148	57
				Domestic relations law :		
1896..	272	......	64	Effect of adoption of children..............	408	333
				Benevolent orders law :		
1896..	377	. . ..	3, 5	Issue of bonds by benevolent orders........	141	52
				State charities law :		
1896..	546	......	3	Organization of state board................	437	578
				Real property law :		
1896..	547	......	6	Effect of woman's marriage with alien.....	756	805
1896..	547	......	85, 87	Uses and trusts..........................	136	49
1896..	547	......	219, subd. 1	Forms of agreement when whole sum is due.	277	145
1896..	547	......	223	Form of mortgage........................	277	145
1896..	584	......	8	Erie co., bonds for 74th Regiment armory ..	733	792
1896..	898	......	1	Confidential clerks of justices of supreme court.........	145	55

GENERAL LAWS AMENDED, ETC. — (*Concluded*).

Laws of.	Chapter.	Title.	Section.	SUBJECT OF SECTION.	Chapter.	Page.
				Tax law:		
1896..	908	......	4, subd. 5	Exemptions of property purchased with pension money................................	347	265
1896..	908	......	4, subd. 6	Exemption of canal bonds..	80	81
1896..	908	......	4, subd. 7	Religious corporations, exemption..	871	278
1896..	908	......	5	Taxation of lands sold or leased by the state	448	581
1896..	908	......	94, 95	Receipts for taxes......................	489	625
1896..	908	......	123	Purchases by comptroller at tax sales.	283	107
1896..	908	......	188, 189	Lien of mortgage affected by tax sale.......	873	274
1896..	908	......	141	Cancellation of tax sales............	393	323
1896..	908	......	158	Conveyance by county treasurer........ ...	490	626
1896..	908	......	180	Organization tax of corporations	869	272
1896..	908	.....	183	Exemption of certain corporations.... ...	785	817
1896..	908	......	187	Franchise tax upon insurance corporations..	494	680
1896..	908	......	220	Taxable transfers....	284	150
1896..	908	......	222	Lien of tax...........................	284	151
1896..	908	......	225	Refund of tax.........................	284	152
1896..	908	......	226	Deferred payment.....................	284	153
1896..	908	......	230	Appointment of appraisers....	284	153
1896..	908	......	282	Determination of surrogate...............	284	155
				Election law:		
1896..	909	......	5, 6, 8, 10, 12, 18, 19, 32, subd. 3, 35, subd. 5, 36, subd. 1, 58 62, 64, 66, 86, 87, 113, 130, 131, 135-138	Elections in Greater New York...	879	277
1896..	909	. ....	138-141	Renumbered 139-142..................	879	303
1896..	909	......	11	Qualifications of election officers...........	410	385
1896..	909	......	61	Publication of nominations.................	608	716
1896..	909	......	80	Official ballots........................ ...	609	717
1896..	957	......	2	Claim of Murphy against the state........	28	11
1897..	7	......	8	Tennessee centennial...........	85	85

II. Sections of Code of Civil Procedure Amended.

Section.	SUBJECT OF SECTION.	Chapter.	Page.
2, subd. 15..	Court of claims, court of record	36	18
46..........	Judge not to sit when interested party...................	268	141
90..........	Clerk in New York or Kings not to be referee or receiver...	454	595
94..........	Interpreters in Kings county.............................	93	35
203........	Clerks for judges of court of appeals....................	221	100
203........	Offices for judges of the court of appeals	221	100
221, subds. 1, 2.......	Added. Assistant clerk to appellate division, fourth department	367	270
250........	Publication of supreme court reports	474	606
254........	Stenographers in supreme court, Kings county............	661	775
263–290. ...	Inserted. Court of claims	36	14
360.	Interpreters in county and surrogates' courts in Kings county	475	607
361.	Stenographers in county courts...........................	176	71
394.......	Limitation of action against directors of banks............	281	148
542..... ..	Pleadings, when amended of course	470	606
797..... ..	Service of papers	40	20
895........	Depositions where adverse parties are infants or committees.	606	715
1126.......	Jurors in Kings county..................................	405	331
1236.......	Entry of judgment......................................	188	77
1273.......	Confession of judgment by married woman...	88	20
1831.......	Judgment for possession of real property	119	43
1393.......	Property purchased with pension money exempt from execution..	848	266
1538	Parties in partition actions	726	786
1581	Shares of infants..	602	711
1836.......	Costs against executors and administrators	469	605
1926.......	Actions by certain officers.............................	302	174
2323a......	Committee of incompetent person in state institution	149	58
2434.......	Proceedings supplementary to execution, when may be entertained	476	608
2458.......	Judgment creditor when to entertain special proceedings...	189	78
2616	Accounting by executor, etc., of deceased executor........	248	114
2614.......	Who may propound will	177	72
2626.......	Probate, when conclusive as to personalty	598	710
2653a......	Validity of wills..	104 / 701	88 / 783
2660.......	Who entitled to letters of administration..................	177	72
2703.......	Recording will proved in other states	605	714
2704.......	Authentication of will or letters of administration proved or granted in other states.............................	608	713
2732, subd. 15	Added. Illegitimate children, right of inheritance.	87	19
2888.......	Application for ancillary letters to foreign guardian... ...	493	627
2868.......	When justices' courts may be held.	404	330
2990.......	Jury trial in justice's court, payment of fees	146	56
3285a.....	Added. Justice's court in Troy............................	604	714
3314.......	Allowance to jurors......................................	23	9
3398–3441...	Added. Enforcement of mechanics' liens against real property and liens on vessels......	419	545

V. GENERAL LAWS REPEALED.

Revised Statutes.

Part	Chapter.	Title.	Section.	SUBJECT OF SECTION.	Repealed by chapter	Page.
1	8	8	All, except § 15. ...	State comptroller, powers and duties.	418	864
1	8	4	All	State treasurer, powers and duties...	418	864
1	9	2, 8, 4	All...... .	Canal, literature and common school funds	418	864
1	9	6	All........	State mortgages.....................	418	864
1	20	10	All........	Inland navigation	592	705
2	1	2	68	Powers over trust of party interested.	417	518
2	4	1	All........	Limited partnerships	420	568
2	4	2	All.......	Bills and notes	612	758
2	4	4	All........	Accumulations of personal property..	417	518
2	7	2	All.......	Fraudulent conveyances of personal property	417	518
2	7	3	All........	General provisions relative to fraudulent conveyances.	417	518

Laws.

Laws of.	Chapter.	Sections.	SUBJECT OF ACT.	Chapter.	Page.
1830..	179	1, 2	Liens of factors and agents...................	418	542
1830..	184	All........	Literature fund.......	418	864
1830..	242	All	Transfer of state stock	418	864
1881..	102	All.......	State mortgages	418	864
1881..	286	All.......	Improvement of canal fund	418	864
1831..	320	All.......	State finances; duties of comptroller	418	864
1882..	8	1, 2	Literature fund	418	864
1882..	296	All.......	Support of government	418	864
1888..	56	All.......	Comptroller's office, papers relative to canals..	418	864
1888..	279	All.......	Chattel mortgages to be filed	418	542
1884..	284	All.......	Repealed Laws of 1881, chap. 220, § 17.... ...	418	864
1885..	141	All.......	Notice of protest, how given..................	612	758
1885..	260	All.......	Regulating specific funds....................	418	864
1886..	356	All	Loans from canal fund..............	418	864
1887..	2	All... ...	Accepting United States deposits	418	864
1887..	129	All........	Amends R. S., part 2, chap. 4, tit. 1, § 5	420	568
1887..	150	All except § 48....	Loan of money belonging to United States deposit fund	418	864
1887..	152	All........	Lights on vessels navigating Niagara and St. Lawrence rivers and Lake Ontario	592	705
1887..	356	All.......	Harbor master in port of Albany	592	705
1887..	860	All	State loan.....	418	864
1888..	58	All........	Loan commissioners	418	864
1888..	198	All...	Amends Laws of 1887, chap. 150, § 12........	418	864
1888..	287	All	Income of United States deposit fund.	418	864
1889..	112	All.......	Fire protection in Hudson and Poughkeepsie on account of steamboats...................	592	705
1889..	175	All... ...	Speed of steamboats	592	705
1889..	849	All	Damage for collision of vessels..............	592	705
1889..	881	All........	State mortgages......................	418	864
1840..	294	All.......	United States deposit and common school fund.	418	864
1841..	65	All.......	Lights on rafts.....	592	705
1841..	264	All........	Payment of United states deposit loan	418	864

GENERAL LAWS REPEALED — (*Continued*).

Laws of.	Chapter.	Sections.	SUBJECT OF ACT.	Chapter.	Page.
1842..	310	All......	Purchases of land for the state....	418	864
1843..	44	All.......	Transmission of public moneys	418	864
1844..	248	All.......	Speed of steamboats on Hudson river........	592	705
1844..	326	All.......	Duties of loan commissioners.	418	864
1845..	87	All.......	Loan to American Seaman's Friends Society.	418	864
1845..	267	All.......	Reloan of money of United States deposit fund	418	864
1847..	8	All.......	Revenues of common school and United States deposit funds	418	864
1847..	151	All.......	Village fire company.........................	414	456
1847..	209	All.......	Village cemetery............................	414	456
1847..	258	All	Revenues of the literature and United States deposit funds	418	864
1847..	426	All.......	General village act..........................	414	456
1847..	476	All.......	Loan commissioners' accounts with purchaser.	418	864
1848..	162	All.......	Canal department, auditor...................	418	864
1848..	215	All.......	Funds appropriated for canals...............	418	864
1848..	366	All.......	Temporary loan to supply deficits in state treasury..................................	418	864
1849..	69	All......	Registration of chattel mortgages	418	542
1849..	228	All... ...	Claims upon canal fund	418	864
1849..	230	All......	Amends Laws of 1848, chap. 215, § 1........	418	865
1849..	301	All	Revenues of literature and United States deposit fund.........................	418	865
1849..	347	All.......	Copartnership names....	420	568
1849..	382	18	Amends Laws of 1847, chap. 480..............	418	865
1849..	411	All	Life boats....	592	705
1850..	176	All...	Amends Laws of 1847, chap. 426..............	414	456
1850..	337	All.......	Settlement of state loans	418	865
1851..	286	All.......	United States deposit fund; loan mortgages in New York city.......................	418	865
1851..	536	All.......	Revenues of literature and United States deposit fund............................	418	865
1852..	184	All... ...	Amends Laws of 1847, chap. 426.............	414	456
1852..	235	All.......	Amends Laws of 1851, chap. 536, § 4........	418	865
1852..	370	All.......	Amends Laws of 1851, chap. 286, § 1........	485	865
1853..	86	All.......	Charges upon canal fund	418	865
1854..	400	All	Authorizing use of copartnership name......	420	568
1855..	535	8	Amends Laws of 1842, chap. 310, § 1........	418	865
1857..	414	All.......	Amends Revised Statutes, part 2, chap. 4, tit. 1, §§ 3, 17, 23....................·.....	420	568
1857..	416	All	Commercial paper...........................	612	758
1857..	721	All.......	Issue of new state certificates of indebtedness.	418	865
1857..	788	All.......	Auditor of canal department.	418	865
1858..	134	All.......	Legalizing sale of stock on time.............	417	513
1858..	247	All.......	Registration of liens and incumbrances upon canal boats............................	418	542
1858..	289	All.......	Amends Revised Statutes, part 2, chap. 4, tit. 1, § 12..............................	420	568
1858..	314	1, 2	Trustees may impeach assignments.	417	513
1860..	108	10, 12	Rights of passengers when departure of trip is delayed..............................	592	705
1860..	446	All.......	Protection of boarding-house keepers........	418	542
1861..	177	All.......	Auditor of canal department.	418	865
1861..	178	All.......	Amends Laws of 1847, chap. 426	414	456
1862..	476	All.......	Amends Revised Statutes, part 2, chap. 4, tit. 1, § 9	420	568
1862..	482	1, 2, 8, 27, 33	Liens on vessels.............................	418	542
1862..	482	All, except §§ 1, 2, 3, 27, 33....	Enforcement of liens on vessels..............	419	559
1863..	20	All, ...	Acceptance of college land..................	418	865

GENERAL LAWS REPEALED — (*Continued*).

Laws of.	Chap- ter.	Sections.	SUBJECT OF ACT.	Chap- ter.	Page.
1863..	144	All......	Amends Laws of 1854, chap. 400.......... ...	420	568
1863..	429	2	Amends Laws of 1862, chap. 482, § 7	419	559
1863..	432		Duration of lien on vessels navigating St. Lawrence river and Northwestern lake.........	418	542
1863..	460	All......	College land scrip...........................	413	365
1863..	464	All, except	Amends Revised Statutes, part 2, chap. 7, tit. 8, § 2.............................	417	512
1863..	781	§ 9..... All.....	(Error; should have been chap 78,Laws of 1863).	413	365
1864..	117	All.......	Amends Laws of 1847, chap. 426..........	414	456
1864..	229	All.......	Amends Laws of 1863, chap. 450, § 8.......	413	363
1864..	412	All.......	Registration of mortgages on canal boats.....	418	542
1864..	558	All.......	United States deposit fund...................	413	365
1865..	309	All.... ..	Protest of foreign bills........	612	7 8
1865..	569	All.......	Rate of wharfage along Hudson river.... ...	592	705
1866..	70	....	Amends Revised Statutes, part 2, chap. 4, tit. 1, § 1.... ..	420	568
1866..	374	All.......	Amends Laws of 1837, chap. 856...........	592	705
1866..	661	All	Amends Revised Statutes, part 2, chap. 4, tit 1, § 13.......................	420	568
1868..	256	All	Use of partnership name....................	420	568
1868..	462	All.. ...	Special village election....................	414	456
1868..	698	All.......	Discharge of United States deposit fund mortgages........................	413	365
1868..	779	All...	Chattel mortgages executed by railroad corporations	418	542
1870..	291	All	General village law	414	456
1870..	885	All, except § 4......	Hours of labor regulated...................	415	490
1870..	885	4	Punishment for exacting extra hours of labor...	415	506
1870..	488	All........	Negotiability of corporate funds; how limited.	612	758
1870..	539	All........	Liens on railroad bridges and trestlework.....	418	542
1871..	84	All	Negotiable bonds; how made nonnegotiable...	612	758
1871..	258	All........	Protection of harbors in Suffolk county.	592	705
1871..	277	All........	Protection of buoys in Niagara river...... ...	592	705
1871..	688	All........	Amends Laws of 1870, chap. 291.............	414	456
1871..	696	All........	Village cemetery commissioner..............	414	456
1871..	870	All........	Amends Laws of 1870, chap. 291	414	456
1871..	984	8	Duties of factory inspector as to apprentices..	415	490
1872..	114	All........	Special partners may lease to general partner.	420	568
1872..	115	All.... ...	Warrants of auditor of canal department....	413	365
1872..	357	All........	Amends Laws of 1870, chap. 291	414	456
1872..	498	All........	Liens of livery stable keepers and agisters	418	542
1872..	669	All........	Liens on wharves, piers, bulkheads, etc.......	418	542
1872..	696	All........	Amends Laws of 1847, chap. 209.............	414	456
1873..	92	All........	Amends Laws of 1870, chap. 291..... ...	414	456
1873..	397	11	Exemption of firemen from poll-tax..........	414	456
1873..	501	All........	Amends Laws of 1833, chap. 279, § 3..........	418	542
1873..	595	All........	Bonds; how made negotiable..................	612	758
1874..	78	All........	Amends Laws of 1870, chap. 291.............	414	456
1874..	345	All........	Village trustees to publish accounts..........	414	456
1874..	474	All........	Amends Laws of 1870, chap. 291.............	414	456
1874..	628	All........	Amends Laws of 1870, chap. 291.............	414	458
1875..	27	All	Designation of holidays......................	614	760
1875..	149	All	Failure to designate terms of village trustees..	414	456
1875..	181	All........	Village water-works	414	456
1875..	197	All........	Amends Laws of 1874, chap. 345.	414	456
1875..	242	All........	Amends Laws of 1870, chap. 291, tit. 8........	414	456
1875..	339	All........	Amends Laws of 1870. chap. 291.............	414	457
1875..	885	All.......	Arrests in villages without warrant...........	414	457
1875..	392	1, 2, 5, 6, 7	Liens for labor on railroads	418	542
1875..	392	8, 4	Enforcement of mechanic's lien on railroad...	419	559

GENERAL LAWS REPEALED — (*Continued*).

Laws of.	Chapter.	Sections.	SUBJECT OF ACT.	Chapter.	Page.
1875..	514	All........	Election of police justices in villages........	414	457
1875..	570	All........	Amends Laws of 1870, chap. 291, tit. 4........	414	457
1876..	92	All........	Failure to designate terms of village trustees..	414	457
1876..	184	All........	Amends Laws of 1875, chap. 181.............	414	457
1876..	808	All.	Amends Laws of 1875, chap. 514.............	414	457
1876..	317	All........	Amends Laws of 1870, chap. 291.............	414	457
1876..	319	All........	Amends Laws of 1860, chap. 446.............	418	543
1876..	876	All........	Dumping of garbage in Hudson river prohibited	592	705
1877..	16	All........	Amends Laws of 1870, chap. 291.............	414	457
1877..	65	1, 3	Negotiable instruments given for patent rights	612	758
1877..	65	3	Penalty for negotiating patent right notes.....	613	759
1877..	244	All........	Amends Laws of 1870, chap. 291, tit. 8........	414	457
1877..	245	All........	Monthly statements of state officers; finances.	418	865
1878..	59	All........	Amends Laws of 1870, chap. 291.............	414	457
1878..	233	All......	Amends Laws of 1837, chap. 150, § 33	418	865
1878..	249	All........	Amends Laws of 1870, chap. 291.............	414	457
1878..	281	All...	Amends Laws of 1870, chap. 291.............	414	457
1878..	291	All...	Comptroller to compromise judgment	418	865
1878..	315	1–5, 13–15	Liens on account of public improvements.......	418	543
1878..	315	6–12	Enforcement of mechanic's lien on account of public improvements........	419	559
1878..	896	All......	Failure to designate terms of village trustees..	418	457
1879..	68	All	Failure to designate terms of village trustees..	414	457
1879..	86	All...	Amends Laws of 1875, chap. 101.............	414	457
1879..	129	All........	Amends Laws of 1870, chap. 291	414	457
1879..	171	All	Discharge of chattel mortgages.............	418	543
1879..	204	1, 3, 4	Prevention of ice gorges in St. Lawrence river	592	705
1879..	228	All......	Amends Laws of 1875, chap. 181, § 5.........	414	457
1879..	834	1	Amends Laws of 1862, chap. 482, § 3.........	418	543
1879..	834	2	Amends Laws of 1862, chap. 482, § 9	419	559
1879..	836	All........	Sale of goods to satisfy liens of warehousemen	418	543
1879..	887	All........	Confirms incorporation of villages	414	457
1879..	418	All........	Amends Laws of 1833, chap. 279, § 3.........	418	543
1879..	580	All........	Sale of goods and baggage of guests in hotel ..	418	543
1880..	64	All........	Confirms incorporation of villages..........	414	457
1880..	78	All........	Water contracts in villages in Richmond county	414	457
1880..	100	All........	Revenue bonds in anticipation of state taxes ..	413	865
1880..	144	All........	Amends Laws of 1870, chap. 291	414	457
1880..	145	All........	Amends Laws of 1872, chap. 498, § 1.........	418	543
1880..	172	All........	Amends Laws of 1847, chap. 426	414	457
1880..	3 · 5	All........	Amends Laws of 1876, chap. 276	592	705
1880..	235	All........	Costs on arrests in villages	414	457
1880..	292	All.	Amends Laws of 1870, chap. 291	414	457
1880..	395	All........	Regulation of steamers engaged in towing....	592	706
1880..	422	All........	Amends Laws of 1870, chap. 291	414	457
1880..	440	1–4, 10, 18	Liens on oil wells........................	418	543
1880..	440	5–10	Enforcement of mechanics' liens on oil wells..	419	559
1880..	496	All........	Amends Laws of 1870, chap. 291	414	457
1880..	517	All........	Interest on loan mortgages belonging to United States deposit fund	418	865
1880..	533	All	Rivers as public highways..................	592	706
1880..	541	1	Lights on swing-bridges across the Hudson....	592	706
1880..	561	1–4	Use of business name	420	568
1881..	16	All........	Amends Laws of 1880, chap. 533.............	592	706
1881..	17	All..	Failure to designate term of village trustees ..	414	457
1881..	80	All........	Amends Laws of 1875, chap. 27, § 1	614	760
1881..	175	All........	Amends Laws of 1875, chap. 181..........·....	414	457
1881..	249	All........	Amends Laws of 1870, chap. 291.............	414	457
1881..	298	All, except § 2......	Seats for female employes.........	415	499
1881..	298	2	Punishment for failure to provide seats for female employes.................	416	506

GENERAL LAWS REPEALED — (*Continued*).

Laws of.	Chapter.	Sections.	SUBJECT OF ACT.	Chapter.	Page.
1881..	353	All......	Village elections on tax question	414	457
1881..	387	All......	Amends Laws of 1870, chap. 291............. .	414	457
1881..	389	All......	Amends Laws of 1880, chap. 561, § 1........	420	565
1881..	408	All......	Amends Laws of 1880, chap. 235.............	414	457
1881..	425	All......	Amends Laws of 1850, chap. 256.............	420	565
1881..	429	All......	Add § 16 to Laws of 1878, chap. 315	418	543
1881..	615	All......	Civil jurisdiction of police justices in villages.	414	457
1881..	690	All......	Amends Laws of 1881, chap. 615....	414	457
1882..	185	All......	Trustees of personal estates	417	512
1882..	226	All......	Renewal of village tax warrant	414	457
1882..	305	All......	Amends Laws of 1870, chap. 291.............	414	457
1882..	316	All......	Amends Laws of 1870, chap. 291.............	414	457
1882..	324	All......	Debts discharged in bankruptcy.............	417	512
1883..	90	All......	Amends Laws of 1870, chap. 291.............	414	457
1883..	118	All......	Amends Laws of 1875, chap. 514.............	414	458
1883..	153	All......	Amends Laws of 1870, chap. 291.............	414	458
1883..	205	All......	Establishing board of claims; powers and duties	36	19
1883..	255	All......	Amends Laws of 1875, chap. 181.............	414	458
1883..	331	All......	Protection of waters of Lake George and Schroon Lake.........................	592	706
1883..	356	All, except § 3......	Bureau of labor statistics....	415	500
1883..	356	3	Punishment for failure to furnish statistics ...	416	506
1883..	383	All......	Contracts for conditional sale of railroad equipment........	418	543
1883..	421	All..	Amends Laws of 1879, chap. 336, § 1.........	418	543
1883..	459	All......	Amends Laws of 1870, chap. 291, title 8.......	414	458
1883..	465	All......	Restraint of peddling in villages...........	414	458
1884..	60	All......	Amends Laws of 1883, chap. 205, §§ 2, 4, 6, 7, 9 11, 18........................	36	19
1884..	85	All......	Jurisdiction of board of claims as to claim for animals killed	36	19
1884..	129	All......	Amends Laws of 1870, chap. 291.............	414	458
1884..	131	All......	Amends Laws of 1870, chap. 291.............	414	458
1884..	308	All......	Special villages to have power of general village	414	458
1884..	315	All......	Contracts of conditional sale	418	543
1884..	412	2, 3	Investment of moneys belonging to United States deposit fund	418	355
1884..	428	All......	Confirms incorporation of villages...........	414	458
1885..	116	All......	Amends Laws of 1883, chap. 331.	592	706
1885..	136	All......	Protection of waters of St. Lawrence river....	592	706
1885..	170	All......	Amends Laws of 1875, chap. 181.............	414	458
1885..	192	All......	Amends Laws of 1870, chap. 291.............	414	458
1885..	211	All	Amends Laws of 1875, chap. 181.............	414	458
1885..	216	All......	Amends Laws of 1863, chap. 422, § 2.........	418	543
1885..	236	All......	Amends Laws of 1870, chap. 291.............	414	458
1885..	273	All......	Amends Laws of 1862, chap. 482, § 2.........	418	543
1885..	277	All......	Prohibits obstruction of Racket and east branch of St. Regis rivers	592	706
1885..	314	All... ...	Scaffolding for use of employes on buildings..	415	500
1885..	342	1–6, 24, 25	Mechanics' liens on real property............	418	544
1885..	342	All, except §§ 1–6, 24.	Enforcement of mechanics' liens on real property	419	552
1885..	355	All......	Returns on repeal from decisions of board of canal appraisers	36	19
1885..	376	All......	Payment of wages by receivers of corporations.	415	500
1885..	450	All......	Amends Laws of 1870, chap. 291, tit. 8........	414	458
1885..	488	All......	Amends Laws of 1884, chap. 315, § 2..........	418	544

GENERAL LAWS REPEALED — (*Continued*).

Laws of.	Chapter.	Sections.	SUBJECT OF ACT.	Chapter.	Page.
1885..	526	All......	Liens of warehousemen	418	544
1886..	88	All	Amends Laws of 1863, chap. 482, § 2.........	418	544
1886..	151	All........	Hours of labor on street railroads in cities of over 500,000................................	415	500
1886..	204	All........	Amends Laws of 1885, chap. 277..............	592	706
1886..	382	All........	Validity of certain notices of lien............	418	544
1886..	409	All, except first § 21.	Factory inspector, factories and tenements. ..	415	509
1886..	409	First § 21..	Failure to comply with directions of factory inspector	416	506
1886..	410	All........	State board of arbitration and mediation......	415	500
1886..	497	All........	Extension of water mains in villages.........	414	458
1886..	556	All	Amends Laws of 1870, chap. 291, tit. 8........	414	458
1886..	600	All... ...	Amends Laws of 1870, chap 291...............	414	458
1886..	616	All........	Amends Laws of 1870, chap. 291..............	414	458
1887..	63	All........	State board of mediation and arbitration......	415	500
1887..	68	All	Amends Laws of 1870, chap. 291..............	414	458
1887..	244	All	Village fire department	414	458
1887..	245	All	State trust fund.............................	418	865
1887..	289	All	Amends Laws of 1875, chap. 27, § 1..........	614	760
1887..	458	All... ...	Protection and liabilities of owners of stallions	418	544
1887..	461	All	Effect of holidays upon payment of commercial paper..	612	758
1887..	462	All... ...	Amends Laws of 1886, chap. 409..	415	500
1887..	504	All... ...	Powers of villages to raise additional money..	414	458
1887..	507	All... ...	Amends Laws of 1883, chap. 205, § 10........	86	19
1887..	513	All... ...	Amends Laws of 1870, chap. 291..............	414	458
1887..	514	All... ...	Amends Laws of 1870, chap. 291..............	414	458
1887..	529	All, except § 2	Hours of labor on street railroads in cities of over 100,000.................................	415	500
1887..	529	2	Penalty for requiring additional hours of labor on street railroads	416	506
1888..	142	All......	Amends Laws of 1854, chap. 400, § 4.........	420	568
1888..	172	All......	Amends Laws of 1870, chap. 291...	414	458
1888..	229	All........	Centennial of inauguration of Washington....	612	758
1888..	314	All........	Amends Laws of 1886, chap. 116..............	592	706
1888..	316	All........	Amends Laws of 1885, chap. 342, § 1..........	418	544
1888..	326	All........	Deposit of state moneys in banks............	418	865
1888..	342	All........	Amends Laws of 1887, chap. 344.............	414	458
1888..	365	All..	Amends Laws of 1883, chap. 205, §§ 2, 3, 5, 16.	86	19
1888..	437	All........	Amends Laws of 1871, chap. 934, § 3..........	415	500
1888..	452	All... ...	Contracts of villages for lighting	414	458
1888..	457	All	Amends Laws of 1887, chap. 458, § 3.........	418	544
1888..	464	All......	Amends Laws of 1887, chap. 245, § 1.........	418	865
1888..	525	All... ...	Acquisition of land for parks in villages	414	458
1888..	539	All........	Protection of purchasers of coal in cities of over 1,200,000	174	71
1888..	543	All........	Liens on monuments.........................	418	544
1889..	50	All	Amends Laws of 1888, chap. 464, § 1..........	418	865
1889..	65	All	Investment of trust funds	417	518
1889..	68	All......	Amends Laws of 1883, chap. 205, §§ 2, 18	86	19
1889..	136	All	Cancellation of worthless accounts	418	865
1889..	174	All......	Amends Laws of 1880, chap. 78........	414	458
1889..	186	All......	Amends Laws of 1870, chap. 291..............	414	458
1889..	229	All	Amends Laws of 1870, chap. 291..............	414	458
1889..	246	All	Amends Laws of 1870, chap. 291..............	414	458
1889..	375	All........	Village sewer act..........	414	458
1889..	380	All........	Preference to citizens of state as laborers on public works...............................	415	500
1889..	381	All........	Cash payment of wages by corporations	415	500

GENERAL LAWS REPEALED — (Continued).

Laws of.	Chapter.	Sections.	SUBJECT OF ACT.	Chapter.	Page.
1889..	381	2	Penalty for failure to pay wages in cash......	416	506
1889..	385	All	Registration of labels by trades unions........	415	500
1889..	440	All.......	Amends Laws of 1870, chap. 291...........	414	458
1889..	455	All.......	Amends Laws of 1875, chap. 181...	414	458
1889..	487	All.......	Amends Laws of 1858, chap. 314, § 1........	417	512
1889..	507	All.......	Village water rents	414	458
1889..	522	All.......	Salary of marshal of board of claims	36	19
1889..	560	All.......	Amends Laws of 1886, chap. 409...........	415	500
1890..	82	All.......	Amends Laws of 1870, chap. 291...........	414	458
1890..	196	All	Amends Laws of 1870, chap. 291........ ...	414	458
1890..	218	All.......	Amends Laws of 1870, chap. 291...........	414	458
1890..	235	All.......	Amends Laws of 1870, chap. 291	414	458
1890..	236	All.......	Amends Laws of 1870, chap. 291...........	414	458
1890..	371	All.......	Amends Laws of 1887, chap. 504...........	414	459
1890..	388	All, except § 2......	Weekly payment of wages	415	501
1890..	388	2	Penalty for failure to pay weekly.............	416	506
1890..	394	All, except §§8, 13, 20	Inspection of mines	415	501
1890..	394	8, 20	Failure to protect safety of miners a misdemeanor......	416	506
1890..	398	All.......	Amends Laws of 1886, chap. 409...........	415	501
1890..	408	All.......	Amends Laws of 1883, chap. 205, § 2.......	36	19
1890..	527	All.......	Amends Laws of 1875, chap. 181...........	414	459
1890..	543	All.......	Amends Laws of 1870. chap. 291, tit. 8, so as to apply to Westchester county..............	414	459
1890..	569	15, 16	Commissioners of excise; assessors............	481	512
1891..	74	All..... ..	Amends Laws of 1875, chap. 181...........	414	459
1891..	116	All.......	Amends Laws of 1870, chap. 291...........	414	459
1891..	189	All.......	Amends Laws of 1870, chap. 291...........	414	459
1891..	160	All.......	Amends Laws of 1870, chap. 291...........	414	459
1891..	171	All	Chattel mortgages of electric company	418	544
1891..	178	All..	Amends R. S., part 2, chap. 4, tit. 4, § 5	417	512
1891..	181	All.......	Amends Laws of 1837, chap. 150, § 18, and Laws of 1880, chap. 517, § 1	418	365
1891..	194	All.......	Amends Laws of 1879, chap. 204.............	592	706
1891..	201	All.......	Amends Laws of 1875, chap. 181...	414	459
1891..	214	All.......	Amends Laws of 1885, chap. 314...........	415	501
1891..	255	1-5, 10-18	Amends Laws of 1878, chap. 315	418	544
1891..	255	6-9	Amends Laws of 1878, chap. 315..........	419	559
1891..	262	1	Negotiable instruments given for a speculative consideration	612	758
1891..	262	2	Penalty for violation.....................	613	759
1891..	306	All	Amends Laws of 1889, chap. 375...........	414	459
1891..	312	All.......	Amends Laws of 1888, chap. 452...........	414	459
1891..	316	All....	Amends Laws of 1889, chap. 375...........	414	459
1891..	385	All.......	Amends Laws of 1880, chap. 533...........	592	706
1892..	91	All.......	Amends Laws of 1872, chap. 498...........	418	544
1892..	194	All.......	Amends Laws of 1870, chap. 291...........	414	459
1892..	195	All.......	Amends Laws of 1875, chap. 181...........	414	459
1892..	222	All.......	Amends Laws of 1870, chap. 291..........	414	459
1892..	274	All.......	Amends Laws of 1864, chap. 412, § 8.......	488	544
1892..	349	All.......	Amends Laws of 1889, chap. 375...........	414	459
1892..	517	All, except § 5.....	Examination of scaffolding..............	415	501
1892..	517	5	Failure to provide safe scaffolding a misdemeanor...	416	506
1892..	564	All..	Amends Laws of 1889, chap. 375.............	414	459
1892..	593	All........	Amends Laws of 1870, chap. 291...	414	459
1892..	629	1-5, 10-12	Amends Laws of 1878, chap. 315..........	418	544
1892..	629	6-9	Amends Laws of 1878. chap. 315	419	559
1892..	640	All.......	Improvement of streets in certain villages.....	414	459

GENERAL LAWS REPEALED — (*Continued*).

Laws of.	Chapter.	Sections.	SUBJECT OF ACT.	Chapter.	Page.
1892..	667	All, except § 2......	Safety of workmen in mines..................	415	501
1893..	667	2	Failure to provide safety in mines a misdemeanor......................	416	506
1892..	678	All........	Amends Laws of 1886, chap. 409.............	415	501
1892..	711	All, except § 4......	Hours of service on railroads	415	501
1893..	173	All, except § 6......	Amends Laws of 1886, chap. 409.............	415	501
1893..	212	All........	Amends Laws of 1870, chap. 291.............	414	459
1893..	219	All.	Labels of trades unions.....	415	501
1893..	263	All	Amends Laws of 1868, chap. 256.............	420	568
1893..	300	All..	Amends Laws of 1885, chap. 342, § 24........	418	544
1893..	339	All........	Amends Laws of 1892, chap. 667....,.......	415	501
1893..	400	All........	Amends Laws of 1870, chap. 291.............	414	459
1893..	405	All...	Amends Laws of 1864, chap. 412, § 3........	418	544
1893..	422	All........	Amends Laws of 1889, chap. 875...........	414	459
1893..	425	All........	Amends Laws of 1888, chap. 205, § 12........	86	19
1893..	447	All........	Hospitals or pesthouses in villages	414	459
1893..	452	All........	Amends R. S., part 2, chap. 1, title 2, § 68 ...	417	513
1893..	464	All........	Amends Laws of 1870, chap. 291.............	414	459
1893..	473	All........	Amends Laws of 1888, chap. 453.............	414	459
1893..	503	All........	Amends Laws of 1870, chap. 291....	414	459
1893..	617	All........	Amends Laws of 1888, chap. 452.............	414	459
1893..	618	All .	Amends Laws of 1870, chap. 291.............	414	459
1893..	624	All......	Amends Laws of 1875, chap. 181.............	414	459
1893..	662	All........	Amends Laws of 1889, chap. 507.............	414	459
1893..	672	All........	Amends Laws of 1887, chap. 150, § 48........	413	365
1893..	691	All, except § 3.....	Hours of labor in brickyards	415	501
1893..	691	3	Extra hours in brickyards a misdemeanor.....	416	506
1893..	694	All........	Amends Laws of 1870, chap. 291.............	414	459
1893..	715	All........	Amends Laws of 1892, chap. 517.............	415	501
1893..	716	All........	Antimonopoly	388	312
1893..	717	All......	Amends Laws of 1890, chap. 388.............	415	501
1894..	185	All........	Chancery fund......................	413	365
1894..	258	All	Hotel-keepers may detain property of boarders.	418	544
1894..	277	All........	Stone used in state and municipal works......	415	501
1894..	284	All	Amends Laws of 1889, chap. 507.............	414	459
1894..	318	All........	Amends Laws of 1875, chap. 181.............	414	459
1894..	329	All........	Amends Laws of 1854, chap. 400.............	420	568
1894..	378	All	Badges of factory inspectors........	415	501
1894..	418	All	Amends Laws of 1892, chap. 640.... ...	414	459
1894..	420	All........	Amends Laws of 1884, chap. 315, § 7........	418	544
1894..	607	All........	Days of grace abolished......	612	758
1894..	622	All........	Amends Laws of 1870, chap. 385, § 2	415	501
1894..	673	All	Village lighting contract..................	414	459
1894..	678	All........	Amends Laws of 1894, chap. 135........	413	365
1894..	699	All, except § 8......	Sale of convict-made goods	415	501
1894..	699	8	Illegal sale of convict-made goods...........	416	506
1894..	680	All	Establishment of electric-light plant in villages	414	459
1894..	724	All	Amends Laws of 1864, chap. 412, §§ 3, 4.....	418	544
1894..	740	All........	Amends Laws of 1858, chap. 314, § 1.........	417	513
1895..	78	All........	Amends Laws of 1863, chap. 460, § 4.........	413	365
1895..	113	All	Amends Laws of 1888, chap. 452.............	414	459
1895..	145	All...	Amends R. S. part 2, chap. 4, tit. 1, § 12. ...	420	568
1895..	146	All........	Amends Laws of 1870, chap. 291.............	414	459
1895..	154	All........	Amends Laws of 1870, chap. 291.............	414	459
1895..	161	All........	Amends Laws of 1885, chap. 342, § 6.........	418	544
1895..	187	All........	Amends Laws of 1870, chap. 291.............	414	460

GENERAL LAWS REPEALED — (*Continued*).

Laws of.	Chapter.	Sections.	SUBJECT OF ACT.	Chapter.	Page.
1895..	202	All.......	Amends Laws of 1889, chap. 375.....	414	460
1895..	324	All.......	Abolishes office of mine inspector	415	501
1895..	854	All	Amends Laws of 1883, chap. 279, § 3........	418	544
1895..	388	All.......	Amends Laws of 1875, chap. 181...........	414	460
1895..	413	All.......	Amends Laws of 1894, chap. 277...........	415	502
1895..	430	All.. ...	Compensation of village boards of health.....	414	460
1895..	437	All...	Village appropriation for fire parade	414	460
1895..	518	All, except § 7.....	Bakeshops, inspection of, etc.................	415	502
1895..	518	7	Failure to obey directions of factory inspector as to bakeshops......................	416	506
1895..	528	All.......	Amends Laws of 1884, chap. 315, § 7.........	418	544
1895..	529	All.... ..	Amends Laws of 1868, chap. 779...........	418	544
1895..	608	All.......	Amends Laws of 1875, chap. 27, § 1.........	614	760
1895..	670	All..	Deputy mine inspector...................	415	502
1895..	673	1-3	Amends Laws of 1885, chap. 342, §§ 1, 2, 3....	418	544
1895..	673	4	Amends Laws of 1885, chap. 342, § 20	419	559
1895..	743	All.......	Amends Laws of 1870, chap. 291............	414	460
1895..	765	All.... ...	Amends Laws of 1892, chap. 667, § 1........	415	502
1895..	818	All.... ...	Chancery fund	413	385
1895..	879	All.......	Amends Laws of 1870, chap. 291............	414	460
1895..	884	All.	Liens of lodging-house keepers	418	544
1895..	899	All.......	Payment of wages of employes of copartners by receivers.......................	415	502
1895..	925	All.... ...	Amends Laws of 1884, chap. 315, § 7.........	418	544
1896..	166	All..	Amends Laws of 1888, chap. 452...........	414	460
1896..	191	All..	Amends Laws of 1895, chap. 818, § 1	413	385
1896..	209	All.......	Amends Laws of 1870, chap. 291......	414	460
1896..	243	All	Amends Laws of 1870, chap. 291...	414	460
1896..	267	All..	Amends Laws of 1893, chap. 716, by adding new § 3............................	383	313
1896..	271	All, except § 6.....	Examination and registration of horseshoers..	415	502
1896..	271	6	Horseshoers not to practice without registration	416	506
1896..	310	All...	Amends Laws of 1875, chap. 181...........	414	460
1896..	341	All.... ..	Amends Laws of 1870, chap. 291...........	414	460
1896..	329	All........	Amends Laws of 1886, chap. 497...	414	460
1896..	384	All, except § 11....	Employment of women and children in mercantile establishments	415	502
1896..	384	11	Employment of children in mercantile establishments without certificates a misdemeanor........................	416	506
1896..	409	All.......	Amends Laws of 1889, chap. 375...........	414	460
1896..	451	All.......	Amends Laws of 1883, chap. 205, §§ 10, 17.....	36	19
1896..	457	All.......	Amends Laws of 1870, chap. 291...........	414	460
1896..	458	All	Amends Laws of 1870, chap. 291...........	414	460
1896..	522	All.......	Amends Laws of 1870, chap. 291...........	414	460
1896..	528	All.......	Amends Laws of 1883, chap. 279, § 3........	418	544
1896..	601	All.......	Amends Laws of 1884, chap. 315, § 7........	418	544
1896..	663	All.......	Lighting contracts in villages	414	460
1896..	668	All.......	Amends Laws of 1870, chap. 291......	414	460
1896..	673	All.......	Amends Laws of 1895, chap. 518...........	415	502
1896..	682	All.......	Amends Laws of 1878, chap. 315, § 18........	418	544
1896..	683	All.......	Amends Laws of 1880, chap. 533	592	706
1896..	788	All.......	Liens on stone, etc	418	544
1896..	789	All.......	Amends Laws of 1893, chap. 691, § 2	415	502
1896..	915	All.......	Amends Laws of 1885, chap. 342, § 5.......	418	544
1896..	923	All.......	Amends Laws of 1870, chap. 291............	414	460

GENERAL LAWS REPEALED — (*Concluded*).

Laws of.	Chapter.	Sections.	SUBJECT OF ACT.	Chapter.	Page.
1896..	931	All, except §§ 5, 6....	Labeling and marking convict-made goods....	415	502
1896..	936	All, except § 5......	Protection of persons employed in the construction of buildings	415	502
1896..	936	5	Neglect to protect persons employed on building a misdemeanor.........................	416	506
1896..	978	All	Village contracts for water....................	414	460
1896..	982	All, except § 6......	Free employment bureaus...................	415	502
1896..	982	6	Free employment bureaus, charging fees a misdemeanor	416	506
1896..	991	All........	Amends Laws of 1886, chap. 409	415	502
1897..	148	All........	Amends Laws of 1896, chap. 271, §§ 3, 4, 6....	415	502

VI. SECTION OF CODE OF CRIMINAL PROCEDURE REPEALED.

Section.	SUBJECT OF SECTION.	Chapter.	Page.
75, 76, 77........	Police justices in villages	414	460

INDEX.

See, also, Asylums: Poor.

Lightning Source UK Ltd.
Milton Keynes UK
UKHW012130180219
337529UK00012B/1407/P